CANADIAN
THEATRE
HISTORY

selected
readings

NɘW
CANADIAN
READINGS

SERIES EDITOR
J. L. GRANATSTEIN

Titles   currently   available

CANADIAN
THEATRE
HISTORY

selected
readings

Edited by
Don Rubin
York University

COPP CLARK LTD.
Toronto

ISBN: 0-7730-5542-8

publisher: Jeff Miller
managing editor: Barbara Tessman
editor: Bay Ryley
design: Susan Hedley, Liz Nyman
cover: Valentino Sanna
typesetting: Marnie Benedict
printing and binding: Metropole Litho Inc.

Canadian Cataloguing in Publication Data

Main entry title:
Canadian theatre history: selected readings

(New Canadian readings)
Includes bibliographical references.
ISBN 0-7730-5542-8

1. Theatre - Canada - History.   I. Rubin, Don, 1943–   .   II. Series.

COPP CLARK LTD.
2775 Matheson Blvd. East
Mississauga, ON
L4W 4P7

Printed and bound in Canada

1 2 3 4 5   5542-8   00 99 98 97 96

FOREWORD

○

Canadians today have come almost to take for granted the existence of theatre. The large cities have thriving theatre communities, skillfully producing the best contemporary and historical domestic and foreign works, and even the smaller cities have their own little theatres, regular touring companies and, through television, access to a wider world. Don Rubin's extraordinary collection of articles on the history of theatre in Canada reminds us forcefully how very recent this phenomenon is.

Well into the twentieth century, there was scarcely any Canadian theatre. An aspiring actor had to leave Canada to train and work, and playwrights, wherever they might have existed, could not get their work produced. The Dominion Drama Festival began to change this, as did the growth of little theatres in a few cities. The Canadian Broadcasting Corporation's radio network soon provided an important outlet, the Stratford Festival raised the standards, and in the mid-1950s the Canada Council's arrival ushered in a brave new world. The resulting explosion in Canadian theatre was simply extraordinary.

The articles collected here tell this story, to be sure, but because the range is so broad we learn that nothing is ever an unmixed blessing. Yes, the DDF was critical—but why were the adjudicators almost always foreigners? Of course, Stratford and the Canada Council were important, but the former reinforced only the British tradition while the latter seemed unwilling to venture very far into support for alternate theatre. And what was it about Canadians that allowed them to see skilled playwrights live under the subsistence level?

That there are writers who are prepared to challenge the orthodoxies of their times is the best sign of vigorous life. Don Rubin's digging has produced both the orthodox and the radical, and his efforts to show the roots of Canadian theatre today will allow students to understand the theatre's past and present in ways hitherto impossible.

J.L. Granatstein
General Editor

CONTENTS

o

○

My aim in putting together this first sourcebook in Canadian theatre history has been to create a history of anglophone Canada as seen through its theatre. When Jack Granatstein first suggested the idea, I knew that a sufficient number of essays existed to make the project viable. But by the time I stopped looking for the essays, manifestos, interviews, letters, and personal statements that finally make up this collection, I was overwhelmed by how much extraordinary material there was and by how far back in time it went. The real problem for me was not what to include but what to leave out.

The fact is that until now there has been no basic text for Canadian theatre courses, no place to find the essential theatrical documents that have shaped and continue to shape our understanding of who we are as a people. For those reading some of these documents for the first time, a few things may surprise: the strong and continuous influence of the Irish literary movement on the evolution of Canadian theatre in the twentieth century, the stubborn and continuing dream of creating a true people's theatre in Canada as well as a centralized or at least a touring National Theatre, the influence of foreign visitors such as William Butler Yeats, Michel Saint-Denis, and Harley Granville-Barker on Canadian theatre practice and attitudes, the long history that theatre in Canada has on both a professional and an amateur level, and the lengths to which some of our artists (especially our playwrights) have gone to awaken national consciousness.

There are ongoing debates to be identified in the volume as well. Among them, the proper role of government toward the arts, the historical influence of the Stratford Festival, the role of the regional theatre movement in the development of a community-based theatre profession, the influence of the alternative theatres in the development of Canadian playwriting, and the fragmenting perspectives of the New Alternatives in the evolution of a contemporary multicultural and multi-visioned Canada.

Among the key documents to be found here, most appearing for the first time since their original publications, are: B.K. Sandwell's important 1911 essay, "The Annexation of Our Stage"; Vincent Massey's 1922 analysis of the problems facing Canadian playwrights, "The Prospects of a Canadian Drama"; Merrill Denison's controversial 1929 essay "Nationalism and Drama"; John Coulter's 1938 article for the American magazine *Theatre Arts Monthly*, "The Canadian Theatre and the Irish Exemplar"; Robertson Davies' 1951 study for the Massey Commission on "The State of Theatre in Canada"; and Tyrone Guthrie's 1954 meditation, "Long View of the Stratford Festival."

Included as well are major essays and statements by leading postwar cultural analysts and theatrical thinkers including Stratford's most consistent and perceptive critic, Nathan Cohen, *Globe and Mail* theatre critic emeritus Herbert Whittaker, former head of the Canada Council and philosophical provocateur Mavor Moore, playwrights George Ryga, Michael Cook, Rick Salutin, Sharon Pollock, Margaret Hollingsworth, and Tomson Highway, cultural commentators Peter Hay, Susan Crean, and Alan Filewod and, published for the first time, the full text of the "Gaspé Manifesto," a 1971 call by Canadian playwrights for a fifty percent Canadian content quota in subsidized theatres.

In this a complete collection of the important readings in Canadian theatre history? Not at all. No attempt has been made to deal with the francophone theatre, its history, development or influence on anglophone Canada or anglophone theatre thinking. That would be a project in itself and one that not only goes far beyond the mandate of this work, but which would have easily doubled the size of the volume.

As well, one would have liked, especially in the early material, more essays from women, First Nations peoples, and those away from central Canada. Most of these gaps are not so much omissions as they are simply reflections of Canada's socio-historical realities. The fact is that our national theatre history has already been rewritten several times over the last three decades; perhaps as "new" older material emerges, it will be rewritten yet again. It is hoped that this volume will provide those in the field with materials to build on.

I would be remiss not to thank a number of people for their involvement in this project. Obviously the idea would not have gotten off the ground without the vision of Jack Granatstein, one of this country's most original and perceptive historians; Jeff Miller and Bay Ryley at Copp Clark who didn't know when we began how large this field was, and whose advice and goodwill were continuously appreciated; Anton Wagner, Robert Fothergill, Judith Rudakoff, and Ross Stuart, my theatre studies colleagues at York University, who read and commented on various versions; my energetic and enthusiastic editorial assistant Catherine Matzig who will one day make her own contribution in this field; and, of course, my own fiercest critic and essential pagan, my wife, Patricia Keeney who, along with me, learned much from this material.

Finally, I should like to dedicate this book to the memory of two people who never stopped fighting for the cause of a culturally independent Canada and especially for the cause of Canadian playwriting. Both of them died too soon: playwrights George Ryga and Michael Cook. The battle continues, my friends.

THE ANNEXATION OF
OUR STAGE, 1750–1916

THE THEATRE IN CANADA
(1750–1880) ◇

J.E. MIDDLETON

○

*In 1914, a multi-volume history of Canada appeared under the general editor-
ship of Adam Shortt and Arthur G. Doughty called* Canada and Its
Provinces: A History of the Canadian People and Their Institutions.
*With one hundred contributors, the series covered a wide range of subjects.
The twelfth volume dealt exclusively with Canadian culture and included this
essay by J.E. Middleton on early theatre in Canada.*

British army officers have been inveterate devotees of private theatricals.
Do we not remember one of Lever's Irish captains forgetting to "wash up"
and appearing on dress parade in the Moorish make-up of Othello? That
was in the toddling days of the nineteenth century. The remarkable dramatic revival in London which began with Garrick around 1750 had its
effect in kindling enthusiasm in every direction. For a hundred years at
least tender subalterns were expected to be "up" in Portia, Desdemona and
Rosalind, whatever became of their drill. Even commanding officers occasionally laid aside their dignity to play the part of stern fathers.

Theatricals became an army tradition, like "peaking oars" in the navy.
It is not surprising, therefore, that the regiments at the outposts of the
Empire, such as Halifax, Quebec and Montreal, should beguile the tedium
of garrison duty by elaborate "productions" in which society revelled.
Scores of these amateur efforts were made from 1820 onward. One of his-
toric importance is recorded in detail in Forster's *Life of Charles Dickens*. On
Wednesday evening, May 25, 1842, the gentlemen of the Coldstream

---

◇ *Canada and Its Provinces: A History of the Canadian People and Their Institutions
by One Hundred Associates*, vol. 12, ed. Adam Shortt and Arthur G. Doughty
(Toronto: Glasgow, Brook & Company, 1914), 651–61.

Guards presented in the Theatre Royal, Montreal, *A Roland for an Oliver*, *Two O'Clock in the Morning* and *Deaf as a Post*. The stage manager was Dickens, who appeared as Alfred Highflyer, Mr. Snobbington and Gallop. The novelist said in a letter to his biographer: "I never saw anything so perfectly touch-and-go as the first two pieces." The story of the frolic is told by "the inimitable" with a flaming self-satisfaction which is in itself a delight.

Another glimpse at military drama takes us twenty-two years forward, almost to modern times. The irrepressible Frances Monck records, under Friday, October 21, 1864, a benefit performance at Quebec by the officers of the 25th Regiment for the Canadian Military Asylum. After dancing on the previous evening with "Dr Tupper, the Premier of Nova Scotia," and approving of him, she writes: "We drove to the 25th Plays. They took place at the Music Hall. As you know, there is no theatre at Quebec. They never replaced the burnt-down one. The actors were soldiers of the K.O.B.'s and acted so very well with such nice voices. The women's parts were done by men. The house was crowded and very demonstrative. . . . Capt. E. said when Col. C. at Montreal is acting and does not know his part, he walks up to the Prompter and says in a loud, hoarse voice: 'What is it?' He acted an Admiral, wearing his moustaches and walking with a cavalry strut."

So much for Quebec and Montreal. Captain Moorson said of Halifax in 1830: "There are no regular public assemblies at Halifax. A Theatre conducted by amateurs is opened five or six times during the season, but a dearth of female performers renders it not peculiarly attractive."

It might be said with some reason that Canada's infant drama was nurtured on pipe-clay and cradled in a sentry-box.

But the whole range of amateur theatricals ancient and modern is of very little moment in examining the status of the drama in Canada. In general it is true that only the playing of trained professional actors and actresses ever approaches the artistic and interests the general public. The proof of the pudding is the eating: the proof of the acting is the box-office receipts. Men and women who are willing to pay to witness amateur performances may be moved by sympathy, or social considerations, ennui, or even despair: seldom are they clamorous to enter because of the fineness of the acting. In one sense, therefore, the Earl Grey competitions for amateurs could have but little influence upon the growth of dramatic art in Canada, nor could they form in any appreciable degree the taste of the community. We do not look for supreme attainment in the young women who decorate china for amusement. We go to the man who has lived with his technique for a lifetime, whose colour-box is not a toy, but a means of self-expression.

While, therefore, it may be entertaining to glance at the stage gambols of the gentlemen amateurs who wore the king's scarlet in British America, it may be more profitable to turn to the professional stock companies who were willing, men and women, to tempt Fortune with borrowed eloquence, to tread in sock and buskin the rocky road to success, to live on short commons in Vagabondia.

Albany gossip of 1786 records the arrival in the Hudson of a company of English comedians, six men and four women, under a Mr Moore. There was no enthusiasm in Albany for Englishmen, least of all for English actors. The

Declaration of Independence was only ten years old. It is specifically stated that the party after a few unpleasant days went north to Montreal, doubtless by way of Lake Champlain to St Johns, thence by road to Laprairie, nearly opposite Montreal. There is no Montreal record of their performances, but it is known that they had in their repertoire *The Taming of the Shrew, George Barnwell, The Countess of Salisbury* and *Venice Preserved*. For these facts we are indebted to a remarkable series of newspaper articles by Frank T. Graham— clipped, pasted and bound in octavo cloth. The book is called *Histrionic Montreal*, and probably the copy in the Carnegie Library, Toronto, is unique.

Albany and Philadelphia were the theatrical bases of supplies for Canada. Indeed, Canada has always been indebted either directly or indirectly to the United States for her drama. Even the English plays and players go to the Dominion today by way of New York. Nor is this a cause for complaint. It is a natural condition.

In 1804 a Mr Ormsby, a Scottish actor, went from Albany to Montreal and established a theatre in the loft of a building in St Sulpice Street. It was opened on November 19 with *The Busybody* and *The Sultan*. A year later Lambert reports a performance of *Petruccio and Katherine* when the play was rendered ridiculous by the intoxication of Katherine, which was all too apparent.

But in 1808 a Mr Pigmore and his company visited Canada. Here is a description by Lambert of the genial impresario, whom we may salute with due respect: "We met Mr P. in a huge sleigh near Trois Rivières. He was wrapped up in a buffalo robe, a *bonnet rouge* was on his head, such as the Canadian peasantry wear, a wampum belt was buckled around his waist, and Indian moccasins were on his feet. With his red face, he appeared like one of the ancient French landed proprietors or like one of the half-breed chiefs. He had some three or four persons with him whom he called his 'company' and was then *en route* to play at Quebec."

In general the theatrical history of Quebec is that of Montreal. When possible the metropolitan companies served the Rock City. Otherwise Quebec society depended upon the garrison amateurs.

J. Bernard played in Montreal in Mr Alport's company in 1829, the piece being Mrs Inchbald's *Lovers' Vows*. Bernard, the son of a naval officer, was an actor of no inconsiderable ability. He returned to England and was the associate of such gay sparks as Sheridan, Selwyn and Fox, and attained immortality by being elected secretary of the Beefsteak Club of London.

As an additional proof of Canada's dependence upon the United States for theatrical pablum, no plays were presented during the War of 1812–14. But at 2 College Street, Montreal, on February 18, 1818, a theatre was opened by John D. Turnbull and his company. Another house in Notre Dame Street began business in 1821 with C.W. Blanchard as manager. Blanchard three years later had a circus in Craig Street, where he gave equestrian drama. But the first real house of entertainment was the old Theatre Royal, erected in 1825 near Bonsecours Market at a cost of £7500. John Molson was the chief shareholder, and Frederick Brown, the tragedian, was manager. The theatre opened on November 21, 1825, with *The

Dramatist by Reynolds. Brown's reputation was excellent and his company intelligent. Thenceforward the travelling "stars" made Montreal a port of refuge. Thomas Hamblin played *Hamlet* with this company, and then came the greatest Gloucester in the history of the stage, Edmund Kean. In Albany Kean had offended the tender sensibilities of the Americans and had had a hard time. Montreal must have seemed like a paradise to him. He presented on July 31, 1826, *Richard III*. On August 2 he appeared as Shylock, the following night as Othello, and on August 9 as King Lear. His success was a notable one and he was honoured by a public dinner.

One need but mention Clara Foster, who in 1829 sang for Montrealers *The Dashing White Sergeant*. Dickens enthusiasts will recollect this as the title of the song that Mrs Micawber was wont to sing when "home with her mamma." James H. Hackett played in Montreal in 1831 and Charles Kean in 1833. Thomas Ward, the lessee of the theatre in 1836, had in his company John Nickinson, who afterwards became manager of a Toronto company of special excellence. In this season William Dowton, the English comedian, appeared as Sir Anthony Absolute, Falstaff and Sir Peter Teazle.

Passing over the Rebellion years, during which there were no performances, we come to the engagement in 1840 of Margaret Davenport, an "Infant Phenomenon" who at the age of twelve played Richard III, Shylock, Norval and Sir Peter Teazle with amazing power. In later years she created the part of Camille in America.

Another famous engagement was that of J.B. Buckstone, who played on September 9, 1841, in his own piece *A Kiss in the Dark*. Buckstone was one of the "characters" of the English stage and for years was a prominent figure at the Haymarket in London.

In 1844 the old Theatre Royal was torn down to make way for the Bonsecours Market. During the last season before its demolition Macready appeared in *Richelieu*, *Werner* and *Macbeth*. The engagement was only moderately successful.

In 1852 the new Theatre Royal in Côté Street was opened with J.W. Buckland as manager and Mrs Buckland as the leading lady. The piece on July 15 was *The Rivals*. Other plays heard that season were *The Heir at Law*, *London Assurance*, *The School for Scandal*, *The Lady of Lyons*, *The Ladies' Battle*, *The Country Squire* and *She Stoops to Conquer*.

Dion Boucicault appeared in 1853, Charles Mathews in 1858 and Barry Sullivan in 1859. Of the erratic genius and ready wit of Sullivan all play-lovers are aware. On one night in Montreal while playing Richard III he gave the lines, "A horse, a horse, my kingdom for a horse," with special fervour. Suddenly a man in the gallery shouted, "Would an ass do?" "Yes," retorted the actor, thoroughly aroused. "Come to the stage door."

The Prince of Wales, afterwards King Edward VII, was in Montreal in 1860. He and Adelina Patti made a first appearance contemporaneously. The prima donna sang to enormous audiences in a special building constructed for the purpose in St Catherine Street.

During the seasons of 1863 and 1865 John McCullough, the tragedian, was leading man of the Montreal Company. The Holman Opera Company came in 1871 with Alice Oates as chief soprano, and W.H. Crane in the cast. In 1876, on May 25, E.A. Sothern made his Canadian début as Lord Dundreary.

Since that time, when the present system of moving whole companies instead of "stars" from place to place began to become effective, Montreal has had the best that England and the United States could afford. The old Royal was deposed, for first-class companies, by the Academy of Music, and later by His Majesty's in Guy Street. Stock companies still flourish, generally during the summer months. A French company plays in St Catherine Street East during the whole season.

It is interesting to note that in the old days the theatrical season began in June and ran through till August. It was not uncommon for heavy tragedy to be played when the mercury was in the nineties. Perhaps our fathers were less worried about the weather than we are. This generation would shudder at the prospect of *Virginius*, *Macbeth* or *Hamlet* in the scorching heat of a Montreal midsummer.

Before 1830 there was a theatre in Toronto. Frank's hotel at the corner of King Street and Market Lane had a large low-ceiled room which was used for dramatic performances. The place was reached by an outside stairway and would be contemplated with horror by a modern building inspector. The proscenium was narrow and low and the scenery was makeshift, but the companies of Mr Archbold, Mr and Mrs Talbot and Mr Vaughan were welcomed. Dr Scadding tells us of the appearance of Mrs Talbot on one evening in *Pizarro* and *Little Pickle*. Other plays produced in this house were *Barbarossa, or The Siege of Algiers*—two garrison men formed the "army"—*Ali Baba, or The Forty Thieves*, *The Lady of the Lake* and *The Miller and his Men*.

The backsliding of a Wesleyan chapel in King Street gave the drama a better opportunity. The building having been abandoned by the denomination, it became, in 1833, the Theatre Royal, where for a number of years the players had reasonable accommodation. Generally there was a close relation between Montreal and Toronto in dramatic matters. John Nickinson and his wife, who had played in Montreal, took the Royal Lyceum Theatre in 1852, and until 1858 won a deserved success. The travelling "stars" did not fail to come, and some excellent performances were given. In later years Mrs Morrison, daughter of the Nickinsons, an actress of marked ability, was the lessee of the same theatre, which was situated in King Street. Up to the day when travelling companies began to replace the old system the Nickinsons, father and daughter, were the most important of a long line of managers. Charles Albert Fechter was in Toronto in 1868 playing a round of Shakespearean parts. On one occasion there was some difficulty with the company and some of the actors refused to go on. *Hamlet* was the bill. Bernardo entered before the castle with the famous salutation, "Who's there?" There was no reply. He repeated the question twice. Then came a voice from the "gods": "Darned if I know. Go on with the play." Toronto today is well served with theatres and patronizes them with great liberality.

Actors came occasionally to Halifax from Boston. Some others, just out from England to try their fortunes in an American tour, sojourned at

Halifax and strutted their brief hour with reasonable satisfaction to "a cheerful and convivial people." But there particularly the Garrison Dramatic Corps, like everything else military or naval, held always a first place in the affections of society. Of late years the Maritime Provinces have been fairly well served, but not so well as they might be. Summer stock is generally popular in the East.

Winnipeg in 1870 was only the germ of a city. But the Theatre Royal was established by the First Ontario Rifles in the rear of a store belonging to Mr Bannatyne. On December 16 the regimental company played a burlesque in three acts, *A Child of Circumstances, or The Long-lost Father.* So the West, opened up under other and more favourable conditions than those attending the opening of the East, had for its entertainment the same meek and lowly beginning—soldier boys playing in a room behind a shop. A year later an amateur dramatic club was organized, and ever since amateur acting has been a common and pleasant social diversion in the Queen City of the Plains. The first important professional engagement was that of the McDowell Company in 1879. Since then Winnipeg and the Great West have fared as well as could be expected, St Paul and Minneapolis being the American base. In like manner the coast cities depend upon Seattle and San Francisco.

A book of some rarity dealing with early theatrical conditions in Canada has been acquired lately by the Archives at Ottawa. In 1861 Captain Horton Rhys of the English army made a wager. In pursuance of its terms he and Catherine Lucette, a Covent Garden soprano, toured the Eastern States and Canada, acquiring within six months a net profit of £500. Rhys, in addition, seems to have acquired a persistently bad temper. He wrote an account of his experience.[1] It is in a sense a literary curiosity, for the author has a villainous style. Further, it is plainly inaccurate, and it exhales a snobbishness gloriously complete. The book is amusing in the serious parts and deadly serious in the humorous parts. Perhaps it deserves some slight attention on this account.

The Canadian part of the tour began at Quebec in the Music Hall on July 25, 1861, under the patronage of Colonel Munro, C.B., commandant, and the officers of the garrison. The band of the 39th Regiment assisted. On the programme was a one-act sketch by Captain Rhys, a series of operatic airs sung by Miss Lucette, and a "Ballad, by desire" entitled *Ever of Thee.* Those familiar with the works of Artemus Ward, a contemporary, will remember his occasional bright references to this piece of musical sentimentality.

Rhys found the Music Hall "a wretched contrivance, rent 40 dols. a night," but, as he also said the River St Lawrence at Quebec was three miles wide, one may be politely incredulous. The *Mercury* said that his facial power and volubility of speech placed him beyond criticism—"as an amateur."

In Montreal he appeared at Nordheimer's Hall; in Kingston, at the Sons of Temperance Hall. He was at Belleville, Peterborough, Cobourg, Port Hope, Hamilton, Niagara Falls and London, and cursed the accommodation everywhere. But he did fairly well, picking up the money, and glowering upon the country.

His experience in Toronto was amusing. He had forwarded from Kingston to the Hon. George Brown of the *Globe* an order for some posters.

When he arrived the order had not been executed. "I was not in a good temper," he says. "After some five minutes' conversation in the *Globe* office with a hungry-looking, bald-headed individual in his shirt sleeves, and nails in mourning, I desired to see the Honorable Brown himself. Much to my surprise, I found that he stood before me. He said that owing to the printers in general being constantly 'done' by the 'travelling profession' they had determined on giving no more credit."

It is extraordinary that Captain Rhys should have felt aggrieved, for in an earlier portion of the book he himself asserts: "Actors in Canada are a little too much of the Fly by Night order to hold a high Social status."

But of course there was a vast gulf fixed between a professional actor and a gentleman amateur, with his name in the Army List, "travelling incognito on a wager."

Cynics say that any one can write a play, but that scarcely any one can sell one. Canadians have been writing in the dramatic form for years. Perhaps Charles Mair began it in 1880 with *Tecumseh*, a drama, duly heroical and embalmed for our inspection in printers' ink. Others who have essayed the impossible include J. Mackenzie, who wrote *Thayendanegea*, a historic-military drama, John Hunter Dewar, author of *De Roberval*, Sarah Ann Curzon, who dramatized the story of Laura Secord, and L.O. David, whose play *Le Drapeau de Carillon* is well worth reading. Frederick George Scott and William Wilfred Campbell, known generally for their lyrics, have each essayed the poetic drama. W.A. Tremayne has written plays to some purpose. His *Lost Twenty-four Hours*, produced by Robert Hilliard, was a New York success.

One might give a list of Canadian-born players who have attained distinction in the profession, but nearly all of them had their training in the United States and are to all intents American rather than Canadian actors. Even Margaret Anglin, the most eminent of our stage women, looks to Broadway for her highest felicity, and should do so. There is no Canadian Drama. It is merely a branch of the American Theatre, and, let it be said, a most profitable one.

NOTES

1. *A Theatrical Trip for a Wager: Through Canada and the United States*, by Captain Horton Rhys (Morton Price), author of *Tit for Tat, Folly, All's Fair in Love and War*, etc. etc., London, published for the author by Charles Dudley, 4 Agar Street, West Strand, 1861.

STARS OF OTHER DAYS
(1875–1900) ⬦

HECTOR CHARLESWORTH

o

One of Canada's major theatre critics and cultural commentators during the first half of the twentieth century, Hector Charlesworth (1872–1945), wrote for a variety of Toronto newspapers including the World, *the* Empire, *the* News, *the* Mail and Empire, *the* Globe, *and the* Globe and Mail. *From 1926 to 1932 he was the editor-in-chief of* Saturday Night. *In his later years, he published three volumes of memoirs. The following is an excerpt from his 1925 memoir,* Candid Chronicles.

Of all the stage doors in America, the one (with the exception of that of the Metropolitan Opera House, New York) that is richest in associations is probably that of the now disused Grand Opera House, Toronto, the walls of which have been standing for fifty years though the interior was burned in 1879. There are a few other theatres as old in various American cities, but the associations are greater in connection with "the Grand," because it was the one theatre where nearly all the noted artists of the quarter of a century from 1875 to 1900 appeared, and the weather-beaten door that still remains, has opened and closed on their comings and goings. And so when I pass it I think of Adelaide Neilson, Irving, Terry, Patti, Edwin Booth, Coquelin, Bernhardt, Modjeska, Mary Anderson, and a host of idols of other days who had stepped across its dingy threshold. A sinister atmosphere hangs over the old theatre now, for within its walls its millionaire manager, Ambrose J. Small, was possibly murdered in 1919, and the mystery of his disappearance has never been solved.

It was here that the radiant Adelaide Neilson came in 1879 to re-open the theatre, renovated after the fire; and it was in front of this stage door

---

⬦ *Candid Chronicles: Leaves from the Note Book of a Canadian Journalist* (Toronto: The Macmillan Company of Canada, 1925), 339–41.

that the students of the University of Toronto took the horses from her carriage and drew her to her hotel. This demonstration, absolutely spontaneous, proved as great an advertisement, that managers subsequently worked up similar demonstrations in connection with lesser stars until the public commenced to jeer.

There was, until a few years ago, another theatre in Toronto of much older associations—the Royal Lyceum Theatre, which, when burned in 1922, was used as a mattress factory, and earlier still as a spoon factory. It was there that Clara Morris, a native of Toronto, afterwards celebrated as an emotional actress, made her first appearance on the stage as a child in pantomime. There also Mrs. Charles Walcott, one of the most distinguished of comédiennes, made her début, under the direction of her father, John Nickinson, who was manager of "The Royal." It was there I saw the first play that I remember, some time in the early eighties. It was a very crude affair called *Uncle Josh*, but its author, the late Denman Thompson, later built it up into *The Old Homestead*, the most popular and successful of all American plays except *Uncle Tom's Cabin*. In the seventies Thompson ran a not very reputable saloon and dance hall on Bay Street, Toronto. He had been a variety actor and was anxious to get back into the profession, so he began with a one-act rural sketch in which he played the role of Joshua Whitcomb, a Yankee farmer. By the time I saw it it had been expanded into a full-length play. The episode in it which remains most vividly in my memory was afterwards turned down when the piece became *The Old Homestead* and a highly moral entertainment, praised from many pulpits as a sermon against drunkenness. Uncle Josh was seen praying at the bedside of a poor woman; and during his devotions her drunken husband came reeling in. Uncle Josh abruptly rose from his knees, picked the bully up in his arms, and threw him out of the window; the property man dropped a box of glass behind the scenes to make an effective noise; while Uncle Josh knelt down and with much demonstration resumed his prayer. To a boy of ten, this episode seemed the pinnacle of humour.

THE DRAMA IN CANADA ◇

FREDERIC ROBSON

o

The Canadian Magazine *dealt with a range of cultural issues from "The Psychology of Gossip" to "The Canadian Militia," and "The Indian Tribes of Labrador." Writing in its May 1908 issue, Frederic Robson noted the growing popularity of theatre across the country but criticized audiences for their interest in only "namby-pamby novelty."*

When the late Sir Henry Irving was playing in Montreal some years ago a newspaper reporter, on the pretext of urgent business, slipped past the secretary and begged the privilege of an interview.

"Canada is familiar ground to you," remarked the reporter by way of breaking through the personal hedge.

"Fondly familiar," replied Sir Henry with his quaint smile, "I have seen this Canada, yours and mine, its plains and all those pictures through the mountains on the coast. Some day you will crown it all with a national drama, that's what you need next, a Canadian drama."

Unfortunately the Arts do not follow close in the waggon tracks of the pioneer, but we must know that pioneering is a past institution in a large section of Canada and yet we have given but few serious thoughts to the establishment of a national art and particularly that section with which the present article attempts to deal—the drama.

Any reader who has followed at all closely what the world is doing in all the branches of its life must have gathered that there is a distinctive English drama, one peculiarly French, Italian or German, and possibly a drama of more recent creation or adaptation that may pass under the name of American. But up here in Canada, we have, so far, to take the crumbs from our masters' tables. Canadians cannot be called a nation of theatre

◇ *The Canadian Magazine* 31 (May–Oct. 1908): 58–64.

lovers. Religious sentiment which once placed the theatre as an accompaniment of the downward path is of too recent existence to be suddenly uprooted by newer ideas and cast aside as unworthy. It is hard to turn a people from bitter opposition to mere scepticism in one generation. Harder still to make them the champions of the thing they once despised, but it is being done, and who can gainsay it?

With the weaning away from old ideas the new generation has come into a new belief that after all, the interpretation which the stage gives to stories of life is the most expressive we have yet found, and that in its transmission from the footlights to the auditor it does not carry the poison of a plague.

Granted, then, that the sentiment toward the theatre in Canada has undergone a change, the question comes—"Has any benefit accrued to the theatre?"

The influence has tended, one must admit, to a numerical increase in theatres and theatre-goers. Discrimination has not kept pace.

A new public, sons and daughters of a generation that tore the theatrical pages from the foreign magazines and burned them, lest they reach the eyes of the children of the home, have tossed aside tradition. They don't believe there is any harm in the theatre, and so they rush helter-skelter to the playhouse as soon as the white and gold doors are open. It doesn't matter what is inside. The idea is to get there and "take a chance." They little think that they are making the theatre what it is, that every sneer at the character of a play they have been disappointed in, is a jibe at their own folly. The public love to be "taken in." It is as true of theatrical management as it ever was of Barnum. You can draw a "house" with the *Broadway Maids*, which every man buying a ticket knows to be a fraud, when empty benches would greet Shakespeare, which every man in town knew before hand would prove a treat. It is one of the little corners of human freakishness which can some day stand explanation.

There has been a lapse of many years since Mrs. Morrison's playhouse in Toronto featured Fanny Davenport, but in the intervening time, who would say that there has been an appreciable advance in public theatrical ideals?

Surely the theatre is not to blame. If a public demanded *The Pilgrim's Progress* in four acts there would be a dozen managers able and willing to serve them with the allegory. If you do not see it at your local theatre it is a fairly accurate law to take, that the public of your own town does not want it.

"The uplift of the stage" is generally little more than a patronizing phrase glibly turned off the tongues of people who know nothing of its practical problems and at heart care less.

There is only one person who can uplift the stage, and that is the man or woman who lines up opposite the box office, but in nine cases out of ten, that man thinks so little of the quality of his amusement that his opinion is rendered negative or positively harmful.

It may strike the reader as very strange that the greatest dramatic works ever written, those of William Shakespeare, which would seem to require a trained mind to fathom them, are scorned as uninteresting in the best educated centres of Ontario, while they are taken up with eagerness by the farmers of the West and the miners of the Canadian mountain towns.

The further a people get from rock bottom primitive virtues, the further from simplicity of thought, the more they desire namby-pamby novelty in their amusements.

And there is plenty of proof that veneer in the heart demands veneer in religion, in friendships and amusements.

A strange contrast comes to mind that places the point of differing dramatic taste in a highly educated community and one rugged, simple, and without the frills of up-to-dateness.

As most people who have travelled through the West know, the theatres of the plains and through the mountains are not generally the lovely creations we have in Toronto and Montreal, and the travelling actor from Fort William westward must put up with inconveniences of no light order.

A Toronto actor, at one time head of the Conservatory's elocution department, was perhaps the first man to preach Shakespeare in the wilderness. In the face of opposition he set out with a small company, fought against ill-luck and misunderstanding and finally succeeded in establishing himself and his company as the recognized attraction of Western Canada. For six or seven years he brought the classic drama almost to the prairie door. Small audiences in this town or large in the other, adverse sentiment or plaudits, he prosecuted his classic mission, playing Shakespeare at every chance. And success came at last where it would have been denied in the East. And why? Was it not that the quiet customed people of the prairies and mountain towns, with loves and hates unfettered by imitation of others or what others did or said or had ever done, felt that in *Hamlet*, for instance, was given them a lens whereby their eyes beheld the philosophy of their own lives. Would it not be accurate to say that the peasant, full-blooded and with good intelligence, might gain vastly more from Shakespeare than the prince of keener intellect, but more pampered tastes? That is why Shakespeare "goes" in the west of Canada and the south and west of the United States while it falls flat in the middle districts; and these same middle districts of both countries generally claim a fair preponderance of discrimination and correct taste.

Since it is impossible from the smallness of the population and the widely scattered cities and towns to maintain companies in Canada playing only to Canadians and governed by Canadian taste, impossible for many years to have a Canadian "stage" or a Canadian drama, it would seem that the means of bringing Canadian dramatic taste up to a higher level and securing proper food to sweeten and make the taste a contented one, must come from a new direction. Formation of amateur societies is disputable as a remedy. Amateur societies meet so often for fun and vanity, so seldom for hard work. Earl Grey has done much to clear the way for better things. His annual competitions for dramatic societies encourage original and skilled work from amateur actors and playwrights the Dominion through. Happily His Excellency's idea is not "to reform the stage." He aims rather to encourage amateurs to interest themselves in the interpretation of plays purely for the personal benefit accruing from such efforts.

American theatrical managers regard the Canadian circuits as among the best paying on the continent. Take Kingston, Ont., a place regarded as one of the best one-night stands on the continent. London too gives a good paying audience; Hamilton turns out well; likewise Toronto and Winnipeg and Calgary and New Westminster, Vancouver and Victoria.

The same line might be followed through Quebec and the Maritime Provinces. So that it may be taken that the money of the Canadian theatre-going public is looked upon with desiring eyes by managers and syndicates in New York city, that centre where North America's dramatic diet is prepared and served out.

To take a hypothetical case, suppose that by dint of an educational campaign throughout Canada on the theatre and its proper function in a community people were brought to believe that the theatre was a Temple of the Drama and not a whirligig with hand organ music and fun for grown-up children, the dramatic horizon might quickly be swung round from murky skies to sunshine. The people would stay at home until a worthy production came to town, then flock to it until the sign of "Standing Room Only" would be a feature on the night of the true drama. And how long do you suppose the managerial lords would be in opening their eyes to the new conditions? The correction of public taste is an immense task, but it can be done and the first element that must be called upon is the Canadian newspaper. Why could not every newspaper boasting of independence of its business office, and these are not a few, come boldly into the field for a more abundant showing of brains at the local theatre and fewer of the travesties that pass before the public's eyes under the name of comic opera and melodrama. Why could they not do this? The newspapers are one of the theatre manager's greatest aids in getting the public's money. It isn't the display advertisements set up in a heavy-face that draw the crowds; it is the advance notice.

Nearly every newspaper gives in return for theatre tickets and advertising contracts, a certain amount of space to the local theatre manager in the news columns, wherein the latter is allowed to say almost what he pleases about a coming attraction, and the newspaper shoulders the responsibility for the accuracy of his statements.

For instance, pick up even our most reputable Canadian papers. There in a prominent place you see: "Greatest treat of the season—Mr. Blank, manager of the Blank opera house has completed arrangements for the appearance in this city of the famous operatic star—Miss Blank—in that most brilliant comedy of the season, So and So. The original cast has been retained, and the company will number 100 people. New York papers proclaim Miss Blank as the cleverest comedienne that has appeared on Broadway since the days of Miss So and So." Most of which the newspaper man knows is grossly exaggerated. Every newspaper editor who admits such copy must know for all intents and purposes his paper in printing such stuff is giving, not the statement of the advance agent but its own. If the *Daily News* or *Herald* of this city or that uses those advance notices without any advertising caption then these papers are backing up every word that is used.

Let one courageous newspaper begin the work of refusing to print advance notices that it cannot vouch for, and a score will follow—for imitation in journalism is not the needle in the haystack.

Unfortunately for Canada, dramatic critics are not to be plucked from every maple tree. Even were they abundant and possessed an appreciative sense, with good knowledge of dramatic technique and good means of expression, what newspaper would want them? How many newspapers would stand for candid criticism of the local theatre's offerings? Possibly ten in the whole Dominion. How many newspapers in the Dominion, no matter how willing to slash unworthy "shows," have at present dramatic columns of any appreciable value to readers? Possibly three.

If we can't have a Canadian stage for a while, let us do the next best thing: Tell the theatrical manager that we have changed our idea of the purpose of the theatre, and will only attend when that purpose is recognized and respected. Shakespeare should have no monopoly of the theatre. No, let us breed more Shakespeares, and to do that the stage should be open to every playwright so long as his ideas are good and his purpose sound.

And let the newspaper look to itself and do its part. Banish the false advance notice. Criticize the play when able to criticize—if not able, then let it alone: say nothing more than that it pleased or disappointed. Let all those harping on the theatre's degeneracy look to themselves and learn whether or not they are giving the dramatic toboggan a good start down hill. The theatre-goer who remains away from the play of merit does as much to kill all merit on the stage as the one who turns out to the melodrama or frothy comic opera.

It is *your* support that will lift up or drag down the present standing of the drama in Canada. It is *you* that this institution, possible of incalculable benefit to any country, looks in the present day for the nod of approval or the scowl that will determine the calibre of its future.

THE ANNEXATION
OF OUR STAGE[*]

BERNARD K. SANDWELL

o

Another major figure in Canadian cultural criticism during the first half of the twentieth century, Bernard K. Sandwell (1876–1954) was theatre critic for the Montreal Herald *(1900–14) and editor of* Saturday Night *(1932–51). In this essay written for* The Canadian Magazine *in 1911, he expressed his concern over the continuing control of Canadian professional stages by foreign syndicates and trusts.*

Some months ago I was discussing with a very intelligent and apparently somewhat talented Toronto girl the question of a theatrical career.

It was not my fault. I did not raise the subject, and never would. I know perfectly well that I know nothing about a theatrical career, except that some of the nicest people I ever met were in process of going through it. I know nothing about any career, as a matter of fact, except that of journalism, of which dramatic criticism is a small and unremunerative by-path. But a great many people still believe that a dramatic critic spends his entire time, when he is not asleep or sitting in an orchestra chair (or both), in associating with players and stage managers and authors in that glamorous realm known as "Behind the Scenes." They look at us as if they saw us "trailing clouds of glory" from that loftier sphere as we walk along the street. And they come to us for information about the perils and rewards of acting and the hygienic effects of tights or decolletage on a draughty stage.

I repeat that I know nothing of all these matters, and never discuss the question of a theatrical career if I can possibly help it. It does not matter how the discussion here alluded to arose, nor how it terminated. The point of interest about it lies exclusively in one remark of the intelligent Toronto

[*] *The Canadian Magazine* 38 (Nov. 1911–April 1912): 22–26.

girl, which, when I thought it over later, seemed to embody the protest of a young nation against the present condition of its stage.

"Do you know," she said, "that if it were possible to pursue a theatrical career here in Canada, in my own country, I would enter upon it tomorrow? As things are, the chief cause of my hesitation is the fact that I must go to a foreign country in order even to get an engagement; that I must play most, if not all, of my time in that foreign country; that I must make New York my headquarters, go the rounds of the New York managers, rehearse in New York, act the plays that New York wants, and by the time I get anywhere in my profession everybody, myself included, will have forgotten that I ever was a Canadian. It isn't fair!"

And is it fair, when you come to think of it?

If this Toronto girl had desired to take up any other art known to humanity, she could have practised it to her heart's content in Toronto, and if she were clever enough she could have made a good living at it, and could have remained with her own people all her life. Doubtless she would have had to study abroad; but that does not denationalise one. As painter, as writer, as musician, as sculptor, as poet, she could have held an honoured place in the community and helped to build up the culture of the nation to which she belonged. Only as actress was she obliged to expatriate herself. The nearest she could have come to that in Canada was the poor and unsatisfactory and half-way art of "recitation." And by the way, there are a lot of clever Canadian girls wasting their time on this infantile pursuit and announcing to bored audiences that "Curfew shall not ring tonight," who would be giving good impersonations in the legitimate drama if the way thereto did not lie beyond their means, beyond their courage, beyond the limits of their country and the helping hands of their friends.

There was a time when our brightest young people of both sexes and all vocations used to drift across to the big American cities. We have changed all that in every other walk of life. One must need big scope, indeed, if the Canadian field is not big enough now. There will always be a certain number of vaulting ambitions to whom leadership among ninety millions of people is more alluring than leadership among nine millions; and these will continue to drift across the line (except in so far as they will more and more go to England) until Canada is numerically, as well as potentially, one of the great nations of the earth. But I am talking about the ordinary people, who go in for an artistic career because they like the art and not because they expect to win undying fame. There are many such to whom the high-pressure life and dollar-saturated atmosphere of the big American centres is repellent, who would rather earn two thousand a year in Toronto or Montreal and save a fifth of it, or bring up a family in comfort, than earn five or ten thousand in New York and have to spend every cent of it in keeping up appearances. And there are some (and the number is growing as our national consciousness grows) who would rather be in Toronto or Montreal just because they are among their own people, because of a certain flag and certain songs, and because of a tune that is played at the end of the show and that brings everybody to his feet. Let us not wholly overlook or despise this latter class.

Canada is the only nation in the world whose stage is entirely controlled by aliens. She is the only nation in the world whose sons and daughters are compelled to go to a foreign capital for permission to act in their own language on the boards of their own theatres. The only road to the applause of a Toronto theatre audience is by way of Broadway. The Montreal girl who wants to show her own people that she can act must sign an agreement with a New York manager.

Is it not time that Canadians bethought themselves of this matter and took steps to amend it? I am not concerned to denounce the American theatrical trusts, syndicates, or whatever you like to call them. They have done good work for the American stage, and in the present state of economic development in the United States they are the only machinery by which a large part of the country's theatrical business could be carried on. What is chiefly wrong with each and every one of them is that they are all aiming, not at giving better shows or even at doing better business than their rivals, but at putting their rivals out of business. None of them can get it out of their heads that the theatres of the United States should be one vast monopoly, and that anybody who is trying to get a share of the theatrical trade should be exterminated. That is bad for art and bad for the United States; but I am not concerned even with that. The Americans are quite competent to look after it themselves.

What I am concerned with is the fact that Canada is included in the area for which these vast organisations are fighting; that Ontario is as much tributary to the offices on either side of Broadway as is Minnesota, and that British Columbia is parcelled out like New Jersey. It was against this condition in matters of trade that Canadians revolted, at considerable self-sacrifice, but with excellent ultimate results, a generation or two ago; and, though our utilitarians are too blind to see it, it is quite as bad for our national life that our arts should be administered from foreign soil as that our industrial needs should be supplied by aliens.

Americans with whom I have discussed this matter pooh-pooh the idea that there is any need for a separate Canadian stage. Imbued with that sublime continentalism which still prevents most of our neighbours from seeing that there can be anything on this continent that does not arise out of the Declaration of Independence, they assure us that if there were a Canadian stage it would merely be a feeble imitation of the American. They tell us that our mentality is the same as their own, that our social and economic conditions are the same, that our plays and our acting (if we had any) would be the same.

Under all these broad assertions there is a stratum of truth and a stratum of untruth. It is true that at the present time we have no plays of our own, for the excellent reason that we have no machinery for producing them; and it is true that we manage to rub along with the supply of plays that our neighbours send us, for the equally excellent reason that we have to. It is true that we are, like the Americans, very new, rather crude, very materialistic and a trifle pleased with ourselves. But we are not Americans, in spite of the fact that we live in North America. We are not, as the Americans are, upon this continent for the purpose of carrying out certain vast experiments, of testing certain far-reaching theories concerning man, property and the State. The Americans decided to abandon all the traditions of the Old World as being outworn and useless; many of us Canadians (I speak in a hereditary sense) are here because we did not believe in those experiments, and because we did not want to abandon the traditions of the Old World; and all of us accept the best of those traditions, the social and economic and political traditions developed in the British Isles, as being amply good enough for the conduct of affairs in our particular section of this continent. The American mind looks on American life as an inventor looks on a new machine, which he has just completed, and the workings of which he finds absorbingly interesting; he is quite sure that if he doesn't like the way it runs he can fix it up. The Canadian mind does not conceive of Canadian life as a thing absolutely apart, quite new and different; but rather as a part of the natural development of the human race, as a section of Life in general. Conceived in that way, it is much too big and automatic a thing to be tinkered with. The popular American play deals with trusts and civic "rings" and new "fake" religions and the tariff and the income tax and the Supreme Court and the Senate. The popular Canadian play does not exist, but I cannot imagine any Canadian wanting to put the Cement Company or the Manufacturers' Association or a Montreal alderman or the Winnipeg segregation district or the Farmers Bank into a play; we are interested in all these subjects, but not in that way, not as subjects of art. And if we are not profoundly interested in our own problems when they get on the stage it is preposterous to expect us to be interested in those of the American Republic.

As a matter of fact, our difference from our neighbours in point of theatrical taste is becoming obvious to us already, however unwilling they may be to see or admit it. The performances which make the deepest impression upon a Canadian audience, out of those which Broadway kindly permits us to see, are those which are nearest to the best English standard; those which make least impression are those which are most acutely American. "The Nigger" [an American drama by Clyde Fitch], sent up here by a centralised management, which does not know Canada from Kansas, merely disgusted Canadians. "The City," undoubtedly the strongest play that the United States has produced, made but little impression. I am far from declaring that our taste is identical with that of England; that were as foolish as to assert that it is identical with that of New York. There is much about the English drama that rather wearies us, chiefly its eternal concern with the leisured few and contemptuous disregard of the very existence of the working many. One reason for the enormous success of "The Passing of the Third Floor Back" in Canada, and to a lesser extent in the United States, too, was the fact that it dealt with people who were not socially superior to everybody in the audience. But the English drama is our drama to a far greater extent than is the American, and the more the American stage neglects the English drama and exalts the American, the more will Canadians have occasion to revolt against the monopolising of the Canadian stage by American bookings.

One of the first things to be done for the rescue of the Canadian stage from this unpatriotic condition is a thing which is beyond the power of

Canadians to promote, except as some of the more influential of us can make representations to the dramatic authors of Great Britain. This is the abolition of the practice of selling the Canadian rights along with the American rights to the same New York producer. It is at this moment impossible for Canadians to see any one of half the most important plays produced in London in the last ten years without the consent of Mr. Frohman, while the other half are controlled by other gentlemen only a little less conspicuous on Broadway. Mr. John Edward Hoare, in a recent article on "A Canadian Theatre," named six leading English dramatists, four of whom are absolutely unknown to Canada, while the other two are known only by comparatively early works—Galsworthy, Granville Barker, Besier, Arnold Bennett, Barrie, and Pinero. Barrie is the great drawing card of the British drama on this continent; and Mr. Frohman owns Barrie for America, body and soul, pen and output. He owns most of Pinero. As to who owns the other four I do not know; but I do know that if they have any commercial value for America their Canadian rights have been sold long ago. The chief hope for Canada would lie in the possibility that the new English writers may have no American value, the American public being too absorbed in its own drama to pay much attention to anybody else. In that case there would be a possibility of some enterprising Canadian securing the right to give their works in Canada alone—a possibility which would be contingent upon his being able to find theatres to give them in and people to perform them.

Canada is becoming a large and theatre-loving country in these twentieth century days. It should not be difficult to persuade the English dramatist that it is worth his while to hold back his Canadian rights when handing his American rights over to a Broadway producer, and to sell the former only to somebody who will undertake to give him a certain number of performances in the Dominion. For if the American contempt for English plays goes on increasing, and the Canadian appreciation of them remains constant while the Canadian theatrical field continues to grow, we shall end by having the more profitable half of the continent so far as the English author is concerned. And as soon as the Canadian performing rights of everything worth performing are no longer held in the grip of Broadway, there arises the possibility of a Canadian producing business, specialising on plays which the Canadian public want, and, at the same time, affording the opportunity of Canadian employment to my young Toronto friend who started all these wandering thoughts. In ten years we shall have as many theatre-goers in Canada as the United States had when it produced Edwin Booth—for the percentage of theatre-goers to population is treble what it was in those puritan days. Is it possible to believe that we shall still be an appendage of a foreign stage, that Canadians who seek to follow one of the noblest and most national of arts will still have to seek permission in a foreign city, of an alien "trust," in order to do so?

THEATREGOING,
CHRISTMAS 1913 ◇

RAYMOND MASSEY

○

A well-known stage and film actor, especially in the United States, Raymond Massey (1896–1973) grew up in Canada. Brother of Vincent Massey, a future governor-general, he recalled his theatre-going experiences as a teenager in this excerpt from his autobiography, When I Was Young.

There were two theatres in Toronto that booked the Shubert and Klaw and Erlanger touring shows from New York. These bookings also included tours of English stars direct from London. The Princess and the recently built Royal Alexandra would both be open for continuous seasons of nine months and more, with the best plays of Broadway and the West End of London with the top stars playing in them. In one year, I saw Otis Skinner, Nat Goodwin, David Warfield, Nazimova, Holbrook Blinn, Martin Harvey, John Drew, Ethel Barrymore, George Arliss, William Faversham and Tyrone Power, the elder. It was the heyday of the "road." There was no indigenous professional theatre in Canada at that time. Although father didn't go to the theatre and my stepmother didn't want to, he staked me to quite a few plays when I was home.

In one miraculous week during the Christmas holidays of 1913, I saw E.H. Sothern and Julia Marlowe at the Princess Theatre in *Hamlet, Romeo and Juliet,* and *Macbeth*; and at the Royal Alexandra, Forbes-Robertson and Gertrude Elliott in *Hamlet, The Passing of the Third Floor Back* and *Caesar and Cleopatra*. Both Hamlets were wonderful and the prince was played with full poetic values by men with voices like violoncellos. Each star was in his sixties but that didn't trouble anyone. The new style, a youthful Hamlet

---

◇ *When I Was Young* (Boston and Toronto: Little Brown, 1976), 85–89.

with the psychological gimmicks and the Freudian overtones—such as perhaps my own performance—was still in the future. Sothern and Marlowe
certainly would not have satisfied current demands that Shakespeare's ill-
starred lovers, Romeo and Juliet, be played by naked children, but they
gave delight to audiences of 1913.

I was riding on a cloud that week. My father had seen *The Passing of the
Third Floor Back* in Toronto years before with mother. It was the only stage
play he had ever seen, and he had loved it. It was a contemporary morality
play by Jerome K. Jerome, who also wrote *Three Men in a Boat*. Nowadays
such a play would be laughed off the stage but I shared father's enthusiasm.
He made me tell him all about it when I got home from the matinee. I think
he couldn't bear to see it again, or any play for that matter. If mother had
lived, it might have been different.

Sir Johnston Forbes-Robertson and his wife, Gertrude Elliott, had just
completed a short season of nine of their great successes at the Shubert
Theatre on Broadway and the repertoire had been reduced to three plays
for the road. Lady Forbes-Robertson retained the role of Ophelia rather than
that of Gertrude which she would have played magnificently but Sir
Johnston wisely thought his Ophelia must have a balanced maturity. After
all, when Hamlet is in the mid-sixties, he can't address such lines as
"Nymph, in thy orisons, be all my sins remembered" to a child with a lol-
lipop! The third play in the road repertory was *Caesar and Cleopatra*, which
Bernard Shaw had written for the Forbes-Robertsons a decade previously.
In this revival the stars were superb. Shaw had supplied them both with
fresh characters which they played with astonishing skill. This play made a
deep impression on me.

Fourteen years later, my first starring engagement was with their
daughter, Jean Forbes-Robertson, in a revival of *The Constant Nymph* in
London.

Sitting in the balcony of the Royal Alex, watching the Shaw play, I
hoped the future would hold many more such enchantments. I lay awake
that night hoping that while I would be busy making and selling binders,
mowers, harrows, plows, cream separators and the like, there would be
plays I could see like *Caesar and Cleopatra*, *Romeo and Juliet* and *Hamlet*. But I
didn't think of acting in them. I was going to try to be like my grandfather,
an implement man.

There were two burlesque theatres in town. The Gaiety played the
Columbia Circuit shows. Father did not include the Gaiety in his program
of drama for me but for 40 cents I would surreptitiously pursue my studies
of the burlesque art form. I was well rewarded for my clandestine patronage. Burlesque in those prewar days was lusty and honest bawdry at its
comic best, before the strip-teasers ruined it and replaced laughs with leers.

Burlesque bore no comparison to any other form of entertainment anywhere. It was really "only in America"; it was unique. It died because it lost
its honesty. But what fun it was while it lasted! Vaudeville too was at its
zenith then. At Shea's Theatre twice daily there were ten good acts, with
headliners like Nora Bayes and Houdini and often "legit" stars such as

David Warfield slumming in a dramatic sketch for ten weeks of variety. In a scant ten years the movies would obliterate live vaudeville.

Then there was the old Grand Theatre which always seemed to be showing an Irish musical with Chauncey Olcott. It also booked the great magic shows such as Thurston's and the good old melodramas. I doubt if any melodrama ever offered at the Grand could top the case of its manager. Ambrose Small, the charred remains of whose body were found in the furnace of the theatre. The crime was never solved.

For a city of about three hundred thousand, there was good theatre of every kind in Toronto.

The theatre wasn't exactly forgotten at school. Beside horses, Mr. Powell and I had another common interest. He was as stagestruck as I. But whereas I was merely a fanatical theatre-goer, he had ambitions for a stage career. He had confided to me in June, 1914, that he thought he would give schoolmastering one more year and then try his luck as an actor in England. He knew a number of people in the English theatre, actors and producers, and he was a talented amateur actor himself. It wouldn't be too risky a venture. But he never made the attempt for he died of wounds in 1918 after four years of active service with the Gunners.

In my last winter term at Appleby, Mr. Powell staged an ambitious production of Goldsmith's *She Stoops to Conquer*. The new gymnasium, to replace the old one destroyed by the fire, was not yet complete and we performed the play in the Oakville Town Hall to two capacity houses of paying customers. This was the second production of the Appleby Dramatic Society, the first having been an attempt at a Victorian farce called *Ici On Parle Français* in the old gym, which nearly put an end to theatre at Appleby. Even doting parents admitted that not only was our effort bad, it was "godawful." Like some other minor disasters in my past, the production of *Ici On Parle Français* left me in a state of shock. A merciful amnesia has blocked all memory of what was in truth my first encounter with the theatre.

She Stoops to Conquer was a much different experience. I knew the play, having seen Annie Russell and Oswald Yorke act the Hardcastles, father and daughter, in their repertory of the two Sheridan comedies and Oliver Goldsmith's play which had come to Toronto the previous year. When Mr. Powell had suggested *She Stoops* for our winter term production of 1914, it seemed a perfect selection. Mr. Powell worked with his cast for the entire term and although the majority approached the production with some reluctance, suspecting that the project was an English class in disguise, Mr. P's enthusiasm was so infectious, and his skill as a director so effective, that all misgivings were soon dispelled. He himself played Squire Hardcastle to perfection, supported by another master, Mr. Price, in the part of the Squire's crony. A boy named Aubrey Turquand gave a comic performance of Tony Lumpkin which character can easily become an egregious bore. The rest of the cast was adequate. The female parts were played by boys on the assumption that the eighteenth-century belles of Goldsmith's comedy had very large feet and spoke in husky contralto tones.

It happened that the McKenna Costume Company of Toronto possessed the wardrobe of a company that had been marooned at the Grand while touring in an Irish light opera. As it was an eighteenth-century period piece, we were at least properly garbed.

I cannot say that my first stage appearance (I refuse to count *Ici On Parle Français*) fired me with any theatrical ambition. I played Young Marlow and I wasn't good. I loved the theatre but I preferred to be out front. I couldn't stand not being a "pro." This feeling lasted through my subsequent amateur stage experience.

It was June, 1914, and suddenly my schooldays were over. The last cricket match had been played, the last prefect's meeting had been held in Mr. Guest's study, and John Harlan was chosen to succeed me as head prefect.

I had been in Toronto three days writing my Honour Matriculation exams and then in Cobourg for a day where I had been invited to ride an entry in one of the jumping classes of the Horse Show. The owner of my mount was a horsey old lady, a friend of my brother's. To console me for a poor performance (I had a fall), she took me to tea at a nearby farm with some friends of hers.

"Their name is Tracy and they won't have been at the horse show. They only like working horses. You'll meet a perfectly lovely girl who's staying with them. She's from Buffalo."

The young lady from Buffalo was the most beautiful creature I had ever seen. She had a musical voice. Tall and dark, she had eyes like my mother's, big and far apart.

Her name was Katharine Cornell. All my life I have automatically forgotten the names of people I meet but hers was an exception. Miss Cornell, at Mrs. Tracy's request, took me to see the cow barns that housed the Guernsey herd, the pride of the Tracy farm. Miss Cornell and the cows evinced a mutual disdain.

Miss Cornell asked me what I was going to be.

"I think I'll make farming machinery or something."

She looked through and beyond the cows. "I'm going to New York next fall. I shall become a professional actress. On the stage."

With that pronouncement, so calm and determined, I knew that the cows and grandfather and the family business were not for me, not for the long pull anyway. Somehow, somewhere, sometime, I would be a professional actor and act with Katharine Cornell . . . on Broadway.

That dream remained my secret for a long time. Twenty-six years later I starred with Kit Cornell on Broadway in the first of three plays.

IBSEN IN WINNIPEG
c. 1914 ⋄

RUTH HARVEY

○

From 1907 through the early 1930s, the 1798 seat Walker Theatre in Winnipeg was western Canada's largest and most opulent theatre. Built by C.P. Walker and affiliated with the Theatre Syndicate in New York as its northern-most stop, many stars were seen there in everything from Shakespearean classics to Henrik Ibsen's avant-garde dramas. The following is an excerpt from Curtain Time, *recollections of growing up in this Winnipeg theatre family, written by Walker's daughter, Ruth Harvey.*

"Ibsen!" mamma would mutter to herself, much as papa would exclaim "actors!" " I wish he'd never been born!"

When we heard that, we knew she had another play to read. Sometimes it seemed as if half the people in town were writing plays and bringing them to her to criticize for them. Papa thought it must be an awful chore, but my mother said that actors ought to be the very last to turn up their noses at would-be playwrights, because it was an old theatre saying that—

> Every dog has his day,
> And every actor has his play.

So mamma, conscientious and hopeful, read carefully every play that was sent to her—even the hand-written manuscript of a tragedy in five acts of blank verse about Boadicea. This one caught my interest because I was just beginning British History at school, and I asked mamma if Boadicea had a blue bottom.

"A blue what?"

⋄ *Curtain Time* (Boston: Houghton Mifflin, 1949), 250–55, 291–94.

"Bottom," I repeated. "The ancient Britons used to paint their bottoms blue. Does the play tell that Boadicea had a blue one?"

"The play doesn't give a hint of it," mamma said. "I think it would be cuter if it did. But perhaps it wouldn't suit blank verse. I don't believe there's any use suggesting it to the author."

She always wrote polite and detailed notes of appreciation to the authors, adding the advice that they take every opportunity to go to the theatre and so improve their knowledge of stagecraft. Papa laughed at this, saying it was a crude way of drumming up trade, but mamma was sincere. She loved to read plays, but she had no use for plays intended only to be read, for closet drama. She bristled when, for example, anyone said it was better to read Shakespeare's plays than to see them acted. A play, to her, was a score for actors; if it wasn't that, it wasn't a play at all. People who wanted to write plays ought to go to the theatre to learn, she said, and her chief complaint about her amateur playwrights was that they wrote as if they had never seen a play later than Dion Boucicault.

But then Nazimova came in a repertory of Ibsen. Within a few months mamma was reaping the harvest.

"It is amazing," she would say, waving the latest manuscript, "how they can get so much of the gloom with none of the technique."

Or: "They all end now with a door slamming."

"Ibsen!" she would snort, sometimes adding viciously, "I wish he had died before he wrote *Ghosts!*"

Then we knew the Doctor had written another play.

The Doctor was a really arduous playwright. At first he had seemed like the others, willing to write one play and let it go at that, but then Ibsen had come to him like a revelation—Ibsen and Ibsen's Oswald. He was inspired to put his knowledge of medicine into drama. The prospect for plays was almost illimitable—there were all the ills that flesh is heir to. The organs were just waiting to be dramatized. The lungs had already been used superficially by a layman in *La Dame aux Camellias*. But no matter!— there were plenty of others to choose for protagonists. The heart, no longer the old-fashioned seat of the emotions, but a physical thing and malfunctioning. The liver, diseased. The gall bladder, with stones. The stomach, with ulcers. Better still, rare diseases, exotic ailments, entrancing curiosities for the connoisseur. And they would not be given the vulgar comic treatment that Molière, who hated doctors, had given them. There would be no slapstick or horseplay, no burlesque physicians with their servants bearing oversized lancets and vials and clystères. It would all be proper and serious, for Ibsen had shown him the way.

In his first play the hero was stricken with locomotor ataxia. But that was just a beginning. Pathology abounded in plots that the Doctor fitted swiftly into three acts. They weren't great plays, but they weren't dull. Mamma read them all with morbid fascination, and retold them with relish to papa at dinnertime. Papa was appalled. He said he wouldn't dare read them, that they would make him ill. I believe he was right. He had a horror of physical pain, and one play of the Doctor's would have been enough to send him to his bed with no definable symptoms but with a fearsome general feeling of impending doom. If mamma had been at all neurotic she would never have survived them, and we noticed, when the Doctor had begun to work on some diseases more than usually horrible and contagious, that mamma would no sooner return the manuscript than she would rush an order to the store for chloride of lime for the garbage cans and have the maid flush down all the drains in the house with a strong solution of carbolic.

One day in the very midst of this Ibsen era along came a play from a new author, and when mamma opened the envelope she began to grin.

"Listen to this, Con," she said. "This is refreshing. It's called *Tinkling Bells in the Haunted Valley*. Now that's a promising title!"

She didn't look into the manuscript but set it on the table and regarded it speculatively, as if it were a puzzle that she wanted to work out for herself.

"It doesn't sound a bit Ibsenish. It wouldn't be another *Doll's House*. Or another *Ghosts*. *Tinkling Bells in the Haunted Valley*? . . ."

Suddenly her face fell.

"It might . . . Lord, I'll bet anything it's just another *Peer Gynt*!"

Occasionally, afterwards, I would hear mamma repeating that title and chuckling over it, and of all the plays sent to her then this is the only title I can remember. And it was all I ever knew of the manuscript. But I still feel, as mamma did, its ridiculous fascination. Every once in a while I find myself thinking about it—*Tinkling Bells in the Haunted Valley!*—and wondering what on earth it was about.

Mamma couldn't do much to help these amateur playwrights except to cheer them, give them a little advice, lend them books on the theatre, and furnish them with the names of New York producers to whom they might submit their plays. Now and again, through her recommendation, she could get an especially good one produced by local amateurs.

But mamma did do a great deal for amateur actors. The English tradition of amateur theatricals was strong in Canada. Every town of any size had at least one flourishing club devoted to putting on plays and one amateur operatic society, and each year these groups gathered in one of the larger cities of the Dominion to compete for the trophies awarded by the Governor General. Mamma's first try at directing amateurs was with a production of Planquette's melodious old opera, *The Chimes of Normandy*, and it carried off the musical trophy in the competition. The town was rich in well-trained singers and instrumentalists, and mamma could give their performances some of the finish and vim of professional productions. A series of other light operas followed. Then plays, for the University Dramatic Society and other groups—plays by Barrie, Henry Arthur Jones, Björnstjerne Björnson, Granville-Barker, Lord Dunsany. For years hardly a season passed that she did not direct at least one ambitious amateur production, sometimes several.

Mamma got on well with amateurs. For one thing, she never felt superior to them—she considered that she was an amateur director herself. For another, she never tried for too subtle effects and she geared her direction to the experience and abilities of her players, as well as taking her acting materials into consideration when she selected a play. The choice of a play was a ticklish business. A certain type of society comedy—high comedy carried not so much by action and situation as by sparkling dialogue—seemed to have an irresistible charm for amateur play-reading committees. This was something mamma deplored and she would try tactfully to steer them from that course. She hadn't the half-educated idea that a bad tragedy is more worthy than a good comedy. She respected high comedy so much that it irked her to see it done by most amateurs, for she thought it was far too difficult for them.

"When they try to play one of these smart comedies, their only idea for stage business is to light cigarettes and puff them, and they turn their backs to the audience and mutter all their lines upstage," she would complain. "They think then they are being modern and subtle, when they're just being fidgety and inaudible."

It was dull for the audience, she said, but the players were having a lovely time. They liked to dress in elegant clothes and say the bright, epigrammatic lines. It made them feel chic and witty. Oh, well, some good might come of it. Playing witty rôles might eventually help to improve their everyday conversation. That idea was not without its precedent. After all, there had been the case, in the time of Charles the Second, of the actress who insisted on playing only virtuous rôles—and was very near being kept chaste by it. . . .

)

. . . Papa never forgot the first time he had gone to New York and suggested to a manager there that he send his company to Winnipeg.

"Winnipeg!" The manager said it with disbelief and derision. "How do they get there—by dog sled? What do they play in—an igloo?"

Now my father's booking chain of theatres stretched across the prairies into the foothills of the Rockies and companies from New York could move from Minneapolis into the circuit through the towns of the Red River Valley, and so north to Winnipeg and on through western Canada, playing Regina, Saskatoon, Lethbridge, Calgary and Edmonton. And now that there were cities enough to warrant the expense of an ocean crossing, more and more English companies embarked on trans-Canadian tours. The West was young, cheerful, prosperous, and eager for the theatre. The smaller towns were no longer one-night stands. Each was well able to support even a very expensive production for a half-week, and in Winnipeg a company played for a full week, often for two weeks. Our seasons were booked solid from August to June.

This circuit represented the northern limit to which touring companies traveled. It lay on the edge of wilderness, with nothing beyond it but a scattering of villages, then forest, tundra, Hudson's Bay and the Arctic Ocean. Winnipeg, its most eastern city, was two thousand miles by rail from New York, and twice as far from London. But there was no need then to go to New York or London to enjoy the theatre. The shows came to us.

In two typical seasons, from 1912 to 1914, my father's red date books shows a great variety of entertainment. Among the stars who came to our theatre then were Maude Adams, John Mason, Blanche Bates, Raymond Hitchcock, William Crane, De Wolf Hopper, Madge Kennedy, Margaret Illington, May Robson, Chauncey Olcott, Holbrook Blinn, William Faversham, Lenore Ulric, Lewis Waller, Sir Johnstone Forbes-Robertson, Laurence Irving, Mrs. Pat Campbell, Marie Tempest, Cyril Maude, Otis Skinner, Mrs. Leslie Carter, William Hodge, Fred Stone, Elsie Janis. . . .

If you had been living in Winnipeg during those two years you could have seen comedies, dramas, farces and tragedies. There had been new plays and old: *Bought and Paid For, Polly of the Circus,* Maeterlinck's *The Blue Bird,* Shaw's *Pygmalion,* Barrie's *Peter Pan.* And plays by Wilde, Pinero, Henry Arthur Jones and Clyde Fitch. There had been many productions of Shakespeare: Mantell had played *King John, Macbeth, King Lear* and *The Merchant of Venice*; Faversham had come in *Julius Caesar*; Madge Titheradge and Lewis Waller had brought *Henry the Fifty* and *Romeo and Juliet*; Forbes-Robertson had played *Hamlet.* To the thousands of youngsters who saw these productions Shakespeare was no longer a school task. It was poetry and color and drama. The plays had come alive.

And in these same typical seasons our theatre had offered plenty of music. There had been a procession of musical comedies and comic operas, from Gilbert and Sullivan to *The Merry Widow, The Prince of Pilsen, The Chocolate Soldier, Naughty Marietta* and *High Jinks.* Sometimes these musical shows would have some famous star like Elsie Janis or Raymond Hitchcock; sometimes they were road companies, but they were well cast and produced and many younger players rose to fame in them. (For instance, I have forgotten who played the lead in *The Quaker Girl* in New York, but I remember the delightful girl who played it in the "second" company that came to us. She was slender, honey-blonde, and very young. Her name was Ina Claire.)

In those same two seasons we had Grand Opera, too. An American Company came with several Verdi operas and the *Bohemian Girl* and *Martha.* The fine Quinlan Grand Opera Company from London stayed at the theatre for two weeks and presented fifteen operas: *Aïda, Faust, Samson and Delilah, Tales of Hoffman, Lohengrin, Tannhauser, The Flying Dutchman, The Mastersingers, Tosca, Madame Butterfly, La Boheme, Rigoletto, The Girl of the Golden West,* and *Louise.* The Minneapolis Symphony Orchestra came to the theatre each spring for a series of concerts, and sprinkled through the season were many recitals, among them ones by John McCormick, Nordica and Maggie Teyte.

Moreover, theatregoing was not expensive. A $2.50 top was a high price scale. My father believed in keeping prices down and you could always get into the gallery—as he intended when he planned the theatre—for twenty-five cents!

So it had been going on for years, and so it would continue for many years longer. But I have cited these particular seasons because they, perhaps more than any others, represent the very heyday of the Road. And because they also mark the end of an era. . . .

MARGARET ANGLIN:
STAR OF CANADA ◊

S. MORGAN-POWELL

o

Theatre critic for the Montreal Star *from 1907 to 1942, Samuel Morgan-Powell was a formidable critic at a time when Montreal was a regular stop for Broadway tryouts. An active supporter of Canadian talent, he recalled in his 1929 memoir,* Memoires That Live, *the enormous talents of actress Margaret Anglin.*

Canada has not yet learned that the practice of scoffing at native artists is no longer fashionable. There are a few Canadians who have made their way in one branch or another of the world of art and who have met with general recognition through the Dominion. But in the main the charge of neglect must stand. There are too many proofs to permit of any argument that it is unjustified. The excuse that the population of the country is not sufficiently large to permit of an artist attaining success here is, of course, fatuous, but it is still advanced by many people. What they would say to any rejoinder that artists who have established their claim to recognition beyond any point of doubt find indifference when they come to their native land once more, it is difficult to discern. Yet the spectacle has been witnessed repeatedly during the past forty years of Canadians who have won distinction abroad coming home only to find their own people studiously cold, or unappreciative, or chillingly indifferent to their work.

This attitude cannot but reflect upon the capacity of Canadians to appreciate art in its various manifested forms. If our cleverest authors, painters, sculptors, actresses, singers and instrumentalists, after hard work and notable achievement, come back to us and are met with a reception that

---

◊ *Memories That Live* (Toronto: The Macmillan Company of Canada, 1929), 76–88.

indicates nothing so clearly as doubt, it is not surprising if they metaphorically shake the dust of Canada from off their feet.

The case of Margaret Anglin is one of the most striking instances of our neglect of great talent among our own people after that talent has been established and proved in a dozen brilliant ways beyond our own borders. Miss Anglin for many years has been certain of a hearty welcome and intelligent appreciation of her work and art anywhere on the North American continent outside of this Dominion. Yet she is a native of Canada, and has always held her own country in affection. She has won the plaudits of the Australian theatre-going public. (And in this connection it may well be noted that Australia, with a much smaller population, shows a very much keener appreciation of good drama than we do in this country.)

Miss Anglin is popular, personally. She has many friends here, and of Montreal, where she spent her girlhood and was educated, she retains many vivid recollections, and has renewed many school-day friendships on her all too rare visits to that city. New York has always loved her. Boston has delighted in her art. California has given her tempestuous welcome when she has appeared in Greek tragedy in the magnificent open-air theatre at Berkeley. Only Canada could never be bothered to attend the theatre to see her. The fact is inexplicable,—painfully so. It is an unpleasant reflection upon Canadian taste and judgment.

For Margaret Anglin has been a brilliant actress. I say that advisedly. It is not merely an expression of my own opinion. It is also the opinion held by the greater number of the most experienced dramatic critics on this continent; and it is endorsed by many of the most experienced artists on the English-speaking stage. Some have preferred her best in comedy; others in tragedy. But of her brilliance all have been convinced, and to her versatility all have borne testimony,—a testimony won by hard and unrelenting study, painstaking effort, indefatigable devotion to her art, and a courage that survived many disappointments and triumphed over many obstacles.

If Margaret Anglin attained a position of great distinction on the stage, she has had Canada to thank for absolutely nothing. This country never gave her the slightest encouragement; it has never even given her the satisfaction of a general recognition of her success. She triumphed in spite of all that. The fact is one that may well give Canadians who claim to be devoted to the advancement of art cause for serious thought.

The story of Miss Anglin's career affords the best possible refutation of the oft-repeated calumny that success on the stage cannot be achieved by legitimate means. Her success was won by merit only, without the aid of influence or of any extraneous favourable circumstances. She worked every bit of the way up the ladder, and she attained success because real merit cannot be kept down in the theatre, if the artist has perseverance.

Whether it is lucky to be born in a building devoted to the passage of a country's laws is a moot point, but Miss Anglin enjoys the unique distinction of having been the only Canadian ever born in the Houses of Parliament in Ottawa. Her father was Speaker of the House in 1879, and her arrival was the occasion for a great deal of good-natured celebration around the quarters of Mr. Speaker. She was educated in a Montreal convent, and on the occasion of her last professional visit to Montreal, in 1914, she paid a visit to her old school and renewed acquaintance with some of the nuns still there. When and why she made up her mind to be an actress, I have never been able to ascertain, but she admits that the idea was present from her earliest recollection.

She went straight from the convent to the Empire Dramatic School in New York, then run in connection with the Empire Theatre, and after a very brief period of study there she was fortunate in attracting the attention of the late Charles Frohman. It was the custom of the school to give performances from time to time which were largely attended by the prominent producers of the day in search of promising new material. Mr. Frohman, a keen judge of latent talent, made no mistake when he offered a girl of eighteen, with but a few months of dramatic study to her credit, the role of Madeleine West in his touring production of "Shenandoah." She jumped at the chance, and so began a career which was to see a wide variety of work and an equally varied succession of triumphs—on the stage of the old Academy of Music in New York, 1894.

That was the beginning,—an auspicious one for a young student, but also one that put her on her mettle and was in the nature of a severe and trying test. Miss Anglin was fortunate in her early years in that she served under several exacting taskmasters, all of them men of wide knowledge and unquestioned talent, whose companies proved valuable schools of experience for the young and ambitious artist. For Miss Anglin was ambitious, though she never seems to have entertained any foolish ideas about a sudden rise to fame overnight. That sort of thing generally takes place on the screen—and at Hollywood.

James O'Neill gave her the first Shakespearean role she ever played—Ophelia, at twenty, and then Virginia. She was in E.H. Sothern's company also; and then the keen-eyed Richard Mansfield engaged her for the part of Roxane in his production of "Cyrano de Bergerac," which will still be recalled by many as one of the notable artistic triumphs of the 'nineties in New York.

Five years after Frohman had picked her out for the Shenandoah part she returned to his banner, this time as leading lady in his stock company at the Empire Theatre,—an organization which did a notable service to dramatic art in America and through whose ranks many of the most prominent and successful actors and actresses on the American stage passed at one period or another of its existence. Miss Anglin remained at the Empire for four years, and during that time she naturally had a very varied and useful experience in strongly contrasted roles.

It is a curious fact that even then she was not decided herself as to whether she liked comedy or tragedy best, or in which special métier her particular talent found best expression. Henry Miller, with whom she became acquainted in 1903, evidently thought highly of her ability in every direction, for with him she appeared in such widely different plays as "The Devil's Disciple," "Camille," "The Aftermath," "The Taming of Helen," and

"Cyntina." Her greatest successes were achieved in roles calling for subtle comedy. She had the poise, the keen intelligence to differentiate between obvious methods and refined methods, and a very appealing feminine touch that remained with her throughout her career and has always been one of the charms of her individual art.

Very wisely, I think, Miss Anglin did not disdain stock engagements. She played in stock in San Francisco, and thus obtained experience in roles such as "The Marriage of Kitty," "The Lady Paramount" (Henry Harland's exquisite comedy), and "The Second Mrs. Tanqueray." When she returned to New York it was with a broader art, a wider command of the subtleties of histrionics, and a greater confidence; also, a repertoire which enabled her to discuss terms with producers and managers on a much more satisfactory basis than she would otherwise have been able to do.

Then came the engagement that brought her name most prominently before the theatre-going public of America and gave her national fame—that of Ruth Jordan in "The Great Divide." In it she renewed her partnership with Henry Miller, and that partnership was destined to bring both of them a very substantial meed of prosperity. A brief engagement with Lena Ashwell, the well-known English actress, in which she and Miss Ashwell alternated the roles of Lady Eastney and Mrs. Dane in "Mrs. Dane's Defense," served still further to enhance her reputation by virtue of the comparison it instituted and the brilliant character of her acting in both roles.

More than a year with "The Great Divide" took Miss Anglin all over the continent in a comprehensive tour, and after creating the role of Helena Ritchie in the play "The Awakening of Helena Ritchie," she made her first venture outside this continent and set sail for Australia, where she was accorded an enthusiastic welcome she had never experienced in her native land, and where she played a highly attractive repertoire and first indulged in her dream to interpret Shakespearean heroines.

It was as Katherine in "The Taming of the Shrew," and as Viola in "Twelfth Night," that Miss Anglin first appealed to Australian audiences. Mr. Williamson, the famous Australian impressario, reported that her acting revealed a remarkable ability to bring out everything that is most womanly in Shakespeare's heroines, and that her public responded cordially to her appeal.

Miss Anglin's return from Australia marked the end of one definite phase of her career and the beginning of another, destined to reveal still more vividly the breadth of her artistic range and unplumbed depths in her command of histrionic resources. The Greek theatre had been built at Berkeley, California, and its directors were looking round for an actress to interpret classic roles from Greek drama on the occasion of its opening. When their choice fell upon Margaret Anglin, it is an impressive tribute to her talent that no dissenting voice was raised in the ranks of her own profession. There were other actresses with wider experience and equal gifts available, but she combined with experience and talent an indefinable quality of poise and of vocal resource that seemed to mark her as pre-eminently qualified to portray the ill-fated heroines of Greek tragedy to American youth.

Those who have seen Miss Anglin since then at Berkeley will agree with me that for any actress to undertake the task of presenting Greek drama in the vast auditorium, in the open air, under conditions as nearly as possible approximating to those which obtained in the days of Sophocles, was a very daring, courageous thing to do, making tremendous demands upon physical and imaginative qualities and challenging to the utmost the very limits of her artistic equipment. Yet Miss Anglin did it again and again with emphatic and unqualified success. She was the reverse of declamatory in her methods. Some people considered her too restrained in her reading of Greek tragedy. But always the quality of authority was there, the quality of inspiration, of an undercurrent of passion held in reserve, that lent to her portraits of the Greek heroines a tremendous value of tragedy and an irresistible human appeal. And it was in this human appeal that the basic secret of her success lay.

Whether as Antigone, as Medea, as Phaedre, as Electra, or as Clytemnaestra, Miss Anglin made the role stand out with a sombre strength, a vivid, startling, arresting dominance, a sheer beauty of tragic magnetism that silenced all minor criticisms. That the figure of one woman should be able to hold the attention of thousands in a tremendous open air auditorium for three hours is a remarkable tribute to that woman's genius, to her great and commanding gifts.

Miss Anglin seems to have alternated—whether by accident or design, I am unable to say, for I have never discussed that point with her,—comedy and tragedy in her work, for from the Antigone of Sophocles to Barbara Milne in "The Rival," and the delicious romantic comedy of "Green Stockings," is a very far cry indeed.

And that brings me to a problem I have not yet solved to my satisfaction,—what is Margaret Anglin in reality, comedienne, tragedienne, or both? I have seen her in comedy; I have seen her in tragedy; and I confess I am at a loss to say in which she impressed me as accomplishing the most distinctive artistic performance. Perhaps, all things considered, there was a slight balance in favour of comedy. Her Viola was an adorable figure of the most fragrant romantic quality. Her Rosalind was the very spirit of Romance walking in the Arden forest paths, pure woman, and pure fascination all through. Yet her Cleopatra was of the very essence of tragedy, a figure so fraught with the atmosphere of impending doom one hesitates to say the woman who could thus portray her was a better comedienne than she was an interpreter of the spirit of tragedy in drama.

It is a very rare thing in the theatre to find an instance such as Miss Anglin's work presents of so evenly balanced an art. Her greatest satisfaction has been in playing Shakespeare, but the responsibilities involved in the presentation of a Shakespearean repertoire almost broke her down in 1914, and she never assumed them again.

When she appeared in Canada in January, 1914, she was worn out by the heavy strain of a long season of management on tour, and the perfectly abominable weather that prevailed, which prevented many people from braving the elements, tended still further to act as a depressing influence.

Yet she gave such memorable performances of Shakespeare as none who saw them will willingly forget.

She was the pioneer of the new style of mounting and setting Shakespeare, as exemplified in the noble scenery of Livingston Platt, with its dependence on rhythm of line and of lighting subtleties. Moreover, she was a great stickler for the text. She would tolerate no trifling with Shakespeare or the Greeks. She retained, as far as possible, the textual exactitude and the original sequence of scenes. She absolutely refused to "star" anybody in the cast. She preserved the true Shakespearean balance; and she emphasized, as no other individual Shakespearean interpreter has emphasized them here on this continent, the beauty of Shakespeare's comedy roles and the essential fragrance of romance embodied in his comedy heroines.

Margaret Anglin brought to bear upon all her work at all times the keen intelligence of a woman who did much thinking on her own account. She was a close student, a woman of strong character, of authoritative but quiet personality, of rare distinction in style, and of unfailing personal charm. Her voice was, and still is, a wonderful organ, alike in its range, its timbre and its capacity for delicate nuances of expression. Happily married into a noted family of actors, she has led a life of retirement when away from the stage. I believe that if she could ever have flung off for a brief space the atmosphere of ultra-refinement that surrounds her, she might have achieved the greatest artistic triumph of her life. But that is only an impression. She has done much notable work; she has brought distinction to her art and fame to her name; and she is an artiste of whom Canada ought to be more than proud.

section

2

STIRRINGS OF INDEPENDENCE,
1916–1929

THE BIRTH OF THE
NATIONAL THEATRE ◇

ARTHUR BEVERLY BAXTER

○

On Friday evening, the 12th of November, in the year of our Lord nineteen hundred and fifteen, the Canadian National Theatre was opened at Ottawa.

A few hundred yards away a list of casualties from the front was bulletined at a newspaper office.

Incongruous?

No.

This war has made the Canadian National Theatre not only possible but imperative.

French literature seems to have sprung from the Revolution—English literature received new life after Waterloo. In the agony of the present conflict, Canada has given birth to a national consciousness.

Five years ago Canadians assumed they were British, smiled in patronizing superiority at the non-progressiveness of England, accepted without a murmur the drama, literature and business ideals of the United States and were rapidly degenerating into a nondescript republic with money as its uncrowned despot and a patriotism that thinly coated a smug but virile egotism. Canada was prosperous. Canada was making money. She had not learned that in national life there is nothing so impoverishing as wealth.

Then—Europe's siesta came to a sudden and rude end. Great Britain was at war with Germany.

Shaken, bewildered, stunned, Canadians heard the words and a great thrill electrified her people from Ocean to Ocean.

Great Britain is at war with Germany!

It was not England, it was not the British Isles—*Great Britain* was at war.

◇ From *Maclean's Magazine*, Maclean Hunter Publishing Ltd., February 1916.

A mighty shout rose from the forests of Eastern Canada, and echoing on the Ontario lakes, sped over the Western prairies with throbbing clarity.

"By the living God, we're British!"

Canada had found herself.

And what of the Canadian National Theatre in all this? Canada must seek national expression through the arts or her travail will have been in vain. Without artistic outlet she cannot grow. On the success or non-success of the Canadian National Theatre, largely depends the future of Canadian drama. It shall be for our artists of pen and brush to say whether or not they can rise to the heritage left them by the lads who fought back to back at St. Julien that Canada might live.

There is no question of it, the Canadian Government has done an extraordinary thing—whether through good humor, or deep insight, or political purposes, no one can tell, not even the Government itself—but it has made the most radical movement toward national art that has ever taken place in the Dominion.

It has handed over, lock, stock and barrel, a beautiful auditorium in the Victoria Memorial Museum, to the Drama League of Ottawa for the production and fostering of Canadian drama.

The Drama League is an organization, which has its headquarters in the United States and exists for the purpose of helping worthy theatrical productions to secure patronage and to educate the public to the enjoyment of high-class art. A branch of the league exists in Ottawa and also in Toronto. So far the activities of the league in Canada have been confined to bulletining its members about various plays that have crossed its path.

But the Drama League of Ottawa has gone one step further. It has determined to soar beyond the limitations of an unsalaried press agent. It has decided to foster the infant Canadian drama, whenever the stork drops it into the "cradle," which is the title bestowed upon the Canadian National Theatre by its sponsors.

The league is fortunate in having efficient and influential officers. The Hon. Martin Burrell, who, in his undramatic moments, is Minister of Agriculture, enjoys the distinction of being the Honorary President, and is one of the few honorary officers that the writer has met, who takes a really intelligent interest in his organization. He claims utter ignorance of things dramatic, but exhibits rather a knowing air when doing so, that leaves one to suspect vast treasure houses of theatrical lore beyond the veil of modesty. I rise for an amendment—the first two syllables of Mr. Burrell's portfolio should be dropped—I move that in future he be known as the Minister of Culture.

The president is one of the Canadian writers who enjoys international distinction—Mrs. Madge Macbeth. She is a woman of energy and a woman of brains. Combined with these gifts she possesses a sense of humor, and a good deal of personal charm. A woman with these qualities is liable to do anything. Mrs. Macbeth decided to create the Canadian National Theatre, and to make the Ottawa Drama League a genuine force in the Dominion's artistic growth. She worked hard and unceasingly. If the theatre should succeed it will be a monument to the self-sacrificing toil of that lady.

For the opening of the Canadian National Theatre, the Drama League showed its good sense by securing Granville-Barker, the famous British producer, who happened to be in New York, to perform the opening ceremonies.

Mr. Barker has a youthful vigorousness about him that is very attractive. He is tall, and good looking, but considering the wonderful things he has accomplished is the most unpretentious and unstagey man that one could well imagine, though he is by no means unimpressive.

He gives the impression that he is fond of walking. Somehow, one pictures him as doing ten good English miles along a good old English highway in the good old month of October, just as a preliminary to a good old English dinner. From an intimate association with some of the theatrical magnates and playsmiths of New York, I should say that Granville-Barker is the very antithesis of Broadway's conception of an actor and producer. He did not wear any diamonds, nor even an artist's tie. Considering that he has been closely connected with Bernard Shaw in several of that gentleman's dramatized cynicisms (in fact Shaw satirized Barker in "Fanny's First Play") he has retained a fresh and wholesome humor that is far more Chestertonian than Shavian. Nor did he exhibit the well bred languor that is affected by certain intellectuals of the Oscar Wilde School—he was well bred, but vigorously so. I don't know anything about Mr. Barker's antecedents, nor do I wish to inquire because I am sure that it would be discovered that his ancestors were Hibernian,—and Ireland already claims so many big literary minds that have graced the world of English literature.

All of which does not directly concern the inception or the opening of the Canadian National Theatre, except that Granville-Barker was the opening.

Few of the audience will ever forget the quiet and sincere plea that Mr. Barker made for a national artistic consciousness. Perhaps it seemed doubly impressive because he represented the best on the English stage, and a few of us knew that within a very few weeks he would be back in England, rejoining the colors. It was not the address of a theatre-soaked manager whose mind never soared beyond the confines of the box office, nor was it the airy pendantry of some theory-soaked professor of dramatic art who sought to prove the drama a hectic and exotic plant beyond the gaze or understanding of the herd.

"The theatre is a pretty rotten affair. That is true, ladies and gentlemen."

It was a simple enough statement, but in these days of sloppy sentimentality, when the American theatrical journals are endeavoring to prove that burlesque chorus girls are earnest, high-minded young women whose sole object is to do their part in the general uplift of the drama, and when they are constantly idealizing and heroising everybody and everything theatrical—the blunt admission of Mr. Barker's was more startling than the mere words can indicate.

"To-night," he went on, "there are literally millions of people on this continent, inside theatres. Most of them I should say are between the ages of fifteen and twenty-five, at the age when they are most keenly susceptible, mentally, and at a time when their sexual emotions are most impressionable. And what of the plays which they are seeing? It is a kindness to describe at least seventy-five percent of them as harmless and vulgar."

"The theatre," said Mr. Barker, "is the school of expression, the school of manners. The ancient Greeks made statues of magnificent manhood that all might see and emulate. Is it any wonder that we breed such human makeshifts?"

According to Granville-Barker, we are all natural artists, though some of us are dull and inarticulate. We start to act as soon as we leave the cradle. The boy of six is found in the corner issuing commands to an imaginary regiment whilst his younger sister is endeavoring to soothe a refractory grandchild. When a business man stepped into his motor to keep an important engagement with a fellow financier, he planned the scene as he drove along—what he would say, what the other man would reply, the answer he would give, the argument the other would have—of course, sometimes the other man would spoil the scene by not taking up his cues properly, and sometimes he would act his companion off the stage. Speaking generally, it may be said that successful men are good actors.

"Acting is not pretending," said Mr. Barker, sounding a more serious note, "it is the interpretation of something that you have assimilated. We all dramatize our lives."

He made an urgent plea that the theatre should always remain an institution for the people and by the people. The least progressive period in the theatre's history was when it became an amusement of the aristocracy as in the time of Charles II, and ceased to be an artistic outlet for the masses. Mr. Barker has great faith in the public's ultimate choice being for the best.

"Some people, he said, "think that Hamlet is a poor play because it is popular. If you will have patience the good will always outlive the bad."

He gave a good natured warning to the Drama League, when he assured them that "you cannot spread art over a community like butter," and urged them not to confuse good drama with "high-brow." The greatest danger of movements to uplift the drama was snobbery.

It was not until near the end of his address that Mr. Barker made his first reference to the great world tragedy being enacted on the stage of Europe. He urged that when the war was over, it would devolve on the arts and imaginative sensitiveness of our people to seek in other nations and in ourselves that which was most Godlike and uplifting. As a nation we must seek for self expression, we must develop a beautiful sense of the imaginative so that we may distinguish between the false and the true.

It was an inspired challenge to our patriotism, and it came from a man who recognizes his duties as a British citizen to such an extent that he is preparing to give his life if it should be required in the great war; but it came from a man whose vision still sees clearly the universal brotherhood of man, and who calls to the poetic arts to fuse the warring peoples to a divine, harmonious whole.

Mr. Barker looks upon the theatre as something more than a slaughter house wherein to kill an evening.

The question is:—How far will the Canadian National Theatre go towards the ideal set for it by Granville-Barker?

It would perhaps be more kind to wish the enterprise God-speed and not criticize; but there are two or three factors which point as great difficulties in the path of the theatre's prosperity.

It is the League's intention to produce Canadian drama by amateurs, with amateur stage management. (The word amateur is not used in a patronizing sense, but in its true meaning of one who follows the theatre for the love of it, not for the remuneration.) Amateurs can produce plays like "She Stoops to Conquer," and operas like "Pinafore," because they have been played so long that their rendition has become standardized, but a new play!—That is infinitely more difficult. The most experienced stage manager in New York will admit that he cannot pass final judgment on a manuscript until he has seen it played. A new production is invariably tried on "the dog" before it is seen by the critics.

Granville-Barker in private conversation with two or three of us, said that a national theatre is useless without twenty thousand dollars a year subsidy. Undoubtedly the Government should go one step further and, if they cannot see their way clear to a subsidy in these times, at least appoint a competent professional stage manager and coach—with a square jaw.

It would be a great deterrent to national drama if this enterprise should fail. And certainly if our mute inglorious Shakespeares who get their first chance in Ottawa, are to receive the maximum of cooperation, their plays should have the benefit of production by competent and salaried stage management.

Plays are invited from authors, anywhere in Canada. If possible those that are worthy of it will be produced, and those that are rejected will be criticized in a constructive manner. Not, by the way, like the great Keene, who once received a new play by an unknown author, read it, and sent the following epistle back with the manuscript:

> "My Dear Sir:
>   I have read your play.
>   Oh, my dear sir!
>   Yours truly,
>   (Signed) John Keene."

Another drawback to the National Theatre is one that could easily be remedied before the final equipment is completed. The stage is neither high enough nor deep enough. Should the league ever want to produce opera even on a very small scale, it would find the present dimensions of the stage quite inadequate.

Who is to be the first Canadian playwright?

Arthur Stringer has been proclaiming the abundance of Canadian material for plays. Perhaps he will oblige us with a drama.

Stephen Leacock ought to be good for a sentimental comedy—and incidentally there is no book that portrays the Ontario small town better than the "Sunshine Sketches," written by that academic humorist. Leacock would probably make all his characters talk Leacock, though—a fault that he would have the honor of sharing with Bernard Shaw.

The best prospect for a real creator of drama (in our humble opinion) looks to be Robert Service. He has the strength and the vision. If he could acquire the stage technique, Service ought to do wonders.

But playwriting requires technique, a delicate, elusive mastery of action, suspense and dramatic values. It is not easy to acquire. We have many excellent Canadian authors; perhaps with the aid of the Canadian National Theatre some of them may become masters of the drama.

The Canadian National Theatre is a serious undertaking and should be the concern of every one, artist and artisan, poet and preacher, capitalist and politician.

Canada must seek artistic expression. It is the law of nations, and the law of individuals and the law of Nature.

From Reading Gaol, Oscar Wilde wrote to his friend Robert Ross:

"On the other side of the prison wall there are some poor black, soot-besmirched trees that are just breaking out into buds of an almost shrill green. I know quite well that they are going through. *They are finding expression.*"

Canada is writing her *"De Profundis"* now.

Out of the depths has come the Canadian National Theatre.

PLAY-WRITING IN CANADA *

HARCOURT FARMER

○

In discussing Play-writing in Canada, one is tempted to remark that the subject can be disposed of simply and swiftly—there is no playwriting in Canada. But this would be a cheap and obvious thing to say; moreover it would be unfair. And it would be too close a critical reflection on our individual selves. The machine can only function when each part acts in co-operative accordance.

Because there does not already exist a powerful growing movement in Canadian dramaturgy is no reason that such a thing *cannot* exist. We must not discourage ourselves (or other drama-producing countries) by admitting that since native drama, to all intents and purposes, *non est*, such a deplorable condition must perpetually prevail. Literary and actable plays will be written in Canada when there is a demand for them; not before.

Music and painting, poetry and general literature, all occupy places of definite social permanence and artistic importance here. They are recognized as necessary vital factors in the country's development. As such, these branches of expression are receiving earnest attention, expert and otherwise, from men and women who really have the national welfare at heart. There are Canadian composers and interpreters, Canadian painters and sculptors, Canadian poets and Canadian authors. Where are the Canadian playwrights?

By "Canadian playwrights" I don't mean persons of Canadian descent, who, migrating to New York or London, have written popular successes. Any competent literary workman can do this, irrespective of nationality. The result is simply a commercial product, not in the least fashion typical of the author's own country. I mean persons of Canadian descent, or adop-

* *Canadian Bookman* 1, 2 (April 1919): 55–56.

tion, who have written plays the subject-matter of which deals with some intrinsic part of Canadian life, past or present; and whose plays are directly artistic representations of Canadian life, or interpretations of Canadian temperament.

I am the first one to admit that this is a rough and ready way of arriving at a working definition. But, for the nonce, it can serve.

In discussing some points regarding plays in general and Canada in particular with an eminent Montreal merchant, I heard him give vent to this: that the boundary-line between Canada and the United States is, for all artistic purposes, a thing of fancy; it doesn't exist. All American art appeals to Canadian people, *ipso facto*, and there's an end on't. Pressed, the eminent merchant admitted that Toronto has produced some native musicians to whom musical America paid instant homage; admitted, too, that certain Canadian painters were more highly regarded in Boston than certain nameless American artists; and finally, conceded, but without enthusiasm, that Canada was a young country and political comparisons were in bad taste.

The man was speaking relatively, of course, but the unfortunate part of it is this: his opinions are shared by more Canadians than I would care to attempt to estimate. His attitude is excusable. He doesn't know any better. But that is no reason why others should accept his conclusions as final and binding.

As a matter of accuracy, the boundary-line between Canadian art and American art is very clear and very well defined. But it is not as inelastic as (for instance) the line drawn sharply between New York art and Chicago art. There are boundaries all over the place. That's the trouble.

Playwrights and dramatists do exist in Canada, to my knowledge, because I have personally met all of them—the whole three. There may be others lurking in the fastnesses of Granby, or cunningly aloof in the social whirl of North Bay, disguised as citizens. If this writing will bring them out into the open, it will have served its purpose.

In a fairly close (and eager) examination of the work of these three Canadian playwrights, I failed to find any trace of the spirit which, to my mind, should inform such work—the spirit I have sought to define above; national interpretation in terms of individual expression through drama. Their plays dealt with (a) obsolete and unpractical morality; (b) Wall Street machinations; and (c) a touching effort to dramatize the Monroe Doctrine. In the plays of (a) the locales were variously London, Paris, New York, and Lisbon; the characters, as can readily be imagined, ran the racial gamut; and the result was pathetically nondescript. In the plays of (b) the scenes alternated between Chicago, New York, Pittsburgh, and Cuba; the characters were exclusively American. (Imagine an American writing a play about Canadians!) In the plays of (c) the action transpired in San Francisco and New York, to and fro for five acts; the characters were British, American, German and one Irishman.

These three dramatic plumbers are well-known and enjoy pleasant reputations. They may or may not be clever dramatists; that is beside the point, and, with a sense of happy relief, I leave such decisions to others. The point is, that in a total of some twenty plays, the product of these writers, all of them Canadians, appears not one play that can be accurately and reasonably described as a Canadian play.

There is an obvious line of demarcation between the dramatist and the historian. It is necessary to recall this fact (I apologise) because there are several Canadians who have written some very interesting historical chronicles; but, in the compositions of this character that I have been enabled to glance at, there has been a sorry absence of dramatic technique. So that, for the purposes of present discussion, we may consider that we have two groups of Canadian playwrights: the people who are versed in Canadian history and unskilled in dramatic construction, and the people who are expert playwrights while being ignorant of Canadian history. The class to which Canadian Letters must look for the provision and development of the true Canadian drama will have to be composed of the blended best of the other classes.

In justice to the two classes let it be urged that their unsatisfying production has been induced from within rather than from without. They have not put forth a Canadian play, because they had no motive for doing so. There is no Canadian theatre, in the sense that there is an Irish theatre and a Russian theatre and a Swedish theatre. Our playwrights can hardly be blamed for unwillingness to write under such disheartening conditions. Practically speaking, there is no demand for Canadian plays, accordingly there is no supply. Yet this will not always be so. In its early days the Irish theatre indicated a similar barrenness and apathy; but it was only the prelude to bigger themes to follow. The Irish playwrights have built their drama out of Ireland and the Irish; and in the process have indicated with remarkable success the possibilities that lie in the creation of native plays.

Canada teems with workable material for a hundred good plays; there are great figures of the past; there is the fascinating epoch when Champlain and Beauchasse and Pontgravé held the stage; there is the lyrical story of Jeanne Mance; there is the magnificent figure of the Indian—who will be the first to tell in terms of drama his romantic history? Longfellow has given us a hint in "Hiawatha," and it seems curious that no Canadian has had the enterprise to write the tragedy of the Indian for the stage.

In drawing attention to the wealth of subject-matter to be found in the Annals, I do not wish to be classed with those who hold that native plays must inevitably be based upon historical events. There are great clashes and conflicts in our own day; which, in due course, will find their way into dramatic form. But objectivity is necessary. I think we have sufficient detachment to write artistically and sanely about the happenings of yesterday; but the great war is too near to us. Its splendors and pathos concern us presently as men and women, not as dramatists. Still, it is the hope of many that, with the passing of time, a play will come out of Canada that will make the world of letters marvel.

It is encouraging to note the increasing interest shown in the drama of other countries by leading Canadian art and literary societies, especially in Montreal, Toronto, Winnipeg and Vancouver. Papers are read, lectures are given, discussions held, and the consequence is a lively sincere effort to bring the drama into line with the sister arts. Members of these societies know more about the modern drama today than they did a decade ago; and they appear to be putting their knowledge to practical use. In this there is not merely unit development; there is that necessary vital impetus which the drama must have if it is ever to occupy its proper place here. Men and women (particularly the women) are discovering that there is room on the platform for a speaker on the drama. And, in this connection, may it be mildly suggested that it is not wholly necessary to depend on New York and Boston for advice in the constructional development of the drama in Canada. Occasional expert help we must have. But let it be complementary to our own work.

It is one thing to discuss plays and playwriting and another thing to write plays and stage them. The formation of Stage Societies in the chief cities of the Dominion (there is already one in Montreal) would serve as a useful and practical extension of the work being done amongst the purely literary societies. A co-operation between the two branches would work wonders, provided there was a ready agreement that all those concerned would work toward the common objective—our own plays in our own theatres.

YEATS SPEAKS ON
THE THEATRE ⬦

WILLIAM BUTLER YEATS

○

Irish poet and playwright William Butler Yeats (1865–1939) was in Toronto on 2 February 1920 for a lecture at the University of Toronto. The next day, the Globe *ran the following report outlining what Yeats saw as the developing connections between the Irish and Canadian theatres.*

William Butler Yeats, the Irish poet and dramatist, cast the glamor of his personality over a select audience assembled in the Hart House Theatre, University of Toronto, last evening, when he delivered a lecture on "The Theatre of the People," under the auspices of the Players' Club.

He told of how, twenty years ago, Lady Gregory Synge and himself had set out to establish a people's theatre on purely poetical lines after the style of Shakespeare and Sophocles, but the enterprise failed. He said the Abbey Theatre of Dublin was a real theatre for all classes of the people: it was patronized by workingmen, shopkeepers, pot-boys, clerks and lawyers and doctors. The plays took their subject matter from the life of the people and depicted men and women who were characteristically Irish.

Mr. Yeats said the play that drew its characters from society had been overdone and was not sufficiently varied, whereas the plays based upon the life of the common people had a wider range. The players were also drawn from every class of the community, not from the educated class only.

Speaking of the difference between the country and the city audience, Mr. Yeats said the one was imaginative and subjective, while the other was practical and objective. Twenty years ago, he said, the country people of Ireland were in much the same state as the English people were in the time

---

⬦ *The Globe* (Toronto), 3 Feb. 1920, 9. Reprinted with permission of *The Globe and Mail.*

of Shakespeare. The town people were practical and wanted a play to prove something. The people of Dublin wanted him to take up propagandist plays, but these were always rejected.

In conclusion, Mr. Yeats said as he was "getting an old man" he would like to occupy the remaining days of his life in producing poetical plays for a select audience in a theatre that would hold only about fifty people. He would seek to attain only beautiful effects and would throw naturalism overboard. He believed that such a theatre would have an elevating effect upon the professional stage. If he had seen the Hart House Theatre before preparing his lecture he would like to have talked of what it was possible of doing for the drama in Canada.

THE PROSPECTS OF A
CANADIAN DRAMA *

VINCENT MASSEY

○

Vincent Massey (1887–1967) and his wife Alice Stuart Parkin conceived and carried through the building of Hart House and the Hart House Theatre at the University of Toronto (named for his grandfather, the industrialist and philanthropist Hart Massey). An amateur actor who would later rise to become Canada's first native-born governor-general, Massey's interest in theatre was partly based on his belief in its social power. His skills as an analyst of the art were also acute, as this 1922 Queen's Quarterly *essay shows.*

Some fifteen years ago a distinguished playwright, Mr. Henry Arthur Jones, in a rather melancholy lecture on the condition of the stage, laid down what he regarded as the four corner-stones on which national drama must needs be built if it were ever to rise above the nineteenth century morass. Mr. Jones' arguments were, at the time, entirely sound, but they are now interesting for another reason. If we examine them we find that since 1906, despite the critics, we have made progress towards better things. It would be interesting to inspect the four "corner-stones" in the light of the last few years.

The first of the four is stated to be the establishment of definite and continuous relations between the drama and literature. The divorce of literature and the drama, as every student knows, persisted, save for the short interlude of Sheridan and Goldsmith, from the Restoration Comedy until the period of Wilde and Shaw. The successful playwrights were not men of letters, nor were their plays literature, and conversely, the men of letters were not successful playwrights, as witness the long line of lifeless unplayed plays that grace the published works of nineteenth century novel-

◊ *Queen's Quarterly* (Oct.–Dec. 1922): 194–212.

ists and poets. Shelley, Scott, Keats, Coleridge, Wordsworth, Dickens, Thackeray, Browning, Tennyson and Stevenson all wrote plays, but with the possible exception of Tennyson's *Becket*, produced nothing that is playable. It would be interesting for some student of literary biography to discover if these men looked upon the theatre as a serious institution, or whether they did not look on it rather as a toy abounding in childish conventions. If this was their attitude—and the nineteenth century stage would make it forgiveable—it was natural that they should neglect to study the stage themselves, should accept a technique at second-hand, and fail to produce living plays. In a letter to Sidney Colvin Stevenson makes a remark, which might well provide the key to the problem: "No," he exclaims, "I will not write a play for Irving, nor for the devil! Can you not see that the work of falsification which a play demands is of all tasks the most ungrateful? And I have done it a long while—and nothing ever came of it." If a man regards the technical exigencies of a great craft as falsification we cannot wonder at his failure in it.

It is only in recent years that the literary craftsman has come to regard the drama, after a long estrangement, as the highest and most difficult form of his art, and the happy result of this change of view is that the modern stage play may be what the contemporary play of one hundred years ago seldom was, a readable as well as a practicable piece. On the other hand, we have rediscovered the fact that a play may be written with a literary finish and still be a play. It is also more likely to be a play that will live. Mr. Brander Matthews' observation on this subject, like many truisms, deserves repetition: "Only literature is permanent."

Mr. Jones' second corner-stone covers the relations between the drama and morality. Of late, in this sphere, we have made a most encouraging advance. Mr. Shaw's crusade against the false conventions, of course commenced the sanitary destruction of prejudice and cant. Other playwrights followed in this work, and Armageddon completed the task. The theatre is now fairly rid of the false morality that applauded the polite indecencies of the stage, while it labelled as immoral the efforts of the dramatist to deal honestly with the fundamental passions of men and women. In England the censorship is all but gone, and the Lord Chamberlain and Mrs. Grundy have left the stage together—duly chaperoned let us hope—while *Blanco Posnet*, long outlawed as sinning against the Holy Ghost and domestic morality, is now licensed to be played, and may one day be regarded as the powerful religious tract that it really is. Even in Canada, where false puritanism is not yet extinct, the process of emancipation has proceeded at a feverish pace. It is unfortunately still true that municipal censors will permit the performance of plays, the general effect of which is overwhelmingly evil, so long as the legs of the ladies are adequately encased; but in an appreciable degree our public taste has been purged of prudery. A sufficient evidence of this may be found in a recent article in the organ of a great religious denomination, traditionally not given to a libertine attitude towards amusements, in which the modern theatre was upheld as a "moral light-house," and Ibsen's *Ghosts*—long suppressed in England—as an example of its beneficent illumination.

In the establishment of the third of Mr. Jones' four "corner-stones"—the maintenance of right relations between the drama and the sister arts—we may not have succeeded so well. The drama, that is to say, the contemporary drama, during the last century, was, of course, hardly an art at all. It was a form of popular entertainment. And the drama, to most people in Canada, as well as elsewhere, is still simply "the show." If "girl-and-music-plays"—as the technical phrase has it—are intended by kindly managers to minister to the needs of the "Tired Business Man," it is obviously to be assumed that most of the population are business men, and that all of them are *very* tired. But there is a reaction against this cynical folly. The movement to recover the stage in the name of art is succeeding. Even in the commercial theatre the drama is being slowly rehabilitated as a fine art—or, in a new sense, as a synthesis of all the arts—while the non-commercial theatre shows the movement in full career. A retrospect of fifteen years will give us ground for hope.

The fourth and last condition that Mr. Jones lays down is the establishment of a proper relationship between *author* and *actor*. The achievement of this may well seem impossible. In the English theatre there seems never to have been a reasonable balance between playwright and player; in fact, there has been an age-long feud between the two, in which one has always eclipsed the other. During the golden age of the Elizabethans, there were relatively few actors whose names have survived. The same is true of the Restoration drama. On the other hand, the period that produced the great men, Kean, Kemble, Macready, and that which produced Irving, were barren of great plays. Individual virtuosity today has obviously a baneful effect on drama—the play cannot but suffer when it is distorted into a frame for the histrionics of a single actor whose name appears on the posters in letters five times as high as that of the man who "only wrote the play." The "star-system" is still with us—and with a larger proportion of fixed stars than even the heavens can boast—and the profitable "long-run" prevails, until actor after actor becomes little more than an animated automaton, and play upon play, good or bad, is exhausted and flung away like a sucked orange. No native drama can arise in Canada, or in any other community, while this system remains unchallenged, and the dramatist is compelled to produce either a safe popular success or nothing. Is there any hope? Perhaps not in the near future, but during the period we are considering—the last fifteen years—the free theatre has been created—or rather introduced in the English-speaking world (for it existed elsewhere long before), and the new theatres, where the play is the supreme consideration, and a critical audience is trained to appreciate a changing repertory, have met with enough success, both in the professional and amateur spheres to lend, even on this vexed subject, a note of confidence.

So much for an effort to suggest very briefly that an eminent critic's indictment of the English-speaking drama, in 1906, is no longer borne out by the facts. Indeed, from the annual volume of excellent plays, written and produced, from the mass of experiment in dramatic production, and above all, from the awakened popular interest in the theatre, in all its aspects, one can conclude that we are witnessing a genuine dramatic renaissance. The twentieth century may well see the supremacy in the arts return to the drama after too long an absence.

The subject of these notes, we must not forget, is the drama in Canada. It is, of course, almost as easy to be witty about the Canadian drama as about the Canadian navy. They each, at the moment, may seem to represent a well-meaning but rather insignificant effort to complete our national equipment—to suggest a pious aspiration rather than reality. The Canadian drama, as a matter of fact, at present represents perhaps no more than twelve or fifteen produced plays. On this slender foundation what can be built? The inquiry has all the romance of an uncharted voyage into unknown seas.

Let us commence with the Canadian theatre. In the theatrical world we are—as I am afraid in some other things—a province of New York. We take thankfully and with necessary docility the dramatic diet which a group of New York gentlemen, with Old Testament names, choose to send us. Their estimate of our palate is patent to all who read the hoardings. The only reaction against this domination of Broadway is the "Trans-Canada Theatre" scheme to bring out English companies for Canadian tours. This plan, however, seems not unconnected with an all-British propaganda. I am not quarrelling with such propaganda, but propaganda and art do not harmonize. Little good will come of the substitution of one form of mediocrity for another. We may hate the product of Broadway, but if it is to be replaced by English importations, let it be only by the best that England can give us.

In the commercial theatre in Canada there is at present little hope. In a few large cities, in North America, or in Europe, managers are being astonished to find that art "pays." On Main Street everywhere, however (and North Main Street unfortunately crosses the forty-ninth parallel) there is still too uncritical a public to accept good plays unless they have the sanction of age and tradition, and a comforting familiarity. The local theatre, therefore, accepts unquestioningly what is sent it by the wise men in Broadway, or St. Martin's Lane, who are skilled in knowing, not perhaps so much what the public really wants, as what it is willing to accept. The public, as a matter of fact, doesn't exactly know what it does want, but the manager—as also indeed the editor and the politician, too—is seldom prepared to give it a gentle lead to better things.

It is, however, of slight avail to rail at the cynical manager; it is wiser to remember that without a wide process of education art will not be a vendible commodity, save to a few, and that progress will only be gained by our own active concern with the process of education. We must create our public, and the instrument of its creation will be, of course, a new Canadian theatre. It is obvious if the commercial theatre lies beyond our scope at present, that a theatre of some kind there must be for our national drama; a theatre is the very condition of its existence. If plays are essential to the fortunes of a theatre the converse of the axiom is equally true. The drama cannot flourish apart from the theatre any more than religion can survive divorced from a church. By a theatre I mean, of course, something more than the material equipment of stage and auditorium. I mean as well the company of actors and craftsmen that make the modern theatre community, just as the church is composed of a body of believers and is not merely a fabric of wood and stone.

On the relation of the theatre to drama the history of the Irish movement is most illuminating. Almost the entire body of modern Irish plays, which have so enriched the modern stage are traceable to the stimulus of the national theatre in Dublin. When Lady Gregory and Yeats and Edward Martyn held their first performance, in May, 1899, their materials were comparatively meagre. As the little movement went forward and grew to greatness in its permanent home in the Abbey Theatre in 1904, the interest in playwriting grew tremendously. From 1900 to 1910, under the new spell, sixty-two original plays were produced by the Irish Players, many of which have won an assured place as classics. It was the Abbey Theatre that gave to the dramatic world the great figure of J.M. Synge.

Lady Gregory herself writes in her published account of the Irish dramatic movement:

> It is the existence of the Theatre that has created play-writing among us. Mr. Boyle had written stories, and only turned to plays when he had seen our performances in London. Mr. Colum claimed to have turned to drama for our sake, and Mr. Fitzmaurice, Mr. Ray, and Mr. Murray—a National schoolmaster—would certainly not have written but for that chance of having their work acted. A.E. wrote to me: "I think the Celtic Theatre will emerge all right, for if it is not a manifest intention of the gods that there should be such a thing, why the mania for writing drama which is furiously absorbing our Irish writers?"

The record of the Gaiety Theatre, Manchester, under Miss Horniman's régime, tells the same story. In three years twenty-eight new plays were produced under the influence of "The Gaiety," and a school of playwrights called into being which has exerted a lasting influence on the modern English drama.

The theatre is essential not only for the obvious reason that men and women cannot be expected to write plays unless they have some hope of seeing them acted, nor simply because of the stimulus which the existence of the theatre provides, but because the playwright can hardly be expected to produce good plays unless he has had some actual experience of stagecraft. The last place to gain this experience is from the stalls, because all the devices of playwright and stage manager, in the nature of things are calculated not to *inform*, but to *deceive* the auditor. An apprenticeship "behind stage"—at any work (even that of shifting scenery might be a useful avenue to knowledge because it leaves the mind free to think) is of value to the playwright's technique. Shakespeare and Molière are the classic examples of dramatists who knew the "show business." Goethe was a successful theatre director. And, to quote modern examples, the Russian dramatist Tchehov was produced by the Moscow Art Theatre, and Stanley Houghton by the "Gaiety," while John Drinkwater, St. John Ervine, and Lenox Robinson learned their knowledge of craftsmanship as the managers of theatres. Eugene O'Neill, the most important figure in the American drama, learned to write plays as one of the Provincetown Players in New York. To turn to Canada, it is significant that the one playwright to write an important play that has been produced in a professional theatre, is Mr. Carroll Aikins, of British Columbia, who operates a playhouse of his own.

The writing of plays is commonly thought to be a simple matter, although one can dispel this illusion very easily by a practical test. There is a story—which is not apocryphal—of a certain professor, who was on the verge of a nervous collapse, and was warned by his doctor to indulge in no mental effort whatsoever. He spent the period of enforced rest in writing a play, and later presented his composition to a distinguished actor-manager, rather tactlessly explaining the circumstances of his dramatic adventure. The only comment he received was in the form of a congratulation on his having so loyally obeyed his doctor's orders.

A play is a most exacting form of literary composition. There is no other form where the mechanical requirements are so rigid. The writer of verse, if he becomes weary of the restrictions of his craft, can resort to *vers libre*, without the risk of outlawry; the novelist has long since burst the bonds of form, but the playwright, if he expects to see his production performed, must abide by unchanging laws and employ unalterable methods, and these he can only learn by a familiarity with the instrument on which he plays—the theatre.

If then we are to have a Canadian drama we must have a Canadian theatre in which to produce it. The ideal is, of course, the repertory theatre, on the model of those which, from time to time, have been founded to give to the drama the freedom which commercialism denies it. Miss Horniman's theatre, in Manchester, the "Gaiety," was the first in Great Britain, and its aim was simple. It was to be:

A repertory theatre with a regular change of programme, not wedded to any one school of dramatists but thoroughly catholic, embracing the finest writing of the best authors of all ages and with an especially widely open door to present-day British writers, who will not now need to sigh in vain for a hearing, provided only that they have something to say worth listening to, and say it in an interesting and original manner.

This aim was to be accomplished by a permanent Manchester Stock Company of picked first-rate actors; by efficient production; and by popular prices.

Such a playhouse as the "Gaiety," with a permanent professional stock company, and a full season of production could hardly be supported as yet even in the largest Canadian cities. But failing such a theatre, what can we expect to serve as the workshop for the playwright, to give him his experience and the vehicle for his ideas? Will the amateur dramatic movements now flourishing in half a dozen of our cities serve the purpose?

The "little theatre," to use the American generic term for the experimental amateur theatre, commonly suffers from two evils; preciousness in art and instability in finance. The evils are inter-related. Little esoteric groups of amateurs removed from any serious financial responsibility to their clientèle, will easily fall a prey to some prevailing fad, and will seek to impose it on their audience. If the commercial theatre errs in trying to give the public what it wants, the amateur theatre makes the frequent mistake of giving its public what it thinks it ought to want, and the amateur theatre, like a certain type of expert in another sphere, is often sublimely confident that food to be wholesome must be unpalatable. Such a policy spells disaster, both artistic and financial. The drama—let it be never forgotten—is a popular art, and must make a popular appeal.

The neurasthenia of little theatres is, of course, almost proverbial. Their many vicissitudes and frequent early demise may sometimes be due to a commendable boldness in experiment, but they cannot provide the young author with any substantial co-operation. In an American city, I visited recently a little theatre which has had several successful seasons to its credit. Its auditorium seats about one hundred. Internecine warfare, however, has led to the secession of a group of furious insurgents, who established a rival theatre on the next floor in the same building, seating about sixty. The rebel theatre, to the visitor, appeared superbly oblivious of the well-meaning, but futile efforts of its rival; the senior playhouse was benevolently patronizing towards the upstart. If these theatres survive their estrangement one can imagine this process of subdivision continuing with further civil wars, until ultimately the actors outnumber the audience. The temperamental theatre can be of little permanent aid to the new playwright. But the free theatre need not be temperamental. It may exist, as many do, to give its audiences a catholic repertory of plays, avoiding, in their production, fads and whims, and the fallacy that an art theatre is a place where one can be edified, but not amused. It can be organized efficiently, not necessarily with a professional company, but most certainly with a seriously professional atmosphere and the spirit of discipline. Such are the essentials of permanence. If its direction is wise, the free theatre can call into being a public that will support it independently of private benefaction or state control.

The free theatre must never forget its duty to the playwright. It must do more than play good plays well; it must seek out new plays and, if they are worthy of performance, pay for them. Excellent plays may, of course, be written for nothing, but sustained, consistent and serious work must not be expected until free theatres are both able and willing to give some compensation for the time and energy involved in dramatic composition. It may be some time before a dramatist can live in Canada on the proceeds of his craft; but if, before long, a writer of good plays cannot derive some economic return for his labour, we do not deserve to have a native drama. Art, it is true, cannot be measured in gold, but society owes to the artist that his wares shall have a material value, and this is the only way in which society can sincerely show its recognition of worth. The commercial theatre, of course, offers the playwright a most lucrative career. The free theatre if it is well organized, should be able to offer him at least a reasonable remuneration.

There are now several well organized community theatre movements established in Canada, but none as yet fulfills the conditions of a repertory house. That will come in time. In the meantime, as an experimental workshop, the most significant theatre is that of Mr. and Mrs. Aikins in the Okanagan Valley, British Columbia. There is no time now to describe the work of this tiny playhouse, the house-parties of devoted amateurs—in the old and finer sense of a debased word—who do everything, from the writing of plays to the shifting of scenery; the journeys of these "Orchard Players"—as they are called—to give performances through the valley country each year; their conscientious study of the technique of production and their research into all the problems of the theatre. From this centre of experiment one can expect significant things to develop.

The Canadian repertory theatre will not grow without sorrow and travail on the part of its creators, but the effort that must be made will be the guarantee of its permanence. We are accustomed to think of the Abbey Theatre (if I may return to this subject for a moment) as the easy and spontaneous expression of Irish feeling. On the contrary, it was the outcome of painstaking unselfish effort. Its founders incurred in turn the hostility of the Church, the apathy of the Government, and even the suspicion of the nationalist movement itself. They were obliged to undergo the humiliation of important actors from London and an English director, and of accepting a subsidy from an English benefactress. The public were long indifferent, and the audiences so small that Lady Gregory, adopting a device from the stage itself, on a disappointing night, used frequently to step out of the theatre, when the lights were low, and reappear from the lobby, ostensibly as a new member of the audience each time. But the Abbey met with ultimate prosperity and became the fountain head of the greatest native drama—in the English language at least—since the time of Elizabeth.

We have dealt with the Canadian theatre. What of the plays? Of these we might have had greater doubts twenty years ago, than now. We are reaching that happy stage when men of letters can find a career in Canada, and our national hall of fame in future should represent a smaller proportion of repentant absentees. There is no reason to believe that our authors would be any less ready to embrace the drama than were their Irish contemporaries, given the same opportunities of expression. As a matter of fact, nothing would seem to be easier than the diversion of literary talent into the dramatic sphere. The lure of the stage with its traditional mystery, and the charm of its illusion, seems to be felt no less by the flapper, bowing in obeisance before the current matinée idol, than by the middle-aged citizen who privily plays at the making of a comedy with the joy that is found in forbidden fruit. There seems to be abroad at present what our American friends would call a dramatic "urge."

There is promise, too, in the slender volume of plays which Canadians, up to the present, have produced. Carroll Aikins' Indian tragedy *The God of Gods* has won excellent criticism. Miss Pickthall's dramatic poem *The*

Woodcarver's Wife has great beauty, although it may be condemned to the library because of its limitations as a practicable play. Mrs. Henry Osborne, in her satirical comedy *The Point of View*, produced last spring in Ottawa, shows distinct facility. Mr. J.E. Hoare has written one or two studies of city life that have been successfully staged in Montreal and in Winnipeg. Mrs. Isabel Ecclestone Mackay has produced one play of the Grand Guignol type, a clever tour-de-force, and has written others of even greater distinction that await production. Dr. Duncan Campbell Scott in his *Pierre* has given us a little play of great beauty. Mr. Merrill Denison, an actor and all-round theatre craftsman, has written one or two promising sketches that are distinctly "of the theatre." Of the manuscripts that lie in many writing desks—possibly in office desks as well—nothing can be said. Some of them that have seen the light have the stuff of the theatre in them. Others would demand demigods for actors and an archangel as a stage-manager.

On the subject of Canadian dramatists, an obvious question is this: "Can a system of training aid the development of playwrights? On such a point we have instantly an issue, dividing on international lines. Under the English tradition where the individual is left to his own destinies, the answer is naturally "no." In the United States, however, where the virtues of mechanical instruction and applied formulae are apt to be overrated, one would expect the question to be answered in the positive, and we find that Messrs. French, for New York, publish a modest work entitled *How to Write a Good Play*, neatly bound in cloth, and sold for $1.75! A more serious American authority on this subject, however, Professor G.P. Baker, who operates in his famous "No. 47 Workshop" at Harvard, what might be called a dramatic clinic for graduates, believes in the value of formal training in dramaturgy. Professor Baker says in one of his books: "The dramatist is born, not made. This common saying," he continues, "grants the dramatist at least one experience of other artists, namely birth, but seeks to deny him the instruction in art granted the architect, the painter, the sculptor and the musician." Professor Baker's "Workshop" was founded ten years ago, and has done most useful work in training students in the craft of the theatre, including the technique of play-writing. Its contribution to the general knowledge of production is considerable, and several of its graduates are successful professional playwrights, but the head of this school himself lays no claim to having *created* dramatists. The function of the "47 Workshop" has been rather to instruct promising students of the drama in the rules of their craft. This service it performs most admirably.

Technical training of all kinds has become a fetish on this continent. We too often forget that the only sound foundation of any professional career is an education in the humanities. Once the mind has been liberally endowed and thoroughly trained, then the formulae, the rules of thumb, the tricks of the trade, whether it be law, journalism or the theatre, can be acquired without the danger that they be mistaken for genuine principles. It has been suggested that our universities give a place in their curricula to dramatics. If this be done, let us accept Professor Baker's own advice, and restrict such a subject to graduates in arts.

It is well to remember, however, that not all the education or the technical training in the world can make a playwright. Mr. William Archer, with the wisdom derived of long experience and keen observation, has said what is probably the last word on this subject:

> ... If any part of the dramatist's art can be taught it is only a comparatively mechanical and formal part—the art of structure. One may learn how to tell a story in good dramatic form; how to develop and marshal it in such way as best to seize and retain the interest of a theatrical audience. But no teaching or study can enable a man to choose or invent a good story and much less to do that which alone lends dignity to dramatic story-telling—to observe and portray human character.

Now to turn to a more difficult subject: the materials of a Canadian drama. What are its essentials? Must the plays be by a Canadian? Must they be about Canada? They must surely have something more than Canadian authorship. Sheridan and Goldsmith were Irishmen, and yet one cannot think of *The Rivals*, or *She Stoops to Conquer* as being the forerunners of an Irish drama. On the other hand, they need not be about Canada. The scenes of Dunsany's plays are laid—most of them—in a land and in a period of his own devising, and yet they have a whimsical admixture of pathos and farce which is as Gaelic as the *Will of the Saints*. A leader in a local journal said recently that the Canadian drama must exhibit a "Canadian point of view." This dictum, I would suggest, only postpones the solution of our problem. It is the struggle to discover a Canadian point of view that creates the artificial Canadianism that is an offence against honest art. We know the Canadian of the lady-novelist—a combination of Jack Canuck and a conventional figure on a war-memorial. He is always a "strong, silent son of the prairies," or a "child of the Northland." He bears the same relation to the real thing that the conventional stage Irishman does to a figure in a play by Synge. No arbitrary set of rules can be applied to a play to make it Canadian, and no standard set of virtues can be made to personify Canada. Local colour cannot be applied externally like paint or whitewash. The colour must have been woven unconsciously into the very warp and woof of the piece. Our native drama will express the spirit of the country when our playwrights set themselves honestly to interpret the life about them. Its Canadianism will then be automatic and inherent.

We shall find, however—indeed we know it already—that Canada is a unit only in a political sense—otherwise it is still a magnificent abstraction. In the elements out of which the drama is made—manners and social customs and atmosphere—there are several Canadas, for a country so scattered geographically, and composed of so many types, diversified in their origin, is bound always to reveal great provincial divisions. There is little in common between the atmosphere of Maria Chapdelaine and Moosejaw—between a peasant farm in Northern Saskatchewan and commercial Montreal, between a Hudson Bay post and an Ontario city. Our schools of drama, and our repertory theatres, too, will inevitably develop on sectional lines. The forces of geography are too strong for the growth of a national drama in the strict sense. It would be comforting, of course, to feel that whatever the diversities of material, a characteristic feeling, manner or style, was possible that could be called Canadian. But if we develop a Canadian style it will not be discovered from an analysis in the laboratory; it will be produced spontaneously by the artist's conscientious performance of his task. In the work of the "Algoma School" of painters we have something, almost indefinable, which can be called Canadian. A similar quality equally subtle will be characteristic of the Canadian drama.

There is, of course, no end to the choice of material which the Canadian dramatist has before him. One inexhaustible and characteristic subject of study is the immigrant, and his emotions of hope or disillusionment, the romance of the old world which he brings to the new, the local colour of another country (out of which we so soon "Canadianize" him). But the important thing to remember is that there is drama in all human relations— a potential play behind every door. The amateur playwright's tendency in the selection of a subject is to choose something that appeals to him as being dramatic. But the quality of drama lies not so much in the subject as in its treatment. Your Canadian play may possess the most exciting atmosphere—forest fires, mounted policemen, logjams without end—or it may abound in all the romantic figures from the history-books from Champlain to Laura Secord, and yet remain nothing more than dully theatrical. On the other hand, it may turn on the daily round of a farm house in Alberta, or deal with the simple folk of Mr. Leacock's *Sunshine Sketches*—(would that he had not abandoned this field!) and possess the essentials of real drama. The amateur dramatist might well learn a lesson from Elizabeth Baker's play *Chains*—the first of the modern English realistic school. This study revolves on the decision of a London city clerk to emigrate to Australia, and the frustration, by his wife's family, of his desire. Nothing else is introduced into the whole three acts, and yet the movement of the piece is uninterrupted and the interest of the audience is sustained throughout. It is an intensely dramatic play.

There is a danger which the Canadian dramatist must avoid—the peril of the didactic. Synge touches it in one of his prefaces: "The drama is made serious," he says—"in the French sense of the word—not by the degree in which it is taken up with problems that are serious in themselves, but by the degree in which it gives the nourishment not very easy to define, on which our imaginations live." In this passage there lies a useful warning. With the growth of popular interest in the drama there is a tendency to use the play as a medium of propaganda. We are familiar with the morally elevating play that our fathers thought safe. The old melodramas, *The Social Glass, Ruined by Drink*, or *Ten Nights in a Bar-room*, are, of course, now robbed by circumstances of their original value. But there are plays in plenty which commit the same sins against art—plays to teach children the value of soap and fresh air; plays to teach farmers the importance of consolidated schools and the evils of scrub bulls; and there are plays to aid home missions, or to stop cigarette smoking, to stimulate patriotism, and to do a number of things, in the interests of health or morals, for which the drama was not intended. Perhaps from our double foundation of Puritanism—drawn from Scotland and New England and a strength in most respects—we have derived a certain weakness for preaching. But the drama may be elevating without a trace of "uplift." A play must not point a moral and the plays which really give us the "uplift"—in the original sense of this degraded word—are the plays which "nourish the imagination." The *Beggar's Opera*, as its prologue says, contains not an honourable man nor an honest woman, yet with its sheet beauty of colour and music and the clean wit of its satire its influence is incomparably finer than the most moral Sunday School pageant, in which a set of allegorical abstractions, called "social service" and "foreign missions"or what you will, ultimately overcome another set of allegorical abstractions labelled perhaps the "drink traffic" or "heathen religion."

Synge has said—and the student of the drama need never apologize for quoting him—"on the stage one must have reality, and one must have joy." This sentence should be painted on the door of every Canadian playhouse. If he believes in reality the Canadian playwright will avoid the faintest suspicion of false sentiment; he will think dispassionately. If a drama is to develop dealing with Canadian life we must view our own civilization with a critical eye. Its faults, its virtues, its peculiarities must be understood and interpreted as Stanley Houghton interpreted those of middle-class Manchester. This argues a detachment of mind and a critical faculty that are slow to grow in a new country. The very fact that the word criticism here generally carries an unfavourable connotation, shows how little it is understood. Our playwrights and our artists generally must acquire this faculty if they are to understand the people about whom they write; it is humiliating that we had to leave the first real interpretation of French Canada to a European. And our audiences, too, must acquire intellectual detachment if they are to appreciate a critical treatment of our national failings. *The Playboy of the Western World* caused riots in Dublin until the Irish public learned to tolerate a realistic treatment of their eccentricities. What would happen to a dramatist who produced a play in Toronto dealing, however sympathetically, with the failings of the Orangeman?

Synge asks us to put into our plays joy as well as reality. Here is a more difficult matter. There is joy in the Irish plays because they faithfully reflect the Irish character. For the same reason Manchester gives us a photographic sordidness, and from the New York schools of playwrights we are apt to receive a wealth of smart cynicism. We Canadians are not a joyous folk—we are rather serious, or sometimes even solemn without being serious at all. Whether gaiety will be characteristic of our new drama no one can say, but it is certainly one of the functions of our theatre to teach us how to laugh—how to laugh unthinkingly and irresponsibly, and to be less professional or academic, or businesslike, in our moments of relaxation.

Inquiry into the metaphysical causes of artistic movements is, as a rule, both fascinating and fruitless. It is idle to speculate as to when a native drama in Canada will develop. The Americans, with many years advantage of us, have still to produce a school of playwrights with more than a local or transitory significance, and plenty of theories there are to explain the absence or to forecast the advent of an American drama. The writer of a recent work points out that great drama has always arisen while states are passing through an Imperialistic phase, and quotes such examples as Periclean Greece, Elizabethan England, and France under the Louis. He then points out that, since the American people are now in a state of reaction and industrial Imperialism, the new drama may be expected at any moment. We may agree with the premise, but the conclusion is less convincing. Some one else observes that the drama is preeminently a thing of action; that Canadians are men of action—practical people—and that the drama should be their natural artistic medium. But unfortunately we are too much given to action. The drama or any other art needs reflection and observation, and these require more time than is available in a community that still is apt to confuse mere activity with accomplishment, and to regard being busy as an end in itself. More leisure is surely one condition of any considerable artistic effort in Canada—either more leisure is indeed, or, at least, the proper use of what we have, and that is another way of saying more education, for well-employed leisure is the final test of an educated people.

But art must wait for education; it is the duty of art to educate, to create its own public. The Canadian drama must use what audience is available and build upon that. The question of the audience should present no difficulty. The education of the playgoer is being carried on now by countless groups of amateurs. Already the demand for the play exceeds the supply; and no competent amateur players in Canada need fear a half-filled house. But I should like, even at the risk of making a rather bold conjecture, to suggest that the free theatre may find its audience reinforced from an unexpected source—the cinema. The popular instinct for a show, inherent in most people, is now being greatly stimulated in this country, and for the time being is being satisfied largely by the moving picture; possibly 150 000 Canadians visit the picture theatre each day. But the power of the cinema itself cannot be permanent unless it should develop a form of art definitely suited to this vehicle of expression, perhaps a type of pantomime adapted to the limitations of a medium where there can be no speaking—one cannot say. But there seems little hope of such an advance. The artistic genius of Los Angeles has been devoted not to scenarios, but to the camera, and the content of the "movies" shows but little improvement, although occasionally a really great artist like Charlie Chaplin may be thrown up from amongst the sensational mediocrities that dominate the screen. When, however, the last mechanical sensation has begun to pall and the most expensive spectacle commences to look cheap, the audience will be left to the filmed novel or play, distorted for the purpose of the screen—which in the vernacular is "canned art"—or it must be contented with instructive films which are not art at all. Is it too much to expect that as the spell of the cinema fades its good-will may so to speak pass to the theatres, if theatres there be to receive it? After all, the power of the drama lies in the contact of the human actor with the human crowd across the foot-lights. For this the screen at its best is a pale substitute. Here lies the opportunity of the Canadian free theatre, and the Canadian playwright to turn competition into reinforcement. There are difficulties, plenty of them. There is the question of finance, and here the cinema has a great advantage. But the public is after all prepared to pay for what it wants, and the real task is how, without the sacrifice of art, to satisfy its wants. So the problem is one for the artist rather than for the business manager. He has before him a dangerous course. On the one hand lies the stark rock of pedantry; on the other, the shoals of cheap popularity and sentimentalism. But of these two perils the former is the greater. If a "movie-bred" audience clamours for its "sob-stuff," let the playwright remember that Euripides was not afraid of the emotions; if the gallery sigh for the "slapstick" let him not forget that Shakespeare gloried in buffoonery. The playwright need not fear to evoke either tears or laughter so long as he is an honest artist.

If advice can be given to Canadian authors it will be found in Yeats' simple message to the Irish authors issued by the Abbey Theatre: "A play to be suitable for performance at the Abbey," he says, "should contain some *criticism* of life, founded on the experience or personal observation of the writer, or some *vision* of life, of Irish life by preference, important for its beauty or for some excellence of style; and this intellectual quality is not more necessary to tragedy than to the gayest comedy." Such counsel has a universal application. If it be followed I have faith enough in the Canadian artist to believe that he can give us plays that men and women will want to see, and will be the better for seeing. The theatres for these plays are in the making; an audience awaits them; the stuff from which the plays are to be made lies close at hand. Whether our drama will lean towards poetic beauty or realistic truth, or satire—that cannot be foretold. But if our dramatists are both good Canadians and good artists their plays will have in them the essence of Canada, and will embody the spirit of the country, whatever that may be, and Canada will be the richer for them.

HART HOUSE THEATRE [◇]

MERRILL DENISON

o

Invited by Roy Mitchell to Hart House in 1921 to be its designer and art direc-
tor, Merrill Denison (1893–1975) also became one of the period's foremost
dramatists. Born in the United States but raised in Canada, Denison regularly
attempted to debunk idealizations of the great Canadian north, as his 1923
article from the Canadian Bookman *demonstrates.*

In the February issue of *The Canadian Bookman* the development of the little
theatre movement, which grew, finally, into Hart House Theatre of the
University of Toronto, was traced from the early productions of the group
later known as the Arts and Letters Players to the plans that had been
developed for a Little Theatre and Independent Art Gallery combined.
When these had reached a definite form and were virtually under way, all
work had to be abandoned because of the war.

It is unfortunate this happened. It is hard to believe that the theatre
could not have carried out its work better outside the collegiate walls. The
Canadian university is not sufficiently distinguished for the warmth and
enthusiasm of its human atmosphere to have become even the foster
mother of any creative art undertaking. But the movement had created too
intense an interest to come to a full stop, no matter what happened to its
building plans, and Mr. Vincent Massey, who was in charge of Hart House
for the Massey Foundation, believing that it should not be allowed to die,
made it possible to include the present theatre and to equip it so elaborately
that it is easily the most perfectly equipped little theatre in America—one of
the best in the world.

Hart House, which is the students' activities building of the University
of Toronto, is designed in the manner of English Collegiate structures,

---

◇ *Canadian Bookman* (March 1923): 61–63.

around a quadrangle. The original intention, I believe, was to put a small lecture hall under the quadrangle and when later the thought of enlarging this into a theatre grew, partly through the existence of a Players' Club in the University, but mainly through a desire on Mr. Massey's part to give an adequate home to the little theatre movement, Roy Mitchell was called in to design and supervise the installation of its technical equipment.

The theatre is not connected with the other parts of the building used by the undergraduates, but is reached through two separate entrances on the south side of the building—one of these leading back stage and the other into the auditorium, which is reached through a long corridor. At the back of the auditorium is a good-sized foyer and along one side of it a promenade. Off the foyer are cloak rooms and in it a very interesting collection of theatrical mementoes and a book stall.

The auditorium is an ideal size, seating about 450 people in easy, comfortable chairs, and the whole has been kept very simple and restrained in design, the only relief being found in the decorative treatment of the lighting fixtures, the dark notes struck by two reading pulpits which emphasize the front wall and the applied ornamental crest of the Players' Club on the seat ends.

In front of the proscenium opening is a forestage, at a slightly lower level, from which large portals lead, at either side, through the raked piers flanking the main opening, to the forestage wings. The proscenium is about thirty by fifteen and the stage twenty-two feet deep; large enough to put on almost any production. In "Alcestis" a cast of over seventy was used.

Back stage the equipment is very elaborate. There are seven dressing rooms, all more comfortable and roomy than those ordinarily found in a commercial theatre, storage and lamp rooms, and upstairs a green room, the costume rooms and the director's private office. There are wind, thunder, rain and noise machines; carpenter, hardware and paint benches designed as interlocking units which may be used on stage for raised platforms, terraces, stair landings and so forth. The loft is equipped with a complete set of lines, and above the forestage is a narrow gallery on which lights may be hung.

The theatre is so equipped that all costumes can be designed and executed in the theatre workshops; all scenery, designed, built and painted on the stage; all properties manufactured there.

While such an equipment is enough to make any theatrical craftsman interested in experiment, incoherent at the thought of using the theatre freely, it is the lighting equipment which is truly extraordinary. There are only two or three theatres in America with as complete or as large a stage switchboard. It has more than sixty switches with an elaborate system of interlocking dimmers by the use of which any group of lights or combination of lights may be controlled at will, dimmed gradually or rapidly, or fixed with any desired intensity of light. The number of wall and floor pockets, used for plugging in wiring connections at various points around the stage, and the forestage projecting gallery gives great mobility. Almost any grouping, control and variety in color is possible. The lamp room is well stocked and includes large flood lights, spot and baby spot lights and troughs. There is a permanent cyclorama or sky cloth hung on rollers without which it would be impossible to obtain any feeling of depth or distance in outdoor settings.

The only real disability from which the theatre suffers is due to the absence of a fly gallery or loft. An afterthought in the general scheme of the building, the theatre had to accept what space was left for it and the stage, unfortunately, is bounded above by the terrace of the quadrangle and below by the top of a drain down which runs an old and, except when it overflows, forgotten creek. It is impossible to swing scenery overhead and in lighting a production it is necessary to hang all lights from the overhead maze of lines and leave them hung until the production is closed. There is no chance of changing the media which determines the quality and color of the light during a show nor is there any chance for experimentation except with each succeeding one. It is necessary to wait before profiting by mistakes; they cannot be corrected immediately.

The first production was a double bill in November, 1919, including Dunsany's "The Queen's Enemies" and the "Farce of Monsieur Patellin," under the direction of Roy Mitchell, the leading force in the little theatre movement in Toronto. A man with a great flare for the theatre, a natural ability to gather around him an enthusiastic group of workers in all phases of stage craft, who submerged their individualities to the work as a whole, he was a far more able technician than he was an acting director.

During his two years at the theatre continual experimentation was carried on. Certain of it, had it been carried further, would have produced far reaching results. The first use in America of Appia neutral colored screens with color applied through the light instead of paint, was made in Alcestis with results that showed great possibilities for the use of this technique. In Rostand's "Romancers," and in "Cymbeline," these experiments were carried further with especial attention paid to the development of a surface which could be as easily applied as the cotton scrim usually used on flats of scenery, but rid of its smooth monotony.

Among his outstanding productions were: "The Chester Mysteries," played during Christmas week. It was set most beautifully by J.H. MacDonald and marks in many ways the high point of Hart House achievement up to the present time—beautiful and moving, a reverent, dramatized Church service. "Matsuo," a grim, powerful tragedy from the Japanese, set by Arthur Lismer, in which Basil Morgan and Nella Jefferis did a superb piece of acting. Shaw's "You Never Can Tell," and MacDonald Hastings' "The New Sin," both set by Lawren Harris, the latter being a particularly fine interior set. "Alcestis," "The Romancers," set by the writer. "Cymbeline," set by the writer and Arthur Lismer, in which Lorna McLean first attempted, with success, a heavy role. "The Trojan Women," "Love's Labor Lost," Ben Jonson's "The Alchemist"—a show few professional companies would dare attempt—a bill of three Canadian plays were among the remaining productions of the first two years.

It is impossible to do justice to the people connected with the theatre— the artists, musicians, actors, carpenters, lighting and stage crews whose brains and efforts counted for so much. Arthur Lismer, Lawren Harris, A.Y. Jackson, J.H. MacDonald, all of the group of seven, contributed their skill and ability to the problems of setting the lighting. Charity Mitchell and Jocelyn Taylor took care of the costumes and properties. James Cowan, William Johnson, P.A. Deacon, Colin Tait and many other undergraduates worked like galley slaves shifting scenery, doping flats and hanging lights.

In the company of actors were: Basil Morgan, the dean of the non-professionals in Toronto; Nella Jefferis, whose "Alcestis" was one of the fine things of the theatre; Dixon Wagner, a character actor of great ability; Capt. Larkin, Ernest Morgan, Leslie Reed, Hodder Williams, Prof. Dale, Charles Thompson, Heasell Mitchell, Elizabeth Forgie, Audrey Hart, who has since begun a promising professional career, Walter Bowles, Vincent Massey, Lorna McLean, Madelaine Galbraith . . . Healey Willen was the musical director.

The theatre had its by-product, too. "The Goblin," the Canadian humorous magazine, which has had such a meteoric journalistic success, had its inception back stage in Hart House.

At the end of two years Mr. Mitchell resigned and was succeeded by Bertram Forsythe, an English actor and playwright. In valuing Mr. Forsythe's directorship it is imperative that one realizes the tremendous obstacles under which he has worked. Unknown and knowing no one in Toronto, essentially an acting director, he succeeded a brilliant technical director, and found himself the innocent inheritor of much disaffection and ill feeling. The manner in which he has carried himself and the theatre through a difficult and trying two years is a great tribute to his personality, and intelligence.

Held to the most rigid economy, playing a season's bill which lacked the interest of other years, without the competent technical assistance his predecessor had, his work must be judged in the main from the standpoint of acting—which has steadily improved under his directorship.

The season of 1921–22 included Dunsany's "Night At An Inn," Barrie's "Pantaloon," Mr. Forsythe's "Playbills," a Georgian masque and "White Magic," Chesterton's "Magic," Ibsen's "Rosmersholm," the "Chester Mysteries," differently done from the preceding years, and "The Tempest." The last was set by Frederick Coates in an interesting and posteresque manner, and was clearly the best production of the year. Here Mr. Forsythe really found himself, and the productions of the present season have been on the same high level, although one finds a certain monotony in the treatment and settings. The last production, Masefield's translation of "The Witch," was one of the best things ever done at the theatre. It was more the type of play such a theatre should so and the settings and lighting were more in the mood of the art theatre than the previous three plays.

While many of the company of Mr. Mitchell's time have been working with other groups, a number have remained and many new ones been added. Lorna McLean, Madelaine Galbraith and Pouff Acklow have developed tremendously under his training, while Monro Greer, Ivor Lewis, Henry Button, Francis Coombs, Grace Webster, Dorothy Walker—all capable people—have been added. Mr. Coates as the Art Director of the theatre, has done some very fine costume designing, executed by Mrs. Letchford. Mr. Reginald Stewart is the present Musical Director.

It is difficult to estimate, as yet, with the nice precision one would like, the worth of Hart House Theatre, Toronto. Regarded as a purely local achievement which has suffered from its inception from a variety of hindering influences ranging from a storm sewer to the University of Toronto, it ranks as the only successful artistic creation to survive the deadly mixture of Scotch and U.E. Loyalist Puritan provincialism and appreciative sterility which curses the intellectual atmosphere of Toronto. It is one of the few local accomplishments to which the travelling Torontonian, away from the home grounds, may point with pride.

As a Canadian institution it has exerted a stimulating influence on other community theatres throughout the country. It has pointed the road. The example of a finely equipped little theatre, in actual operation, has made it easier for other groups to crystalize and give a definite form to their aspirations. It may have piqued the local pride of other cities, too, and created aspirations where there were none before.

Observing the work of the group of people connected with the theatre, from one production to another, one feels that it is of great value as a training school for acting. A capable and sincere company has been formed which is assuredly non-professional rather than amateur. The manner of production, however one may object to the interpretation or the choice of play, is always capable and is always free from the faults which make so many amateur dramatic efforts ridiculous.

These words of praise may be said and written without any qualification whatever. Viewed in the light of its attainments, against a background which is, in the main, a dull and ordinary gray, Hart House Theatre stands out full of color and vigor. Considering that it has fought against the general apathy and indifference and lack of understanding with which any attempt toward indigenous artistic creation is received in Toronto, there is something quite magnificent about it.

But a critic, unless he be an unmitigated scoundrel or a poverty-stricken typewriter tapper, forced to express opinions on subjects of which he knows nothing for his daily bread, must pay to the thing he discusses the compliment of treating it seriously and sympathetically.

When one realizes that Hart House is equipped in such a way as to make it the finest theatrical experimental laboratory on the continent, one feels that it is falling far short of its possibilities; that it should be doing infinitely more than it is. While it may be contributing something to the theatre in Canada, which is not a very difficult task, it is certainly contributing nothing whatever to the theatre, as, for instance, the Provincetown Players or the Theatre Guild are.

Most people will consider it a fantastic flight of the imagination to picture Hart House entering the same class as the Theatre Guild, but there is no reason why it should not try to do so. Actually it should occupy a place in the North American theatre between the two and it should not rest satisfied until it has done so.

Today Hart House has reached a point of mediocre excellence which would lead one to believe that growth was at a premium, were it not for the fine production of "The Witch" made last month. It marked the first break in a succession of imitative offerings based on imitations of itself; a routine, acceptable to its audience, but one which was leading nowhere. Its repertoire has been that of any stock company whose main worry is in the box office and which judges the success of a play by its receipts.

The writer may take the business of the theatre too seriously; perhaps he does, and, if that is the case, there is nothing more to be said. It seems to him, however, to be the most ample, varied and richest means of expression the race has ever developed. With the theatre as a medium the artist can use forces far beyond the range of any single art, for he must embrace literature, music, sculpture, painting, architecture—life itself.

The theatre is in a state of flux, far reaching changes are taking place in its technique and purpose; it is going some place, and Hart House is situated so that it might help and give direction to its growth. Experiments could be carried on there, which would permeate and influence the world of the theatre as the great German and Russian experimentalists have, if the controlling influences in Hart House did not insist that it exist for its audience alone instead, as is proper in a theatre of this type, of the audience existing for the theatre.

The vast field of lighting in the theatre is virtually unexplored. Only tentative experiments have been made, even in the Continental Theatre, but these experiments lead one to believe that when the possibilities of mobile colored light, which may be changed in chroma, value and hue with the mood of the play, not only on stage but in the auditorium itself, are fully exploited, a revolution, now dimly felt, will occur in stage expression. At the present time the theatre is working with electricity in the terms and with the limitations of the kerosene lamp.

These experiments must be carried on. The insatiable desire for progress that marks a developing art demands it and Hart House is the only place on the continent where they can be carried out. It has the opportunity to contribute something, be it ever so little, to the world, by honest, fearless craftsmanship, and yet it has been satisfied for two years to confine itself to competition with the uptown and downtown stock companies.

Hart House Theatre should be the most dynamic force in the artistic life of Canada, it should be a focal point for the creative life of the country, to which all art would find itself irresistibly drawn and from which, in turn, would pour out a vital flood of artistic achievement. That this is not the case is clearly due to the lack of courage and vision and imagination of its controlling Board of Syndics and the sterility of the University which surrounds it.

Any director, no matter who he may be, what his abilities are, or his initial enthusiasm, will find himself powerless against these two atrophying influences.

CANADIAN PLAYS FROM
HART HOUSE THEATRE◇

VINCENT MASSEY

○

In 1926–27, Vincent Massey edited two volumes of Canadian Plays from Hart House Theatre. *His introduction to the volumes is enthusiastic as well as perceptive.*

This volume is the first of a series in which will be published the plays which have been written by Canadian authors and produced in Hart House Theatre, Toronto. Among those whose names appear in the first two volumes, the reader will find represented a large proportion of the playwrights in Canada whose work has enjoyed actual production. These make a slender company. Our native drama, as far as volume is concerned at all events, has not yet passed beyond its early infancy. It may seem strange that the drama, the most ancient of the arts, should be the last to develop in a new country such as ours, but the reason is not far to seek. The drama is inseparable from the theatre. The great dramatic movements in all ages have been led by men with a practical knowledge of stagecraft—men of the theatre itself. Plays, after all, must be written for the stage and must live on the stage. The purely literary play, composed for the library, is, as Mr. Granville-Barker has put it, like a ship built for the harbour. But what of the theatre in Canada? Our theatres are under alien influences. We accept in the main what Broadway sends us and a Canadian playwright who waits to see his play in a commercial playhouse is the very symbol of unconquerable optimism. If the drama is to take its place beside the other arts that are now expressing and enriching Canadian life, it must be through the development of the amateur theatre throughout the Dominion. Out of our play-

◇ *Canadian Plays From Hart House Theatre*, vol. 1 (Toronto: The Macmillan Company of Canada, 1926), v–vii.

producing societies—groups of workers such as are now established in Ottawa, Toronto, Winnipeg and Vancouver—have come what we possess of Canadian plays, and on the perpetuation and the spread of this amateur movement will depend the growth of what we can call a real national drama. Let us welcome therefore every group of men and women who come together to "do a play," whether they use a theatre, a church, a school or a barn for their purpose. There is no finer form of communal effort than this, in which everyone, whatever his or her calling, can find a place. Through such endeavours the community, too, can recover something of the art of amusing itself, which is almost lost in this age of machine-made entertainment. But above and beyond all this, through the effort to act in plays and to produce plays, will come the desire to *write plays* as well— plays that are Canadian—not self-consciously Canadian because the dramatists are good Canadians. They will be good plays, too, because they may have been given mechanically a Canadian "atmosphere," not because they may deal with Canadian politics—but Canadian because their authors, as workers in the theatre, will know the stuff of which plays are made.

Will our drama lean toward poetic beauty or realism or satire? From this first group of plays from Hart House Theatre, it is difficult to conjecture. In mood and in treatment, they cover a wide field. We have poetry in Mr. Aikin's play, *The God of Gods*. Mrs. MacKay has given us a sketch in the manner of the "Grand Guignol." *Trespassers* is a social comedy. *Pierre* and *The Freedom of Jean Guichet* are domestic tragedies. *The Translation of John Snaith* presents a philosophy in dramatic form. Irony is the motif of Mr. Borsook's play, social satire that of Mrs. Osborne's; while, in Mr. Denison's work, we find *genre* studies conceived with a sure sense of dramatic values. One element is missing—that of farce. Is this by accident, or are we, after all, a serious—even a solemn folk? There is one element, however, common to all these plays and that is an underlying sincerity. And it is this quality together with the richness of material, which lies at the hand of every Canadian playwright, that makes it not only an obvious duty, but a great privilege as well, for Hart House Theatre as often as possible, to produce plays by Canadian authors. It is not too much to expect that given the support of a public, both discriminating and loyal, the amateur theatre in Canada will give birth to drama really Canadian in spirit and, therefore, worthy of Canada.

THE SARNIA IDEA ◊

○

The following unsigned piece appeared in the Toronto Globe *in November 1928. It was written by Lawrence Mason (1882–1939), music and drama critic for the Toronto* Globe *and* Globe and Mail *from 1924 until his death.*

The Drama League in Sarnia had its origin just a year ago in a small dramatic reading club which met once a week at the homes of the members. The membership was limited to 25, a number which might be comfortably accommodated in private houses. One-act plays were read aloud, different members reading the separate parts in costume, and going through the action of the play as well as possible with one or two rehearsals. The members were divided into three groups, one group each week forming the audience, another group giving the play, and a third meeting early to rehearse for the following week's performance. These meetings took place under the direction of Mr. H.A. Voaden and it was through the inspiration of his guidance that the club finally gave way to a much larger organization.

It was at first suggested that the club present three one-act plays to an outside, invited audience, the parts being read as at the private weekly meetings, but when the invitation list was drawn up it was soon seen that no private house could accommodate so many. A hall was engaged for the evening, and with the stimulus of a real stage to work on, the questions of lighting and curtains and properties developed to such proportions that a small admission had to be charged to cover expenses. The plays, which were finally memorized and not read, were: "Followers," by Harold Brighouse; "The Land of Heart's Desire," by W.B. Yeats, and "Suppressed Desires," by Susan Glaspell and George Cram Cook. The whole presentation was received with such enthusiasm that a greatly expanded Drama League was formed, and preparations immediately begun for the presentation of another bill late in the spring. A League membership fee of $3, to

◊ *The Globe*, 3 Nov. 1928, 22. Reprinted with permission from *The Globe and Mail*.

cover the one performance last year and three this, was charged, and two hundred members enrolled immediately.

Almost an entirely new group was chosen for the late spring production and this new material was shaped by Mr. Voaden's untiring efforts into a very creditable cast. The plays produced were: "The Knave of Hearts," by Louise Saunders; "Brothers-in-Arms," by Merrill Denison, and "The Monkey's Paw," by W.W. Jacobs.

With the departure of Mr. Voaden for Toronto, the League suffered a severe loss, and for a while the hope of a Little Theatre in Sarnia was almost abandoned. However, with the enthusiastic enrolment of members that had taken place, it seemed unfortunate that so well patronized an undertaking should be given up. Local directors were appointed, and rehearsals for the autumn production were begun in June.

LAST MONTH'S PRODUCTION

On Monday and Friday nights of last week the autumn production was publicly presented and won wide commendation for its workmanlike soundness and artistic excellence. No detail had been neglected, immense care and skillful endeavor had gone into the lengthy preparation, and the result was as smooth and finished a performance as one could wish. The play was Shaw's "You Never Can Tell," a very considerable undertaking for any company. Costumes, properties, settings, music, and even the ladies' hairdressing were strictly "in period," all the designing and executing or selecting and adapting being done by League members. The success achieved shows very impressively what can be done by sincere community effort rightly guided.

The only theatre available is the auditorium of the old Collegiate Institute, now a public school, which the Board of Education has very kindly placed at the disposal of the League, outside of school hours, in recognition of the essentially educational character of the work being done. This stage has been extended and remodified and enables the League to carry on until the much more satisfactory quarters in the new Collegiate are ready for use. The transformed auditorium is called The Community Playhouse, and seats about 300 people.

An interesting bulletin of the League's activities and opinions, called The Community Playhouse News of the Sarnia Drama League, is issued periodically to members and circulated widely among similar groups in neighboring towns. As a consequence, representatives of Little Theatre groups in London, St. Thomas and Detroit attended the performances of "You Never Can Tell."

"THE SARNIA IDEA"

The underlying idea or purpose, or the ultimate aim or ideal, in this Drama League activity remains to be set forth. It is not, of course, original with or peculiar to Sarnia. Lethbridge, Alberta, reached the same point years ago, and so did Vancouver, Regina, Moose Jaw, Saskatoon, Winnipeg, and many other Western centres, to say nothing of Ontario. It is here called "The Sarnia Idea" because of the fine way in which it has been formulated and worked out in that comparatively small-sized Ontario city, largely through the vision and influence of one very gifted and devoted enthusiast, Mr. H.A. Voaden, head of the English Department in the Sarnia Collegiate Institute before he moved to Toronto.

The Sarnia Idea, then, is not the presentation of "amateur theatricals" for profit or just for fun, as a pastime. It aims at remedying the drawbacks in the existing theatre situation, so far as professional companies and "the road" are concerned; and beyond that, it aims at forwarding a National movement with deeply important implications.

Towns that are on the regular route of the travelling road shows fare badly enough nowadays, but towns that are off that beaten track are in a truly deplorable plight. Motion pictures and inferior "barnstorming" outfits or cheap vaudeville have the field to themselves, all being unsatisfactory in quality and steeped in undesirable United States propaganda. The only hope lies in a movement of the people themselves, for their own liberation and betterment.

A CANADIAN RENAISSANCE

The Sarnia group is strong in educated, cultivated people, of high ideals and enthusiasms, and with remarkable ability and eagerness for hard work in overcoming obstacles in order to reach worthwhile objectives. The most prominent people in the city are glad to place their special knowledge or talents at the service of the movement. Five months of hard work lie back of last week's production, in which sixty or eighty people engaged with unflagging zeal and earnestness.

If this is the situation in Sarnia it must be so elsewhere. There must be this same sincere desire for better things in the drama, for self-expression and self-development, for contact with the great realities of aesthetic experience. The great need is for effective leaders, but Sarnia has shown how to "carry on" even after the loss of the most indispensable director.

The Sarnia Idea is that the movement shall broaden out from town to town, finding occupation and interest for thousands of people who now do not know what to do with their leisure time, building up public appreciation and demand for plays of literary and artistic merit, and the various Little Theatre groups interchanging their views and productions, thus promoting progress for all in the right direction and on the highest plane.

The next step would be the uniting of the many scattered organizations in a Canadian Drama League, which would maintain standards, pool knowledge for the assistance of beginners, encourage the writing and performance of native original plays, establish strong ties with the British Drama League, resist the infiltration and dominance of United States influence, and promote the development of a national consciousness and a national culture. The practical utility of such a Dominion-wide association would be incalculable in maintaining a library and lists of plays, in found-ing new groups, in providing directors or technical experts, in adjusting dis-putes, and in other ways too numerous to mention.

Mr. Voaden sees Ontario and Canada as on the brink of a great renais-sance in artistic activity, like the Elizabethan or Periclean Age, which will give us a National Drama as the "Celtic Renaissance" gave one to Ireland. Whole busy communities will take a prime interest and an active part in high artistic endeavor. Generous rivalry will stimulate each town to emu-late its neighbors, for the Sarnia movement shows that there is everywhere a deep-seated craving for this aesthetic nourishment, this higher than merely material vocation. Metropolitan centres can hardly imagine the intensity of this feeling in "underprivileged" outlying communities, but when it finds its fulfilment in "The Sarnia Idea," the result may well be a new renaissance, with Canada taking the lead in showing the world a whole nation vitally concerned with the great things of the mind and spirit.

A NATIONAL
DRAMA LEAGUE ⬦

H.A. VOADEN

○

*Educator, director, playwright, and cultural animateur Herman Voaden
(1903–91) sought to create a national theatre and drama through a number of
initiatives including a National Drama League. He argued for the concept in
this December 1928 piece from* Canadian Forum.

The great renaissance of the drama in Europe, which began in the late nineteenth century was seriously interrupted by the war. The lighter forms of
amusement became popular. America, like Europe, was preoccupied with
revues, musical comedies and movies. Just before the war the road system
began to go to pieces. The one-night stand became increasingly unprofitable
and smaller cities were no longer served with drama. The development of
the star and the long-run plans of presentation resulted in inferior and
unequal companies being sent on the road. This only increased the dissatisfaction expressed against the commercial theatre from all quarters.

The reaction against these conditions commenced on this continent
even during the war. America was a step removed from Europe and did not
feel immediately the impact of the new drama. Indeed it was not until a
new generation of stage technicians and playwrights had grown up that
anything significant was done. In 1916 the Provincetown group was
formed, bringing to light Susan Glaspell and the phenomenal genius of
Eugene O'Neill. Other repertory theatres were established, notably the
Neighbourhood Playhouse, the New York Theatre Guild, and more lately,
Eva Le Gallienne's Civic Repertory Theatre. Morris Gest brought the
Chauve Souris and the Moscow Art Theatre to America, giving new colour

⬦ *Canadian Forum* 9, 99 (Dec. 1928): 105–6.

and impetus, to the movement. Artists, designers, musicians and dancers rallied to the new theatre. Amateur and semi-professional little theatres were formed in all the large cities, doing splendid experimental work. The American Universities, after the example of the brilliant pioneer activities of Professor George Pierce Baker at Harvard, now of Yale, began to train skilful technicians to lead the movement, both in the writing and production of plays. Plays were written reflecting the life of the people. The University of North Carolina encouraged the creation of a drama closely associated with the lives of the folk.

What part has Canada shared in this unusual development? In a few of the largest cities, little theatres have been established since the time of the war. These have done fine work in production and have given occasional opportunities to the few playwrights whose plays have enjoyed actual production. Yet for the most part, Canada continues to suffer from the same dearth of good drama that the United States experienced during the war. She has few leaders in the theatre. The Canadian Universities give no recognition to dramatic activities in their curricula. If leaders are desired they must be sought in most cases from such American institutions as Professor Baker's School of Drama, or the Carnegie Institute of Technology. Second-rate road shows and third-rate movies are vehicles for an unwelcome American influence. Indeed, with our long frontier and scattered civilization there is a very grave danger that the pressure of American influence will in time override our national and British character. Geographically and culturally we are becoming one unit with the United States. In following the American precedent of standardizing life and turning our energies into material channels we are losing our spiritual integrity and that creative energy which alone can maintain and develop our independent national character.

Fortunately there are signs of a change. There is a feeling that the theatre has a deeper purpose to express, a finer message to bring; that it must be given new force and prominence in Canadian life; that it must bear a closer relation to our ideals and activities. The time for colonial dependence and slavish imitation is gone in art, as in politics. Canada has a definite part to play in the world. The artists, notably the Group of Seven, were among the first to strike out boldly. They carved new materials out of our landscape and evolved a different technique to handle them. It is probably true that the painters are the heralds always of wider and more far-reaching artistic developments. They make us artistically aware of a new scene. This new scene must produce its effect on character, and both scene and character are immediately at hand for the novelist, poet, and dramatist.

The movement of the Group of Seven has centred in one city, Toronto. Creative talent is developed best on the basis of the efforts of various community or artistic groups, each inspired with a single idea. It was so with Antoine's Free Theatre, the Manchester School, and the Irish Players in Dublin, to mention only three examples. In each of these cases memorable plays were written, and memorable productions were staged. The hope of Canada lies in the development of similar experimental theatres and dramatic groups in many Canadian cities, each group inspired with a high artistic ideal and determined to give opportunity to creative talent, both in staging and play-writing. There are signs everywhere apparent of a quickening of activity in this direction. Little theatres are springing up in great numbers. Many of them are abortive in character and poorly led. The great need is for an organization to encourage the formation of these new groups, to guide them in the direction of artistic activity and to point the way to a distinctly Canadian drama.

Such an organization should be initiated on a provincial basis. Ontario, with its numerous towns and cities so close together, will perhaps be the starting point. When a number of other provinces have followed her example their provincial associations can be affiliated in a Canadian drama league. This larger league would connect the activities of the various provinces and give unity and strength to the task of creating a new culture in Canada. The reason for starting with the province as a unit is apparent. The work of the association would consist in sending out organizers to help in the formation of new societies, guiding the course of those already formed, providing member societies with full library assistance, loaning sets of worthwhile plays to them to be read or acted, sending to them producers and technical advisers, arranging for conferences, play-competitions, lecture tours, and exhibitions, and affording expert criticism of plays written. Most of these activities could be more easily carried out through provincial organizations than a national league. The national league would handle only those phases of the work that were outside the scope of the provinces.

Canada is probably on the eve of a great renaissance in her art and literature. She is unshackled by the past. She looks only to the future. With untold wealth, power, and idealism, she is ready to create a new and important culture. All that has been done before in prose and poetry, music, painting, and sculpture is only a preparation for what is to come. There is no more logical focussing centre for this new renaissance than the stage. The modern stage speaks with an orchestra of languages. The author is only one of a larger circle of artists, designers, and musicians. Never before has the theatre held such power, richness, and opportunity. The release of creative energy will come in the theatre when popular interest and enthusiasm have been aroused to the highest pitch. With communities all over Canada creating a native and proper culture, with the dramatic activities of these communities skilfully guided by provincial and national organizations, with the soil prepared for the writing and production of new drama, a Canadian Renaissance in art and literature is assured.

THE ULTIMATE
NATIONAL THEATRE ⬦

RUPERT CAPLAN

o

CBC Radio producer and director Rupert Caplan was closely connected with the developing Montreal theatre. In January 1929—just a month after Herman Voaden's call for a National Drama League—Caplan underscored the importance for theatre to be rooted in a sense of community.

The world of the Little Theatre in Canada is at the spring and there is rosy promise of buds swelling and of fertile earth newly turned. Signs of life— birth—growth—are everywhere:—in Vancouver, Winnipeg, Toronto, and Ottawa. In Montreal one may detect a whiff of recurrent but as yet theoretical persistence.

Collectively our little theatres are important beyond measure because they build the foundation for more mature creative theatres and develop an audience for the Ultimate National Canadian Theatre.

They should be tended and encouraged because they are the only means under existing economic conditions by which worthwhile drama can be brought to us. The essential difference between the little theatre and the frankly commercial theatre is, first, the type of play given in the little theatre has the virtue of being grounded in the very life of the community, and, second, there is the advantage of permanence and continuous production in the little theatre. It has a programme which brings a certain definite number of performances to its audiences each year. The commercial or speculative manager on the other hand, may drop any play, no matter how fine, if it does not show an immediate profit, and he may go through a whole season without producing a play because "conditions aren't right." One may fairly ask right for whom?

⬦ *Canadian Forum* 9, 100 (Jan. 1929): 143–44.

From the standpoint of the audience a community theatre implies a playhouse permanently established where a spectator can always go with the assurance of seeing "fair" plays of the present or past acted with sincerity and intelligence, and staged with proper appreciation of the mood of the play. The place of such a theatre should be in every community that has grown up culturally or wherever there are enough adult-minded people to form a reasonable audience.

The post-war increase in little theatre activity in America is amazing. There are at present at least 500 active producing groups in existence. It is true they vary in standards of production, in importance of plays chosen, and in numbers of productions given. They vary in ability, maturity and size (and this applies to our Canadian Little Theatres as well) but there they are and still growing. And whether these Little Theatres have turned out good actors or not, they are nevertheless showing attractive and often beautiful productions that breathe sincerity and keen understanding of the combined arts of the theatre.

There is not a city of twenty-five or fifty thousand population in this country where a beginning of an organization towards an ultimate national theatre could not find a supporting audience, granted that the appeal was not too limited or "arty" at first, that an expert artist director was in charge, and that the project was managed in a business-like way.

We are not concerned here with the groups that have never risen above the standards of the old aimless social dramatic clubs—Montreal unfortunately seems to be the happy hunting ground of a dozen or so of these groups.

In Europe and the United States there already exist a number of playhouses so far removed from the commercial theatre by ideals and organizations as to merit the rather exalted title of "Art Theatre" and to us in our humble beginnings there are many fruitful lessons to be learned from their experience, their repertoires, and their methods of organization. They found their birth out of a period of discontent, of revolt against the influence of the business theatre, and of amateur enthusiasm.

There are in Canada a few very promising Little Theatres; at least two significant organizations exist—The Ottawa Little Theatre and the Toronto Hart House Theatre.

The Ottawa Drama League have built a beautiful playhouse of their own; nothing could better indicate the position they have assumed in the life of their community than the fine theatre that has been built for them and the magnificent support accorded them. Their programme for this season calls for the production of at least six plays, each play running for a week. The seating capacity of the theatre is about 500 and the house is practically "sold out" for the entire season by subscription.

The Ottawa Little Theatre grew from the most unpretentious amateur beginnings, and with the Toronto Hart House Theatre has emerged as a permanent foundation for the advancement of the creative and combined arts of the theatre.

In Montreal a group known as the Community Players (perhaps one of the first little theatre groups in Canada) failed to materialize out of auspicious beginnings. Their failure was, in my opinion, the result of a lack of inspired and autocratic direction. But as I have indicated, there is still promise in Montreal for the establishment of a community theatre.

It is nice to think that these various theatres in Canada may have cleared the way for that Canadian dramatist who is somewhere in a remote village or in some college hall striving to express himself greatly in drama.

WHAT IS WRONG WITH THE CANADIAN THEATRE? ⬦

H.A. VOADEN

○

In June 1929, the Globe *carried this specially commissioned article by play-wright and teacher Herman Voaden. Its import was explained in an introduction by the paper's theatre critic, Lawrence Mason.*

Much though The Globe's critic has written in these columns about the fascinating subject of the New Stagecraft or the Modern European Art of the Theatre, numerous questions received at this desk show that there is still need of further enlightenment on this inexhaustible topic, and so Mr. H.A. Voaden, Head of the English Department at the Central High·School of Commerce, Toronto, was invited to write an article for this page expressing his own views on the matter. Mr. Voaden has made a special study of the modern stage, both abroad and in the United States, and is also well known as a Little Theatre director in Sarnia and Toronto, as a valued helper and speaker in many Ontario towns which are endeavoring to launch a Little Theatre, and as an important influence in the fruitful efforts now being made to link Little Theatre productions with the Province's educational system. His article follows:

WHAT IS WRONG WITH THE CANADIAN THEATRE?

The use of the term "Canadian Theatre" immediately raises a question: Have we a Canadian Theatre? Our commercial theatres depend almost entirely upon "road" and stock" companies from the United States and Great Britain. This means that the strength of the Canadian Theatre rests with its amateur and semi-professional groups. Unorganized as these are, it

---

⬦ *The Globe*, 22 June 1929, 22. Reprinted with permission from *The Globe and Mail*.

is difficult to estimate their numbers. Probably there are between forty and fifty Little Theatres or dramatic societies in Canada and several hundred church or social groups producing one or more plays of less important character each season. What fundamental criticism is to be levelled at these amateur groups, particularly the Little Theatre societies which should be assuming the leadership in giving a definite status to the Canadian Theatre?

A FUNDAMENTAL FAULT

The outstanding criticism is a lack of strong individuality and originality. There is a tendency to play safe and to merely imitate other Little Theatre groups in the production of plays current a number of years ago in London and New York. An example of this is the number of times that "Outward Bound," in itself a fine play, has been performed in Ontario of late. Few amateur societies will stake their reputations on playing for the first time in Canada, or on this continent, plays important in the history of the theatre, or noteworthy as examples of current continental stagecraft. Few are willing to give opportunities for production to aspiring native playwrights.

Perhaps we have too much production and too little study and knowledge of the drama as a literary form which has its antecedents in ancient cultures, and to which important contributions are being made in many countries throughout the world today. To the writer's knowledge no Canadian Little Theatres have small experimental halls, or drama workshops, where historical material and new plays, either foreign or native, can be tried out.

NEGLECT OF NEW ART OF THEATRE

But the failure of the Canadian amateur theatre to achieve anything noteworthy—its lack of imagination and originality—is in no way so clearly exemplified as in its neglect of the principles and practice of the modern Art Theatre. Exception must, of course, be made in the case of productions by two or three Little Theatre groups, and particularly those by Hart House Theatre, Toronto.

The artist in the theatre, it has been said, is a new sign, unknown to Shakespeare or Molière. His coming to the theatre is, perhaps, the most important factor in the history of the twentieth century stage. Space does not permit a thorough discussion of the Art Theatre. For long it existed chiefly in the imagination of stage designers like Appia and Craig, and colorists such as Bakst.

The movement toward realism, toward the drama of ideas and social problem plays, produced, however, an inevitable reaction. The pioneers of the new stagecraft, who were at first forced to give their attention to the classics, have in later years found new material to work with, notably the expressionistic drama of Germany, the curiously intense plays of O'Neill, such as "The Hairy Ape" and "The Emperor Jones," and the innumerable fantastic and poetic pieces that are now being produced in so many Art Theatres.

THE ART THEATRE BRIEFLY DEFINED

Simply stated, the Art Theatre seeks to avoid the dull literalism that so often characterizes the treatment of realistic plays. The representation of detail to secure the illusion of reality, especially in exterior scenes, has long been found to be well-nigh impossible. This is particularly true of the Little Theatre, where the audience is so close to the stage as to make the old conventions of painted back-drops and irregularly cut wing-pieces ridiculous. Here the principles of the Art Theatre, carefully carried out, are the salvation of the production. One or more simple tree or other designs may suggest formally and simply the idea of the scene; or by an effective use of light and shadow, aiding, perhaps, this stylized concept, the atmosphere of the scene may be achieved. The difficulty with the more formal method of staging is that it implies a degree of stylization in the acting of the play which is apt to be at odds with the human and emotional forces of the drama.

The same principles apply, perhaps to a lesser degree, to the staging of interior scenes by modern methods. Here again there is no attempt to reproduce on the stage all the objects and details of the original scene. Rather these details are simplified and those forms and lines that will be true to the emotional mood of the play are accentuated. Thus, if the play has the feeling of dignity, tall candles and windows might be used, and all other objects eliminated or underscaled to contribute to a fundamental impression of dignity. It will be seen that the adoption of such a principle opens up new vistas in the staging of plays. Once freed from the tyranny of literal representation, the director and artist have unlimited scope for originality and imagination in their staging. They need be true only to the inner spiritual significance of the play.

In a recent production of "Riders to the Sea," for example, the writer draped grey curtains and used a few simple objects to suggest an Irish cottage. Then he centred a tall arch with a platform and steps and a high wall of grey pylons, to suggest the theme and mood of tragedy. Against this the body of the drowned son was placed. The lights in the foreground were dimmed at the end of the play, and even the light on the body died out to the sound of the "keening" as the mother knelt, lonely, in her sorrow. Thus, on a small stage, the play was presented with a richness of imaginative suggestion which no realistic stage setting could secure. Here was truth to the inner meaning of the play, to the sombre and majestic forces that sweep through it.

METHODS OF THE ART THEATRE

A brief discussion of the actual methods and elements employed in the Art Theatre will be helpful. The general tendency is to break away from the "picture frame" type of setting. Here one imagined the fourth wall of a room removed while one "peeped" in at the actors. The latter moved about in a bright blaze of light with all shadows "killed." In avoiding this harshness and artificiality in feeling, curtains are used extensively in the Art Theatres.

They lend a certain softness and emotional quality. When dark and tall they convey an impression of dignity or shadowy distance. If grey or neutral in tone, they form an admirable medium to reflect light of any color.

Quite as important as this use of curtains, however, has been the discovery of the cyclorama or "horizont" in place of the old-painted back-drop, to give the illusion of distance for any exterior scene. This is, of course, simply a curtain or plaster wall neutral or broken in color. In Germany today the cyclorama is being ever more subtly used, to suggest a neutral boundary or background for the action of the play, of an immense void.

Then in place of the old scenery consisting of "flats," which were painted and repainted many times to represent actual scenes, screens are used, following Gordon Craig's suggestions or elements painted or "stippled" in neutral colors against which lights play to establish a definite mood or emotional rhythm. Thus in the remarkable production of Gordon Craig's "Macbeth," seen recently in Toronto, no painted scenery was used at all with the exception of one "drop," obviously a Broadway interpolation quite out of harmony with the symbolic and imaginative character of the play and its settings. The settings for "Contract" and "Antony and Cleopatra," the last two productions of Hart House Theatre, which were designed and executed by Mr. Lowrie Warrener, similarly avoided painted scenery, and employed decorative panels in the one case and the rhythmic play of color, light and shadow in the other, to suggest atmosphere.

In their determination to avoid interruptions in the emotional current of plays consequent on long waits while scenery is being shifted, the Germans, always progressive in matters of the theatre, have built elaborate sliding, revolving and "wagon" stages. Those who have seen performances at the "Volksbuhne" or Reinhardt's "Deutsches Theater" in Berlin have doubtless been amazed at the smoothness and dramatic power obtained by these gigantic mechanistic stages. Yet such devices are apt to defeat their own ends. Even in Germany there has been a reaction from mechanism in stage settings, particularly toward the use of lighting as a vital emotional force in plays. Experiments have been made in the use of lights as setting, through the projection of scenery. But the strength of the Art Theatre lies, finally, in the simplicity, sincerity and imagination that it employs in its treatment of scene.

PERILS OF THE NEW MOVEMENT

Obviously such a revolutionary art of stagecraft is beset with dangers and pitfalls. This has been the case with the production of that unique group of plays written in Germany since the war and roughly termed expressionist drama. In their determination to escape from the bounds of realism, the young German dramatists produced plays that were vivid and chaotic. The staging of these was often powerful, but was for the most part unnatural and unconvincing. Even in the case of such a great artist as Craig, one cannot but feel that aesthetic quality is often at variance with the natural human emotional note of drama. It may still be maintained with justice that acting is the life-blood of the theatre. Too often today it is neglected. But there is no reason why the theatre should close its doors to beauty and imagination.

Perhaps the greatest factor in the success of the New York Theatre Guild has been its insistence on a high standard of acting, combined with its practice of the best principles of modern stagecraft. Similarly the failure of the Stratford-on-Avon players to give complete satisfaction was largely due to the fact that, while their ensemble acting maintained a fairly high level, their methods of staging were inadequate and largely conventional. This was particularly noticeable in the production of such a play as "The Midsummer Night's Dream," where their presentation lacked the enchanting spontaneity of the Heidelberg performances in the old castle courtyard, or the spirituelle magic of Reinhardt's Berlin and New York productions.

SOME SUCCESSFUL EXAMPLES

Perhaps the most consistent and artistic exponent of the new stagecraft is the Russian, Pitoeff, producing in Paris. For example, Andreyev's play of circus life, "He Who Gets Slapped," he staged with a background of black curtains, with narrow scarlet ribbons looped from the proscenium arch to indicate a circus tent. The actors made their entrances and exits from behind a huge circus poster, which was changed from act to act to indicate change of scenes. In their admirable book, "Continental Stagecraft," MacGowan and Jones refer not only to this production but to a performance of Tchekhov's "Uncle Vanya," where "slender birch trees formally spaced against a flat grey curtain" indicated a Russian countryside. A recent despatch from Paris deals with his production of Tchekhov's "Three Sisters" and his method of presentation, "eliminating all, except the essential, giving the idea of a scene rather than its detail, using curtains in the backgrounds and deep pools of shadow in the lighting."

One can only mention the once-famous Leopold Jessner of the State Theatre in Berlin, and Robert Edmond Jones, the American designer whose settings were seen in Toronto this winter in connection with the American Opera Company presentations. The most remarkable figure in the theatre today is the internationally famous Max Reinhardt. While capable of many styles of production, he shows in his work a steady tendency not only to do away with the old artificial type of scenery and to make full use of the new lighting and stagecraft, but to proceed a step further and break away from the proscenium-frame type of production altogether. He is presenting his actors on a simple platform-stage or letting them mingle with the audience as in the remarkable production of Buchner's "Danton's Tod" seen in New York last year. Here the actor presents himself frankly as such and establishes a direct and immediate contact between himself and the audience. The same tendency to eliminate scenery was apparent in Jacques Copeau's presentations on the noted stone stage of the Vieux-Colombier in Paris.

The possibilities of such a method of presentation are unique, particularly when it is seen in its relationship to the reunion of the drama and the church in terms of vital spiritual power as they were in the times of Greece and in the Middle Ages. Not only Reinhardt's impressive "Miracle," but his production of the medieval "Everyman" or "Jedermann," before the cathedral in Salzburg illustrates this point. No one who has been present at this pageant of the human soul enacted in terms of a religious faith prevalent centuries ago can fail to perceive the power that the liberated theatres has today, as of old.

AN APPEAL TO CANADIANS

Surely we in Canada cannot ignore these unique and far-reaching changes that are taking place in the world theatres. If our stage is to save itself, it must be no longer the scene for the actor and producer in the narrow sense of the term. It must enlarge its vision and scope to embrace the playwright, the student, the thinker, the poet, the musician, the designer and the artist. More Canadian artists are especially needed. In Europe the greatest achievements in the theatre have been made by artist-directors, like Pitoeff, who represents Craig's idea of the master director, or through the close cooperation of artists and directors like Reinhardt and Stern, Jessner and Pirchan in Berlin, and Welchert and Sievert in Frankfurt. Surely the remarkable native work being done by many Canadian painters should lead to the establishment of the new philosophy and technique of stage design in Canada.

Moreover, our native playwrights should discover new materials in character, motive and action, particularly in the direction indicated by our painters. It is unfortunate that there is no progressive school of the drama in Canada to afford training for our leaders in the principles and technique of the new stagecraft. In the United States these are now established in connection with the larger universities, and academic credit is given for work done with them.

Our amateur theatres also suffer from lack of organization and the strong guidance and encouragement which the British Drama League, for example, affords its two thousand member societies. But what we need above all is courage: the determination to be no longer merely imitative, but to proceed with originality and imagination, knowing better what is being done outside Canada, and striking out along new paths in stagecraft, with a firmer will to recognize and develop our own native drama.

VISIONS AND REVISIONS, 1929–1945

NATIONALISM AND DRAMA [*]

MERRILL DENISON

o

In the 1929 Yearbook of the Arts in Canada, *playwright Merrill Denison was asked to speculate on the state of theatre in Canada.*

I find writing about the Canadian theatre or drama depressingly like discussing the art of dinghy sailing among the bedouins. There is so little to be said on the subject save to point why there is none. Depending on one's expository habits this can be done tersely, as in the case of the bedouins, by saying "there are no dinghys because there is no water," or at appalling and splendid length by re-examining the geology of the Mediterranean basin and recalling all the flood-mythology one can remember. The same procedure applies to Canadian dramatic writing. One may simply say "There is no Canadian theatre, and it is impossible to believe there ever will be one," or one may examine, at length, the soil conditions under which a theatre flowers, and establish, one by one, the reasons for its absence from this country. True, there are exceptions. Just as there must be the occasional pond or river on which some bedouin has launched a raft and hoisted a sail, so there have been Canadian plays. But the generality holds good. The exceptions are acknowledged to protect oneself from pointless future argument.

It is not at all surprising that there should be no Canadian drama. One's surprise comes from learning that anyone could have seriously believed there ever could be a Canadian drama. Let it be noted to the credit of the mass of Canadian citizenry that but a small fraction of its number has ever concerned itself about the matter. It has been a fancy of a very special and narrow group which, for want of a better name, may be called intellectuals. This description is not exact. In a country where national intentions are so confused and amorphous as in Canada, the term "intellectual" broadens its

[*] *Yearbook of the Arts in Canada,* ed. Bertram Brooker (Toronto: Macmillan, 1929). Reprinted in *Canadian Theatre Review* 8 (Fall 1975).

conventional embrace to include many who simply believe in bigger and better tariffs, and group literature, painting and the drama among the native industries which ought to have protection, whether it will do them any good or not.

A belief in the possibility, or desirability, of a Canadian drama seems to have sprung partly from the national consciousness born of the war, partly from the reputed charms of the Abbey Theatre in Dublin, and partly from an inherent American appetite to flavour with real and worthwhile purpose the Little Theatre movement which followed the war and preserved some of its social charm and atmosphere. In short, this dream of a native theatre is a product of that introspective patriotism that recognizes nationhood most easily in folk songs and native dances, an imitative creative impulse and the uplift. Of all the mirages discovered in the dust of Imperial conferences, none seems a greater illusion than this idea of a Canadian theatre. The analogy of dinghy racing may be violent, but it is sound. Without some of the objective conditions present, neither is possible.

If these statements seem harsh and sweeping, consider for a moment the nature of the world's great theatres. None has ever existed save at the capital centre of a people. Perhaps you challenge this fact by citing the Commedia dell'Arte, the provincial theatres of Germany, the Abbey Theatre of Dublin, the Manchester Theatre. The challenge is not an important one. These theatres have existed and have done important work, but all of them, once they caught the eye of the metropoli, have rushed to it as fast as their little legs would carry them, and have been submerged in it. The theatre, and hence the art of writing for the theatre, is at once the most primitive and the most sophisticated of all the arts. Nationally, it is the most centrifugal of the arts. It flourishes only at the vortex of a culture. Painting, literature, music, sculpture, may conceivably spring into being in the provinces, flower independently of the capital and finally exert an influence on the latter. Such does not seem ever to have been the case with playwriting or the theatre.

Some ten years ago, a thoughtful attempt, inspired by the success of the Irish renaissance and by the writings of Gordon Craig, was made to challenge this apparent law. All over America little theatres sprang into being. The movement was often promoted by sincere artistic purpose. There is no need to belabour, here, their history. They survive and serve a useful purpose, but of their lofty intentions not a wan shadow remains. They exist only where economic conditions have killed the metropolitan theatre. Their creative impulses were never anything much but a pious hope. It is held by some that they exerted a splendid influence on the public taste. I doubt it. If my own acquaintanceship is any guide, and there is no reason it should not be, I recall far more people bored to death by the little theatre than were ever inspired by it. Its notable achievement was the introduction of O'Neill, Lee Simonson and Robert Edmond Jones to the theatre, but it might be argued that these men were first a product of Baker's 47 Workshop at Harvard, and that the Provincetown owed its success to them rather than the other way about. In passing, one notes Maurice Brown and Paul Green, both men who have contributed something to the American theatre. With these exceptions, the little theatre movement has been diverting rather than creative. I do not question the claim that it is an excellent institution, nor that there is a place for it on this continent, which includes Canada, but I do say that its history confirms the law suggested, that the art of the theatre flowers only at the cultural centre of a people.

How does this affect Canada? Very directly I would say. Having no distinct culture, we naturally lack a cultural centre. Because Toronto is the seat of the country's largest university, and because the branch houses of British and American publishing firms are located there, the impression is rooted in many minds, most of them in Toronto, that it is the cultural centre. A detached observer would rather choose, I think, to describe it as a provincial capital. Possibly the best possible of all provincial capitals, but still a provincial capital. Seeking its cultural focus, whether Canada turns to New York or London for the food that nourishes the spirit and warms the soul is a point that need not be argued here. We all know anyway. Certainly, all Canada turns to one or the other, excepting French Canada whose aesthetic sun is Paris. Leaving aside French Canada, as every English speaking person is forced to do when discussing Canada in the lordly, comprehensive way I am here, our culture is one of two kinds. Either it is colonial or American. In a discussion of the theatre, it does not seem to matter much which. In either case the possibilities of a native theatre are nil. We are the provinces and our theatre is either that of London or New York, and since New York is nearer than London it will presumably be New York. In relation to the New York theatre each Canadian city is in exactly the same position as its American counterpart in point of distance and population. Another reason that leads to the belief that our theatre is New York is the observation that a Canadian audience watching any genre American play such as *First Year, Craig's Wife* or *The Show-off* recognizes the commonplaces of his everyday life, while 75 percent of the same audience will recognize in parallel English plays an alien society.

Having disposed of the native theatre to my own satisfaction, we now approach the question of a native drama, and hence the dramatist. Unlike the novelist, who may see his creative work in terms of life, the dramatist must always see life in terms of the theatre. No great play was ever written for publication. It was created to be played, and until this consummation, it is still a chrysalis. The playwright writes for a definite theatre unless, of course, he is practicing or amusing himself. For this reason anyone writing plays in Canada will have the London or, more probably, the New York theatre in mind, and the moment either of them embraces him he will promptly embrace it. Having embraced it, even if his sense of being Canadian is strong, he will not struggle long against having his national identity submerged in that of the city that has crowned his brow.

There is, of course, no reason why playwrights should not come from Toronto or Winnipeg as from Chicago or Iowa. As a matter of fact they have. The 49th parallel has no occult grudge against the drama. Nor is there any reason why a Canadian should not write of a locality he knows. If he is capable enough, and his theme interesting, his plays will find production. But they will not be Canadian in any national sense. If finely done they will bear the earmarks of a Canadian locale, as plays written against the background of California or North Carolina are flavoured by them. If the plays are folk plays, they will be very similar to plays written about similar people living under similar economic conditions on similar soils of the United States. For convenience sake, the theatre may recognize these plays as Canadian, as they now classify certain plays in text books as "middle west" or "North Carolina." The distinction, as far as the world of the theatre is concerned, will be entirely geographic. Should the playwright in Canada choose to write social comedy or satire, the result will be the same as if he had chosen to write of people of similar social and economic position anywhere in the States. Life in Cleveland and Toronto is identical. To differentiate the allegiance of his characters, the playwright must have God Save the King played off stage. Those who stand are probably Canadians, but even this test is not a sure one. Search for a distinctive Canadian subject and you are confined to the life centering about the vice-regal establishment at Ottawa and around the gubernatorial mansions in the provincial capitals. I have no doubt that one could build a cheerful and amusing play in this milieu, and I suppose it would furnish an interesting commentary on colonial Britain the world over, but I have no illusions that it would prove palatable in Canada or interesting out of it. I can think of two other plays that could be written around Canadian problems and which would possibly find an interested and attentive audience in England but would result in the dramatist taking up permanent residence outside Canada. In other words the two or three indubitably Canadian plays that might be written would never find a welcome in a Canadian theatre even if there was one.

The fact that there is none will come as distressing and discouraging news to but few people. Personally, I can see no need of one. Until the national intentions of Canada are greatly clarified, the theatre would at best be an artificial graft supported with as great travail of the spirit and the purse as a native orange industry. But there is this to say about a native theatre: in a discussion of none other of the arts are the realities of our cultural pretences brought so sharply into focus.

SYMPHONIC EXPRESSIONISM OR NOTES ON A NEW THEATRE*

H.A. VOADEN

o

By the 1930s, playwrights such as Herman Voaden felt confident enough in their artistic visions—in this case Symphonic Expressionism—to articulate them for a wider public.

THE PLAY

The new theatre waits the playwright who will conceive and project his theme in beauty of word, light, color, movement and sound. It had been demonstrated that poetry, painting, dancing, music, sculpture and architecture are capable of vital translation to the theatre and powerful expression within it in conjunction with each other. When the composite artist-playwright appears he will use all these! He will create the new symphonic language of the stage. He will usher in the new theatre.

What shall we produce until he arrives? Shakespeare, the Greeks, romantic and poetic drama, abstract and expressionist pieces written since the theatre began to escape from "the banality of surfaces"—all supremely great drama, in which language sweeps in powerful rhythms, in which characters rise above individual types and become universally significant. We shall have to take liberties with script, of course. Most of these were written with the literal word in dominant control. The script must be newly orchestrated, stripped of extreme naturalness and enriched with movement of color, light, dance and music wherever these new voices will add to the beauty and power of the theme.

---

* *The Globe*, 17 Dec. 1932, 5.

THE PRODUCER

He must be thoroughly familiar with the orthodox traditions of acting and directing. He must be able to make the playwright's idea vital in clear characterization and strong situations.

But this is not enough. He must be master of the plastic, arts, musician and choreographer. In him all the contributing voices are blended and unified. In his own mind and imagination he achieves the synthesis. In his direction he is master conductor with an orchestra of many instruments held in even control. He projects the new expression.

LIGHT AND COLOR IN THE NEW THEATRE

Fluid, positive light and color are essential instruments in the new theatral orchestra. Each sentence in lyrical or rhythmic speech has a definite cadence, a definite emotional flow. A sequence in a paragraph or dialogue has a similar rhythm, a similar dramatic rise and fall. The artist-producer will evolve light and color forms, light intensities, and color progressions to parallel these speech cadences, these dramatic crescendos and decrescendos. In any emotional moment light and color will be contributing factors equal in importance to the actor's voice, the actor's or dancer's movement, and the musician's music.

MUSIC IN THE NEW THEATRE

Music, color and light begin where words leave off. They lift the spirit in agonized exultation: they speak with sublime pity and humanity. The playwright and producer will use them with this in mind.

Aside from its employment in climaxes and preludes, music will be used, like color and light, as an agent in the accenting of sentence cadence and dramatic movement. It will be an important element in the spiritual enrichment of the new expression.

SPEECH IN THE NEW THEATRE

The playwright's dialogue is the anchor which holds the theatre to realism. If the dialogue is naturalistic the theatre cannot escape. As it becomes more poetic, rhythmic, spiritual, it lends itself to freer and more lyrical interpretation. On this plane, if handled with skill and imagination, it can join the other arts in the new stage expression. It may become more abstract; the words, as in much recent expressionistic writing, may be merely symbols for "behind-life" states. Here its alliance with the other arts is inevitable. Or, again, we have the singing or chanting of words, where speech is merged in music. The last step is the elimination of speech from the theatre altogether, leaving the composite expression to the dancer, musician and artist.

Exponents of the new method have been accused of desiring such a theatre. But this is not true; they do not wish to lose the explicit power of the spoken word. Yet they are entitled to insist that the actor is no more essential to the new theatre than the musician, artist or dancer, and that without him the theatre would still have an integral existence of its own.

The important thing is that speech in the new expression is only one of the many elements in the theatral language. The problem for the new playwright and director is to utilize it for its virtues of significance and narrative statement, while at the same time keeping it sufficiently lyrical, so that it merges with other voices in a new rhythmic utterance.

MOVEMENT IN THE NEW THEATRE

Naturalistic dialogue compels naturalistic movement and gesture.

Lyrical speech brings opportunity for a corresponding freedom in movement. The new stage language demands the formal and elevated movement of ritual, or the free exuberant expression of dancing. If the functions of actor and dancer are separated, both are possible. The actors can move as ritualistic figures, speaking with presentational freedom and power, while ecstatic and outspoken physical expression is left to dancers, moving separately or in relation to the actors on a space stage.

Perhaps more ideal is the combination of both functions in the actor-dancer, whose movements would be ritual or dance, as the play-theme demanded. Here, again, the theatre probably must wait for more complex abilities. But the actor-dancer is the solution to the problem of unity in the projection of the composite speech. He would react sensitively to an accompaniment of music, color and light. He would fuse them with the words he speaks and, the movements he makes. In him the theatre would at last gain its complete freedom and its complete composite power of statement.

THE NEW AUDIENCE

Does the new theatre await an audience equally sensitive to all manifestations of beauty and equally appreciative of all voices in the theatral orchestra? Surely not. The new playwright and director will have many arrows in their quiver, and some at least are bound to strike home. To those vulnerable on all fronts, the wounds will be grievous indeed.

CONCLUSION

In a world fraught with dissatisfaction and haunted with a sense of spiritual inadequacy the theatre remains a repository for great hope, vision and belief. To youth it never gives dusty answer. The ideal of a symphonic expression is difficult of fulfilment. That is its challenge. Let us bring to the theatre the solidity and power of sculpture and architecture, the glory of painting, the spiritual immediacy of music. Let us restore to it the greatness of poetry, dance and ritual it once knew. Let us combine these in new plays written and produced in a language richer and more complete than heretofore evolved.

MEMORIES OF THE DDF [◊]

DAVID GARDNER

O

Actor, director, theatre administrator, historian, and former theatre officer of the Canada Council, David Gardner (b. 1928) was one of the few Canadians asked to be an adjudicator by the Dominion Drama Festival (DDF). In Betty Lee's history of the DDF, Love and Whisky *(1973), he recalled the experience.*

"I enjoyed it. I loved doing the research, I liked the communication with people. A great deal of lobbying went on, but one had to keep one's sense of humour about that and realize that such coercion goes on in the professional theatre as well. It goes on in any endeavour. How about government lobbies? But an adjudicator had to keep himself as pure as possible through all that and call the shots as he saw them. I was invited around a great deal but made it a rule not to attend a cocktail party before a play, though I'd be happy to attend the final night's party after it was all over. I was most interested to meet groups after each performance but that was after the fact. I didn't want to meet the performers before the play. That wouldn't be fair. I wanted to see the play with no preconceived ideas. If I met an actor at a cocktail party before I saw him on stage, for example, I could have said oh my gosh this man isn't acting at all. The man is simply being himself—though to be yourself on stage is to act rather well.

"Yes, there was sometimes coercion, but usually there was great kindness and warmth and people understood the attempt to keep one's integrity. I would want to read the play over during the afternoon of a performance so I often ate alone. But that was also because I wanted to keep myself as uncluttered and as well rested as possible. I would say it was tough work.

◊ Reprinted with permission from *Love and Whisky*, by Betty Lee (Toronto: Simon & Pierre, 1982), 243–47.

"I had some strange experiences, of course. I particularly remember my adjudication in Newfoundland in 1961. I arrived at some airport in the middle of winter with snowdrifts fourteen feet high, to be met by nobody. There was a call over the public-address system that a cab was waiting for me. I got into the cab and the driver said we were going to go to Corner Brook. We drove and we drove through a valley of snow. I saw nothing but snow for 50 miles. The taxi bill was $32. I had $35 in my pocket. I said, Jesus, what a welcome to Newfoundland. I was put up at the Bowater Hotel. Nobody met me in the lobby and there was no note in the box and I smelled sulphur in the air from the paper plant. Well, I thought this is a great welcome, I suppose someone will get in touch. I went to bed about 11:30 p.m. then suddenly the phone rang and someone said 'oh, you're here, we heard you've checked in, good, come over and have a drink.' I told the person I was in bed and he replied 'well, get your clothes on.' So I did. When I got to the room, the man who had been talking to me promptly handed me an envelope and said 'here's what you're supposed to say about this play on Thursday night.' I said thank you very much, took the envelope, put it in my pocket and said I would be very pleased to read it Friday morning.

"The man grinned and said, 'oh, you're a fighter are you?' I said yes, I was a fighter. 'Oh,' replied the man, 'well, you're too young to be an adjudicator.' I said perhaps you're right, but I think you should decide after you've seen me adjudicate. Well, said the man, what do you think about this play and that play? I said I think that, that, and that. Why? Oh, then, you know what you're talking about. I hope so. Then I asked about the arrangements for adjudication. I wanted to see the theatre. The man said no, the first thing the next morning you get your photograph taken with the manager of the Bowater Paper Plant. I said, fine. But then I want to see the theatre and backstage and the arrangements for my little desk and I want to see the room I can write in. There would be no room for me to write in. I told them I wanted a room to write in. Would I have to write in the theatre with all those guys sitting around watching? Or have you got the whole week written out for me?

"Ha, ha. You're to have supper tomorrow with so and so from a group and we have cocktails every afternoon at four. I said thanks very much, I will turn down all those things. I will see you at the party at the end of the week. Oh. Well, who would introduce me at the theatre tomorrow night? Nobody. Go and introduce yourself. I said I would not do it. Why? Well, I said I wanted someone to go on and say this is Mr. Gardner. If I go on and say I am Mr. Gardner, who is to believe me? Okay, they would get someone to do that.

"Well, the festival started. The first night, it was J.M. Barrie's *Mary Rose*, not one of my favourite plays. I tore it to shreds. I had a heckler all through the adjudication, a man sitting in the front row who was very drunk. So I heckled back and said come on up and we'll all adjudicate together. It was a real battle. The entire week was a battle. The next day I was invited to lunch on a Bowater boat that was frozen into the harbour on an angle. I said I'd go to that one because I was supposed to meet all of Newfoundland's officialdom. I was the adjudicator, right? Well, there was a head table plus a lot of small tables and I was put as far away from the head table as possible. As a matter of fact, I was put at a table with my heckler, who happened to be a drunken millionaire who lived in Newfoundland. We had a marvellous luncheon. At the end of it we even liked each other.

"I said to him, shall we fight those bloody sons of guns up there at the head table and he said, why not. Give them hell the whole week. They've been used to running things here, so give them hell. And I did. Every night I gave adjudications as hard and as crisp as I could. But by the end of the week I think I had won people over. On the Thursday night, the group that had won the regional festival every year for the past six years came in that afternoon and went away that night. They didn't stay for the Final night, they were much too busy and confident. The performance was terrible and I said so. Also I learned they were all on pep pills. As a matter of fact, I mentioned in my adjudication that it looked as though the company was on drugs. Well, that was earth-shattering and at the end of it the man who had given me the envelope that first night said "you can tear it up, you did it better than I did." I said I hoped so.

"On the last night, I reviewed the final play then I went away and came back twenty minutes later and recounted my entire impression of Newfoundland from beginning to end. I talked about the insular attitude, the choice of repertoire which was entirely British repertory. That I would never have known I was anywhere near to the North American continent and so on. I asked them to join Canada. This, apparently, was all being taped. After saying all that I added that I was supposed to hand out some silverware. First award to this, so and so award to that. I give it to this company even though it doesn't deserve it. The standards were superb but the morality and intent behind the production and the creativity was nil. However, it was the best English repertory production of the week.

"Then the Lieutenant-Governor of Newfoundland got up to speak. He said he had a prepared speech but that he was going to tear it up. What was the point? Mr. Gardner was a courageous young man and it had been a most stimulating half hour. Straight from the shoulder you might say. So, straight from the shoulder back, he had to say he didn't agree with a lot of things that had been said. But Mr. Gardner had given everyone food for thought, so go in peace. That was Newfoundland. It was rough, but I remember it with a great deal of affection. It's interesting that the ones who told me to go to hell in the beginning were the ones who drove me to the airport."

THE WORKERS' THEATRE
IN CANADA *

E. CECIL-SMITH

○

*The essentially middle- and upper-class orientation of the Dominion Drama
Festival (and the Little Theatre Movement in general) was challenged on
numerous occasions by the Worker's Theatre Movement and the Progressive
Arts Clubs that sprang up across the country during the Depression. In a letter to the editor of* Canadian Forum *in 1933, Ed Cecil-Smith, one of the leaders of the Worker's Theatre, demanded that the magazine recognize such
groups. The following month, the* Forum *printed an entire article by Cecil-
Smith.*

The Editor, *The Canadian Forum*

Sir:

Mr. Archibald Key, late of the *Drumheller Mail*, has contributed an interesting but Utopian essay to your issue of September, under the title, "The
Theatre on Wheels," in which he attempts to bolster up his hope that the
Little Theatre movement is again on the make in Canada, as in other countries' (sic).

Of course, the readers of your journal, being normal human beings,
probably realize just as well as I do that the artificial stimulus given to this
movement by His Excellency, the Governor-General, is no sign of health, no
sign of life—quite the reverse. I shall not strain this point, because it is easy
to see in Mr. Key's article how the wish gives birth to the thought.

It is interesting to note, however, that Mr. Key, in his effort to hew a
line for the theatre of his dreams, has come very close to describing a new

---

* The first selection is reprinted from *Canadian Forum* 14 (Oct. 1933): 39; the second
selection is reprinted from *Canadian Forum* 14 (Nov. 1933): 68–70.

theatre which is actually springing up all over Canada; a theatre which does not depend on Broadway, nor on London, nor on the Dennison Company for its inspiration. I refer to the Workers' Theatre.

Except for the fact that the September issues of *Masses* and *The Canadian Forum* were out on about the same day, Mr. Key might have received his inspiration from reports of two tours undertaken this summer by the Workers' Theatre groups of Toronto, and several others being planned this fall by the Toronto and Winnipeg groups.

Here is the new Canadian dramatic movement in very truth. A drama rooted in the lives and struggles of the toilers of Canada's shops, mines, farms, and slave-camps. Plays written in the heat of life by the same workers. Mass recitations and plays presented by worker-actors who understand what they are doing because they can live the very parts they take.

Believe me, Mr. Editor, there is no George French nor Dennison Company tripe put on by these groups. Life to these Canadians is too serious to worry about polite bedroom scandals, or the ridiculous cavortings of a flat-footed detective in pursuit of *The Black Ace*.

"The Theatre on Wheels" it is indeed. When six actors and a solitary suitcase, containing all the properties and costumes needed for seven plays, pack themselves into a small roadster for a tour, they cannot depend very much on the elaborate fakery that has been built up by the capitalist stage to fool tired people into believing they are seeing a real play.

No indeed, the play itself must be so strong that it grasps the very guts of the life of the audience. This must be the key to the growth of a Canadian National Stage. We must learn to recapture the secret of Shakespeare and the Elizabethans; we must make the very audience a part of the company of actors.

This is what the Workers' Theatre is beginning to do; not so well as it should yet, but still a beginning. This is what the Little Theatre can never do and why it must remain for ever sterile.

No, if Mr. Key really wants to be associated with the growing, living, pulsating stage in Canada today, he must not pin his hopes on the "Dramateur" movement, if this means following the bankrupt line of the Little Theatres. He should, on the other hand, see what he can do to help the miners of the Drumheller valley establish their own Workers' Theatre group. There is plenty of room in the mining fields of the West to have a permanent group of this kind with a theatre of its own for experimental work.

In your notes on contributors, you credit Mr. Key with being opposed to the Alberta coal operators. Here is a chance for such a man, interested in the stage, a writer of several plays, to not only show his opposition to these murderous operators, but to translate this into action.

What about it, Mr. Key?

> Yours, etc.,
> E. Cecil-Smith
> Toronto

ɔ

During recent months there has sprung up across the country something which gives observers and participants alike the hope and belief that there now exists a future for the Canadian stage, beyond the drab and dreary prospect held up for it by the amateur dramatics of the "Little" theatre, or the church stage. This is the Workers' Theatre movement.

Very Canadian in the problems with which it has to deal and the difficulties which it must overcome, this new movement does not cut itself off from the international scene in the way which the nationalistic amateur "drama leagues" must do, in order to prove its Canadianism. Its themes, its plots, its stage difficulties and technique, its authors and its players—these and many other things clearly stamp it as truly Canadian.

The very name of this movement indicates just what it is. It is not a theatre for the workers, but a theatre of the workers. These two things are very different. There are plenty of examples of the establishment of theatres and dramatic troupes by organizations such as the British Labour Party which were calculated to give the working class the opportunity of seeing the best, or not-quite-the-best, of the classical and bourgeois dramas. Such is not the function of the Workers' Theatre. It is the outgrowth of the past four years of crisis in Canada and the whole capitalist world, and the growing realization on the part of many workers that something must be done about it. But this must be a propaganda stage! Quite so, but because the content of the play is class content there is no justifiable reason to suppose that the art and technical side is to be forgotten. Quite the reverse is true, as a rapid survey of this movement will show.

Faced with certain very definite limitations set on it by the lack of funds with which to hire large theatres, and the extremely important task of reaching the greatest possible number of workers, the Workers' Theatre has gone about its work in a manner which shows that it has a great future before it, even though at present it is comparatively small and suffers many of the ailments of youth. To a very great extent its work is, and will remain, on the open stage and even out of doors. This has meant the development of different forms of dramatic presentation, in the finding of which this new theatre is growing strong.

At the present moment its forms can be roughly divided into three categories. First there is the mass recitation, a form unknown to the Canadian stage in the past. Secondly there is the short agitational-propaganda sketch, which form borrows much from the school of symbolism, and is very effective in getting over an idea in short time, and with the least amount of costumes and properties. Neither of these forms absolutely demands the use of scenery at all.

The third grouping includes those plays, short and long, which utilize the methods developed by the "realist" school and develop their themes in a manner more similar to that in general use on the North American stage.

In the past year and a half, and particularly during the current year, a great many of these plays, sketches and mass recitations have come into use, approximately 70 to 80 percent of which are written by Canadians. A very few examples of these could be given to show the general trend. Possibly the most effective mass recitation yet written in Canada came from the pen of a young Montreal worker, Sidney Nicholls. This takes as its theme the murder, during an eviction this March, of unemployed Nick Zynchuk, who was shot in the back by a Montreal police constable, and the subsequent attack on the 20 000 workers who came to his funeral, by hundreds of police. Presented first at the memorial meeting for Zynchuk, this piece received immediate and enthusiastic response. It has since been used from one end of Canada to the other, and is very valuable in rousing workers to the need of organizing themselves against police terror.

These mass recitations generally call for a cast of from five to eight people, and are performed in a standardized Workers' Theatre uniform of black sateen blouse and trousers, set off by a bright red neckerchief. This uniform is calculated to be effective before any type of backdrop, or at an open air meeting. Under the second grouping can be mentioned *War In the East*, by an undergraduate of the University of Toronto, and *Unity*, by Oscar Ryan, Toronto worker. In the former the symbolism was carried a little further than has been done by many of the other sketches or plays. This was really a short, four-scene play, dealing with the attack on Manchuria and Jehol by the Japanese imperialists. In the first scene of this the stylized characters, Mikado, Capitalist, War Lord, and Priest wear masks which aid the slight costumes (top hat, priest's cassock, and so forth) in showing that they represent forces, rather than individuals. Throughout these agit-prop sketches, the only properties or costumes used are very simple, such as a helmet and baton to indicate a cop, uniform cap and gun to indicate a soldier, top hat, white gloves, spats and cane for the boss, etc. These are worn with the uniform black blouse and trousers. Characters representing workers are dressed as in the mass recitations. Wherever such exist, lights and stage sets are utilized, but are often done without.

Unity was written for and first produced at a mass meeting on May first, held in Hygeia Hall, Toronto. This meeting was called by a conference including Labour Parties, Socialist Parties, C.C.F. clubs, Labour Defence League branches, and Mass and Cultural Organizations of workers, and was really representative of the Toronto working class. This sketch was a high-light of the evening and has since been produced elsewhere. Under the classification of the "realist" dramas, perhaps the best so far produced was the work of a Toronto electrician, H. Francis, and entitled *Looking Forward*. This is a two-scene play, depending for its strength entirely on the dramatic development of one family, more particularly the father, who begins as a more-or-less satisfied relief recipient, bringing home a sackful of over-ripe groceries from the Pogey house, and ends up with the determination to demand a decent unemployment insurance scheme. This was written for the recent National Congress on Unemployment and was presented, along with other plays and sketches, at the congress in Ottawa. There are other promising playwrights being developed by this movement, possibly a round dozen already, but the start is only just being made. In the department of the play-writing alone, a good future is in prospect for this theatre.

At the present time there is being written collectively a presentation to be put on in a large Toronto theatre during November, which will call for more effort than the Workers' Theatre has had to put into any previous performance, and may well be expected to mark another high spot in the young life of the movement. This will be put on in conjunction with a campaign being launched by the Canadian Labour Defense League against section 98 of the criminal code.

But what of the activities of this movement on the side of producing and staging these plays? This also is nothing of which it need be ashamed. As our example, let us take the Toronto Workers' Theatre group, a section of the Progressive Arts Club. This is the oldest of six such groups set up by the PAC, from Halifax to Vancouver, and admittedly its activities are probably more extensive than those of other groups, but at least it is an indication of what is being done. During the Summer which has just past, this group has undertaken three tours, besides making a number of other trips. The first tour was through the Niagara Peninsula, during which they were able to take part in helping the cannery workers of St. Catharines in their strike for better wages. The second took them as far west as Windsor. To the performance in this latter city there came a number of working class writers and intellectuals from Detroit, who expressed the opinion that there was nothing of this sort in their city.

The third trip ended at Ottawa at the unemployment congress, mentioned above. In these tours the Workers' Theatre were well received by the audiences everywhere, and the messages of their plays and sketches were well understood. It might be interesting to record that in those places where the audience was overwhelmingly made up of those elements termed "Anglo-Saxon," such as at London, the response and reception was the best of any. Another thing of interest lies in the fact that in some of these towns, such as Gananoque, the audience had never before seen a dramatic presentation of any kind, with the exception of movies. Thus the Workers' Theatre is getting to people never even reached by the bourgeois stage, whether professional or amateur.

Besides these three tours, the group has had very many bookings in Toronto and the vicinity, which have taken them to practically every working class hall and camp in the neighbourhood. Trips to other cities have also been undertaken, particularly to Hamilton and Stratford. At the former place, the Workers' Theatre assisted a similar organization known as the Rebel Arts Guild in a dramatic evening which included a five-scene play by a Hamilton worker.

At Stratford, last month, the group was not only faced by the largest audience which it has been privileged to play before, but also the largest gathering that ever collected under one roof in that city. Close to 3500 people jammed in to the old Brooks plant to see them, and to judge by the applause and remarks passed afterwards, appreciated them greatly. The only advertising for this affair was done by one or two placards, and by word of mouth. For all these performances, it must be remembered, rehearsals are carried on under the greatest difficulty. Even now, when a headquarters has at last been secured, they must rehearse in a small room, about 20 by 12 feet. Previously to that even smaller quarters were utilized. Anyone who has had any dramatic experience will well understand what this means.

This movement is not only developing its own writers, but also its own directors and actors and stage directors. They are not content, however, with the director knowing how to direct, the actor knowing how to act, and the writer knowing how to write.

Believing that the widest possible knowledge of the whole of the stage technique and tradition is necessary, they are arranging a series of weekly lectures, conducted by their own members, and such professionals and experienced people as they can interest, to cover as wide a range as possible. Further than this, the first steps have already been taken for the establishment of what are termed Workers' Theatre supporters clubs. These will meet once a month, consisting of such workers as are interested in this movement, together with the playwrights and the actors. At these meetings, new plays are rehearsed, others are presented, and the whole is followed by a discussion which is calculated to bring forward the greatest possible number of vital suggestions about the plays, sketches, and so forth, so that all can learn from it, writers, audience and actors. This method is not usually practised by other dramatic organizations in Canada, and must be considered a new and important step in the development of our drama.

Due to a limited amount of publicity which this movement has obtained in the pages of *Masses* and a few other publications, but more particularly due to its activity in all the struggles of the Canadian workers, a very considerable interest has been aroused in the movement from coast to coast. At the present time, the secretary of the Workers' Theatre in Toronto is in touch with people in more than sixty cities, towns, and villages in Canada, who are either asking for plays, or for information as to how to establish their own groups. This excludes the six cities in which the Progressive Arts Clubs are located, and well indicates the probable growth of the movement. When the movement is able to establish even one permanent theatre of its own, say in Toronto, the perspectives in front of it will be infinitely greater. By that time it should have won the support of many of the more proficient professional actors, directors, and technicians in Canada, who in the past have been slow to come to it. This is due undoubtedly to ignorance of the existence of the movement, or to an under-estimation of its importance.

"The predominant ideology of any society is the ideology of the ruling class in that society." This Marxist axiom remains as true as ever, but it must be remembered that there are other classes in capitalist society, besides the capitalist class. There is the petty-bourgeois class—roughly anglicized as the lower middle class. This class has its own ideology in Canada. Many of its exponents are well known to readers of *The Canadian Forum*. There is another large class in society today, the working class. Its class ideology is known as Marxism, and many of its exponents are now in jail. The supporters of the Workers' Theatre believe that this movement expresses one of the facets of the ideology of our class, which is growing more conscious of itself every day.

I have ignored a very important aspect of the Workers' Theatre, and that is its international aspect, and its growth in other countries. I hope that the readers of this journal will be sufficiently interested to learn of this, and that the editors will allow me space to deal with it in a future issue.

CANADIAN THEATRE IN THE 30s: A NEW KIND OF ARTS ORGANIZATION [◇]

TOBY GORDON RYAN

○

Among the people most active in the Worker's Theatre Movement was Toby Gordon Ryan and her husband, writer-critic Oscar Ryan. She recalled Canadian theatre life in the 1930s in her 1981 memoir, Stage Left.

A NEW KIND OF ARTS ORGANIZATION

I was excited by my contact with the Progressive Arts Club. I met some very interesting people there. They were eager to pioneer a new kind of arts organization. Here, I felt, was the logical place to start a theatre—a social theatre that would reflect the times, that would contribute, in a theatrical way, to the protest movements then developing for civil rights, for jobs, for unemployment insurance, for union organization.

Once this idea crystallized in my mind, the group I immediately thought of, and which had left such a deep impression on me, was Prolet-Bühne. It became clear to me that this was not a time for a theatre in a special building, waiting for audiences to come and see plays. The times called for a theatre which would, as PAC was clearly doing, *go to its audiences* and speak to them directly about what was going on and what they could do about it.

The Depression not only affected workers in their jobs. It was so all-pervasive that even the students on the campuses joined the battles for a better

◇ *Stage Left: Canadian Theatre in the Thirties* (Toronto: CTR Publications, 1981), 3–32, 36–37, 43–46.

future. At the University of Toronto, the newly-formed Students' League took part in awakening protest movements. Out of this socially-aware student organization came Jim (actually Jean) Watts, Dorothy Livesay and Stanley Ryerson. They had some student theatre experience and were anxious to become part of it.

Thus, this nucleus, and some additional young men and women, became the Workers' Experimental Theatre. In the writers' group of PAC, we now had people ready and anxious to provide plays suitable for a mobile theatre for the times.[1]

○

The Workers' Experimental Theatre (soon abbreviated to Workers' Theatre) had very little organization. All of us acted, directed, collected props, built and painted whatever little scenery there was, scrounged rehearsal space.

We had no money but many good friends and helpful organizations who wanted to see our theatre flourish. The Ukrainian Labor-Farmer Temple Association (ULFTA) on Bathurst Street welcomed us to their hall for rehearsals. Sometimes we could use their stage. It was not always available as the organization had a tremendous culture program of its own which included music, dance and theatre.

When the stage was not available we used a dressing-room downstairs. Unfortunately, it was close to the men's washroom. It got to be very funny after a while to have our very serious dialogue about war, about unemployment, punctuated by flushing toilets and a small audience of bewildered men who couldn't imagine what we were so intense about. Nevertheless, we were deeply grateful to the organization for giving up some of their space to us.

The Jewish Labor League had a hall on Brunswick Avenue. They, too, helped us by allowing us to use their quarters from time to time. We rehearsed in large rooms in private homes. We used any available space we could find, providing it was free. In this way we built our repertoire of short plays and mass recitations and prepared them for performance.

We borrowed some ideas, at first, from the Prolet-Bühne. They were an excellent prototype for what we wanted to accomplish. In this sense, my seeing this fine troupe in New York helped Workers' Theatre to aim for high standards of presentation. We later created some of our own techniques to suit our situation.

Our actors wore simple black pant-and-blouse outfits, to which were added pieces of costume (hats, kerchiefs, aprons, gloves, etc.), to identify specific characters. We constructed flexible one-piece stage settings which could be put up quickly anywhere (and were portable) to identify locale. We had small props, which actors could handle easily and which helped the audience to identify character and situation (wooden rifles, canes, four wooden poles which could be turned into a prison cell, etc.). This made our theatre extremely mobile and one that could be taken anywhere on short notice.

We played in workers' halls, outdoors on trucks or on bandstands in parks. We played for trade unions, Workers' International Relief, the unemployed councils, Canadian Labor Defense League branches, Labor League, Ukrainian, Finnish, Macedonian and other ethnic organizations, May Day celebrations, concerts of cultural enrichment.

We charged a nominal fee for performances, just enough to cover expenses.

On the whole, we were kept very busy and participants found it exciting to pioneer this very special social theatre for a very special time.

A little extra spice was added to our rehearsals when they were visited frequently by three hefty men in overcoats and fedoras who stood at the back and watched us at work. It was fairly easy to identify them as police. At first, these visits were rather intimidating, as they were meant to be, but as time went on we simply accepted the harassment as a fact of life in the thirties. . . .

○

We played, for the most part, in workers' halls—some with a proscenium stage and backstage facilities, others with just a slight rise from the floor platform. Everywhere the people in charge of these halls greeted us warmly when we arrived to set up and rehearse our program. They stayed to help in any way they could to make the performance as effective as possible.

For many of our ethnic audiences, our visit was the first experience with a theatre doing English plays that were direct and contemporary.

As a travelling troupe without funds, we depended on local people to put us up and feed us and this was one of the more delightful aspects of our tour. We got to know and were treated royally by many kind, warm people in the cities we visited, people who often were on relief themselves but shared their food with us and gave up the most comfortable bed in the house. They were delighted to entertain the young roaming actors. We were very touched by their hospitality.

For Jim, I think, this was a very special experience. She had never come into such close contact with ordinary working people. I recall the first night she and I shared a room in a Ukrainian home. We climbed into an ample bed and under a mountainous, soft featherbed such as many Europeans enjoy. But it was summer and very warm. The two of us, practically submerged under this down-soft cover, laughed most of the night every time we realized what a picture we must have made with just our heads showing from the billows of bedclothes.

For our late supper that evening we were honored guests. We were treated to large bowls of thick cabbage soup and delicious black bread and butter, plus a very tasty home-made coffee cake for dessert. My background had prepared me for the lovely meal. But for Jim this repast was a first and I must say she enjoyed it thoroughly. All these pleasant experiences made us feel truly like a roving people's theatre.

It was summer. All of us enjoyed the outdoors. As we went from city to city, we would stop near water, have a swim and do a little sunbathing, then continue on our way refreshed. The memory of the six of us, working and playing together, and the receptions we were given, on and offstage, are still fresh and pleasurable.

One of the highlights of this tour was our participation in a cannery workers' strike, while we were playing St. Catharines. The workers were, for the most part, immigrant women whose wages and working conditions were pretty dreadful. Union organization was the issue and most labor bodies in the city were supporting the strikers. Since jobs were scarce, the company was able to recruit scabs to replace striking cannery workers.

An appeal was made at the concert where we performed for support for that night's picket line to block the entrance to the factory. The plan was to move a freight car in front of it so that the strike-breakers would be prevented from entering.

We had already entertained the women on the picket line with some of our plays. The police had been out and had watched our performance. After the concert we too responded to the appeal for help and joined that night's picket line. We were later taken to the police station and given a strict deadline to leave town. The police criticized Jim Watts for being there because she was a university student who "should have known better." We were all questioned, but they really went after Jim.

The next morning we read that the mayor had described us as out-of-town "agitators." He threatened dire consequences if we didn't leave. We took his advice and left. We still had the greater part of our tour to complete.

This incident must surely have been a first time for a theatre company to be given such importance in our country.

In addition to playing for audiences on tour, we also tried to meet people in various towns and cities who were interested in forming local workers' theatres. We tried to help with advice, scripts and general encouragement in the short time at our disposal.

Our repertoire for the first tour, as reported in *Masses*, consisted of seven short plays:

- *Solidarity, Not Charity* — a one-acter taken from the U.S. *Workers' Life.*

- *Eviction* — a mass recitation written by two members of Montreal PAC about the murder of Nick Zynchuk.

- *Farmers' Flight* — one-act play, Montreal PAC.

- *Labor's Love Lost* — one-act satire, adapted from U.S. *Workers' Theatre* magazine.

- *Meerut* — mass recitation on the trial and sentence of the Indian trade union leaders, by the WTM of England.

- *Joe Derry* — written by Dorothy Livesay, member of PAC, for the tour.

- *War In The East* — a play in four scenes on the war against the people of Manchuria and China, written by Stanley Ryerson, member of Toronto PAC. . . .

EIGHT MEN SPEAK

The high point, the most challenging experience in the life of the Workers' Theatre, was the production of *Eight Men Speak*. The script was a co-operative effort by four members of the PAC Writers' Group—H. Francis (Frank Love), Mildred Goldberg, Oscar Ryan and E. Cecil-Smith.

The play was in six acts and called for a cast of over thirty. We had to find additional actors to augment the small Workers' Theatre company. We approached the Unemployed Council for help. The response was terrific. We didn't know there were so many single unemployed men interested and excited about being in a production of this kind.

I was impressed with the loyalty of these young men who, in spite of their own desperate situation, came regularly to rehearsals. It was, for them, no easy matter. Since the single jobless received no state assistance, they had to spend much of their time lining up for mission or soup-kitchen meals, and then finding a place to bunk, especially in the cold weather. None thought of dropping out. They were real troupers.

It should be remembered that most of the men had never acted before; many of them had not even seen a live play on a stage. It meant learning in rehearsal as they went along. What marvellous, diligent students they were! When they were not involved in a scene, they sat and closely watched everything else as it took shape, so as to learn and improve their own skills.

In view of all these circumstances, I would say the production of this play was a great achievement. Oscar, as co-author, describes how this all came about:

"*Eight Men Speak* resulted from a very critical civil rights situation in Canada. In 1931, eight leaders of the Canadian Communist Party were arrested in simultaneous raids across the country. It was the culmination of a period when people were being picked up on the street, in their homes, at meetings halls, simply because they had no visible means of subsistence; in other words, they had no jobs. Many had no homes, so it was common practice for policemen simply to pick them up and take them to police stations, and sometimes rough them up.

"It was a very violent period with wholesale and sustained attacks on civil rights across the country. The climax, of course, was the arrest of the Communist leaders. But even this outrageous Section 98 violation of civil liberties was peaked with the attempt to murder Tim Buck, national leader of the Communist Party, by firing shots into his prison cell at Kingston Penitentiary.

"At the time I was publicity director for the Canadian Labor Defense League. Its principal objective was repeal of Section 98 of the Criminal Code, under which almost anybody could be arrested for almost anything—doing anything or doing nothing. It was introduced at the time of the 1919 Winnipeg General Strike by Arthur Meighen.

"We in the CLDL felt that something had to be done to rouse public sentiment against Section 98 more effectively than through leaflets, mass meetings, petitions and other traditional ways.

"We thought, *Why not have a play?*

"I took our proposition to the Progressive Arts Club writers' group. We discussed the possibilities. Would we be able to produce a script and mount it in a hurry—immediately? Four of us volunteered to write it collectively. We worked out a sketchy outline, and assigned scenes and acts among ourselves. Within a few weeks we had the first scripts to read, discuss and revise.

"At first, our intention had been to do a dramatized mock trial in a large theatre. But we wanted something with greater impact. We felt it needed intensity, color, conflict, theatricality. We added blackouts and mass recitation and some light humorous elements. We introduced, I think fairly effectively, new staging effects which were not then commonly employed in Canada, but had been pioneered in some of the European experimental theatres. We soon had a script ready to put into production. That's where Workers' Theatre took over.

"Jim Watts directed the early rehearsals and, when the load became too big, turned over the job to me but continued as assistant. Rehearsals were held almost daily. Our cast, many of them unemployed, could not afford carfare; they walked to and from the rehearsal halls each time.

"There was one performance—December 4, 1933—at the Standard Theatre on Spadina at Dundas, in the heart of the city. Some 1500 people crowded in. They were a tense and exceptionally responsive audience. Again and again and again throughout the evening people cheered and applauded and cried out their support. The final curtain brought a sustained ovation, an emotional outburst. For audience and actors alike, it was a rare theatre experience not soon forgotten.

"We decided on a repeat performance. No sooner did we announce it than the police threatened to cancel the theatre's license. The owner backed down."

Eight Men Speak's premiere received only scant critical reviews from Toronto's daily papers, which were more interested in political hysteria than in production values, especially after the banning.

Frank Love, another co-author, recalled:

"I was surprised that the press should not be impressed (by the production) even though they disagreed, but why weren't they stirred by it? I remember one girl, she came from a fairly well-to-do family. She was working as a secretary and she was a very knowledgeable girl. She told me she was never so stirred in her life. Too bad it couldn't have been put on again and again to see the reaction from more people. When we announced a second performance, the whole university was down there buying tickets. But nobody else got a chance to see it. I don't know whether they would have been stirred by it or not. If they would have, maybe this was a good technique to follow again."

○

In a foreword to the first printed edition of *Eight Men Speak* in 1934, Ed Cecil-Smith placed the ban in its political context:

"Why are the Canadian authorities afraid of this play? Why do they move heaven and earth to prevent it being presented for a second time? Why has the order gone out from the Ontario parliament buildings that any theatre which is rented for the showing of *Eight Men Speak* shall at once lose its license? Why did the Winnipeg police and the Manitoba government swoop down on the Walker Theatre and remove the license the day before the play was to appear there?

"The answer is not far to seek. It lies in the essential truth of every word of these six acts. These things which are dramatized in the following pages must not be allowed to be played in public, if the government concerned can do anything to prevent it. . . .

"It was played to a house seating 1500 which was sold out long before the curtain was scheduled to rise. It received an ovation from the working class audience which was reflected by scare headlines in the bourgeois press. The Toronto Police Commission held secret sessions and consulted the crown attorney and city solicitor to see what legal action would be taken against the authors, producers or actors. For fear of dragging the facts to light in an even more public manner, these upholders of law and order decided not to make such a frontal attack.

"By methods well known to capitalist lawyers and lobbyists it was finally decided that the attack should be made by the provincial inspector of theatres with a perfectly safe threat of license cancellation.

"While these discussions were going on in secret, there was an enormous demand that the play be repeated. Owing to a difficulty in securing a theatre (it was only possible to rent one for one night a week) the Standard was again rented for January 15, 1934. Two days before this the manager of the theatre was hauled to the office of the inspector of theatres and given the ultimatum. He at once broke his signed contract with the PAC. . . .

"It was finally disclosed that Prime Minister R.B. Bennett himself had been sent a copy of the stenographic report of the play by the RCMP. He could not understand, he is quoted as saying, how on earth the Toronto public ever allowed this play to be produced at all. So now we find that this attack on the freedom of the stage and the freedom of criticism of the government has a very highly centralized beginning.

"In other cities and towns, plans went ahead for presentation of *Eight Men Speak*. In fact, since the ban was pronounced in Ontario, it has actually been presented in part on at least six occasions, and never once has the government dared to prosecute the producers or actors. . . ."

○

This production was a turning point for me, as well as for others in Workers' Theatre. As a member of the cast, I was reminded again of how potent an art form theatre can be.

The audience reaction was very emotional—cheering, laughing, booing—as their involvement grew. There was active rapport and participation between actors and audience, such as I have always believed good theatre should have. Without this, theatre becomes an exercise in escape and one never knows what the audience is feeling, or whether they are even entertained.

I believe good entertainment in the theatre includes audience involvement—whether they are moved to laughter, or to tears, or caught up in mystery and revelation.

I began thinking at about this time that it was no longer enough to do short plays which appealed only to particular people. It wasn't enough any more to have simplistic characterizations and situations. We had to go further.

It occurred to me therefore that it might be possible to combine two kinds of theatre into our organization in order to appeal to many more people. Such a theatre could devote part of its time to short, mobile plays which could be taken out to various audiences. But the greater part of our effort would be given to longer scripts, still concerned with contemporary social themes, but which were more complex in production and in the development of characters and ideas.

I wanted to draw on people who seriously wanted to study their craft and who would work at developing themselves as actors and directors. It would obviously take more time and effort to produce such plays, plays which would speak to the major issues and conflicts of the times in a deeper, more theatrical way. It did, though, seem possible to reach out to newer and broader audiences with a theatre of high artistic standards, innovative in technique and in subject matter.

N O T E S

1. See *Eight Men Speak and Other Plays of the Canadian Workers' Theatre* (Toronto: New Hogtown Press, 1976).

THE CANADIAN THEATRE *

H. GRANVILLE-BARKER

○

One of England's leading men of the theatre, writer-producer-actor Harley Granville-Barker (1877–1946) visited Canada many times during his long career. One of those visits during the 1930s was as an adjudicator for the Dominion Drama Festival. His impressions and hopes for Canada were revealed in this essay for Queen's Quarterly *in 1936.*

It is impossible to prophesy. It is not easy to evaluate what is happening at the moment. But one of the privileges, and penalties, of advancing age is a perspective which allows one to interpret the more immediate past. Looking back over the past forty years of drama in England, it may be said that from the early nineties to the years just before the war was a time of honourable achievement and even higher hopes. Since the war most admirable and vital work has been done, work of wider extent, of a more varied promise.

Among the early hopes of the present century was that of seeing the drama in England recognized and organized and placed beyond the danger of relapse to insignificance, unworthiness and neglect; recognized as one of the major arts, and as a thing, therefore, whose well-being was of importance to a civilized state; organized because more than any other art the drama depends on organization. A theatre is a factory. The production of a play is the assembling of a number of individual products, diverse and akin,—the dramatist's, the actor's, the scene-designer's, the musician's. Each of these may be a delicate and will be, moreover, a human and uncertain thing, not made to measure and standardized like the parts of a motorcar. The production of a play is to be thought of as the final, though ephemeral, unifying and setting in motion of these various and elusive things,—a nice process.

◇ Reprinted with permission of *Queen's Quarterly* Volume 43, No. 3, Autumn 1936, 256–67.

What should we say of a man who set out to manufacture motor-cars in any sort of factory he came across, with any sort of machinery which happened to be on the market, and with a staff engaged and dismissed at haphazard? That is a hopeful proposition compared with the chances—not simply of putting plays on the stage,—anyone can learn to do that more or less well,—but of something very different, of cultivating the art of the drama in a theatre not permanently organized for that purpose.

Thirty years ago in England our hopes were high for the establishment of a national theatre. The name did not matter. It rather frightened some people. They saw in it another monument of bureaucracy. But the essential thing for the drama as it then stood was to establish it; to give it a home where its work could be done for its own sake first and then for the sake of the public; to enable its directors to take long views; to remove it from the ranks of cut-throat competition, from the need to make the greatest amount of money in the shortest possible time—which, whatever may be its benefits to commerce, is most unbeneficial to any kind of art. Those hopes came to nothing. The moment passed and, while some of the plays survive, the drama of that day, seen as a whole, is almost as if it had never been.

The drama which is alive in the theatre, apart from the recording of the play on the printed page, is inevitably the thing of the moment, but only in the sense that many important activities are, like journalism, politics, statesmanship, education, medicine, even religion. Each has its ephemeral aspect. But that does not prevent us from providing them with institutions which will give them dignity and stability and permit them to establish traditions, so that the passing generations, free to initiate new departures, to add new structures of their own, may yet have a tried foundation upon which to build. To compensate for what is inevitably ephemeral in it, something of that sort is what the theatre needs if it is to fulfil its social and artistic ends. Without it the workers whom it needs, though they may be attracted to its service, cannot be held there. For no man, once he has left his youth behind, likes to feel that his life's work is to consist in ploughing the sands. That hope is alive again in England. Whether it will materialize now no one can tell. There are great difficulties in the way. But, looking back, we can see why, thirty years ago, it failed. The appeal that it made was too narrow. Its sympathies were too restricted. The drama of that day was not yet healthily and deeply re-rooted in English soil.

And now, since the war there is a change. It is a very remarkable phenomenon, this sudden spread of the love of drama among the people. It is not confined to any one country. And nowhere is it so remarkably and healthily manifest as in the Dominion. What, however, is notable about it is that it is not a mere love of spectacle, of sitting passively to watch an alien performance,—that is satisfied, and amply, by the cinema, at its best a most entertaining thing. And it was freely said that the cinema would kill the drama. But the very contrary has proved true. The cinema has hit the commercial theatre very hard indeed. I use that term "commercial" not in the least reproachfully. Commerce in the drama can be as honest a commerce as any other, and predominantly is. But its business is money-making; and at that the cinema easily beats it. But in this very fact and in what has followed from it, in the refusal of the drama to let itself be overwhelmed by the cinema, or crippled by the professional theatre's difficulties, lies the proof that the love for it is not a mere love of spectacle, but something both more active and innate. The fact is that if the whole of the commercial, professional theatre were swept away, the drama would still survive. There are places in Canada where the theatre has actually been swept away. And some of the competitors in the recent drama festival have never sat as audience in a theatre in their lives. That is a truly significant thing, and a thing to rejoice in. For in virtue of it, we are down to the level of the soil with firm ground under our feet. Here is a simple and healthy and entirely natural attitude towards a simple, natural and healthy art.

And this is the thing which has been lacking till now in all the English-speaking communities which have come under Puritan domination, which have therefore been taught to regard drama as an exotic and rather unwholesome, if not actually immoral pursuit. Now upon many things, and upon this among them, there is much to be said for the Puritan point of view. But the logic of it is to abolish the drama, and that cannot be done. It was abolished for a while in England in the seventeenth century, but it rose up again and, what is more, it rose only to justify many of the worst things they had said about it. What they repressed was at worst a fairly wholesome entertainment; what arose twenty years later was a debased and unwholesome one. It were better—after all the proof that has been given us—to accept the instinct for dramatic expression as something innate in people, something which will out. Better, then, let it find the natural channels of expression.

A most hopeful sign that a Canadian national drama is waiting to be born is this, that there were actors in the drama festival who had never seen a play professionally acted in their lives, had never learnt to think of the theatre as a mischievous thing and actors as queer, unreal, outlandish folk, but who take drama as a perfectly natural means of artistic self-expression, and have found in their own remote towns audiences who will take it so too. That was the first thing to achieve, a right attitude to the drama, and it has been achieved in Canada. It has been shown that the thing is rooted in the soil, and it has already shown a very pretty and promising spring flowering.

But rich as its flowering already is, no one can pretend that it is as yet much more than this. Are there to be any ripe and enduring fruits? Who is to say? We cannot look with certainty even into the immediate future, but we can see something of its possibilities in the mirror of the past.

Look for a moment back to the England of the sixteenth century, and to the birth of the Elizabethan-Jacobean drama, to the circumstances which went to its making, and to what it meant to the England of the day, to what English-speaking men and women have owed to its spiritual nourishment ever since. We must allow for the great difference in external circumstances here and today, but, so allowing, we may yet see in that mirror how a Canadian drama might come into being, and what it might mean to the people and the country. The England of that day was a nation still in the making. The Tudors had established political unity; and in peace and under a rule of unified law the cultural harvest of the Renaissance, flourishing for a century or more in Italy, could be enjoyed. It was the age of Erasmus and Cabot and Thomas More. And More's young friend, Heywood, wrote some charming little plays. But they and the rest were academic, not very vital, not things rooted in the soil. It was the day of the student, the classicist, the learned poet still. The popular theatre was there, but it was little better than mummery, a common, rather despised, and neglected thing. For fifty years and more the English Renaissance was postponed by the Tudors' resolve to preserve religious unity too. Tyranny in that matter was approved. Toleration was a Utopian dream. At least we have not had that tragedy to go through. But with the settlement under Elizabeth, men's minds found something like freedom. The desire for self-expression possessed them, and one of the chief results of that was the Elizabethan drama. Much of this present desire for self-expression is a reaction from the bitter discipline of a war which was fought, after all, to justify freedom and our ideals of self-government. Not all of it is. Things are not so simple as that. But it is worth remarking that this desire has found its widest expression among the free peoples.

Three facts went to the production of the Elizabethan drama. The first was the academic drama. In the schools and universities students still learnt rhetoric, and the chair of English literature at Edinburgh is still called the chair of rhetoric. The acting of plays was a compulsory means to that study. The second was the troups of professional mummers and clowns: they were the "rogues and vagabonds" unless they were in the service of some great lord, as the best of them took care to be. Then they wore his livery and went free. And the third was the remnants of the old popular religious drama, for which the reformed church had no use. But the people had loved it. They had acted in it themselves, and they hungered for it still.

Out of those three elements and the prepared responses to them the Elizabethan drama was made. It naturally centred in London. For now the country was at peace, all ambitious young men began to come there. They came from far distances too, these young poets and would-be actors. The distances of the England of those days were, when it came to travelling, the distances of Canada at the present time. When the Barnabe Barnes came from Yorkshire and Daniel from Somerset and Marston from Shropshire, it was much such a journey as has been made by an enthusiastic company of young competitors at the drama festival of 1936 who chartered a Ford car or two, and made their way from Vancouver. Gallant fellows! And it took two days' hard riding for a certain young man from Stratford-on-Avon to gain London. And if, for the first time, he had to walk, he did not do it in much under a week. But there were other factors. Have you ever thought of the particular combination of circumstances which—the capital fact of his genius apart—was needed to produce the Shakespeare of the greater plays? Had there been no theatre for him to learn his business in he would be for us the poet of *Venus and Adonis* and possibly of *Love's Labours Lost*. Had the wish of the Puritan City of London prevailed, and the public theatres been closed, we might at most have had *A Midsummer Night's Dream* and the politer comedies.

It was the prevailing will of the great lords in the Privy Council—asserted with some difficulty too—of the statesmen of the time, Essex and

Hunsdon, Walsingham, Cecil and Southampton, who valued literature and the arts and wished the people to have their theatre; it was the will of the Queen herself, and of James, who took the players under his own protection and made them members of his household—it was this deliberate policy which enabled Shakespeare to teach his fellow-countrymen their country's history in *Henry IV* and *Henry V*, to show them in *Caesar* and *Coriolanus and Antony* what the Roman Empire would have to be, if it was to be. And he taught them, in *Hamlet* and *Lear* and *Macbeth*, to think and feel greatly; to pity profoundly and love deeply—qualities every bit as necessary in a people that means to be great.

How much of the imaginative spirit which sent Englishmen adventuring upon the seven seas is embodied in the literature and drama of that age. It did not create that spirit in them. But it made that spirit articulate. And here the drama,—with its direct appeal to the people, its combination of emotional and intellectual appeal, was at that particular moment of the making of the nation, the moment when the faith by which it was to live for the next few centuries was being determined,—the drama was at that moment a most important thing. And when certain communities of Puritans, who abominated the drama, set out westward a generation later, with, so to speak, a pickaxe in one hand the the Bible in the other, if they could possibly have replaced certain merely legalistic books of the Old Testament by certain plays of Shakespeare, their harsh spirit by his humaner spirit, it might have been a better thing for them and their descendants even until this day. A happier thing certainly. And it is good for people to be happy. No one, if he comes to think of it, will underestimate the part that can be, and that is for good or ill, played by literature and drama in the spiritual life of the nation, especially when that nation is at a formative adolescent, impressionable age.

In this case of sixteenth and seventeenth century England, those things did not happen by accident, by the mere blind play of commercial forces. Shakespeare did not write *Coriolanus* and *King Lear* to earn his living. He had to earn his living; but that was an incidental consideration. There were far easier ways of doing it than that. Nor did the Lords of the Council, these Elizabethan statesmen, make it possible for him, indeed, actively encourage him, to write because it was a good financial proposition, even though incidentally it may have been. They did not reason the thing out. But their imagination served as well, and they had faith in its dictates. Being imaginative men themselves they felt that what the England of their day needed was this spiritual stimulus. And that saw to it that the men who could give it to her should be enabled to do so.

The moral of this is that Canadians have the makings of a Canadian drama under their hands today. Whatever you may do, you will not reproduce that miracle. No one can promise a Canadian Shakespeare. Yet how are we to know that his birth is not recorded in the columns of some Ontario or Quebec or Alberta or Vancouver newspaper this very day? Even if the harvest were only a Jonson, a Massinger, or a Beaumont or Fletcher, its encouragement might still be worthwhile. But it is clear that sooner or later a decision will have to be made about the business. Judging of the quality of the product as it has been exhibited, the decision will come soon. For the one thing that such a movement as the drama movement will not do is to stand still. It has been brought to its present state. If it is merely held there for three or four years then, like all such spring flowers, it will begin to fade away. It will, in more positive terms, disintegrate. And for a demonstrable reason. The best of these actors, the most promising of these dramatists, who now do this work casually, incidentally to their other work, will begin to find their true vocation in it. And if they cannot find opportunity to fulfil that vocation here, they will drift away to New York or London or to Hollywood where they will feel that they can. This is bound to happen. And Canada will lose them, will lose this much of the spiritual and intellectual strength she herself has bred. Incidentally they will lose themselves. For in those alien places they will almost certainly become aliens. They will be subdued to the colour in which they work.

It would be impertinent to counsel the laying of the foundation stone of a great Canadian National Theatre, a material theatre, tomorrow. Yet about ten years back, when the London scheme for a national theatre showed some signs of renewed life, there was an open competition for architectural designs and plans for a building. It was won by a Canadian architect, Mr. W.L. Somerville, of Toronto. He won because he had so admirably faced the practical issues of the problem. The practical problem must be faced for what it is. The drama and the theatre that is wanted will not automatically come into existence by the operation of the rather discredited law of commercial supply and demand. Fortunately there is proof that it will not. Supply and demand in this matter have shown during these past few years that Canadian drama is a poorly considered item in the calculations of the honestly money-making theatres of London and New York. That is our good fortune. And what seems their good fortune is, from this point of view, their ill fortune. For the real difficulty in the way of establishing an "organized" theatre there is that they have so much already that they cannot be persuaded that they need it. But the need for it can be expressed in the nutshell of a metaphor; you may have the best bookshops possible, full of the latest fiction and with a sprinkling of popular classics. Yet no statesman who thinks in terms of his country's intelligence would suppose that to be compensation for the non-existence of a public library.

The problem is to be faced for what it is—its cultural aspects, its true economics, the problem as a whole; questions of finance allowed their due place, but now with the whole thing reduced to terms of crude profit and loss. For almost as much as the quality of the best artistic product in the Dominion drama festival has been the extraordinary good sense of the organization of it, in which is to be discerned the guiding hand, the kindly tact and real wisdom of Colonel Osborne. No statesman today can be content to neglect this problem, which is the problem of the nourishing or starving or, even worse, if it is left neglected, the poisoning of the imagination of the people. Other problems press on our rulers daily. The world is too much with them indeed. But there are the elder statesmen, and the statesmen temporarily out of office. We may commend this uncontroversial matter to their attention. And surely, this is a matter worthy of statesmanlike attention, worthy of the attention of the statesmen of a free country, since they depend, as we all depend, on the spiritual, moral and intellectual qualities of the mass of the people. And who, looking around the world today, will contend that our free institutions themselves can be certain to survive in the face of efficient dictatorships and obedient masses, unless we become as efficient in our own way by faithfully pursuing our very different ideal, which is to make each individual, man and woman, worthy of his freedom and fit to choose his rulers and from time to time to judge them. That cannot be done, it is a commonplace, by an ignorant or morally debauched mob.

If we neglect the education of the people we are preparing our own destruction. That is a commonplace too. It is still, perhaps, not quite so common to recognize what the limits of education are. There is the limit of time which can be given to it in school and university—that we see. But limitation in the acquiring of knowledge? Take up the daily paper. It contains a hundred subjects upon which, if we were directly ruling our country, we ought to have knowledge and opinion. But about nine-tenths of our knowledge is next to nothing, and our opinion not worth having. We must delegate the matters to our elected rulers. But finally we shall have to judge whether they have done right or wrong. And here is where the case for cultivating our imagination comes in.

Imagination is not a royal road to a knowledge of facts, nor is there any, but it is, in some sense, to an appreciation of them, and to a knowledge of men. It will not be, if it is debauched and impoverished by yellow journalism, cheap fiction, poor plays. But if the plain citizen, the ordinary man and woman, can be offered instead good fiction, sound drama,—the real world and the meaning, the right and the wrong of it, and, above all, the honesty and dishonesty of the people who run it, can be brought home to simpler folk, they will come into first-hand contact with these great affairs by contemplation of their equivalents in the mimic world of fiction or the theatre. What finally matters in our dealings with public men or private? That one should be a good judge of character, should know the plausible from the honest man. The art of the drama is, above all else, the art of the exhibition and interpretation of character, of character in action. And there are lessons to be learnt from it. The dramatist's, the poet's, the novel-writer's business is to bring home the truth to his hearers in the guise of a parable; an old and divinely honoured method. It is no paradox to say that in the Roman plays of Shakespeare a key will be found to the politics of Empire. It is plain truth that if you have been stirred and enlightened by the storm scenes of *King Lear* you will be better fitted to deal with the problem of the unemployed.

And it is in this world of the imagination, guided in it by the "choice and master spirits" of the ages, that men and nations learn to know themselves, and to realize what they can be and do and hope to become. The material achievements of the Dominion of Canada have already been great and they will be greater. But unless intellectual and spiritual achievement ever keeps pace with them they will not finally be of real account in the world's history. The drama can but play its own part in this spiritual achievement, and it need not be a negligible part.

THE CANADIAN THEATRE
AND THE IRISH EXEMPLAR ✧

JOHN COULTER

○

Irish-born playwright John Coulter (1888–1980) felt that one possible model for the emerging Canadian theatre to follow might be the Irish Literary Movement, as he explained in the American magazine Theatre Arts Monthly *in 1938.*

It is as well to say at once that I speak of the theatre in Canada as a visiting Irishman from London, England. As such I am not an unbiased observer, and for reasons which will presently appear I had better make this remark the subject of a little preamble. I confess, therefore, that my notion of values in the theatre was powerfully and permanently affected by years of regular attendance at the Abbey. Week by week I sat there, "all mouth and eyes," watching with delight and wonder while the life I knew, the dreary secular life of Irish parlors and kitchens and farms and pubs, was turned by the Abbey playwrights and players into parable, lovely and rich and lively dramatic parable. Tragic plays there were, showing the Irish to themselves as noble persons of heroic breed; and plays full of extravagant fun and high spirits, revealing us to our surprised and flattered selves as a humorous and witty race; and plays of savage satire or irony at which we stared in angry astonishment—Irish mugs in Irish mirrors. In short, nearly all the plays I saw were Irish, flowering from the soil of Ireland and deeply rooted in it. And I was naive enough to assume that the plays of other countries were similarly rooted, that they were similarly a means, and a most potent means, for the imaginative criticism, portrayal, interpretation of national life and character.

✧ *Theatre Arts Monthly* 22 (July 1938): 503–9.

That naive assumption did not survive. I went to London. In London I looked with some incredulity or befuddlement at the plays in the West End. What shocked me was the spectacle of a theatre doing supremely well what seemed to me supremely not worth doing. I thought of it as a theatre which had lost touch with life and reality, or which made false whatever touch it had for the sake of a flashy theatrical artifice reflecting the improbable manners and doings of worthless creatures without roots in any soil. There were, of course, many exceptions; but that sort of play seemed to me to rule the West End stage.

With these contrasting types of play went contrasting styles of acting. In the Irish theatre the criterion of excellence was the ability of the players to recreate local scene and character on the stage with sincerity and simple truth. In the West End theatre it was ability to register personality, to exploit the box-office appeal of a star actor as a saleable asset through plays which were primarily "vehicles." Conflicting styles, based on conflicting ideals. I was biased in favor of the Irish ideal. I had no doubt at all of its superior value and vitality as an art. I thought that as an art it was going on in the right direction from a point at which the commercial theatre had lost its way. And that was the bias with which I looked at the theatre in Canada. It remains with me, and has been strengthened by what I saw and endured in the competitive rigors of one season of the Dominion Drama Festival.

Now the theatre in Canada virtually is the amateur theatre of the Festival. The professional houses are not all dark, and there are stock repertory companies such as the Holden Players whose winter stand is in Winnipeg and whose summer theatre is at Bala in the Muskoka Lakes. But it is the amateurs who not only hold the fort effectively against the competitive attack of cinemas, radio, flood-lit sports and the like, but go on generating such enthusiasm for the arts of acting and production that, from my own conversational contacts, I might well have deduced that every other person in the Dominion was in some way associated with the movement, and that most of them were actively rehearsing or producing or organizing a production, with or without a speculative and ambitious eye to the numerous Festival laurels: the medals, the certificates, the Sir Barry Jackson trophy, the Bessborough trophy itself.

This outbreak of acting and producing is not confined to the big towns; it is epidemic also in the little villages from the maritime provinces to the mining and lake-shore settlements in the north, and extends out west across the prairies and on over the Rockies to Vancouver and the Pacific Coast. Indeed it is one of the few elements common to the otherwise heterogeneous life of the Dominion. Here, in this nation-wide enthusiasm for dramatics regarded both as an alluring form of education and as an exciting pastime, is a disinterested cultural activity, organized and directed as such but in practical effect exerting a political influence, in the sense that is interpenetrates the whole structure of Canadian society and draws together its diverse communities of race, language, vocation and religious or political creed. In the geographical and racial conditions which make precarious the cohesion of widely scattered provinces within the Dominion—part French in language and tradition and part British, plus sections derived from every other European and Asiatic nationality—any activity which promotes community of interest is of political importance. And that is part of the Festival Theatre's importance to Canada, though not an ostensible or consciously exploited part. Not consciously exploited, yet I cannot think it mere coincidence or accident that the crowning trophy of the Festival was presented by the Governor General whose name it bears, His Excellency Lord Bessborough, and that not only Lord Bessborough but his successor in the viceregal office, Lord Tweedsmuir, should encourage the movement by direct personal interest as well as by official patronage.

I do not know how deeply or how far this unifying influence has gone. Its results cannot be spectacular. It is true that the French-speaking section is still something of a festival within the Festival. It is true that adjudicators and spokesmen for the Festival are still impelled to advocate means of mitigating even the sectionalism within the movement. But it is also true that the award of the Bessborough Trophy is for the best production in the Festival presenting a play in French or in English, and this is everywhere accepted as but another and a fair way of saying: for the best *Canadian* production.

Another and more direct way in which the Festival can help in the making of Canada is by itself becoming Canadian. There, when I try to assess its potentialities by my own standard and the bias I have described, lies the edge of my argument. In a sentence: Canadian theatre is excellent theatre but not yet specifically Canadian. (And if I were asked: What virtue is there in becoming specifically Canadian? Why not aim at the ideal of internationalism in the theatre at least? I should reply that in my belief the way to internationalism in the theatre as in all else lies through the prior achievement of the greatest degree of nationalism. It is an organic growth outward from a core which is the individual himself, in this case the individual playwright.) Meantime, as I am glad to admit, the arts of acting and production have been lifted in Canada to a level—shown at its highest in the Festival finals—a level which I have never seen surpassed by amateurs, even in Ireland where play-acting is less an art than an instinct.

I remember that the two runners-up who tied for second place in the 1937 finals as adjudicated by Michel Saint-Denis, gave finished performances that would have passed the professional standards of Broadway or Shaftesbury Avenue. They were: the Strolling Players of Vancouver, in excerpts from *The Barretts of Wimpole Street*; and the Dramatic Club of the University College Alumnae Association, Toronto, in an act of *The Cradle Song*, directed by Edgar Stone. I remember how Michel Saint-Denis had difficulty in deciding that certain others were not also deserving of a share in the tie, notably the Vancouver Little Theatre for its production of Neil Grant's *The Last War*. And I remember how he spoke of the acting of the Strolling Players under the direction of Colin Laurence as impressive, and described the production of *The Cradle Song* as "almost perfect."

There come to my mind, too, happy recollections of performances by Canadian actors, some of whom drew from Michel Saint-Denis the significant compliment that "they knew what acting meant, and could sometimes find the whole truth of a character or a situation in a single gesture or phrase." I can here but name a few of them, well known in widely separated parts of the Dominion: Gay Scrivener, Florence Castonguay, Eunice Alexander, May Fletcher, Betty Boylen, Irene Henderson, Belle Greenberg, Agnes Muldrew, Nancy Pyper. And among the men: Ivor Lewis, a master of character acting; Joseph Plante, Colin Laurence, Jules Ross, G.A.P. Arnold, Frank Rostance, John Greer, James Pryce, Eric Aldwinckle, and that gentle and diffident character-comedian whose genius should be known beyond the bounds of the Dominion, H.E. Hitchman.

There is plenty of evidence that Canadian groups are well aware of what is being done in the contemporary theatre of Europe, as well as of America, and are themselves eager to share in every form of stage experiment. I think particularly of Herman Voaden's Theatre Studio Group and of Toronto's socially-conscious and propagandist Theatre of Action directed by David Pressman, who has great skill with untrained players and a most alert sense of theatre. Eager experiment. Excellence of production and acting. These are everywhere in evidence, yet for me they do but mark what I deem a major failure of the movement in Canada. For in spite of the existence of the Festival organization in every part of the country, promising to give likely plays at least a fair chance of production; in spite of encouragement by the Festival committees through offers of medals and cash prizes— the writing of Canadian plays still muddles incompetently along, far in the wake of the other arts of the theatre. I am afraid it is not admitted that the most potent of all the theatre's activities is the expression of what is characteristic in the life of the community through plays written by, for and about the people of the community. There is a deplorable lack of good plays that can be called in any specific sense Canadian.

As an effective answer to this criticism it might be said that my insular outlook prevents me from seeing that Canada is not a small island like Ireland but an enormous stretch of continent; that its people are not an indigenous racial unit inheriting well-marked characteristics and immemorial traditions susceptible of dramatic treatment; that there is in Canada, as yet, no such thing as Canadians, in the sense that there are Irish in Ireland. To which I should reply that the Canadian, as a national type, is at least emergent. And, assuming some virtue in the national ideal, I should argue that this emergence might be helped if playwrights, actors and producers north of Niagara would turn their eyes from Broadway and look around them at a place called Canada. In the streets of Canadian towns, on the prairies, in the lake settlements and mining villages, a hundred grand plays are waiting for Canadians who will write them. And for an earnest of what can be done, look at the plays of Merrill Denison. In the short comedies of his collection called *The Unheroic North* there was the beginning of authentic Canadian drama. There were the first fruits of a harvest which still waits to be gathered. The sooner what Denison started and left undeveloped is carried forward again by himself or others, the better for everyone in the movement.

A play by Mrs. Bicknell, presented at the 1937 Festival, and dealing with the struggle of prairie farmers against disaster, was a courageous effort to do what is needed. It was called *Relief*. Mrs. Bicknell is a farmer's wife, she wrote and directed her play, and her husband and some neighbors along with herself composed the cast. And, like her, other playwrights have done a little gleaning here and there. But it has been a gloomy gleaning of rather bitter fruit. For it is true that amateur playwrights, determined to be serious, often forget that true comedy can be as serious as tragedy, and that gloom, depression and disillusion are not even essential elements of tragedy. There is inviting subject-matter for plays in prairie droughts and crop-failure, in mining disasters, in the poverty of the slum dwellers of city streets or country shacks, but accurate reporting of misfortune or disaster or accident is not enough to make a play; and indeed what is dark and grievous in the actual circumstances of life has no rightful place on the stage till it is transmuted by art into the very different category of the tragic experience.

I think such a reminder worth offering, and yet, as I make it, I reflect that inexperienced and maybe potentially good young Canadian playwrights are still working without adequate help of a criticism, a philosophy, a point of view. The plays which they see performed for the Festival are frequently plays which they would do better not to see at all: plays chosen because of their success in the professional productions of Broadway or Shaftesbury Avenue, even plays of the kind I have described as "vehicles" and which only the special gifts of the actor for whom they were devised can make tolerable. (I do not, of course, deride the plays and productions which succeed in the commercial theatre; I merely say that success in that field is of itself no reliable guide to suitability for amateurs. It can, on the contrary, lure them into fearful folly.) Indeed I have sometimes been tempted to stand up in the theatre and shout a protest, angered at the ineptitude which could waste good acting and good producing on plays manifestly unsuitable or unworthy; plays dealing with people and circumstances of which the actors plainly knew nothing whatsoever, or plays in which all truth of conduct or character was sacrificed to some trumpery plot leading to a situation supposedly effective in the bad sense of the word "theatrical."

My best wish for the theatre in Canada is that to its other excellences it should add a few playwrights, writers of integrity and vision, who would themselves give it conscious outlook and purpose by providing plays, and by helping to formulate a criticism and philosophy analogous to that by which the reading committee of the Abbey Theatre made the Irish drama not only Irish but of universal significance. There is already the beginning of a school of Canadian playwrights, whose talent, however, is as yet not matched by instinct or wisdom to direct it. They want the big spectacular success. Their eye is on the big money and the big name of success on Broadway or in London's West End. They have not yet learned the paradoxical truth that the most effective way to keep an eye on Broadway is to keep on looking attentively at the life passing under your own nose in your own home town. They have not seen that it is by a sort of transfusion of vitality from plays rooted in the life of small-town streets or country soil that even the commercial theatre of Broadway is periodically revived. That is the lesson of *Tobacco Road* and *Of Mice and Men* and *Our Town*. It is the lesson which Brian Doherty of Toronto was quick to learn when he sensed the dramatic possibilities of Bruce Marshall's gentle parable of life in a Scottish town, *Father Malachy's Miracle*. It is the lesson of Mazo de la Roche's *Whiteoaks*.

I wish there were in Canada a reading committee of such insight and sympathy and such authority that young playwrights would consult them and be guided by them as were the young Irish playwrights by the Abbey committee. I wish such a committee had available a little theatre, adequately endowed as it should be by government grant, or by public subscription, a theatre like the Abbey in which Canadian plays of promise could be given production. It could so easily come about that such a theatre, from even the smallest spark at first, could in the end generate such light and heat as would set afire the imagination now dormant in Canada's potential writers for the stage. There is no adequate reason why such a theatre should not be established and maintained as a centre of all the arts of the theatre, with one or two repertory companies like the Abbey companies, who would play Toronto, Montreal, Ottawa, Quebec, Winnipeg first of all, and thereafter make a circuit of smaller towns for one or two-night stands. I wish. . . . But what's the use of wishing! Go find a gold mine! And though there are in Canada gold mines (but not in any venture of the theatre!) I am not myself likely to find one, nor to persuade those who do to make possible the fulfilment of such a dream—of a Canadian theatre for Canada.

A TOUR ACROSS CANADA [✧]

MAURICE COLBOURNE

O

Barnstorming by foreign stars was a way of life clearly on the way out in Canada by the end of the 1930s. The following article was written for the New York Times *by the British star Maurice Colbourne (1894–1965) in 1940.*

Well, we have done what we set out to do. I suppose that is something. Barry Jones and I took what has come to be known as the Colbourne-Jones Company across Canada and back on a sort of voyage of discovery to see whether the theatre still existed in territory that was a profitable and happy hunting ground ten years ago.

Let me say at once that we found the theatre. But it was moribund. Frankly, I do not see how the patient is going to survive. It not only cannot afford the drastic new treatment which any sound doctor of the theatre would prescribe but it lacks at present even the will to live. I will mention later some of the patient's more pathetic and irritating symptoms.

I think no company, certainly no company from across the Atlantic, has made the trans-Canada trip for seven years. Our trip, however, had nothing to do with the war. We conceived it in March, were spurred on by the emotion evoked by the royal visit in May, planned it through the Summer and carried on despite the war. I believe we wanted to make the trip simply because, after seven years' absence, we were homesick for yes, the wide open spaces, the Rockies and even subzero cold!

We were quite a party. Thirty-nine, to be exact, with three productions wedged without many inches to spare into two eighty-foot baggage cars. Our plays, "Geneva," "Tobias and the Angel" and "Charles the King," were selected for their variety as plays. They formed a sort of gigantic triple bill.

We were very proud of our production of them, everything being brand-new and a little bit better, we thought, and still think, than it had been in London. The three plays involve twenty-one scenes and 199 costumes.

We were due to sail on Sept. 30, but the sailings, first of one ship and then another, were cancelled, leaving us nothing to do but stand by packed and ready to sail at twenty-four hours' notice. We eventually sailed on Oct. 6. The only thing was to take the delay light-heartedly, in the spirit of the man who objected to the blackout and the closing of theatres on the ground that Londoners could stand being bombed but not being bored. One member of the company threatened to put in for a rise in salary if we were torpedoed and she had to remain afloat for more than a week.

But all this, as Charles Frohman was fond of saying when anything had happened that he wanted to forget, "is yesterday." Let me come to today when the tour is over; and to "Geneva"; and to Shaw.

The symptoms of decay in the theatre through Canada seem to me, as I look back on this instructive tour, fourfold. First, the theatre is a matter of habit, and in Canada people are losing the habit. Our audiences were mainly of people old enough to have acquired the theatre habit before the almighty film flooded the world, and these people would think nothing of driving more than 200 miles to see the plays. But in the minds of the ordinary person of 20 or 30 years, the fact that a first-class company in a first-class play was in town tonight simply, speaking generally, did not register. As for the growing generation, a party of pupils from the Montessori School in Calgary came to see us, and when the curtain rose they whispered to each other, "Technicolor!" Nor even after the curtain fell finally could they be persuaded that we were real people and not some new film process.

Secondly, not all but the majority of the few remaining theatres in Canada are not only in a state of varying dirt and disrepair backstage but, what is much more important, their auditoriums and general appointments in front are so dilapidated or uncared for that patrons have to overcome a long-established repugnance to their one and only local theatre before they will go and see a play in it. We have heard legitimate complaints from patrons concerning six of the theatres we played in. And we only played in ten all told. Of the remaining four, three are normally now used as picture houses, which is equivalent to saying that they are clean and attractive. The remaining one deserves an honorable mention: it is the Royal Alexandra in Toronto.

Thirdly, there is the competition with the pictures, and the pictures have won. The people one meets are quite sincere when they say that they are starving for plays, but unfortunately they are few in number and speak only for themselves. The rest also are starved of plays. But they are not starving for them. They have found a cheap, handy, comfortable diet of something else instead, the diet of pictures, with which they appear perfectly content and feed on with alarming regularity once or twice a week.

Fourthly, the harm done to the theatre by the Little Theatre, though incalculable, is, I am now convinced, great. What is wanted from the Little Theatre if it is to justify its existence is a band of enthusiastic playgoers instead of groups of (in the main) astoundingly self-satisfied would-be play-performers. Too often self-expression is only a polite name for exhibitionism. Amateur means lover, and the least a lover of the theatre can do to show his or her love is to go to the theatre on the increasingly rare occasions when the real theatre comes along. But the amateurs are generally too busy amateuring.

Barry Jones was asked to broadcast to some 150 Little Theatre Groups in the vicinity of the city where we were playing. He compiled with a very fine talk about the theatre and the Little Theatre. Not only was the effect on our box-office negligible, if any, but the instigator of the broadcast displayed his love of the theatre by wanting free seats. And what is to be said of the lady who drove me to a Little Theatre reception given in our honor and gayly explained en route that she couldn't possibly come to "Geneva" because she was so busy rehearsing, or of the Little Theatre which produced its own play in the very week in which we, the only English company to visit the city in seven years, were due to appear? Nothing printable.

The trouble with the Little Theatres is that their necessarily inexpert acting alienates even their own audiences, who are kept to heel largely by a kind of social blackmail. The general and unfashionable public instinctively is too wise to be drawn into the pretentious net of Uplift. But the damage is done, for to them a play comes to mean a dull thing to be avoided, like the plague.

Nevertheless the tour all in all was a success. Our business might have been very much worse, and our audiences, we have reason to believe, were more than satisfied with what we gave them, and that is the great thing. I would like to think that my own play, "Charles the King," was our strength and stay, but it is a play that simply eats up money, and it was undoubtedly Bernard Shaw's "Geneva" that took us safely across the continent without financial loss.

Since New York is due to form its own opinion of "Geneva" on Tuesday I will say nothing here that may prejudice that opinion either way, I being at this stage prejudiced in its favor to the nth degree. But perhaps I can without offense summarize what I wrote about it in "The Real Bernard Shaw," because when I wrote I had no axe to grind, never dreaming I would ever be playing in "Geneva" or be in any way associated with its production in New York. I cannot quote from the book verbatim because the war makes it difficult for books to reach one from across the sea on time, and I have not yet seen a printed copy. I remember remarking, however, that what struck me about "Geneva" was its author's Olympian fairmindedness, and the resemblance of the second act to a symphony with rich sweeping orchestration.

What astounds me about G.B.S. now, even more than his perpetual youthfulness of mind, is the amazing sureness of his handwriting. A letter from him which reached me this week is before me; the script might be that of a man of 38 instead of 83. Perhaps some one would like to reproduce a bit of it, one day, so that people can see what I mean. Only we shall have to be careful. Shaw knows everything there is to be known about the laws of copyright, and these things sometimes make him angry. And, though he looks strokable at 83, he can still be angry. Indeed, as his young countryman, John Stewart Collis, has rightly said, "Whereas Shaw's beard used to be redhot with anger, it is now whitehot with rage."

section 4

GOVERNMENT INTERVENTION, 1945–1967

TOWARD A CANADIAN THEATRE ✧

JOHN COULTER

o

John Coulter's increasing interest in and commitment to Canada was clear in this essay written for the Canadian Review of Music and Other Arts *in a 1945 issue.*

By Canadian theatre we mean the dramatic activities of people in Canada. In that sense Canadian theatre already has a history. It has grown and is growing. Its forms include stage, film and radio. Film and radio flourish on public funds, and as show business. Our particular concern is with the stage.

In Canada the stage is all but exclusively amateur, the professional houses being now mostly dark, and kept so for commercial reasons. But amateur stage is everywhere active, in big cities and small frontier settlements alike. It is our most potent form of disinterested activity, artistic and recreational. It has been able—as instanced by the pre-war meetings of the Dominion Drama Festival—to draw together in friendly rivalry the otherwise diverse elements of race, language, vocation and religious or political creed which make up our emerging national community. That is the point to which Canadian stage had grown. We believe we are about to pass beyond it.

We believe the move forward will be made in every Province of the Dominion, all sharing a common plan but working it out with whatever adaptations may seem appropriate to the special conditions of each Province. The local dramatic societies are the competent judges of these conditions, and obviously it is for them to decide what practical method

✧ *Canadian Review of Music and Other Arts*, 4, 1 and 2 (Aug./Sept. 1945): 17–20.

suits them best within the general scheme—a scheme to be determined by a meeting of representatives from all parts of the Dominion.

We in Ontario should begin now to find out what is most practicable for our own part of the country: a scheme capable of embodiment, as at least an element, in the wider plan. And we think that, for us, what is needed is a drawing-together of all our hitherto scattered dramatic groups in a Provincial theatre organization, provided with a home—buildings, equipment, personnel and a policy. Stages and platforms on which shows have in the past been presented will still be available, but augmented in many places by the new community centre buildings which—unless the movement is grossly mismanaged—will have stages and auditoriums where local and visiting companies may play the district. But the necessary fulcrum of extended dramatic activity in Ontario is now a central theatre, a building of modern design and equipment with workshops for mounting and dressing shows, premises for a play library and a school of theatre arts.

A Provincial theatre council—as a constituent member of the Dominion theatre council—would be in charge of general policy here, and the practical work would be done by a professional staff and a permanent company of players. The council would be representative of all the Ontario drama "regions." The professional staff would include, with clerks and crews, directors, stage designers and teachers, who, when needed, would travel to outlying societies as advisers or coaches. The permanent company of players would be drawn, as far as practicable, from the best of Ontario's actors and from the students of the dramatic school. They would perform a chosen repertory of plays in the central theatre, and later would tour the Ontario circuit and the theatres of the other Provinces. During the weeks of this tour by the permanent company, regional companies and the companies from the other Provinces would come in and play their shows in the central theatre. This would be part of an exchange system. It could in the end provide a continuous season of productions here and across the Dominion.

Since the theatre at its best is a reflection in terms of dramatic art of the characteristic life of the community, the writing of Canadian plays, hitherto neglected, will be fostered. New plays that are good enough for production will be produced. That assurance may speedily change the aspect of playwriting in this country. There are already a few Canadian authors who, with a competent stage inviting their work, could in time make the plays of the Canadian theatre not only of importance to Canada but of universal significance. It happened so at the Moscow Art Theatre. And at the Abbey Theatre in Dublin. There is no certainty that it could not happen in Canada.

To finance building and endowment is, we think, the joint duty of the Federal and the Provincial governments. It seems to us not outrageous to expect that the Federal government will yet provide a fund to be shared by Provinces who are themselves willing to contribute. (We recall the extensive theatrical activities, up and down the British Isles and in many countries abroad, conducted since 1934 by the British Council—a branch of the British Foreign Office—with the bill footed by the Treasury. And we wonder has anyone the effrontery to suggest that the British Treasury has merely been spending enormous sums of public money on manifest tomfooleries? We prefer to think that the British—politically the wisest and most mature of peoples—have understood long since the significance of the stage in this modern form of goodwill diplomacy.)

Meanwhile, Ontario is not lacking in citizens who could make possible an immediate start upon the planning and preparations for building. What is needed here, as elsewhere in the Dominion is, first, discernment and complete conviction in the dramatic groups of the need and importance of the movement, then clear statement of plan and purpose. The rest is chiefly an affair of expert modern promotion.

For the moment all must of necessity be tentative, outline and suggestion merely. But that is proper to beginnings. As a local beginning we propose that the drama societies of our own district, Toronto, should meet. They should clarify for themselves a plan which could at least provisionally be the plan for all Ontario, and an integral part of a Dominion plan. Later the groups in other Ontario regions should be called in to consider this plan, with representatives from other Provinces welcomed as observers. These other Provinces might at the same time be holding similar gatherings. Out of this, if we had practical sense and the enthusiasm or passion to accomplish what is possible though difficult, Canadian theatre might again move forward toward maturity.

THE THEATRE IN CANADA:
A NATIONAL THEATRE? ✧

H.A. VOADEN

o

Can the Canadian theatre ever achieve real maturity without government sup-
port? Writer-educator Herman Voaden discussed this question in a 1946 issue
of Theatre Arts Monthly.

Will the Canadian theatre emerge as an important national theatre, with a
significant literature of its own, by its own unaided efforts? Or can this be
achieved only by government assistance? The principle of subsidization has
been accepted for three generations in Canada. In 1863 [sic], the isolated
provinces joined together to form a Canadian confederation reaching from
sea to sea. At that time Canadian statesmen subsidized the railroads, fling-
ing bands of steel across a continent to bind together a country that was
geographically not a country. For decades the tariff has subsidized and protected the Canadian manufacturer and worker.

One reason for this subsidization is the presence of an overwhelmingly
great power along three thousand miles of our border, exercising powerful
attractions, both material and cultural, which, while not baneful in themselves, are sometimes prejudicial to Canada's interests as a united nation.
The Maritime Provinces belong geographically to the New England States.
Quebec is a world in itself, with separate language, religion and civil war.
Between Ontario and the west lie 500 miles of rock and tree wilderness,
spanned for half a century by rail and only recently by air and transconti-
nental highway. The west is closer to the American west than to Ontario; a
great mountain barrier makes British Columbia geographically a unit with
the Pacific Northwest.

✧ *Theatre Arts* 30, 7 (July 1946): 389–91.

The necessity of preserving and fostering Canada's nationhood has compelled an extension of the principle of subsidization in the last two decades to include government support for the two mechanical media of information, entertainment and culture—the radio and film. The Canadian Broadcasting Corporation is supported by considerable government funds as well as an annual license fee. The National Film Board is also supported liberally from public funds.

Both of these great national organizations, under independent boards or commissions, are playing a significant part in the development of Canadian character and art. The CBC has recently commissioned two operas: *Transit Through Fire*, a radio opera, and *Deirdre of the Sorrows*, a full-length work. The music for both was written by Healey Willan, one of Canada's most distinguished composers, and the librettos by John Coulter, well-known Irish-born Canadian playwright. The CBC has also presented many programs of music by other Canadian composers. It has sponsored fine Canadian radio-play workshops, notably the Toronto series, Stage 44, Stage 45 and Stage 46, under the direction of Andrew Allan. Canadian playwrights, actors, directors, composers, players, singers and conductors are making a genuine contribution to Canadian culture and receiving a good living as a result of the effort of this government-subsidized organization.

In the same way the National Film Board, in its animated films, its films on folk music and handicrafts and its series on Canadian painting, is interesting itself in the arts of Canada. It is making a significant contribution in the field of the documentary film with its *Canada Carries On* and *The World in Action* series. It is employing first-rate musicians, artists and theatre workers in increasing numbers.

Finally there is a measure of government support for the visual arts in the annual grants that are made to the National Gallery at Ottawa, which has purchased an admirable collection of Canadian paintings and sculpture and circulates exhibitions nationally and internationally.

The artists of Canada wish to extend the services provided by the CBC, Film Board and National Gallery and to add to them national services in music and the theatre. In the "Ottawa Briefs," these and other proposals were made by sixteen national cultural organizations of the country. In 1944, nine delegates from these societies appeared before the Reconstruction Committee of the House of Commons and pointed out that the creative arts stand in a key position in the economy of the whole nation and that there is great need for a wider distribution of cultural advantages at present available only to the few. "Millions of persons living in Canada have never seen an original work of art nor attended a symphony concert or a professionally produced play. . . . On the other hand, thousands of professional, creative minds enjoy a field so limited that they are forced into activities unsuited to their talents." They urged the use of the arts as ambassadors of goodwill abroad.

They made three basic proposals. The first was that a government body should be set up to promote the arts, working in conjunction with the CBC, Film Board and National Gallery. The second was that the government should provide grants-in-aid to assist in building hundreds of community centres across the land, and spend annually the equivalent of a dollar per person to help maintain these centres and provide library, theatre, music, art, film and educational services for them. Thirdly, they made specific recommendations for the encouragement of the arts, including a national orchestra-training centre, state and regional theatres, a national library, the improvement of industrial design, national competitions in music and the arts and national prizes and scholarships.

Members of the delegation were successful in selling their basic idea of decentralization of the arts and wider distribution of cultural advantages to the parliamentarians. They were praised because they sought the good of the community rather than profits or earnings. They were hailed as a new kind of pressure group. Now strongly organized as the Canadian Arts Council, they are pressing with increasing public sympathy for the implementation of their proposals. In connection with the United Nations Educational, Scientific and Cultural Organization some sort of commission of national bodies in these fields will be set up to make possible the interchange of educational and cultural information and services with other countries which are members of UNESCO. Community-centre organizations are mushrooming by the hundreds, and a National Arts Board is being urged as an immediate necessity to provide cultural services essential to support and vitalize programs for these centres, as well as for UNESCO export.

If these plans materialize the Canadian theatre will experience a renaissance in the years to come. Through hundreds of halls and new community centres across the country, theatre, concert, opera and ballet troupes will circulate. The best of them will be sent abroad. In this tremendous upsurge of activity a new theatre literature will be born.

But should these fine schemes fail? What then will be the prospects for the Canadian theatre? Will it be able to pull itself up by its own bootstraps?

Apart from Toronto, Montreal and two or three other centres, the commercial or road theatre in Canada is dead. Distances are great, attempts made during the past year by Canadian theatrical producers to arrange schedules for professional troupes across the country have not been successful. It has been necessary to use school auditoriums and other halls not designed for the purpose; arrangements have been made for bookings in former theatres now showing movies, but these have not been satisfactory.

The decline of the road, a long process which was completed in the Thirties, was matched by a tremendous increase in amateur theatre activity, the whole movement encouraged by the Dominion Drama Festival. Chiefly through the efforts of Colonel H.C. Osborne, Chairman of the Festival, seven or eight thousand dollars was raised annually and the services of an outstanding adjudicator were secured, who travelled from the Maritimes to British Columbia judging Regional and Provincial Festivals. The winners in these Festivals were brought to Ottawa for a National Festival in the late spring. The Festivals performed a unique service, not only in arousing public interest in the theatre, raising production and acting standards and encouraging native playwriting, but also in cementing national unity and a feeling of common citizenship.

With the war it was necessary to abandon the National Festivals. Local festivals were continued in the western provinces, especially in British Columbia and Saskatchewan. Through the activities of the Summer School in the Arts at Banff, and the leadership given by the Departments of Education or the Extension Departments of the Universities in the four provinces, dramatic activity actually increased during the war in Western Canada. It flowered in the Western Canada Theatre Conference, which was formed in Banff in the Summer of 1944. This important organization has already taken steps to encourage playwriting, to coordinate and improve drama festivals, especially in the matter of adjudication, to improve the construction, equipment and lighting of school and community stages and generally to prepare the ground for a National Conference and National Theatre in Canada.

In the east the story is different. Only one university, Queen's at Kingston, maintained a summer school in drama during the war years. A second university, Western at London, Ontario, last year offered drama and play production courses for the first time. Hart House Theatre was closed for the duration. Many established groups and new organizations did splendid work in entertaining the troops, some continued their program of productions for civilian audiences, a few carried on the vital task of sponsoring new Canadian plays and experimenting with non-commercial plays and techniques.

In London, Ontario, and Montreal the theatre held its place and won new laurels for itself. In Toronto in the spring of 1945 the first move was made to form an Ontario Division of a National Theatre. At the same time a Toronto Civic Theatre Association was set up. This Association while not completely successful in its initial efforts, is making some progress, and in April sponsored a Drama Festival.

The general picture after the war already shows a big increase in amateur theatre activity. Regional drama festivals will be held this year in many parts of Canada, and the officers of the Dominion Drama Festival plan to launch the Festival on a national scale in 1947.

Out of the National Festivals may emerge, in a year or more, a National Theatre Conference, and in time, perhaps, a National Theatre with regional theatres and professional repertory troupes. It is possible that the process may be accelerated by a large contribution from a private foundation or benefactor. But there is an increasing conviction on the part of many theatre workers in Canada that this process will be a slow one and that it will not achieve the hoped-for results.

These protagonists of government support claim that if Canada is to become a world cultural power, as important in the arts as she is now in trade and industrial production, she must subsidize not only the radio and film, but the visual arts, music and the theatre as well. They maintain that only then will the theatre reach its true stature as a humane, civilizing instrument, expressing and enriching the life of a young but potentially great nation.

DORA MAVOR MOORE AND THE NEW PLAY SOCIETY (c. 1946) ◊

MAVOR MOORE

○

Actress-teacher-animateur Dora Mavor Moore (1888–1979) began the New Play Society in Toronto in 1946. The first professional theatre to be started in Canada after the war, its early days were recalled in her son Mavor Moore's autobiography, Reinventing Myself.

For all of Dora Mavor Moore's devoted years of preparation, the New Play Society was an improvisation. That the lecture hall in the Royal Ontario Museum had just become available as a public theatre was serendipity. That it was the only mid-city venue neither stigmatized by an amateur past nor already unionized by professional stagehands was coincidence. But she was pressing her luck when she immediately mailed out a brochure soliciting $10 subscriptions for six plays in the next three months without knowing what they were going to be.

Beyond opening with J.M. Synge's *The Playboy of the Western World*—to link the NPS in the public mind with Ireland's Abbey, the people's theatre she saw as a model for Canada—she had only a welter of possibilities, none of them Canadian. But even *The Playboy* was uncertain. The publisher's Toronto agent, a novice named Mona Coxwell whose specialty was helping by impedance, discovered after rehearsals began that all North American rights were tied up in a forthcoming Broadway revival. Permission to proceed was granted only after Andrew Allan gallantly flew to New York to argue that two nights in backwater Toronto was no threat to an all-star Broadway run. Confident that the Broadway production would sink itself

◊ Reprinted with permission from *Reinventing Myself: Memoirs* (Toronto: Stoddart, 1946), 155–64.

with commercialism while hers in the defiant spirit of the Abbey would make history, DMM allowed none of this pother to interrupt rehearsals.

Through the immediate fog her objective was clear: a professional company versatile enough to perform anything—the classics, challenging works from the international repertory, and Canadian plays, when they came. They would come, she believed, only if there were companies capable of putting them on well. Defining "professional" and "Canadian" would have to wait. Had Aristotle not framed the laws of Greek theatre after the event? But to mount such a series, back-to-back, with only a month to organize plays, directors, performers, technical resources, and advance publicity called for ad-hockery of a high order.

In her circle of believers was an experienced Danish actress, Karen Glahn, who offered to direct Strindberg's *The Father*—not yet seen in Canada—as the second production. To close the series at Christmas she could revive one of the medieval Nativity plays she knew so well. *Lady Precious Stream*, the Chinese classic in English translation that she and I had seen in London, would tie in nicely with an exhibition of chinoiserie planned by the Royal Ontario Museum if she could borrow costumes from the Chinese community. I proposed Somerset Maugham's *The Circle*, to demonstrate that Canadian actors (especially with Jane Mallet in the lead) could trump American actors in English. DMM, similarly convinced that Scottish plays were more likely to find an audience in Toronto than in New York, wanted to include James Bridie's London hit, *Mr. Bolfry*, in which the Devil drops in on a Highland manse. That would give the NPS the cachet of a North American premiere in its inaugural season. Telegrams flew back and forth between Toronto and Glasgow, but for all Bridie's willingness *Mr. Bolfry*, like *The Playboy*, was locked into a Broadway option. (The flowering of Canadian drama in the next two decades owed much of the belief of British and U.S. literary agents that Canada was part of the United States.) All the last minute I suggested instead something all too aptly called *The Wind Is Ninety*.

This bill was announced, then immediately revoked. As *The Father* opened and I joined the fray as production manager, the succession was in disarray.

The hoped-for costumes from Chinatown for *Lady Precious Stream*, scheduled next, had not materialized. We had been upstaged by a professional Chinese troupe stranded in Toronto by the war, who rounded up every costume in town for their five-hour production of *Wang pao ch'mau*—which turned out to be the Chinese original of *Lady Precious Stream*. In desperation we invited the Chinese actors to accompany their costumes into the Museum Theatre and present their epic over two nights. I then made a virtue of necessity by announcing the event as part of "our plan to include in each series of plays a drama of another land, when feasible and practical in the original tongue." When Andrew Allan later offered to direct Eugene O'Neill's *Ah, Wilderness!*, following *The Circle*, he deftly rationalized the whole chain of flukes in a program note: "Having opened its first season with plays Irish, Swedish, Chinese, and English, the NPS continues quite suitably with an American play."

This juggling act, performed while I made a living from teaching and radio, was an experience so traumatic that 37 years later the memory of it caused me to explode with laughter during a solemn meeting in Ottawa. The assembled heads of the federal cultural agencies had just been told by a crisp assistant deputy minister of finance that we must each hew to "a five-year plan, with no ad-hockery!" When he took umbrage at my laugh, I quoted in self-defence the economist John Maynard Keynes: "The artist cannot be told his direction; he does not know it himself." "That," said the technocrat, his eyes narrowing along with his mind, "is what has got to change." He was soon elevated to the rank of deputy minister.

As far as the public knew, the launch had been a success. But inside, as soon as the NPS hit water, the cry was "All hands to the pump!"—starting with the family.

Before my arrival brother Francis had helped to rig and light the Museum Theatre stage. (After completing his interrupted education in engineering, Francis escaped to Montreal and another hotbed of ad-hockery—the aircraft industry.) Brother Peter, a major in the army he had joined at 17, was now demobilized, demoralized, and thus available as an overqualified stagehand. He was also our truck driver once he got his civilian driving licence—which was not until after the night he borrowed my car for a toot and bounced it off a telegraph pole. The police sergeant on duty turned out to be an old comrade-in-arms, who let him off with a sermon and strict orders to get a licence yesterday. As a dramatist, I was much struck by this proof of the power of coincidence. (Peter soon returned to the army, for which his stage management skills proved invaluable in several theatres of war.) Meantime the old homestead with its single bathroom and four bedrooms, two of them the size of closets, accommodated mother and three sons, daughter-in-law Dilly—once more the costume maker—and whoever stayed overnight on the couch. Dilly and I moved out as soon as our furniture arrived from Vancouver and we found an apartment to put it in. This was only just in time; the house on Ridelle had become a reasonable facsimile of Santa's workshop.

The extended family came from all quarters. Half the Village Players were backstage workers, well aware of the mission impossible expected of them. Electrician Jack Richardson, for example, was given $50 to build a switchboard for the Museum Theatre. Well-wishers with clerical skills, underemployed actors among them, attended to the paperwork; interning lawyers and tyro accountants kept us more or less legal. Everyone built sets, made props, distributed posters, and swept the stage. Word that the hive was humming soon spread to Montreal and Ottawa. Before long prodigal sons and daughters of Toronto began to trickle back from New York and London. When Mary Pickford's young nephew John Mantley arrived from Hollywood to find his roots, everyone could see that there was indeed a family tree.

They came to share in an experiment, but their agendas were far from alike. Some hoped for an art theatre, others a commercial theatre, a political theatre, or an avant-garde theatre. Some sought an apprenticeship in acting, stage management, or teaching. Some were anticipating television. Most needed pocket money, which was all they got at first: $15 per production, rehearsals included, or sometimes $5 a night, the till permitting. Even this pittance was often in arrears, and I became expert at writing abject apologies laced with vows to mend our ways. How these diverse interests were to be held together on a continuing basis, let alone a five-year plan, was never discussed. There was too much to be done today.

Casts and crews had to be selected and persuaded to sign on, supplies purchased, letterhead printed, advertising space booked—all without any form of capital. Government grants and tax-deductible donations were unheard of. Corporate angels remained in the sky. For offices and set construction we had to cadge space from sympathetic small businesses. For rehearsals we leased a brightly lit hall from the School of Radiant Living, whose adherents covered the walls with invocations to Relax and Unwind on the Stairway to Heaven. This ambience was in marked contrast to our infernal grotto in the Royal Ontario Museum, reachable only through haunted galleries under 24-hour guard after the rest of the building was closed for the night. For months we were even refused permission to erect a modest sign outside to tell the public what was going on inside.

But it was precisely this crazy disparity between ends and means. I think, that bound our diverse enthusiasms together. Compared with the magnitude of the challenge, the slim resources of the challenger seemed absurd.

My mother was now almost 60. My feelings toward her, as colleague, vacillated daily between awe and exasperation. The source of both was her insistence on inspiration by example. From long experience we knew each other's strengths and weaknesses and divided the labour, regardless of title, with almost telepathic understanding. Yet whenever I or others close to her wavered in commitment, she took aim at the conscience as unerringly as Eros ever did at the heart. Her method was to throw herself into the breach. Did this curtain need hemming? She would attend to it. Was there no one to peddle brochures in the lobby? She would do it. People did things at her behest that they felt better for doing but afterward could hardly believe they had done. When DMM reached 85, Lister Sinclair said of her: "She taught us by showing, not by telling. She always showed us never to get angry or impatient, except with pessimism and a put-down; but with people who said things cannot be done, or were not worth doing, she showed us how to be very angry indeed."[1] Her irreverent sons, contributing to her meagre income, labelled this her Dora and Goliath Act. But her passion for human fulfillment coupled with her self-denial had an irresistible appeal to idealists. When the Village Players voted to form a professional company, the 22-year-old Donald Harron, still a struggling student, had been reluctant to go along. Yet within a month he agreed to play Christy Mahon in *The Playboy*, because (he told his fiancée) "Mrs. Moore is risking her frilly shirt on this venture and I can't let her down."[2]

If the pay, at first, was token, her dedication to professionalism was not. In her eyes being professional had to do with a pledge, not a wage. The Village Players had freely chosen to become initiates, and now she was providing the same free choice to others. The vow, once taken, must be respected regardless of the pay scale. She had been trained in a tough school: North American theatre before the advent of protective unions. I heard her once refuse to release from performance an actor whose father had died. "The only death that keeps you off the stage," she told him firmly, "is your own." She considered art less important than life, but one of life's most important justifications.

In the program for *Ah, Wilderness!* Andrew Allan explained why so many radio personalities of the day—Bernard Braden, Barbara Kelly, Jane Mallett, Tommy Tweed, Claire Murray, Budd Knapp, Ruth Springford, Lloyd Bochner—were ready to accept such uncompromising terms:

> Canadian radio drama, for its vitality and for the polish of its production, has been the admiration of American critics for several seasons. But the director of tonight's performance and several members of the cast he has brought with him believe firmly that no important work can be done in either radio or films unless it is based upon the legitimate theatre—performance by living actors before a live audience.

Yet the public was reluctant to admit Canadian theatre into the major league as readily as it had Canadian radio. When young Nathan Cohen made his critical debut reviewing *Ah, Wilderness!*, his ambivalence was explicit: "A brisk, professional affair that Broadway producers would have envied. It was the best-acted, best-directed amateur production we have ever seen in Toronto."[3] But this was the last time Cohen called the NPS amateur. Within four months he would speak of "that level which made the NPS a fine and splendid Canadian theatre repertory: professional in the best sense of the word."[4]

Other reviewers at first took refuge in the usual Canadian blend of praise and prudence: "made what may well be a contribution of durable value" or "its chief value is in the training of young players." Soon, however, came a note of rising surprise: "Its excellence was astounding" and "another of those surprisingly polished performances which, in the New Play Society's to-date short existence, have given it a remarkable prestige."[5] But the elder statesman of Toronto critics, *Saturday Night* editor B.K. Sandwell, was still wrestling with the paradox a year and a half later:

> The Little Theatre can command, in any place where there is radio production, a body of players who, while they have to perform in an amateur way, do so with professional skill and in a professional spirit. The New Play Society is one of the new type of Little Theatre organizations, though there is another contributing factor to its air of competent professionalism, in that a number of its members have had experience in playing to the armed forces in the last war. . . . The society has the enormous advantage of being able to fill the house and turn people away at practically every performance.[6]

We were well into our third year, receiving national coverage and the odd review in New York's *Variety*, before Sandwell worked his way out of his Little Theatre box to reach a delicate 50-50 compromise: "The performance was of a quality much superior to some of the touring companies stemming from Broadway, and equally comparable to a number of the better visiting productions."[7]

There was good reason for critical caution in the beginning when professionalism was a target more often missed than hit. Onstage, vigorous acting and obvious space limitations allowed us to get away with simple decor and basic technology; but in the office amateurism was rampant. We were all learning on the job, because there was nowhere else in the country to learn. With neither time to plan ahead nor money to hire expertise and proper equipment, the whole company was running on spontaneous combustion. When *The Coventry Nativity Play* opened on December 20, as the final production of that first 1946 season, we were all exhausted—as much from fumbling the can as from carrying it.

We awoke next morning expecting to read our obituary in the *Globe and Mail*. But critic Colin Sabiston, identifying himself as "a methodical atheist," recorded the event more like a Herald Angel: "Never in the history of Toronto's theatre has there been an evening of more concentrated beauty.... You will say: 'I have been to the theatre and have seen a miracle.'"[8] A more methodical atheist might have uncovered a more remarkable miracle. Like crazed revellers writing their New Year's resolutions in blood lest they change their minds the next day, we had announced a second season of six plays, with the number of performances increased from two to three.

The truth was that the NPS was as unprepared for a second season as it had been for a first, and my own participation was increasingly problematic. In the months ahead I had commitments at the United Nations requiring periodic stays in New York. We had six weeks to line up plays, directors, and casts, having promised "one British, one American, one European, one classical revival, one foreign-language presentation, one 'free-choice'—to be Canadian when first-class plays are available."

For the foreign-language slot we had invited L'Equipe, the Montreal troupe directed by the meteoric Pierre Dagenais, to bring its production of Sartre's *Huis-Clos*—to mark the first time a francophone Quebec company had ever appeared in Toronto. But our only firm undertaking was to open with Bridie's *Mr. Bolfry*, the Broadway production having been postponed. In fact, Bridie himself had put a cork in it, strenuously objecting to the producer's plan to drain the Scotch out of his dialogue. We immediately saw a parallel with the self-determination of Canadian theatre.

O.H. Mavor/James Bridie had more than a familial interest in his cousin Dora's fragile venture. Three years earlier he and two friends (one a physician and one a dramatist, reflecting his dual personality) had founded the Glasgow Citizens' Theatre. The Citizens' basement auditorium in the old Royal Scottish Academy of Music was far more commodious than ours in the Royal Ontario Museum, and their operation—with Tyrone Guthrie among the directors—more ambitious. But the growing pains were similar. When I sent Bridie one of our flyers, he replied:

> I'm so ashamed, in the face of the latter, of our penny bazaar
> Citizens' Theatre printings that I won't send you any of them....
> Our own outfit, with an empty till and a stupid and often hostile

local press has managed to lift itself, mainly by pulling on its own bootstraps, into a position of some honour and glory. . . ."[9]

He was, in fact, subsidizing the Citizens' with his lucrative West End comedies. And it was *Mr. Bolfry*, with Alistair Sim as the Reverend Mr. McCrimmon debating Raymond Lovell as the Devil, that had secured his reputation as a major British playwright. (Shaw sent him a postcard: "I was glad to know that if I had done nothing else for the drama I had at least made the production of such stunners as Bolfry possible."[10] Giving the North American premiere to Toronto was a gesture of solidarity.[11]

On the personal front I should have known what I was letting myself in for when I took on Bolfry. From playing the Devil on radio I had learned the exquisite thrill it held for a clergyman's son. But Bolfry was a more dangerous assignment: his adversary McCrimmon was a man of the cloth. I was about to do battle with my father, with my mother directing the proceedings. Bridie took refuge in theatrical advice:

> I don't know if there are any acting tips I could usefully give you. The high spot sermon by the Devil was considerably cut for the London version—I think the Ten Commandments came out—but it has always been played in full elsewhere & has managed to hold most audiences. I've never seen a satisfactory Devil. If we revive the play I think we'll go for another ego of the parson, i.e. He will look like McCrimmon in shiny caricature. . . .[12]

For McCrimmon we lured another veteran into the underpaid fold: Scots-born Frank Peddie, onetime British India hand now practising law to support his addiction to the stage. Peddie was older and shorter than I, with the stocky build and gnarled face of a boxer turned amiable in middle age; so we made Bolfry a caricature of McCrimmon's idealized youth, dressed in identical clerical black except for scarlet socks. We restored the Devil's Ten Commandments—a declaration of war on God's Ten—and on opening night I sailed through them so proudly that when the maid (Ruth Springford) cued me for the rest of the sermon ("What will happen if you win this War?"), I dried up. Turning to McCrimmon, I ad-libbed, "What do *you* think?" Peddie angrily returned the serve—"God has struck you dumb!"—and waited. I recovered only by summoning memories of other apocalyptic sermons from my childhood. But *The Star*'s word-drunk theatre critic Augustus Bridle caught me at it: "If Mavor Moore's father, once curate of St. James here, could have heard his son in this play, he would have seen him brilliantly impersonate a legendary, spookish Mephisto-cleric. . . ."[13] How did Bridle guess my model? Could he tell I had not yet found the devil in myself?

I had presence of mind enough to write a note in the program forging a link between Toronto and Glasgow, "where works by Scottish dramatists may obtain a hearing, and where Scottish actors and actresses may make their own kind of contribution to the theatre of the world. We of the New Play Society are working, with your help, toward a theatre of this kind for Canada." But I was soon hoist with my own parallel. When Fletcher Markle returned from New York to direct William Saroyan's *The Time of Your Life*, a

Pulitzer Prize winner, we were immediately accused of abandoning Canada and selling out to Broadway.

The illustrious cast added weight to the charge that we were "going commercial." Radio's Lorne Greene, John Drainie, and Frank Willis joined us for the first time, as well as stage professionals Alex McKee and Robert Christie. ("There are no small stages," growled Markle, adapting Stanislavsky to our theatre. "There are only big actors.") But Saroyan had actually refused the Pulitzer Prize on the ground that commerce has no business patronizing art. Markle and I saw his unconventional hymn to underdogs as an invitation to be ourselves, not to get on the bandwagon. And in this regard Markle believed Canadian audiences had a thing or two to learn:

> The present day theatre is said to be suffering not from lack of audiences but from a lack of real theatre people. This is an American remark, about American theatre. . . . But here in Canada we seem to be caught in the truth of this statement in reverse. We have the actors and workers of the theatre . . . our actors are in the habit of acting. It is to be hoped that those who can make up our audiences will form the habit of coming to the theatre.[14]

Torontonians had long since formed a theatre-going habit: visiting imported productions at large roadhouses such as the Royal Alexandra. The existing audience, we now realized, would not easily be diverted from that habit. Canadian theatre was by definition alternative theatre, and we must develop an alternative audience.

NOTES

1. In "A Tribute to Dora Mavor Moore," St Lawrence Centre, November 30, 1971.

2. Quoted in Martha Harron, "A Parent Contradiction" (Toronto: Collins, 1988), 87.

3. Toronto Wochenblatt, December 18, 1946.

4. Canadian Jewish Weekly, April 10, 1947.

5. Rose Macdonald, Telegram, October 12, 1947; Colin Sabiston, Globe and Mail, October 28, 1946; Pearl McCarthy, Globe and Mail, December 7, 1946; Rose Macdonald, Telegram, November 23, 1946.

6. B.K. Sandwell, writing as "Lucy van Gogh, in Saturday Night, September 1947.

7. Sandwell, Saturday Night, March 1949.

8. Sabiston, Globe and Mail, December 21, 1946.

9. O.H. Mavor, letter to MM, December 23, 1949.

10. Quoted in Ronald Mavor, Dr. Mavor and Mr. Bridie, 116.

11. Ernest Rawley of Toronto's Royal Alexandra later tried to bring the Glasgow Citizens' Theatre to Canada. In September 1950 Mavor/Bridie wrote to DMM: "Tyrone Guthrie was very keen that we should go to Canada and perhaps Australia next year but the matter has not yet come before the board. I doubt whether we could undertake it. . . ."

12. O.H. Mavor, letter to MM, January 1947.

13. Toronto Star, February 21, 1947.

14. Program note, The Time of Your Life, March 20, 1947.

TOWARDS A
CANADIAN THEATRE [*]

GEORGE BRODERSEN

○

The development of a Canadian audience is the subject of this interesting 1947 essay from the Manitoba Arts Review.

It has become something of a commonplace to speak of the theatre as the Cinderella of the arts of Canada; but most commonplaces contain at their heart at least a core of truth. Certainly, by comparison with some of the other arts, the criticism is reasonably valid. There are few Canadian playwrights or actors who are as well known in their field as Grove in the novel. Birney in poetry or Lorne Harris in painting. The other arts, if they have not yet reached the ball, are at least on their way; Cinderella alone remains among the ashes.

Is this merely a sign of national impotence in matters theatrical, or is there some deeper and more hidden cause? For the fact can hardly be denied. Certainly on the surface there is no reason why the Canadian theatre should be the undernourished, puling infant that for the most part it is; day to day existence in Canada, while perhaps lacking the raw material of great tragedy or the polished urbanity which leads often to high comedy, is at least an existence vital and challenging.

Perhaps the answer is most easily to be found from a brief consideration of what theatre involves. More than any other art, theatre means communication—the transference to the audience of the concepts of the author, through the medium of the actors' characterizations, patterned, modulated and illumined by the director. Fiction, poetry, painting, music even, have this in common; they are essentially individual arts, created by the individual

[*] *Manitoba Arts Review* 5, 3 (Spring 1947): 18–23.

and needing only the response of an individual brain to have achieved their purpose; and despite man's faint groping for some wider form of world organization to replace the nation state, this is still in essence an individualistic age. But the art of the theatre needs an audience, and not merely an audience of one. It requires visual contact between actor and spectator, the rapport established among the members of the audience, the bond of interest and emotion stretching across the footlights. For this reason radio plays, which have been among the more successful products of recent Canadian writing can hardly qualify as theatre: even with the still far off advent of television the situation will remain the same.

Theatre then demands an audience. But it is almost another commonplace to say that there is no audience for theatre in Canada. How far this is really true is a matter of opinion and a matter of faith; but there is evidence to support it, there are reasons to account for it. In the first place the communication that theatre demands is a two-way affair; it demands co-operation, and active co-operation from the audience. And this means that an audience, to play its full part in a performance, cannot sit back and allow itself to be uncritically amused. It means hard mental work, often hard emotional strain; those, for instance, who saw the Margaret Webster production of *Othello* in 1944 in Winnipeg may have experienced then and still recall the feeling of complete exhaustion, mental and physical, caused in those who had been following the performance fully. But only too often the average audience goes to the theatre uncritically, willing to be amused with little— which is often all they get—, and unwilling to do the hard work that is really involved. In addition Canada really has hardly any well equipped theatres; those that have not succumbed to the depredations of the movie moguls from Warner to Rank have fallen beneath the hammer of the wreckers' gang; all that remain are converted, and usually inadequate and inappropriate concert halls, or else antiquated and prehistoric barns through which blow the ghosts of a great but antediluvian tradition. But comfort for either audience or actor is there none. And when one can see Lana Turner in comfort for 58 cents, one will not go to the discomfort of the average Little Theatre for 75 cents; particularly if one has also to work. For man is differentiated from—one hesitates to say raised above—the best not only by his reason but also by his laziness.

What then is to be done about it? How can one attract an audience to the Canadian theatre? There are two schools of reply. The first, and it must be admitted the easier, is that of John Holden in a recent interview in the Winnipeg Free Press. Mr. Holden, a Christmas visitor to the city where for several reasons he and his company of players were successful occupants of the Dominion theatre in the days of its legitimacy, claims that to get an audience into the theatres of Canada all that is necessary is to give the public what it wants and it will come. Perhaps this is not as simple as it seems; but let that pass. But in effect it means that a menu of murder mysteries in which the criminal is obvious to everyone except the detective, from his very first entrance, and pseudo-psychiatric excursions into the realms of abnormal psychology as the main course, with a spicy dessert of bedroom farces straight from Broadway. In other words the pabulum of the Canadian theatregoers is to be the raw material of "B" grade Hollywood movies. If we are content with this, well and good; but in that case we may as well give up the future of the Canadian theatre as blighted and hopeless; Cinderella will remain an old maid and a poor relation.

The other approach is harder, much harder:—but much more enduring. It is simply to consider the small group of confirmed theatregoers in Canada as responsible and intelligent adults who are willing to face the challenge of ideas and the impact of individual thought; it is to see them as a leaven which by active, even missionary interest, will slowly bring in the stragglers by the roadside, and convince them that there are higher things in theatre than *Life With Father*, that there are more important things in theatre than a commercially successful long run, that the essence of theatre is a challenge which goes deep into the intellectual and emotional natures of all who participate. To pander to the instinct for ease and the instinct for comfort—both mental and physical—is merely to prostitute a vital art and to act unworthily of a mature and adult people.

This means then that the first stage in the education of an audience for the Canadian theatre is to habituate them to the best, which in effect means the classics of all ages and all cultures. It is at least significant that there is a marked swing back to the classics in many of the most honourable theatre companies abroad: the success of the recent Old Vic visit to New York with a repertory including *Henry IV, parts 1 and 2, The Critic*, and *Oedipus*, or the current venture of Eva La Gallienne into repertory with *Henry VIII, Androcles and the Lion*, and *John Gabriel Borkman*, are cases in point. Inside Canada the same forces are slowly germinating in both east and west, and the schedule of the New Play Society in Toronto is an object lesson to all other semi-professional, semi-amateur groups, with its inclusion of such plays as *The Playboy of the Western World*, and *Ah, Wilderness*.

In the long run, however, the educating of a Canadian audience to demand the best in scripts and the best in acting may prove to be not quite so difficult as might at first be thought. For man, despite his laziness, is also a seeker and an idealist, and can recognize the best, when it is pointed out to him. Perhaps we might also produce in time a crop of Canadian critics of the theatre, capable of recognizing a good new play when they see one, because they have a knowledge and an experience gained from handling the best of other days. For the critic of the theatre has a very definite place in the theatrical hierarchy, and of first rate current theatrical criticism we have as yet produced only a microscopic quantity. There is hardly a paper in the country,—with the notable exception of *Saturday Night* in the days of Nancy Pyper,—with an accredited theatre critic on its staff; movie critics of course we have, and the occasional radio critic; but theatre critics are as rare as a chinook in Winnipeg. Add to that the too prevalent habit of theatre reporters of merely listing the names of the actors as gleaned from the programme, and calling this criticism, and the outlook is bleak. Theatre coverage there is in plenty, for the activities of the amateur theatre groups make news of social if not of artistic import; theatre criticism there is none.

Wordsworth claimed that the poet must create the taste by which he is to be judged; the same is true to an equal extent of the actor, the director and the playwright, particularly in Canada where there is no longstanding tradition of theatre to fall back on. What then is the state of affairs back stage?

Practical theatre in Canada today may be considered from three aspects; the amateur, the commercial and the professional. Obviously the amateur theatre in number of members and in the amount of productions is at present by far the largest section, and there can be no denying the very high level of work done from time to time by such groups as the Montreal Repertory Theatre, the London Little Theatre, Workshop 14 in Calgary, the Crescent Players in Moose Jaw, or the Vancouver Little Theatre. But there are many besetting weaknesses in the amateur movement today. First there is a tendency to split up into groups too small for really effective production work at the amateur level, a tendency which often leads to rivalry and petty jealousies, to backbiting criticism and gossip; only too often amateur theatre groups are formed of what might be designated "theatrical friends," who visit the performances of rival groups, intent on seeing all the faults and steadfastly refusing to recognize any of the merits. There are few Canadian settlements, whatever the size of the city, large enough to support more than at the most two sound and strong amateur groups.

Equally most of the groups are handicapped by lack of training; it is often said that one learns to act by acting, and to a certain extent and up to a certain level this is true, but any actor's performance is bound to be influenced by his whole approach to the actor's craft, by his whole philosophy of theatre. And this needs acquiring and comes most easily by training; such key matters as the complete projection of a character on the stage can hardly be successfully carried out by the externalized methods of the average amateur actor. The trouble here is largely a matter of time; few groups either can or will spend the time in rehearsal or the effort in concentration at rehearsal and in production that any finished performance demands; any characterization needs time to grow and develop, and this cannot be done in the average three weeks of spare time rehearsal which is almost all that most groups allot. A further weakness and difficulty, closely related, lies, as has been suggested, in the choice of play; the slick Broadway farce, the airy nothings of Thornton Wilder, the empty nothingness of drawing room comedy whether English or American need above all things subtlety and finesse; the false pointing of a line, a weakness in tempo can shatter the crystal bowl to fragments; in particular, they need years of experience. It is a fallacy to think because the Lunts can play for years in *O Mistress Mine*, a pleasant little piece about the minor pleasures of adultery, that this is fit meat for the Prairie Butte Little Theatre. After all the Lunts are the Lunts and not the local station agent and schoolteacher.

The other main besetting weakness of the amateur movement is something often quoted as one of its major virtues—the competitive instinct engendered by the orgy of festivals which bedevil the world of the theatre for half of every season. Not that there is anything against festivals as such; indeed the chance offered by such institutions as the Dominion Drama Festival, this year revived after a lapse of eight years, to gather together talent from all parts of the country for a week of theatre is an admirable and valuable experience. But why make it competitive? A series of critical comments on performances by a competent adjudicator is clearly of value, both to the individual members of casts and to the audience at large, and is a stage towards the creation of the taste by which the theatre we hope for in the future is to be judged; but why should the poor adjudicator, harassed as he is by a round of social obligations and cocktail parties, and bowed down by the strain of watching three different performances a day for a week, be forced at the end of his days of tribulation to award prizes to the best play, the best actor and the best actress? At best, these awards are sops to vanity; at worst they are the seeds of dissension and jealousy. If a festival must be competitive, the only course is to demand the same play to be performed by each contestant; then at least some sound standard of judgment could be applied; but then the festival would not pay. Surely better still is the type of non-competitive festival organized among themselves by the four western universities, an innovation full of hope for the amateur theatre in Canada.

Turning now briefly to the other branches of theatre in Canada today, the commercial and the professional, a clear cut distinction must be drawn between the two. By the commercial theatre is meant the touring "second company," operating usually out of New York and presenting only too often second rate performances of third rate plays. Fortunately for us in the west, the advent of such companies is confined almost entirely to the east; distances are too great to allow of an invasion of the prairies in this way. But only too often the road show, as must have been obvious about three seasons ago in Winnipeg, with a few exceptions, is tawdry in the extreme. The commercial theatre is in theatre to make money and for no other reason; hence its prices are as high as or higher than any self-respecting audience will pay, and its productions as primitive as it can get away with. After all, that is one of the main props of successful commerce. The professional theatre, on the other hand, while intent on making a living out of the theatre, has higher aims and higher ideals. It regards the theatre as primarily an art and not a business; it regards these plays which are best artistically as the plays which it must produce; it pays as much attention to the small parts in a play as to the "leads"; above all it regards teamwork and co-operation among the company as of infinitely more importance than the possession of top name stars. For those interested in and practising professional theatre there is a constant struggle to interpret the play as the author conceived it, to present it honestly and faithfully; they are aware that much of the "glamour" of the theatre is merely fake tinsel, that it is a career of constant strain and continuous concentration,—like marriage, not to be lightly undertaken.

In the field of the genuine professional theatre much has happened in the past year. Both in Toronto, with the New Play Society, and in Vancouver with the Everyman Theatre, a start has been made along these lines. Both groups are working with very similar aims: to perform the best plays of all ages and of all nations; to train into a closely knit ensemble of players a group of actors capable and versatile enough to perform these plays; perhaps above all, to hold in Canada much of the talent which would otherwise be attracted to the United States or to Europe. Both groups believe firmly that before anything as highflown as a Canadian National Theatre can come into being there must be a living and practising theatre; that this depends on a supply of trained actors, directors, stage technicians, but equally on a trained body of critical opinion and an enlightened and intelligent audience. Both groups believe also that, by their very existence, they can stimulate the writing of first class Canadian plays, plays written about Canada for Canadians by Canadians. So far the main effort of the Canadian playwright has been directed towards the somewhat limited field of the one act play, probably with an eye on the amateur movement and its drama festivals, and perhaps also enticed by such competitions as those sponsored annually by the Western Canada Theatre Conference; but there are signs of a change. One has only to consider such plays as Elsie Gowan's *The Last Cave Man*, to be produced this season through the west by the Everyman Theatre, Gwen Pharis's second full length play *Stampede*, produced last spring by the University of Alberta and again in revised form by the Banff School of Fine Arts, Mavor Moore's *The Fox of Bay Street*, a satire on the Toronto business man, which Toronto has so far failed to produce, or Lister Sinclair's as yet unproduced, *The Man in the Blue Moon*, a modern and highly individual melange of *Everyman* and *Peer Gynt*, with a little Thornton Wilder thrown in for good measure.

Half a century ago, creative theatre in the English language seemed numbered among the lost and dead arts; then came Shaw, with caustic wit and incisive reason creating a revolution, Wilde scattering epigrams which eclipsed the wit of Congreve, and Synge restoring the theatre's rightful heritage of poetry; a generation ago, on a pier in Provincetown the American theatre, sired and fostered by the genius of O'Neill, sprang Phoenix-like from the ashes of an Elizabethan past. Today, the Canadian theatre is in the throes of birth; much depends on the response of the average intelligent Canadian whether the infant be stillborn or have a chance of maturity.

○

THE ORDER IN COUNCIL

P.C. 1786

With growing pressure on the government to become actively involved with the arts, letters, and sciences, Prime Minister Louis St. Laurent established a Royal Commission in 1949 to investigate the field. Chaired by Vincent Massey, its published mandate was clear.

Certified to be a true copy of a Minute of a Meeting of the Committee of the Privy Council, approved by His Excellency the Governor General on the 8th April, 1949.

The Committee of the Privy Council have had before them a report dated 7th April, 1949, from the Right Honourable Louis S. St. Laurent, the Prime Minister, submitting:

That it is desirable that the Canadian people should know as much as possible about their country, its history and traditions; and about their national life and common achievements;

That it is in the national interest to give encouragement to institutions which express national feeling, promote common understanding and add to the variety and richness of Canadian life, rural as well as urban;

That there exist already certain Federal agencies and activities which contribute to these ends; including the Canadian Broadcasting Corporation, the National Film Board, the National Gallery, the National Museum, the Public Archives, the Library of Parliament, the National War Museum, the

---

◇ The Robertson Davies section is taken from *Royal Commission Studies: A Selection of Essays Prepared for the Royal Commission on National Development in the Arts, Letters and Sciences*; recommendations on the theatre and the order in council are from *Report: Royal Commission on National Development in the Arts, Letters and Sciences, 1949–51* (Ottawa: Edmond Cloutier, 1951).

system of aid for research including scholarships maintained by the National Research Council and other governmental agencies; and

That it is desirable that an examination be conducted into such agencies and activities, with a view to recommending their most effective conduct in the national interest and with full respect for the constitutional jurisdiction of the provinces.

The Committee, therefore, on the recommendation of the Prime Minister advise that:

1. The Right Honourable Vincent Massey, P.C., C.H., Chancellor of the University of Toronto.

2. Arthur Surveyer, Esq., B.A.Sc., C.E., D.Engn., LL.D., Civil Engineer, Montreal.

3. Norman A.M. MacKenzie, Esq., C.M.G., K.C., LL.D., President, University of British Columbia.

4. The Most Reverend Georges-Henri Lévesque, O.P., D.Sc.Soc., Dean of the Faculty of Social Sciences, Laval University.

5. Miss Hilda Neatby, M.A., Ph.D., Professor of History and Acting Head of the Department, University of Saskatchewan.

be appointed Commissioners under Part I of the Inquiries Act (Chapter 99 of the Revised Statutes of Canada, 1927) to examine and make recommendations upon:

(a) the principles upon which the policy of Canada should be based, in the fields of radio and television broadcasting.

(b) such agencies and activities of the government of Canada as the National Film Board, the National Gallery, the National Museum, the National War Museum, the Public Archives and the care and custody of public records, the Library of Parliament; methods by which research is aided including grants for scholarships through various Federal Government agencies; the eventual character and scope of the National Library; the scope or activities of these agencies; the manner in which they should be conducted, financed and controlled, and other matters relevant thereto;

(c) methods by which the relations of Canada with the United Nations Educational, Scientific and Cultural Organization and with other organizations operating in this field should be conducted;

(d) relations of the government of Canada and any of its agencies with various national voluntary bodies operating in the field with which this inquiry will be concerned.

The Committee further advise:

1. That the Commissioners be authorized to exercise all the powers conferred upon them by Section 11 of the Inquiries Act and be assisted to the fullest extent by the officials of all appropriate departments and agencies;

2. That the said Commissioners adopt such procedure and methods as they may, from time to time, deem expedient for the proper conduct of the inquiry and sit at such times and in such places in Canada as they may decide from time to time;

3. That the Commissioners submit interim reports from time to time as they see fit or as they may be directed by the Governor in Council;

4. That when, pursuant to the powers conferred by Section 11 of the Inquiries Act, the said Commissioners have authorized and deputed any qualified person as a special Commissioner to inquire into any matter within the scope of the aforesaid inquiry as may be directed by the said Commissioners, any person so deputed, when authorized by Order in Council, shall exercise the same powers which the Commissioners have in accordance with the Inquiries Act (Chapter 99 of the Revised Statutes of Canada, 1927);

5. That the Commissioners be empowered to engage such counsel, staff and expert assistance as may be required for the proper conduct of their inquiry;

6. That the said Commissioners be directed that a record should be made of all the evidence given before them or before any special Commissioner in the course of the inquiry;

7. That the Commissioners be directed to report to the Governor in Council; and

8. That the Right Honourable Vincent Massey, P.C., C.H., be chairman of the Commission.

N.A. Robertson,
Clerk of the Privy Council.

A DIALOGUE ON THE STATE OF
THEATRE IN CANADA

Along with its final report, the Massey Commission published a series of "studies" by distinguished thinkers in various fields. The major theatre study was done by Robertson Davies (1913–95), then editor of the Peterborough Examiner. Davies chose to submit his report in the form of a dialogue.

(Note: I have revived the characters of *Lovewit* and *Trueman* who, in a pamphlet on the conditions of the English theatre in 1669, have already shown themselves admirable assistants of this sort of work. R.D.)

Lovewit is seated in his study. To him, Trueman in haste.

Trueman: Good morning, Lovewit; I am lucky to find you at home. You have heard the news?

Lovewit: That we two are to prepare a memorandum on the state of the theatre in Canada for the Royal Commission? It came to me by the morning post. What a chance to speak our minds!

Trueman: My dear fellow, you must contain yourself. A memorandum to a body of such solemnity and dignity will be no place for your jokes and your flights of exaggeration.

Lovewit: What, honest Trueman? Do you suggest that His Majesty's Commissioners are so far outside the bounds of common humanity that they cannot relish a joke now and then?

Trueman: I did not say so. But I have seen some of the petitions and memoranda which have been presented to them already, and they are, as the schoolboy said of the works of Matthew Arnold, "no place to go for a laugh." Indeed, I wonder if we can come up to the standard of sobriety which they have set.

Lovewit: Why, my dear fellow, it will be the easiest thing in the world. We will put down what we want to say in some form congenial to ourselves—as it may be, a dialogue—and when it is done we will send it to a bureaucrat or a public relations counsel to be translated into the proper style, for this language of official documents is not one which any artist can master.

Trueman: No literary artist would dare to touch it, for fear some of it would stick, like pitch, and ruin him. We must have plenty of tabulation of points, labelled (a), (b), and (c). And we must make a pretty show of numbers, and even Roman numerals—But no; numerals look unbusinesslike, and our age wants its artists to be as businesslike as possible.

Lovewit: And rightly so. But to be businesslike, and to make a parade of the apparatus of business are different things. We will be businesslike, and the press agent shall make the parade.

Trueman: I know a needy, pragmatical fellow who, for a trifle of money, will supply us with a rare show of statistics to prove anything we choose to say, and these shall provide us with appendices to drag at the tail of our memorandum, and give it weight.

Lovewit: And I know an astrologer who has foresworn the casting of horoscopes and now gives all his time to making pie-charts for business houses.

Trueman: Oh rare! The press agent, the pedant, and the astrologer shall give our memorandum the modish air of a modern state paper. But if it is to have any sense in it, Lovewit, we must provide it.

Lovewit: You are right. And to talk sense about the theatre demands a high degree of self control, for it is the Temple of the Passions, and too often its devotees allow the passions to escape from the temple and invade their conversation.

Trueman: Let us resolve, here and now, to be as sensible as we can in what we say about the Canadian theatre.

Lovewit: To avoid special pleading—

Trueman: Ay, and to avoid also that pitfall of those who talk of the theatre—I mean what George Jean Nathan so aptly calls "ersatz profundity."

Lovewit: Agreed! And yet never to forget that the theatre is an art, or a compost of many arts, and that it must be treated at all times with love. For he who makes the theatre his harlot, or his little-regarded companion of the evening, or his school-mistress, will never know her to enjoy her fairest favours. They know her best who love and serve her best.

Trueman: I suppose, for a beginning, we must answer those who question whether the theatre exists at all in Canada, in any form which deserves careful consideration. Yet it seems to me that it exists here, as it does everywhere in the world, in those centres of population which are big enough to support it. For whatever the enthusiasts may say, not everyone wants the theatre, and of those who want it, not all want it on the same level.

Lovewit: True, for the moving-pictures supply the wants of thousands of people who would seek their entertainment in the theatre if no movies existed. But the theatre they would demand, and get, would be the theatre of windy melodrama and domestic comedy. In some countries the theatre can, and does, compete with the movies in providing this sort of fare, but it cannot be said to do so in Canada. The failure of many a Canadian travelling company, jaunting from town to town by car, and putting on its show with borrowed furniture, under the auspices of some local service club, is due to this alone: it is doing badly what the movies do much better. And when Canadian actors who have engaged in such pursuits say that Canadians are indifferent to the theatre, they delude themselves. The fact is that Canadians are indifferent to bad theatre.

Trueman: I am glad to hear you say so. For it appears to me that Canadians are as responsive to first-rate work as any other people. A Canadian audience may sometimes be naive; it may be a little behind the times when confronted with the latest confection from New York or London. Sometimes we are a little provincial. But we are by no means stupid.

Lovewit: I agree. And I may tell you, Trueman, that I have myself been an actor in London, and I have known London audiences to be naive, old-fashioned and provincial when confronted with something they did not understand. And need we suppose that a New York audience is any different? Their treatment of some fine plays certainly does not suggest it. I am with you: Canadians are as quick as anyone to recognize and applaud what is first-rate. Their reception of fine foreign artists has shown it.

Trueman: It must be said, however, they they have not yet put the stamp of unmistakeable approval upon any theatre artist of their own who has not first gained some recognition abroad.

Lovewit: There are two answers to that. Perhaps they have not yet found an artist of the theatre so plainly of the first rank that they choose to acclaim him. And also it is almost out of the question at present for a Canadian theatre artist to be seen in all parts of the country and thus to gain national acceptance. Monsieur Gratien Gélinas hopes to try the experiment soon. If he succeeds as well in English as he has done in French, he will be the man.

Trueman: True: but it is not our task to prophesy. The artists of *Les Compagnons de St-Laurent* are also working on a very high level, but while they act in French their fame will be confined to Quebec and to that very small part of the English population which knows French well enough to follow a play with pleasure—a proportion, I may say, which is even smaller than it professes itself to be. But in the English-speaking theatre who have we?

Lovewit: There is no one. And it is impossible to say how much the fame of Fridolin and *Les Compagnons* owes to the fact that their audience is a compact one compared with the audience which English-speaking actors face. No one doubts their ability, but it must be allowed that they are fortunate in not having to establish their celebrity in all ten provinces.

Trueman: We are agreed, then, that Canadians who care for the theatre at all are warmly responsive to first-rate theatre. And let us be generous in our definition of first-rate theatre: a classic thoroughly understood and finely presented, a display of virtuoso acting in a play of modest merit, a fine piece of ensemble work in a play of Tchekov or Ibsen, a farce played with skill and gusto—any of these may, in its degree, provide that special pleasure, that sense of exhiliration and fulfillment which first-rate theatre can give. For make no mistake, friend Lovewit, the theatre is a vigorous, living, and in a certain sense, a coarse art; it is vulgar in the true sense of the word. I am always suspicious of theatre-lovers who insist that they can only endure the finest plays performed to perfection. There are many kinds of excellence in the theatre, but all are recognizable by the completeness of the special effect which they produce upon the audience and by the unmistakeable deep satisfaction which they give.

Lovewit: Do you think that this completeness of effect is often achieved in the theatre in Canada?

Trueman: Sometimes, certainly, in the performances of the professional companies which visit our big cities.

Lovewit: Ah, but they come to us from England or from the United States; we cannot count them.

Trueman: No, but we must not overlook them, for they provide examples for our native actors, and in the theatre, as in all arts, example is of the utmost value to those who would reach a high level of achievement themselves. The pity is that they come so seldom, and visit so few of our cities; for this reason we lack the constant inspiration of theatrical work on the highest level. It is an economic problem, of course. When the Old Vic visits New York it cannot come to Canada without losing money. When Gielgud brings us *Love for Love* he does so at a money sacrifice, and the unfamiliarity of the play keeps people out of the theatre.

Lovewit: There you touch upon a point which we must not neglect. We have said that there is an audience in Canada for any sort of first-rate theatre. But there is one class of theatrical work which must be excepted, and that is the performance of unfamiliar classics. You spoke of *Love For Love*; our Canadian education is so poor in quality that virtually no Canadian who is not a university graduate in English has ever heard of its author, much less felt any anxiety to see his works on the stage. There are great realms of drama closed to us for this reason alone. In England, and to a very much lesser degree in the United States, it is possible to see plays performed which are out of the common run. But we Canadians are an illiterate people in this respect, and we fear the unknown as only the ignorant and the intellectually lazy can fear it. This is a matter, my dear Trueman, in which our country desperately needs reform.

Trueman: You will start no quarrel with me on that score, and I am as good a Canadian as yourself. I think it may fairly be said that except for two or three comedies of Shakespeare, *She Stoops To Conquer* and Sheridan's *Rivals* and *School For Scandal*, and two or three Ibsen bogies, a classic is rarely performed in the English-speaking theatre in this country.

Lovewit: An Australian told me recently that before he was eighteen he had seen twenty plays of Shakespeare performed, more or less ably, by the company which Alan Wilkie maintained in that country. This experience has enriched his life in a fashion inexplicable to most of our countrymen. Have you ever asked a group of Canadian schoolteachers, professionally engaged in teaching Shakespeare, how many Shakespearean plays they have seen on the stage?

Trueman: I confess that I have shrunk from such depressing investigation.

Lovewit: Their answers would sadden your heart and chill your blood, I promise you. What can they know about Shakespearean drama if they have never experienced in it its proper form? Who attempts to explain the works of Beethoven if he has never heard an orchestra play them?

Trueman: You need not confine your pity to schoolteachers alone. I think it very likely that a majority of Canadians of good education—as education goes here—and good financial estate, have never seen a Shakespearean play performed.

Lovewit: As far as the classics of the theatre are concerned, we are a nation of ignoramuses, and the oft-advanced excuse that because we do not know what we are missing we are none the worse for it, seems to me to be a disgraceful evasion.

Trueman: That brings us back to what I said a short time ago: I think that one reason why we slight the classics is that we lack the example and the tradition which is wanted by those who tackle them.

Lovewit: Tradition! You have hit it!

Trueman: Do not mistake me. A weight of tradition may be as great a handicap as none at all.

Lovewit: But a genuine, living tradition is constantly renewing itself, and the theatre, perhaps more than the other arts, relies upon a living tradition. The theatre has its relics and its apostolic succession, you know, and among actors reverence for the great ones of the theatre's past is a living and potent force.

Trueman: Your phrase "apostolic succession" catches my fancy. Will you not clarify what you mean?

Lovewit: With pleasure, if you will allow me a personal reminiscence. When I was a young and unimportant actor at the Old Vic I had several conversations with Ben Webster, who was himself of a great theatrical family; he told me how, when he and May Whitty, his wife, were touring on this continent on the fifth of Sir Henry Irving's visits, they helped to cheer the last hours of an old member of the company, Henry Howe, who died when they were in Cincinnati; "Evergreen" Howe was born in 1912 of a Quaker family, and when he wanted to go on the stage he asked advice of Edmund Kean. Webster told me of Kean's surprise; "Why, cocky, you're a Quaker!" When Howe said that none the less he wished to act, Kean thrust his face into the boy's and rasped, "Well, cully, can you starve?" . . . I tell you this story because, as I sat in awed admiration at the feet of Ben Webster, a man with roots deep in the theatre's past, I seemed, through his kindly acceptance of me, to reach back into the past, through Evergreen Howe, to Kean himself. That is tradition, Trueman. I do not pretend that it made me a better actor, but it gave me a sense of the wonder and nearness of the great past which made it impossible for me ever to give the theatre less than my best, whatever that best might be. And that is the thing which our Canadian actors cannot get, although I know how powerfully many of them desire it. They want the living tradition, and as yet there is no one to give it to them.

Trueman: Acting, as a profession, is still in its infancy in Canada. We might hope for the establishment of a native tradition if there were not strong forces working against it. But to earn a sufficient income as an actor in Canada is possible only to a score or so of people. The remainder must work as radio actors in order to live.

Lovewit: And in saying that you explain many of their deficiencies. Radio acting makes no demands upon the body; an actor whose body is untrained will never make his mark upon the stage except in a limited range of roles for which he is perfectly suited. He will be lucky if he rises above mediocrity even in those. Acting in the classics, or in a modern play which is not realistic in manner, is impossible for him, for he does not know his business.

Trueman: I suspect that you do not consider radio acting as real acting.

Lovewit: Radio, unaided by the stage, has not produced a single actor of the first rank. The microphone imposes too many limitations. Emotions must be expressed in such a manner as to agree with the machine, for the machine is the final arbiter. The speech of even the best radio actors is unsuitable for the stage, without radical change. And what passes for sincerity in radio has nothing to do with the larger sincerity which is demanded of an actor who must fill a theatre with sound. Yet this is the work by which most of our actors have to live.

Trueman: Do you consider that in general it makes bad actors of them?

Lovewit: Not of the wise ones. The encouraging fact is that many of these young men and women take great pains to learn to act well on stage. They train their bodies and their voices. And when they have the chance they act in a way which gladdens the heart.

Trueman: Do you refer to their performances in the summer theatres?

Lovewit: Yes, and anywhere that they have a chance to work under conditions which are in any way conducive to real artistic effort. I have seen them in classical plays, in commercial plays and in musical comedies and revues. They are not numerous, but there are enough of them to give us a theatre if they could live by it.

Trueman: Ah, but as soon as they had reached a certain level of excellence they would get offers from the Stages and we would lose them.

Lovewit: We would lose a few of them. But there are others—some of them among the best—who would stay here. For patriotism in the arts is no less common then it is in other spheres. If they had a chance at a respectable livelihood and an honourable way of life, they would stay, and they could give us a truly fine theatre.

Trueman: While such people exist it cannot be said that we are without the means to create a theatre. But so far we have said nothing of the theatre which exists widely everywhere in Canada, and flourishes triumphantly in some parts of it.

Lovewit: Our amateur theatre? Yes; if it flourished on such a scale, proportionately, in the U.S.A., news of the prodigy would have been spread to the uttermost ends of the earth. For where else in the world will you find a national amateur theatre movement comparable with our Dominion Drama Festival?

Trueman: It is one of Canada's cultural glories, but Canada characteristically does not know it. The Dominion Government is indifferent to it, and hundreds of thousands of citizens either know nothing of it, or are profoundly misinformed about it. It receives no penny from the public purse. And yet it engages the attention of much of the ablest artistic talent of the country, and it provides, in its final yearly festival, a week of drama which has won the sincere admiration of extremely able professional men of the theatre, who are brought here to judge it. I cannot think of any other country in the world where a comparable effort would be so persistently snubbed by the Government. Even on the lowest level, its publicity value to the country is enormous. The libel that Canada hates the arts is more strongly supported by the resolute official slighting of the Dominion Drama Festival than in any other single matter.

Lovewit: Do not grow too heated, my dear fellow. It may be a blessing in disguise. The artist who is slighted by his Government is at least not under his Government's thumb. But more of this later. The curious fact, in my estimation, is that in Canada the amateurs are so much better off then the professionals.

Trueman: It is a fact that some of the large amateur societies own fine theatres and have a good deal of money to spend on presenting their public performances. Such a group as the Little Theatre of London, Ontario, which owns a handsome, full-sized theatre, supports a studio for experimental work, gives assistance to promising young people, and employs several persons to attend to its business all the year round, is a brilliant exception. The average amateur theatre group works in a hired hall, pays its way from year to year, and in the course of time acquires a wardrobe and some scenery. If, at the end of a season, it has paid its bills and still has enough in hand to finance some of the preparatory work for the season to come it has done well. And in addition to these groups of average success, there are struggling groups which often cannot make ends meet.

Lovewit: Lack of merit?

Trueman: Very often, but in some cases it is because they present unpopular plays which they think should be seen. In large cities there are also groups of poor people who, as they act for poor audiences, never have quite enough money. But a few of them do work of artistic value, for all that.

Lovewit: When you speak of "artistic value" in an amateur performance do you mean the same thing as when you use that phrase of a professional performance?

Trueman: Such a phrase cannot have a constant value, like a bar of gold of a fixed weight. But you are right to take me up in that way. When speaking of the amateur theatre one must beware of sophisticating one's standards.

Lovewit: You agree with me, then, that the amateur theatre must be judged by the same standards as the professional?

Trueman: I agree that the best amateur work must be judged by the same standards as the best professional work, for it has earned that compliment. When judging the work of amateurs who plainly are not the best one must use one's common sense, and some measure of charity. Do not forget, Lovewit, that I am a Canadian playwright, and I have seen my plays acted by professionals, good amateurs and bad amateurs; if I had judged them all by the same standard I should not be here to collaborate with you now upon this memorandum, for I should have slain the bad amateurs and chopped them into messes before the astonished eyes of their friends and relatives. When one has said that they, too, are God's creatures one has said absolutely all that can be said in their defence.

Lovewit: You speak as if there were no bad professionals.

Trueman: A bad professional will bedaub your play with his own egotistical nonsense, but he will leave something of its original substance. But your bad amateur will ravish it and dance upon its corpse without any comprehension that he is doing it a disservice. But let us talk no more of bad amateurs. My gorge rises.

Lovewit: Speak then of the good amateurs. Do you think that they ever surpass the professionals?

Trueman: I will not say that they cannot do so: I say only that I have never personally seen them do so. I have seen here in Canada some fine, sensitive work by amateur actors, but it has always seemed to be lacking in the qualities which fine professional work possesses. The tragic purgation by pity and terror; the comic glory of laughter; these have never been present in their full and unmistakable power.

Lovewit: Are you not a little unreasonable? These amateurs must earn their bread by other work; how can they have the same energy to give to acting that professionals have, who do nothing else?

Trueman: You do not deceive me, Lovewit; you are joking. Of course what you say is half the explanation. But the real fact is that the amateurs lack the imaginative power which the professionals bring to their work. I have seen very capable amateurs; they have some technique of body and voice, and they have a certain amount of flair. But they have not the copious imaginative power which in the gifted professional actor illuminates everything he does and, in his great moments, raises acting from a craft to an art.

Lovewit: Yet there is truth in what I said. The actor does no work during the day, and why? Is it because he is idle? No: it is because a creative or interpretative artist needs long periods of leisure in which to prepare for the work which he is going to do. Foolish people envy him this leisure. They think how lucky he is to be paid for three hours' work a day. Yet if he is to work at the necessary pitch of intensity during those three hours, he needs the whole day free to prepare for it. It is in this respect that the amateur is at a permanent disadvantage. However seriously he may take his acting, he cannot give all of what is best in him to it. And thus he remains an amateur. Yet for all this it must be said that the best Canadian amateurs are very good indeed.

Trueman: So good that if there were a professional theatre here in which an honourable livelihood could be made, many of them would be in it, and might achieve heights of which they have not dreamed.

Lovewit: Do you think so? I too have seen a good deal of amateur work here, and the point which has depressed me about it is its old-fashioned quality.

Trueman: You mean that it lingers still in the realistic, understated mode which was popular in the 1920's? That is true.

Lovewit: The best actors of today have adopted a more robust style, and have left understatement to the movies, the radio and the amateurs. How thrilling the robust style can be, even in a movie, has been amply illustrated by Sir Laurence Olivier in *Henry V* and *Hamlet*. But amateurs are desperately afraid of what they call "ham." Now if they only knew it, "ham" is one thing they can never be, for "ham" is robust acting from which intelligence has been removed. If they are never robust, how can they be hams, stifle their intelligence as they may?

Trueman: Very often our amateurs remind me of Roy Campbell's comment on some South African novelists:

> You praise the firm restraint with which
>   they write—
> I'm with you there, of course:
> They use the snaffle and the curb all right,
> But where's the bloody horse?

They make a fetish of restraint when what they need is to cut loose.

Lovewit: Aha, but there you touch on what I believe to be a vital point. One can only cut loose in an act of artistic creation if one is in it up to the neck. The amateur theatre, at its best, still continues to have strong social implications. Qualities which have little to do with good acting—fairness to others, team-play, and the like— are given an exaggerated value there. For social reasons the good actor must not soar too far beyond the level of the mediocre actor. And although we must respect the ideas which lie behind such behaviour, they have nothing to do with great art.

Trueman: Precisely so, for art is undemocratic and unsocial in much of its working. Nothing so cruelly and irrevocably separates man from man as the existence of unmistakable artistic talent in one and the lack of it in another. And no one is more ruthless in his subjection of others to his needs than the great artist who is engaged in an act of creation. In the amateur theatre these facts must be kept in restraint as much as possible or the amateur theatre would cease to exist. But in the professional theatre they are the ordinary facts of existence; every professional accepts them, and they do not, in themselves, cause any friction. Though actors are, in the main, unusually genial and charitable toward one another in their private relationships, they recognize when they are at work that the superior and the inferior artist do not stand upon an equal footing. The amateur theatre is too close to private life for that.

Lovewit: It is really very simple. It is the economic factor which puts everything in perspective. The professional has his value and all his colleagues know it. The amateur has no unmistakeable means of determining his artistic worth.

Trueman: Yet if we say these things in our memorandum will not the Commissioners think that actors are mercenary dogs who judge a man only by the fee he commands?

Lovewit: We may trust them to understand the matter in the way we meant it. After all, it is true in every kind of professional work that the big rewards—be they money, or honour, or public acclaim—go usually to the man whose talents give him the best claim to them.

Trueman: There is always one way in which the first-rate amateur can rid himself of his disabilities.

Lovewit: You mean that he can become a professional?

Trueman: Yes, and it may be said that the amateur who does so is in little danger of falling prey to that cynicism about his work which wrecks the careers of many professionals who have gone on the stage at the earliest opportunity. Two theatres which have exercised an incalculable influence on modern drama began as amateur theatres: I mean the Moscow Art Theatre, and the Abbey Theatre of Dublin. They were born of a great love of the theatre; when the time came to break with the disadvantages of amateurism they faced that risk bravely. But during their years of professional greatness they never lost the fresh approach and the devotion of the good amateur. And it may be said that the Theatre Guild of New York had its beginning in the amateur Provincetown Players. Our Dominion Drama Festival proves to us every year that there is the raw material of a professional theatre in Canada which might rise to very great heights.

Lovewit: Well, let us suppose that such a devoted group of amateurs as began the Moscow Art Theatre were to try its luck in Canada; could it exist in one of our big cities?

Trueman: It might, if it had adequate financial backing. Don't forget that Constantin Stanislavsky was a man of wealth. In my opinion, it would take three years for such a group to reach a point where it could pay its own way. Most of the theatrical ventures which I have had a chance to watch in Canada have died from a combination of two diseases: they were not good enough, and they were not wisely financed. The two diseases are interlocking, for lack of money leads to bad work, and bad work keeps money out of the theatre.

Lovewit: Just a moment; I am an Old Vic man, as you know. Lilian Baylis was never discouraged by lack of money.

Trueman: Lilian Baylis was a financial genius; she also owned a theatre and thus had one large tangible asset; and she worked in a country and a city where the theatre counts its lovers in millions. The Canadian companies of which I speak are in a different position. If I were forming a Canadian theatre company the second man I would engage would be the best business manager I could find. And I would not seek to establish a company in one place; I would travel.

Lovewit: But have you not heard the moans of those who have travelled already? Where is there for them to play? In school auditoriums, which have no space for scenery, no adequate lighting, and stages which might better be described as niches in the wall. There are also town halls, skating rinks and armouries. Theatres are few, and many of them are barn-like edifices, impossible to fill and as uncomfortable, in their way, as the school auditoriums.

Trueman: But if the theatre in Canada is to wait upon the establishment of well-found playhouses in every small city and large town it will wait until the crack of Doom. For—get this through your head, Master Lovewit—the theatre is not first a thing of bricks and mortar, but of players and playwrights, and if first things are to come first the inconveniences of the existing halls must be met and overcome.

Lovewit: Pray do not hector me, my dear friend, for I present difficulties only to draw you out.

Trueman: Your pardon, honest Lovewit. But when I hear it suggested that a play cannot be done well without a perfect theatre—meaning some version of the peep-show theatre of the past two hundred years—I cannot contain my choler.

Lovewit: Arena staging might be tried. Fine things have been done in that manner.

Trueman: Yes, and there is our old friend the fit-up—the portable stage equipment. And the depressingly educational appearance of school auditoriums could be relieved by an imaginative portable false proscenium. For a great step is taken toward stage illusion by any means which conceals from the audience that it is in the assembly hall of the Podunk Collegiate and Vocational School, where it has succumbed to boredom so often in the past.

Lovewit: I really do not see why a well-equipped and artistically respectable company should not travel in a circuit, as the players did in eighteenth century England. Indeed, when one considers the success of Community Concerts in Canada, one wonders if circuits might not be financed on a similar subscription plan. They would have to take in many small places, to cut the cost of travel but that would be desirable.

Trueman: An advantage of such a plan would be that, as with Community Concerts, the audience and the money would be assured, and the company would be able to judge its expenses with its eye trained upon its income. So long as it kept the confidence of its audience, it would have little to fear.

Lovewit: And it would keep the confidence of its audience so long as it could provide first-rate theatrical entertainment.

Trueman: That is the nub of the whole matter, for as we cannot repeat too often, more theatrical ventures are killed by their own lack of merit in a year than are killed by the neglect or malignity of the public in ten. I said that the second man I would hire, if I were charged with the task of establishing such a venture, would be a first-rate business man. The first man, and the keystone of my arch, would be a first-rate artistic director.

Lovewit: You would be hard set to find him.

Trueman: Men of capacity are hard to find in all walks of life. He would have to be a man of fine taste, yet with a keen sense of what his audiences could be persuaded to like. He would have to keep not only his actors, but his directors, designers and technical people up to the mark. He would have to listen at all times to his business manager, and he would have to possess a good knowledge of business himself. He would have to provide, like Stanislavsky or Lilian Baylis, inspiration, instruction, succour, rebuke and a focus of faith for all who worked with him, and he would have to provide the public with a figure-head whom they could trust and admire.

Lovewit: You ask for a paragon.

Trueman: No; merely for a man big enough for a big job. Such people are not common, nor are they cast in one mould. Can you think of three people more apparently different than Stanislavsky, W.B. Yeats and Lilian Baylis? And our leader here, whoever he may be, will be like all of them, and yet not like any of them.

Lovewit: Come, Trueman, we agreed to stick to common sense. You are talking as though our Canadian theatre would be the work of some single remarkable figure.

Trueman: Perhaps I am wrong, but I do not think so. Such a leader would collect about him the admirable single talents which exist in our country now, but which have no focus. If I write a play, to whom can I turn for an opinion which will content me? And you, Lovewit, who direct and act with a certain taste and discretion— is there anyone for whom you are ready to give your utmost, and whose banner you would follow through good times and bad? Canada has plenty of theatrical talent which is very nearly first-rate, and which would be so if it could find a catalyst—a messiah—call him what you will.

Lovewit: If we sent a memorandum to the Commissioners saying that we want a messiah they may take us for madmen—

Trueman: I doubt that. The Chairman of the Commission is a notable patron of the drama, and the other Commissioners, being persons of cultivation and noble spirit, must love it too. Let us say that we need a messiah by all means, and I am sure that they would unite in the Song of Simeon if he were to appear.

Lovewit: Trueman, restrain your Celtic emotion! Any suggestion that the Commissioners are ready to sing a *Nunc Dimittis* will undo us utterly! To imply that a Commission is ready to depart, even in peace, is inexcusable impertinence! What they want from us, I venture to say, is concrete suggestion. What, in short, can the Government of Canada do about the theatre in Canada?

Trueman: It could do several things. It could give reputable travelling companies, composed of Canadians, a special favourable rate on the Canadian National Railways, by making some suitable arrangement with the railway authorities. The haulage of a company and the quantity of scenery is a formidable consideration for any theatrical venture.

Lovewit: That would be a practical benefit certainly.

Trueman: And it might induce provincial governments, at a dominion-provincial conference, to relieve reputable Canadian companies of the burdensome amusements tax which the provinces now levy.

Lovewit: True, for it seems unjust that the native theatre should be expected to tack onto every ticket of admission an extra charge which is not used for the furtherance of the theatre or any of the arts. If there is a case for such an impost upon any form of entertainment—which I am disposed to doubt, for it is discriminatory, and I shrewdly suspect that it has its root in a puritanical dislike of merrymaking in general—there is surely none upon the Canadian theatre, which deserves well of its country and its country's governors.

Trueman: Well, there we have two benefits which might be conferred.

Lovewit: Both, it may be said, are negative: they let the theatre companies off certain expenses. They do not plainly give them anything.

Trueman: And that, in my opinion, is as it should be. For you may as well know, Lovewit, that I oppose giving artists money from the public purse except under the most unusual circumstances: lessen their burdens, but give them no cash.

Lovewit: For the reason, I suppose, that I spoke of earlier: the artist who gets nothing from his Government is not under his Government's thumb.

Trueman: Precisely. If the theatre is to have a patron today it must be the Government, for the Government now takes the means of patronage from private persons. But Government patronage, unless it is of the negative, unobtrusive sort which I have mentioned, or unless it operates under special safeguards, can become severely repressive in its influence. Let us suppose that some governmental scheme for a National Theatre were set at work in this country within the next five years: at every election economies are promised and the National Theatre would come under fire. That would beget a spirit of nervous tension and servility among the artists and administrators of the National Theatre which would make first-rate work impossible.

Lovewit: Alas, yes! And can you not imagine some Member of Parliament complaining bitterly in the Commons every time the National Theatre performed a play about people whose morals were not identical with those of his constituents? Or if he saw an actor from the National Theatre whose dress displeased him, or who wore his hair at a length deemed unbecoming in a servant of the state?

Trueman: Our elected representatives are already heavily burdened with public business: let us not lay upon them the responsibility of overseeing a theatre, as well.

Lovewit: There may come a day when a Canadian theatrical company has unmistakeably earned the right to be called a National Theatre. By that time it will have its traditions, its method of work, its individual style, and its faithful and appreciative public. If the nation chooses to offer support to it, it can accept upon honourable terms, and insist that it be allowed to know its own business better than the noble tribunes of the people. For although I am a democrat, Trueman, I do not believe that people who know nothing about the arts should be allowed to make life miserable for those who do.

Trueman: Because I am a democrat, I thoroughly agree with you. And I agree, too, that a National Theatre cannot be brought into being simply by the expenditure of public money. It must grow. Set up a National Theatre, and remove it from money anxieties by a state grant, and in ten years it will have become a pension scheme for the artistically worn out, the incompetent, and the faddists.

Lovewit: Either that, or a new playground for the professional do-gooders. Never forget those well-meaning enemies of art. They are the people who will not allow the theatre to be its own justification. The theatre is educational and recreative. But it is not so primarily. It is first of all an art, and it is as a form of art that it stands or falls. Let people get their hands on it who regard it as means of spreading some sort of education dear to themselves, or who think that it is a social medicine, and you will kill it as dead as a doornail. But let the theatre develop freely and gloriously as an art, let it present classics and good modern plays, let it ravish the souls of its audiences with tragedy and comedy and melodrama, and it will educate and recreate them more truly and lastingly than the zealots think possible. The car of Thespis must not be turned into a travelling canteen, dispensing thin gruel to the intellectually under-privileged.

Trueman: Yes, if the theatre in Canada is to develop into anything of worth it cannot afford short-cuts. It must take the long way, in order that it may have time to learn not only its own business, but the special tastes and needs of our people. It is superficially attractive to think of a National Theatre created by Government fiat, but I fear the consequences. In our country officialism is splendidly developed; the art of the theatre, though promising, is no match for it. Officialism and public interference might well prove too overpowering, and the result would be a National Theatre continually engaged in a losing fight with essentially inartistic influences.

Lovewit: By the bye, my dear friend, we must be careful of our use of that work "artistic" in our memorandum. Through no fault of its own it has acquired overtones of preciousness.

Trueman: Yes, we must make it clear that we employ the word "artist" in its true sense of "maker." The artist is he who creates. And he must be as little as possible hampered by people whose work is not to create but to complicate, obfuscate, worry and destroy.

Lovewit: We are agreed then, that the Canadian theatre should thoroughly learn its job before there is any talk of a National Theatre? Even though its way may be hard?

Trueman: Most certainly. Nor must we forget that to many people the words National Theatre mean a building, probably in Ottawa. Now unless such a building is a centre from which travelling companies go on tours through the length and breadth of Canada, it is a foolish extravagance. A theatre is not a thing of bricks and mortar. If a djinn from the Arabian Nights were to whisk the Shakespeare Memorial Theatre from Straford and set it down in Ottawa, with all its equipment, we would still be without a National Theatre. But if we can develop even one company, acting in a tent or in school halls, which can move Canadians to tears and laughter with the great plays of the past, and with great plays of the present (including perhaps a few of their own), we have the heart of a National Theatre.

Lovewit: The emergence of such a company would be an interesting phenomenon; I have sometimes wondered if criticism would have any considerable part in shaping and polishing it.

Trueman: Informed criticism could do much, but informed criticism is an uncommon thing in the periodicals of our country. If a critic is to be of any use to an artist, he must understand and love the art he criticises, and he must be deeply versed in its literature and its tradition, as well. He must know at least as much about the art as one of its practitioners. The hack critic, the mere reviewer, the reporter given leave to editorialize, is of no positive value and can be a real danger if he is himself a malignant or frustrated man.

Lovewit: Our attitude toward criticism is too deeply affected, I fear, by that of the U.S.A. There a critic is too often employed merely to give his opinion on a matter which he has not studied deeply, because he is a wit or can pass for a wit. This style of criticism is dangerous at its best, and when imitated by men of meagre gifts it is execrable.

Trueman: A fine critic is himself something of an artist, and he may, in some cases, encourage an art or even bring forth new developments in it. One of the principal tasks of every good critic of the theatre is to memorialize great performances and events in its history; part of his genius is to know when these events occur, for they are not always obvious. But it is to be feared that most critics serve the theatre as a flea serves a dog—as an irritating parasite which may at times bring the dog into derision.

Lovewit: Do you speak as a playwright whose work has, at times, been scorned?

Trueman: It may be that I do, but that does little to lessen the truth of what I have said. To have one's work condemned is unpleasant but not insupportable; to have one's work condemned irresponsibly is gall and wormwood. I think that the newspapers and periodicals have a duty in this matter which many of them neglect. But a growing theatre will make them repair their neglect.

Lovewit: I suppose the case of the Canadian playwright must be considered in any complete view of the Canadian theatre. I am told that a great many people in Canada write plays, and yet comparatively few Canadian plays are shown upon the stage. Are the majority so bad?

Trueman: Because I am a Canadian playwright myself I must be careful how I answer you. Only a few of these manuscripts have come my way, and the thing which astonished me about them was not that many were bad, but that several were near to being very good. People whose judgement I trust, who have acted as judges in playwriting competitions, have said the same thing to me often, and they have better cause to know the facts than I. But in order to write a play one must be not only a person with some degree of literary skill, but a theatre craftsman as well. One must know not only how people talk, but how to make them talk in such a way as to complete a piece of action in two and a half hours without too much padding, or too much jumping about in the plot. One must consider the actors, and give them opportunities to show their own special skill as distinguished from your own. One must know how to build up a speech to a climax, and then how to get down from the climax without tumbling. One must not introduce characters who do not help to carry forward the story, for actors cost money and must not be wasted. And above all, one must beware of the wrong kind of subtlety, for the delicate shades which give distinction to a novel have no place in a play: the subtlety of the playwright lies in quite another direction—not less than the novelist's, but different.

Lovewit: Aha, you touch upon something which I have often thought, and you must forgive me if I interrupt. It has occurred to me many times that the radio has a weakening effect upon many admirable Canadian writers who occasionally write plays. Radio drama being—let us not mince words—an enfeebled echo of the real thing, encourages the sort of subtlety of which you speak. When a speech can be whispered into a microphone with such immediacy of effect that the listener may almost fancy himself sitting in the larynx, if not in the heart, of the speaker, the writer is tempted to try effects which are quite lost when transferred to the stage. But because unthinking people admire what they regard as subtlety, and condemn breadth of effect, these ineffective devices are attempted again and again.

Trueman: It is this very thing which makes it so hard to put a good stage piece on the radio. A broad effect in radio is merely confusing. Alas for those who beat the drum on behalf of radio drama, the mind's eye is imperfectly hitched to the mind's ear. Hence the Procrustean "adaptation" which is necessary to crush a play into an hour's length, and make it endurable to one sense alone.

Lovewit: Not all Canadian playwrights, of course, suffer from the baneful influence of radio writing, but some of the most potentially brilliant of them do so.

Trueman: You interrupted me in my discourse upon the things which a playwright must know. He must be able to tell a story, with a certain richness of embellishment which it is the fashion of the day to mistake for thought, entirely in dialogue and action, usually without shifting his scene from a single place. He must—

Lovewit: My dear fellow, please do not tell me any more of the things that he must be able to do. We do not propose, after all, to write a treatise on the playwright's craft.

Trueman: Very well, let us say merely that it *is* a craft and that it must be learned. The best way to learn it is to write a play and see it through rehearsals and in performance. But as it costs quite a lot of money to give a play a production even in the amateur theatre, this cannot happen very often. The next best way is to see a lot of plays, and to learn from them. That can only be done where a theatre exists. I am quite sure that a robust Canadian theatre would bring forth a large body of Canadian plays, some of them good enough for export.

Lovewit: Hm. Do you think that people abroad would be interested in Canadian plays?

Trueman: Lovewit, you disgust me! Is not the theatre of the civilized world interested in plays by and about Russians, Norwegians, Frenchmen, Swedes, Hungarians, Italians, Belgians and even—God bless us!—Irishmen and Scotchmen? Are Canadians so cut off from the charity of God and the indulgence of mankind that they alone are of no interest to their fellow-beings? Take my word for it, if the plays are good enough, the world will like them.

Lovewit: Hm. I am reminded of the story of a gifted young woman who asked a celebrated orchestral conductor if her sex would prevent her from getting a place in a first-rate orchestra. No, said he; you will manage it if you are able to play twice as well as any of the men. Canadian plays will have to be very good indeed to break through the prejudice which exists against them, on the ground of their origin.

Trueman: I will confess to you that the agent who hawks my plays in England keeps mum about the fact that I am a Canadian. He says that it would work against him. Nobody thinks that there is anything odd about an Englishman or an American writing a play, but apparently it is still considered unpropitious for a play to come from Canada. Still, I think that the prejudice will be overcome and that we shall see Canadian plays performed abroad— when we have the playwrights capable of bringing that about.

Lovewit: It seems to me unlikely that we shall have plays which will command the attention of the outside world until we have a national drama which has roused and stirred us on our own soil.

Trueman: Agreed. Nevertheless, I like to look forward to that day, when-ever it may be. For I like to think that Canada will have a proud place among the nations, and I fear that her integrity, her good sense, her honest dealing and her indisputable political genius will not suffice to gain it for her. Think: do you know of any nation that the world has considered truly great which has not had one or many manifestations of great art? Canada will not become great by a continued display of her virtues for virtues are—let us face it—dull. It must have art if it is to be great, and it has more real vitality, in my opinion, in the art of the theatre than in any other save music. And I think its theatre is potentially just as good as its music and perhaps better.

Lovewit: I agree, but art cannot be compelled. It will not flourish here sim-ply because we wish it.

Trueman: But we can remove some of the hindrances which lie in the way. I agree with you that the offer of prizes for plays, and establish-ment of scholarships for talented writers and actors is not the Government's responsibility, but the Government might change its ideas about taxation as it affects writers; if royalties were treated as capital gains, which they are, rather than as profits, which they are not, it would help the writer to improve his posi-tion when he has a stroke of good fortune. A writer, surely, deserves well of the state? He exploits nothing but his own tal-ent; he does not impoverish the land; whatever he creates he cre-ates out of nothing which anybody else wants. And yet his creations give pleasure, and in special cases they may reflect hon-our upon his native land. I do not suppose that the Ministers of Finance and National Revenue are conscious of the existence of authors in any real sense. Yet to the author who, after years of work, a stroke of good fortune brings a considerable sum of money, it sometimes appears that these gentlemen are simply waiting to swoop upon him and despoil him. Canadian authors who are worth their salt do not want subsidies and handouts, but they would like a chance to build up a sufficient estate to permit them to live by writing alone, and to take the time necessary to do their best work.

Lovewit: Very well; let us turn from the authors to the actors. Should promising artists of the theatre be given state scholarships in order to study abroad?

Trueman: I would rather make it possible for them to study at home. The establishment, now, of a National Theatre would be a great mis-take; we do not know enough to ensure the success of such an undertaking. But the time is ripe for the establishment of a Theatre Centre, where all the arts of the theatre could be studied and practised under expert supervision, and where our excellent amateurs could find the polishing they need to make them good professionals, as well as the inspiration to carry them beyond their present limited artistic vision. Government assistance in establishing such a centre would be public money well spent.

Lovewit: A centre? A school, you mean?

Trueman: No, a practical theatre studio, not a drama school. I would strongly recommend a centre based upon the Old Vic Theatre Centre in London; Sweden has copied it, and we could find no better model. Furthermore, I have the assurance of its director, Monsieur Michel Saint-Denis, that he is willing and indeed eager to help in the establishment of such a centre here. What better model than the Old Vic Centre? What better advisor than the director of that centre and one of the ablest men of the theatre in the world today? If anything is to be done, Saint-Denis is your man; and it isn't every day that people of his quality offer to help a struggling art in a new country.

Lovewit: How is such a theatre centre financed?

Trueman: By fees from each student, and by a government grant which, in the case of the Old Vic Centre, is £5000 a year. Call it $25 000 a year for Canada, and a trifle for what it would do.

Lovewit: And who would head such a centre?

Trueman: It would have to be a man with some experience of such a place, and I am sure that Monsieur Saint-Denis would help us to find him.

Lovewit: And he would be our messiah?

Trueman: Perhaps: or our John the Baptist. Or even a thoroughly competent minor prophet would be a blessing. And when such a centre, and its students, were sufficiently strong we might think about a National Theatre. If the Government wants to help us, let them help us in this way: let them make it possible for us to *learn*. But as you see I am mistrustful of any sort of direct state patronage of the arts when the artists are not in a strong enough position to make conditions.

Lovewit: France, to name only one country, has had national patronage of the theatre for nearly three centuries.

Trueman: Which means that such patronage began in an age when it was in effect personal patronage by persons deeply concerned about the theatre. Our modern bureaucracies are not rich in such enlightened patrons, and our succeeding ministries are almost antiseptically free from them. The *Comédie-Française* was a product of the spirit of its time, and it had its roots in a strong popular theatre. When we have a strong popular theatre here, it will be time for us to think about a national theatre. We live in an age of ever-increasing socialism, as you know, and it is good socialist practice to take over a going concern.

Lovewit: You are not to be shaken, then, in your belief that Canada does not need a National Theatre?

Trueman: Have I been talking all this while in vain? Of course I believe that Canada needs a National Theatre, directed by competent artists of the theatre, and so highly esteemed by our country and by the civilized world that it can, literally, run its own show and be under no obligation to cringe whenever a contumelious parliamentarian knits his brows! I want Canada to have a National Theatre which is one of the proudest possessions of the state, and not a drag upon the public purse! For the theatre is one of the arts which can maintain high standards and still pay its way; it is a truly popular art, and the people will support it when it is unmistakeably of the first quality. I want a National Theatre in Canada as soon as we have developed a fine native theatre which has learned to support itself by its own efforts, asking from the Government a very little money and a few favours as assurances of goodwill. I want, in short, a National Theatre with its roots in the country, nourished by experience, craftsmanship, and a noble ideal of what a theatre should be!

Lovewit: Honest Trueman! Give me thy hand! I have but dissembled my agreement in order to provoke this splendid rage in thee! Pardon this tear! 'Tis but an ebullition of joy!

Trueman: Enough for one morning. Come, let us to the cocktail lounge where we may drain a bumper to the future!

Exeunt arm in arm.

THE THEATRE

Clearly summarized in the final Report *issued in 1951, the Massey Commission's thinking on theatre covered a wide range of subjects, from amateur theatre to theatre buildings, from a national theatre to the problems of touring. The overall* Report, *whose major recommendation led to the creation of the Canada Council, and established the principle of government subsidy to the arts, was a landmark in Canadian theatre history.*

(From the correspondence of Samuel Marchbanks)

To Apollo Fishhorn, Esq.,

Dear Mr. Fishhorn:—

You want to be a Canadian playwright, and ask me for advice as to how to set about it. Well, Fishhorn, the first thing you had better acquaint yourself with is the physical conditions of the Canadian theatre. Every great drama, as you know, has been shaped by its playhouse. The Greek drama gained grandeur from its marble outdoor theatres; the Elizabethan drama was given fluidity by the extreme adaptability of the Elizabethan playhouse stage; French classical drama took its formal tone from its exquisite, candle-lit theatres. You see what I mean.

Now what is the Canadian playhouse? Nine times out of ten Fishhorn, it is a school hall, smelling of chalk and kids, and decorated in the Early Concrete style. The stage is a small, raised room at one end. And I mean room. If you step into the wings suddenly you will fracture your nose against the wall. There is no place for storing scenery, no place for the actors to dress, and the lighting is designed to warm the stage but not to illuminate it.

Write your plays, then, for such a stage. Do not demand any procession of elephants, or dances by the maidens of the Caliph's harem. Keep away from sunsets and storms at sea. Place as many scenes as you can in cellars and kindred spots. And don't have more than three characters on the stage at one time, or the weakest of them is sure to be nudged into the audience. Farewell, and good luck to you.

March 4, 1950.   S. Marchbanks.[1]

o

1.   We think it appropriate first to pay tribute to the many thoughtful and scholarly briefs on drama which we have received reminding us of the eminent place which the drama has held in the long history of the arts, and of its relation to the sister arts of poetry, music and the dance which not infrequently reach their final perfection when associated in dramatic performances. Indeed, the tragic drama of Fifth Century Athens demanded and concentrated for its needs the full cultural resources of a highly gifted people, in poetry, in music, in the dance, and in philosophic and religious thought; from the tragic theatre and its supernal themes stemmed the arts of the Athenian sculptor, the painter, the architect, in a manner to be repeated only once again at the second flowering of the human spirit in Renaissance Italy. The drama has been in the past, and may be again, not only the most striking symbol of a nation's culture, but the central structure enshrining much that is finest in a nation's spiritual and artistic greatness.

2.   The point need not be laboured: many of man's greatest artistic achievements, from Aeschylus to Bach and from Euripides to Wagner, have been cast in a dramatic mould. This great heritage is largely unknown to the people of Canada for whom the theatre, where it maintains a precarious existence, is restricted to sporadic visits in four or five cities by companies from beyond our borders, to the laudable but overworked and ill-supported efforts of our few repertory theatres, and to the amateur companies which have done remarkable work against remarkable odds, largely for their own private pleasure. In Canada there is nothing comparable, whether in play-production or in writing for the theatre, to what is going on in other countries with which we should like to claim intellectual kinship and cultural equality.

3.   Although it is quite evident from the representations made to us across the country that there are considerable regional differences in the prosperity and effectiveness of the theatre in Canada, and although there are many evidences of a lively interest in the theatre, we have found fairly general agreement throughout the country on the following critical points:

(a) Canada is not deficient in theatrical talent, whether in writing for the stage, in producing or in acting; but this talent at present finds little encouragement and no outlet apart from the Canadian Broadcasting Corporation which provides at the moment the greatest and the almost unique stimulus to Canadian drama. The C.B.C. drama, however, is an inadequate substitute for a living theatre.

(b) Facilities for advanced training in the arts of the theatre are non-existent in Canada. As a consequence, our talented young actors, producers and technicians, revealed through the excellent work of the Dominion Drama Festival, must leave the country for advanced training, and only rarely return.

(c) Except in the few largest centres, the professional theatre is moribund in Canada, and amateur companies are grievously handicapped, through lack of suitable or of any playhouses.

(d) There is no National Theatre in Canada and nothing at present to indicate that there will be one. Although witnesses and other authorities on this matter differed in their conception of what a National Theatre should be and of how it should be brought about, there was wide agreement that it should be one of our cultural resources.

4.   In spite, however, of these many difficulties and obstacles the picture of drama in Canada is not at all one of unrelieved gloom. There still remain in Montreal, Toronto, Ottawa and Vancouver active theatre companies which have been able, consistently or periodically, to maintain professional levels of production and to preserve at least a limited public taste for the living theatre. In the person of Gratien Gélinas we have in Canada a man of the theatre who with rare vigour combines with equal distinction the qualities of the playwright, the producer and the actor. *Les Compagnons de St-Laurent*, maintaining both a school of dramatic art and a professional company of which any country might be proud, are well known not only in the Eastern parts of Canada but in the United States. The Western Stage Society, a professional non-profit company centred in Saskatoon, has shown that an enterprising company can do much even with very limited facilities for drama; in its first eighteen months this Society twice toured Saskatchewan and played in 140 cities, towns, villages and hamlets in whatever quarters could be found. The Canadian Repertory Theatre in Ottawa produces a play a week throughout the season, giving great pleasure to its supporters and saving Ottawa from the dubious distinction of being the only important capital city without a theatre. There are other professional or semi-professional companies, notably in Toronto, which appear from time to time, and there are, of course, many hundreds of amateur groups, some of them of genuine distinction.

5.   Probably the most encouraging aspect of the drama in Canada is the work of the Canadian Broadcasting Corporation, which has fully demonstrated that we suffer from no lack of playwrights, of producers or of actors where opportunity exists for their abilities. Throughout Canada we have heard, from drama groups and from persons competent to speak on these

matters, warm tributes to the freedom, the imagination and the artistic integrity of the C.B.C. productions. We were told in Vancouver, for example, that the Canadian actor would not find it possible to continue were it not for the C.B.C., and in Montreal that the C.B.C. has created a renaissance of dramatic art in Canada. It is possible that our Canadian society will always produce more young people of talent in the arts, letters and sciences than we are capable of absorbing; but it is apparent that, at the moment, for our young playwrights and actors who are eager to remain in Canada if they can make even a meagre living, the C.B.C. almost alone offers any opportunity.

6.   There is undoubtedly in Canada a widespread interest in the theatre. We have mentioned earlier the astonishing number of amateur dramatic societies; and even indifferent plays presented by visiting companies of no great distinction from abroad have been sold out weeks in advance. A first-rate company of players could probably maintain themselves profitably in Canada for as long as they wished to stay. From the evidence of the many briefs presented to us, and from the accounts we have heard of packed theatres in any centre where a play, whether amateur or professional, has been presented after the long absence of the living theatre, it seems apparent that there is in Canada a genuine desire for the drama.

7.   Nothing in Canada has done so much for the amateur theatre as the Dominion Drama Festivals which, apart from the war years, have been held since 1933. This nation-wide movement has created and has sustained interest in the theatre and has been directly responsible for the appearance of hundreds of theatre groups; it has also been a powerful agency in bringing together, in understanding and in the sharing of common purposes, companies of players from all parts of Canada who differ, it may be, in language, in background and in resources, but who are joined in the strongest of unions, an enthusiasm for a common and a pleasurable objective. We have been impressed by the warmth and the extent of evidence agreeing that the Dominion Drama Festival is now established as an important national movement and as a valuable unifying force in our cultural life.

8.   To make its work fully effective, however, the Dominion Drama Festival needs help in meeting recurring and increasing deficits (now borne by private donations), and in extending its activities. The Festival decided in 1950, as an act of faith to put itself on a full-time basis and to engage a staff to work throughout the year on Festival activities; but there are urgent needs for a central office with a library of plays, for trained organizers and directors, and for assistance in securing adequate theatres. Drama groups throughout Canada, moreover, have pointed out to us the almost impossible financial problem involved in sending a company of players over great distances to compete at the Festival. Last year (1950) the Festival was held in Calgary; only two groups in Nova Scotia expressed any interest in it, and no company east of Quebec City was in fact represented. We are informed that many local dramatic societies are now reluctant to enter the Festival since if they win their regional festival they cannot attend the national com-

petition; some local companies of amateurs also feel that they cannot compete on equal terms with companies of professional actors; and although the Festival undoubtedly reveals each year the best dramatic work in Canada, it has grown somewhat remote from the smaller dramatic societies many of which originally it helped to bring into being. Other societies husband their resources by restricting their local productions in order to travel to the Dominion Festival, if successful; as a consequence, it becomes an indirect cause of curtailing productions in certain areas. We found widespread agreement that it would be a serious setback to our national understanding if for financial or other reasons acting groups in Canada are compelled to abandon the Festival, or it if must restrict its further development.

9. In Canada the writing of plays, in spite of the few vigorous creative writers who have found encouragement in the C.B.C., has lagged far behind the other literary arts. We have been informed that there is little writing for the theatre in Canada because of our penury of theatrical companies; these are few in number for lack of playhouses for which there is no demand since our people, addicted to the cinema, have rarely the opportunity to know the pleasure of live drama professionally presented. It has been universally true that the play-writer must have a vigorous, living theatre for which to work; for this, radio drama is no substitute and indeed, we are told, habitual writing of scripts for radio broadcasting purposes, though a skill in itself, may ruin a writer for the theatre where the dramatist must know how to use movement, gesture and stage-craft in composing his work.

10. Although the field of formal education lies outside the competence of this Commission, we have noted with interest that increasingly drama is recognized in the school curricula of most provinces, notably in Western Canada, as a valuable means for attaining some of the objectives of general education. Throughout the country, too, drama and the arts of the theatre are receiving increased attention from educational authorities and voluntary organizations concerned with adult education. A few Canadian universities have full-time departments of drama, and in such summer schools as the Banff School of Fine Arts much excellent work is being done. But nowhere in Canada does there exist advanced training for the playwright, the producer, the technician or the actor; nor does it seem rational to advocate the creation of suitable schools of dramatic art in Canada when present prospects for the employment in Canada of the graduates seem so unfavourable.

11. We mentioned the lack of playhouses in Canada and on this subject we have heard much throughout the country. We are told that amateur companies are severely restricted in their activities by the almost insurmountable difficulty of finding adequate rehearsal quarters and suitable theatres for their productions; only five or six amateur companies in Canada have a permanent house of their own with reasonably adequate lighting and other stage equipment. Professional companies seldom venture to go on tour because the few remaining legitimate theatres in Canada are so widely separated that the costs of travelling are prohibitive. For a variety

of reasons, economic, sociological and aesthetic, the legitimate theatre which thirty years ago flourished throughout Canada has disappeared. (In passing it should be noted that the varied companies who appeared in the innumerable Canadian "Opera Houses" of the last generation included everything from distinguished acting to burlesque and vaudeville, and that few of them were indigenous to Canada). The local theatres could not compete with the moving-picture, and after standing vacant for longer or shorter periods were taken over by the great motion picture companies which not infrequently found it necessary to demolish the theatre stages in their plans for conversion. We have been repeatedly informed that the theatre could be revived if only federal subsidies could be secured for the erection of suitable playhouses throughout Canada and for part of the travelling expenses of Canadian professional companies. We have also been told that a chain of legitimate theatres throughout Canada would make possible tours of competent professional companies from abroad, thus providing a stimulus to Canadian actors and playwrights and a useful example of the wide gulf separating the interested amateur from the competent professional who has been thoroughly trained and apprenticed, learning his craft under the goad of sternly skilful direction and of ruthless competition. There is no doubt that the expenditure of adequate sums of money could restore suitable and numerous playhouses, but whether this would mean a renaissance of the theatre in Canada has been sharply questioned. *Les Compagnons de St-Laurent* agreed with the Western Stage Society that the construction of theatres and halls on the grand scale is not necessary or advisable but that much could be done to make existing accommodation more suitable for theatrical performances if competent advice on this matter were available from a central agency.

12.   Repeatedly at our sessions throughout Canada the question of a National Theatre was discussed. Almost invariably the view was expressed that a National Theatre should consist not in an elaborate structure built in Ottawa or elsewhere, but rather in a company or companies of players who would present the living drama in even the more remote communities of Canada and who would in addition give professional advice to local amateur dramatic societies, a procedure which, we understand, has been made effective in the Union of South Africa where the problems were essentially similar to our own. The permanent company would be principally engaged in bringing the theatre to all communities in Canada where facilities for presentation exist. It has also been suggested that many Canadian cities and towns now lacking an adequate playhouse would find it practicable and desirable to make suitable provision for the regular appearance of the national company of players. These would not only present plays of a high professional level of performance but would give counsel to local dramatic societies in acting and in stagecraft. It would no doubt be desirable for gifted amateur actors of local societies to appear in minor or even in major roles with the professionals, to the great advantage and pleasure both of themselves and of their community. The members of the permanent company would also be available, in the theatre off-season, as directors of sum-

mer theatres or as instructors at summer schools of the theatre; and the permanent company could appropriately represent Canada at international festivals of the theatre. The brief of the Governors of the Dominion Drama Festival adds that such a permanent company would also "encourage writing for the Canadian theatre and provide an opportunity for presentation of Canadian plays."[2]

13. If there were such an outlet and such a goal for young Canadians gifted in the arts of the theatre, it has been suggested to us that it would be advisable and necessary to make provision in Canada for the more advanced training of young artists discovered by the Dominion Drama Festival and by other amateur and professional organizations. Such an advanced school, if established, should be closely associated, we were told, with one of the Canadian universities so that students could conveniently receive both the specialized training in the theatre and the general training in language and in the liberal arts essential to their careers; and the advanced school should give instruction in the kindred arts of opera and ballet.

14. As part of the school of the National Theatre it has been proposed to us that there should be a well-designed and adequately-equipped theatre which would include suitable studios for advanced instruction and experimentation in stage-craft, costuming, make-up, lighting, and in other technical skills. It would, of course, be disastrous to conceive of the National Theatre merely as a playhouse erected in the capital or in one of the larger centres; but it seems apparent that the national company of players would require a base for their operations and that the advanced school should have adequate quarters for instructional purposes and for performances. The playhouse of the national company would no doubt serve as a model for communities throughout Canada proposing to construct theatres as municipal enterprises, and its staff would be competent to advise dramatic societies throughout Canada on all theatrical matters.

15. A National Theatre has been strongly advocated as the logical and essential sequel to the progressive scheme of development which has been created through the work of voluntary organizations but which at present leads nowhere. Such a theatre, it has been argued, would provide a goal and an outlet for the young persons of first-rate ability who each year are trained in the amateur or professional groups, in universities and summer theatres, or who have won distinction at the Canadian Drama Festival and who now, apart from the very few who can find work with the C.B.C. or with a repertory company, must leave Canada or abandon the theatre as their life work.

16. We must not, however, give the impression that the views of those Canadians competent to speak on the drama in Canada are unanimously in favour of the immediate establishment by one means or another of a National Theatre. Indeed, the dangers inherent in attempting to establish and to operate an agency for the advancement of national culture directly

under government control have been expressed to us wittily and with force in the Special Study on "The Theatre in Canada" which was prepared at our request by a well-known Canadian writer and actor. By this authority on the Canadian theatre, and by others who share his views, it was suggested to us that the Government of Canada at the moment should do no more than make possible for Canadian companies of players easier and less expensive means of travelling throughout our vast distances. The suggestion was made, too, that the Federal Government, in the course of one of the Federal-Provincial Conferences, might suggest to the Provinces that they consider the possibility of relieving non-profit dramatic companies of the amusement tax which the provinces now levy. The point was made to us, in general, that the burdens now pressing upon drama in Canada should be lessened, but that there should be for Canadian drama no direct contribution of public money.

17.   The argument went on to suggest that government patronage of the arts, unless it operates under special safeguards, can become severely repressive in its influence; if a governmental scheme for a National Theatre, for example, were set at work in this country within the next five years, at every election when economies are advanced the National Theatre would automatically come under fire. Dependence upon government support, in this view, would give only a precarious existence to a National Theatre in Canada and would make first-rate work impossible. This argument adds that there may come a time when a Canadian theatrical company will have unmistakably earned the right to be called a National Theatre. By that time it will have its traditions, its methods of work, its individual style and its faithful and appreciative public. If at that time the nation chooses to offer support to it, it can then accept this support upon honourable terms, insisting, however, that it be allowed to conduct its own business in complete independence.

18.   As we have observed, to many people the words "National Theatre" mean a building, probably in Ottawa; but unless such a building is a centre from which travelling companies go on tours throughout the length and breadth of Canada, it would be a foolish extravagance. If the Shakespeare Memorial Theatre, we were told, could be transplanted bodily from Stratford-on-Avon to Ottawa-on-the-Rideau, with all its equipment, we would still be without a National Theatre; but, "if we can develop even one company, acting in a tent or in school halls, which can move Canadians to tears and laughter with the great plays of the past, and with great plays of the present (including perhaps a few of their own), we have the heart of a National theatre."[3]

19.   We have come to share the conviction, expressed to us by representative drama groups throughout the country and with particular force and clarity during our sessions in Vancouver, that the theatre has now reached a critical point in its development in Canada. We were pleasantly and appropriately reminded of the tide in the affairs of men which taken at the flood leads on to fortune, and it was demonstrated to us with skill and knowl-

edge that we are now witnessing in Canada a full-flowing tide of interest in the theatre. There is great activity on the part of local drama clubs and societies; drama festivals, in spite of many difficulties, culminating in the Dominion Drama Festival are flourishing; training and experience in the theatre are now given in schools and universities throughout Canada; our few repertory companies have held the pass; the C.B.C. has revealed something of our native talent in the arts of the theatre, and it may be expected that the still unknown potentialities of television will provide great opportunities for our playwrights, actors and producers.

20.   It seems to us that the time is now opportune for the provision in Canada of the modest help from federal sources which will permit these varied activities of the drama in Canada to find their logical outcome and their fulfilment. The manner in which we believe this help can properly and effectively be given we shall propose in Part II of this Report.[4]

NOTES

1. From the correspondence of Samuel Marchbanks, reprinted by permission of the copyright holder, *The Peterborough Examiner*.

2. The Governors of the Dominion Drama Festival, Brief, p. 9.

3. Robertson Davies, Special Study, *The Theatre in Canada*, p. 25.

4. Chief among the Commission's many recommendations was the creation of an arm's length government agency "to be known as the Canada Council for the Encouragement of the Arts, Letters, Humanities and Social Sciences to stimulate and to help voluntary organizations within these fields, to foster Canada's cultural relations abroad, to perform the functions of a national commission for UNESCO. . . ." From the Massey Commission *Report*, p. 377.

THEATRE NEEDS MORE
THAN A PAT ON THE HEAD ✧

JOHN COULTER

o

Not everyone was impressed with the Massey Commission report. John Coulter responded with something less than enthusiasm in this piece from a 1951 issue of Saturday Night.

"Live horse and you'll get oats." In my native country that saying was the cynics' comment on hopes certain to turn sick. In my country of adoption any hope that public funds might be adequately used to help fledgling theatre find its wings is already a sick hope. "Grow strong, Canadian theatre, strong enough to fly without help, and maybe you'll get help." It's a rich joke.

With such encouragement can't you see the township thespians laughing and laughing and then scrambling up the haystack to spread their costume wings and soar? Yet this is the sum of the encouragement which Canadian theatre will find in the Royal Commission's two volumes of several hundred-thousand well-considered, coolly reasonable, suitably unexcited and oh-so-unexciting words.

In brief, the Commissioners' report that there's much interest in theatre in Canada but no adequate professional means of nourishing it, and that this interest is manifest and nourished principally through the activities of the DDF. (The distinction is not stressed between the theatre as a form of creative art; a part of commercial entertainment industry gambling with "risk capital"; and as the social pastime known as amateur theatricals with overtones of cultural prestige.)

What, chiefly, does the Commission recommend as public assistance to theatre? That, through appropriate voluntary organizations, some money

✧ *Saturday Night*, 11 Sept. 1951: 12, 28.

should be spent on "the underwriting of tours" of Canadian productions, and in providing awards for young people "whose talents have been revealed in national festivals." If, to the triumphant justification of incorrigible optimists, these so reassuringly unextravagant recommendations are acted upon, what should be the practical effect?

Probably that the DDF should have some assistance in its annual struggle to keep off the rocks; and that a few amateur or semi-professional companies of players who, by persistently disregarding every precept of economic sanity, and by dint of feeding on their own substance, had managed to survive through several seasons, should be helped to tour their shows here and abroad; and that a few talented young people would be helped to go abroad for training as theatre artists (to be contentedly employed afterwards in what Canadian theatre?) Live horse and you'll get oats.

The tone of these remarks may suggest that, in my opinion, the commissioners have not correctly interpreted the attitude to the theatre of the tune-calling Canadian taxpayer at large. On the contrary, I think their interpretation discouragingly correct. And that is evidently also the opinion of Mr. Robertson Davies, who prepared for the Commission a special study of our theatre.

Mr. Davies offers his opinion in the form of a dialogue, at times mildly ironic but always amusedly aloof and urbane. Surely he is in danger of bitting his tongue when he publicly bids himself, "restrain your Celtic emotion." He reminds us that one Canadian of genius could bring Canadian national theatre into existence, as Yeats and Stanislavsky and Lilian Baylis brought national theatre into being in their native lands.

I used to think and say so myself. Now I add a conditional clause—*if* the Canadian public were as ready for such a Messiah as were the Irish, Russians, British. Even so, the task of the Canadian should be enormously more difficult, since in Canada there are so many Canadas, so many racial and national elements still far from constituting what the milkman would call a homogenized Canadian people. I suspect that the appearance of such a genius is an expression and product of the public's need and readiness for him. I am not sure that we are ready. Or maybe we don't know our own brat—prodigy I mean—when we see him.

Having thus played John the Baptist to our coming Messiah of the theatre, Mr. Davies turns a sceptical, wary eye on the horde of theatrical roadgraders now busy in the wilderness preparing the way. No bonuses for them! Mr. Davies is for helping them in a merely negative way. "Lessen their burden," he says, "but give them no cash." Good old hard-headed, puritan-pioneer stuff! As to the small brass tacks, he would have railway fares reduced for touring companies, and would relieve them of paying amusement tax. He would encourage competent criticism, and would offer oats to the horse if only, unfortunate nag, he can keep on the road long enough to earn and eat them. Let Canadian theatre "thoroughly learn its job" before looking for help to learn it. (I wonder had the Abbey Theatre thoroughly learned its job when Miss Horniman kept it in existence by presenting it with the theatre, recently burned down.)

But what might be happening today, had some enlightened million-aire—or body of citizens corralled by an omnipotent Women's committee—offered a ten-year lease of a suitable small stage to, say the New Play Society of Toronto who, during several seasons, had proved its ability to learn and do its job. (The job of staging plays which were a flowering of Canadian life in terms of theatre.) "But if we can develop even one company," says Davies, "which can move Canadians to tears and laughter . . . we have the heart of a National Theatre." I suggest that in the work of the NPS, for one example, we had for several years the heart of a National Theatre, thumping away for all it was worth, but nobody thought of providing it with a theatre to go on thumping in.

GROWING TIP

The Commission, and Robertson Davies, seem scared that governmental support of theatre is necessarily stultifying through interference in the theatre's artistic affairs: a notion with which I don't agree. Because this year I have seen it disproved. One of my most piquant observations in England was of the spirited, enlightened sponsorship of the "growing tip," the advance guard, in all the arts by the British Council and the Arts Council. The Commissioners do, however, recommend the setting up here of a sort of amalgam of these Councils, a Canadian Council. If such a Council should, in fact, be set up, and *if it were composed of the right people*, the nose-bag might soon be on our skinny horse.

I spoke of the mild irony and the danger of tongue-biting in some passages of the Special Study. "I suppose," says Mr. Davies, languidly, "the case of the Canadian playwright must be considered in any complete view of Canadian theatre." Delightful! The playwright as a mere afterthought of theatre! But the irony missed its mark or was badly blunted on the hard pre-Cambrian bosom of the Commission. There's no recommendation for succor of the playwright. Let the seed of theatre strike root in the stony ground if it can! A little artificial manure might work marvels.

I am myself sure that the history of theatre in Canada is not likely to differ greatly from that of theatre everywhere else: theatres have never been theatres but at most theatrical museums till they became playwrights' theatres.

The Special Study suggests that authors, who may work for years to earn one financially profitable production, should not be taxed as though the money when it comes were the average earnings of each year. The Commission takes no specific notice of this eminently reasonable and just suggestion. Nor does it make any recommendation toward finding a way by which even a selected few of Canadian plays should at last be made available to all Canadian producers. I suggest, and have several times publicly suggested, that whether they are a good "publishers' risk" or not, at least the plays which win the DDF awards as best Canadian-written plays in the Festival, ought to be published year by year.

CANT PHRASE

"Ought to be . . ." Why, ought? Manifestly there's no ought about it, unless the arts are genuinely of importance to Canada. Are they? Or is "the importance of the arts" merely a cant phrase to be archly mouthed at public meetings and privately repudiated with a wink? To compel an answer to that question is at least one of the justifications of the Commission's work. We shall have the answer, delayed since that notable morning when the question was first asked on Parliament Hill in the once famous Artists' Brief— we shall have the answer when we see what action, if any at all, is taken on even these paltry recommendations.

Meanwhile, as for theatre people who can't endure to be half-timers of the theatre, they may still sing: Oh Canada, how much longer do you expect us to stand starving on guard for thee? The horse hears only the same old promise of oats and responds with the lifted tail, and with tail and mane a-flying goes neighing off on glinting heels to the bursting bins, across the border.

THE MASSEYS AND
THE MASSES [*]

TOM HENDRY

o

More than twenty years after its release, the Massey Commission Report was still being debated. From the pages of the Canadian Theatre Review *(1974), Tom Hendry (b. 1929), co-founder of the Manitoba Theatre Centre, looked back to the* Report's *assumptions.*

To understand how, at a time when even so conservative a body as the Canadian Labour Congress has begun making something more than polite noises about the necessity for national independence for its constituent bodies, the Government of Canada can go on paying out millions of tax dollars yearly to organizations dedicated to the continuation of the most abjectly colonial repertoire policies, one must take a careful look at the roots of present policy. A cursory reading of books like Betty Lee's *Love and Whiskey*, a skin-deep portrait of the D.D.F. with a number of valuable chapters on Canadian theatre history, indicates that the "old-boy" network of accommodations around which is constructed the present shambling structure of Federal participation in the arts stretches back to pre-War days, to the thirties when only exalted visitors, such as Governors-General, had the time or the background to take an interest in the arts in our country. Vincent Massey, who was eventually to chair the Royal Commission which recommended the establishment of the Canada Council, was more than slightly involved in the launching of the Dominion Drama Festival under Lord Bessborough (whose wish it was ironically to have the Festival as a showcase for Canadian plays), and in that organization's continuing fortunes. The degree to which he became the intellectual prisoner of thinking which saw only the voluntary organization as the vehicle for the decentralized distribu-

[*] *Canadian Theatre Review* 3 (Summer 1974): 6–10.

tion of Federal subsidy is reflected within the Massey Report itself and in the eventual terms of reference suggested to the Council which was its child.

To understand the enormous leap which the Federals must take from a responsive stance in the area of the arts to one that is truly responsible—a leap which they must take if they are ever to recapture the initiative in the area and bring some degree of order and—dare one say it—justice to a scene which has become a gigantic mutual back-scratching exercise for the privileged, one must also examine carefully the proximate articulation of cultural policy as it affects the performing arts: I refer of course to the recommendations of the Massey Commission and the phraseology of the Act of Parliament setting up the Canada Council.

In its report of May 1951, the Royal Commission on National Development in the Arts, Letters and Sciences made, among others, the following recommendation:

"That a body be created to be known as the Canada Council for the Encouragement of the Arts, Letters, Humanities and Social Sciences to *stimulate and help voluntary organizations within these fields* (italics mine), to foster Canada's cultural relations abroad, to perform the functions of a national commission for UNESCO and to devise and administer a system of scholarships."

In amplification, the Royal Commission recommended "That the Canada Council, without limiting its freedom to advance the arts and letters, the humanities and social sciences in Canada, and to promote a knowledge of Canada abroad in the ways and by the means which it will judge appropriate, give consideration to the following proposals:

(1) The strengthening by money grants and in other ways of *certain of the Canadian voluntary organizations* on whose active well-being the work of the Council will in large measure depend. (Italics again mine.)

(2) The encouragement of *Canadian music, drama and ballet* (through the appropriate voluntary agencies and cooperation with the CBC and NFB) by such means as the underwriting of tours, the commissioning of music for events of national importance, and the establishment of awards to young people of promise whose talents have been revealed in *national festivals of music, drama or the ballet.* (Italics again mine.)

(3) The promotion of a knowledge of Canada abroad by such means as foreign tours by Canadian lecturers and by performers in music, ballet and drama and by the exhibition abroad of *Canadian art* in its varied forms." (Italics mine.)

The Canada Council Act of 1957, which became the Statutory embodiment of much of the Commission's recommendation, eventually translated much of this into:

"The objects of the Council are to foster and promote the study and enjoyment of and the production of works in the arts, humanities and social sciences and in particular without limiting the generality of the foregoing, the Council may, in furtherance of its objects:

(A) Assist, cooperate with and enlist the aid of organizations, the objects of which are similar to any of the objects of the Council.

(B) Provide through appropriate organizations or otherwise, for grants, scholarships or loans to persons in Canada for study of research in the arts, humanities and social sciences in Canada or elsewhere or to persons in other countries for study or research in such fields in Canada.

(C) Make awards to persons in Canada for outstanding accomplishment in the arts, humanities or social sciences.

(D) Arrange for and sponsor exhibitions performances and publications of works in the arts, humanities and social sciences.

(E) Exchange with other countries or organizations or persons therein knowledge and information respecting the arts, humanities and social sciences, and

(F) Arrange for representation and interpretation of *Canadian* arts, humanities and social sciences in other countries."

The terms of reference are sweeping and wide, but it is interesting to note the degree to which the focus on things Canadian which characterized the Royal Commission's recommendations has been neatly removed in framing the governing Statute. Certainly those who, over the years, have administered this Act have done so in terms of the letter of the law, as eventually framed, not in the spirit of the prescription the Massey Commission recommendations sought to be, with regard to the encouragement of native Canadian *creation* in the arts. Certainly in the case of the organizational thrust of Recommendations and Statute, they have been diligence itself in respecting both spirit and letter. One cannot believe that administrators as sophisticated and civilized as those the Council has had as ornaments to its staff, were not aware of the probable thrust in a post-Colonial situation of organizational thinking in terms of repertoire and Canadian creation. One had only to look at the stock-in-trade of Stratford, of the Symphonies, of the DDF, of the major dance groups to realize that precious little of Federal subsidy would go to Canadian creators if the distribution of subsidy was to be entrusted to such organizations as existed in 1957, the year the Council got into business, and such organizations as would likely come quickly into existence. Assuming that the Council and its administration understood what would happen, one finds it equally hard to believe that they did not in fact welcome a continuation of the colonial period in repertoire and further, did not, by their financing and encouragement make such a period of retardation possible. The defence always given here is that by its system of individual awards, the Council is able to funnel subsistence directly to the creator, whether or not he is of interest to performing bodies; try rationalizing *that* one away to the composer who still cannot get his works played, the playwright still effectively locked out of the best-financed theatres, the choreographer still denied access to our finest dancers.

In its first year (1957-58), the Council established a pattern which, sixteen years and perhaps one hundred million dollars later, still lays its heavy hand on grants policy. Thus, in the field of music, of $230 000 given that first year, exactly $5000 given to the Canadian Music Council went identifiably to support the Canadian music which the Massey Commission recommended the Canada Council be formed expressly to support. The remainder—a generous 99 percent—was channeled to organizations whose interest in the Canadian composer was, and remains, peripheral and capricious, but whose awareness of themselves as cultural bastions of a colonial class structure continues impeccable to this day.

In the 1957–58 field of theatre and ballet, of $250 000 given,

- $100 000 went to the National Ballet (for support of what might be termed most kindly "traditional" repertoire); $20 000 went to the Royal Winnipeg Ballet (ironically most of it for original material) and $80 000 went to the Stratford Festival and its then wrong-side-of-the-blanket sister group, Canadian Players, mostly for tours of Shaw and Shakespeare.

- Of the $50 000 remaining, only $15 000 given to Le Théâtre du Nouveau Monde for a tour of Dubé's *Le Temps du Lilas* can in any way be viewed as support to the Canadian Drama which, again, the Commission had recommended the Council be formed to support and encourage. Apart from the help to the Royal Winnipeg Ballet, native expression in dance was in no way helped by the actions of the Council.

Why was no leadership given by the Council when the performing arts twig was thus bent? One can only assume that the administrators who recommended the grants, the Council members who assented to them, were in fact sympathetic to the only predictable results of such policy—the laying of the foundation of two decades of colonial repertoire in the performing arts, the denigration, in practical terms, of the Canadian creator, and the perversion of, for generations, the natural inclination of Canadian interpretive artists for works reflecting directly the Canadian reality. Apart from the apparent sympathy in 50's Council leadership circles for the colonial route, one notes that by accepting the primacy of the delivery system—the voluntary organization dwelt on so lovingly by Commission and Statute—and the responsive stance such an acceptance dictated, the Council abdicated from the beginning any pretence of leadership. From the beginning what was good for the National Ballet was automatically assumed to be good for the Canada Council; whether or not this coincidence of interest—out of which grants, Council memberships, advisory posts, consulting fees and all sorts of goodies flowed depended on all sorts of nebulous qualifications characterized as "quality," "excellence," "lasting worth" and other terms made meaningless by any application to art. (Show me any generation's "excellence" and I will show you, in 99 percent of the cases, the next generation's junk, kitsch and schlock.) Further, the application of these meaningless and dubious yardsticks was in the main made by "advisors" who were recruited from the ranks of the already-subsidized, and who, thus had an important stake in shutting off or diverting potential competition. The fact that the whole process was presided over, in terms of the Arts Section secretariat, by the late Peter Dwyer, a vastly civilized Oxford graduate who had served with great distinction in the British Secret Service, and whose values were firmly internationalist when dealing with English-Canadian cultural aspirations, helped considerably to ameliorate the worst excesses of a system based upon genteel venality. But given the structure and aims of the Council, it is doubtful if Dwyer or anyone else, even had they so wished, could have prevented its rapid takeover by its initial clientele.

The program and direction set out were approved by a Council composed of such average, representative Canadians as Samuel Bronfman (Montreal), Major-General Georges P. Vanier (Ottawa), Eric Harvie (Calgary) and E.P. Taylor (Toronto) among others. I was told in all seriousness by a Council officer in those days, that very rich people were sought for the Council in the hope that they would develop a loyalty thereto and, on their death, leave large chunks of money to its Endownment Fund, the interest of which then provided the operating wherewithal. This democratic, representative Council and its Secretariat sought advice from arts professionals such as Herman Geiger-Torel (Canadian Opera Company), Budge Crawley (Crawley Films), Walter Homburger (Toronto Symphony), Raoul Jobin (Paris Opera and Metropolitan Opera), Michael Langham and Tom Patterson (Stratford Festival), Richard MacDonald (Dominion Drama Festival), Herbert Whittaker (*Globe and Mail*), Gwyneth Lloyd (Royal Winnipeg Ballet) and Jean-Louis Roux (Le Théâtre du Nouveau Monde). Of these, only the last two had ever been associated with Canadian work, but of the whole lot only Budge Crawley, Herb Whittaker and the man from the Paris Opera didn't get a grant that year.

As it began, so it has continued. Them that has, gets; them that exists, controls. And what is wrong with this? The question may be asked, "Why shouldn't a constituency control the body whose actions vitally affect their fates?"

The answer is, of course, that the constituency has altered but the manner in which it is represented and administered has not. The same group of organizations existing in 1957 has remained in control of Council policy ever since. Perhaps it was true in those days to ask: why commit money to the generation and production of Canadian work? Who wants to put it on anyway? Now, of course, all this has changed and in effective terms the heart of the Canadian performing arts lies with the creator not the quasi-commercial delivery system, the voluntary organization which will put on anything for which it discerns there is an "acceptable" market. Granted that some years of technical re-adjustments lie ahead of us as these organizations bring themselves into line with changing reality. And none of this is meant as a criticism of the large organizations. What they were formed to do, they frequently did well. But things have changed around them and the organizations have not. This year's Stratford season is probably no worse and no better than many other seasons. It is the climate around the Festival which is different. The very last dinosaur on the very last day before it died was still a well-designed animal which brought the relationship between mass and economy of brain-size to its finest point ever. But the next day, it died. Because the climate around it had changed, and the dinosaur had not.

CANADA, TRIUMPH AND
A TENT, 1952–1953 ◇

JAMES FORSYTH

○

Tyrone Guthrie (1900–71) first came to Canada in 1930 to produce an histori-
cal series for radio, "The Romance of Canada" by Merrill Denison. About the
same time, he met Dora Mavor Moore in Toronto who, two decades later, would
be instrumental in convincing him to come back to Canada to help launch the
Stratford Festival. Guthrie's biographer, James Forsyth, recreates that extraor-
dinary period which led to the opening of the Stratford Festival in 1953.

Tom Patterson, the "small voice out of the everywhere" was a physically
small man with a big idea. He was born in Stratford, Ontario, completed his
education in the University of Toronto and was now a publicity man in the
employment of *Maclean's* the publishers. And being a publicity man in a big
city of a big nation he was trained to have big ideas. He was, according to a
close friend, "well up on Civic Administration; and the best authority
around on Municipal Sewerage but he knew Hell-all about Theatre." Yet he
wanted to provide his birthplace with a theatre.

There was a practical reason behind this fanciful desire. Stratford had,
as the heart of its economy, the great railway workshops. He had seen what
cruel things had happened to his home town when its economic heart came
under threat during the 1930s Depression. And now, in the 1950s, the new
railway engines were to be diesel engines. The Age of Steam with its roar-
ing giants was over; and the great Stratford workshops were under threat of
closing down. If they did, the heart would go out of Stratford. What to do?
Then he got this big idea.

His town was not only called Stratford, a river—well, almost a river—
ran through it, called the Avon. The wards of the town were called Falstaff

---

◇ *Tyrone Guthrie: A Biography* (London: Hamish Hamilton, 1976), 221–31, 245–47.

and Romeo and there was a street called Hamlet. If Stratford-upon-Avon in England could be a bonanza town for the tourist trade, why could not Stratford-on-Avon, Ontario, be also? It did not seem to occur to him that the other Stratford was the birthplace of someone with even more universal ideas than he—and that that was quite a draw for the public. His idea became an obsession and he began to be a very positive nuisance, promoting it in the face of all sorts of "wise" opposition. It was about this time that John Coulter directed Guthrie's attention to what was going on around Stratford.

Patterson's persistence got him a committee and at its head a citizen who had a big heart, a stubborn resoluteness and a strong streak of religious rectitude—Dr. Harry Showalter. A man neither to be pushed into foolish dreams nor panicked out of proper ones, Showalter ran a highly successful business dealing in non-alcoholic beverages. One of these was called Kist. (The great publicity gimmick for this product was a shop-front banner which all its Stratford purveyors displayed, "COME IN AND GET KIST.") Tony Guthrie blessed this beverage with the name of "Château Showalter," and had every reason eventually to bless the man.

It is of interest in the Guthrie history that before ever he came on the scene, Olivier (unbeknown to him) was almost brought in. The Committee authorized Tom Patterson to spend $125 to get himself down to New York, where Sir Laurence Olivier was performing. By sheer native push he was to get through to the great man and convince him that it would be great for him to lend his name, and perhaps his presence too, to this New World Stratford Shakespeare Festival. But even Tom Patterson's push was not enough to get through the defences thrown up around the world star. He came back from New York defeated.

Then came an unpredictably helpful result of all the talk and rumour. Some Shakespeare enthusiast from Edinboro, Pennsylvania, came to Stratford and to Tom Patterson, when Tony Guthrie was still in Edinburgh, Scotland. He was in hope of a job in what the papers said was a new Shakespeare Festival Theatre. There was not much hope of a festival at the time, let alone a theatre. There was not even a job in it then for Patterson. So he took the man along to meet his friend Mavor Moore, son of Dora. As Mavor was in the middle of setting up the TV in Toronto, there might be some job with him for an enthusiastic arts man. Whether the man got a job or a return ticket to Edinboro, Penn., does not concern us; what does is that Tom Patterson got together with the Mavor Moore family. Tom did not really know which way to turn. "Have you talked to my mother about the idea?" Mavor Moore said. Tom had not. So Mavor directed him to her office. And this is where Guthrie in 1952 reaped from seeds sown in 1931—when via James Bridie's introduction he had met that vital lady of the Toronto theatrical scene—Mrs. Dora Mavor Moore.

It became obvious to her that Patterson knew very little about what she knew so much about—Theatre. What he needed for his project was not so much a "star" like Olivier, but a "name" director. The name she had in mind was Tyrone Guthrie, the brilliant young man who had produced "The Romance of Canada" and who she knew had done wonders now with her cousin in the old country. It was after this visit from Tom Patterson that she sent off the cable to John Coulter, and the letters to him and Guthrie.

When she got Guthrie's more than favourable reply, she summoned Tom Patterson to her office again. "I have the man you want, and I know that he is interested—Tyrone Guthrie." She had the right to expect an excited reaction. What Tom Patterson said to her was a non-committal "Fine." Because what he said to himself was, "Who the hell's Tyrone Guthrie?" And it was not till he had had time to nip into a public library and look Guthrie up that he enthusiastically responded. She suggested that he should put a call through right away to Guthrie at his home in Ireland. That was when the ancient, upright telephone rang in the high hall at Annagh-ma-Kerrig. And after answering it Tony did literally fly out the next day.

Now that Tyrone Guthrie was coming, one thing about that telephone call worried Patterson. He had nervously told him what he could, about town, the site, etc. Then the question of a fee was mentioned and Patterson had more cause for nervousness, because nobody had given him any authority to offer anything. He found himself mentioning a figure of say $500. What he did not know was that, just before he mentioned the figure, some leprechaun on the Irish line cut them off. When they got connected again everything else was briefly agreed and Tom Patterson rang off under the impression that the great man was coming for $500. He wasn't to know that he would have come for $5.

So, "Doctor Guthrie" was due to arrive (in 1950 he had been made an honorary Doctor of Law at St. Andrew's University, Scotland, and, in Canada, he enjoyed this form of address which so ran in the Guthrie family). Tom Patterson was sent to the airport in a small Volkswagen, with instructions to look for a "tall wraith of a man" with an almost military haircut and eyes as piercingly observant as Leo Tolstoy's. (The Mavors had been friends of the Tolstoys.) Off the plane came a whole posse of tall men answering this description. It was a deputation of Canadian Mounties in civilian clothes. But one tall figure, bare-headed and in "best blue," did not move off with this police posse. Little Tom Patterson, feeling like David in the approach to Goliath, got near enough to identify the Anglo-Irish giant.

The talk about the project started so immediately and went off at such a spanking pace, that by the time Dr. Guthrie was trying to compress himself into the small Volkswagen, Tom Patterson was surprised by—and comforted by—the banality of, "Jesus Christ!—my luggage!" "Never mind. I'll fix it," said Patterson. And the little bespectacled Canadian impressed Guthrie by the alacrity with which he did so. This was a more youthful and zestful member than usual, in Guthrie's experience of committee members. He would have been impressed too by the economy with which Patterson fixed his Toronto accommodation for the night. He had gone to Dora Mavor Moore in despair: "I haven't got the cash to put him up in a respectable hotel." (If he had known Tony Guthrie beyond the pages of *Who's Who* he would have known that Guthrie was happiest at a Y.M.C.A. or a two-star hotel with the one-star bill.)

Dora was not keen to get stuck with more than the $25 of that telephone bill. But she was not going to see the visit spoilt on its very first night. "He can come to us—for tonight anyway." "To us" was to one of the oldest wooden-built houses in Toronto; built in 1814. When Guthrie first entered it, he said, "It reminds me of my mother's home." Indeed there were ways in which the matronly authority of Mrs. Mavor Moore would remind him of his own mother; the same intelligence, warmth, and impatience.

Next day Tom Patterson drove Dora Mavor Moore and Guthrie the 125 miles or so out to Stratford. And all the way his ranging eye would be telling him—because he was a fateful man—that this was "his way" to travel. In fact there was something dreamlike in a journey which began as they left the Toronto suburbs with a sign which said "Islington," and that they should roll on through open corn country of the county of "Perth" to reach "Stratford," north of "London," passing through a hamlet called "Shakespeare." In Stratford, the bridge which spanned the Avon carried a "Waterloo" road; and around the verges of the Avon waters there were great willows which would have been at home on the banks of the Cam or the Isis. It was rather like a dream. On the way, he got to know Tom Patterson, and Patterson got a whiff of Guthrie common sense and Guthrie command. In the embarrassing position of having taken a wrong turning and having lost his way in his own native territory, Patterson stopped at a gas station to ask the way, "No," said Dr. Guthrie, firmly. "Takes two to find the way when lost. *I'll* ask the questions, *you* listen to the answers."

Without delay he met the Committee. And using to the full the aura of exotic authority brought all the way from old England, and speaking to keen but theatrically innocent folk who looked eminently responsible and responsive, he had the courage to tell them that they had better call the whole thing off now if they were not prepared to find a lot of money and, for the first year, lose most of it. Also, he was not for a moment prepared to commit himself to their proposed Festival if—Tom Patterson had the Guthrie eyes fixed on him—if they were just thinking of it as a good promotional gimmick which would bring busloads of tourists from Detroit and make the shopkeepers' cash registers ring to a merry tune. *However* (and one can hear the Guthrie nasal intake of breath and the pause for effect) *if* they were prepared to do something of such significance, in the Art of Theatre, and the presentation of Shakespeare, that the above would merely follow as a by-product of other aims more spiritual—both for the benefit of Stratford and the Canadian nation as a whole—*then* he would do what he could to realize Mr. Patterson's dream; and to see it through with them.

It was a thrilling moment. Yes, they would. Then Yes, he would. The project was "on."

It was a heavenly July evening and all were forgathered to end the day in the elegant house of engineer Mr. Alf Bell and his dynamic architect wife, Dama. This was on the other side of the Avon from where he had been shown a sort of public park bandstand. This bandstand had been the first choice of Tom Patterson, as the place where the plays might be played. But after the Guthrie address this could only be referred to apologetically. No, a special site must be chosen; theatres from the "tin" to the tented must be talked of; but for the moment he must recross the Stratford, Ont., Waterloo bridge and get some sleep. They crossed it. And not for the first time on that historic day Tom Patterson had a red face. At the Windsor Hotel, where he had booked Dr. Guthrie in, there was not a sign of a soul. True, it was late, but an empty reception desk and no night porter? "Not to worry," said the Doctor and strode up to the derelict desk. There he thumped not the reception bell but the cash register. And he persisted in thumping it till a bleary-eyed night porter, with a limp, came into the hall, saw the giant, and with understandable alarm said, "What y' doin?" Purpose firmly but quietly explained, the Doctor from England was shown up to his room and the nervously exhausted Tom Patterson drove back over the Avon to his parents' house. There was no sign of exhaustion in the Doctor. He came back downstairs, struck up an acquaintance with the lame night porter, and talked till 3 a.m., no doubt quietly provoking his companion by his questions into the answers that gave him a rundown on the town and what was going on. In the quiet Stratford night the sound of the "lonely moose" hooter on the great trains could remind him of the great railway town it had been; and also of his own Canadian National Railways days. Things had definitely taken a fateful turn.

In the remaining days of this first visit he had time to see the town; and liked what he saw. It was large enough to have the necessary core of imaginative and intelligent people to get things going. It was small enough to feel itself to be one community. Theatrically it *could* be his chosen community; for his sort of Theatre—they were the sort of people who would respond to his benevolent tyranny. His Canadian friend, Robertson Davies, later wrote of him:

> His greatest gift was not specifically theatrical; it was that power to discern what was best of each one of a group of widely differing people and to use them in a common cause, which is characteristic of great leaders in politics and the church. . . . Let no one suppose that I underestimated his powers as an artist. . . . But it was this power as a leader that pulled us through, gave us a faith in our own abilities.

The immediate things that had to be decided within these limited days were choice of site and type of theatre. For a moment, in the Canadian air, in the morning sun, his love of festival and the extravaganza almost tempted him back to the pageantry of an open-air affair. Standing on the slope of the park at tree-top level to the willows, with swans and the Avon waters of the lake some hundred yards away, he had talked of barges, island stagings and . . ."No! Quite nonsensical," he checked himself. He was not going to settle for the open air, noisy birds, even train whistles, and uncontrollable children off. This was not what he had come here for. It had to be a new theatre constructed to the old recipe of playhouse for which Shakespeare wrote the plays. But the high cost of bricks, mortar and labour daunted him; and it petrified Patterson. He knew, in a way Guthrie did not know then, that the whole town was by no means behind him. By the time the milkman (who was to become one of the world's best front-of-house men) had done his own unofficial public opinion poll—during his milk-rounds—it was pretty obvious there would be as much opposition as support. Also, the next-door town of London considered that it could show a much better history of theatrical activity, and if Guthrie was coming to pioneer theatre, why not in London? (The name, at that point, would have been no recommendation to Guthrie.)

With various forms of structure under discussion, they drove Guthrie the three-hour journey back down to Toronto. Further talks went on with Dora and her son, Mavor Moore. She offered to be helpful in suggesting who was who in the recruiting of Canadian company. And Rupert Caplan of the Montreal days also offered the same help. Both offers were accepted. But, although Guthrie wanted the whole concern eventually to be entirely native to Canada, he knew that the North American public was not going to flow to that little township out there, just because it happened to have some parallels to Stratford, England, or some crazy new Canadian Shakespeare Show. Of course he knew that Canadians were used to jumping in large cars with packed picnic hampers, and to travelling huge distances in order to see something spectacular. But it was essential, he thought, to go back to the sort of idea which sent Patterson after Larry Olivier. There had to be, in the package offered the public, at least one "name," one worldwide star. He, or they, should come and play as the nucleus of a Canadian playing company. But before one approached any star, one would have to know wherein he was going to play.

Guthrie the nomad, Guthrie of the tent, spoke of tents. Mavor Moore remembered that, outside Toronto, there was the Summer Theatre of the Melody Fair. They played musicals in a big-top tent. They were playing one now. Again they bundled into the little Patterson car. They paid their way into the Fair's big top. They sat right through the performance of the musical. Guthrie sat totally silent, entirely observant. The show was over. They drifted back to the parking lot, then Dr. Guthrie turned back, looked at the tent from all possible angles again. They waited for him to come to the car. As he got his long legs in, he broke the silence: "The tent's the thing." All the Guthrie loves were coming together in the one place: tents, theatre, trains, pioneering and an adequate community with much Scottish—and Irish—blood in its veins.

With this decision made about the tent, Patterson and he went back up to Stratford. There they prepared to face a full committee meeting in formal session in the Town Hall. In the Windsor Hotel, Tom Patterson began to go from awe to laughing admiration of the man. For he now could see how unstuffy he was and how his own people, of pioneer stock, would warm to the Doctor's "wicked" humanity. "Christ!" he heard come from the bathroom—where he thought the splashing meant his guest was washing his face—"I've washed the clean one!" Travelling lighter than light was a Guthrie art, and he had recently blessed the technological age for the invention of the nylon shirt. He now travelled all over the world with only two: one on, one off. He was now left in the summer heat with the soiled one (and he was a great shedder of perspiration). To buy a new one would outrage the Guthrie sense of economy. So, Rise above it!—on went the soiled one. On their reconnaissance runs round Ontario they would stop at a petrol station for "gas" and—with the discipline of a punt-dweller—the great Doctor would resort to the toilet, wash through the dirty shirt and then, as they drove away, drape it out to dry in the baking hot back of the car.

Off they went to the Town Hall and when the Doctor stood up to speak—to the shock of some and the delight of most—he threw off his jacket, apologized for the soiled shirt and cracked right into action. Speaking with urgency and wit from notes written on the back of a cigarette packet, these were the requirements he laid down:

1. Theatre to be on the site he had indicated, on the park slope overlooking the Avon's lake.

2. Theatre to be specially designed and its fabric—at least at first—to be not bricks and mortar but canvas: a pavilion to the Art of Theatre.

3. The stage within the tented shell to be specially designed and the designer to be Miss Tanya Moiseiwitsch; who should work in conjunction with a Canadian architect.

4. Somebody here—"Not me—not my business to be your agent"—should go to Britain on "a shopping tour" to get us an international star. Suggestions—Alec Guinness (brilliant actor now a "name" and a world star through the film screen).

Having established the principles of his tyranny, he swept off to visit Rob and Brenda Davies, in Toronto, saw his godchild of the Davies brood, and flew off home. And so ended the first visit. There was planned to be a second visit to audition and recruit company and to see architect about tent. Also a third on which Judy should accompany him.

Before he left, Harry Showalter had seen to it that Dr. Guthrie was rewarded with a respectable fee. Showalter had raised the necessary cash by the simple expedient of not asking but telling specific fellow citizens that they would give such and such an amount; and, now they had seen and heard Guthrie, they did. This alone shows the infectious enthusiasm Guthrie left at work in Stratford while he got back to his Edinburgh Festival commitments, and with fascinating news for James Bridie. . . .

. . . The first night came. The cars rolled up all day. The evening came, the crowds poured in. The Governor-General, Vincent Massey, honoured the occasion. The young volunteer ushers, in black slacks and white shirts, moved slickly about their business. They had been thoroughly drilled by the milkman-turned-house-manager (Norman Freeman) and briefed by Guthrie with the words, "Yours is the show before the show; the eyes of everyone will be on you." They moved like naval cadets putting the ship to sea; got people aboard and seated with courtesy. Trumpets blew. The red geraniums were in place round the tent. A yellow pennant—present from Stratford-upon-Avon, England—floated from the top of the tent. A gun fired. The play was on. Guinness took the stage, as Richard III.

"Now is the Winter of our discontent made glorious Summer. . . ."

They loved it. They came, not like a sophisticated London audience to make comparisons, they came to see something to them quite new; and, with the feeling of festival, and pilgrimage, they were prepared to enjoy what they were offered. What they were bowled over by was the colour and the quality of the costumes, the props, banners; the sheer professionalism and the movement of it all coupled with the eloquence of the language. There was a quality about it that nobody but the informed minority had expected way out there in Ontario. This theatre was probably going to play to 1500 people a night. Guinness's personal triumph was followed on the very next night by Irene Worth's triumph as Helena in *All's Well That Ends Well* (a character Guthrie came to believe was Shakespeare's finest female creation). *All's Well* was in modern dress. But this too was taken as no upsetting innovation; everything was so much of an innovation.

It had worked. The bookings were good. All the doubting Thomases were defeated and the Festival was obviously now something the Stratford community could be proud of. Also, Guthrie had proved his theory that Shakespeare would be in vital communication with audience on this sort of stage and in that sort of auditorium. There were snags of course. For instance rain *could* stop play if it drummed down on that canvas roof, but this was an on-going concern and the tent was not to be forever. Was this what his whole career had led up to? And would Guthrie, the nomad, stay? Would the tent really give way to bricks and mortar?

Guthrie, typically, was soon on his way. But the next year was planned. He would stay till the Canadians totally took over and no longer depended on talent from the old country.

RUMOURS OF A FESTIVAL
(c. 1952) ◊

AMELIA HALL

o

Was there professional theatre in Canada at the time of Stratford's launch? Yes there was, thank you very much. Actress Amelia Hall's (1916–84) post-humously published autobiography, Life Before Stratford *(1989), confirms this fact.*

I do not recall when I first heard rumours of a Shakespearean Festival to be started by a man named Tom Patterson in a little western Ontario town called, appropriately enough, Stratford. When I read the brief newspaper report, I thought, "Probably some nut with money" and visualized a little man with a white beard.

I put it out of mind until another newspaper story indicated that Mr Patterson and his Stratford backers had succeeded in interesting the great Tyrone Guthrie in the project. Furthermore, Dr Guthrie was coming to Canada to meet with these wild-eyed idealists.

On July 16 of the previous year, while we were into the second week of *The Importance of Being Earnest* at the Straw Hat Players, the Toronto *Telegram* reported a press gathering to hear Guthrie on the contemplated Stratford venture. The newspaper described Guthrie as a "tall, ramrod of a man, fifty-two," and added, "he sounds like a realist as well as an artist."

It must have been some time in November 1952 that the phone rang down in the CRT's Green Room and a youngish voice announced that he was Tom Patterson and could he and Dr Guthrie come to see us? I said we would be most gratified, and I would acquaint the actors with the facts and make a list of those who wanted to be interviewed. Tom Patterson sounded quite jolly. Where was my rich old gentleman with the long white beard?

◊ From *Life Before Stratford: The Memoirs of Amelia Hall* (ed. Diane Mew) pp. 255–58. Toronto: Dundurn Press, 1989. Reprinted with permission.

They came while we were presenting *The Three Sisters*. I heard that they saw some of the production. Too bad that the physical presentation for *The Three Sisters* fell so far short of the standard for which we had become justifiably famous.

I met Tyrone Guthrie in the schoolroom that we had arranged for his use. He came toward me grinning and saying, "You don't look at all as you did when I saw you in Muskoka." That had been when I was playing Lady Bracknell, and we had not known he was there. He, Tom Patterson, and I chatted, and I saw the model of the stage that Tanya Moiseiwitsch had designed for Stratford. The meeting was most happy, informal, and invigorating. The two plays they had decided to present were *Richard III* and *All's Well That Ends Well*. They were planning to recruit Canadian actors as far as possible for the supporting roles and hoped to secure the services of Alec Guinness and Irene Worth as the two leading actors.

Not all of our actors went to see Guthrie. Bill Hutt did, and George McCowan, and I don't recall who else. George, I believe, was later made an offer but did not accept. Bill and I were the only two who were interviewed on the CRT premises who went that first year. But of our old CRT actors, Eric House was in the company that first Stratford season.

A letter was sent to me on December 22, 1952, from Tom Patterson, signed by Mary Jolliffe:

Dear Miss Hall:

Thank you for coming to see Dr. Guthrie. He asked me to say what a pleasure it was to meet you.

You are one of a very small group of actors whose cooperation at Stratford we should particularly value; and whom we regard as potential leading players in our Festival Company.

At the same time, until our program is finally fixed, and until Mr. Cecil Clarke (Dr. Guthrie's Assistant Director) arrives, we cannot finally decide the casting.

Knowing, however, that your professional services are in considerable demand, we do not want to lose you because we cannot make an immediate offer.

Would it be too much to ask you not to accept engagements for the ten-week period beginning June 7 without first letting us know?

Years later Dora Mavor Moore told me that Guthrie came back from Ottawa to tell her: "I have found just the actress to play opposite Alec!"

Cecil Clarke put in an appearance in Ottawa in March 1953. Lynn Wilson, our property mistress, recalled the event: "One cold grey morning in 1953 I'd come to the theatre, just by chance, extra early, to find a sorry little man (blue with cold) tugging at every locked door of LaSalle Academy. I felt a bit like a St. Bernard, so grateful he was to be rescued. I always believed that's why I was asked to go to Stratford; that cold little man was Cecil Clarke." Cecil Clarke had arrived in Canada to organize the physical side of the productions and to hire the artists. He came to my house and offered me the role of Lady Anne in *Richard III*. Before he left, standing in the hallway, he asked if I would be willing to stand by to play Helena in _All's Well_, if Irene Worth decided not to come. I agreed, and Mr. Clarke asked me to keep the offer confidential. I did not tell even my mother.

When he got back to Toronto, Cecil Clarke sent me a letter, written on paper with a real letterhead, "Stratford Shakespearean Festival of Canada Foundation."

> I would like to confirm with you that we wish you to play the part of Lady Anne in _Richard III_. _All's Well That Ends Well_ has provided us with a problem, now that Irene Worth is definitely coming out to play Helena. Would you be prepared to play the Widow in this play? It is not a bad little part and I think that you will find that you will be able to do quite a bit with it. . . . Rehearsals will start the first of June at Stratford, and the season opens July 13 with _Richard III_. As soon as I know whether you agree to play the parts suggested, I will get Mr. Tom Patterson to get in touch with you with regard to terms.

Of course, I replied that I would be delighted to play any role they suggested. In this next letter, Cecil Clarke wrote: "I am delighted to have your letter and to know that you will be with us. I will arrange costume fittings in Toronto on your way through to Stratford. You have a beautiful costume as Lady Anne."

And thus it was that, after _Victoria Regina_ closed on May 23, within a week I was plunged into rehearsals for one of the most exciting and momentous events in the Canadian theatre. The rest, as they say, is history.

But let us remember that history correctly. Some thirteen years after that first Stratford season I was flying back from the west and happened to leaf through the Air Canada magazine _En Route_. In it was an article on the National Ballet of Canada, and there I read that when Celia Franca came to Canada to try to form a national ballet company, the Stratford Festival had not yet been born, there were "no opera or professional theatre companies, . . . and no Canada Council to supply government financial support." All of that is true, except the four words "no professional theatre companies."

In a Toronto newspaper I read recently, "There was no television, no Canadian Opera Company, no permanent drama companies across the country. There was, indeed, virtually no professional theatre except in summer stock terms." That is just not true! The Canadian Repertory Theatre had been in existence for two years by the time the National Ballet was founded in 1951, and the Stage Society for one year before that. The CRT was playing a thirty-five-week season each year and paying a living wage to everybody concerned. This does not make the fantastic achievements of these other artistic groups any less admirable. But let us at least get the record straight.

A LONG VIEW OF THE
STRATFORD FESTIVAL ◇

TYRONE GUTHRIE

ɔ

A series of books commemorating the first three Stratford seasons was pub-
lished under the names of Tyrone Guthrie, Robertson Davies, and others who
had been instrumental on the artistic side in those early years. The following
extended meditation on Stratford's future by Guthrie appeared in the second
volume of the series, entitled Twice Have the Trumpets Sounded.

I am aware that the greatest single factor that has enabled the Festival to
establish itself has been completely outside the control of those concerned. I
refer to the fact of its timeliness. However carefully the Festival might have
been organized, however brilliant the performances might have been, it
would have availed nothing if there had not been a public hungry and
eager for the kind of fare that was offered.

Now here I am going to venture some opinions of a general nature
about a vague entity known as "Canada," and a group of my fellow creatures loosely grouped together under the heading "Canadians." I am aware
that it is fatally easy, and often fatally unwise, for visitors to land out with
assertions based on their own early impressions of a new environment.
Europeans never stop handing out information about "America" and even
advice to "Americans," based on the evidence gathered in a week's visit to
New York. And this kind of nonsense is a two-way traffic. I never stop listening to confident generalizations on the question of Irish Partition from
lively visitors who have just flown in from Chicago, motored west through
blinding rain to see the farm where Grandma was raised, then after lunch,

---

◇ *Twice Have the Trumpets Sounded: A Record of the Stratford Shakespearean Festival in*
Canada, ed. Tyrone Guthrie, Robertson Davies, Grant Macdonald (Toronto: Clark,
Irwin & Company, 1954), 152–72.

not on the farm but in an hotel, have motored south through blinding rain to see Grandpa's tombstone, getting back to Dublin in time for dinner at the Shelbourne. If they are "serious" they spend a day in Dublin "doing" the well sign-posted Joyce relics, including some surviving Joyce relatives, after which they feel equipped to tell the world all about Ireland. It does not occur to them to visit Belfast. Belfast is "ugly"; Belfast is obsessed with Business; Belfast people have the most ghastly accent; they are "common"—you've only to be in Dublin five minutes to be told all that as an absolute fact. Similarly, lively visitors to Scotland from overseas spend a week at the Edinburgh Festival where they meet Gregory Peck, some delightful opera singers from New Jersey, Thornton Wilder and the Catholic Archbishop of Saint Louis. Then, after a coach trip, in blinding rain, through the Trossachs, a coach trip, in blinding rain, through the Scott Country (tea at Abbotsford), a steamer trip through the Kyles of Bute, in blinding rain, they feel—and who wouldn't?—equipped to issue press statements upon Scottish Nationalism, Scottish dialect, Scottish vigour, Scottish decadence, the economic plight of the Highlands, the future of Scottish Football and, of course, the influence of the Scottish climate.

And yet . . . and yet.

What do they know of Ireland, Scotland or even Canada, who only Ireland, Scotland, or even Canada, know? The confident generalizations of lively visitors obviously are not the whole truth. But the whole truth on such matters just is not accessible. It just is not possible to assimilate completely so large and complex a unit even as Ireland, let alone Canada. Therefore I shall not be too apologetic. I do not ask to have my generalizations accepted as The Truth; merely as impressions based upon a limited but first-hand experience.

A large number and a wide variety of Canadians are becoming more and more conscious that in many important respects Canada is a very dull place to live in; that economic opportunities are immense but, having made enough money to live comfortably, there is comparatively little in Canada to nourish the spirit. And yet the economic opportunities are making it possible for an ever-growing number of people to have a considerable amount of leisure, and are making it possible for an ever-growing number of people to be expensively and elaborately educated. They are equipped with money, leisure, and an awareness of "culture" for which there is therefore a large demand but, as yet, a very small supply.

Many people are also aware that a rich Canada will be a powerful factor in world affairs, an important influence in human development. Power and influence carry responsibilities. To shoulder such responsibilities adequately Canadians will have to be more than just materially rich.

It is fairly evident that with increasing riches and comfort the pioneer vigour of body and spirit soon decays. Spiritual simplicity rarely outlives hard conditions. Peasant virtues of thrift, honesty, industry certainly can and do survive transplanting into more sophisticated conditions, but they only survive by adaptation to the new environment. Such adaptation, in broad terms, is what I believe the term culture ought to mean.

Canada, therefore, at the present moment is a "sellers' market" for culture: the demand is greater than the supply. That is why the Stratford Festival was hailed with such enthusiasm, why it has had such striking economic success, why it has become—out of all proportion to the size of the undertaking, or its quality in relation to similar Festivals elsewhere (Salzburg, for instance, or Edinburgh)—"important," a symbol of a new spirit in Canada.

It is against this background that the Governors of the Festival must plan its future.

ɔ

The central point of planning seems to me to be the choice of programme.

The first year we concentrated solely on the production of two plays. Rightly, I think. Even so we bit off almost more than we could all chew, so difficult was the job of starting from scratch. Finance was the toughest problem, since not unnaturally people were chary of offering large sums to further a project which, however admirable in intention, did not look at all likely to be solvent or offer any guarantee that it would even be artistically creditable. Then there were all the building problems; then those of booking and advertising; then those of accommodation not only for a cast and staff of about a hundred, but for the nightly influx of theatre-goers—two thousand people most of whom wanted an evening meal, and about half of whom wanted bed and breakfast. In other words there was a sizable job of administration which had to be tackled by people most of whom had no previous experience of what they were undertaking; and none of whom had a really clear idea of the results expected.

On the theatrical side, there was a company to be recruited and welded into some kind of artistic and moral unity; that was comparatively easy because of the great goodwill of the actors. It was more difficult to set up a mechanism for making the costumes, properties and accessories, so that again there should be some artistic cohesion. The Professional Theatre had never had very firm roots in Canada. There had once been a fine market for visiting stars and touring companies; but resident companies had never, so far as I can gather, operated upon any considerable scale. And the Amateur Theatre, which has for the past thirty years done a fine job in keeping "live" Theatre alive, never operated in a manner that made possible the existence of theatrical workshops and warehouses which could supply what we needed. We were in this respect like real pioneers. Most of the things we required were not to be had by sending to a store and buying them. We had to get hold of the raw material, set to and make them.

To get the theatre built, to get the plays on, and to provide the mechanism for administering the season, fully occupied all available energies the first year. Nevertheless some of our visitors felt that if they made the pilgrimage to the plays, it would be nice if Stratford offered them a little more to do. They complained that a tour of the Railway Works, the Mausoleum, the Hospital, the Sewage Disposal Plant and the "Y," though fascinating, was not enough. And we agreed.

So the second year we determined to extend the Festival's range of attractions. We mounted three instead of two productions. In addition there was an interesting exhibition of contemporary Canadian painting, and another of theatrical art, comparing decors and architecture in the theatres of many different epochs and parts of the world. There was also a two week's Seminar conducted by senior members of the Festival company and staff. Applications for this considerably exceeded the numbers of students who could be taken; and it should be possible to develop this branch of the Festival's activity interestingly and usefully.

Unfortunately putting on three plays in quick succession nearly broke the back of the production staff. In theory *Oedipus Rex* was to be a simple production. The cast was comparatively small. Each of the actors would wear only one dress. There were very few properties. The play was short and would require far less rehearsal than a large Shakespearean effort. That was in December 1953; in Ireland; on paper.

By March it was clear that we had made a slight underestimate of the work. Masks would be required; and if the Chorus were to be any good it would need a very great deal of rehearsal indeed. However the mask difficulty was not insurmountable; there had been a similar problem with the armour for *Richard III* the year before; and the Chorus could be rehearsed, just like the fight at the end of *Richard*, for an hour every evening. No difficulty really, if one had a Sensible Plan.

What we had failed to foresee was that the effort of putting on three plays is much more than one third greater than the effort of putting on two. Had we all been fresh there would have been ample time to prepare *Oedipus*. But everyone was tired. Tired people take longer to do anything than fresh people. The effort to keep up to schedule made everyone more and more tired. Tiredness made everyone prone to colds. *Oedipus* got on only through a barrage of catarrh and by the skin of its teeth. But a lesson has been learnt. Without a much larger staff, which in present conditions would be extravagant, two productions are as much as can be prudently undertaken.

o

The dramatic programme will continue to be classical. We conceive it to be the most useful function which the Stratford Festival can perform. In the first place a classical programme is the indispensable training ground both for the practitioners and connoisseurs of any art. In Canada, except at Stratford, there exists at present no other opportunity to present a classical programme on any considerable scale. There have been, and will be more, classical productions of merit but for economic, as well as artistic, reasons it is most unlikely that, except in Festival conditions, there can be productions on the scale which we have been able to present; or that, for some years,

another theatre will exist in Canada with the particular intention of presenting a planned series of big classical plays.

There is in Canada a remarkable supply of gifted actors. The Dominion
Drama Festival, The Canadian Broadcasting Corporation, which has a particularly distinguished dramatic record, and more recently television, and a
growing number of small professional theatres have given them opportunities to get experience. A young actor in Toronto at the present time has, in
my opinion, a better chance to earn a living, than he would have in London
or New York, where the market is grossly over-supplied and where the
pressure of competition is stifling. But while in Toronto, Montreal and other
Canadian centres the economic opportunity is good, the artistic opportunities are rather limited. Chances to act upon the stage before an audience are
rare, the quality of stage productions, though rapidly improving, is not as
yet equal to the standard in London or New York. There are lessons which
can only be learnt in front of an audience, which films, radio and T.V. can
never teach. For instance, one of the most important weapons in an actor's
armoury is to know how to "feel" an audience; to react to the audience's
reaction. This is partly a matter of instinct, but also largely of experience.
And such experience is not one of the things which a studio can supply.
There are technical lessons too which radio and film acting cannot teach—
notably how to declaim. The microphone is inimical to declamation. But in
the theatre it is essential not merely to make oneself audible at some distance, but to have at command the full range of the voice from a whisper to
a shout. Radio and film acting can often be subtle and interesting but it is
always a matter of fine shades, small effects; it is as though a painter were
always obliged to work on a tiny canvas with a strictly limited palette.
There is no opportunity for the sweeping bold strokes, the thunderous
attack, the effects of violent contrast, the large-scale deployment of temperament which display the actor's art at its most exciting. These effects can
only be employed in a theatre, in front of an audience and in plays of some
range and scope.

Stratford, as I see it, should provide an outlet for frustrated gifted
"hams" who for the greater part of the year earn bread and butter in the
studios. After a period of bashing around in big stuff they will return to
their microphones in better heart and with a bit more knowledge of breath-
control and audience-control. After a period of living with, in and for
Macbeth or *Lear* or *Peer Gynt*, or even *All's Well*, they will return with a better
sense of proportion to commercial serials and all their other chores. And, if
they are fortunate enough to work in a theatre, they will return to more intimate and "realistic" plays with the refreshment and relaxation which can
follow only from a change.

But naturally the Stratford Festival should not be run primarily for the
benefit of the actors. I mean only that the actors' benefit is, in long term, the
playgoers'. More widely experienced, better equipped actors mean better
performances.

But, further, I think that in Canada the audience too needs to be trained
for the Theatre. If you never get anything but margarine, you lose the taste
for butter. For many years people have got into the way of accepting radio

and the films as the only means of dramatic expression; they have grown to accept the standards of commercial entertainment as the only standards which exist. They are like people who for years have never read anything but newspapers or who for years have never looked at a picture except the illustrations and advertisements in magazines. They are highly and intelligently critical of technical efficiency, but they forget that there are whole ranges of ideas, whole fields of expression, of the most profound and universal significance, which never "get into the papers," which for one reason or another are considered "un-commercial."

I take it that a Festival such as Stratford should assume that the large majority of its patrons are theatrically inexperienced but are not therefore unintelligent. Their judgment, if unsophisticated, will be all the fresher. If they have bothered to come some distance, and have paid quite a high price, to see a play, most of them will, I imagine, be prepared to give to it their serious critical attention. So they must not be played down to. The programme must be chosen from plays which may be held to have some significance, which have something serious to say (all great comedies are serious; seriousness and fun are not antithetical), which enshrine some universal truth to human experience.

Now judgment of contemporary plays, even by very gifted and experienced people, is constantly shown to be fallible. All too often their swans are geese. Moreover the taste of experts is apt to be far too advanced for ordinary playgoers. The only possible assurance in this matter is to choose plays which are agreed to be significant not merely by contemporary judgment but by that of good critics over a considerable period of time, work in fact which has survived the ins and outs of mere fashion and has been held in respect by several generations of critics. In other words, works which have become Classics.

Now the Festival was originated with the idea that it should be primarily a Shakespearean occasion; the theatre and stage have been designed primarily for the production of Shakespeare. They are not, in my opinion, architecturally suitable for the kind of plays written for a proscenium theatre, and that includes the Classic Drama since the second half of the seventeenth century. But I hope that the policy of the Festival will not exclude all plays other than those of Shakespeare. Though the greatest, he is not the only great playwright of his epoch; and the stage is not, in my opinion, unsuitable for many kinds of drama besides the Elizabethan. It is my hope that, while Shakespeare continues to be the mainstay of the programme, other suitable and significant works may frequently be given. There are dozens which would otherwise hardly ever be produced on the American continent, and which are infinitely more illuminating and rewarding on the stage than on the shelf. In this respect we of the English-speaking world are like the possessor of the finest collection of pictures in the world. A very few of them are on the walls; a large number, of no less excellence, are kept in store and are never seen by anybody.

If the Governors were in general agreement about the merit and suitability of a new play, I greatly hope that they would back their fancy and give it a showing. It must be remembered, however, that the risk of such a step—financial and artistic—is very great. While a too cautious policy in the Theatre is a slow death by pernicious anæmia, an over-adventurous policy leads to sudden death in embarrassingly public circumstances—a fatal seizure at mid-day in the Market Place.

It may be asked, why—if the programme is to be classical—the plays hitherto chosen have not been those which are considered the greatest. Why, for example, choose such an obvious doubtful starter as *All's Well That Ends Well*, or such an obvious lightweight as *The Taming of the Shrew*? The answer is two-fold. First, we have thought that one essential of the programme was contrast; that in a programme which included *Measure for Measure* and *Oedipus Rex*, the third play should be less inclined to stir the emotions than to tickle the ribs. Second, and even more practical, the box-office success of a theatrical undertaking depends less upon the choice of play than upon that of the leading actor. This may not be a Good Thing, but in my opinion it is a fact. A Star Name not merely attracts customers to see this particular actor, but it is a kind of guarantee that the whole enterprise is likely to be of good standard. So far Stratford has been fortunate in getting two leading actors of this extremely limited top class, but the programme has had to be chosen to suit their personalities and inclinations. This is quite as it should be. It would be unwise to announce the production of, for instance, *King Lear*—a play which we have been urged to do—unless we first knew that we could command the services of an actor whom we thought attractive to the public, suitable to the part, and who was eager to play it.

Since the inception of the Festival, those responsible for its programme have been under quite a barrage of requests for the "better known" plays of Shakespeare. I am not quite sure what this means. Perhaps it means the plays which are most often produced. *Hamlet* is the play which has been the most often produced and, surprisingly, *Romeo and Juliet* comes next. Hamlet too, as a character, has been the subject of more books in English than anyone who ever lived, with just two exceptions: Napoleon Bonaparte and Jesus Christ. Perhaps the "better known" plays are those which are fullest of the kind of quotations which find their way into the propaganda of insurance companies and car manufacturers, and which Ethel reproduces in chain-stitch and Aubrey in pokerwork. *Hamlet*, again is easily first in this category ("For thine especial safety"); *As You Like It* ("seven ages") and *The Merchant of Venice* ("quality of mercy") are runners-up. Or perhaps the "better known" plays are those which appear most often in the Exam Syllabus, and consequently are most vigorously pumped into the young. Though I do not know which these are in Canada, I am in a position to know what they are in Britain: *Macbeth, Julius Caesar, Twelfth Night, Midsummer Night's Dream, The Merchant of Venice, As You Like It*, and *Henry the Fifth*. I cannot for the life of me find any reason for the choice of this particular group. All seven are great works of art; none of them, in my view, is a bit suitable for study in class by people under sixteen. But, granted that they may be, why is *Macbeth*, for instance, preferred to *Hamlet*, or *Julius Caesar* to *Coriolanus*? But there it is. These seem to be considered the most suitable for schools, and therefore are possibly the "best known" of Shakespeare's plays.

While the choice of programme must continue to be governed by the exigencies of casting, I should have thought that to show some of the less familiar plays, the ones that scarcely ever get a professional showing, was one of the valuable functions of a Festival. The unfamiliarity of these plays must by no means be taken to imply that their quality is inferior.

The Festival has also been given quite a number of lectures on the moral standards of the plays chosen. *Measure for Measure* and *All's Well* were both faulted for not being "pleasant." Granted that everyone has a right to his own opinions, artistic or moral, I suggest that to expect Shakespeare to be a moral propagandist is entirely to mistake the man. The greatest critics, though they are wildly at odds on many matters, speak with one voice on this point: they agree that Shakespeare's pre-eminence is due to the miraculous understanding he shows of human nature. He is concerned to interpret his characters but not to draw moral conclusions about them. Moral judgments imply bias, incompatible with the impartiality, the all-embracing sympathy which gives to Shakespeare his godlike stature.

There is not a single one of Shakespeare's plays which is entirely "nice," or which is not calculated to put "ideas" into the heads of impressionable people. Those who are afraid to admit the nastiness latent in every human creature had better stay away from Shakespeare. I guess they are fully entitled to wage war on what they regard as evil, but I sincerely trust that they never succeed in establishing the sort of moral censorship which existed in Victorian England. We laugh nowadays at Dr. Bowdler, but it is still all too possible for otherwise rational people to allow themselves to be worked into a high state of moral indignation over the supposed impropriety of what conflicts with their own standards not of moral but merely of conventional behaviour. Mad results follow, a sort of moral McCarthyism, the most illiberal and vicious thinking and action in the name of purity and virtue.

꙯

A classical policy is open to the objection that it makes no provision for the production of new plays. And I have heard it argued that a Festival which offers no encouragement to Canadian authors has no right to consider itself a Canadian institution.

This argument does not seem to me to be sound. It is true that, if the policy at Stratford is only to do classical plays, then the Canadian dramatist does not receive the direct encouragement of performance and royalties. But he does stand to gain in several indirect but important ways. First, it will do his plays no harm if, when they do get performed, there are players at hand who have received the more various and far-reaching experience which only a classical programme can provide. Secondly, it will do his plays no harm if they meet an audience whose imaginative range and critical capacity have been extended by some first-hand acquaintance with classical performance. Thirdly—and this I suggest with humility because I know very few of the Canadian plays—I cannot conceive but that a Festival of Classics done in Canada will be a useful exemplar to contemporary Canadian dramatists. Any dramatist of quality, no matter how revolutionary, how "original," his work may be, can learn valuably from the classics of dramatic literature. And he can learn only so much from reading. It is as important for him to see performances of the Classics as it is for him to see performances of the work of his contemporaries. I cannot therefore agree that a Festival of Drama at which only classical plays are given would have nothing to offer to Canadian dramatists.

Possibly a Festival's claim to be a Canadian institution might be based upon the fact that the company of actors was overwhelmingly Canadian. I don't know. I don't know how far it may be possible to interpret a classical play in a distinctively Canadian way. I am not even quite sure that there is a distinctively Canadian way of doing anything. I am not even sure, despite innumerable legends in support of the idea, that there is a distinctively British, French, Jewish or Chinese way of doing anything. And perhaps Canada—apart from French-Canada—has not been settled long enough for distinctive habits of thought, feeling and expression to have grown out of the effects its climate and its soil have had on the inhabitants. Anyway it is hardly conceivable that an environment so vast and various as the Dominion of Canada could ever, even a hundred years ago in the period when the ideas of Nationality and Nationalism were most flourishing, have produced a single distinctive national type. And surely it is even less likely to be produced now, when, under the pressure of modern industrial development, all geographical and ethnological differences are being ironed out, and when the whole tendency of the age is towards greater and greater standardization.

Nevertheless it is desirable that Canadians should try to assimilate classical works of art as part of their own heritage, not just regard them as imports, acquired at second-hand from overseas. And I think that this assimilation is one of the things that the Stratford Festival ought to be most concerned to assist.

Shakespeare is in one sense of a local Warwickshire dramatist. A great part of his magic derives from the wonderful, and often wonderfully inappropriate way he uses his own youthful environment as the basis of his imaginary world. The wood near Athens, for instance, where Lysander, Demetrius, Hermia and Helena have their adventures, does not attempt to suggest the rocks and olive trees near the real city of Athens; but evokes rather the image of the beech and oak woods of Warwickshire. The house where Olivia lives in *Twelfth Night*, with its chantry, its orchard, its buttery hatch, is a Warwickshire manor house, far, far removed from anything which might be expected in a realistic Illyria. But Shakespeare is, of course, far more than a local dramatist. His ideas have a universality and a truth to common human experience which far transcends geographical boundaries. Northumberland, for instance, is, in dialect, landscape and occupation, just as different from Warwickshire as is Western Ontario. Can there, therefore, be any good reason why, with the common bond of the British language, Shakespeare should not seem as indigenous to Western Ontario as he does to Northumberland?

The process of assimilation will be easier if a style of performance can be found which does not emphasize the English-ness so much as the universality of Shakespeare's work. This will be easier still if the universality can be clearly related to current ways of speaking and behaving.

Naturally this does not imply that all the plays should be given in the speech and manner of that myth, the Common Man. That would just be an absurd style for Shakespearean performance. The great personages of Shakespeare can no more be reduced to the level of the Common Man in Canada than they can be in England. In *Coriolanus*, for instance, the whole play is based on the utter contempt of the chief character for the Common Man. The whole point of Great Personages is their difference in character from the Common Man, whom they resemble only in species. In England a good performance of Shakespeare is a presentation of characters who, while in no way reduced in stature, are still recognizable as people like ourselves, still part of the current scene. So it could and should be in Canada.

Some of the plays are more easily related to contemporary manners than others. *Henry VIII*, for instance, is concerned with a particular historical context and has only a remote connection with any other environment or group of people. Inevitably this is so with all the historical chronicles. But many of the tragedies and romances are amazingly independent of details of period or environment, and are consequently more adaptable to transplantation.

Our production at Stratford of *All's Well* made no attempt at setting the play in any realistic or identifiable time or place, but it did attempt to relate the people and the story to contemporary life. I think, from the cordiality of its reception and the evident appreciation of its humour, that the artists did establish some correspondence between the characters they played and the sort of people who are familiar to all of us in daily life. And this, I hope and believe, had the effect, not of reducing the play to a commonplace and journalistic level, but rather of suggesting the exciting and romantic possibilities of real life.

Now, while I hope that performances of the Classics at Stratford may seek to have a distinctively Canadian flavour, I trust that this will not give rise to too narrowly and exclusively "National" a policy. The result of such a policy is formidably exemplified in the Abbey Theatre in Dublin. In its earlier days, under the guidance first of Lady Gregory, then of Yeats, then of Lennox Robinson, there was a continuous attempt to train the company in more various and important material than just Folk Plays. The Folk Plays, however, were always more popular because they were so much better done. The actors, absolutely brilliant in the portrayal of an environment which they knew well and in dialect which was their own, never rose above a rather feebly amateurish level in classical or foreign works. Consequently the Folk Plays began more and more to dominate the repertoire, and the players began less and less to bother about extending their technical, imaginative and intellectual range. Then about twenty-five years ago, in return for a very small subsidy from the State, the Abbey Theatre agreed to submit to various political conditions. The chief one was that any actor, before being allowed to speak English in the Abbey company, must pass an exam in the Irish language. The programme now laid even greater stress than before on the production of new plays by Irish authors dealing with Irish life. That was reasonable enough, and inevitable in a period of long-suppressed ebullient Nationalism. But unfortunately the Free State saw fit to impose a severe moral censorship, and the Chairman of the Abbey Board is now neither a literary nor a theatrical man; he is a politician. The result is that the quality of the productions has declined to a level entirely pedestrian and commonplace. Here and there are good individual performances when a player of talent is happily cast. But in general the theatre has lost almost all cultural importance. Where once it was remarkable throughout the whole world, it is now no longer a centre even of national interest. There can, in my view, be no real pull-up in quality until players and audience are both willing to submit to a course of training in works more demanding and far-reaching, and until the policy of the theatre is less narrowly and provincially national.

While we may agree that it is impossible to define what is, or is not, distinctively Canadian; and while we may hope that the Theatre in Canada may not develop in too isolationist a manner, yet we must remember that what a creative artist needs almost more than anything else is an attachment to a particular environment, usually that in which he was brought up as a child.

Again and again one sees in the work of the greatest artists how their strength is derived from geographical roots. Think what the Warwickshire countryside has done to Shakespeare's poetry, or the Athenian to that of Sophocles. The novels of Hardy or George Eliot are saturated in the atmosphere of their author's environment. Ibsen is inescapably the product of Scandinavia; Chekhov, Turgenev, Tolstoi, Dostoevski are unthinkable except against a background of Russia. Although there are some striking instances to the contrary—T.S. Eliot is one, Henry James another—in general it is his childhood's background, where his most impressionable years were spent, which form the background of a mature artists' work.

Canadian artists, if they are to thrive, must express what the Canadian climate, the Canadian soil and their fellow-Canadians have made of them. It is vital for their health as artists; and it is no less vital for the health of the community that those with artistic talents should contribute to its life, instead of taking the first opportunity to escape to places where their gifts are welcomed, understood, respected and even rewarded with money.

It is not always remembered by practical people that, although writers, painters, musicians and the like often display a maddening incapacity to deal with combine harvesters, or to answer letters, or to save money, yet they are not necessarily on that account to be written off as Long-haired No-Goods. They are the voice in which one epoch speaks to another. What is remembered now of the Medicis except through the works of art which they commissioned? The lyrics of Robert Burns are made of far more enduring material than the girders of the Forth Bridge. Long, long after the Canadian railroads have crumbled to dust and are no more than a garbled legend, or, worse, a file in some antiquary's records, a song or a picture from this epoch will speak for us, whose maker is now neither celebrated nor rich nor valued in any way, because we simply do not recognize the power of survival, the liveliness, of what he is making.

It is important, therefore, that Canadians should be able to express their own environment, not only for the artists themselves, not only for the community now, but for posterity. And I think that something of Canada can be expressed even in terms of classical drama, the roots of which may be far removed in time and place. These works, can, I think, be *interpreted* into a Canadian idiom, given a Canadian style.

THE THEATRE *

HERBERT WHITTAKER

o

Theatre critic for the Montreal Gazette *from 1935 to 1949 and for the Toronto* Globe and Mail *from 1949 until his retirement, Herbert Whittaker (b. 1910) was an enthusiastic observer of the Canadian theatre scene from his early work as a designer and director with the Dominion Drama Festival. After World War II he reported on the increasing professionalism of Canadian theatre. In 1957 he contributed this essay.*

The subject of Canada's theatrical culture is a delicate one. Rather than recognize the uncomfortable fact that this country has just the kind of theatre it deserves, no more, no less, Canadians are apt to take the stand that they have no real theatre.

The excuse is that this country is taking its place in the world in an age dominated by mechanical mass media, which provide much of what is necessary in entertainment and communication. There might even be an impression that theatre, as the world has known it since the Greeks at least, is a dispensable art form.

Such gloomy views are shared by the complacent, who are thus absolved of any shame or blame for the poor condition of theatre at the present time, and by the desperate ones, who bewail the condition but find themselves in the minority.

But the truth is that Canada has a theatre and has always had a theatre of sorts. The instinct for theatre is a natural one and, indeed, an inevitable part of the complex structure of human expression. The need to enact

---

* *The Culture of Contemporary Canada*, ed. Julian Park (Toronto: Cornell University Press–The Ryerson Press, 1957), 163–80. Reprinted with permission of Herbert Whittaker, founding chair, Canadian Theatre Critics Association.

events, symbolic or actual; to exhibit the gift for enacting; to speak through others to your world—these are as deeply rooted as is the instinct to record action or establish truth by repetition.

It is preposterous to think that a mere half-century of electronic development could wipe out such instincts in one group of people, no matter how isolated they might be.

Canada's future theatre will be unique in that it must attain full flower after the arrival of substitutes which seemingly hamper theatrical cultures in other parts of the world. More than that, it will probably use the mechanical media to strengthen its position. There is evidence of this turn about-face already, for the radio has brought independence to the Canadian actor and television is making him more prosperous. Both win him wider audiences than he has known in the past, making him, as an actor must be, a recognizable figure.

Furthermore, the kind of independence allowed him by these substitute forms, so useful where the potential audience is spread out thinly across a continent, is giving him identity and self-recognition. These the Canadian actor has lacked in the past for two reasons. First, the theatre had been supplied from beyond the borders of the country, and the presence of local actors in a company indicated only that the management has not been able to afford the fully imported product. Secondly, the actor has not found in acting at home enough satisfaction, enough of a guarantee of his professionalism. He must be accepted abroad, with no label of local origin, before he quite accepts himself. His audiences have shared this view with him, generously, labelling him as a gifted amateur until he has been away and come back with the sign of approval from more knowing audiences.

This is the inevitable outcome of a theatre which has always been supplied from abroad, from three major sources beyond our boundaries. England, the United States, and France have not only set our standards of theatre for us but have also supplied the plays and players. To this day our dramatic literature is still almost entirely borrowed.

If Canada had only one major influence to contend with, a rebellion of sorts might have taken place many years ago and an assertion of independence made. But when Canadians turn from the style or manner of France or England, as being too formal or too deeply rooted in an old culture, they have been able to associate themselves with the young vital theatre of the United States. Conversely, when the melting-pot world to the south makes too crude an exhibition for our tastes, we can just as easily swing over to embrace the more dignified forms of the mother countries.

It may yet prove that the years which brought professional theatre into a decline in Canada were the greatest boon to us, though at the time they seemed to be the desolation of our hopes. A brief examination of the development of theatre in this country since its introduction from abroad strengthens that point.

A picture of the various forms and degrees of theatrical culture here is very close to being a picture of general Canadian development. It is not a flattering likeness but the resemblance is unmistakable. Canada, it seems, has always had the kind of theatre it needs, deserves, and wants. We will not go back to the days which casual historians used to dismiss with such a phrase as "before the white man came." That theatre did exist among the early inhabitants of this part of the continent is best testified by an examination of the various rituals as described by early travellers from Europe. Cast but an eye upon the Indian masks of the British Columbia tribes, which stand comparison very well with the masks of the Greek theatre, and you may be assured that the instinct for theatre was as natural here as anywhere else, even if the recording instinct that produces a national drama is evidently not.

But modern Canadian theatre, to which we must limit ourselves in so brief and easy a summary, established no relationship with existing forms when it was set in motion by the first colonists.

The first modern theatre in this country, then, was garrison theatre. One of the first productions would have been that of a new and scandalous comedy by a contemporary Frenchman named Molière. The play was *Tartuffe*, and Quebec City was rehearsing it almost as soon as was Paris. Meeting with some of the same forces of censorship as attended its Parisian performance, that Canadian première was cancelled.

Garrison theatre was staged by the officers and their wives for their own amusement, rather than for the entertainment of the troops. Later, professional actresses took over for the officers' ladies when the performances were thrown open to the townsfolk. That indefatigable amateur actor, Charles Dickens, played with such a double cast during a visit to Montreal.

But between *Tartuffe* and Dickens' appearance in *Every Man to His Humour* one cannot see a strong determination on the part of the nonmilitary settlers to have a representative theatre. It must have been about this time that the first newcomers from Europe started off on their plaint that Canada has no theatre, a cry undiminished even today. But the truth of the matter is that more materialistic frontiers have been of first concern to the people arriving in this part of the New World. They still are.

It is also true that many of those colonists were refugees seeking a new freedom from the decadent toils of European civilizations, as they saw it. Puritans have always recognized and damned the evils of self-exhibition and the insidious delights of the playhouse. In a country already bleak, these hardy forebears did not have to campaign very energetically against that particular ancient evil. The difficulty of gathering an audience in a country so sparsely populated did much to discourage it, and curfew conditions existed in the more populous centres. But the garrison theatres were beyond the censure of the stern forefathers of the hamlets.

It is but an affirmation of the natural place of theatre in life to say that Canadians eventually did get theatre—for the small population, great distances, and inclement weather combined with both the Puritan veto and the materialists' disinterest to make the country an unlikely one for such a crop.

But grow that theatre did, and by the nineteenth century there were audiences for the English touring companies, out to pick up American dollars even then, and for the American companies which included most of our Eastern centres on their theatrical circuits.

As the country grew more prosperous and better settled, the small new towns included assembly halls of one sort or another among their public buildings. In Ontario, there sprang up a chain of opera houses. These establishments are rather deceptive in name. For the most part, they were second-story jobs of wooden construction, located over the city hall, the post office, or the library. But theatres they were, and no mistake. Each had a box office at the top of the stairs and rows of chairs facing the stage. And each stage was fitted with a handsome roll curtain. Behind this proud banner of theatre hung other drops, often interchangeable, and in some of these theatres the slots for the old-fashioned wing pieces can still be seen. Not all of these opera houses were plain plank affairs. Some of them were highly ornamented. A balcony ran around three sides of the hall, and this was decked with ornamental plaster—even cupids can be seen. Chandeliers varied in elaborateness, but there were always chandeliers.

In the bigger, older centres, full-fledged theatres sprang up from their own foundations, and those in Montreal and Toronto rivalled anything in New England. Few of these theatres are still in existence. Fire took its toll and office-builders snatched at valuable space. When the theatre was menaced by the motion-picture makers, however, in the second and third decades of the twentieth century, there were still many legitimate theatres for the buying.

The houses still-standing had served the visiting companies and the stars, when those luminaries appeared over the horizon. Such visitations were modest enough at first. A player of name would come attended by a manager only, at first, but later such exalted beings protected their reputations by bringing their chief supporting players, at least a suitably gifted and attractive leading lady, or leading gentleman, and a villain or two. Later they were to come with whole companies, with elaborate mountings and full wardrobes. Then the situation started to become top-heavy and to crumble under its own weight.

The list of great figures of nineteenth-century theatre who appeared in Canada, and appeared regularly, is quite surprising. The English tragedian, Macready, for instance, played in Canada, and so did the Booths and the Barrymores in their day. Sarah Bernhardt was banned by the Bishop of Montreal, and did splendid business as a result. Edmund Kean was proud to have been made chief of a tribe of Canadian Indians and wore his feathers with delight. The noble company of Sir Henry Irving and Ellen Terry were praised by us, and after them, their tradition was upheld by such disciples as Sir John Martin-Harvey and Sir Johnston Forbes-Robertson. Up from the United States came, regularly, Mrs. Fiske, Southern and Marlowe, the Scottish Shakespearean Robert Bruce Mantell, and Genevieve Hamper, George Arliss, Guy Bates Post, and Otis Skinner. The list is long and many coloured; it serves to demonstrate that Canada was a profitable territory for the players in those days.

They were all part of what was called "the road." They were its chief glory, and one of the first causes of its downfall. As their names became famous, these stars claimed bigger and bigger salaries. Often those salaries were paid at the expense of the supporting company. The competent actors with whom they had so proudly surrounded themselves were supplanted by less efficient, less expensive players. The public started to recognize the difference, and the dramatic critics pointed them out, flattering the celebrities the while.

That decline is first noted about 1910, but this did not mean that an end to the professional theatre was in sight. The stock companies flourished when the "road" came on bad days. Some of them became local institutions of dignity and wide support, and we may be sure that comparisons in the press often favoured the well-entrenched local company. Some of these enterprises were definitely thread-bare, or became so in later years, but many were worthy and conscientious bodies, with the public's best interest at heart in bringing outstanding modern drama to Canada as soon as possible—after it had been recognized and acclaimed in London or New York. Of these, Vaughan Glaser's company is perhaps best remembered, for it played for six years in succession in Toronto, from 1921 to 1928, but others gained respect and patronage to match, including Cameron Matthews' English Players, Charles Hampden's British Players, the English Repertory Company, and the New Empire Company. Other cities had their favourites, too, if not as many as Toronto.

In the summer seasons, when everybody in town—or at least, all the carriage trade—was presumed to have gone to their country homes, the stock companies sometimes went on the road, to visit the smaller centres. These smaller cities greeted them as successors to the old barnstorming troupes. It is worth noting that among those barnstormers were to be found the first Canadian professionals. A notable example of these were the famous Marks brothers, who played all through the country.

What happened to the Canadian theatre in the second decade of the present century was not a disaster unique in itself. The same catastrophe was to strike the American "road" and even the English provinces, to a certain extent. With the stars asking too much money and the booking agencies realizing less and less profit, a fatal blow was delivered when the railway costs went up. Touring became almost an impossibility, for distances were great and became greater as the towns big enough to support the companies proved to be fewer and further apart. Costs of productions also rose as standards went up.

By the late 1920s the motion-picture industry had become firmly entrenched, financially and in public esteem. The distributors of films bought up all the available theatres and built lavish new ones. The new theatre owners proved unwilling to rent their properties to the old-fashioned competition. Why should they, when the motion pictures were offering better and better entertainment, attractions which never declined in standard when seen in a small, out-of-the-way centre?

The loss of the legitimate theatre was noted and bewailed. It might have struck thinking Canadians as a greater loss if the country had evolved its own dramatic literature before motion pictures became coherent and started to talk. But what difference did it make if, instead of being supplied with American and English entertainment by rail, they were now supplied with the same commodities in tin cans? And all parts of the Dominion were equally served? The method of presentation was certainly less exhilarating, but the bill of fare was much the same.

When radio took hold of the country, it proved a little more stimulating to the thin line of Canadians huddled along the border of its southern neighbour, as if in an effort to keep warm. For the Canadian Broadcasting Corporation was soon set up to save Canada from the vulgar excesses of American commercialism, and also from its vulgar successes. There was a new hope born for the Canadian drama, and to a certain degree this hope was realized by Canadian writers, who found for the first time a theatrical medium which was interested in their ideas. The public accepted this and got some satisfaction from the high standards in radio drama achieved later under Andrew Allan and Esse Ljungh of the CBC. And, when it came to comedy, that public could always tune in across the border. Perhaps the sense of achievement was felt more particularly by the participants in this development. A new acting profession centred around the CBC studios in Toronto. There were new names known: John Drainie, Budd Knapp, Tommy Tweed, Frank Peddie, Jane Mallett, for instance, and they were known across the continent.

But the outlook for the legitimate stage was bleak. The English companies had petered out after the last noble tours of Sir John Martin-Harvey and the later, equally gallant attempts by Barry Jones and Maurice Colbourne. The American companies never ceased to flow entirely, for the Royal Alexandra in Toronto is maintained as a successful touring house even to this day and Montreal's His Majesty's, although owned by film people, has survived to become Her Majesty's once again. But the flow was certainly limited and no longer trickled across country.

The theatre instinct, however, showed up elsewhere, and in a humbler, more indigenous form. When imported theatre receded from the land, Canadian citizens took a hand at last. Amateur dramatic societies had never been wholly absent from the Canadian scene since the days of the garrison theatres. Now they flourished mightily. An enterprise uniting them, called the Theatre Guild of Canada, had been attempted, but it proved premature. The more serious groups rallied around the banner of the governor general, who set up the Earl Grey Musical and Dramatic Trophy Competition, in operation as early as 1907. Five such competitions were held before the dramatic part of this first festival, for such it was, collapsed in 1911.

But the Little Theatre movement, as it was later to be known, did not collapse. It grew apace after World War I. The Ottawa Drama League was launched in 1913, and the Players Club of the University of British Columbia started in 1915. The Players Club of the University of Toronto began in 1916. From this latter group sprang the celebrated Hart House Theatre, and the Right Honourable Vincent Massey, later the first Canadian to become governor general, was a member of it, as was his actor-brother Raymond.

The vice-regal Massey was responsible for building Hart House Theatre in 1919. Soon there were dramatic societies and clubs all across the Dominion, some of them conceived on a lofty plane—such as the Montreal Repertory Theatre, founded by Martha Allan in an effort to supply the need for a theatre operating in both French and English. Hart House itself became the home of a notable theatre group and only in the last ten years (starting 1946) has been turned over to University Theatre. Although their names were not to be as widely sung as the first radio actors, the Hart House players—Ivor Lewis, Frank Rostance, and Nancy Pyper among them—were recognized as having theatrical distinction.

It was not until 1933 that a form of national theatre emerged out of all this chaos of good intentions. Again the help was to come from a governor general. In 1932 the incumbent of Rideau Hall, the Earl of Bessborough, summoned representatives of leading theatre bodies to Ottawa. The Dominion Drama Festival was established then, with regional competitions held the next spring. The first D.D.F. finals—for this Festival was also competitive—were held in Ottawa in May 1933, with the late Colonel Henry Osborne of Ottawa as president.

With a brief, and not altogether creditable, abstention during World War II, this Dominion Drama Festival has been in operation ever since. At last, Canada had its own theatre, sporadic and unprofessional as it was. Several generations of actors, who would have swelled the ranks of the profession had there been one, maintained themselves by other occupations during the day and play-acted, most seriously, by night. The visiting adjudicators, almost invariably brought from England, were surprised at the standards reached by players and producers.

There were many changes as the D.D.F. organization grew and expanded. Today there are thirteen regions, some of them subdivided with preliminary competitions necessary to weed out the entries. When it started operations again, after the war, the Festival was open to amateur and professional players alike, playing full-length plays with full theatrical accoutrement. When its growth gave rise to financial difficulties, a commercial backer for the enterprise, a distillery, was found.

It is impossible to underrate the importance of this still basically amateur competition in surveying the picture of theatre in Canada today. Where a new professional theatre is emerging, the deeper roots go back to the Dominion Drama Festival and its member bodies. Where the professional theatre is yet to emerge, the amateur companies carry on. Whatever the future of the Canadian theatre, the Dominion Drama Festival will continue for a long time, one feels, in its present state of usefulness. Perhaps later it will dwindle into the village drama of other countries, but for years to come it will very likely continue to serve—bridging the wide spaces between theatrical centres and the long months between tours. It must continue to serve as schooling and opportunity for the fledgling actors, directors, and designers.

Nevertheless, the Dominion Drama Festival is something of a sieve for talent. The sporadic effort, the change in personnel, the lack of continuing energy—because working for it cannot be a full-time job—these are as much part of the Festival as its sporting spirit, its excitement, and its camaraderie. Some notable adjudicators have brought their wisdom to it—including Harley Granville-Barker, J.T. Grein, Michel St. Denis—but their good advice has seeped away in the constant change of personnel of a

Festival. Groups do not return to the finals many years in succession, and when they do return their personnel have generally changed.

For all the inadequacy of the Dominion Drama Festival as a firm supporter of theatrical tradition and of standards in this country, it is certainly out of the Festival rather than out of the long-gone stock companies and visiting touring companies that the present professional theatre springs. But that new development is as much fed by the Canadian Broadcasting Corporation radio drama and television as by any legitimate force, amateur or professional.

The CBC is a body closer in structure to the British Broadcasting Corporation than to any of the American networks. It combines commercial sponsorship with government control in a manner which would be deemed impossible beyond its borders. Its influence on Canadian theatre has been enormous since it was established in 1936 to succeed the Canadian Radio Broadcasting Commission, in operation since 1932. Most of the people who would have turned to theatre for expression turned to the CBC as the only mildly creative medium paying a living wage at the time. Their contributions, fitting narrowly into a structure basically that of a civil service, have been important. We have spoken of some of the radio actors who emerged, and the radio producers. When the CBC plunged into the vastly more expensive medium of television in September 1952, new names emerged and new places were created for the workers in theatre arts.

One is tempted to say that Canada has the kind of radio and television it deserves, too, for while its programs and policies are much criticized, it steers an often admirable balance between entertainment and education, achieving neither most of the time but missing by narrower and narrower margins as it gains confidence.[1] It has encouraged writers, it has encouraged directors, and it has given actors and artists new strength. It has also enriched the selective segments of the Canadian public with special artistic treats. Its main weaknesses are timidity, lack of imagination, and fear of vulgarity. But it was designed to provide a chain of high-power stations across Canada and to unify a scattered country—just as the Canadian Pacific Railroad was established with Confederation—and it serves this major purpose. Canadians from sea to sea share its news broadcasts, its hockey reports, its symphony concerts, and its Stage Series, and are as one.

Let us turn now to that new development, the Canadian professional theatre as it appears today. Without the Stratford Shakespearean Festival, now entering its fourth year, that picture would still look grim—for the influence of this body can be felt pulsating behind most other theatre ventures, directly or indirectly influencing them. With it, the picture is bright, edged in gold and full of the happy, even if false, perspective of glorious vistas.

Started in 1953, twenty years after the Dominion Drama Festival, it is a curious outcropping of native innocence, sporting spirit, and simple faith in help from abroad, all sound Canadian characteristics. The dream of a Stratford, Ontario, citizen, Tom Patterson, it was backed by a notable community effort and guided by a superb general, Tyrone Guthrie, the six-foot-four Irish director who mustered the acting talent in Canada by some clairvoyant means, augmented it with talent from England, which has included Alec Guinness, Irene Worth, James Mason, Douglas Campbell, and Frederick Valk, and gave Stratford three smashing summer seasons in a tent which houses a superb free-form Elizabethan stage designed by Tanya Moiseiwitsch, top designer of the English stage. The plays have been *All's Well That Ends Well*, the Festival's most spirited achievement, and an exciting *Richard III* (1953); an impressive *Oedipus Rex*, masked and ritualistic, a wildly farcical *The Taming of the Shrew*, and a less successful *Measure for Measure*, which needed the Guthrie touch, being directed by the director's first production head, Cecil Clarke (1954). Gurthrie's next production at Stratford was *The Merchant of Venice* (1955), starring Frederick Valk. Then Dr. Guthrie turned over his position of director to Michael Langham, who had directed a most commendable *Julius Caesar* that same year. Mr. Langham revised the company slightly and staged an impressive *Henry V* and a full-text, dullish *The Merry Wives of Windsor* for the 1956 season, winning much respect for his mingling of English and French-Canadian actors in the former. And Stratford proudly accepted the invitation of the Edinburgh Festival to take a production there in August of that year, the first English-speaking company from abroad to be honoured by the major arts festival in Britain.

Dr. Guthrie's connection was not broken entirely. He rallied the company for a 1956 invasion of Broadway, repeating his 1952 Old Vic production of Marlowe's *Tamburlaine the Great* and importing Anthony Quayle, actor-director of the Stratford-upon-Avon Memorial Theatre, as its star. Dr. Guthrie also prepared the revival of his *Oedipus Rex*, which shared the Edinburgh's Festival Hall stage with Mr. Langham's *Henry V*.

At the end of 1956 the familiar tent was dismantled and there rose on its site a $1 500 000 building, designed to carry out the circular form of the original. Thus Canada's Stratford could claim, as Stratford-on-Avon and Stratford, Connecticut, can not, a theatre devoted to those principles of Shakespearean staging first preached by William Poel before the turn of the century. The opening play in this long-awaited theatre was *Hamlet*, given first on July 1, 1957, with Christopher Plummer as the Prince, under Michael Langham's direction. Dr. Guthrie returned to produce the season's second play, *Twelfth Night*, with the Irish actress, Siobhan McKenna, as Viola.

Both of the Stratford excursions abroad have been perhaps overstressed in importance, but Canadians depend desperately on approval from relatives and friends, a colonial attitude which can only be cured, presumably, by winning that approval from which may develop a critical opinion of what the country needs for itself. Stratford's Festival has already done this to a greater extent than any other enterprise. That fine, sad little comic, Gratien Gélinas, affectionately nick-named Fridolin, rode out of Montreal, after years of original revues, to tackle Broadway in *Tit-Coq*, in 1951, and was beaten back within three days. The CBC annually marches off with American radio awards, and the documentaries of the National Film Board are highly regarded by all the people who regard documentaries highly. But Stratford's Festival succeeded in attracting both national and international admiration, praise, and press coverage.

The effect of Stratford was tremendous. The actors who played at Stratford became overnight the aristocracy of their profession. Before them, the radio actors were the national leaders. Now the new names were Donald Harron, Barbara Chilcott, Eric House, Lloyd Bochner, Donald Davis, William Hutt, and William Shatner. Among their ranks were some who had made the jump from radio drama, players like the distinguished Eleanor Stuart, Lorne Greene, William Needles, and Robert Christie, all playing star roles at Stratford. And to their ranks were added the names of the British actors who joined the company: Douglas Campbell from the Old Vic, Antony Van Bridge from the Young Vic. There are also such young Canadians as have been brought back from outside to appear at their national festival: Frances Hyland, Richard Easton, Douglas Rain, and Christopher Plummer, a compelling young classical actor who is Stratford's first real Canadian star as Henry V.

The Stratford Festival is clearly the dominant force in Canadian theatre today, bulwarked by its appearances on Broadway and Edinburgh and by a moving little documentary, *The Stratford Adventure*, made by the National Film Board. Around its theatrical core have been developed a Music Festival and also other attractions: 1955's *Tale of a Soldier*, which introduced the French mime, Marcel Marceau, to many American and Canadian audiences; 1956's *Rape of Lucretia*, a Canadian *première*; and Montreal's Théâtre du Nouveau Monde, whose Molière farces were popular side attractions for 1956. A film of Guthrie's *Oedipus Rex* has also been made with plans to film the First Folio at Stratford.

Out of the Stratford Festival has emerged The Canadian Players, another Tom Patterson idea, brought to vigour under the direction of the pugnacious Scottish actor, Douglas Campbell. This company carries platform drama to the country, dispensing with scenery and period costumes. Its first venture, Shaw's *Saint Joan*, had Mr. Campbell's wife, Ann Casson (daughter of the original interpreter of the role, Dame Sybil Thorndike) as Joan. The second season found first Frances Hyland as Joan, then Norma Renault, with the company adding another play to its repertory, *Macbeth*, starring first William Hutt, later Mr. Campbell. Prominent members of the company have also included William Needles, Bruno Gerussi, Roland Hewgill, John Gardner, Ted Follows, and Ameila Hall, all of them contributors to Stratford. Their third tour consisted of *Peer Gynt* and *Hamlet*, with a second company taking out *Man and Superman* and *Othello*.

One could say that The Canadian Players emerged from Stratford as easily as one could say *Tamburlaine the Great* did, but to say that Toronto's Crest Theatre did would be an overstatement. This fine repertory theatre started in January 1954, after Stratford's first season, by which it was undoubtedly inspired, but its origins lay closer to the grassroots of Canadian theatre.

It is safe to say that summer is a very good time for professional theatre in Canada. Stratford is a summer venture which looks as if it might become a year-round venture. The Crest Theatre, too, had its beginnings in a summer company. And a number of summer theatres have nourished a modest professionalism in the land, among them the now extinct John Holden Players, who acted at Bala, starting in 1934; the longest lasting one, the Brae

Manor Theatre (1935) launched by Madge and the late Filmore Sadler at Knowlton, in Quebec's Eastern Townships; the Mountain Playhouse in Montreal, started by Joy Thomson; the Peterborough Summer Theatre; the Niagara Falls Summer Theatre; the Garden Centre Theatre at Vineland; the Niagara Barn Theatre; and the Red Barn at Jackson's Point. They have a precarious existence, but they have kept audiences entertained and actors working and learning.

Two of the summer theatre operations, those at Gravenhurst and Port Carling in the Muskoka Lake district, were operated by the Davis brothers, Murray and Donald, who after half-a-dozen years opened the Crest Theatre in Toronto as a full-fledged repertory. They emerged, as many of their company did, from the ranks of university actors at Hart House Theatre, having learned their trade under the direction of Robert Gill. Other university theatres, from the Maritimes to British Columbia, have made their contributions to this growing professional theatre, as well as trained audiences for it.

The last and perhaps greatest impetus to this professionalism came with the introduction of television to Canada. Where radio launched the Canadian professional actor, television has given him a recognizing audience and a better salary. It carries him through the winter months, the months between Stratford.

So there we have the various contributing factors which go to help establish a Canadian professionalism in the theatre. Conditions for a native-born theatre were never more promising in the history of the country, although it is better not to compare these conditions with those of other nations yet. Now who is missing? The playwright.

The writing of plays is surely the most subtle and most difficult of creative tasks, for it depends on so many ingredients which change daily. A play is not truly a play until it is interpreted by players, and good ones are necessary. It is not proved as a play until it has played before audiences. Up to now, Canadian writers have not had sufficient reason to believe that their plays will receive a proper hearing in their own country, although various organizations, such as the pioneering, prospering New Play Society, the Jupiter Theatre, and the Crest Theatre, have staged the works of Canadian playwrights. But the revenue a professional writer can expect in the country he knows and is writing about is very small at best; for the playwright it is almost infinitesimal. Robertson Davies, most popular of the Canadian playwrights, commands much more as a novelist and humorist. Other playwrights—Merrill Denison, Joseph Schull, Patricia Joudry, and Stanley Mann—must either go away or turn to other fields, if they depend on their writing for their living. But television lets the playwright work not too far away from the medium of his choice, and so there is hope there.

That is the one commodity common to all branches and members of the Canadian theatre today—hope. The dark days of the century can now be seen to have served an important purpose. Canadians were thrown back on their own resources. Canadians are a people trained to think of themselves as sitting atop the greatest natural resources in the world, smugly wearing the label of The Country with the Greatest Future. In the theatre, as in many other fields of development, that future is upon us now. What emerges in the next few years will be of greatest importance, if it matches that which has emerged in the past decade or so. If Canada has come slowly to its theatre, it may have come wisely. The theatre it evolves may now be able to draw what it wants from the three older cultures and add what it needs beyond that to provide a strong and true expression of its own kind of life and its own kind of people. If Canada reaches for the theatre it deserves, it must find new forms and new ideas, perhaps even a new language. As a theatre growing up in the twentieth century, aided and abetted by the mechanical media of showmanship instead of opposed by them, it should certainly be worth watching for and waiting for, although the waiting period has been an uncommonly long one.

NOTES

1. See "Is TV a Threat?" a symposium
   in *Queen's Quarterly*, LXIII (Summer
   1956), 265.

THEATRE TODAY:
ENGLISH CANADA ◊

NATHAN COHEN

○

Theatre critic for the Toronto Star *from 1959 until his death in 1971, Nathan Cohen (b. 1923) achieved a national and international reputation for his forthright views and incisive analyses of theatre which he saw as part of a larger sociocultural dynamic. Throughout his career he questioned the influence of the Stratford Festival on the development of an indigenous Canadian theatre, as this selection from the* Tamarack Review *in 1959 demonstrates.*

Theatre as a mirror and critic of the moods, tones, idioms, paradoxes, virtues, and inadequacies of life on a thinly-populated, four-thousand-mile sub-Arctic strip; as a concentrated artistic statement with a persevering dynamic; as a body of imaginative work with themes and standards—in short, theatre as something of value to a discerning public has never counted in the life of English-language Canada. Nor is it likely to in the reasonably foreseeable future.

On another level, however, as a negotiable commodity in the market of show business, theatre is not as unimportant as it used to be. Non-existent just a dozen years ago, Actors' Equity now has a membership of over a thousand in Toronto alone. The establishment and rapid expansion of the television industry in Toronto has brought to this city hundreds of people from all corners of the country, and from England and Middle Europe, with theatrical skills, aptitudes, and hopes.

The press coverage is considerable. In 1959 the hiring of new drama critics by the two afternoon Toronto papers unleashed a heated promotion campaign. The progress of Canadian artists away from home and the state

---

◊ *Tamarack Review* 13 (Autumn 1959): 24–37. Reprinted with permission of the estate of Nathan Cohen.

of the lively arts at home are editorial staples, usually in confident vein. The major magazines try to include at least one article in each issue dealing with the lively arts; stories with a live theatre slant invariably get priority. The grants of theatre subsidies and scholarships by the Canada Council are reported faithfully as are all its emoluments.

Indeed, we have now reached the point where Canadian businessmen will invest in local entertainments and locally-originated shows, not from charity or a sense of guilt, but for the hard-headed purpose of making money. Toronto backing led to the production overseas of Ted Allan's *The Ghost Writer* (called *The Money Makers* over here). John Steele obtained Bay Street sponsorship for a tryout of Patricia Joudry's *Three Rings for Michelle*, and also for the Arts Theatre performance in London, England, of her *Teach Me How to Cry*. Glen Frankfurter and Len Peterson had responsible business support for their Lansdowne Theatre venture.

The climate for theatrical activity has changed, no doubt of that. Twelve years ago, for a Canadian mounted and enacted show to run a whole week, to a total audience of fifteen hundred people, was an occasion of magnitude. Today productions staged, performed, and sometimes even written by Canadians may occupy a theatre for as long as three months. In 1957 the Freedman-Morse presentation of *Salad Days* stayed thirteen weeks in the 425-seat Hart House Theatre in Toronto. A year later it was brought to the 800-seat Crest for a run of nine weeks. A much more astonishing record was registered by the production of *My Fur Lady*, which after a nine-week run in Montreal toured Canada triumphantly for close to two years.

Specifically considered, the professional theatre in English-language Canada breaks down into the Stratford Festival, which functions one third of the year; the Canadian Players, a two-unit touring company; the Crest, a theatre which uses local talent exclusively; two summertime musical companies (Theatre Under the Stars, Music Fair) which go in for American leads; a clutch of summer theatres; and a handful of independent managers who specialize in musical revues (*After Hours, Clap Hands*) and the first Canadian performance of minor New York and London successes (*The Fifth Season, Visit to a Small Planet*, and *Salad Days*). And there are a few theatres—the Royal Alexandra in Toronto, Her Majesty's in Montreal—which depend primarily on American road attractions to keep their doors open.

For all practical purposes, our professional theatre is confined to the area in and around Toronto. There is no equivalent to New York's Broadway or London's West End, no geographic centre inside the city, but the bulk of the operations exist somewhere in Toronto, and Stratford and most of the summer theatre groups fall within a hundred-mile radius. Toronto is in fact the centre of all the performing arts in English-language Canada, from television and film production and live theatre to ballet, opera, radio, and both pop and serious music. With its wealth and population (nearly a million and a half people in Greater Toronto) it is the one community able to accommodate such a diversity of artistic efforts.

Aside from the Stratford Festival, which has a national vested interest status, and Theatre Under the Stars, whose losses are underwritten by the city of Vancouver, the other theatre enterprises are in perilous health.

The summer theatres have a fantastic mortality rate. Typical is the Red Barn Theatre, which in nine seasons has changed management eight times. The Crest, founded in 1954, has lost annually an average of $30 000; launched as a private concern, it has latterly been reorganized as a non-profit enterprise to qualify it for Canada Council and charitable foundation bounty.

At the end of its second season Music Fair is so far away from recouping its initial quarter-of-a-million-dollar investment that its return in 1960 is gravely in doubt. The Canadian Players has never made any profit; its existence depends entirely on the goodwill of Lady Eaton. With the road circuit for American attractions shrinking, both the Royal Alexandra and Her Majesty's stay open shorter and shorter periods. It is no secret that the first has been put up for sale, and that the other will be converted into a motion-picture house or parking lot at the first attractive opportunity.

The lot of the independent producers is equally sobering. What moneys Mervyn Rosenzweig and Stan Jacobson made in Toronto on *The Fifth Season* they lost on *Uncle Willie* and *Out of This World*; they have now retired from the game. Terry Fisher's attempt to turn the Avenue Theatre (now a parking lot) into a house for American touring plays and intimate musicals backfired disastrously; he too has left theatre for good. The producers of *My Fur Lady* tried to double their income with the revue *Jubilee*. They lost an amount conservatively estimated at $50 000—every cent, actually, that they made with *My Fur Lady*.

The inception of a new professional group among us takes place in a neon glare of publicity and fervent affirmations of a glowing year; its passing generally goes unmarked. In the last twelve years (the period this essay is concerned with) there have been many such deaths. Totem Theatre in Vancouver lasted two seasons. The Stage Society in Ottawa and its successor, the Canadian Repertory Theatre, held on for five years. The greatest number of fatalities has been, of course, in Toronto. Jupiter Theatre was with us for three years. Melody Fair, the first tent musical in Canada, subsided shoddily in its fourth season. The Lansdowne Theatre appeared and expired in less than a month. The Earle Grey Players, which pre-dates the Stratford Festival in the performance of Shakespeare by at least five years, now limits itself to a tour of the schools. The oldest of our professional companies, the New Play Society, is in hibernation. Once each year it crawls out for its durable and highly profitable revue *Spring Thaw*.

The magic of the Stratford Festival works only within a carefully circumscribed box-office circle. People will gladly come to Stratford; they will not suffer Stratford to come to them. In 1958 a Festival touring company played in London, Ontario, Montreal, and Toronto prior to a visit to New York's Phoenix Theatre. The American response was kind but desultory; the Canadian welcome was so poor that ambitious plans for a permanent touring company were dropped at once.

The Canadian Players is no luckier when it comes to the larger Canadian communities. Its last appearance in a Toronto theatre, in December 1957, was a financial catastrophe. The same thing happened in December 1958 when it came to Montreal for two weeks.

People inside the trade will tell you that the live entertainment Canadians like most is the intimate revue, a collection of songs and sketches, preferably with a satirical bias. The continuing popularity of *Spring Thaw* and the wild triumph of *My Fur Lady* (although it had a fragile story line) seem to confirm that view.

Actually very few revues end in the black. After a rousing season at the Red Barn, producer Brian Doherty gathered his cast and the best of the summer material and came to the Royal Alexandra for a two-week stay preparatory to a trans-Canada tour. The engagement ended abruptly; the tour never materialized. A dissident group from the NPS staggered along for six weeks with *Fine Frenzy* (forced runs are a commonplace in our professional theatre), but the idea of presenting the show annually collapsed. Besides *Jubilee*, the following revues were casualties in 1959: the Crest's *This Is Our First Affair*, the Stratford-sponsored *After Hours*, and in Montreal *Poise'n'Ivy*. Even *Spring Thaw* has begun to lose favour: during the last month of its 1959 edition the cast played to half-empty houses.

One way to attract audiences to home-grown shows in Toronto is to schedule them to be taken abroad as samples of our culture. The Crest did excellent business with *The Glass Cage*, written for it by J.B. Priestley and later taken to London, England where it soon foundered. Then of course there were the Stratford-incubated *Tamburlaine* and Gratien Gélinas's *Ti-Coq*. They played to turnaway crowds before their unhappy excursions to New York. (Indeed, the peremptory rejection by American critics of *Ti-Coq* so inflamed the national ire that Toronto recalled it for another, and even more lucrative, engagement. A good deal was said then about *Ti-Coq's* appealing to all Canadians, English speaking and French, and about its artistic merit. It is worth noting, then, when someone speaks about closer cultural relations between our two main language groups, that *Ti-Coq* has never been performed, or publicly considered for performance, by any English-language amateur or professional company.)

The preceding information makes one thing clear: as a business speculation the professional Canadian theatre stands on very shaky feet. It is possible, if the right combination of ingredients is found, to have an occasional long-run show and to make some money from it. But such events happen seldom, and the amount to be made is not really great.

A few more statistics will round out this part of the picture. There is not in Canada a single person who earns a living as a playwright, or who has any practical hope of doing so. Nor is there anyone, aside from a few people attached to the universities, who earns a living as a director. Finally, of all the people listed with Equity, only a hundred—mostly men, by the way— are employed in the theatre the entire year. For the others, acting is a part-time, a secondary occupation.

Shortly after the Second World War, something happened in Toronto which suggested the beginnings of a vital, indigenous English-language theatre for Canada. In 1947 Mrs Dora Mavor Moore, a onetime actress with the Ben Greet Players and drama teacher, and her son Mavor set up the New Play Society. Their aim was to develop "a living Canadian theatre on a permanent, but non-profit basis." They proposed to draw their people from the versatile, bustling colony of radio actors with the Canadian Broadcasting Corporation, and from Mrs Moore's students and the campus of the University of Toronto.

Their theatre was the concert-hall of the Royal Ontario Museum, an elongated, acoustically-poor basement auditorium with a match-box stage, a cement floor, no flies, no wing space, and pitiful lighting equipment. The first season's repertoire was a conglomeration of classics, recent Broadway hits, controversial modern works, and new Canadian plays.

From the outset it was manifest that the NPS would blaze no trails and match no Broadway or West End goals in respect of production values. The settings were shabby, makeshift; the direction and acting shrieked practical inexperience. But in terms of a powerful inquiry and emotionally true projection of a play's basic qualities the NPS speedily asserted its worth. There were, in particular, productions of *Juno and the Paycock* and *The Time of Your Life* which gave playgoers, conditioned to expect the worst of Canadian actors, a stunning opportunity to find themselves engaged by that life on stage which comments thrillingly and perceptively on the reality of life.

The need for a Canadian orientation was innate in the NPS, partly because of the Moores' temperament, and also because the breezes of a belated nationalism were at last rustling through the tiny world of our arts. As the NPS took firmer hold, original works were presented at every opportunity. Some—Lister Sinclair's *Man in the Blue Moon* and Andrew Allan's *Narrow Passage*, for example—were utterly worthless. Others—Mavor Moore's spoof of the familiar Canadian vices, *Who's Who?*—were theatrically ingenious and had a legitimate frame of reference. A few, while not critically outstanding, nevertheless deserved serious attention. Morley Callaghan contributed a moving study of a young man's rootlessness in *To Tell the Truth*. Ulster-born John Coulter delivered *Riel*, a biography which drew a strained but daring parallel between Canada's one truly mythic figure and Joan of Arc. Harry Boyle dug into his bag of personal observation to tell, convincingly and modestly in *The Inheritance*, a conflict of two generations of farmers in Southern Ontario after the First World War.

The result of these activities was the creation for the NPS of a growing and intensely loyal audience. Shows started to run a week instead of a few nights, a fortnight instead of a week. The calibre of production improved, erratically. Word of mouth spread the message that here was something special, a company with a mission and the will to carry it out. However bad, each show had a contagious excitement. Very often the NPS overreached itself ludicrously: the staging of *Riel* was scandalous; *King Lear* was presented with just five days of serious rehearsal, and with an actor in the title part still suffering from laryngitis. But it really did not matter. There was passion in the NPS, an artistic focus, and an elated rage for identity.

Meanwhile an explosion of theatre occurred at the University of Toronto. Its fuse was Hart House Theatre. This admirable playhouse, a gift from the Massey family in 1919, was at first a haven for coteries of amateurs. These people were sincere and not entirely talentless. But the atmosphere was hot-house, the gardeners not that knowing, and the seeds they planted proved barren. Following the war the university's Board of Syndics decided to bring in a full-time director whose task would be to put on shows with student personnel. That too was in 1947. The director, Robert Gill, immediately found himself surrounded by a group of young men and women literally lusting to serve him. They plunged into every play he scheduled with a burning quality of personal involvement. They entered into bad plays (*Winterset, Jason*) with the same zeal they had for good ones (*The Seagull, Romeo and Juliet*). They throbbed with a craving for self-expression through theatre, and offered themselves as raw material, eager to be shaped and given a controlled and continuing energy. Doing four shows a year with Mr Gill was not enough. In between his productions they did their own, or they rushed to the NPS, sometimes to do leads, more often to appear as walk-ons and extras. From their strivings came the summer theatre company, the Straw Hat Players, founded by Murray and Donald Davis, and from that followed a period of significant summer theatre expansion.

In the main these companies (at peak there were about a dozen, and in many of them the performers doubled as crewhands) found their plays in the standard British and American repertoire. But not altogether. The International Players of Kingston, Ontario, which invited audiences to come on a "pay-what-you-like" basis (the plate was passed around after the second act), gambled with a new play, *Fortune, My Foe* by Peterborough editor Robertson Davies. His comedy about a Canadian professor who loathes this country but loathes even more the idea of living and working in the United States was an instant conversation-piece. Delighted by the reaction, the company next season did a second but less eventful Davies play, his historical comedy-drama, *At My Heart's Core*. But of course it was not the plays, but the manner of their doing, which generated excitement.

It would be missing the point to describe the curious thing going on as the hammering out, the crystallization of a true style. Rather it was a conscious groping after style, a disorganized but conscious attempt to make use of inner resources, impulses, and homegrown attitudes chiefly by young people born and raised in Canada, or who had spent their formative years here. To put it negatively, these people simply didn't want to reproduce American and British plays according to American and British models. They wanted to put their own stamp on them. To put it positively, theirs was a teamwork approach in which the mainspring of attack was a resolve to realize the author's intention in the light of their Canadian experience.

To do this they emphasized forthright characterization and emotional interplay, clean, efficient movement, and distinct speech—a speech free of mid-Atlantic accents and inflections and which had nothing in common either with Oxford or Mayfair English or the dialect-flavoured intonations of Bronx, midwest, and Mississippi American.

The quest drove them, moreover, into an investigation of organic principles of production, into the notion of an aesthetic unity involving the set, the performances, the lighting, so that the production itself should be of a piece in which all elements soundly fitted and harmonized.

At some point in all this rash of thinking and doing, the point began to take hold that plays dealing with the life around them, and with the circumstances which nourished and inhibited it, were essential to their quest, for it was only through such plays that the style they were trying to uncover could find its real vocabulary, a style which would be peculiar to them and which Canadian audiences would recognize as belonging to this country. Manifestly it would have to be a flexible style—capable of receiving and absorbing all other cultures—but plainly it would have to be rooted in Canadian attitudes and currents. Each play, whatever its artistic virtue, put director, actors, and audiences on their own mettle. There were no precedents to follow in playing or watching, no alternatives to judge by. The farmer in *The Inheritance* had Scottish forbears, but had fashioned a way of life decidedly his own. The intellectuals in *Fortune, My Foe* had British origins, but no duplicates in contemporary British life and drama. To interpret them tellingly, to give their behaviour and struggles a valid meaning and a sense of reality received and perceived, the director, his cast, the writer had to look around them, digest what they saw and heard, and make use of that information.

Let's not exaggerate the scope and extremity of these trends. In all they represented a small cultural groundswell, the start of a feeling, the beginning of a rude and scattered irrigation of a hitherto sterile world. Loosely, one may compare what happened to an off-Broadway eruption. There is a sudden surge of actors, writers, directors, designers, who seem to be much more populous than they are, but who bring new stirrings with them, who want to or are forced to challenge the establishment, and who have a numerically tiny but partisan and vociferous following. The difference, of course, is that in the United States people are drawn to a heartland; for all its deficiencies, there is an alliance of sorts between art and commerce on Broadway. No such magnet existed in Canada—only a void waiting to be filled. But the ingredients were forming, taking shape, staking claims, moving to a goal. Toronto was the logical home, and the hour was favourable. By 1952 the NPS, which had already toyed with the idea, was seriously considering the establishment of a permanent company. The Davis brothers had already taken the first steps toward getting their own theatre.

Then in July 1953 occurred what so many people call the Stratford miracle, the organization of a Shakespeare Festival on a big-league scale and with devastating impact in the park of a small railroad town in Southern Ontario whose one preposterous link with Shakespeare's birthplace was its name.

Were the Festival part of an energetic, entrenched, diversified theatre scene in Canada its consequences would have been beneficial, or at any rate not as harmful as they have turned out to be. As it is, the Festival inflamed two chronic, understandable but thoroughly dangerous Canadian yearnings: the itch to win international glory by excelling, in some branch of the arts, the two big brothers—Britain and the United States—in whose shadow we must always stand; and the passion to bypass the apprentice stage of culture and metamorphose overnight, from an instant, quick-frozen state, as it were, into a full-fledged artistic maturity.

The Festival began with several assets. Foremost was the theatre, lovely and luxurious, with a three-sided, seven-level stage (tent-enclosed originally, but later given a permanent shell). The Canadian audience came unfettered by traditions and preconceptions. There was a well of Canadian actors to nourish the British and British-trained leads who had come to help the venture get started (Alec Guinness, Irene Worth, Michael Bates, Douglas Campbell). It had one of the world's finest designers in Tanya Moiseiwitch and a flamboyant showman in director Tyrone Guthrie. Finally, there hung over everything a grand determination to bring new impulses and a more generous vision to bear on the display of Shakespeare's infinite genius.

But by the second season, it was apparent the Festival had its full share of liabilities. The open stage had its tyrannies no less repressive to Shakespeare than the proscenium arch; furthermore, it was inflexible, and did not allow for various kinds of production. The stage demanded a "go, go, go" treatment of a play, and accented visual richness (provided for by costumes more lavish than the most lavish settings) and spectacle at the cost of all else. Great actors could appear in this theatre, but great acting was impossible in it, and so was the development of a true ensemble style.

There were other disappointments. The well of Canadian actors proved exceedingly shallow; not only was the number of actors to choose from limited, but so was their calibre. In any event the practical intention, despite claims otherwise, was to use stars (a Hollywood actor, James Mason, was brought in the second season to star in *Oedipus Rex* and *Measure for Measure*) and to play safe with novelty of presentation. In effect Stratford was teaching an uncritical audience that Shakespeare's plays had no depth, but were just blueprints for pretty pyrotechnical exercises. The words were totally trivial, the characters mere wax figures, all to be juggled about at the director's caprice.

What has happened since proves that these liabilities are inherent in the Festival structure. It has evolved into a cultural equivalent of the Canadian National Exhibition grandstand show, an anti-artistic extravaganza. It was that dreariest of all successes, something which had made its mark by being dull in a new way.

Seemingly, the immediate effect of the Festival was to give our theatre a much-needed push. There was a spurt of activity. In 1954 the Davises opened the Crest. The NPS imported a director from England and gave him a permanent company to work with. Tom Patterson, who started the Festival, and Douglas Campbell set up the Canadian Players as a means of keeping a nucleus of the Festival company together the rest of the year. Independent groups with professional aspirations mushroomed. One took over the Royal Alexandra Theatre to stage the Leo Orenstein comedy, *The Big Leap*. A theatre-in-the-round was started in Halifax; Totem Theatre was born. Summer-theatre managements planned longer seasons. All prepared for the rush of audiences. The lean years were over. At last the feast!

In fact the audiences proved indifferent and there was a subtle but important change in the theatrical atmosphere. For one thing, although Stratford had made theatre respectable, it had not made it popular, only popular as a social event. For another, the impact of Stratford as a circus was to convince people in the theatre that the drive to a Canadian character was so much rubbish. The Crest Theatre decided that the look of a show was the big thing, that and a West End outlook. The shows offered by the Crest became deliberately British in content and expression—*Richard of Bordeaux* and *Lord Arthur Savile's Crime* were characteristic vehicles. As remarked before, the NPS was caught up in the vogue for things British. As well, it became heavily production-conscious.

The panic feeling induced by the bad box-office was augmented by a crisis in the supply of actors. For one thing, television was by now well-established, and paid more and reached larger audiences. For another, actors preferred the prestige of being invited to play in Stratford which after all paid the best wages, offered the most congenial working conditions and the longest tenure of employment. Players took work with the Crest or the NPS between engagements, to catch the attention of TV producers, or to be seen by Stratford scouts.

Above all else the proselytizing and nationalistic feeling, which envisioned theatre in Cánada as both a social and artistic medium, coming together, synthesizing, wavered and died. One last effort was made to reverse the trend. The New Play Society, disenchanted by its brief flirtation with West End thinking, hired the Avenue Theatre for an all-Canadian season. At least two interesting shows were tried—Donald Harron's dramatization of the Earle Birney novel about a Schweik-like soldier *Turvey*, and Mavor Moore's musical based on Voltaire's *Candide*—but the spirit was gone. The New Play Society now gave the impression of having been passed by in the sudden rush.

To speak, then, of a professional theatre in English-language Canada with a personality, a vigorous present and a promising future, is mere wishful thinking. We have perhaps a score of good actors—trained mechanics whose chief asset is that they can blend into the American or British theatre scene with a minimum of difficulties. We have a few, a very few, good directors. We have no writers seriously qualified to write for the professional stage or with any interest in making contact with the public. All we really have is a pocket-sized commercial theatre, pretty well limited to one city, anarchic, rampant with the speculation, waste of talent, and aimlessness which marks Broadway and the West End, but with none of their healthy buttressings and impulses.

True, until a generation ago we didn't have even that. After the talking pictures and the depression wiped out the community opera houses and the resident stock companies, theatre in Canada became an amateur's monopoly. With a few exceptions, the pre-war Theatre of Action in Toronto and Montreal Repertory in Montreal, that theatre and its prime symbol, the Dominion Drama Festival, have always been abysmally unadventurous.

In that sense no doubt the present condition must be accounted an improvement. But a scattering of performers and playhouses does not comprise a living theatre. The way things are going now, we may find ourselves, in just a few years, with only the Stratford Festival to prove that there is, or ever was, a professional theatre of sorts in Canada. The rest is likely to crumble into thin, fugacious particles, swept away on the wind, with actors repairing to the greener pastures of New York and London and with writers pouring out their efforts for television where they will be swallowed up in an hour and forgotten in a minute. The whole thing could well dissolve before our eyes like the Cheshire cat, leaving behind only the Festival as the ghost of a grin.

For those of us who love the theatre the prospects are gloomy. But in the twentieth century, with so many alternative entertainments available, theatre for its own sweet sake is a mere chimera. There is no obligation for the community to support it, or for the state to maintain it. The theatre must create a place for itself that will gain it devotion and respect. In Canada this it has failed to do. It may be that, being such a small country, the idea of a theatre of our own was always an illusion. Or it may be that a later, a more principled, less easily influenced generation of actors and writers will rekindle the flame. Still, one cannot help wondering what our theatre might have become if the Stratford miracle had not occurred—that miracle which has been such a blight.

A THEATRE FOR CANADA $^\diamond$

MAVOR MOORE

o

Mavor Moore (b. 1919), author of over a hundred produced plays, musicals, and operas, was able to express an "insider's" view of the development of the Canadian theatre in a 1956 article in the University of Toronto Quarterly.

In the *Elegant Sayings* of the Tibetan Lamas it is written:

Not to be cheered by praise,
Not to be grieved by blame,
But to know thoroughly one's own virtues or powers
Are the characteristics of an excellent man.

By this standard Canadians are often thought to be past praying for in any creed. We look in the mirror and there is nothing there. Some sceptics have even suggested we have no mirror—that is, none or few of the arts reflective of our character, as these arts have reflected the character of other nations past and present. We own the world's most famous blank face.

Now this may be considered no serious matter for anyone but the owner of the face, and indeed his concern with it is often inferred to be more cosmetic than cosmic. Much breadth and ink are spent in controversy about the real nature of the face, most of it about as profitable as sorting maple leaves in a high wind. It serves only to obscure the paramount issue: that face is also a *tabula rasa*, and it is perhaps the most propitious on this distracted globe. Therefore the pattern that emerges on it, whether by accident or design, is of considerable consequence not only to ourselves but to our fellow men.

The importance of the Canadian pattern to the rest of the world remains, perhaps, to be demonstrated decisively, but its importance to Canada is now being generally if belatedly recognized. The travels to

---

$\diamond$ *University of Toronto Quarterly* 26, 1 (Oct. 1956): 1–16. Revised version.

Broadway and Europe of our Stratford Festival Company, the journeys of our opera and ballet companies and other groups, have focussed national attention on the Canadian theatre as never before. Individual artists in the field of literature, music, and the theatre (including mechanical theatre such as film) have long before this made international mark, but never before have large groups bearing the country's name carried our reputation thus far afield. As we observe that thousands of intelligent and influential people in other countries judge Canada on the basis of theatrical representation, it dawns on even the most philistine that our achievements in this arena may conceivably be of serious moment to the country as a whole and not merely to a dilettante few.

The Canadian theatre, therefore, like the stock-market, is bullish these days, and shares in our great national debate: whether to take the bull by the horns or the tail. Shall we lead the monster in our own way, or hang on while those with more experience chart our course for us? Surely the answer to this question should depend neither on dogmatic nationalism nor careless opportunism but on where we want to go, the value of that goal to ourselves and to all men, and our shrewd estimate of the wish and capacity of others to get us there.

Both pro and con factions in the "Canadianism" controversy have helped becloud the atmosphere. The case for a distinctively Canadian culture has been kissed half to death by preciosity and chauvinism: by those who limit culture to the hot-house variety, and those who find the entire catalogue of human virtues singularly Canadian. And more often than not, earnest friends of the cause have fallen prey to a subtle booby-trap: desperately wishing us to be accounted civilized, they have accepted as the indices of civilization those jaded activities esteemed by a few older countries, and scorned the genuinely fresh impulses among us which might, ironically, have produced the recognition they seek.

This twin longing for both self-approbation and approval by the Board of Experts from Out of Town has caused much schizophrenia; as when a "Canadian" company from Stratford visits New York in a play by a sixteenth-century Englishman, staged by an Irishman, designed by an Englishman, music by a Scot, stage-directed by an Australian, and the two leading roles performed by an English actor and an Australian actress. Should we welcome this outside help, or should we spurn it on the grounds that it is not native, even if the native product is less impressive? And what is a native Canadian: how long does it take to become one of us? Is it impertinent of Mr. Douglas Campbell, that fine Scots actor, to call his group "The Canadian Players," or is he conferring an honour by joining us? Is it a cause for national shame that our "National" Ballet requires an English director, our Opera Festival two German-born mentors? Or is it the only course of sense, once it is decided we need these things in a national way, to import skilled artistic labour? And what is a Canadian play: can it be a play about Wales by a born Canadian (Mr. Robertson Davies' *Jig for a Gypsy*) or a play about Canada written by an Irishman (Mr. John Coulter's *Riel*)? Is there a Canadian dialect of the English language? and if so would it be more or less provincial to use it? Should we not then perform Shakespeare and the classics in our native idiom instead of imitating the current speech fashions of London? Or would this be laughed at in Edinburgh? And so on.

These inquiries are the staple of discourse among the dedicated from bohemia to suburbia. But while they are by no means inconsequential from the political point of view, they are so loaded as to defy any answer but the dogmatic and emotional. As I hope we shall see, the important issues cut across these false antitheses.

These who decry a concern with Canadianism are likewise beset by the weeds of dogma and have patent self-tripping booby-traps of their own. There is, for instance, the still widely held if less frequently expressed theory that we are essentially an inarticulate people: too busy, too practical, too athletic to bother with such fripperies as self-expression. Let others with more time to waste entertain us if they will (and all arts are here assumed to have entertainment as their sole function), we are bent on more serious pursuits—for example, the production of whisky, tobacco, and hockey-players. As an otherwise genial stockbroker put it to me: "We're acting out history in this country; we haven't got time to stop and talk about it." It seems no cure for this strong-silent fixation to suggest that from the Roman Empire to the Russian vigorous peoples have proved able to handle both activities without undue strain, or that since human fulfilment involves all man's capacities the two may not be unrelated. If we are indeed inarticulate and uncommunicative we lack the distinguishing mark not only of Canadians but of *homo sapiens*, and should defer not to superior countries but to superior creatures like the bee. At the very least, a Canadian theatre would be a contradiction in terms, not merely a parasitic foreign body.

A corollary of this fixation is the old truism that Canada is a geographical monstrosity in which all the lines of communication run north and south, so that resistance to the American tide—even if desirable—is bootless. Thus Mr. Morley Callaghan in *Maclean's Magazine*: "The wonder of it is that those who are trying to create an anti-American spirit in this country [Mr. Callaghan so labels his opposition] don't take the time to look at a map and then hold their heads. . . . In effect now, we are an island in an American sea." But the inference does not follow. True, the big battalions often win; but God is sometimes not on their side at all, and in fact is reputed to have once aided David against Goliath. The recent actions of some of the United States entertainment unions in curtailing the growing use of Canadian performers in that country suggest that the wrong conclusions may have been drawn from the geographical fact. We can look at the map without holding our collective head; we can even feel it throb with the challenge of so large and amiable a sea to conquer.

The same misconstruction can be placed, and often is, on our ties of another kind to Britain: that we are a cultural appendage even though physically removed. The fallacy should at once become apparent when we remember that Britain has never hesitated to lead—not follow—the entire continent of Europe and indeed parts of the world even more remote than we from her, and that Scotland has never hesitated to lead England. Are we by definition somehow less capable? It is often lamented that we have "no traditions" in the arts, or none except those taken over (sometimes literally) from our friends and neighbours. But if we lack the good old traditions, neither have we—yet—the impedimenta of the bad old traditions and we are in an excellent position to furnish some new ones for everybody. It is more blessed to give than to receive, even to rich old uncles.

Another favourite argument advanced against a national culture consciously sought is that "all art is international." This view is put forward in the best intellectual circles as if it had the combined authority of the United Nations and Mr. T.S. Eliot. We are told that every nation's culture is built by wholesale borrowing, and the fewer the barriers the better; and—by a deft bit of sophistry—barrier is extended to include one's own culture. It is pointed out that English culture first flowered greatly when Chaucer embraced French and Italian influences; that English music reached new heights under the German Händel, and so forth. We are assured that in this modern age, when boundaries melt away in the face of unprecedented travel and communication, we have less excuse than ever for narrow "nationalism." Are we to seek Canadianism at the very time nationalism is everywhere outmoded?

This lofty argument conceals a neat verbal play: the word *inter*national is used to mean *supra*national, so that *exchange between* nations (a multilateral, dynamic process) is translated into the erection of *absolute standards* (that is, unilateral, static values) for *all* nations. We are apparently to believe that a picture is best painted by pouring all the colours into one pot and shaking thoroughly before application. But the world's culture is not, praise heaven, one amorphous grey, but a rich and varied pattern; call each of the colours "national," "regional," "ethnic," or what-have-you, the separate colours must exist before a pattern can be made of them.

An important sense in which all creative art *is* supranational, is, of course, that it does not conform to the structure of our political states. It is, in fact, a human characteristic, not belonging to any particular group of humans. But it is rash to pretend that art can be abstracted from its various local habitations to the extent that it can be given a set of universally applicable laws—though rash theorists are never lacking. The impulse to create is universal among men (perhaps even the cardinal characteristic) but it has never yet been demonstrated that a single set of rules or conventions for the production or evaluation of works of art is adhered to by all men. In fact the reverse would seem true as well as desirable: the more the merrier. And even the fact that some conventions are more widely adhered to than others, or of longer sanding, should not beguile us into clothing them with universality or—as is often the case—divine immutability. In our theatre, this beguilement takes the form, for instance, of the belief that the sole adjudicator for our Dominion Drama Festival must have as his principal qualification a knowledge of theatrical convention elsewhere, preferably in Europe; the assumption being that the same rules hold good everywhere, and that his ability to judge an entry's relevance to our own environment has nothing to do with the case. The essence of conventions is surely that they are changeable—and ought to be changed—when and where they are no longer viable. Are we rather to fit our lives to the convention?

There is a strong current of world opinion which apparently feels we should. No less an authority than the Education Officer of the British Colonial Office, Mr. W.E.S. Ward—a man of vast experience in the clash of old and new cultures—generalizes:

> What usually happens is that a foreign culture appears attractive to the people and for various reasons they desire to acquire it. When the British and other provincials set themselves to learn Latin and the Roman way of life, they did so not through any legal compulsion, or through any legal prohibition of their mother tongue, but because the new ways opened up to them opportunities of social, economic and political advancement. In other words, it paid them to learn Roman ways.

Almost the same words are often applied today to French Canada in relation to the rest of the country, and to Canada as a whole in relation to the United States and/or Britain. And Canadian writers and performers who go abroad thus justify their adoption of more "advanced" dialects and ways. In plain terms, this is an invitation to join the Club That Matters, with the added inference that only a fool would decline.

Mr. Ward, like others who swallow this dangerous piece of humbug, is the victim of a grand illusion. He is confusing scientific and technological superiority with cultural superiority. Changes in the field of the arts are only occasionally a matter of "advancement," and these occasions have to do with technical developments only. Has painting "advanced" since Michelangelo, or drama since Sophocles? Did it honestly "pay" the Incas to learn Spanish ways? Naturally any country which is technologically on top considers its way of living the best available and any move towards it an advance; and it is very easy for anyone wishing to justify the propagation of that way to plead "internationalism" and accuse those who oppose of obstructive "nationalism." In fact, however, the positions are nearly reversed: he who strives to preserve and develop distinctive arts is the broader humanitarian, he who seeks assimilation and conformity the narrower. At the moment the Canadian sculpture receiving most attention from the rest of the world is the carving of the Eskimos; the day they abandon it for copies of Rodin will not mark an advance.

But there remains the brave optimist who tells us to be of good cheer, for no outside influences *can* reach us. Thus Mr. Thor Hansen, distinguished representative of a large oil company in Canada (American-owned):

> Culture is something you cannot buy, something you cannot import, something you cannot learn or produce at will. A writer, an artist or musician cannot sit down and say "Now I will produce culture." Culture is something that evolves out of the simple, enduring elements of everyday life; elements most truthfully expressed in the folk arts and crafts of a nation.

Miss Margaret Aitken, the columnist and Member of Parliament, calls these "wise words to allay all those fears" (about foreign pressures). They seem to me not only not wise but among the more naïve I have ever read. Mr. Hansen and I cannot have shared access to the same history books. Does he seriously believe that any group is *not* subject to influences other than the "simple, enduring elements" of our own local "everyday life"? Did the Spanish have no effect on South America, the British none on India? Has he never met a Canadian Indian and asked him what happened to his folk arts and crafts? Do Africans acquire a taste for radio and television by a sort of internal combustion? It may well be that any writer, etc., who is daft enough to announce as he sits down to create "Now I will produce culture" may fail to do so: it seems to me a stupid way to begin anything. But this does not prevent artists (amateur and professional) from producing culture, and unless we have been grossly misinformed they have been doing just that for thousands of years. The simple elements of everyday life may not endure at all unless pains are taken by someone to see that they do. Mr. Hansen is mistaking the soil for the fruits thereof, or at best the roots for the flowers. Culture, I suggest, can come to a country in all the ways he says it cannot and more besides. And while it is true the wish or the will cannot alone produce a culture, the desire and the will to move our creative life in a certain direction is a big help in getting there. One thing is sure: if we fail to move it ourselves others will more it for us, because we cannot stand still culturally any move than we can politically or economically.

A nation is the focal point for the common habits, desires, and aspirations—political, social, economic, cultural—of a group of people. A geographical area is a nation only to the extent it succeeds in representing these, a vigorous nation only in so far as it nurtures and develops them, and a worthy member of the world community only in so far as it devotes its increase to the common good. It will not achieve these ends by self-abnegation.

○

Of all the arguments adduced against self-determination, however, perhaps the most persuasive is that we are, as a people, so like the British and/or Americans that the differences are negligible and are bound to become less. Mr. Callaghan again:

> What is involved here is all that shapes a culture—the economic forces, all the methods of production and distribution, the way people dress and eat, the songs they sing, the games they play and above all the language. When you try to resist these forces by sheer acts of will [see above] you can be "different" all right. Young Canadians, for example, could start wearing togas and sandals. But nothing truly indigenous can come out of it. Cultures don't grow in this style, anyway; they grow like cabbages.

Mr. Callaghan has as deliberately chosen an absurd figure for his example of wilful difference as he has carelessly chosen one for culture: I should hate to be a partner in his farm, where cabbages fend for themselves. But let us examine this theory that nothing indigenous can come from a conscious attempt to be different.

There are actually hundreds of ways in which our daily lives differ from those of our neighbours, from political parties to newspapers to television to divorce and back again. They may not be as obvious to us as the differences between ourselves and the Japanese; but let us remember that to many westerners all orientals are indistinguishable. It depends where you sit. Saying that things Canadian are not different often means only that when we look at Canadian life through British or American spectacles, we see only what is compatible with those lenses. We see what we are looking for. It is this ingenious device that gives rise, for instance, to the complaint—as frequently lodged by ourselves as by incomers—that we have "no theatre" in Canada. Not a different theatre, notice, but no theatre, or "none to speak of." Not finding theatre of a kind one is accustomed to, or has been taught to believe is the only sort God recognizes, one not unnaturally assumes there is none of any kind, remaining blind to the considerable activity of a kind one does not think to look for. Toronto, for example, is a larger television production centre than either London or Paris. I once met a Parisian lady in New York who complained of the absence of "true" theatre there!

The upshot of thus borrowing the cultural yardstick along with the culture is that whatever it does not measure is presumed to be not worth measuring. It is not only different but thereby indifferent. Without our own yardstick, we surrender our rights along with our responsibilities and enter a new period of colonialism, our tastes dictated by others more sure of theirs than we of ours. It is no excuse, either, to plead that others' tastes are already formed (and thus available as a standard), while ours are only aforming. We may feel that the Americans, the British, the French know for sure what criteria to apply to a novel, a painting, a play; but even if this were true their criteria could not be static: they might change tomorrow. The truth is that we have much that is discernibly Canadian, but like the stepmother when the prince's emissary comes to call, we send little homebody upstairs in the belief she doesn't qualify. And yet our Cinderella may be the very girl the prince is looking for.

It would be a dull world if the rest of mankind were as overmodest as we. By occidental standards an oriental singer can scarcely sing at all: he can produce neither a "proper" tone nor quality nor can he sustain a pitch without wobbling. But to sing our kind of music is not what an oriental singer is trying to do. And if he had thrown away his own values and embraced European models, European music itself would be the sufferer, for it is now being fed and transformed by eastern influences. To look someone else in the face and say "Yes, I admire your way of doing things, but your situation is not quite mine and for myself I prefer another way"—this is not the mere childish perverseness rightly parodied in Mr. Callaghan's image of sandals and togas, but a healthy adult attitude. When the French impressionist painters revolutionized the techniques of painting they did not first denounce da Vinci and Rembrandt as fakes; they simply looked at things in a new way themselves and found a sincere mode of expression for what they saw. Fools among the critics and the public may have fought over whether the traditional or the new methods were "superior"; time's wisdom now allows us to enjoy both. Without the "differences" we should be the poorer.

This perhaps argues that we should cling to whatever already-established standards we have; but does it also argue that we should consciously try to be different while in the growing stages? Well, let us take a look at the formative stages of some of those cultural models nowadays held up for us to imitate.

There is a fallacy—supported mainly by teachers and professional critics, I am sorry to say, who have a vested interest in their own knowledge—that new art is invariably built upon the old. The brick-layer likes to think he knows all about building, and resents the rise of the cement-pourer. Now while a great many artists have wrought fine things out of old cloth (especially antiquarians like Morris), it is nonsense to suppose that mastery of old techniques will automatically produce something worthwhile, or even that it is the best way to begin. It is not infrequently the worst. It would be truer to say that those now considered great masters were flouters, not followers of tradition. And it is astonishing to discover how many of those we think of as representative of their time and place in history were thought in that time and place to be not only radical but *incompetent*.

Those who find our own local customs deplorably amateur might recall, for instance, that Shakespeare was long and widely held to be talented but illiterate and unskilled. His contemporary Ben Jonson was generally judged his superior, largely because he followed the classical masters; and Jonson himself, though an admirer of Shakespeare, regretted his inability to "blot" his own lines and his lack of classical training. A century and a half later Voltaire considered him inferior to Dryden. Dryden agreed:

> Our improprieties are less frequent and less gross than theirs (the Elizabethans. . . . Malice and partiality set aside, let any man, who understands English, read diligently the works of Shakespeare and Fletcher, and I dare undertake, that he will find in every page either some solecism of speech, or some notorious flaw in sense. . . . But the times were ignorant in which they lived. Poetry was then, if not in its infancy among us, at least not arrived to its full vigour and maturity: witness the lameness of their plots, many of which were made up of some ridiculous incoherent story . . . either grounded in impossibilities or so meanly written, that the comedy neither caused you mirth, nor the serious parts your concernment. . . . Those who call theirs the Golden Age of Poetry have only this reason for it, that they were content with acorns before they knew the use of bread.

Dryden, to do him justice, genuinely loved "the divine Shakespeare," and perhaps for this reason undertook to "correct" many of his plays—in the belief that with the best of intentions the Elizabethan simply did not know how these things were done. "The critic was willing to concede greatness of soul to Shakespeare," writes Spencer in his *Shakespeare Improved*, "but *neither a civilized taste nor a competent craftsmanship.*"

Germany is renowned for her music. Who would you say epitomized that genius: Bach? Mozart? Beethoven? Wagner? The leading German critic of Bach's day wrote: "His compositions are devoid of beauty, harmony and clarity of melody." Or Mozart, if you prefer: "Nobody would overlook the talented man in Mozart; but I have never heard a single profound expert praise him as a correct, much less a perfect composer." Beethoven they found "harsh and ugly," and bitterly scolded him for breaking the rules. The violent antagonism aroused by Wagner's operas is too famous to need repetition. The point is not that these critics were wrong—this needs no labouring—but why they missed the boat: they falsely assumed that intentional infidelity to the "rules," or rather fidelity to much deeper impulses, was the result of inability or ignorance!

Closer to our own times, here is the distinguished critic of the London *Observer* writing ten years after George Gershwin's "Rhapsody in Blue" was first heard: "No American composer of importance has appeared (with the possible exception of Macdowell, who is dead), which is not surprising when we observe that none has been recognized by the Americans themselves." Change the nationality and the quotation might well be from the recent London *Times* symposium on Canada. But the explanation for this condescension is so pertinent to our own situation that I must include it here as given by David Ewen, the American critic:

> The truth is that while many of us acclaimed the Rhapsody in 1924 for its charm, originality and native traits, few of us realized how truly important this music really was. Those of us who had spent a lifetime in concert hall and conservatory were somewhat pedantically disconcerted by its technical lapses. . . . We were right about those faults—they strike us anew each time we hear the work. But what we failed to realize at the time was that the Rhapsody had qualities that no deficiency in technique could kill; and the most important of these qualities was its vitality. . . . However much Gershwin was praised by critics and serious musicians when he was alive, such praise was inevitably tempered with reservations: he was talented; he exerted an influence; his music was both entertaining and exciting—but both he and his music were of ephemeral importance. A handful of years is, obviously, too short a period to measure anyone's posthumous importance. But one thing is reasonably sure about Gershwin's: it is by no means ephemeral.

The latest episode in this story is the immense and unique success in postwar Europe of Gershwin's opera "Porgy and Bess," which despite its abysmal picture of American life has proved the ablest of all United States ambassadors and firmly enthroned its composer as the great American artist the London *Observer* failed to observe. Forgotten are his contemporaries who slavishly learned their correct lessons; they failed to learn the most important of them all: that live things are not created out of dead tissue.

In Canada we have had one superb chance to learn this lesson, but we seem to be poor pupils. Perhaps the sole product of our art and imagination to have made a recognizably Canadian dent in the world's consciousness to date is the painting of Tom Thomson and the Group of Seven. Mr. Vincent Massey tells the tale in his *On Being Canadian*:

> We, of course, know the facts, how a group of gifted artists a generation ago *turned their backs on Europe—quite deliberately*—and surrendered themselves to their own environment, striving to uncover its secret. The inevitable happened. The Canadian landscape took possession of them. They abandoned the methods and techniques which were alien to Canada, and recorded its beauty faithfully in the clear lights, bold lines and strong colours which belonged to it. They had to struggle against strong opposition, those pioneers, among colleagues and the general public as well, but opposition is better than indifference. It produces an argument, and the pioneers won their case and achieved recognition. In Canadian painting, the revolutionary of a generation ago has become the "old master" of today.

From Shakespeare to Thomson the so-called incompetents have triumphed in their vitality and overthrown the sterile patterns of other places and other times. Mankind is a creative being, and he must keep on creating or wither away. Correctness, obedience to dead rules—this way sterility lies. Said the *Magazin der Musik* of Vienna in 1787:

> The works of Kuzelich remain alive and are welcomed everywhere, but Mozart's compositions do not unanimously please. He has *a decided inclination for the unusual.*

Anybody here know Kuzelich?

ɔ

The case of Shakespeare is particularly interesting because he is the most important playwright in Canada. Thanks to him our theatre has achieved a fame denied it when performing the works of mere local authors: our Shakespeare Festival at Ontario's Stratford has brought acclaim to Canadian actors and to their British mentors in the directing, designing, and other departments, has emphasized the apparent lack of Canadian playwrights, and has brought to a head—as it continues to have British supervision—the whole issue of imported help.

Even though in its past (fourth) season the festival hired no foreign stars, it is believed by many that its success has been due largely to our having the humble good sense to copy the masters. The same might be said of three other important theatrical enterprises: Vancouver's Theatre under the Stars, which produces American musicals; Toronto's Crest Theatre, which produces mainly British and American revivals (three Canadian plays in three years) under the guidance of an English administrator, director, and designer; and Montreal's Théâtre du Nouveau Monde, which has made its greatest reputation playing Molière. (A classic, of course, is the heritage of all of us and may become our own in a freshly imagined version). But there is a pivotal ambiguity in the policy of imitation: what is to be imitated?

Dryden, in a moment of rare moving candour, said of his attempts to improve Shakespeare: "... but I fear (at least let me fear it for myself) that we, who ape his sounding words, have nothing of his thought, but are all outside."

In other words, what is really most valuable in Shakespeare, as in all great creators, is in the strictest sense of the word inimitable: a personal vision of life and the vitality with which it is expressed. The rest—the "sounding words," the tricks of presentation, what is often called "technique"—is inessential. If anything is apparent from history it is surely that the impulse comes first, the technique for implementing it only afterward, in fact as a result. Forms per se are bound to be empty and hollow things if they are divorced from the inspiration that sought them out. If it is the form we imitate, we shall deservedly end up with a carbon copy of someone else's personality, recognizably Canadian only in its weakness.

The excuse that is usually given for repeating the successes of other lands and for bringing in outsiders to show us how these things are done in the best circles is that the public is pre-sold on them; that whether we like it or not Canadian audiences are in tune with the British or American product and its standard. This belief is not quite supported by the facts. The two most popular theatrical productions in both French and English Canada have been entirely Canadian in cast, script, music, design, and direction— and it is noteworthy that the principal contributors to neither had training abroad: the play *Ti-Coq*, which ran for nine months in Montreal in French, and the review *Spring Thaw*, an annual Toronto affair which this year ran for almost four months. No imported production has ever run for so long. Coincidentally, the author of *Ti-Coq*, the remarkable comedian Gratien Gélinas, first made his name in review, which would seem to indicate a Canadian fondness for this form. I believe the reason for its popularity is that it provides an audience with an experience it cannot get at plays or films from abroad; its very local topicality allows it to belong to its audience in a way impossible for outsiders to achieve. (The fact that it is a minor form of theatre elsewhere should bother only those who choose to borrow foreign definitions of "theatre.") Certainly it has permitted us to develop satire to a keener edge than other forms so far; and perhaps our proximity to the United States will afford us exercise in that direction. The Irish have proved the sharpest satirists of the British scene.

But—it may be argued—it is all very well to say that Canadians will attend Canadian shows; how can we hold up our heads until we can compete in the world market on that market's own terms?

The irony of this position is staggering. New Yorkers and Londoners consider us hicks (when they do) precisely because we meekly accept the worst they have to offer as holy writ. It is not obvious that, if they are as bright as we seem to think, by the time we catch up to their present modes they will be ahead again? The styles we have so much admired and copied will already be out of date, probably retired by a new style from some country which had the wit to recognize and believe in its own. The attention lavished on Ontario's Stratford has proved at least that when we do something new and vital on our own soil the world will turn to look. It should be plain to all that the world will not turn aside to notice how well we imitate what they can do better and already take for granted.

But wait! Did we not just now confess that Stratford owed much if not all to imported help? And other prominent ventures too? Let us finally examine the nature of that contribution.

There have been two giants from abroad in recent times whose presence among us has galvanized our artistic life: John Grierson, the first head of the National Film Board, and Tyrone Guthrie, the first director of the Stratford Festival. It is of the utmost importance that we realize just what it was they brought: they were both notable, before they ever came here, as *tradition-breakers*. Non-conformists in their own societies, they brought as their most precious baggage their iconoclasm. To each of them—and I remember well the first conversations Dr. Guthrie held when he arrived in Toronto that fateful July five years ago—the appealing thing about the Canadian situation was the opportunity to create something new: the *tabula rasa* I have spoken of. Each saw in Canada the resources both human and economic to realize their visions without the encumbrance of tradition. And both created something here it would have been impossible to do elsewhere. The unique thing they brought with them was a bounding idea, and the unique thing that met them on arrival was Canada's capacity to project it: it was the meeting of these two forces that produced the explosion.

If proof were needed that it was the spirit of newness which mattered, it was surely provided by the success of Dr. Guthrie's Stratford presentations compared with the failure of his production of *Tamburlaine*, which was a frank attempt to recreate a production he had made previously in England (it rehearsed here for only two weeks) on a traditional stage.

Does this mean that we should go out of our way to eschew skills brought here by a host of other new Canadians and visitors? I think it means rather that we should use *all* skills that serve *our own ends*. We should be grateful for all the know-how we can get which is prepared to produce creative power by uniting with our inspiration instead of stifling it. In this sense we cannot learn too much. The more we become aware of the infinite variety of creative techniques in the world, the less extravagant credence we shall place in the divine perfection of any one of them. And the greater value we shall place upon our position of freedom to develop our own. To learn that little Denmark has a ballet which is distinctive but the envy of dancers everywhere; that China has comedians whose miming is quite unlike our own version of comedy but still manages to convulse occidental observers; that Japan has a film industry second in size only to that of the United States; or even that Hottentots like their eggs rotten—all this should give us the courage to be ourselves. We do not need to put on the dog, of whatever breed; and to do so is to throw away not only our dearest advantage, but one of the world's best hopes.

The measure of the newcomer's usefulness as a member of our national community and the larger international community must be his grasp of this fundamental point. It has little to do with his clinging to skills acquired in other places to fit other situations, and everything to do with his readiness to toss them out, like excess baggage, on the exciting journey of exploration we are taking here. In brief: we should embrace as brothers all those willing to make one with us, and reject with every means at our disposal all those who come attempting to impose on a new land what has been fashionable in an old. We should also do battle with their accomplices among us who, flattered by acquaintance with celebrities, belittle their countrymen in a tragically mistaken effort to curry favour with the élite. Both of these species are barnacles on the ship.

Last year the United States itself had an opportunity to give substance to an enterprise similar to our Stratford Festival. With all their know-how they muffed it. Wrote the *New York Times'* Brooks Atkinson of the Stratford, Connecticut, Festival:

> It would be appropriate to begin the new enterprise with a new idea, as the people in Stratford, Ontario, did three years ago. In Ontario they are still keeping the idea fresh with the *Julius Caesar* they opened there on June 27. But the *Julius Caesar* at the Connecticut Stratford is still dreaming wistfully of Sir Henry Irving and Sir Beerbohm Tree.

Too many Canadians still cannot see the pinewoods for the Beerbohm Trees.

What matters in the long run is not that we are Canadian, but that *because* we are Canadian we have an unparalleled opportunity to contribute something new and vital to a world that needs and wants it, and expects it of us. If we miss the chance, our face in history should be not only blank but red.

TRENDS IN CANADIAN
THEATRE◇

THOMAS B. HENDRY

o

Written for the American theatre journal TDR *in 1965, the following article is less a look at trends in Canadian theatre than it is an early study of one of the country's first regional theatres, the Manitoba Theatre Centre, which was co-founded by Tom Hendry and John Hirsch (1930–89).*

During the past ten years, a theatre modelled more on European patterns than on anything to be found in North America has arisen in Canada and has established itself in the principal cities—Vancouver, Winnipeg, Toronto, Montreal, and Halifax—from coast to coast.

This European look is not surprising: of 11 Canadian Artistic Directors, five are European by birth, three are French-Canadians whose first influences in professional theatre came from France, and only three are English-speaking Canadians whose first experiences in theatre were "North American"—of these, one has been strongly influenced by observation of the English repertory system and a second by the work of the Berliner Ensemble; the third is a rugged individualist who runs Canada's only frankly profit-seeking producing organization. All the other theatres are non-profit organizations administered by professionals under the guidance of volunteer Community Boards of Governors.

A major pressure toward non-profit operations is the existence of the Canada Council, a non-political body created by the Government of Canada in 1957, but allowed to operate autonomously on the revenue from a $50 000 000 endowment fund. The Council has concentrated its institutional support of the performing arts in the area of non-profit community-based organizations. Recently, the source of the Council's money was altered

◇ *Tulane Drama Review* 10, 1 (Fall 1965): 62–69

somewhat when a $10 000 000 unconditional income grant was made by the Government of Canada. The length of time during which this money will be spent has not been announced, but it is assumed it will be three years.

At the moment none of this recent windfall has been committed, so that for the purposes of discussion I will use the Council's pre-1965 income of $3 085 000, which is disbursed in the following areas: grants to arts organizations and individual artists, $1 370 000; grants to individuals and organizations concerned with the humanities and social sciences, $1 215 000; administrative costs, $500 000.

During the fiscal year ending June 30th, 1964, 18 theatre, ballet, and opera groups received from the Canada Council a total of $578 000 in grants ranging from $1000 to $86 500. Each grant is made on the basis of the facts of the particular case and no rules of thumb which would indicate reasons for the size of the grants are apparent.

An interesting feature of national subsidy comes to mind when one examines the total subsidy picture in Canada. The same eighteen organizations which received the Canada Council's $578 000 also received provincial subsidies totalling just under $500 000, municipal subsidies totalling just under $250 000, and private subsidy totalling just over $550 000, for a total of almost $1 900 000. During the same period their earned income was just short of $3 650 000, and the entire group sustained deficits totalling about $200 000.

Taking these facts into consideration, certain questions come to mind: 1) Was the provision of federal assistance the catalyst which liberated the assistance funds in other areas? Which came first? 2) Does the provision of federal subsidy provoke a move "into opposition," as it were, in the provincial, municipal, and private sectors? This seems possible, since three organizations domiciled in Quebec, the province most jealous of its identity, receive $88 000 from the Canada Council and $179 000 from other sources; three similar organizations in English-Canada received $105 000 from the Canada Council and slightly over $210 000 from other sources. Regional location does not seem to affect the desire to spread the possible influence-effect of subsidy. 3) Are there discernible patterns in subsidy? The broad pattern seems to be one-third federal, one-third provincial, one-third private. However, out of $550 000 given by private sources, only $16 000 was given to organizations in the Province of Quebec; the difference was made up by provincial and municipal giving. It is probable that in the United States, if a decision for subsidy is made, the pattern will eventually approximate that of English-Canada, rather than French-Canada. Twelve theatre, ballet, and opera companies in English-Canada receive operating subsidies:

From the Canada Council	$414 000	30%
From provincial sources	258 000	19%
From municipal sources	165 000	12%
From private sources	532 000	39%
	$1 369 000	100%

Despite the eloquent arguments of many who feel that private giving is the cornerstone, my own experience indicates that it is the receipt of a grant from the Canada Council which sets the seal of approval on a given group and tends to make subsidies from other sources more likely. The Council's prestige in matters of discretion—it has backed only one "loser" of any consequence during eight years of operation—is such that givers tend to breathe more easily when writing out checks to organizations known to have continuing Canada Council support. If nothing else, the existence of the Council has created a set of standards which others have tended to accept.

This is not entirely to the good, because it tends to create and perpetuate an artistic Establishment which receives Council support and therefore drains off a high percentage of the other support available. In the present situation of the performing arts in North America, still a long way from reaching anything like a popular audience—such as that enjoyed by films—many consider that anything is beneficial which tends to concentrate available resources into limited areas where these resources are most likely to do some good. This is arguable, and will become increasingly so as the regional spread of the performing arts continues in Canada.

THE COMPANIES

The Canadian professional theatre has its roots in the between-the-wars and post-war amateur theatre. Almost all of the people now in charge of theatres in Canada received their basic experience in amateur companies, which were particularly receptive to the attentions and participation of European immigrants who brought with them a consciousness of European theatre values, to add to that of those who, after a period in the French-speaking Canadian amateur theatre, went to France for training. All of these people found a natural focus for their aspirations in the work of Tyrone Guthrie who, in 1953, founded the Stratford Shakespearean Festival in Stratford, Ontario, the world's most gorgeous summer stock operation and our most successful and internationally influential theatre.

Stratford created a model for indigenous Canadian theatre: a non-profit organization, unconcerned with the values of New York, unashamedly using imported personnel where Canadian expertise was lacking, equally unashamedly welcoming subsidy support in return for placing its destiny—at a policy-making level—in the hands of a volunteer citizen Board of Governors, and representative of the community in which it found itself. In 12 years there has been little deviation from this pattern.

One learns in examining the affairs of theatres to avoid comparisons, especially on a methodological and operational level, but certain broad generalizations are possible in discussing organizations which, in detail, are found to be as different as day and night. In general, the theatres of Canada: 1) Depend to some extent on subscription sales to identify and organize their audiences, or are moving rapidly towards doing so. 2) Play a 25–30 week season in their home city, out of which they do some touring. 3) Have effected some form of liaison with educational authorities, on whom they depend to supply some portion of their audiences. 4) Mount consecutive productions rather than repertory seasons. Here Stratford and the Neptune

Theatre, in Halifax, are notable exceptions, but in general it has been found that Canadian audiences demand a greater range of versatility than the Canadian actors whom most theatres are able to afford are yet able to supply. 5) Present a broad spectrum of dramatic material ranging from the blandly pseudo-avant-garde (*Oh, Dad!*) through the conservative classics—*École des Femmes* (*Taming of the Shrew* for English-speaking audiences) to the frankly commercial (*Les Oeufs de l'Autruche*, *The Gazebo*), with a sprinkling, particularly in French, of original work (*Klondyke!*, *All About Us*.)

A consideration, in terms of repertoire offered, of financial data will give an idea of the reception accorded the Manitoba Theatre Centre over the seven years since its inception, during the first five of which I served as co-founder (with John Hirsch) and first Administrator.

The Centre is the most successful of the Canadian regional theatres and in terms of general quality is, in my own biased opinion, slightly inferior to the Stratford (Ontario) Festival, which I put first among the group, and in most cases equal to the Minnesota Theatre Company.

The theatre is situated in a city of 450 000, which has very large ethnic minorities who simply refuse to go to the theatre. The reachable population, we estimated, was closer to 200 000. We were fortunate in having in Winnipeg a Jewish community of approximately 25 000, who provided the firm audience-foundation upon which we built the theatre.

Examination of the financial data (see table 1, pp. 256–57) will suggest some of the problems encountered in founding and expanding this type of operation. The theatre was a natural outgrowth of the Winnipeg community. Both Hirsch and I were residents (I was born there; he arrived from Hungary in 1947). To say we were not influenced by Broadway is a large understatement: I saw my first professional play during our second season, when we engaged a fully-professional cast for *Look Back in Anger*.

Examination of the repertoire discloses a naïve attempt in the early years to include plays we imagined would be box-office successes; eventually we moved to a different set of standards and simply presented plays which interested our Artistic Director both in themselves and as components of a list of plays he felt ought to be presented in any community. Some may quarrel that this sets up, in theatrical terms, a "Five-Foot-Shelf of Books" concept, but it is similar to a concept held by Max Reinhardt, who had fairly good ideas in general. Also, we tried to choose plays which our Artistic Director felt we could do justice to in production quality.

In general, in the early years, we were dealing with an audience which knew nothing of theatre. Our general public-relations approach to the community attempted to satisfy three main aims: 1) to convince the community that attendance at a theatre, like reading, writing, wearing shoes, or eating with cutlery, was a good civilized thing to do; 2) to convince the community that the Centre had their theatrical best interests at heart and that we could be relied upon to give them their money's worth in a responsible manner; 3) to convince the community that there were certain jobs, such as supplying the "illustrations" for those young people studying drama, that only a professional theatre could do really well.

At the time of its founding, the Centre had two assets—a 15-year lease on a theatre in fairly good operating condition, and $7000 in the bank. By the time we had mounted our first fully-professional season, during the fall, winter, and spring of 1961–1962, our beginning budget had grown 400% and, in a small way, we had gone into the fund-raising business.

Even while raising money, we attempted to extend our area of communication with the community. We did not solicit donations. We sold memberships of varying value, treated our Members as shareholders, sent them regular information, and invited them to the theatre to hear speakers like Tyrone Guthrie.

Throughout the Centre's existence those involved have carried out very heavy speaking schedules among service clubs, youth organizations, and church groups. Indeed, in the very early years we re-hired even artistic staff, to some extent, on the basis of their willingness to speak frequently and without fee, on behalf of the Centre. As the quality of work upon the Centre's stage has improved and knowledge of its existence has permeated the community, the need for this kind of activity has lessened somewhat. To a great extent it has been replaced, as a missionary activity, by tours to high schools by Centre companies presenting excerpts from plays which are being studied as part of the curricula.

As the community has become more aware of its need for the Centre, both earned income and subsidy have steadily increased. Expansion of the budget has been steady. 1963–1964's unfortunate over-expansion has been corrected, and because the theatre is thoroughly rooted in the community what might have proved, in another operation, to be fatal has only created a small setback. To compensate for last year's difficulties the Centre sensibly decided to cut back on touring activity, which in Western Canada is a source of steady loss.

The Centre is the country's leading regional theatre and is watched closely by other theatres. As the Centre continues to consolidate its position and to re-occupy areas from which it has temporarily withdrawn, it is probable that—in terms of scope of operation—it will become even more of a model for the others to follow and that as a result many theatres still to be founded in Canada will, like the Manitoba Theatre Centre: offer a "major subscription series" comprising a broad spectrum of theatrical experience; operate small studio theatres which can eventually house original work not yet ready for the main stages; co-ordinate their work with that of educational authorities; operate some form of School of Theatre Appreciation, designed to up-grade audience taste during the formative pre-teen and teen years of a young person's life; accept the need for sizable subsidy from the outset; seek, through many forms of proselytizing activity, to establish contact and continuing communication between the theatre and its community.

Because the amateur movement in theatre in Canada is still well established and widespread, there are a number of cities which have a nucleus audience capable of being rapidly expanded, and a population large enough to provide, during the theatre's early years, sufficient ticket sales to sustain the theatre. Experience in Winnipeg, Halifax, and Vancouver indicates that

TABLE   1   *MANITOBA THEATRE CENTRE
GROWTH CHART
(of a theatre operating in a city
of 450 000)*

	1957–58	1958–59	1959–60
October:	Remarkable Mr. Pennypacker	A Hatful of Rain	Solid Gold Cadillac
November:	An Italian Straw Hat	Blithe Spirit	Tea & Sympathy
December:	The Crucible	Teach Me How to Cry	On Borrowed Time
January:	Alice in Wonderland	The Glass Menagerie	Reclining Figure
February:	Misalliance	Born Yesterday	Look Back in Anger
March:	Death of a Salesman	Ring 'Round the Moon	Volpone
April:	The Rainmaker	Diary of Anne Frank	Teahouse of the August Moon
May:	Arsenic & Old Lace	Of Mice & Men	Anastasia

INCOME:			
Season Tickets	$ 7 200	$15 500	$ 19 000
Casual Tickets	29 000	26 000	26 300
Sundry & Rent	10 650	16 700	5 000
Canada Council	—	—	10 000
City & Province	—	—	7 300
Private Aid	4 250	5 500	25 400
Total Income	51 100	63 700	93 000
EXPENDITURE:			
Production	25 130	30 100	54 000
Promotion	5 954	12 200	18 800
House & Admin.	15 316	23 200	25 700
Studio & School	—	—	4 200
Tours	—	—	—
Total Expenses	46 400	65 500	102 700
NET:	$ 4 700	–$ 1 800	–$ 9 700
Performances	47	63	84
Subscribers	700	1 300	1 800
Attendance	15 000	32 000	44 000
Budget Increase		41%	57%

Note: 1957–58 figures represent combined results of M.T.C.'s two predecessor organizations—
Winnipeg Little Theatre (amateur) and Theatre 77 (semi-professional). All sums are in Canadian
dollars.

MANITOBA THEATRE CENTRE
GROWTH CHART (cont.)

1960–61	1961–62	1962–63	1963–64	1964–65 (Budget)
Mister Roberts	Lady's Not for Burning	Bonfires (Revue)	Private Lives	Hay Fever
Gaslight	Speaking of Murder	Once More With Feeling	Pygmalion	All About Us
Streetcar Named Desire	Playboy of the Western World	Enemy of the People	The Hostage	Mother Courage
Biggest Thief in Town	Arms & the Man	Mrs. Warren's Profession	Midsummer Night's Dream	Taming of the Shrew
Dark of the Moon	The Boy Friend	Pal Joey	Little Mary Sunshine	Irma La Douce
Juno & the Paycock	Separate Tables	Summer of the 17th Doll	Five Finger Exercise	Heartbreak House
Visit to a Small Planet	Thieves' Carnival	The Caretaker	The Gazebo	Who's Afraid of V. Woolf
The Fourposter	Look Ahead	A Very Close Family	Cat on a Hot Tin Roof	Typists & Tiger
$40 100	$ 54 500	$ 62 200	$ 89 000	$102 000
33 900	69 500	84 400	85 300	76 000
16 300	15 500	8 400	14 500	23 650
17 000	30 000	33 000	35 000	35 000
11 500	14 000	33 000	34 500	45 000
22 800	31 600	34 400	41 000	52 000
141 600	215 100	255 400	299 300	333 650
64 200	112 000	128 300	155 500	172 500
18 800	34 100	46 600	52 000	37 800
50 500	60 000	63 400	92 700	89 900
4 500	12 300	17 600	19 500	25 500
3 100	4 600	10 300	29 000	7 300
141 100	223 000	266 200	348 700	333 000
$ 500	–$ 7 900	–$ 10 800	–$ 49 400	$ 650
120	224	258	280	240
2 700	3 200	3 800	4 200	5 100
64 000	112 000	125 000	135 000	110 000
37%	78%	20%	32%	–4%

more than 10% of the reachable population is willing to become theatre-goers if properly and vigorously asked to do so—always provided that the quality of work is satisfactory, and improving.

The very strength of the amateur movement is, to some extent, inhibiting the spread of professional theatre, but mostly it is felt by default. Our lack of potential artistic directors and business administrators is a far more serious reason for the present pause in expansion.

The increased resources which will flow into our theatres, thanks to the Council's recent $10 000 000 increase in funds, will eventually have the effect of keeping in Canada many of the talented young people who, until now, have gone abroad to seek careers in theatre. Among them we will surely find those we need.

Our acceptance of European values, and of the people who bring them, together with the—to them—familiar atmosphere we are creating leads me to believe that, for a time, we will be able to continue to count on importing the largest percentage of our artistic leadership in theatre. This leadership, if past experience is any criterion, should provide the human resources to bridge the gap until the day arrives when young Canadians, who from their formative years have grown up in an easy and natural relationship with responsible professional theatre, come along and take over.

STRATFORD AFTER
FIFTEEN YEARS ◇

NATHAN COHEN

O

A close look at the Stratford Festival's first 15 years by the man who was probably its fiercest critic.

Buy the end of its 15th season, the Stratford Festival has become completely mythologized. Michael Langham, who followed Sir Tyrone Guthrie (then Mr. Guthrie) as its artistic director, has bequeathed a bumper estate to his handpicked heirs, Jean Gascon and John Hirsch.

In the Festival's first year, the programme consisted of two plays, *Richard the Third*, and *All's Well That Ends Well*, and 16 recitals. The season, which began July 13, was set for five weeks, and went a week longer. The total attendance was 68 000. The expenditures came to $157 000.

Look at things now. The tent which originally enclosed the pie-shaped auditorium has given way to a permanent building, the world's first indoor circular playhouse. The Festival also owns the Avon, a proscenium arch house with a thrust stage. Between them, the Festival and Avon are valued at $4 million, and are noteworthy for their equipment and comfort.

The 1967 season began June 12 and concluded October 14. The last month was reserved for performances, followed by question and answer periods, for groups of high school students from (mainly) Ontario and Quebec, and from other parts of Canada and the U.S. Four productions were given in the Festival theatre: Shakespeare's *Antony and Cleopatra*, *Richard the Third*, and *The Merry Wives of Windsor*, and Gogol's farce about provincial Russian bureaucracy in Czarist times, *The Government Inspector*. Three more productions—*Colors in the Dark*, a new play by James Reaney,

---

◇ *Queen's Quarterly* 75, 1 (Spring 1968): 35–61. Reprinted with permission of the estate of Nathan Cohen.

and two operas, Mozart's *Cosi Fan Tutte* and Britten's *Albert Herring*—were done in the Avon.[1]

The final programme under Mr. Langham's stewardship also included a series of solo and orchestral concerts on eight weekends in the Festival theatre, two weeklong seminars in which many distinguished Shakespearean exegetists took part, book exhibits, and a retrospective display of posters, programmes, costumes and models describing one hundred years of Canadian theatre.

For the 1967 season the budget came to $1 700 000. The attendance was just over 400 000. The total personnel, including actors, stagehands, costumiers, painters, carpenters, boxoffice, promotion, clerical and so on, reached 500 at the peak period. There is a permanent staff of 45.

When the Festival was launched, Stratford was a rural community of some 20 000 people with a dying industry as a railroad spur. Shakespeare has brought it prosperity in the shape of 14 new businesses giving 3500 jobs and, to date, $5 million in tourist income.

The Festival company is the only Canadian performing arts group with a genuine international reputation. It has appeared in Edinburgh (1956), New York (1956, 1958), and Chichester (1964). It has been featured on Canadian television (Peer Gynt, 1958, and *Henry the Fifth*, 1956), on American television (*The Afflictions of Love*, 1963, presented in seven American cities), and on Telstar. It has been shown on films (*Oedipus Rex*), and is the subject of a widely-seen National Film Board production. It has been recorded. Its Gilbert and Sullivan company appeared throughout the United States (1960–61–62), and briefly in London, England, 1962 with *HMS Pinafore* and *The Pirates of Penzance*.

In theatre circles abroad, the Stratford Festival is a Canadian's card of entry. I have been asked about it in such unexpected places as Skopje in Yugoslavia and Bangkok in Thailand. In Tokyo, a Japanese actor wanted to know how his performance of Cyrano de Bergerac compared with Christopher Plummer's in Stratford. In Hong Kong, an English language clerk in the Communist Book Shop struck up a conversation. He knew three things about Canada. It was "a satellite of the American imperialist warmongers." The Peking Opera had performed in Vancouver and Toronto, over the objections and conspiracies of the State Department, and was warmly welcomed by "the progressive and peaceloving forces led by the determined workers." And finally "you have a respect for your classics of culture, such as your Shakespeare."

At home, the Festival's influence is extensive. Its success, following on the Massey Commission report of 1951, helped to oil the way for the formation of the Canada Council. It has stimulated an interest in professional theatre across the country. It has encouraged several ambitious performing arts ventures, although such organizations as the Canadian Opera company, the Royal Winnipeg Ballet and the National Ballet of Canada preceded it on the scene.

The best evidence of its secure position is that, in 15 years, the attendance level has dipped below 80% only once, in 1957. On several occasions it has exceeded 90%.

For years now the Festival administration has braced itself for signs of a crucial decline in public interest. The boom in Shakespeare in North America was expected to wane after the quadricentennial. But enthusiasm keeps growing. The United States now has 11 Shakespeare festivals, amateur and professional, and all doing good business. The best-known, the American Shakespeare Festival of Stratford, Connecticut, although notoriously mediocre, has just had its best season in 12 years.

At Stratford, Ontario, the box-office for the 18-week season came to $1 215 000, an increase of $21 000 over 1966. In view of the quantity and diversity of the programme, this figure does not tell the entire story. Clearly however the crisis did not materialize.

Not everything undertaken or blessed by the Festival transmutes into gold. Along with survival, expansion, the establishment of a music programme and an opera company, the shows for students and the tours, there have been setbacks, miscalculations, misadventures, blunders and failures of nerve.

In 1956, after Sir Tyrone Guthrie filmed his production for the Festival of Sophocles' *Oedipus Rex*, the Stratford Festival foundation announced a plan, in conjunction with Leonid Kipnis productions, "to film the entire first folio of Shakespeare, using the same Festival stage productions as the interpretive basis . . . with the purpose of putting on permanent record the work done at Stratford, and of making films available for art and educational distribution on an international basis."

Oedipus Rex was shown at the Edinburgh and Venice film festivals, and subsequently in a few "art cinemas" and on CBC-TV. That was the last heard of the project, even though making film records of Shakespeare productions for the stage has become commonplace since then.

That same year, 1956, Mr. Langham's first as artistic director, the Festival offered a *Henry the Fifth* in which the French characters were played by actors from the Montreal French language theatre. Granted the stunt nature of the casting, it indicated a pattern for the development of a company expressive of our dominant cultural strains and impulses, and therefore capable of a genuine originality of interpretation. The use of these actors could also be expected to whet the Stratford playgoers' interest in the French language theatre of Canada.

That was not how it turned out. During the season, the Théâtre du Nouveau Monde, many of whose members were in *Henry the Fifth*, gave three performances at the Avon of a trio of Molière farces. They were poorly attended. In 1958 TNM returned for a short, and again ill-attended, engagement with one of its prize attractions, *Le Malade Imaginaire*.

Nine years passed before a Montreal company was invited back. It was the TNM once more, this time with a version in English of the company's brilliant rendition the season before in French of Strindberg's *The Dance of Death*, but using the same director, Jean Gascon, and the same leads, Denise Pelletier and Gascon.

Ten years passed after *Henry the Fifth* before French language actors again appeared on the Festival theatre stage. What brought them back was the same play, *Henry the Fifth*. Some were also used in the first part of *Henry the Sixth*.

The only person in the Montreal theatre with a continuity of involvement is Jean Gascon. After being invited back to direct a few plays he was appointed an associate director, with opera as his chief area of responsibility. He has worked a number of times at the Avon and the Festival with the TNM's chief designer, Robert Prevost.

Such is the sum of the French language Canadian theatre's participation in the Festival. The 1967 season, with its centennial overtones, was bereft of any activity attesting, concretely or symbolically, to the essential fact of our state existence except for a few programme and picture specimens in the Canadian theatre exhibit.

An arrangement with Clarke, Irwin and Co. to bring out an annual Festival volume ended in 1957. A plan for the Toronto *Daily Star* to record excerpts from the productions and distribute them to Ontario's secondary schools was called off after the third record. Negotiations to make recordings for commercial distribution have not materialized. A programme to sponsor play contests with the Toronto *Globe and Mail* was cancelled, in 1961, following the results of the first competition. That same year marked the termination, after four seasons, of an international film festival.

The company's reception when it goes on tour is altogether curious. As an example, in 1956, when the company participated in a pre-Broadway tryout in Toronto of *Tamburlaine the Great* ticket sales were excellent. But two years later when it played Toronto, Montreal, and London, Ontario, with *The Two Gentlemen of Verona* and a Canadianized version of *The Broken Jug*, while again on the way to New York, apathy prevailed. In both instances, too, the New York appearances had to be cut short. Nor did the Stratford connection do anything to boost interest in New York of *Love and Libel* (from Robertson Davies' novel, *Leaven of Malice*) and *Moby Dick*. Again, an annual tour of the major Canadian universities in special Shakespearean programmes was attempted once, in 1962, and has not been heard of since.

During its tour last year under Festival Canada auspices, the company played to sell-out or near-capacity houses in the east, but met lack of interest in the prairies and in Vancouver. To add to the paradox, the Festival company outdrew the National theatre of England in advance orders for their simultaneous runs at the World Festival of entertainment in Montreal in late October.

As noted, the Festival is by its nature a summertime activity. Even stretching that period to four months has caused problems. Obviously it is not feasible for the company to function in Stratford the whole year. For some time efforts have been made to form a connection in another city which would enable the company to continue to work as a unit during the so-called regular season, roughly October through April, in a theatre which would be to the Festival company as the Aldwych in London is to the Royal Shakespearean Company of Stratford-on-Avon.

At first glance, Toronto would seem to be the logical choice. It is close by; 40% of the total Festival audience comes from Toronto. But it was feared the familiarity might damage Festival sales. In addition there was the competition from the large number of visiting shows that make Toronto next only to Los Angeles and Chicago as a major touring theatre centre.

Attention turned to Montreal, where English language theatre is moribund. But the English language community is a minority, lethargic in cultural matters. The municipal government showed no interest in proposals for a liaison between the Festival company and the TNM.

The next selection was Winnipeg. This seemed ideal on several counts. The Manitoba Theatre Centre, launched in 1959 by John Hirsch and Tom Hendry, had evolved into an exemplar of what a regional theatre should be. Its audience had grown with it in numbers and sophistication. It had critical prestige and popular support. The city itself was far from the touring circuits. Many Stratford principals had appeared auspiciously in Manitoba Theatre Centre productions (unlike Stratford, the Vancouver Playhouse and Neptune theatre in Halifax, the MTC does not have a permanent company). The auguries were good.

So much for augury. After two consecutive productions in 1966— *Nicholas Romanoff*, a new play by William Kinsolving, and the aforementioned *The Dance of Death*—the trial marriage came to an unceremonious and abrupt ending. The causes for the breakup are not important. At any rate, now the MTC is pursuing a similar, and so far more compatible, relationship with the Shaw Festival, and the Festival company has been renamed the Stratford National Theatre of Canada and will be housed for six months of the year at the $45 million National Arts Centre in Ottawa, scheduled to open in 1969 or 1970.

In 1964, amid fanfare emphasizing the bold and artistic character of the project, the Festival launched a cycle of Shakespeare's plays about the kings of England. The cycle would be presented, not as they were written, but in chronological historical order, beginning with *Richard the Second* and ending in 1967 with *Edward the Fourth* (the second and last part of John Barton's adaptation of the *Henry the Sixth* trilogy) and *Richard the Third*, the play which had opened the Festival in 1953.

But when the 1967 programme was announced, *Edward the Fourth* had vanished from the list. It had been dropped, it was formally explained, because of the discouraging response the season before to *Henry the Sixth*. For the most part the news was carried without comment, or with an audible sign of relief. William Leonard, the drama critic of the Chicago *Tribune*, summed up the general attitude when he wrote (Aug. 13): "It takes courage to scuttle a prestige production that has been planned for several years. It also takes common sense. No matter how much work or money goes into a show, it is no good if the public refuses to buy it."

During the Festival's infant years, drama courses were given, at first to anyone who enrolled, and then only to company members, in voice, movement and mime. Perhaps because the National Theatre School began to hold its summer semesters in Stratford, and there was an overlap, perhaps because of the actors' burden of work, perhaps through lack of interest, the classes eventually stopped. To fill the void, a workshop policy was introduced in 1965 for both the drama and opera companies. The long range aim is to have them work on specific assignments which, hopefully, will develop into something worth showing in public.

Some of the Festival's difficulties may be due to the frequent absences of its artistic directors. This was especially true of Sir Tyrone Guthrie. In a quieter way Mr. Langham[2] also spent a good deal of time away from Stratford and Canada generally, as much as four or five months of each year (in 1965, he was away all year, but that was a sabbatical).

The mythology of the Stratford Festival draws its strength and tenacity from four basic assumptions:

1) The Festival theatre is one of the best and most versatile in the world, but primarily represents the flowering of a truly faithful way to stage Shakespeare and the entire corpus of the classical drama;
2) The Festival company is outstanding for its teamwork and quality of excellence on every level;
3) The Festival has avoided stagnation and sloth by pushing the dramatic art along new and significantly modern trails, and is imbued with a strong "here and now" consciousness;
4) The Festival has uncovered a large hitherto stay-at-home public with a readily available interest in the performing arts, and is educating them painlessly and perseveringly in the enlargement and deepening of their sensibilities.

Myths, as we know, are often based on the way people want things to be, rather than as they are. The falsehoods are more comfortable to live with, easier to assimilate. The Stratford Festival is an ideal demonstration of how such wish fulfillment works, and where it leads in the malformation and adulteration of value judgements.

Far from being moderately true, all four propositions describe an arc about 180 degrees wide of the reality. Far from showing the opposite side of the coin to the commodity theatre, the Stratford Festival is an apotheosis of that theatre's vision of itself in vindication. It expresses just how the David Merricks and the Emil Littlers of the world envisage themselves "artistically" in the temple of their most sanctified, and feverish, fantasies.

That the Festival is nevertheless held in such esteem gives us a good look into the stage of culture in a society of consumer leisure and affluence, and into the character of the phillistinism prevalent in the technological age, not just in the mass media but in the world of academe.

What can be said unequivocally about the Stratford Festival is that it has one of the most attractive theatres in the world, and one of the loveliest locations for it.

Begin with Stratford itself. The town has lost none of its relaxed, rural quality. People are friendly. Restaurant prices are reasonable. There are none of those souvenir shops and pseudo-Shakespeare and cosy, fake period houses which disfigure Stratford-on-Avon. Then go to the park, superbly landscaped, with the Festival theatre standing on the side of a hill. Directly under it is a field where youngsters often play softball. A few yards from the field, on the other side of the winding road is a creek, the Avon of course, which bifurcates Stratford. Trees and tables, judiciously spaced, line the bank on the theatre side. Swans and cygnets move serenely in the water, ignoring their viewers. If the weather allows it, people sit at the tables with their box lunches and dinner. Or they flop down in the grass. Or they just walk. A few go boating.

The sense of informality and unruffled calm is enforced by the theatre's own appearance. When the tent was dismantled and replaced in 1957 by a concrete block and steel shell, architect Robert Fairfield took pains to adhere to the tent-like contours and figurations. The building has an inherent carnival appearance, accentuated by the coronet at the apex of the roof and the mast from which flutter the Festival pennant (the abstracted S) and the Canadian flag. The lobbies are spacious. Despite their spareness, they have no trace of austerity.

What gives the Festival its true singularity of course are the seating arrangements and the stage. The auditorium and balcony are semi-circular, with 16 descending tiers downstairs, and seven upstairs. Altogether there are seats for 2176 people. The furthest row is just 60 feet from the stage.

From rear to front, that stage projects 34 feet into the orchestra audience. Four steps from the audience floor lead to the primary playing area, quite small really, 18 feet wide by 14, with a trapdoor. Another step leads to an inner playing area just 15 feet wide. The second area has six columns supporting a balcony on either side of which are stairways that lead to and from it, with landings and doorways at their halfway point.

Like the inner playing area, the balcony has a doorway at the rear. The balcony also has adjacent windows. In addition to the other entrances, two tunnels rise from under the auditorium onto the concealed room on a floor above and behind the balcony.

The shape of the Festival theatre marks the culmination of a campaign which began in England in 1894 when actor-manager William Poel organized his English Stage Society and began to present Shakespeare in halls and yards rather than in the orthodox playhouse and in the conventional way. Poel was obsessed with the need to rescue Shakespeare, as Bernard Shaw said in an article in 1923, from "the scene painter, the costumier, and the spectacular artists generally. [Shakespeare's] plays were presented in mutilated fragments, divided into acts with long waits between, in which form they were so horribly boresome, being most unintelligible, that only the most powerful personal fascination could induce playgoers to endure him."

The crusade to emancipate Shakespeare gained momentum after World War II. One of the younger open stage ideologists was Sir Tyrone Guthrie. His Edinburgh Festival production in a church of the Scottish morality, *The Three Estates*, convinced him of its practicality.

When the invitation came from Tom Patterson, who had conceived the idea, to advise on the organization of an open air Shakespeare festival (estimated annual budget, $30 000), Sir Tyrone recognized a splendid opportunity to demonstrate the value of the open stage to the world. He persuaded the committee to proceed instead with a closed-in tent theatre with a stage which his longtime colleague, the scene designer Tanya Moiseiwitsch, would create, and to make the Festival a top-level affair. The organizers had been daring little and dreaming small. He mesmerized them with prospects of a world exposition.

Sir Tyrone was specific from the outset that he was not interested in a duplication of the Globe, or any of the other Elizabethan playhouses, about which, anyway, we know only by documents and drawings made from unreliable memory. What he sought was a stage which embodied the conventions of the Elizabethan stage, and would be free of the picture frame "where illusionary effects are prepared as a surprise behind a curtain."

In such a theatre, he wrote, in what is still his best article on the subject (*Shakespeare Survey*, Vol. 8), there would be no interruption in the continuity of the action. The actors could come in and leave from several directions. The director would have a much easier time grouping the players and negotiating the flow of movement. The money saved on sets could be spent on rich and handsome costumes.

The advantages Sir Tyrone cited included far more finesse in the delivery of the speeches—since the open stage automatically accommodates a much larger quantity of people in the same area than a proscenium theatre could, there would be an immense contraction in space—and a much greater degree of intimacy between the performers and the audience. Such intimacy would make the audience feel that, with the actors, they are engaging in a ritual, an incantation. Each spectator becomes a member of the same congregation as the actor, attending the same service. Not all plays, Sir Tyrone added, would suit an open stage. "The plays of Congreve or Sheridan, for example, of Wilde, Pinero or Barrie were written for the proscenium stage and so should be produced."

Now, to a large extent, the need to build a new type of theatre to convey the freedom of Shakespearean stagecraft rests on several question-begging premises.

After all there is no evidence that the Globe, roof or unroofed, or for that matter the Court or the Fortune or the Blackfriars, that is to say the Elizabethan theatre, was the perfect physical environment for Shakespeare's true spirit.

It has to be remembered too, but very seldom is, that there is no support for the contention that the theatres in Shakespeare's day were all wooden O's, of the same shape. Surely the playhouse for which a Ben Jonson and an Inigo Jones did their masques, with their emphasis on scenery and extravagant effects, must have been very different from, say, the one for which Jonson wrote *Volpone* or *Bartholomew Fair* or *The Alchemist*, or Marlowe his *Edward the Second* and *Tragical History of Dr. Faustus*. Nor was the Globe the only theatre for which Shakespeare wrote.

The buildings of that period, clearly, were much like the plays themselves: makeshift. That also applied to Shakespeare's audience, a weird mixture of court folk and rabble. Just as it is true that we can never really know what the style of acting was like in Shakespeare's time, so as an audience we can never really react as the Elizabethans did. Nor can we be forced to feel like them.

Beyond that, no proof exists that you need a new type of theatre architecture to abolish sets and to achieve that uninterrupted continuity of action deemed essential to the Shakespearean dramatic form. Even in Poel's day his colleagues, Harley Granville-Barker and W. Bridges-Adams, proved that the effect could be obtained by an alternation of flats and curtains or by placing the action on and around a bank of interlocking steps. This was demonstrated time and again between World Wars I and II. Even in the United States, where Shakespearean performance has always been a hit-and-miss affair, such designers as Norman Bel Geddes, Mordecai Gorelik, Lee Simonson and Robert Edmond Jones illustrated this point.

How useful is the open stage? How adaptable? Aside from Shakespeare's, what kinds of play can be done in the Festival theatre? Evidently the Greek classics don't belong. Sir Tyrone's antiquarian interpretation of *Oedipus Rex* (played by James Mason in 1954 and Douglas Campbell in 1955) left no discernible impression. None of the Greek plays has been done, or even considered, since.

Presumably the open stage would lend itself to the other Elizabethan dramatists. After 15 years, we don't know, since none have been done. Not Jonson. Not Marlowe. Not Webster. Not Dekker. Not Middleton. Not Heywood. Not Beaumont and Fletcher. Not Chapman. Not Ford. Dryden, too, has been ignored.

Goldoni has yet to find his way into the Festival theatre, and Goethe, and Ibsen, and Lessing, and Buechner (although a production of *Danton's Death* was planned and then, because of casting problems, abandoned). Of the great French playing hits only Molière has been tried, with *Le Bourgeois Gentilhomme* in 1964.

Needless to say, Wilde, Congreve, Barrie and Pinero and Sheridan have been excluded, Shaw too. But Wycherley was tried, with *The Country Wife*.

Among 20th century playwrights only Chekhov—*The Cherry Orchard*, 1965—has been seen on the Festival stage. Since he, too, specifically wrote for the proscenium theatre, displaying his characters in enclosures with furniture and bric-a-brac and against the visible outdoors, he poses awesome challenges to an open stage director and cast.

The problem becomes one of masking the back parts of the open stage, of turning that stage into something it cannot possibly be. Here is the irony. Unlike the picture stage, which is merely neutral, and as it were malleable space waiting to be used, the open stage has a permanent and unalterable identity.

Both the Tyrone Guthrie theatre in Minneapolis and the Chichester theatre have presented a variety of dramas written for the picture stage. The Guthrie theatre has also tried a number of plays from the classical repertoire—Aeschylus' *The Oresteia* in a version entitled *The House of Atreus*, Molière's *The Miser*, Congreve's *The Way of the World*. The Stratford Festival has been more conservative. Besides the writers specified, the only writers to be performed in the Festival theatre have been Donald Jack and Edmond Rostand.

Jack's satire of a free soul, a painter, in a materialistic, conformist society, *The Canvas Barricade*, although not quite as bad as it was made to seem by unsympathetic direction, was a blemished and banal endeavour several removes from life and art. Rostand's *Cyrano de Bergerac*, played by Christopher Plummer in 1962 and John Colicos in 1963, is one of the Festival's greatest successes.

Partisans will tell you that the inefficacy of most types of drama on the open stage proves nothing. Clearly a new type of theatre demands new types of plays, making use of its organic elements. The superiority of the open stage, or if you like the value, will be manifest when these new plays appear.

Paradoxically, the Stratford Festival has been reluctant to find out with the new plays it has commissioned—*The Canvas Barricade, Nicholas Romanoff* (1966), *The Last of the Tsars* (1966), and *Colors in the Dark* (1967). Under the contest's terms, *The Canvas Barricade* had to be shown in the Festival theatre. The other three were done in proscenium theatres, the last two at the Avon.

So far the only play to be written for an open stage with any success is Peter's Shaffer's *The Royal Hunt of the Sun*. Dealing with the Spanish conquest of Peru, it was specifically composed for the Chichester theatre. The critical ecstacy diminished quickly when the play was removed to a conventional theatre, where it was immediately evident that the opulent pageantry glossed over a paper-thin text.

It's enlightening that, like *The Royal Hunt*, *Cyrano de Bergerac* is replete with ceremony, group action and spectacle. For the feature which dominates the open stage, wherever you find it, is the necessity for movement, preferably on a large and lively scale, on all three sides simultaneously. It is no accident that the adjective that appears most often in critics' notices about open stage shows is balletic.

The stage encourages—no, imposes—a form of motion in which action occurs in the mass, by the manipulation and distribution of that mass in shifting and vivid terms. The vividness issues from the picture created by the combination of resplendent costumes and properties—huge carpets, large maps, etc.—and dance-like ensemble mobility.

Obviously, and ultimately, however, the Festival theatre stage stands or falls as a Shakespearean vehicle. If it truly serves as the most nearly perfect medium for his transmission, investing him with the speed and fluidity apparent from the text, releasing the poetry of the language, and capitalizing on the benefits of 20th century engineering and stage lighting—then it needs no other justification.

By the end of the 1967 season (the *Edward the Fourth* fiasco aside) the Stratford Festival company has done all but one of the plays of which he is the unquestioned author: the tragedies, the comedies, the fantasies, the problem plays, the Roman plays, the histories. Several have been done twice: *The Taming of the Shrew, The Merry Wives of Windsor, Twelfth Night*, the two parts of *Henry the Fourth, Julius Caesar* and *Richard the Third. Cymbeline* has not been done at all. *The Two gentlemen of Verona* was given only on the 1958 tour.

The first thing to note is the Festival's bad record with the tragedies. All must be graded as seriously inadequate: *Hamlet* (1957), *Othello* (1959), *Romeo and Juliet* (1960), *Macbeth* (1962), *King Lear* (1964) and *Antony and Cleopatra* (1967).

Equally the Festival has yet to create anything which marks a turning-point or compels a need for a reassessment in the interpretation of Shakespeare—nothing, say, compared to Olivier's *Othello,* or the Peter Brook production of *King Lear* with Paul Scofield, or the inventively tele-scoped version by Jean-Louis Barrault of *Henry the Sixth* at the Odeon-Paris (four and a half-hours long, with one 15 minute intermission, and engross-ing throughout).

The plain truth is that in exchange for the swiftness of scene changes—you can begin a new scene even as the present one is ending, or before—the price exacted by the open stage is considerable and inequitable.

In the new theatre, Sir Tyrone has told us, "every member would be near enough to the actors to see even small shades of expression, and to hear the actors without the actors being obliged to raise their pitch or delay the pace of their meaning."

Even in this day of debased language, press agentry glut, industrial and social science jargon, and anti-intellectualism, it's clear that speech is the heartbeat of Shakespeare's grandeur, the dynamic through which plot and character are revealed, explored and developed. Shakespearean drama is language activated, the tension which holds the fabric of visualized conflict and characterization, the discipline that powers everything in the text. We do not come to "see" Shakespeare, but to "hear" him.

And "hear" him is precisely what is such a problem in the Festival the-atre, since only one-third of the audience can listen to what an actor is say-ing and see the gestures accompanying his speech at the same time and in the same way.

The predicament is not limited to the soliloquies, with the actor circum-navigating the stage from right to left, turning his back first on this group, then that, and then going to the reverse direction, thereby ensuring each section of the audience a fair opportunity to be deprived. It pertains to any passage in which two or more actors take part, and in which what they are saying is more important than what they are doing, which is nearly always.

How do you make sure everyone gets the gist of what is being said (since that is the most you can hope for in the Festival theatre), and what do you do for the others while the actor concentrates on one particular group?

That this deficiency in communication exists, and is crucial, has gone unnoticed, or been scorned, by most of the critics, who sit in the centre of the auditorium, between aisles 5 and 8. Their location in terms of vision and audibility is, as it would be in a proscenium theatre, close and direct.

The general public is less strategically placed. Their situation was described in the *Toronto Daily Star* (June 18, 1965) by Robert Fulford:

> I found myself spending Monday and Tuesday evenings [at the Stratford Festival] in seats close to the outer edge of the audience. On Monday, I was far around the half-circle to the actors' left; on Tuesday, to their right. My seats were not the worst in the house—on both nights there were several hundred people farther off-centre—but even so, they were terrible. . . . For long stretches of the play, I couldn't hear what was being said. Sometimes as much as

half of an important speech was incomprehensible, because the actor was talking in the opposite direction.

Mr. Fulford experienced none of the ritualistic identification promised with open stage production.

Far from being on intimate terms with the actors, I was made to feel ignored and isolated. Far from appreciating the beauties of the open stage, I found myself longing for the old-fashioned proscenium. My motive was no more noble than a desire to see what was going on.

When King Henry and his son Hal played their great confrontation scene, its effect was lost on me. I saw only Hal. I learned later that Leo Ciceri as King Henry was great. I wouldn't know; I saw his back, no more. His back is not eloquent.

When Prince Hal became Henry the Fifth and rejected his old friend, Falstaff, the effect on part of the audience was marvellous— I mean the part which could see Falstaff crumbling under the brutal and terrible words. . . . The rest of us, something like a quarter of the audience, missed the point entirely.

Sir Tyrone's point was that intimacy of an actor-audience relationship is determined by geographic proximity. But that's a fallacy. In the beginning, during the Guthrie tenure and for a few seasons after, much was made of the audience "participating" when actors rushed clamorously down the aisles for the battle scenes, or when principals used the aisles to enter and leave. The actual result was to disrupt attention, making people seated on the aisles self-conscious, afraid they might trip someone, and reminding everyone that they were being asked to subscribe to an illusion in no wise essentially different from that in a proscenium theatre.

One seldom hears anything said now for the open stage theatre as a means of bringing the audience and actor into a ritualistic harmony. When actors use the aisles now at Stratford it's because they have come to see the performance, not to be in it. Some of the permanent Elizabethan features are now seldom used—the trapdoor for example.

The open stage also inhibits intimacy among actors. It becomes impossible to show an intimate scene intimately. The contortions forced on Julie Harris as Juliet and Bruno Gerussi as Romeo in their balcony sequence, the squirming and rotating for the benefit of the audience on all three sides, made the scene offensive.

When the Festival began, many of the things which were bothersome seemed to be due as much to Sir Tyrone's eccentricities as a director as to the theatre. Sir Tyrone's gifts and shortcomings as a director (he is really much better as an artistic director, organizing, stating policy, spotting and using talent, cheerleading) are about equal. Among his felicities those which stand out are his flair for broad comedy and robust violence, and gusto and colorfulness of his massing of crowds into choreographically-imagined and held patterns, and is virtuosity with the apparatus and physical mechanics of theatre production.

Against these virtues one must mention his suppression of those elements in the acting which fail directly to relate to zestfulness and drive, his frequent, arbitrary tampering with the lines and indeed with the whole text, his mawkishness and triteness. For all its virility and energy, moreover, there is a noticeable lack of sexuality or passion, or deeply-felt concern, in his productions. Very often, the lyrical comedy passages spill over from gaiety into a schoolboy's puckishness and nose-thumbing, and the melodrama reduces itself to the sweepings of an eager desire to shock.

The troubles with the Festival theatre stage are built-in. Although a theatre of the round, the open stage theatre is unable to show us Shakespeare in the round. A good many directors have used the stage since Guthrie's day, and the results, while sometimes passably entertaining as exercises in grotesque ballet or carnival revelry, have leaned increasingly toward a meagerness of the spirit and to a preoccupation with beautiful composition. It is no accident that the artistically most laudable productions in Stratford's decade and a half, the two parts of *Henry the Fourth* as directed by Stuart Burge in 1965, also made the least concessions to the stage.

Mr. Burge made a gargantuan effort to force the stage to fit the temper of the plays. He was unable to do it, but in trying at least he compelled us to pay some notice to the sound and the sense of the words and the action, and to Shakespeare's colossal breadth as an artist and warmth of understanding as a human being. For one mark of Shakespeare's immeasurable genius is the degree to which he expresses the prejudices and standards of his age, while transcending them to speak to the world.

The real significance of the open stage is economic and social rather than artistic. To begin with, because it takes up so much less space, it offers one solution to the problem of property acquisition and the cost of building a new theatre. Secondly, because of the supremacy it accords the director, its advent signifies that we have officially entered the era of the regisseur, Gordon Craig's "ubermensch."

The ideological justification of the ubermensch stresses the fact that he and he alone, by co-ordinating everything and giving the result the imprint of his personality, can create "total theatre." Total theatre simply means the manipulation of light, sound, movement, speech, body, and decor to achieve a unity of effect. It does not mean, although this is what is happening and will be the fact of life for some time, the relegation of the stage writer and actor to subsidiary places in the scheme of theatre interpretation—much like the screen actor and author.

Only two men to date have succeeded in fashioning productions in which every detail was fused into the whole, watched over, and guided by a master individual. In both instances, they were their own authors: Richard Wagner and Bertolt Brecht.

o

Here is William Leonard again, of the Chicago *Tribune*, telling his readers what makes Stratford something special:

[It] is an organization that has not grown heavy or sterile with the passage of the seasons. It doesn't have to resort to modern dress productions or other gimmicks to sell Shakespeare. . . . The artistic quality of its presentations is consistently high, and its acting company is recognized as a splendidly knit ensemble. Repertory really can work. Stratford proves it.

Even allowing for the hyperbole inherent in the vocabulary of critical hucksterism, his statements are loaded with inaccuracies. "Modern dress productions," for example, have been presented frequently at Stratford. *All's Well that Ends Well*, as an example, was set in that Austro-Hungarian empire (or Edwardian) period Sir Tyrone favors. He did *The Taming of the Shrew* in a Wild West milieu. Michael Langham transferred *Coriolanus* from ancient Rome to France on the eve of its revolution. He gave us a *Timon of Athens* in which the title part recalled a mid-20th century Greek shipping magnate and Alcibiades, who looked like Fidel Castro, led a band of guerillas direct from the Cuban hills.

There is a second kind of gimmickry Stratford practises, although not peculiar to it. That is the "bright idea" device. The aim here is to turn the play inside out, to make it seem exactly the opposite of what it is. Stratford has done nothing to compare with Maurice Bejart's transformation of *The Merry Widow* into an anti-war piece, but it has come close on occasion, no more so than in the 1966 version of *Henry the Fifth* or the 1967 production of *Richard the Third*.

Considering how far some of Shakespeare's plays have been stretched and twisted at Stratford, it is amazing that they remain intact at all.

Certainly the Festival has made noises and gestures alluding to its alertness to any pitfalls. What we have witnessed most often, however, during Mr. Langham's tenure has been only a helter-skelter island-hopping from one notion to another, without a committed effort to see any of them through, to determine and use their productive possibilities.

The ruthless discarding of *Edward the Fourth*, the retreat from a meaningful continuing association with the French language theatre in Montreal, the collapse of the Manitoba Theatre Centre partnership, the opportunistic engagement of Alan Bates for *Richard the Third*, the failure to commission new operas and to bring some life and creativity to the whole music programme. (What is José Iturbi doing among the performers? José Iturbi!), the studied extinction of the film festival, the refusal to commission new plays for the Festival theatre, all these indicate timidity, conservatism, fear, a hardening institutionalism.

The acquisition of the Avon as Festival property indicates physical growth. But the implied promise that Avon will provide a home for commercially speculative and artistically venturesome or combustible material is scarcely to be taken seriously. So far the most radical show presented there has been the Brecht-Weill operetta, *The Fall of the City of Mahagonny*. Brecht and Weill are certifiably acceptable figures in the cultural system. Everybody likes the *Threepenny Opera*. *Mahagonny* could offend no one, not even with a pointless burlesque of the Last Supper most people didn't notice, or mind when it was called to their attention. The show was a curio, a corpse. No amount of embalming could inject a twitch of breath into it.

The two new plays done at the Avon have been unspeakably poor. Michael Bawtree is not to be blamed altogether for *The Last of the Tsars*. Although he had never written a play, Mr. Langham gave him just six weeks to do it, after having decided to jettison *Nicholas Romanoff* and substitute for it something else using the same actors and costumes. And was *Nicholas Romanoff* so bad that it should have been pulled out in the first place? Having chosen to do it, surely it was less than courageous for Mr. Langham not to stay with it and its author. Subsidized, classical repertory companies are supposed to have the right, indeed the privilege of failure.

But why did Mr. Langham want to do a play dealing with the life of Russian royalty? A play about Cuba or Vietnam or the civil war of the American Negroes and whites, one can well understand. It is, superficially at least, about the here and now and of universal concern. But where is the relevance of the disappearance of the monarchy from the Russian scene? And why such a play a year before the 50th anniversary of its occurrence? And why ignore, both on the eve and during it, one's own 100th birthday?

Perhaps Mr. Langham hoped *Colors in the Dark* would serve that purpose, seeing in it a work of merit by a Canadian, and one moreover that would also be a salute to Stratford, killing two birds so to say, with one show. Mr. Reaney comes from Stratford. The events he describes largely take place there. It is hard to believe Mr. Langham saw merit in his dreary melange of plot, cant and poetic whimsies about the author as a young man. He must have. To think otherwise attributes to Mr. Langham an inexcusable cynicism.

But the real clue to Stratford's health, and whether it has remained clear of smother and stagnation, lies in the attitudes of its audience. There the reaction to the two parts of *Henry the Fourth* in 1965 and *Henry the Sixth* in 1966 tell us all we need to know. Many playgoers complained bitterly at the absence of bravado flourishes and spectacle in Henry. They heartily disliked *Henry the Sixth*, admittedly dull going. Only a fraction of them turned up at the Avon for the uncompromisingly baleful and witty production of *The Dance of Death*. They want familiar shows and fun plays.

To understand what kind of people go to the Festival, and to which it must pay submissive attention, one must realize that the real Festival achievement has been to persuade its public that they need not take Shakespeare seriously. To take him seriously is to relate yourself to his plays for what they have to say, and to readjust your knowledge of the human condition according to their insights.

It makes things infinitely easier to consume them as you would any status commodity. I was not surprised when a businessman told me, and several other people used the same expression, "what a bang" *King Lear* gave him. In the Festival theatre its bitter, searing flames had been tamped down into a cosy fire observed at a safe social and emotional distance. You can be 600 feet away from a stage and be overwhelmed by a play's direct impact. You can be 20 feet away and able to see the actor's most minute expressions and not be affected by it at all.

To respond to Shakespeare truly, however flimsy or frivolous the particular play is, is to be sent tumbling into a world where all is uncertainty
and menace and impermanence. It is to wonder who the face in the mirror
belongs to and what would happen if you put your hand on a hot stove.
Entertainment is not a matter of killing time enjoyably with your friends or
in congenial company. That's not entertainment. That's sedation. And sedation is precisely what most of the people who come to Stratford want, and
get. The form of the theatre determines that the show will have, in the
familiar phrase, "lavish production values." The productions themselves
are not likely to kick the boat. If one looks decrepit (*Henry the Sixth*) or
another that it might be heading for dangerous waters (*Henry the Fourth*,
parts one and two), you just stay away. As Mr. Leonard put it: "No matter
how much money or work goes into a show, it is no good if the public
refuses to buy it."

Recently the Department of Tourism and Information for Ontario
revealed that married couples over 40, with a median annual income of
$10 000 and more, constitute the largest stratum of the Festival audience.
Next came high school teachers and students, who are taking Shakespeare
in their class. Few students continue to go once they leave school or university. My suspicion is that the Festival is much more attractive to students
who want to go into the theatre professionally than to those who have no
such interest.

Basically, when you examine its components, the Festival draws its
attendance from the same stratum of people which supports Broadway, and
for the same reason. It is not an intelligent, selective, receptive or discriminating audience, with an ability to make mental notes for future contingencies, and an awareness that situations of real interest and importance on the
stage must have time to mature in the mind. It is an audience too frightened
to complain that it cannot hear what the actors are saying or too indifferent
to care.

o

"The company," Mr. Leonard reports, "is a splendidly knit ensemble.
Repertory can work. Stratford proves it."

The paradox is that after 15 years the nature of the company, its specific
identity, eludes any definition. It has been suggested that this is because the
style, while taking form, has not yet cohered. It is on the verge of becoming.
Yet it took the National Theatre and Royal Shakespeare companies only a
few years to evolve their styles (and not only in the acting, but in the decor).

But England, it will be objected, is the Shakespearean heartland and is
going through a period of theatrical prosperity, at least in the appearance of
important new interpretive talent. Very well then, let's look closer to home.
The Association of Performing Artists (APA), an American touring company, has been able to achieve a distinct identity for itself in less than eight
years. Montreal's Théâtre du Nouveau Monde, working in thoroughly
impoverished conditions, was able to define its personality in half a decade.

The Charlottetown Festival has found an individual look for itself in just three short summer seasons. Such economically distressed, and only intermittently operative American companies as The Living Theatre, The Open Stage and the American Conservatory Theatre have been able to find their raison d'être in remarkably brief time.

Although the Festival company has a home, its members do not have that community of temperament and purpose, that sense of social and artistic interdependence, which is the essence of style.

One reason why so many Festival productions have been unable to attain an authentic, unifying competence is the absence of a purposeful point of view (as opposed to a fashionable and bogus artistic stance) toward the content and the stagecraft, and their blending. What frequently passes for style at Stratford is really a display of some highly developed stock company skills and teamwork. In all essential aspects, the Festival company is no better today than when it was formed in 1953. Indeed, in some ways it is worse, since many newcomers are influenced by the accretion of bad acting habits developed in the meantime.

Some able guest stars have appeared at Stratford, within the limitations imposed by the stage and the varying quality of the company they have done worthwhile work: Alex Guinness and Irene Worth; Jason Robards, a vigorous and sensitive American who showed as Hotspur how one can act Shakespeare excitingly and accurately without any formal classical training or any instruction in Elizabethan prosody; Paul Scofield; and Eileen Herlie. But, in terms of any influence they have had, they might as well not have been at all.

Over the years too some fine performances have been given by individuals in the company, if you were seated in the right place to see and hear them: Douglas Rain's *King John* and his *Prince Hal*; Guy Hoffman's governor in *Henry the Fifth*; Christopher Plummer's *Hamlet* and *Benedick*; Tony Van Bridge's *Falstaff*; William Hutt's *Richard the Second* and *Justice Shallow*; Leo Ciceri's *Henry the Fourth*; one should mention too the work done by such actors and actresses as Powys Thomas, Joseph Shaw, Amelia Hall, Mervyn Blake, Eric Christmas, Eric House, Hugh Webster and William Needles. These are people of substance, technically accomplished and personally authoritative. They are seasoned character actors, the company's backbone. But for the most part theirs were contributions given as though in a vacuum, without reciprocal sparks from the rest of the company.

At the end of 15 years then the Stratford company consists of three sharply defined elements: a body of able character actors; a sizeable group of mediocre performers who have been with the Festival for a fairly lengthy period of time; and a third group of youngsters, who have either been pushed into parts for which they are not yet fit and as a result have been seriously weakened as artists (Heath Lamberts, Roberta Maxwell, Brian Petchey) or who are undefined and unshaped, and are crying out to be taken in hand.

All three groups are under constant pressure to externalize their movements and speech. This is dictated in part by the conditions of which Mr. Langham issues and to which he has adhered, a tradition that includes a fear of expressing wild and uncontrollable feelings, and of sex as a source of manifestation of the most profound bestiality and nobility, of evil and exaltation.

One symptom of this is that even the Van Bridges and the Hutts and Rains cannot make the speech sound like their natural mode of expression. They handle it as if they were translating, with the speed and agility of UN experts, from a foreign language. Furthermore, even when performing Molière and Gogol, Stratford actors play them in a British vein. Although the accents are mid-Atlantic or as much like that as possible, the attack is very much pre-Suez West End and Stratford-on-Avon. The verve which the company is often credited with comes from the amount of running around they have to do, nothing deeper.

○

Where now the Stratford Festival? It is a vested interest, entrenched. The arrangement with the National Arts Centre in Ottawa solves the problem of a winter home, and all-year activities. Now the federal government, like the Canada Council, is committed to the Festival's permanence.

The Festival was born at a fortuitous moment. The same set of elements and circumstances cannot happen again, as Sir Tyrone has discovered in his obsessive quest for another Stratford "miracle": a middle-class community looking for a prestige event to identify with; an international figure restlessly prowling for an excuse to build a special type of theatre building; an out-of-the-way town scrambling for a gimmick that might attract a few tourist dollars in the summer.

The Festival was an instant triumph because it was an instant advertisement for an attitude that goes with the acquirement of means and status symbols. It has continued to hold its place by virtue of the overwhelming mediocrity of the Shakespeare festivals in the United States, and by its smashing impact, formidable organization, and incessant protestations of being bold, progressive and self-critical. These have made it the most uncritical organization in theatre history, or at least the most intimidating.

The 1968 Festival repertoire, the first organized by Mr. Gascon and Mr. Hirsch, is a mixed bag: *Romeo and Juliet, A Midsummer Night's Dream, Tartuffe* and *The Three Musketeers* for the Festival theatre; *The Seagull, Waiting for Godot*, the opera *Cinderella* and a return engagement of the Royal Winnipeg Ballet for the Avon. The music programme of concerts in the Festival theatre Saturday afternoons and Sunday mornings is unchanged.

There is no real pattern here, and some of the selections are bewildering. Why *The Three Musketeers*? Why the limitation of Shakespeare to *Romeo and Juliet* and *A Midsummer Night's Dream*? Are we to believe that the directors think that the Shakespeare boom finally is subsiding? Do they perhaps feel the Festival is too dependent on him, and the time has come for a principled shift of emphasis? Is the omission of original plays accidental, or a portent?

The whole nature of the drama programme suggests tentativeness and pulse-feeling. Let us put the best construction on it, and theorize that Mr. Gascon and Mr. Hirsch hope to use the 1968 season to get their balance and take stock. If they do that, candidly and comprehensively, then they will admit that the Festival has little value as a vital centre for the interpretation of Shakespeare and the other makers of the dramatic heritage, or as a forum for new voices and impulses. In the same way that it has failed to exercise leadership from within, it has failed to get the public at large to think of the theatre arts as a basic element of their lives and consciousness.

To get the Stratford Festival out of its cul-de-sac demands uncompromising courage of management and a large clarity of artistic vision. It is no overnight process. What we may hope to find out, during the 1968 and 1969 seasons, the length of their contracts, is whether Mr. Gascon and Mr. Hirsch understand what ails the Stratford Festival and have the capability to deliver it from the life-in-death state that now seems to characterize it.

NOTES

1. In addition, the Festival company made a nationwide tour of six weeks during February and March under Festival Canada auspices of *The Government Inspector* and *Twelfth Night*, and appeared for the last two weeks of October at the World Festival of Entertainment in Montreal with *The Government Inspector* and *Antony and Cleopatra*.

2. Mr. Langham, technically, was the Festival's third artistic director. Cecil Clarke, who had assisted in the Festival's birth as production manager and assistant director, was named artistic director for 1954. During the rehearsals for *Measure for Measure*, Sir Tyrone had to take over. With the 1955 season Mr. Clarke was nowhere in sight and Sir Tyrone was again artistic director.

THE REGIONAL
THEATRE SYSTEM ⬦

MARK CZARNECKI

◯

A freelance theatre critic, Mark Czarnecki (b. 1945) wrote regularly on theatre for Maclean's *during the 1970s. This essay is from a collection edited by Anton Wagner entitled* Contemporary Canadian Theatre: New World Visions. *It was published in 1985 in order to give delegates to the World Congress of the International Theatre Institute (UNESCO), an event being held in Canada for the first time, an understanding of the workings of Canadian theatre. This particular essay dealt with the regional theatre movement in Canada from the late 1950s through the mid-1980s.*

Understanding the concept of a regional theatre in Canada is difficult, and in the mid-1980s possibly irrelevant. Despite the idealized portrait of a regional theatre in the 1961–62 annual report of the Canada Council, no formal or legal definition of the term exists—and the distinction between regionals and several other large theatres has become increasingly blurred. By common consent, however, by 1974 a baker's dozen of the largest subsidized theatres across Canada (exclusive of festival theatres such as Stratford and Shaw) were called "regionals." Attempts to assess their common characteristics have foundered, but the history of Canadian theatre since 1945 is largely the story of their ongoing evolution.[1]

FROM REGIONAL THEATRES: A NATIONAL AUDIENCE

Looking back over the decade since the Massey Commission on the arts, the Canada Council in its 1961–62 annual report concluded that huge strides in theatre had been taken, among them the founding of the Stratford Festival

---

⬦ *Contemporary Canadian Theatre: New World Visions*, ed. Anton Wagner (Toronto: Simon and Pierre, 1985), 35–48.

in 1953 and the establishment of Winnipeg's Manitoba Theatre Centre (MTC) in 1958—the model for what were later termed regional theatres. But the gains were insufficient. Particularly elusive was the holy grail of a national theatre accessible to audiences across the country. In this regard the report noted drily, "Stratford reaches that part of a national audience which can pay to get there."[2]

The Council's further thoughts merit quoting at length:

> In a country with the configuration and population of Canada, a truly national theatre is not likely to be created in any one city—however much money might go into a building. Stone walls do not a theatre make nor licensed bars a stage. The essential of a *national* theatre, as we see it, is that it should reach a *national* audience—even if this audience must for convenience be broken down into regional audiences. . . .
>
> A regional theatre must first be situated in a city with a population capable of giving it support and bearing the brunt of its expenses. . . . In addition to a regular season of plays, the company would have to provide productions designed to be taken to small centres within its general area, or to plan one or two regular periods of touring each year with a small repertoire of plays. It would also have to provide theatre for children and, if possible, should organize a school for training embryo actors. . . .
>
> In a decade or so, a fairly close working relationship might develop among them and with Toronto and Montreal. It has been suggested that it might not be impossible with careful planning at the beginning of the season for at least one or two productions a year to be interchanged between two theatres. . . .
>
> If we strain our eyes a little further down the road in this hazy light, we still cannot see in any numbers those essential figures in the theatre landscape—the playwrights of great talent. We can only hope that they are lurking round the corner.[3]

The Council punctuated this general outline with two concrete conditions—strong local support and professional, inspired direction.

In 1985, over two decades later, we can conclude that many facets of that regional vision did materialize: each regional did incorporate some, if not all, of the functions outlined by the Council. Others did not, for complex but definable reasons. Among these, two predominate: an overall cultural bias, in the period under discussion, towards institutions (necessary in themselves but potentially limiting to creativity), and the absence of specific provisions for regionals to encourage the creation and development of new plays.

The first issue is general, applicable to all the arts in Canada, and was addressed by the report of the Federal Cultural Policy Review Committee in 1982 in terms demonstrating that the Council's warnings in 1962 had gone mostly unheeded:

> Federal cultural policy has largely favoured physical plant and organizational development over artistic creativity and achievement. . . .

What they add up to is more an industrial and employment policy than a cultural policy, properly understood. The bricks and
mortar are necessary, but they are not the end product, the purpose
of it all.[4]

The issue of playwriting also has a more general context. Obviously,
problems facing Canadian playwrights as writers—poor distribution, massive U.S. and British or French competition, unconsciously colonized audiences—are shared by non-dramatic writers as well. More specifically,
however, playwrights cannot survive without theatres, as an earlier Council
report made clear: "The Council is of the opinion that living theatre
demands living playwrights and that the Canadian theatre demands
Canadian playwrights."[5] It is curious, therefore, that the Canada Council's
statement of specific aims for regional theatres, apart from encouraging
them to commission plays, does not explore in any detail the organic relationship between playwrights and theatres. Presumably the Council, by
stating that the regionals must have strong local roots, might have felt it
redundant to spell out that those roots would naturally sprout playwrights.

Initially, the regionals did nurture playwrights. MTC under John
Hirsch and Tom Hendry produced their own plays as well as work by Ann
Henry and James Reaney, then resident in Winnipeg. In Vancouver, the
Playhouse under Malcolm Black had great success introducing the plays of
Eric Nicol and George Ryga. No new works by those playwrights, and rela-
tively few by other Canadian playwrights, have been premièred at the
regionals since 1971 (the notable exceptions are Montreal's Centaur,
Regina's Globe and, since the late 1970s, Theatre Calgary).

THE REGIONAL IDEAL: MANITOBA THEATRE
CENTRE AND THEATRE NEW BRUNSWICK

Much of the Council's thinking on regional theatre was derived from
observing the growth of MTC, which also became the ideal for the regional
theatre system in the United States. Having garnered support in Winnipeg
for children's and amateur theatre in the early 1950s, Hirsch and Hendry
amalgamated two semi-pro companies to produce MTC in 1958. Young
people's theatre remained an essential program, and a young company
working out of its theatre school also developed. MTC toured shows
around its region, and became a winter home for many Stratford actors, as
well as National Theatre School graduates. As for programming, Hirsch
stressed the need to educate audiences unused to theatre, gently alternating
light comedy with the occasional classic and always encouraging local playwrights to develop their art within the practical confines of the theatre.

MTC's shining ideals have never been duplicated. In practice, from the
particular viewpoint of regionality, a more influential model for regional
theatres was Theatre New Brunswick (TNB), founded by Walter Learning
in 1968. Both in that capacity, and later as theatre officer for the Canada
Council from 1978 to 1983, Learning has been the most authoritative

spokesman for the generally understood notion of regional theatre (in 1983, he resumed a direct association with the regionals when he became artistic director of the Vancouver Playhouse.) Learning started TNB by persuading towns outside Fredericton to sign up for a tour of the theatre's mainstage productions. This all-encompassing embrace of its region constituted a definition of "regional" more in keeping with the name itself, and one which became more accepted than the far-flung "national audience" concept envisioned earlier by the Canada Council.

TNB's regionality also had significant implications for programming. According to Learning,

> There was no doubt that the organization had to be play-of-the-month. We were the only English-language game in the province. We had to work within the widest possible spectrum, and we had an obligation to the school curriculum. The audience wasn't sophisticated, but it had insight and we couldn't be condescending.[6]

What that meant in programming terms was initially two of the so-called "three C's"—contemporary plays with an occasional classic. Learning did not at first consider the third "C" (Canadian plays) necessary until the late New Brunswick poet Alden Nowlan prodded him into co-writing plays which Learning then produced at TNB. "Three C" programming evolved at other regionals as well and became an accepted rule, one that acquired further official sanction during Learning's tenure at the Canada Council. "If you have theatres operating on $2–2.5 million budgets," said Learning, "part of their function is a lending library—you have to pull out the classics once or twice a year."[7]

Several regionals diverge substantially from that norm. Montreal's Centaur Theatre, for example, produced nothing earlier than Ibsen from the time Maurice Podbrey founded it in 1969 to 1984. The Globe Theatre in Regina, founded by Ken Kramer and his late wife Sue in 1966, began as a community-oriented children's theatre, quickly developing into a populist adult theatre with strong roots in Saskatchewan's past and present. Only since 1980 have classics appeared with any regularity in its programs. Significantly, the Globe and the Centaur are among the most successful regional theatres in terms of attendance and critical reception. And not by chance, both have had long associations with playwrights of stature resident in their respective cities—Rex Deverell at the Globe and, until 1984, David Fennario at the Centaur.

SUBSCRIPTION

In its 1966–67 report, the Canada Council was already asking fundamental questions about the regionals and their audiences. Having noted with approval that a co-production between MTC and the Shaw Festival would "provide larger audiences for not greatly increased production costs," it asked with some concern:

> The question still remains as to whether the regional audiences have been able to broaden in any fundamental way the outlook of their audiences. If the interest of the audience has developed, can plays and productions meet their rising expectations? Can the theatre reach beyond the habitués to an audience as yet almost untouched? Can they find the artists and technicians to carry out their aspirations and meet the demands made upon them? Can they uncover new playwrights of quality and thus provide a social commentary on our own society?[8]

Certainly, the regionals helped develop excellent actors and technicians, but thanks to certain aspects of their infrastructure, the answer to the report's other questions is a resounding no.

First, and most important in that regard, is the subscription season, a concept which came to Ottawa from the Chicago Lyric Opera in 1965 in the person of marketing consultant Danny Newman. Newman is the apostle of subscription—the pre-sale of an entire season, usually with a discount, in order to provide operating capital for a performing arts organization before its season starts. Since the Council was and remains chronically underfunded, it welcomed Newman's ideas and eagerly passed them on to the boards of the new regionals.

Although subscription undeniably works as an economic measure, it can also be detrimental from an artistic viewpoint, especially in theatre. Initially implemented with a conservative opera audience, subscription ignores the basic distinction between theatre—essentially a local, political (in the broadest sense) endeavour—and the other performing arts. By locking theatres into fixed time slots for productions, subscription does cut losses on unsuccessful works—but it also prevents capitalizing on hits, unless a transfer house is readily available. In such cases, the loss is not just economic, since both theatre artists and their audiences are also denied the opportunity to support and applaud a successful cultural endeavour. The result is that economic hedging curtails a community's potential to take pride in and enjoy its own work. Discounting plays has a similar effect: inevitably, an audience urged to buy six plays for the price of five will unconsciously depreciate the value of those works. And although the subscription philosophy calls for one risk—usually a new, i.e. Canadian, play—out of five or six to balance the "safer" classics and contemporary works, many artistic directors do not bother with the risk, and end up downplaying their wild card.

Subscription's shortsighted approach, based on erroneous assumptions, invites long-term programming disasters. The ideal subscription season in theory includes a judicious mix of the three C's. But such a division only raises artistically irrelevant questions of nationality. The basic premise underlying the three C's is a sliding scale of demonstrated worth: the classics by definition have proven themselves over the centuries; contemporary (usually taken to mean "foreign") works have only recently achieved prominence, but sufficiently so to allow them to travel from their countries of origin. That is a sign of universal appeal, perhaps indicating eventual status as a classic, but not necessarily an indication of quality. The epithet "Canadian" is misplaced—the category which should logically follow the previous two is in fact *new* work. In practice, if new work is lucky enough to be produced, it will most likely be produced in its country of origin; hence in Canada such work will be Canadian. But because cultural nationalism is such a contentious issue in Canada, the focus on new work has shifted from its innovative to its political aspect.

The result is that, far too often, *any* work by a Canadian playwright has been bundled into the new or risk category for the purposes of regional programming. That tendency disregards the fact that playwrights such as David French, George Ryga, Michel Tremblay and George Walker should clearly have "contemporary" status since their established work is frequently produced outside Canada. Even though their audience appeal and worth has been verified, remounts of Canadian plays in theatres on subscription are slotted into a category which should include only new work—with the result that their status is downgraded and new work does not appear at all. In short, the belief that balanced subscription seasons give regionals the opportunity to develop new work and take risks is in practice an illusion.

New work undeniably involves risk, whether the work is Canadian or not, but new plays are the lifeblood of theatre—without accepting their challenge, theatre artists wither and die, and so will their audiences. Safe commercial programming on subscription aimed at safe returns does not attract new audiences and kills the interest of established patrons. But given their need to generate box office income, some regionals understandably do not want to take the risk of new work. The problem could be solved if a certain portion of government subsidy were earmarked not for work by Canadian playwrights but specifically for *new* work, irrespective of origin. In practice, as noted, that work will invariably be Canadian. But such a stipulation would also encourage the regionals to break free from subscription blinkers and view established Canadian work in the same perspective as they do proven dramatic literature from abroad.

BOARDS AND BUILDINGS

Several economic developments in the late 1960s resulted in a hardening of fiscal arteries on the boards of regional theatres. That change had its origins in the Canada Council's basic funding philosophy, "partnership in the arts"—the concept that cultural funding should not be dependent on any one source: "The Council believes that the arts community will do best when there are a number of benefactors to which it can turn for help. A monopoly of subsidy from any single source would, in our opinion, tend to squelch the freeness and unpredictability characteristic of the arts."[9]

Such a statement reflects the thinking of governments which do not believe that culture is an absolute good in itself. If arts patronage overall is viewed as an informal consensus among competing vested interests, the inevitable conclusion is that the government is merely a broker for the consumer demands of the public. On the other hand, since the government is itself one of those vested interests, it could naturally expect stronger representation in proportion to its increased public funding. In the early and mid-1960s, at the height of government enthusiasm for arts funding, the federal government clearly identified itself with the artists. The Council even went so far as to withhold funding from Toronto's premier theatre, the Crest, on the grounds that its artistic standards were slackening. In a time of decreased government funding, however, the "vested interest" concept of arts funding would have different practical results.

To the extent that a theatre is funded by individuals or corporations, it might be reasonable to expect that its board members, as in any business, would proportionately represent those social or economic interests—not the wider interest of the community or public at large. Just how those interests would be manifested culturally is easy to define. In its 1967–68 report, the Council noted ingenuously:

> [Music] enjoys a much higher percentage of subsidy from the private sector than any other kind of performing art. . . . Most theatre by tradition is an intimate form of art which must establish a close contact between the actor and his public which it can best do in small houses. It might therefore be thought that private donations to the theatre would be high, but on the contrary we are faced with the paradox that this most intimate of the performing arts obtains, as a percentage of expenditures, by far the lowest level of financial assistance from the private sector.[10]

That has always been true in Canada, and it is also true that the larger the theatre, the more likely it is to receive private subsidy.[11] But the Council saw a paradox where in fact there is none. What the Council does not say is that intimacy—sexual or political—is often socially unacceptable. A non-verbal art like music, which does not potentially deal in ideas, or any vision which might challenge the social or economic status quo, is obviously going to draw funding from organizations with a vested interest in maintaining that status quo.

Yet another trend contributed to the same result. 1967 had been Canada's centennial year, and a favoured centennial project across the country was constructing a performing arts complex. Previously, the Council had made it clear that plays and players came first, buildings later. But after 1967, the success of the arts was increasingly evaluated in terms of their economic impact: "Construction of cultural facilities across Canada during the last decade [the 1970s] partially reflects the perceived need to increase cultural amenities to compete for the industrial location of new companies. . . . The arts also play a significant role in urban renewal, particularly in revitalizing the downtown core."[12]

Buildings and institutions represented visible and quantifiable capital investments which created jobs in construction, administration, technical production, even theatre acting—everything necessary for a vital theatre except the playwrights to create the works and directors of vision to interpret them. With significantly larger capital investments and operating budgets, the perceived wisdom was that such theatres required board members with fiscal acumen. This tendency dovetailed with the Council's promotion of private participation once its own role in the partnership of the arts had diminished.

CRISIS AND RESOLUTION

In retrospect, it is clear that the general direction of the regional theatres was set in the late 1960s and early 1970s. In its 1969–70 annual report, the Canada Council notified its clients that a time of austerity was at hand. The predicted dark age in fact lasted more than a decade: from 1971 to 1980, federal grants to large theatre companies (budgets over $400 000) declined from $1 964 000 to $1 428 000 in constant 1971 dollars—while the number of companies sharing those grants increased from 8 to 13.[13]

One immediate result was a withdrawal of government from its previously perceived role as a patron of culture to a more functional broker role governed by undefined criteria of public taste. The Council likewise shifted responsibility for funding the arts onto the box office and corporate donation: "The idea 'partnership in the arts' can be converted into hard economic facts. It has become clear that unless much more support is forthcoming from private donors, many arts activities will simply not survive at anything like their current levels."[14] The Council's professed "good reason for optimism" in this regard was severely undercut by a statistic in its discussion that "between 1962 and 1971, business contributions dropped from 16% to 7% of total performing arts subsidy."[15] Taking into account just large theatres (over $400 000 budgets in 1971), that figure rose to only 9% by 1980.[16]

As a further austerity measure, the Theatre Arts Development Program, a major incentive for regionals to train theatre professionals, was discontinued in 1969. The Council also announced its intention to crack down on arts organizations with considerable deficits; while acknowledging that they "often attain their standards of excellence by taking severe risks," the Council nevertheless actively encouraged boards to choose financial stability over artistic creativity. At the same time, the federal government refused—and continues to refuse—to allow three- or five-year budgeting for arts organizations to help eliminate crisis financing.[17]

The threat of reduced funding and increased reliance on box office only strengthened the intrinsic conservatism of the regionals' boards. In 1971, an inevitable confrontation between boards and artists insured that most regionals never again mounted provocative theatre.

Throughout the 1960s, the Vancouver Playhouse had led the way in encouraging playwrights, notably Eric Nicol and George Ryga. (Ryga's *The Ecstasy of Rita Joe* and *Grass and Wild Strawberries*, along with Nicol's *The Fourth Monkey*, remain among the Playhouse's most popular productions.)

But Ryga's next play, commissioned by the Playhouse, dealt with the most traumatic political crisis in Canada's history—the murder of Quebec minister Pierre Laporte by FLQ terrorists in 1970 and the subsequent imposition of the War Measures Act on Quebec by the Prime Minister at the time, Pierre Trudeau.

The perspective in Ryga's *Captives of the Faceless Drummer* was decidedly anti-Trudeau, and the board refused to allow production of the play, forcing the resignation of its artistic director, David Gardner. Since then, no new work of Ryga's has premièred in a regional theatre, even though Ryga is one of the most frequently produced Canadian playwrights outside of Canada. Ryga concluded in 1974, "A priority in the future development of theatre in Canada is for the theatrical artists of this country to insist on direct control of theatre institutions subsidized by the state."[18]

Just about the time ossification set into the regionals, a generation of young, innovative Canadian theatre artists, realizing that the established theatres were not sympathetic to their cause, began to create their own theatres. Ken Gass, who founded Factory Theatre Lab in 1970, said:

> [Establishing Factory Lab] was a simple and arbitrary way of escaping the theatrical rut of following fashion. Regional playhouses were (and largely still are) shaping their seasons to reflect fashions of Broadway and the West End. . . . By limiting the Factory to only new Canadian plays, we were forced to abandon the security blanket of our colonial upbringing. We found ourselves in a vacuum without roots and, indeed, without playwrights. The plays soon surfaced.[19]

Aided in many cases by federal make-work grants from non-cultural ministries, these artists founded the so-called "alternate" theatre movement which has produced most of the noteworthy Canadian plays since 1970. This new reality was quickly rationalized into an ad hoc production hierarchy: smaller theatres would take the risks on new work, develop them and, if proven successful, the regionals would incorporate them into their Canadian play slot.

The fact was, however, that the regionals were not just reluctant to try new work on their own: a new work premièred elsewhere had to be complete and guaranteed at the box office before they would venture even a remount. Few regionals were interested in using their stages for the essential tasks of rewriting and improving new work—and the smaller theatres were not funded to do it either. The Lennoxville Festival in Quebec did perform this function during its decade of existence from 1972 to 1982, alleviating the pressure on the regionals to do so. But Lennoxville was a country festival, completely isolated from any community support since it did not reflect any of the life around it. When the festival folded in 1982, none of the regionals publicly accepted its development role. The result has been, as John Gray commented after *Billy Bishop*'s brief run in New York, a hit or miss mentality even more detrimental to the evolution of a play than the commercial jungle of Broadway:

Canadian plays are a minority art form here, a kind of underground process. Tarragon: what's one hundred and fifty seats? Give me a break! If they'd make room for us at the regionals, we could probably become more structured, more formalistic, cleaner. But they don't. Too often, when we do move to the States, we go directly from an underground situation to a tremendously uptown, international one. It's small wonder we have a tough time.[20]

By 1978, the failure of the regional system to incarnate "Canadian" theatre had become so apparent that the Council issued policy statements assigning "priority to Canadian plays, Canadian artists, and the employment of Canadians for senior artistic and administrative positions with publicly funded theatres."[21] The policy was misguided since it addressed the irrelevant problem of nationality, not the crying need for innovative work. And since these guidelines were reinforced only by implicit financial censure rather than specific sanctions, many of the regionals obeyed their letter and not their spirit. In the same report, the Council also announced tighter austerity measures. Little incentive was therefore provided the regionals to change programming which, whatever its artistic merit, rocked no boats and kept their financial gunwales above water. In the same year, a playwright-in-residence program was funded by the theatre office, but few regionals took advantage of it.

Until the mid-1980s, little changed in the regional system. With the exception of the Centaur, the Globe, and Theatre Calgary under the artistic direction of Rick McNair, seasons at each regional were virtually indistinguishable. Walter Learning commented: "A strange paradox arose. The more similar the programming became, the greater the isolation of the individual theatres despite umbrella organizations such as the Professional Association of Canadian Theatres. The artistic directors rarely talked to each other."[22] In fact, this paradox is not surprising—with similar programming and constant economic anxiety, mistrust is natural. Formal links with the major festivals (Stratford, Shaw and Charlottetown) had been dropped, ensuring tighter competition over personnel and properties.

As the regionals became more institutionalized and socially acceptable, membership on the boards increasingly acquired the cachet of opera, ballet and the symphony. Certainly the appearance of conservative elitist theatre with essentially social functions is a fact of cultural evolution anywhere. The most successful example of that process is Edmonton's Citadel, founded in 1965 and still dominated by executive producer Joseph Shoctor. A millionaire impresario, Shoctor is a cultural czar with immense public, private and corporate funds at his disposal. His new, glittering three-stage theatre complex is the envy of regionals everywhere. Shoctor has at least one innovation to his credit—from 1980 to 1984 he dispensed with an artistic director, selecting plays and personnel on an individual basis in his capacity as producer. This role was a natural outgrowth of the tendency at his theatre—and to some extent at most other regionals—towards socially approved entertainment which would increase fundraising and audiences at the expense of artistic vision.

SIGNS OF CHANGE

In 1983 and 1984, the artistic directorships of every regional except the Centaur and the Globe changed hands. But an equally significant development was a revival of touring in unexpected formats.

A key player in this regard was Shoctor. His flamboyant approach to theatre—marked by repeated efforts to mount productions intended for Broadway—is shared by Richard Ouzounian, who became artistic director of MTC in 1980. Together they revived the Canada Council's long-dormant notion of co-producing shows and touring them. Although the Council had hoped that co-production would be put to best advantage with plays of merit that might not otherwise be produced, Shoctor and Ouzounian collaborated on the rock musical *Grease* in 1982 and set up a tour which ended disastrously in Toronto, having barely broken even.

In the spring of 1984, Shoctor took the idea of co-production and touring one step further when he and Montreal impresario Sam Gesser planned a tour for *Duddy*, a musical based on Mordecai Richler's novel, *The Apprenticeship of Duddy Kravitz. Duddy* marked the first time a regional had co-produced with private funds: the musical was aimed at Broadway but died in Ottawa. And, in the fall of 1984, Ouzounian—by that time producer at Toronto's CentreStage—co-produced the world première of Bernard Slade's *Fatal Attraction* with private producers Toby Tarnow and J.P. Linton on a tryout basis for Broadway.

Yet another variant on touring took place in 1984 with a tour of A.R. Gurney's off-Broadway comedy *The Dining Room*, privately produced by Gemstone Productions (Joseph Green, Gordon Hinch, Leon Major). In the spring and summer of that year it was shown as part of the regular season at MTC and Theatre Calgary, and later at Ottawa's National Arts Centre (NAC) and Toronto's St. Lawrence Centre. *The Dining Room* was another milestone: regionals had included in their seasons a production exclusively funded by private money—in other words, the theatres were leasing out their stages and sharing the profits. Some board members at MTC, however, felt such a production had nothing to do with what a regional theatre was about, and publicly expressed concern that it contradicted the mandate of the theatre.

While these innovations were taking place, the English-section of the NAC—after a decade of performing the role of de facto regional theatre in the Ottawa area—also acquired a producer, Andis Celms. His producing role was part of a new mandate for the NAC, which included devoting most of its time to "showcasing" or co-producing works from Canada's regional theatres. To the extent that the NAC uses its vast resources to encourage the regionals to send successful Canadian dramas or innovative works which they might not otherwise attempt, the change in mandate should be beneficial to Canadian theatre as a whole.

There were other tremors witnessed in 1984 in the regional landscape, among them the demise of a grandiose experiment at London's Grand Theatre. There, Robin Phillips, former artistic director of the Stratford Festival, took over a large regional theatre with traditional three C programming and transformed it into a top-quality classical repertory company. The type of programming remained much the same but the individual plays were more challenging: *Timon of Athens* instead of *The Taming of the Shrew*, *The Doctor's Dilemma* instead of *Arms and the Man*. After opening in the fall of 1983, the season faltered at the box office and the board got cold feet, sabotaging the project before it had a chance to prove itself.

Placed at a disadvantage by a looming deficit, Phillips could not fight his board and win. At Theatre Calgary, however, playwright Sharon Pollock won a Pyrrhic victory in a similar confrontation. Pollock had worked closely with outgoing artistic director Rick McNair on her own and other plays. In the spring of 1984, she became the first Canadian playwright of note to be named artistic director of a regional theatre. Then, in a sudden *volte-face*, Pollock resigned, stating that the board had not taken seriously her reservations about the theatre's standards of management. Her resignation did make an impression on the board, however. While searching for a new artistic director, they stated publicly that the appointee would have full power over administrative as well as artistic matters. In January of 1985, Martin Kinch, a playwright and director who had co-founded Toronto Free Theatre in 1972, accepted the post at Theatre Calgary.

Other bright spots appeared on the regional horizon in 1984. MTC and TNB were taken over by James Roy and Janet Amos respectively, both former artistic directors of the Blyth Festival in southern Ontario. Blyth, an extremely successful community-oriented theatre with an all-Canadian mandate, has a strong commitment to new work. Amos has also written plays, and she and Roy are married to playwrights (Ted Johns and Anne Chislett) who both mined the region around Blyth for their best work.

As important as Amos' and Roy's commitment to community and new work is the fact that they will encourage Canadian playwrights to write plays for larger stages. Because the regionals have traditionally thought of Canadian work as risky, playwrights working on new plays were encouraged to minimize the number of characters and limit the physical settings. This gave audiences and critics the impression that their vision was limited—Canadian dramatists, it was commonly felt, were only capable of two-man chamber pieces. However, Theatre Calgary under McNair had gone a long way towards demolishing that myth by providing funds for Pollock, John Murrell and W.O. Mitchell to write large-cast, epic plays if they wished. Amos and Roy also undertook to present large-scale works by their respective spouses which had already proven themselves on the limited Blyth stage. Even in a confined Toronto production, the epic canvas of Chislett's *Quiet in the Land* won it the Chalmers Award for best Canadian play of 1982.

Further good news in 1984 came from an unexpected source when Shoctor re-established the position of artistic director by appointing the British director Gordon McDougall to the post. Among McDougall's 1984–85 offerings were four world premières, three of them Canadian. And in March 1985, Bill Glassco, former artistic director of Tarragon Theatre where he nurtured many Canadian playwrights, was named director of theatre at Toronto's CentreStage.

CONCLUSION

Placed in the 20-year historical perspective of regional theatre, the changes apparent in 1984 were decidedly beneficial to the growth of Canadian theatre. Out of 13 theatres, at least four—the Centaur, the Globe, MTC and TNB—had become committed to rooting themselves in local soil and growing theatre from the playwright up. At Halifax's Neptune, Tom Kerr, formerly of Kelowna, B.C., was gradually shifting his theatre in that direction, while Gordon McDougall at the Citadel promised to continue innovative programming.

These successes occurred relatively late in the regionals' history. The discussion in this essay of how such changes came about has stressed their importance at the expense of the regionals' obvious success in other areas. Thanks to the institutional intent of government funding, for example, most possess a more than adequate physical plant. Although the process of building theatres first and hoping theatrical talent will fill it later is patently cart before horse, it does not condemn the horse to follow the cart forever: the presence of an excellent facility should not be a necessary impediment to the growth of drama. And, simply in terms of statistics, such institutions have enormously enlarged the audience for theatre, just as the Canada Council intended in 1961. At the board and government levels, however, there is cause for concern. Subscription remains the *sine qua non* of marketing. Government and corporate funding continues to flow at an accelerating rate towards the largest institutions and the most conservative programming.

Official disinterest in new work that speaks directly to its audience is a symptom of a national malaise—a lack of confidence in one's own culture, whatever the city, province or region. No matter what the people think, most politicians in Canada do not view culture as an integral part of daily life. Concessions are made to the arts as if artists and their supporters were only an annoying lobby which unfortunately cannot be ignored because of its demonstrable economic clout. As long as regional theatres are funded— whether by government, business or the public via the box office—on other grounds than the necessity for cultural self-expression, their function will remain compromised and their achievements questionable.

NOTES

1. The following is a list of the regionals, with information about stages, touring, young companies, theatre schools, miscellaneous information and projected revenue for 1984–85. Revenue figures are taken from the 1984 Survey of Performing Arts Organisations conducted by the Council for Business and the Arts in Canada.

Bastion Theatre, Victoria, B.C.: McPherson Playhouse, proscenium, 657 seats; Youth Touring Company to schools; Bastion Theatre School; $979 560.

Vancouver Playhouse, Vancouver, B.C.: Queen Elizabeth Playhouse, proscenium, 647; Waterfront Theatre, flexible, 240; Playhouse Acting School; $2 079 750.

Citadel Theatre, Edmonton, Alberta: Shoctor Theatre, proscenium, 685; Rice, thrust, 217; Maclab, thrust, 700; Wheels/Wings touring to schools; Citadel Young Company in Edmonton; Citadel Theatre School; $3 991 290.

Theatre Calgary, Calgary, Alberta: Max Bell Theatre, flexible proscenium, 750; Stage-Coach company to schools; children's acting classes; Extensions Department—play readings, workshops; playwright-in-residence; $2 188 895.

Globe Theatre, Regina, Saskatchewan: Globe Theatre, in the round, 400; all mainstage shows tour to Moose Jaw and Yorkton; Theatre School touring to schools; Globe Theatre School; Alternate Catalogue experimental company; playwright-in-residence; $1 001 755.

Manitoba Theatre Centre, Winnipeg, Manitoba: Mainstage, proscenium, 785; Warehouse, flexible, 230; one Warehouse production tours rural areas; $2 746 200.

Grand Theatre, London, Ontario: Grand Theatre, proscenium, 800; McManus, flexible, 150; $2 543 000.

CentreStage, Toronto, Ontario: Bluma Appel Theatre, proscenium, 894; Hour Company tours to high schools; $3 280 300.

Théâtre du Nouveau Monde, Montreal, Quebec: mainstage proscenium, 850; Inactive.

Centaur Theatre, Montreal, Quebec: Centaur 1, flexible, 255; Centaur 2, proscenium, 440; playwright-in-residence; $1 500 104.

Théâtre du Trident, Quebec City, Quebec: mainstage flexible, 653; $1 275 400.

Theatre New Brunswick, Fredericton, N.B.: Beaverbrook Playhouse, proscenium, 763; all productions tour to 8 towns; Young Company tours to schools; summer company; $1 025 600.

Neptune Theatre, Halifax, Nova Scotia; mainstage proscenium, 521;

one production tours province; Young Neptune to schools; Neptune Theatre School; $1 537 904.

2. Canada Council, *Annual Report 1961–62*, 4.

3. Ibid., 4–8.

4. *Report of the Federal Cultural Policy Review Committee* (the Applebaum-Hébert Report). Ottawa, Information Services, Department of Communications, Government of Canada, 1982, 6.

5. C.C.A.R., 1960–61, 33.

6. Walter Learning, private interview, September 25, 1984.

7. Ibid.

8. C.C.A.R., 1966–67, 22.

9. C.C.A.R., 1973–74, 17.

10. C.C.A.R., 1967–68, 11.

11. Regional theatres are financed by box office receipts and other earned revenue, private and corporate donations and subsidy from the federal, provincial and municipal governments. In 1983–84, the largest regional theatre in terms of revenue, Edmonton's Citadel, earned 40% from box office, 24% from other earned revenue, 6% from private and corporate donations and 30% from government. The smallest regional, Regina's Globe, earned 35% from box office, 9% from other earned revenue, 8% from private and corporate donations and 48% from government. (Source: CBAC survey).

12. "An Economic Impact Assessment on the Fine Arts," Canada Council, 1983, 48.

13. Canada Council, *Selected Arts Research Statistics*, 3rd ed., 1983, 54.

14. C.C.A.R., 1973–74, 18.

15. Idem.

16. *Selected Arts Research Statistics*, 54.

17. C.C.A.R., 1969–70, 57–58.

18. George Ryga, "Theatre in Canada: A Viewpoint On Its Development and Future," *Canadian Theatre Review*, No. 1, Winter 1974, 32.

19. Quoted in Renate Usmiani, *Second Stage: The Alternative Theatre Movement in Canada*. Vancouver, University of British Columbia Press, 1983, 32–33.

20. John Gray in *The Work: Conversations with English-Canadian Playwrights*, eds. Robert Wallace and Cynthia Zimmerman, Toronto, Coach House Press, 1982, 55.

21. C.C.A.R., 1978–79, 15.

22. Learning, private interview, September 24, 1984.

AN APPROACH TO OUR BEGINNINGS: TRANSPLANT, NATIVE PLANT OR MUTATION?[◇]

MAVOR MOORE

o

In 1974, a new national theatre journal, the Canadian Theatre Review, *was founded at York University. York theatre professor Mavor Moore used its pages to look anew at some of the ongoing issues concerning the Canadian theatre.*

In the strict sense, one *founds* nothing; one invents nothing out of thin air. One *finds* a previously unexploited configuration of existing factors, and exploits it. The job of the researcher, in science and technology at least, has traditionally been twofold: to explore possible new configurations, and to unravel the provenance of past ones. In the field of the arts, aside from their technical aspects, we generally leave to the artists themselves the task of exploring new frontiers, while scholarly research is generally taken to mean the study of art history—of how we got here rather than where we might go. That is why in art, as the great filmmaker John Grierson put it, "First comes the need, then the art, then the theory."

The question here is whether our theatre is a European transplant, a native plant, or a sort of American mutation. My question is deliberately rhetorical, because what I really want to do is look not at the historical evidence per se but at the kind of fundamental attitudes about art and society that such simplistic questions presuppose. And I shall use the history of Canadian theatre as a source for illustrations, although the problems are world-wide.

◇ *Canadian Theatre Review* 25 (Winter 1979): 10–16.

I think I first became sharply aware of the existence of such presuppositions in 1949, when Gratien Gélinas' play *Tit-Coq*, after an unprecedented
success in both French and English Canada, opened in New York. What
bothered me was not that the critics didn't take to it, nor even that they
could not recognize what to me were its virtues. It was that they turned its
virtues into vices. What I knew to be deadly accurate about life where I live,
they assumed to be theatrically contrived—like modern Judge Bracks
uncomprehendingly crying "People don't *do* things like that!" The next
thing I noticed was that a good many Canadians believed they must be
right, because, after all, in New York they know a theatrical contrivance
when they see one.

A decade later, when our Stratford Festival had established our own
theatrical competence, the company travelled first to New York and then to
Britain. In both places the productions were admired. But I noticed that the
American critics were careful to praise the performers for their "style," in
which they felt American actors to be lacking, while the British critics
praised them for their "vitality," in which British actors were at the time
considered to be deficient. In other words, the compliment in either case did
no damage to the *amour propre* of the giver. By this time it had begun to
dawn on me not just that Homer nods, but that in some respects Aristotle is
a humbug.

In his book *The Structure of Art*, the American art historian Jack Burnham
makes a crucial point about research, and one particularly applicable to the
performing arts, the products of which are essentially ephemeral.

> It appears that we never perceive the conceptual mechanisms of art
> because art scholarship, upon which most of our knowledge of art
> relies, is directed only toward secondary structures. . . . Historical
> research, criticism, and connoisseurship can never define art; their
> real function is to perform elegantly and gratuitously as pendants
> to the work of art. In other words, they prevent explanation. . . .
>
> As a rule historians try to develop analytical tools covering the
> broadest array of art styles; but as innovation further fragments the
> art impulse, and new and contradictory styles of art arise, histori-
> ans are forced to adopt a variety of approaches. Not too many crit-
> ics or scholars seem to be worried by this situation, although they
> should be. It indicates that all their efforts are directed toward
> explaining the physical evidence of the art impulse, rather than
> (toward) the conceptual conditions which make art objects possible
> under vastly different circumstances.

How difficult it is, then—for all of us—to study incidences of art as they
occur, or have occurred, in societies about which the individual observer has
only a limited knowledge. We are dealing here with cultures, sub-cultures
and counter-cultures—for which the observer's conceptual grid, even when
he is very close to his subject—may be the very thing impeding full comprehension. Sheldon Nodelman, another recent American art historian, details
the consequences:

Not only is the whole matrix of assumptions, values and usages—in which the social institution or work of art under study is rooted—initially unknown to the observer, but . . . his spontaneous interpretations are founded, consciously or unconsciously, on patterns of behaviour and attitude proper to his own culture, and must almost always be wrong. . . .

The reality of the (art) object consists in the full texture of all its relationships with its environment. . . . The observer must scrupulously avoid the imposition of artificial and limiting categories upon the object, and must frame his tentative theoretical model in the broadest and most inclusively relevant terms.

These dire warnings need not deter us from the attempt to study and understand each others' arts. But they do suggest it might be a good idea to look carefully at some of those assumptions and preconceptions. And the Canadian theatre offers as good a laboratory as any.

Perhaps the most dramatic instance of the fallacy of applying inappropriate values occurred at the start of our recorded history. When the Europeans arrived in this part of the world—in the 16th or 17th century or whenever—they sincerely believed that culture was something that had to be imported. In fact, theatre in North America was already by then a sophisticated art. Captain Cook, when he arrived in Vancouver in 1778, found a stage strikingly like that of the Elizabethans and performers of obvious skill. But because there existed no *written* texts, no literary drama of the sort the newcomers were used to, the native theatre was dismissed as primitive, worthy only to be replaced by Shakespeare, Molière, Sheridan, boulevard farces, melodrama, music hall and burlesque. I'm sorry to say that most so-called "white-men" have continued to believe that civilization arrived on this continent with their baggage, and faced a hard struggle for survival unless the supply was continually replenished from abroad. As recently as 1957, the respected *Oxford Companion to the Theatre* described Canadian dramatic efforts as "probably no more amateur than were the first plays of medieval Europe."

Only recently have American scholars bothered to include Canada in their chapters on North American Theatre—again, I suppose, on the basis that since it did not appear on their radar screens it did not exist. It seems not to have occurred to many of them to check out the screen—even when they found it blipping excitedly over the miniscule Francophone theatre in New Orleans while ignoring the much more salient one in Montréal.

But there are reasons for the historic invisibility of Canadian theatre. In the past, Canadian actors went to New York, London or Paris, and chameleon-like became American, British or French. Companies in Canada advertised themselves as "The New York Comedy Company" or as being "direct from Drury Lane."[1] Anglophone playwrights either wrote directly in American or English English or allowed their Canadian-set works to be "translated." When the 1936 Mazo de la Roche's *Whiteoaks* was presented in London, despite its occasional Ontario references it turned out to be about an impeccably English family; in New York it became a play about an

American family headed by a redoubtably New England Ethel Barrymore. The same fate awaited John Herbert's *Fortune and Men's Eyes*; and in Paris its prison was unmistakably French. When published, moreover, a Canadian playwright's work was published (at that time) abroad; to this day Grove Press (New York) will not permit Herbert's play to be included in any Canadian anthology. Now the price of versatility is anonymity. A Canadian artist, whether at home or abroad, was either somebody else or nobody.

But it is not my purpose to make a plea for attention. What I am getting at are the attitudes and presuppositions which inhibit proper study of such phenomena, wherever they occur. The most prevalent of these is the old shibboleth that "All art is international," and the next most prevalent is the equally bankrupt notion that it is "national." As I shall try to show, this is a false antithesis, a case of twin fallacies.

When applied to culture, "nationalism" is at the moment a dirty word applied by established and self-confident societies to the self-realization of smaller and less confident ones—while they blithely label the dissemination of their own values "internationalism." But if art is international, it must first be national—since there must be national arts for there to be an interchange between. Surely this is *not* what the internationalists mean, since they deplore nationalism. Perhaps they mean something more like *supra-national* or *non-national*—not related to borders or political systems. Or they may be searching for some phrase equivalent to Northrop Frye's precept for literature, "a conceptual framework derivable from an inductive study of the literary field." If so, they haven't found it yet.

The lofty doctrine that all art is universal (if I may so amend the internationalist dictum) is based on the assumptions that:

a) there is some sort of universal set of standards or criteria, applicable to all art objects and to which all men adhere;
b) these criteria have nothing to do with local conditions, since they must be portable;
c) the "best" art (whatever that is) subscribes to these standards; and—quite co-incidentally—
d) the values to which I and my peers subscribe are, or ought to be, those of the whole world.

It's not hard to see how we arrive at this egocentre. Standards are merely conventions of measurement and evaluation, and, like all conventions, they change. Nonetheless, from time to time certain sets of rules or criteria find acceptance over a wide area and are elevated into dogma. It behoves its adherents to codify them and promote the code as the One True Faith. Its promoters by now have a vested interest in the code and its critical canons and cannot see straight. The perpetuation of their system becomes an aesthetic end in itself; and like Procrustes they will allow to join them only those who fit their bed. Those who do not are distorted or maimed until they do, or simply turned away.

In a word, the theory of a universal standard is reductive. Its true aim is homogenization. Now Nationalism as a political doctrine may well, as the Internationalists suggest, be both dated and dangerous; the sooner the world resolves its political differences the better for all of us. But in the field of culture such a resolution would be disastrous. In art, variety is more than the spice of life: it is the essence. What is universal is not the forms, but the impulse to create art.

But just as *internationalism* is a misnomer for the universality of the artistic impulse, *nationalism* is a misnomer for the local expression of that impulse. Any artist—anywhere—has the need and the right to see life through his own eyes and to express what he sees in his own way; to reflect his own reality, his dreams and his nightmares, instead of copying the empty shells of forms found suitable by others; to contribute one more variation to the astonishing fecundity of the world's arts. Now this is far from the narrow parochialism and chauvinism usually stigmatized as *nationalism*. Surely it is the homogenizers, those who seek to reduce the number and variety of artistic species (in the name, naturally, of "international standards") who must be charged with narrowness of vision.

Roy Mitchell, the first director of Hart House Theatre, and the only consequential philosopher of theatre Canada has ever produced, wrote in his book *Creative Theatre*:

> The most ancient principle of the arts is that it is better to use what you have, to build with native stone, to carve in native woods. . . .
> Art is a native growth which, to be strong, must arise generation by generation from the soil of its own people.

Mitchell, like thousands of Canadians, ended up an American in the United States, where he is now being recognized as the man who, a decade before Artaud, articulated the modern need for a theatre of passion and movement. Though not entirely a prophet without honour in his own country, he was not appreciated here in his own time, since Canadians had chosen instead to believe the experts from out of town who told them the only way to achieve anything was to join the big-time.

More recently another Canadian philosopher, Marshall McLuhan, has pointed out that when an environment is all-pervasive, as it is in mass-media North America, one needs an "anti-environment," a house of one's own to keep out the sun and the rain. I suspect that both philosophers were showing here their Canadian conditioning. Perhaps it is difficult for those *providing* the environment to understand the need for an anti-environment. This need has always been central to the Canadian experience, as it has for many lesser societies. In the case of Canada, however, it is a *sine qua non*— scattered as we are along a border shared with the biggest entertainment, arts and education factory the world has ever known. The temptation to sit back and be entertained, educated and published at by our amiably prolific American cousins is irresistible to many—especially since we have scarcely got over our deference to British and French culture.

The flavor of our cultural past may become tangible if I cite two quotations regarding our version of the English language; comparable comments could be quoted about our version of French. The first is from an article titled *Canadian English*, written by a leading clergyman in 1857—some time after *U.S.* English was found acceptable in higher quarters. He describes our way of speaking as "a corrupt dialect growing up amongst our population, and gradually finding access to our periodical literature, until it threatens to produce a language as unlike our noble mother tongue as the Negro patua, or the Chinese pidgeon English." I need hardly point out the even-handedness of his bigotry. But 120 years later, we may still find a relic of it in our predilection for English accents on the stage—not only in British plays, where it is entirely justifiable, but in translations of Sophocles, Ibsen and Chekhov.

The second quotation comes from a 1948 article by a Canadian-born American linguistic scholar, on the "culture dependence" (his words) of Canada on the United States and Great Britain.

> In the past 35 years, it has been primarily the United States which, through motion pictures, magazines, books and personal contacts, has kept Canadian English "up-to-date."

I'm sure you notice that he assumes the influence has all been one-way. Certainly he avoids mentioning the hundreds of words from north of the border, both French and English, which are to be found in dictionaries of "American" English.

What seems to be the case is that we are damned if we do our own things and damned if we don't. If our theatre, for example, is to be judged by its compatibility with the approved International Fellowship style, any attempt to be original—that is, to add a new dimension, a new insight, to the world's art—is bound to be seen as a failed attempt to be à la mode. It may very well be that in time to come, the most valuable aspect of the Canadian theatre will turn out to be its difference from that of others; that it will offer the world not only an alternative North American art, but a model for greater diversity in general—because we are a pluralistic society in which no really "national" theatre can exist nor should be expected to.

Even to speak in a general way about "the Canadian Theatre" is therefore to fall into the nationalist-internationalist trap; the label is customarily used to obscure the contents of the can. It is used by nationalists as a battle-cry to ward off foreign influence, and by internationalists (with equal hypocrisy) as a put-down—as in the phrase, "It doesn't have to be Canadian, it has to be good." Misuse of labels by equating the name with the value of the contents is no monopoly of either side.

When a label *is* linked with a value judgement, however, there is a sense in which its value can only be set by the addressee. This is the label which reads: "To Whom It May Concern." Its relevance to others, that is to say, is not at issue. And this is the final point I want to make here about our presuppositions, the blinkers which make it difficult for us to study and evaluate the art of others. Irrelevance to others is not an issue where one is dealing, for example, with a topical revue (an art form in which we happen to excel), which is often the more successful for being relentlessly parochial. I remember Brooks Atkinson, then the critic of the *New York Times*, writing up one of my own revues in Toronto, saying that although he didn't understand the jokes it must have been very good because everyone else was laughing. The same might also validly be said of a public affairs broadcast—not all of us are troubled or excited by the same public issues—or of a shared song, a painting evoking shared emotions, a novel or play the understanding of which demands acquaintance with social or historical context.

But we must note at once that the label "To Whom It May Concern" has little to do with geographical locality or even political nationality, since in the modern world we are often closer to outsiders who happen to share our tastes and enthusiasms. In this day of instant communication, sub-cultures and counter-cultures spread like wildfire over continents, across oceans, around and in-between the established cultures. This means, of course, that "nationality" will scarcely do as a criterion of merit or acceptability; but it also means—and this is too often overlooked—that the so-called "international" or "universal" standard is not the only kind that is portable. There is not *one* universal portable set of values or practices but *many*—and, so far as I can see, the more the merrier!

For the package labelled "For Whom It May Concern," the usual judgmental criterion ("It's good enough to go anywhere") is quite beside the point, and if indiscriminately applied can be highly destructive. The application of some supposed standard of universal fitness, the search for a Lowest Common Denominator ("Will it play in Peoria?") or even a Highest Common Factor ("Will it work in the West End, or Paris, or Broadway?") may bury the very differences which were valuable in the first place. At the very least, it may have the injurious and inhibiting effect of persuading young Canadians, or those in similar societies, that art is something turned out by your betters—that Golden Ages occur only to others in other places and other times than your own.

While nothing can excuse the meretricious hoax that *because* a work of art is regional or parochial (Canadian, Québecois, Swiss, whatever) it is thereby as "good" as anything produced elsewhere, this should not blind us to virtues and values *other* than comparability or compatibility with prevailing fashions—even those with impressive pedigrees. The one sure thing about fashion is that it will change. Studying it is an imperative for scholars; but keeping up with it is a mug's game.

I seem to have only once mentioned the question I posed at the beginning. So I had better make a deathbed repentance. Is Canadian theatre "a transplant, a native plant, or a mutation?" Well, it has its father's eyes, and its mother's chin, and its great-aunt's curly hair—according to them. But isn't it time we began, like properly scientific observers, to study the baby instead of listening to its elders?

NOTES

1. When the first Association of Canadian Theatre Managers was formed in 1906, it held its first meeting, naturally, in New York.

THE DEVELOPMENT
OF SELF-IMAGE,
1968–1995

○

A STRANGE ENTERPRISE:
THE DILEMMA OF THE
PLAYWRIGHT IN CANADA *

THE GASPE MANIFESTO

○

From 19–23 July 1971, a dozen theatre professionals concerned about the development of Canadian playwriting and playwrights met at Stanley House in Quebec's Gaspé as guests of the Canada Council. Hosted by the Council's Theatre Officer, David Gardner, the group—ranging from playwright George Ryga to American literary manager Arthur Ballet—debated methods of support. The result was a controversial manifesto: a call for 50 percent Canadian content in subsidized Canadian theatres. Drafted by playwright Jack Gray, it is published here for the first time.

For the past week the undersigned have been meeting at Stanley House in The Gaspe to consider the dilemmas that face the playwright in Canada.

We have examined the working conditions of the playwright, looked at his economic prospects, discussed practical ways to enhance his professional status and improve his economic lot, and sought ways to enable him to take his proper place in the theatre and in the cultural life of Canada.

What is striking when one examines the condition of the playwright in Canada is the abnormality of the situation in which he works. In most countries and most cultures those who create original material are prized and valued members of the creative community. Really successful theatres demand new work and in fact depend on it for their existence. In the normal situation what people ask for are new novels, new films, new poems, new comic strips, new television programs—and—strange as it may seem,

---

* Conclusions and recommendations of a seminar sponsored by the Canadian Council at Stanley House, 19–23 July, 1971.

new plays. Theatres that matter are based on their own new work, work that speaks to its initial audience in accents that are immediately relevant. The normal situation is that there are new plays, and lots of them.

We believe there is no meaningful Canadian theatre except where our playwrights take a major role in it.

That they have not done so to date is a scandal and a disgrace. Another point that has emerged clearly from our deliberations is that there are no easy ways to get this new work. Playwrights must be encouraged in every possible way to write *their* plays, and theatres must be encouraged in every possible way to produce these works. It is essential, as well, that it be clearly understood by the writers, the producers, the audience, the critics, and all who support the theatre, that support of the playwright, however, generous it is, will not produce instant masterpieces. Indeed, it may not produce masterpieces at all. We can anticipate, however, that if we do as many new plays as we can, as well as we can, we are more likely to turn up the occasional masterpiece. Quality will grow from quantity.

What the Canadian theatre needs now is a constant supply of new work, both from the novice and the established playwright, and in all forms and styles. That means that those responsible for the theatre in Canada, the boards, the artistic directors, the managers, the Canada Council and each of those other agencies that supply so much of the money that keeps our theatre going, must begin, as a matter of priority, to back the playwright in every practical way they can. We believe that the most effective support is that which goes directly to the playwright, enabling him to write those plays *he* wants to write. But no play lives until it is produced for its audience, so that it is essential that there now be a clearly stated policy that establishes that public funds be used, first, to make sure our writers are writing, second, that our theatres are enabled to present these works to our audiences.

An important point that emerged again and again in our talks was the fact that the modern playwright is a multi-media man, working not only for the stage, but also in television, radio and film (and often in other fields as well). The Canadian playwright tends to use all the media available to him, and it is clear that there is an urgent need that all those agencies who are supporting and regulating the various media, the Canadian Film Development Corporation, the Canadian Broadcasting Corporation, the National Film Board, the Canada Council, the Department of the Secretary of State, the Canadian Radio-Television Commission, and so on, should begin to coordinate their support programs for the dramatist to ensure that the best use is made of the funds that are available to support him.

While the theatre today is plagued with many problems, the drama, in all its forms remains one of the most powerful and attractive forms we use. Its place in the increasingly complex world of communications is central, and crucial. We usually learn more from the stories we tell one another than from the sermons that are preached at us, whatever guise they take. While the theatre is in one sense a minority art, and in our own time has been almost swamped in the indiscriminate deluge of the mass media, amazingly it has not gone under. In fact, and even though it is often no longer commercially workable, enormous efforts are made all over the world to preserve, to extend and regenerate it. The modern theatre has reflected the wild unrest and the vitality of our era in its frenetic search for new forms, and yet there is no evidence that this exciting search has affected the innate conservatism of the drama, whose commitment is to certain immutable processes that men experience—to birth, life, death, and by extension to our human emotions, love, hate, greed, ambition and so on.

It is the whole life of man that our dramatists seek to express, in ways that deeply engage our interest and concern. The theatre must deal in such matters to matter; our theatre in Canada must deal with them if it is to make its contribution to our life. What our dramatists want is the opportunity to make this contribution, their contribution, which hopefully will enhance and enrich the lives of all who share in their work.

"The entertainment of decent people," Molière once noted, "is a strange enterprise." It is time our playwrights got on with the strange enterprise. To do this they need drastically improved working conditions. They need wider and more flexible forms of support. They need to know that opportunities exist for the production of their work in all media, and especially in the theatre.

Each of the points that follows seeks, in one way or another, to further these aims.

We recommend:

1. That the Canada Council and the other grant giving agencies make it their policy that the theatre in Canada become predominantly Canadian in content, and that they therefore develop, through their theatre programs, support that encourages in all practical ways, and as a matter of priority, the production of works by Canadians.

   ("Canadian" in this context shall be taken to have the same meaning as that currently used by the Canada Council.)

2. That all Canadian grant giving agencies stipulate that no later than the first of January, 1973, any theatre receiving funds will be required to include in its repertoire at least one Canadian work in each two works it produces, making it clear that among the first criteria for subsidy is the question of the content of the theatre's repertoire, which is to say, what percentage in the season is Canadian work: that the minimum requirement apply to works in each category of a theatre's season (e.g. main stage, studio, workshop productions, children's plays, and so on); and that adaptations of existing stage works not be considered Canadian.

3. A major problem facing the freelance playwright is how to make a living wage sufficient to allow him to continue to work and live in Canada. While all freelancers accept the speculative nature of their calling, the hazards for the playwright are almost unmanageable, and few of our talented people sustain their playwriting careers for very long. Direct sup-

port is currently available to the playwright from the Canada Council in a variety of ways, including short term grants, bursaries and awards. In addition, we understand that the Council is discussing the establishment of a guaranteed income program for selected senior artists.

We feel that the guaranteed income program is of vital importance and recommend that it be pursued, and if possible implemented, and that this be a priority in the Council's planning.

We further recommend that the Council consider the feasibility of making a portion of the awards renewable for playwrights, so that more sustained support can be offered writers who qualify for such assistance.

4. That the funds available to playwrights from the Canada Council be made more flexible. In addition to the grants of various kinds that are currently available, and to the practical aid contemplated in the new Implementation Grants, we suggest that the Council consider making available what might be called *short term production grants*.

   We are thinking here of grants that can be made on an ad hoc, short-term basis to individuals, to small companies, or to groups that are organized for a specific project, to enable them to mount or develop a single production. Such a grant could be made, for example, to a writer to enable him to find or to organize a production of his work in a way particularly suited to his needs. It would also make it possible for the Council to give selective support to specific programs without taking on a commitment to sustain support to a company or group over an extended period.

   We feel that if short term production grants are established, priority in this category should be given to new Canadian works.

5. That the Canada Council (and others who may wish to engage in such a program) set aside funds to enable theatres, universities and other qualified institutions to acquire a playwright either as writer-in-residence, or dramaturge, or literary manager, or pet, that in general such appointments be made only to working playwrights, and that the appointment be made at the request of the theatre, university or other institution, but that the money be paid directly to the playwright.

6. That the Canada Council make available funds to make possible the automatic publication of all new plays by Canadians that have been or are about to be professionally produced. While we wish to see the publication of produced scripts made automatic, we would also recommend that the judging of the publication potential of any other playscript be brought under the Council's theatre section.

7. That the Canada Council recognize the need for a variety of additional services in connection with the development of new play scripts, including their marketing, contracting and general exploitation, and that it consider sympathetically applications from qualified individuals in the various regions who seek the Council's support in the initial

stages of such enterprises. We do not feel that the projected national booking agency can in any way fulfil this function.

8. That since the playwrights of Canada are not currently formally represented in any professional association, that all playwrights join either Société des auteurs or ACTRA, to enable these unions to deal credibly on behalf of the playwright.

Signed by Arthur Ballet (Director of the Office for Advanced Drama Research, Minneapolis, Minnesota); Carol Bolt (Playwright); James de B. Domville (Administrateur, Théâtre du Nouveau Monde); John Douglas (Dramaturge, St. Lawrence Centre); Suzanne Findlay (Associate Producer and script editor, the Canadian Broadcasting Corporation); David Gardner (Theatre Arts Officer, Canada Council); Marc Gélinas (dramaturge, membre du Conseil d'administration des auteurs dramatiques); Jack Gray (Playwright, Acting Secretary-general of the Canadian Theatre Centre); Peter Hay (Drama editor Talonbooks, former dramaturge, Vancouver Playhouse); Tom Hendry (Playwright, former literary editor Stratford Festival, former Secretary-general Canadian Theatre Centre, and former administrative director of the Manitoba Theatre Centre); Jean Morin (Dramaturge, Vice-président du Centre d'essai des auteurs dramatiques); George Ryga (Playwright).

THE CHALLENGE[*]

JOHN C. JULIANI

○

The growing nationalism of the post-centennial years led to more and more attacks on the Stratford Festival—a continuing symbol, according to many, of colonial thinking. When, in 1973, the Festival's Board of Directors yet again turned to England to choose an Artistic Director—Robin Phillips—critics of this lingering colonialism had a clear focus for their attacks, as well as a voice in the newly-created Canadian Theatre Review. *In its first issue,* CTR *published a letter to the editor from director John Juliani (b. 1940) who sought "to avenge the honor" of Canada's "emerging theatrical heritage" by challengng Phillips to a duel. (For the record, the duel never did take place.)*

To The Editor:

I have recently been informed of the appointment of the English stage director Robin Phillips to the position of Artistic Director of the Stratford Shakespearean Festival of Canada.

My initial reaction to this news is a mixture of shock and fury; shock because it is difficult to believe, in the context of recent developments in the Canadian theatre, that the appointment of a non-Canadian as artistic director of the country's major English-speaking theatrical organization could even be conceived much less actually realized, and fury because the insult it represents to all Canadian theatre practitioners is impossible to stomach.

I am quite certain that response in Canada to this betrayal of our theatrical identity at this, perhaps the most crucial juncture in the articulation of that identity, will continue to be forceful and direct. But, however many words of opposition are raised against this irresponsible and retrograde step, they will prove to be insufficient unless they are also voiced by those

◇ *Canadian Theatre Review* 1 (Winter 1974): 145.

responsible for founding the Stratford Festival, viz. the Canada Council and other levels of government.

Since I have little expectation that funding agencies on which the Stratford organization is dependent are likely to exercise such responsible initiative, I am assuming the responsibility personally, calmly, and in all seriousness, to challenge Mr. Phillips to a duel in order to avenge the honor of our emerging theatrical heritage. This challenge has been delivered to Mr. Phillips in the United Kingdom and I await his reply, ready to meet him in whatever form of combat he chooses and in whatever place he should deem appropriate.

CULTURAL POLITICS ◇

PETER HAY

○

The nationalistic attacks extended outwards from theatre to government cultural policy and back again. Vancouver dramaturge (as well as founder of Talonbooks' play publishing program, Peter Hay (b. 1944) was a formidable spokesman for the cause. From CTR 1 *(1974).*

To some it might not come as a surprise that Canada has no national cultural policy. It took major international upheavals to alert us that we had no national energy policy. There has been relatively little discussion—except in emotional terms—about the recent emergence and the long-term impact of cultural nationalism in Canada. Not one of the three or four major political parties on the federal scene have a platform on cultural policy. Apparently the NDP is thinking about drafting one. If so, it may have been shamed into it by the strong stance which has been consistently taken by the Committee for an Independent Canada. The CIC has had the advantage of two nationalistic publishers at the helm: Jack McClelland and Mel Hurtig. And it was publishing that received most attention from the Ontario government's Royal Commission on Economic and Cultural Nationalism. But it does not take a special interest group to perceive that foreign control of our economy produces fallout in the social and cultural sectors as well: these problems are rooted in the same soil. What has not been adequately realized either by politicians or the public is that nationalism is a cultural phenomenon, long before it blossoms politically, [or] bears its sometimes poisonous fruit. How fast this maturation is completed and how edible the fruit turns out to be depends largely on the nation's self-confidence, self-awareness, though also on international forces and events.

Recently there was enough awareness to preclude an American from becoming the police chief in Calgary. Not enough to prevent the appointment of yet another Englishman to direct the Stratford Festival in Ontario,

◇ *Canadian Theatre Review* 2 (Spring 1974): 7–15.

which, from time to time, calls itself the National Theatre of Canada. This suggests that Canadians on the whole have not perceived as yet the causal role played by culture: within the context of nationalistic symbology police seem more important than theatre. But then the whole thought-process along these lines is still very new; the flag which the nationalists wave was invented less than ten years ago. It may be bad news for those who deplore or are genuinely troubled by any manifestation of nationalism, that every sign indicates intensification in this direction. But long before the end of this century, I believe, our perception of priorities will have shifted sufficiently to realize that a country which takes a jealous pride in her national theatre would never advertise for a police chief outside of her borders in the first place.

Part of our present problems stems from that oracle of Canadian constitution, the BNA act, which is silent on the apportioning of cultural responsibilities. Unlike education, resources or communications, culture is not exclusively a federal or provincial matter. This has certain advantages: the arts have access to funding from a variety of sources, including three levels of government, the corporate and private sectors. But such advantages are outweighed, in my opinion, by the result that no one government and no single sector is willing to shoulder the responsibility for the development and survival of a cultural institution. (The National Arts Centre may be one exception.) What happens instead is a kind of game, in which inadequate funds are advanced to cultural organizations by one source solely to elicit further (and perhaps larger) sums from the others. The object is to shame the playing partners into matching grants. One inevitable result is the concentration of funds in a few large organizations instead of having more of them competing for excellence and public attention on a more modest scale. The playing partners (or funding agencies) have managed to spread the responsibility for their investment on the public's behalf thinly enough so that in effect not one of them can be held accountable by the public. The reason I am calling this a game, is because the illusion is created that there are really several sources of money which would account for different areas of responsibility. But, as we all know, there is only one pot of money originating from the public, whether in the form of government taxation, corporate exemptions or direct outlay on admissions.

Most Canadian cities remain one-horse towns, mainly through this policy of putting all the eggs into a basket sometimes too small to hold them. The largest eggs in these baskets during the past two decades have been laid by the federal government, first through the Canada Council and lately as part of make-work programs, such as LIP [Local Initiatives Program] and OFY [Opportunities for Youth]. It is the federal role, therefore, in the development and continued nurturing of Canadian theatre that this essay attempts to understand.

At the root of government involvement in all the arts there are (at least) two profound misunderstandings about the nature of culture itself. As the Latin etymology implies, culture is a process of growth and cannot be established with the instant or short-term results that politicians generally require. Secondly, it has to be nurtured within an environment which may be inimical and unresponsive to the workings of a central government. Insofar as it requires suitable soil and expert gardeners, culture is indigenous in geographical locations that are sometimes unexpected and outright inconvenient for bureaucrats.

Moreover, the supposition that forced irrigation through increased funding is by itself efficacious has been generally proven erroneous. The cultural projects that have been most disappointing and brought the least permanent return to the taxpayer have been those housed in extravagant edifices, requiring large outlays simply for upkeep. The authentic and most successful cultural expression by Indian and Eskimo craftsmen, by individuals working under conditions well below the living standards of average Canadians, has had the least access to public funds.

The Canada Council interpreted its mandate in much the same terms as the CBC: the task of creating a network of professional arts groups in major centres across the country. Where some already existed, it was a question of enlarging them through increased funding; where none did, amateur groups were encouraged (again with money) to hire professionals. Today, every province in Canada has a professional theatre company, except Newfoundland, and the Canada Council is currently negotiating with four groups to create one there. The emphasis lies on accessibility to the widest audiences. That is why the CBC's strongest arguments for ever-larger sums (as at the recent CRTC hearings) are based on hardware: transmitters to reach more people. This is pragmatic in the confederation where everybody is paying for the CBC, and in a democracy where politicians have to be elected. The current crisis that is facing both the CBC and the chain of theatres midwived by the Council is no longer one of accessibility or hardware, but content.

The first instalment in the piecemeal approach towards cultural policy on a federal level was the Canadian content regulations imposed in 1968 on the television and radio industry by the CRTC. Since then, the Secretary of State has also funded policies on film and publishing. A new Performing Arts Policy has been in the works for almost two years; originally promised for last December, it will be an attempt to rescue the larger performing arts organizations from their constant uncertainties and widening deficits through long-term planning. This would be achieved through three or five-year budgeting which might save some of the paperwork and energies spent on annual fund-raising drives, though the latter depends on the amounts that would be made available from the Treasury Board. Theoretically, this new policy—if and when it is put into effect—would free some of the Canada Council's resources to concentrate on smaller groups, individuals and specifically on innovation. But also inherent in the proposed Performing Arts Policy is the failure of the Canada Council to exercise budgetary control over the run-away expansion of major cultural institutions in the country. In some cases, budgets tripled and quadrupled in a period of ten to fifteen years, out of proportion with rising wages and costs, or indeed with any increases in output, whether measured quantitatively or in terms of artistic quality. Audiences, though, have increased dramatically for all the performing arts, and one of the problems with deficit budgeting is that success generates higher financial loss.

While it is both desirable and overdue to remove a number of arts organizations from the brink, as we have recently seen in the case of the
Montreal Symphony, there are consequences that should not be overlooked.
The Canada Council, like its model—the Arts Council of Great Britain—has
been fiercely protective of its political independence. According to its char-
ter, it is accountable to Parliament through the Secretary of State, but as far
as its deliberations and decisions are concerned, it is free from partisan politics and from the government of the day. Well, perhaps not quite. For one
thing, the government has means at its disposal to pressure seemingly independent agencies or even bypass them completely. In 1968, the same year
that the CRTC proclaimed its Canadian content regulations, the Hon.
Gerard Pelletier, then Secretary of State, announced

> the development of a comprehensive cultural policy (which had)
> as its objectives the promotion of a genuinely popular culture and
> cultural equalization—in other words, "democratization and
> decentralization." . . .

Perhaps before anybody understood the precise meaning of such jargon,
warfare erupted between the department of the Secretary of State and the
various cultural agencies. Foremost among them was the Canada Council,
which in those days was in a much greater rut than at present. It proved an
unequal struggle. First came the Opportunities for Youth program, which
made modest sums available to cultural groups all across the country for
summer activities. The criteria were not—as in the case of Canada Council
grants—professional training or contacts within an exclusive artistic community, but inventiveness and financial need of individuals in the larger
context of social experimentation and participation. There followed the
Department of Manpower's Local Initiatives Program, originally designed
as a winter works scheme to ease seasonal unemployment. A much larger
sum of money was pumped into new arts groups, especially theatre, almost
accidentally, especially as the program became year-round. According to
the Pasquill study,[1] in 1971–72 alone more than two and a quarter million
dollars was spent on just theatre groups by LIP, or well over a third of what
came the previous season from traditional sources of subsidy. Only about
$34 000 was given by LIP to what the study calls "professional theatre" or
companies that were presumably established before the program. Or, in
other words, the years of struggle that a regional theatre put in before it
worked itself up to the point of receiving $100 000 from the Canada Council
were rendered ridiculous by the ease with which a dozen unemployed individuals obtained the same sum in their first year.

Pressured by all the established performing arts groups and weakened
by a lack of leadership following the departure of Peter Dwyer, the Council
put forward desperate bids to secure administrative control over cultural
grants from OFY and LIP. Pressure from the same sources spilled over into
an ideological objection against such attempts at "equalization and democratization" as the true meaning of these phrases were becoming abundantly
clear. Understandably so: the profession was reacting (and in some cases,

still is) to a major attack on the definition of its "professionalism," since under LIP anybody receiving a salary, regardless of training, talent or other qualifications, could and did call himself a professional. The matter was complicated by the fact that, theatre being on the whole a low-paying profession with a high level of unemployment, most of the new groups under LIP (and certainly those that managed to survive) were begun by qualified professionals who were either out of work or who were disenchanted by the established theatres. The reaction was also caused by a justified insecurity on the part of the profession about the ambiguities of its own professionalism. As I pointed out in an article at the time, one sometimes feels in Canada that the only difference between amateurs and professionals is money.

The power struggle was settled with the appointment of André Fortier as the director of the Canada Council. As Under-Secretary of State under Pelletier, Fortier was the Council's "enemy"—trying every means within the government's power to pressure a nominally independent crown agency into a new direction, which it was resisting. His appointment resolved the conflict with a bloodless *coup d'état* of classic simplicity. This mutual co-optation meant that the government got its way and the Canada Council in losing an enemy also acquired a strong director with direct access to the government and therefore a chance to influence its future policy.

One could say that this coup was tantamount to the Council's loss of independence. However, this freedom was largely theoretical and illusionary in the first place. The Council's main ideological weapon against the Secretary of State's tactics was an accusation of *dirigisme* or political interference. But it is worth noting in the internal correspondence and minutes of Council meetings at the time (1971–72), that the Council was willing— and almost eager—to trade off its independence in return for greater influence on government policy and a share of the financial fall-out. In other words, *dirigisme* became acceptable as the price to be paid for a larger piece of the cake.

The professional arts groups, which form the bulk of the Canada Council's constituency, were only a beat slower in detecting from which way the wind was blowing. I remember a national conference on arts management held by the Canadian Conference on the Arts at the Banff Centre in November 1971. Speaker after speaker denounced the Secretary of State's declared principles and his OFY program (LIP was still to come). Artistic freedom was the rallying cry. By the time Direction 73 came to be held in Ottawa, April 1973, *dirigisme*, was a dead issue, and many of the same people who had deplored it were now speaking of equalization and democratization as if they had invented the terms. The antonym—élitism—was now being used as the ultimate put-down (by the élite itself) in contexts not altogether dissimilar from words like "revisionist" or "petty-bourgeois" in Communist countries.

But if the government could claim almost total victory in the ideological arena of semantics, at least until the next counter-revolution occurs, the process described above has also conveniently detracted attention from the more formidable bodies that daily threaten to compromise artistic freedom in a real sense. Chief among these is the concept of the Board of Directors, or Bored of Directors as they could be more aptly named for their penchant to dismiss artistic directors and personnel. In theory, the Board of Directors of a non-profit society represents the audience, the local community and the tax-payers. In practice, most Boards are composed of the wealthy and the upper middle classes. In theory, the Board raises money from the private and cor-porate sectors. In practice, as a percentage of total subsidies, private support for the performing arts in this country has has been halved in the decade between 1961 and 1972. In theory, the Board is elected at the general annual meeting, as required by the Societies Act. In practice, most Boards are self-appointed from inception and have a way of perpetuating themselves through relatives and friends. In theory, the Board is responsible only in financial matters and leaves all artistic decisions to artists with the necessary background and expertise. In practice, the Board hires those artists and fires them if it disagrees with their policies, staffing or programming. Then it can hire other artists who will see things the Board's way. It is part of the demo-cratic process (except perhaps in the United States) that a governing body which makes a major error is forced to resign or face defeat at the polls. Judging by the number of dismissals of artistic personnel in Canada during the past few years, Boards must have made quite a few errors of judgment when they hired them. There is no precedent for the Board of Directors of a cultural institution ever having resigned. In principle, Boards are composed of conscientious, hard-working and well-meaning volunteers from the com-munity. In practice, there are good Boards and bad Boards. All Boards are potentially worthy, and all have the power to be anything but that.

If the rationale for the Board is that it represents public responsibility over public monies, it is time to recognize that no Board can ever be truly representative of a community. The closest thing to this would be nomina-tions and elections by the audience. Yet, all taxpayers, regardless of their interest in the arts, contribute to public subsidy. What the Board provides is not representation, nor in most cases, responsibility which they quickly pass on to hired personnel. They are supposed to prevent control of arts organi-zations by any level of government. In Europe, a civic theatre or opera house is directly answerable to the City Fathers, and all artists working in subsi-dized theatres are in effect civil servants. Some will see this as an extreme form of *dirigisme* and potentially damaging to the arts. But, as I have already pointed out, in a democracy all governments are tried every few years by the entire electorate. Boards remain. Given the choice, I find interference from politicians would be greatly preferable to the current situation.

For one thing, politicians would first have to become more educated about the arts and cultural problems, something they can now avoid by del-egating responsibility along with the funds to buffer agencies like the Canada Council, which in turn passes the bucks to other buffers in the shape of Boards. More importantly, artists would then come into direct contact with politicians and through them might become more aware of concerns in the whole spectrum of society, instead of the minute sector currently inter-ested in the arts. One of the tragic consequences of "artistic freedom" as we now have it—especially in English Canada—is the complete isolation of most artists from the political arena where the real aspirations as well as apprehensions of the people *en masse* are expressed. Instead . . . the artist occupying centre stage as prime mover and symbol of society, we have him free to work and live on the fringes in benign neglect, free from the basic benefits of social security that most citizens enjoy, and above all, free to be utterly insignificant to a society which rightly wonders why he needs to be supported, since the majority do not know his work. In other words, artistic freedom, so jealously guarded by a burgeoning cultural bureaucracy, has contributed to the virtual disenfranchisement of the artist who has little voice in matters of public policy. Surely, what should matter most to artists is to matter.

In this regard, the position of writers, entertainers and theatre artists in Quebec has generally been the envy of their English counterparts. No amount of grants can replace popular success, or compensate for a lack of it. A surprising number of Quebecois artists enjoy both, simply because they work in a society which insists on a political definition of culture, as a vital factor in survival. Of course, this does not mean that all Quebec art is doctrinaire. On the contrary, the most popular entertainers profess no political convictions. But it is a political process that makes them popular.

The current challenge to the arts in Canada—and particularly to theatre, which has the widest impact and is best equipped to articulate it—is to understand the political process: what happens when two or three are gathered together in the name of power? I am not talking about the Kremlin or the White House; almost the same can be learned from the way a Board of Directors operates in your local town. Direction 73 was the largest cultural conference ever held in Canada, between three levels of government in the nation's capital, and it didn't even make the National [CBC]. And every arts group in the country has a battery of publicists on its payroll: the arts are daily in the business of manipulating the media. Yet when André Fortier appeared on Jack Webster's open-line show in March of this year in Vancouver, he emerged shaken and rattled by the red-neck onslaught. But where were the artists? There are enough of them working at home to jam the telephone lines—literally the life-lines—to Mr. Webster's little entertainment every morning, until one day he might become an ardent patron of the arts. I am not talking about producing political art, socialist-realist art or socially-redeeming art. But every artist who wants to reach an audience has already committed a political act. The feeling of frustration, of insignificance even when compared to other interest-groups that almost all artists expressed at Direction 73 and at regional arts conferences is caused mainly because it is always more frustrating to be manipulated than to be manipulating. Alexander Solzhenitsyn single-handedly took on the massive state apparatus of the Soviet Union and forced it to a stalemate; most Canadian artists are defeated by a grant-application form. Some of the spokesmen for our theatres think that the greatest threat facing the arts today in Canada is the take-over of the Canada Council and some other cultural agencies by the Secretary of the State. At the same time the major institutions, following the Council's example, are eager to sell out their cherished independence to the Secretary of State or any government agency in return for greater guarantees of financial security. Theirs is a pragmatic approach, even if they dare not confess to enjoying the loss of political virginity.

Meanwhile, at open meetings across the country, frustrated artists are flailing at the Canada Council, as if it were the sole repository of good and evil. At the root of most accusations against the Council's methods of distributing grants, adjudicating applications or even answering correspondence, there is the tacit and naive assumption that these are venial lapses from a state of incorruptible purity and perfection. I think for the time being it would be much healthier if individual artists simply assumed that the Canada Council is a fairly corrupt institution, motivated largely by political considerations and serving pockets or cliques (and not necessary the élite) who have mastered the not-too-complicated rules of grantsmanship. Taking this more or less realistic assumption, one might be pleasantly surprised about some of the better aspects of the Canada Council, including its responsiveness to political pressure. Indeed, there is no reason why individual artists could not use the Council's weight, as cultural organizations already have, to fight their various battles for them, whether on the national or local level. After all, the Canada Council is on the side of artists—all artists in principle, and some artists in practice.

But despite changes under Fortier in the Council's image and style, despite the new Explorations Program and Touring Office, it would not be realistic to expect any institution to initiate major steps which will alter policy. The Canada Council's list of grants to performing arts groups has no rhyme or reason to it. It has simply evolved on a first-come, first-served basis. There is no correlation between dollar value and cultural value, because nobody has been aware that such a correlation is important or even exists. Yet, at a time when there are widespread complaints about the scarcity of money for the arts, especially by the Canada Council, it is legitimate to ask: in fifty or a hundred years' time, what kind of activities of the 1970s will have provided a heritage for Canada—the millions spent on reproductions of Shakespeare and Shaw, or the handful of original plays which would still be surviving, and which were then given a few thousand dollars or nothing in subsidy? The council is lately proud of supporting the so-called alternative theatres, which produce most of the new Canadian works, our future heritage. Its current Annual Report (1972–73) tells the real story: The Tarragon Theatre received $7000 to produce a season of six Canadian plays. The Stratford Festival was given in the same year $460 000. I know that we are talking about two different organizations, perhaps with different requirements. The question is: which is the more important to Canada at this time and in future times? Where should our limited resources go? If a theatre important at one period of development has now been superceded, should it still gobble up the lion's share of the funds? Even if we disregard the difference in plays—whether they are by Canadians or dead foreigners—does the Council believe that actors, directors and technicians working for Tarragon have a smaller size belly or fewer requirements for shelter than their counterparts in more established theatres? Have democratization and equalization produced exactly the reverse, whereby one set of actors earn $65 to $100 a week, but a substantial number of their colleagues elsewhere need $300 a week? Yet salaries are dependent on subsidy, because there are not too many $300-plus wages Tarragon can pay from its $7000 from the Canada Council. And considering the success it had on a shoe-string, would it not be worth seeing for one year what a vital, new company could do with $460 000? And that will only become a possibility once the Council and government have thought long and hard about the correlation between dollars and value in Canadian culture.

NOTES

1. Subsidy Patterns for the Performing
   Arts in Canada, The Canada Council,
   Feb. 1973.

CREEPING TOWARD
A CULTURE: THE THEATRE
IN ENGLISH CANADA
SINCE 1945 ◊

DON RUBIN

o

Appearing in the first issue of the Canadian Theatre Review *was an essay seeking to put the country's evolving nationalism and theatrical maturity into an historical context for a new generation of theatre professionals. The author, Don Rubin (b. 1942), would later revise this essay significantly. For historical purposes, however, the essay appears here in its 1974 version.*

It was the French critic, Ferdinand Brunetière, who spoke of the curious relationship between periods of national awareness, national identity and major periods of dramatic literature. Utilizing in his essay, *The Law of the Drama* (1894), that keyword of 19th century thought—Will—and identifying Will with realization of national selfhood, Brunetière pointed out that

> ... it is always at the exact moment of its national existence when the will of a great people is exalted within itself, that we see its dramatic art reach also the highest point of its development, and produce its masterpieces. Greek tragedy is contemporary with the Persian wars. . . . Consider the Spanish theatre: Cervantes, Lope de Vega, Calderon, belong to the time when Spain was extending over all of Europe, as well as over the New World, the domination of her Will. . . . And France in the 17th century? The greatest struggle that our fathers made to maintain the unity of the French nation was at the end of the 16th century. . . . The development of the the-

◊ *Canadian Theatre Review* 1 (Winter 1974): 6–21. Revised article.

atre followed immediately. . . . I do not see a dramatic renaissance whose dawn has not been announced, as it were, by some progress, or some arousing of the will.[1]

If one can accept Brunetière's theory—and it does seem quite defensible (even the emergence of theatre in the United States only occurred after the recognition of American selfhood following the First World War)—one may just have a significant reference point to enable one to recognize, understand and assess the impressive development of the Canadian theatre since World War II in general and since 1949 in particular.

I think most of those working in fields of Canadian social history would be willing to accept the conclusion of World War II as a starting point for purposes of identifying the roots of current Canadian "nationalism." The reasons are manifold relating most particularly to some sort of national realization in those years following 1945 that Canada did have some viable role to play in the world at large as well as in the economic and social communities of Europe and the Americas.

It was in the wake of this new awareness, that in 1949, Prime Minister Louis St. Laurent put forward to the Privy Council a report suggesting the formation of a Royal Commission whose job it would be to examine national development in the arts, letters and sciences and which would make recommendations as to how the government could best encourage organizations in these fields "which express national feeling, promote common understanding and add to the variety and richness of Canadian life, rural as well as urban."[2]

In the course of its two year study, this Royal Commission, headed by University of Toronto Chancellor Vincent Massey, travelled nearly 10 000 miles, held 224 meetings including 114 public sessions, received 462 briefs and heard 1200 witnesses including submissions from 13 federal institutions, seven provincial governments, 87 national organizations, 262 local groups and 35 commercial radio stations. A Nootka Indian, it was even pointed out, travelled 125 miles to tell them about the vanishing art of his race and how it might be saved. What the Commission ultimately recognized after hearing the same nationalistic cries over and over again was that Canada was fast becoming an empty shell. While it had managed to retain its own government, its own leaders and its own buildings through the years, there was precious little that could be called Canadian in many of those people, and precious little that could be called Canadian inhabiting those buildings. Canada, the report suggested, was losing its culture, its arts, its artists, and its scholars to its friendly neighbour to the south.

"From these influences, pervasive and friendly as they are, much that is valuable has come to us: gifts of money spent in Canada, grants offered to Canadians for study abroad, the free enjoyment of all the facilities of many institutions which we cannot afford, and the importation of many valuable things which we could not easily produce for ourselves. We have gained much. In this preliminary stock-taking of Canadian cultural life it may be fair to inquire whether we have gained a little too much."[3]

The Commissioners go on to point out that "our use of American institutions, or our lazy, even abject, imitation of them has caused an uncritical acceptance of ideas and assumptions which are alien to our tradition. But for American hospitality we might, in Canada, have been led to develop educational ideas and practices more in keeping with our own way of life."[4] Only a few pages later, they make their statement even stronger.

> ... a vast and disproportionate amount of material coming from a single alien source may stifle rather than stimulate our own creative effort; and passively accepted without any standard of comparison, this may weaken critical faculties. We are now spending millions to maintain a national independence which would be nothing but an empty shell without a vigorous and distinctive cultural life. We have seen that we have its elements in our traditions and in our history; we have made important progress, often aided by American generosity. We must not be blind, however, to the very present danger of permanent dependence.[5]

The final report of that Royal Commission was submitted to the Governor General in May of 1951 and was accepted by the government. Not only was it accepted, it was distributed widely, it was read widely, and its most crucial recommendation was soon after implemented:

> That a body be created to be known as the Canada Council for the Encouragement of the Arts, Letters, Humanities and Social Sciences to stimulate and to help voluntary organizations within these fields, and to foster Canada's cultural relations abroad. . . .[6]

As for the Commission's comments on the state of theatrical art in Canada particularly, it was clearly pointed out that "Canada is not deficient in theatrical talent, whether in writing for the stage, in producing or in acting; but this talent at present finds little encouragement and no outlet apart from the Canadian Broadcasting Corporation. . . . Facilities for advanced training in the arts of theatre are non-existent in Canada. . . . Professional theatre is moribund in Canada, and amateur companies are grievously handicapped through lack of suitable or of any playhouses. . . ."[7]

But, the Commission went on to say, from the evidence it was clear "that there is in Canada a genuine desire for the drama. . . . We have been repeatedly informed that the theatre could be revived if only federal subsidies could be secured for the erection of suitable playhouses throughout Canada and for part of travelling expenses of Canadian professional companies." It was also noted that the writing of plays in Canada "has lagged far behind the other literary arts . . . because of our penury of theatrical companies; these are few in number for lack of playhouses. . . ."[8]

The Massey Commission Report then becomes a key to understanding the rapid rise of Canadian arts and arts organizations in the period following World War II. It is the major precipitating factor in the creation of the Canada Council, which, in its turn, was to become the prime mover of arts organizations. And the prime task for the Council, the task it saw as most necessary at the time, was the construction of buildings in which to house "culture" across the country.

For the record, the Canada Council was established by a government act in 1957 "to foster and promote the study and enjoyment of and the production of works in the arts, humanities and social sciences." Financed exclusively in those early years from the death duties on the estates of two millionaires—Sir James Dunn and Izaak Walton Killam—the Council found itself in that first year with some $100 million. Of this sum, roughly half was to be used for capital and building grants to Canadian universities; the remaining $50 million—or, more precisely, the interest only on the remaining $50 million (originally this figure amounted to about $2.6 million)—was to be used for grants to companies in the literary, visual and performing arts as well as to individuals scholars and artists. By 1970, the Council's budget—by that time assisted heavily by annual grants from the federal government—had risen to $32 million. Its grants, in its first 14 years of existence, had totalled some $104 million of which $60 million had gone to arts groups and individuals.

In 1969, the late Nathan Cohen pointed out that "nearly all of the professional theatres we now have in Canada have come into existence since the Canada Council was established. Regional theatres in Winnipeg, Edmonton, Calgary, Vancouver, Fredericton and Halifax . . . the Shaw Festival, the Charlottetown Festival, Toronto Workshop Productions, the Canadian Mime Theatre. . . ."[9]

Cohen went on to point out that these theatres were not actually created by the Council (actually, the one theatre which might be said to have been "created" by Council monies was Toronto's Civic Theatre—a failure; a few other theatres, though, did receive Council funding prior to beginning operations including Theatre Toronto, the St. Lawrence Centre, the Neptune in Halifax, and the Lennoxville Festival in Quebec). Rather, his point was that "conditions appeared in which serious theatre projects have been able, by and large, to obtain help from the Council for their continuation."[10]

Left out of this discussion so far and of equal importance with the Massey Commission Report and the formation of the Canada Council was the establishment of the Stratford Festival in 1952–53. Directed by Sir Tyrone Guthrie in its early years, the Stratford Festival's impact on the Canadian national identity as well as on the Canadian theatrical identity has been staggering indeed. Begun as basically a summer operation, the Stratford Festival's first season consisted of two plays—*Richard III* and *All's Well That Ends Well*. It began in mid-July, ran for six weeks, attracted some 68 000 people and cost $157 000. The Festival today runs virtually 12 months a year, boasts three theatres (its main stage; the Avon Theatre in the centre of the city; and The Third Stage, a quasi-experimental operation begun in 1971 in what was formerly a badminton club) and has a budget of some $3.2 million. The theatre's 1972 season drew 375 000 people to Stratford and brought in slightly over $2 million at the box office. Council support alone to the Stratford Festival (when travelling the company calls itself the Stratford National Theatre of Canada) amounted to $435 000.

Indeed, so significant had Stratford's cultural and economic impact become that by 1972, there were those calling for the theatre to be subsidized not by the Canada Council but rather by the Ministry of Tourism, which was in fact already making grants to the Festival. The argument was that for the Council to cut Stratford's budget would cause severe economic ramifications on the city itself. This being so, Stratford, it was argued, should be funded by some other area of the government. Implicit in this proposition is the Festival's apparent rigidification through the years, its movement from a vital and lively cultural force to an example of cultural petrification (the term "dinosaur" to describe such large theatres has also come into the theatrical vocabulary).

As Nathan Cohen described this tripartite development in the '50s:

> The Massey Report set down as a cardinal principle that the arts are a matter of governmental concern and by so doing, it fundamentally changed the government philosophy on the subject. . . . The Stratford Festival came along two years later to prove the Massey Report's point. . . . The Stratford Festival became the status symbol among opinion makers and intellectuals in Canada of the uses to which the arts could be put to give Canada an independent identity at home and abroad. . . . The establishment of the Canada Council followed inevitably from these events.[11]

Suddenly Canada had a theatre. Suddenly major cities across the country were producing the classic plays from world dramatic literature with professional companies. Actors were being developed, designers were appearing, and newspapers even began hiring full-time theatre critics (both Herbert Whittaker of the Toronto *Globe and Mail*—earlier in Montreal—and Cohen himself began establishing national reputations as professional critics in this same post World War II period). Suddenly, Canadians had an alternative to the second-rate touring companies which had been sent through a handful of major cities for so many years (usually Montreal, Toronto, and Winnipeg). And suddenly, too, Canada had an alternative to the innumerable amateur companies which had for so long provided the country with its major claim to indigenous theatre.[12]

By 1967—the celebration of the nation's Centennial—it had become apparent that Canada had a theatre in its midst and innumerable subsidiary organizations had developed around it. (I am thinking primarily of the Canadian Theatre Centre which had been established in 1956.) The only question existing by this time, though, was one of identity: most of the theatre being produced in Canada was clearly not Canadian. That is to say, it was not a theatre of Canada but merely one which existed in Canada. The element that was obviously missing was the playwright, the writer who could speak clearly, firmly, and intelligently in a native voice. In fairness to those who were writing prior to, say, 1967, it should be pointed out that there had been attempts to create viable Canadian drama. Unfortunately, the attempts—with the possible exception of the annual satirical revue produced by the New Play Society, *Spring Thaw*—were, by and large, depressingly derivitive and dramatically dreary.[13] The few Canadian plays which did have any real success were those which actually achieved their note in other countries such as Mazo de la Roche's *Whiteoaks*, Brian Doherty's *Father Malachy's Miracle*, and Patricia Joudry's *Teach Me How to Cry*.

This, of course, leads us back to the original question of national awareness and identity. It should have become clear by now that the Canadian identity—in theatre and otherwise—was, through this period and up to about 1967, a colonial identity, an identification with world powers whose influence and cultural size rather dwarfed the young giant which was Canada. But I would suggest that when Canada and, in particular Montreal (French language Canada seems to have achieved its cultural identity some years earlier) took upon its shoulders the burden of an international Exposition, the seeds were sown for national introspection as well as for national extroversion. I would suggest that it was in fact during Centennial year, during Expo '67 and in the period shortly thereafter, that the current concern with a viable Canadian national identity was born. For it was during this period that Canada began to realize, that Canadians from coast to coast began to realize for the first time, that, as George Ryga has put it, after a hundred years we were still together as a people, that the country not only had stature and size but that it could have the respect and envy of the world as well. It was in 1967 that Canada set about this task of identification and although that definition was still a negative one (that is, defining itself not so much as what it is but as what it is not ("we are not the United States, we are not Great Britain") it nevertheless set the political and social stage for the chauvinism which has thus far characterized Canadian life in the '70s.

The Centennial too also helped the Canadian theatre in a number of concrete ways, most particularly in the national funding of a great number of new theatre buildings across the country. The St. Lawrence Centre (that phoenix which had grown out of the ashes of the Jupiter, the Crest and Theatre Toronto), although not actually opened until 1970, was nevertheless a Centennial project. So too was the Manitoba Theatre Centre's new glass and concrete home in Winnipeg opened in 1970; the $46 million National Arts Centre in downtown Ottawa which opened in June of 1969; and the Charlottetown Festival Theatre which was launched on the Centennial of the first meeting of the Fathers of Confederation—1964.

Throughout this period, the Canadian playwright, that most difficult of creatures to find and develop was working dutifully away in places ranging from downtown garrets (John Herbert's off-Yonge Street Theatre in Toronto was, in fact, called the Garret Theatre) to quiet West Coast rooms more used to the creation of novels, poems and television scripts than plays (George Ryga, after all, had to be persuaded by Malcolm Black of the Vancouver Playhouse to create his play, *The Ecstasy of Rita Joe* for the theatre's Centennial celebrations). Others were working away within the more refined structures of our universities (James Reaney, author of such plays as *The Killdeer* and *The Sun and the Moon*, was and still is employed as a professor of English at the University of Western Ontario).

There were some, of course, who were determined to write for the theatre directly and who had rather large visions of themselves. It was in the summer of 1969 that John Palmer, a native Maritimer who later moved to

Toronto, decided that what Stratford needed was its own experimental theatre and thanks in part to cooperation from Stratford's then resident dramaturge, Tom Hendry, and director Martin Kinch, the Canadian Place
Theatre opened in a storefront across the street from Stratford's Avon
Theatre. The opening production of the Canadian Place Theatre's first—and
only—season was *Occasional Seasoning* by Larry Kardish, a writer whose fine
play, *Brussels Sprouts* would later appear successfully at the Factory Theatre
in Toronto. Staged by John Palmer, the production was probably most noteworthy for its staging of scenes in corners of the oddly-shaped room thereby
making it almost impossible for all the audience to see all the play at any one
time. Other plays that first season included *The Dance* by Terry Cox and
Palmer's own *Memories For My Brother, Part One*, both staged by Martin
Kinch (Palmer's play opened that fall at Theatre Passe Muraille) and *Anthem*,
an adaptation of Proust's *Remembrance of Things Past* directed by Palmer. Not
so curiously, a few years later, Palmer, Hendry and Kinch would team up
once again to create a similar venture called the Toronto Free Theatre. It too
was to become a home for the Canadian playwright, a place where audiences could enter without charge and where native playwrights could have
their plays staged with a reasonable amount of professionalism.

One could conveniently, though not entirely accurately, date the emergence of the Canadian playwright from the appearance of *Fortune and Men's
Eyes*, John Herbert's powerful prison drama, in New York on February 23,
1967. Though the play had been earlier staged at the Stratford Festival as
part of a workshop and though the play had eventually had an extended
run at Toronto's Central Library Theatre, it was not until the play achieved
its success in New York that serious attention was paid to it (Herbert, in
fact, is still fond of pointing this fact out to chauvinistic Canadians). But if
Fortune becomes one of the first Canadian-authored plays to achieve international note during this period, there is nevertheless a play which
deservedly achieved even greater Canadian note. I would prefer to date the
emergence of the Canadian playwright from the appearance on November
23, 1967 of George Ryga's *The Ecstasy of Rita Joe* at the Vancouver Playhouse.
Featuring Frances Hyland in the title role and Chief Dan George as her
father, David Joe, *Ecstasy* was Ryga's rather wry Centennial gift to the
Canadian people.

A play which ostensibly anatomized Canada's treatment of its minorities
(here represented by the Indian), *Rita Joe* on a deeper level, merely continued
into dramatic form Ryga's earlier preoccupations with the dehumanization
of Western man in general and Canadian man in particular. Concerned
from the time of his novel *Ballad of a Stonepicker* (1962) with the concept of
the "semento" (the word is defined in Ryga's 1962 television play, *Indian*, as
meaning a man who has lost his soul but, on a larger level, it means any
man who has lost touch with the earth), Ryga dramatized once again a tale
of sementos and those who were struggling—but in vain—not to become
sementos in his *Rita Joe*. It remained with him as a conceit not only from
Ballad through *Indian* and *Rita Joe* but it appears again in a somewhat different form in his later *Grass and Wild Strawberries* (1968) and in a still more
subtle form in both *Captives of the Faceless Drummer* (1971) and *Sunrise on*

Sarah (1972). The image of the Indian, of course, that creature of the earth who was gradually being forced into the asphalt societies of the white man, was entirely apt for Ryga's vision. If one is able to see his Indians, his "hippies," and his political and social misfits as symbols for those struggling against becoming "sementos" rather than as sociological facts one probably will have some genuine insight into Ryga's obsessions. ("When Rita Joe first come to the city," ends his finest play to date, "she told me . . . the cement made her feet hurt.")

James Reaney's work is probably next in importance during this post-Centennial flowering of the Canadian playwright. Born in 1926 in the miniscule country town of South Easthope, Ontario, Reaney demands attention if for no other reason than the large body of produced work he has to his credit—nearly 30 plays. Reaney's stage reputation rests primarily on such works as *The Killdeer* (1959), *The Sun and Moon* (1962), *Listen to the Wind* (1966), and *Colours in the Dark* (1967).

A terribly frustrating writer to deal with because his plays come so close to being so good so often, Reaney almost never lets one forget that deep-down he's a literary man rather than a man of the theatre. His works, for all their obvious expressionistic fascination and symbolic sense, constantly betray a self-consciousness which is often self-defeating in terms of production. His plays on stage seem to work their best when they are at their least pretentious, their least aware of themselves as literature. But when the scripts are given literary full-rein, they often disintegrate into allusion, illusion, and ultimately confusion. However, one cannot deny the originality and fascination of Reaney's mind, and he may yet break from his literary consciousness and create a truly viable work for the stage.

The year 1970 for some reason seems to be yet another key year in the evolution of the contemporary Canadian playwright and it was in that year that a new theatre, the St. Lawrence Centre, made what to that time was one of the most positive statements about Canadian dramatists. Under the general directorship of Mavor Moore (his mother, Dora Mavor Moore, had been outspoken about the need to have a true Canadian theatre as early as the Twenties and had also founded the New Play Society in Toronto in 1946), the St. Lawrence was to become, for its first season at least, a home for the Canadian play. Opening its doors in February of that year, with a monumental failure—and deservedly so—called *Man, Inc.*, written by Quebec's Jacques Languirand and followed by Jack Gray's play about the Winnipeg strike of 1919 called *Striker Schneiderman*, the season ended with two staggeringly dull productions—a version of Boris Vian's *Knackery For All* and Barker Fairley's version of *Faust*. Though the quality of the Canadian writing was found wanting, the Centre did at least establish a beachhead if not exactly a fertile garden, for the native writer.

A season later, Moore had left the Centre turning the reins over to Leon Major (Moore was also one of many people who previously recommended Major as head of the new Neptune Theatre in Halifax; when Moore was hired for the Centre, Major was also his first choice as director of the theatre company). It was shortly after Major's arrival that new Canadian plays disappeared almost entirely from the St. Lawrence except in the occasional "studio" productions or in the occasional adaptation such as Betty Jane Wylie's version of Ibsen's *Enemy of the People* set in Saskatchewan, or Peter Wylde's *Three Sisters*.

But if the St. Lawrence Centre was turning away from Canadian writers, other theatres in Toronto, Montreal, Vancouver, Halifax, and even Edmonton began to develop alternative producing houses which were, by and large, devoted to native work in native productions. The spiritual and perhaps symbolic grandfather of the movement—certainly for eastern Canada—was George Luscombe's Toronto workshop productions, but it was Theatre Passe Muraille (even the names showed the desire of these companies to break free of traditional values), a company founded in 1968 at the experimental Rochdale College by Jim Garrard that helped create a genuine movement. Beginning by looking for examples of theatre experiment from abroad (one of TPM's first productions was Paul Foster's *Tom Paine*; another was Rochelle Owen's *Futz*, a play and a production which tested the limits of Toronto the Good's morality laws when the cast was brought to trial—the company won), Passe Muraille moved from the College to a local church building at 11 Trinity Square soon after. In 1970, Garrard left the company to become theatre-artist-in-residence at Simon Fraser University in British Columbia and it was his second-in-command, Paul Thompson, who turned Passe Muraille from simply an experimental house into a Canadian experimental house. Of the 50 or so productions done at Passe Muraille between 1970 and 1973, about 90 percent were new plays by new writers from various parts of the country. And while the production level was never exactly consistent, the plays *were* receiving hearings and the hearings were being greeted rather sympathetically by young Toronto audiences.

In 1970, a second company dedicated to Canadian work, the Factory Theatre Lab, was founded by a young man named Ken Gass, a native Vancouverite who first attracted attention in Toronto with a student production of van Itallie's *Interview* during a high school play festival at York University (Gass was teaching theatre to high school students at the time). Relatively inexperienced at theatre management and organization (the Factory is still one of the more haphazardly-run theatre organizations in the country), Gass nevertheless rented himself a loft above a downtown auto garage and the Factory Lab came into being.

A disciple and a friend of John Herbert, the Factory, in a very real way, was the child of Herbert's own Garret Theatre. Gass had worked with Herbert in Garret workshops and a bit of Herbert's intensity and nationalistic fervour obviously had rubbed off. Herbert advised and encouraged Gass and the Factory—by dedicating itself solely to the discovery and production of original Canadian plays—seems to have virtually assured itself of a niche in Canadian theatrical history. Gass maintained right from the beginning of the Factory's life that Canada did indeed have its own writers. They simply needed the production opportunities. It was an old cry and one that had been heard from the writers themselves. Curiously, it took a theatrical neophyte with a lot of nerve but with not much money to prove this to be true.

The Factory Theatre Lab opened its doors on July 23, 1970 with productions of two short plays, *Act of Violence* by Torontonian Stan Ross and *We Three You and I* by Vancouverite Bill Greenland. Since that time, the theatre has produced about 30 scripts a year in either full production or in staged reading format. Without a doubt, though, the most successful of these scripts has been David Freeman's *Creeps* which opened at the theatre on February 3, 1971.

Freeman, a cerebral palsy victim who decided not to be limited by his affliction any more than absolutely necessary, began working on his play while employed at a CP shelter. When it was finished, it eventually worked its way into the hands of former University of Toronto professor Bill Glassco who had turned his back somewhere along the line on the academic life and had been working as a director in a number of small theatres around the country, the Factory among them. Glassco worked closely with Freeman in developing the new script—a curious cross between the theatrics of Brecht and the naturalistic idealism of Ibsen (the actual structure is Greek, perhaps the most solid of all dramatic structures). The result was a rather powerful statement of life in the CP shelters, a play which anatomized virtually everything from do-gooders and service clubs to self pity. Vicious sarcasm was the play's most obvious tone, but it was combined with moments of ascerbic humour and staggering emotional power to create what must rank as one of the major dramatic statements of the post '67 period in Canada.

Audiences responded strongly to *Creeps* despite its often strident tone and its often crude language. In Glassco's production, the play was movingly acted, beautifully staged and consistently fascinating. Though the conclusion of the play was hesitant and unsatisfactory (when the play was later restaged, Freeman rewrote the ending only to find that the problems he had resolved were replaced with new problems), it nevertheless had the power to hold its audiences and, moreover, to attract and move audiences not only across Canada but in the United States as well. The play was the Factory's most successful production running to sold out houses for nearly six weeks.

But success inevitably breeds problems. It was after the production of *Creeps* that tensions began to appear between Glassco and Gass over the theatre's future direction (the two seemed to be at odds over the theatre's politics). The tensions were resolved by the fall of 1971 when Glassco opened his own theatre around the corner from the Factory. The opening play was a revised version of *Creeps* with the original Factory cast. When the play opened, the new theatre, called the Tarragon, had a virtually guaranteed hit on its hands. *Creeps* ran long enough to ensure Tarragon's success, and Glassco's shrewd business sense, his ability to organize a theatrical structure as well as his own personal access to fairly large amounts of money would make sure the Tarragon remained viable through the next few seasons. But as solid as the Tarragon appeared to be structurally, with the exception of *Creeps*, it was running itself into the ground artistically. One dreary production after the next, one dull play after the next (all Canadian, all new, all awful) threatened to bring Glassco's artistic reputation tumbling down around him. And then came *Leaving Home*.

Written by a 23-year old former Newfoundlander named David French, *Leaving Home*, another play developed around the Greek dramatic structure, another exercise in naturalistic writing, told the story of a Newfoundland family trying to survive—both collectively and individually—within the impersonal social structures of Toronto in the 1950s.

It was *Leaving Home* which, in its way, even more than *Creeps*, was responsible for saving the Tarragon from artistic bankruptcy that first season. It was, after all, the only new play which Glassco had offered which had anything whatever to recommend it. Glassco's judgment, which many had questioned for a time between the closing of *Creeps* and the opening of *Leaving Home*, had been restored.

But even beyond the Factory and Tarragon and Theatre Passe Muraille, Toronto had several other experimental or, at least, quasi-experimental theatres in operation by 1972. Returning to Toronto Workshop Productions, founded by George Luscombe in 1959, this was an ensemble that had offered up through the years a number of original productions at a time when original productions were not considered chic. For this, TWP deserves positive mention here. Yet, it must also be added, that most of TWP's original work did consist of adaptations of foreign literature, particularly American works and American concerns, and, as such, its contribution, while interesting, has not really been all that significant. Also going into operation in the summer of '72 was the aforementioned Toronto Free Theatre begun as still another home for the Canadian playwright by Tom Hendry and John Palmer; and too, the Studio Lab Theatre had been struggling in its own unique experimental way through the years.

But such English-language activity, though heaviest in Toronto, was by no means limited to only one city. John Juliani's Savage God experiments in Vancouver—the Savage God concept actually began in 1966—offered up not only fascinating scripts but fascinating theatrical events and happenings in its years of quasi-regular operation. Then too, the Arts Club of Vancouver was staging plays throughout the same period which were unable to find homes and productions elsewhere. In Edmonton, the consistently sold-out Citadel Theatre found itself being challenged in 1971 by a University of Alberta theatre director named Mark Schoenberg and his Equity company, Theatre Three. Interested primarily in offering Edmonton audiences an alternative to the more popular programming of the Citadel, Theatre Three was staging pieces such as Calderon's *Life Is A Dream*, Genet's *The Maid's* collective creations such as *Christmas in Canada*, new Canadian scripts such as Neil Freeman's *Some Evening Sunshine* (an adaptation of some of Leacock's writing), and even introducing Pinter. With the arrival of English director John Neville for the 1973–74 season at the Citadel and with Neville promising to "Canadianize" and make the Citadel more adventurous in future years, it will be of more than passing interest to see how Theatre Three responds and exactly how it will then define itself within the Canadian "alternative" context.

In Winnipeg, the Manitoba Theatre Centre was reviving its Warehouse Theatre for the production of new plays and student shows. Such an "experimental" theatre was high on the list of priorities for its young artistic director, Keith Turnbull (it's interesting to note that Turnbull's youthful ideas of Canadianization of the Canadian theatre were not really shared back in 1972 by his considerably less "radical" Board of Directors and before 1972 was over, Turnbull, his General Manager Gerry Eldred and his Director of Public Relations, Pat Armstrong had all departed for other companies). Turnbull, when he left MTC, was replaced by one of the Theatre's former artistic directors, Edward Gilbert who, in his first two seasons back in Winnipeg failed to produce a single Canadian script. Whether this indicates a backlash, a return to outdated visions of a regional theatre and its responsibilities is a bit difficult to assess at this point. It is worth pointing out, though, that the same situation had also taken place during the same period of time at Theatre Calgary where 23-year old artistic director Clarke Rogers was fired by his board and replaced by Harold Baldridge, an expatriate Canadian who had been living and working in the United States for 15 years. The obvious difference between the MTC and the Calgary situations, however, was clearly in Baldridge's willingness to think Canadian despite his initial unfamiliarity with the developing Canadian product. In his first season he had the political foresight to schedule a production of *Leaving Home* and in his second season—1973–74—Theatre Calgary was offering *Walsh*, a new script by Sharon Pollack.

By the fall of 1973, Calgary could actually boast two professional companies with the arrival of a new venture called Factory West. An offshoot of Ken Gass's Toronto Factory operation, Factory West promised not only Canadian work but Western Canadian work on its stages. And shortly thereafter came a third professional group called Alberta Theatre Projects.

Other small alternative companies were springing up as well. In Halifax John Dunsworth and Bob Reid were forming their Pier One company thanks to federal LIP grants. In less than two seasons Pier One had staged more than 30 scripts, mostly new, mostly Canadian and, in several instances, the works were actually written by Haligonians. Even at the Neptune, things Canadian began appearing on the tiny stage especially during the 1972–73 season which saw the theatre offering up three major Canadian productions (*Colour the Flesh the Colour of Dust* by Michael Cook, *Listen to the Wind* by James Reaney and *Leaving Home* by David French) in a season of seven. Of course, that kind of programming may have been a bit too adventurous for the Neptune board. Neptune's 1973–74 season only included one Canadian script and its non-Canadian work retreated to such stuff as *You're A Good Man Charlie Brown* and *Harvey*. All of this activity was further increased by the development of Neptune's own Second Stage as a viable producing unit. During its first LIP-financed season, it was Keith Turnbull who took charge of Neptune's Second Stage; season two was under the direction of Michael Mawson. In both years, the Second Stage work was consistently interesting, well-produced and heavily Canadian.

There were other Maritimes' manifestations as well. In Charlottetown, a new winter stock company under the direction of Ron Irving sprung up at the Confederation Centre and in its first season offered up a company-scripted production about drug addiction and an interesting new script by Charlottetowner Tom Gallant called *Amadee Doucette and Son*.

What sparked this sudden interest in Canadian work all across English Canada? To a great extent, one could probably trace this movement directly back to two conferences held in 1971 by Canadian playwrights. In July of that year, the Canada Council sponsored a meeting of playwrights in the Gaspé and it was out of this conference that the original demand for 50 percent Canadian content in our theatres was first heard.

It was only a few months later that Canadian-play supporters again assembled, this time in Niagara-on-the-Lake at the home of Brian Doherty, co-founder of the Shaw Festival, to continue discussions and to debate some further propositions. If nothing else, this second meeting simply solidified the feeling that Canadian theatre needed Canadian plays. The publicity surrounding these conferences, the outspoken statements emanating from them and the sense of community established had innumerable ramifications.

One such as the establishment of a national organization called the Playwright's Circle which was to represent playwrights in dealing with theatres and which would make scripts available. Unfortunately, in its desire to begin speedily, the Eastern-based playwrights neglected to pay proper attention to the other regions of the country and after a series of hurt feelings, the Playwright's Circle lost its Western base which included such writers as George Ryga, Peter Hay and Herschel Hardin.

Yet the Circle survived and, in time, created the Playwright's Co-op, an association of writers who would read new scripts, publish these scripts in inexpensive form, represent writers in negotiations with theatres and meet to discuss issues of mutual concern. In its first 18 months of operation, the Co-op published more than 130 plays, had more than 4500 copies of their scripts purchased and had assisted in nearly 40 productions of scripts they handled. As of mid-1973, the Co-op had a salaried staff of five and was hoping to move into other areas of publishing although financing continued to remain a problem. Founding members of the Co-op included Tom Hendry, Martin Kinch, Carol Bolt, Jack Gray, John Palmer, Len Peterson and Daryl Sharp. Sharp served as the group's first administrative director until the summer of 1973. In the fall, Heather MacAndrew was named to replace him.

And there were still other manifestations of this new-found interest in things Canadian. In the fall of 1972, 21 drama critics and theatre journalists (even the number itself is indicative of the new interest in the Canadian theatre) came together to create a group called the Toronto Drama Bench. Its aims were "to encourage an interchange of ideas relating to theatre in general and the Canadian theatre in particular, and to encourage through its collective efforts respect for the art of theatre, theatre criticism and theatre reporting in both the community and the various communications media." Founding members of the organization included Janine Manatis of *CBC Television*, Urjo Kareda of the *Toronto Star*, Don Rubin of *CBC Radio* and Herbert Whittaker of *The Globe and Mail*. It's also of some note that the Drama Bench's first major project was the jurying of a $7500 cash award to the season's most outstanding new Canadian play. The award—made possible through the Floyd Chalmers Foundation—was originally to be divided between the playwright ($5000) and the producing company ($2500). After protests by various Toronto theatre companies, though, it was decided to divide the latter $2500 among four other playwrights whose plays were also deemed "outstanding." And over the summer of 1973, came the establishment of the Canada Council's Touring Bureau—an organization whose prime task it was to move Canadian companies across the country.

Whether this sudden interest in Canadian drama is a passing fad or whether it is solidly rooted in the newly-awakened Canadian identity is, of course, a question only time will be able to answer. The fact is, though, that in both the 1971–72 and 1972–73 seasons in Canada, more than 200 new Canadian plays received full-scale productions. The figures are indicative of a new awareness, a new interest in Canada and its people. Canadian writers are beginning to speak with their own voices and they're demanding that Canadians listen to them. One can only assume from all this that if the national economy remains viable, if the political situation in the country does not alter too radically in the years ahead, if the Canada Council remains in a reasonable financial position and if Canadians from coast to coast continue to look at themselves and their country with pride, the Golden Age of Canadian Drama may well be at hand. And if it doesn't produce a Sophocles, a Molière, a Shakespeare, or a Calderon, it may nevertheless produce some few works which will have helped to illuminate a rather large corner of the world at a rather fascinating period of time in its cultural and political history.

NOTES

1. Ferdinand Brunetière, "The Law of the Drama," in Barrett Clark's *European Theories of the Drama*, 384–85.

2. *Report of the Royal Commission on National Development in the Arts, Letters and Sciences* (1951), xi.

3. Ibid., 13.

4. Ibid., 15–16.

5. Ibid., 18.

6. Ibid., 377.

7. Ibid., 195.

8. Ibid., 196, 197, 200.

9. Nathan Cohen, notes from a lecture given at York University, Toronto on December 2, 1969.

10. Ibid.

11. Ibid.

12. The impact of non-professional companies, and especially the impact of the Dominion Drama Festival during this period cannot be minimized, but since this essay is primarily concerned with the growth and development of professional theatres, the non-professionals, as important as they are, must be left out.

13. It might be noted here that Barrett Clark, the revered American dramatic scholar, had published a list of "major" Canadian dramatists as early as 1928 in his book, *A Study of the Modern Drama* (Appleton, New York, 1928, p. 466). Among the Canadian dramatists mentioned are Merrill Denison, Fred Jacobs, Isabel Ecclestone Mackay, Duncan Scott, Marian Osborne, H. Borsook, Britton Cook, Carroll Aikins, L.A. MacKay, Leslie Reid, Mazo de la Roche, Lyon Sharman, T.M. Morrow and a gentleman named Merton S. Threlfall.

THE INVISIBLE COUNTRY ◊

S.M. CREAN

Arts critic and cultural analyst Susan M. Crean (b. 1945) sought to define the relationship between national and international culture in her 1976 book on the arts in Canada, Who's Afraid of Canadian Culture.

> I like to think that subconscious Canada is even more important than conscious Canada and that there is growing up swiftly in the country, under the surface, the sense of a great future and of a great separate identity—as Canada.
>
> John Grierson, 1946

In 1967 we awoke to find ourselves celebrating the 100th anniversary of a real country. This country. With money and attention lavished on national festivities as never before, we became aware of Canada as never before. We watched the centennial year unfold, and what we saw was ourselves. For a little while, Canada was visible.

We were all changed by that vision. It was a glimpse of "subconscious Canada," a taste of the excitement, energy, and creativity that lay beneath the proverbial bland exterior and a preview of the cultural and artistic ferment that was to follow. For some, the renewed sense of nationality was exhilarating; for others, it was frightening. For everyone, it raised hard questions about the future of our country, and, above all, highlighted the contradictory nature of whatever might be called our identity: bookstores, newsstands, and movie houses where "Canadian" is a foreign word; *Hockey Night in Canada* with Boston playing Philadelphia in the U.S.; theatre directors and conductors who have to be coaxed to perform Canadian works,

◊ *Who's Afraid of Canadian Culture* (Don Mills, ON: General Publishing, 1976), 7–19.

which they judge for the most part to be immature or second-rate; art galleries built to display imported art; university faculties where Americans outnumber Canadians—in short, an entire culture and fine arts establishment dedicated to the worship and imitation of other peoples' cultures.

"My generation of Canadians grew up believing that, if we were very good or very smart, or both, we would some day *graduate* from Canada," wrote Robert Fulford, the editor of *Saturday Night* and Canada's best-known cultural journalist. In the forties, this was the best Canadians could hope for. Faced with such overwhelming lack of evidence for a sovereign Canadian identity, most commentators have been reduced to babbling about whether we have an identifiable culture at all, and whether we need one anyway.

THE SURVIVAL VALUE OF CULTURE

Such questions, which are common, betray a notion of culture as something akin to "being cultured"—going to the opera and using finger bowls. Individuals who have acquired a taste for the fine arts ("highbrow culture") or who show a proclivity towards "upper-class" speech and manners are said to be cultured. Obviously, people are not born with culture: they "achieve" it through cultivation. The implication is that culture, like moral or religious conversion, elevates the unrefined human condition.

According to this view, culture is an exclusive thing, available only to the few with the breeding to appreciate it—undemocratic to begin with. Some have it and some do not. Most people apparently manage with little or no culture.

But anthropology and ethnology show that the fine arts have their counterparts in all societies, nations, and tribes, and the history of modern art is full of examples of artists borrowing from other cultures (the French cubists from African carving, for example). The ballet, for all its refinement, is no more than an equivalent to the Plains Indian chicken dance. By reflection, realizing that we are all ethnics of some kind, the fine arts may be seen as the institutionalized culture of the European, British, and American ruling classes, endowed with semi-mystical connotations. For the rest of us, sports, domestic crafts, and the host of activities of the masses that are usually identified as leisure pursuits or hobbies are also culture. Bowling is culture, and so is watching TV. Culture includes art; art itself is only a part of culture.

For that matter, leisure is only a part of it too. Culture is a process of communication in which everyone participates by virtue of belonging to the human race. There could be no society without it. Culture is the process whereby groups and individuals share and exchange ideas, perceptions, and experiences; whereby the collective attitudes of a social group, its goals and values, are formed and transmitted to succeeding generations. Going beyond language or shared understanding, culture provides a *modus operandi* for all aspects of social activity, from manners and *mores* to the practical side of everyday life.

Culture enables a group of people to exist together and to operate successfully in their particular situation, and persevere into the future. Each culture develops its own idiosyncrasies and favourite expressions that reflect this particularity. The Inuit language contains 23 different words for snow but no word for art, indicating the importance of being precise about weather conditions in the Arctic and revealing an integrated approach to life that does not separate art from the utilitarian skill of carving tools and utensils. Our culture has a lot to do with what we eat and how we cook, how we arrange our homes, factories, and offices, what we wear. For better or worse, culture programs our children for their roles in life. Culture is not restricted to play; it defines work and play in the first place and shapes the organizations we build around them. Culture is inescapable: cannibals, convicts, even Canadians have a culture, albeit such an invisible one that Canadians themselves are scarcely aware of it. Perhaps that is why, when it is acknowledged to exist at all, Canadian culture is often described as dull and colourless.

OFFICIAL CULTURE

The chief reason why Canadian culture tends to be invisible, especially to Canadians, is that at the very word "culture" our attention is directed elsewhere, usually far from the plane of mundane existence. "Let them eat cake" may well have a metaphysical meaning: give the starving populace a few crumbs of something really special to help them forget they are out of bread.

Within our complex society, people are organized into a myriad of specialized jobs, trades, professions, and vocations. So we have artists and also the "cultural" professionals, those special people who do our culture for us. Culture itself is assigned a special role, set upon a pedestal and venerated with that same peculiar ambivalence with which mankind traditionally worships Woman. On the one hand, culture is glorified, used as a measure of the greatness of civilizations. On the other hand, it is cloistered—pampered, you might say, and treated as an indulgence, an entertainment, or a plaything by those who can afford the luxury and as a status symbol for those who cannot.

In Canada, Official Culture is represented by the arts. They *are* Canadian culture officially speaking, so that when we try to define what this culture must be, the things that are likely to spring to mind are Shakespearean fantasylands, Beethoven and all his works, Mikhail Barishnikov defecting in Toronto and starring with the National Ballet, and Henry Moore's pavilion.

In this context, cultural deprivation could scarcely be called genuine hardship, since culture is really nothing but a frill for ladies and dilettantes with a lot of spare time. Witness opening night at the symphony of the opera when performances of the ritual classics of the past are attended by squads of expensively gowned priestesses (the women's committee) and other devotees who come to see and be seen. Witness also the state occasion at the National Gallery when the Prime Minister or the Governor General officiates at the inauguration of a big exhibition.

The fine arts today enjoy a status not unlike that of the official state religions of the Roman and British empires: they provide spectacles for public reverence on holidays and special occasions. They form the Official Culture, which in many European countries means state culture, as well.

In countries such as the United States, where culture was pretty well left up to the robber barons and their descendants, dominant groups and individuals who possessed the means took it to be their patriotic duty to enshrine their way of life as Official Culture. The leaders of Canadian society, lacking or perhaps unwilling to commit sufficient wealth, were nonetheless determined to build some modest castles of their own. And so, over the last couple of decades, federal and provincial cultural ministries and arts councils have been set up to direct a regular flow of public funds, so that today, with a National Gallery, a National Ballet Company, a Canadian Opera Company, a National Arts Centre Orchestra, and a multimillion-dollar National Arts Centre, Canada may be seen to be keeping up appearances—to have the cultural apparatus that befits a middling power in the "civilized" world.

Considering that, without government subsidies, tickets priced at $5.00 could have cost five times as much, this sounds like a pretty good deal. It is an even better deal for the people who could easily pay the $25.00.

In *The Vertical Mosaic* John Porter first explained how the corridors of political power intersect those of economic power in Canada and are cemented in a network of private schools, Anglican colleges, and restricted clubs. While the cast of characters may change over the years, the convergence of class and power remain unchanged. It is a matter of public record that the same people who direct politics, business, and industry sit on the governing boards of ballet companies, museums, and the CBC, in their spare time. They form a small and self-perpetuating coterie that manipulates culture, that is, Official Culture, as surely as it directs the economy.

Louis XIV's Académie des arts is a good example of how giving art an official definition can lead to political censorship in a highly visible sphere of cultural life. By establishing the pre-eminence of its concept of art over all others while setting absolute standards for training and practice, the Académie succeeded for a time in making ideas resistant to change. And the imposed standards being none other than those of the absolute monarch himself, the academicians were, in effect, policing the arts on the King's behalf.

A standard, which may itself be a work of art, is a model or a measure for comparison. When a standard is invoked to differentiate between other works in order to make a selection, it follows that, the more refined the selection, the more the standard will operate as grounds for rejection. When it came to art, Louis knew what he liked, and he was in a position to commit the resources of all France to the propagation of the kind of art he liked, while effectively denying support to all other kinds. By promoting their own kind of art, the kind found in the repertories of official institutions coast to coast, and by using public assistance to carry on, the controlling interests in our own "academies" are actually enlisting Canadian taxpayers in the suppression of their own culture.

EXCELLENT OR CANADIAN

Critics, academics, art directors, and other culture experts are implicated in this suppression to the extent that they supply the rationale of Official Culture. This ideology is founded on the dogma that Art (meaning the official concept of art) is universal and that there are absolute standards of quality (official standards) by which all art, including art made by Canadians, should be evaluated. Canadian work is good depending on how well it measures up in terms of Art, the art of the grand old imperial centres of Rome, Paris, London, New York and so forth. That, in a nutshell, is the imperialist attitude to culture: "(My) Art transcends classes and national boundaries; (your) Canadian art is provincial."

In matters of taste, as the saying goes, there is no disputing. Likes and dislikes, even when shared by a multitude, are subjective; that is, they are reflections that arise from and are experienced within individual minds. Beauty is in the eye of the beholder. Judgments as to what is good and bad do, however, imply a definite point of view (good or bad for whom?), so that taste, if there is any accounting for it at all, expresses self-interest.

Of course, critics' judgments reflect this self-interest, or bias, too; those who take the stance that their point of view coincides with that of humanity in general (based on some theory of human nature) absurdly presume to project their taste—their self-interest, their bias—on the human race at large.

Of course, humanity does not exist in the abstract but in the concrete humanity of real people, a humanity as richly varied as the whole range of tribes, cultures, classes, and nations that go to make it up. When two or more individuals like the same things and this agreement is secured over time, a standard could be said to exist expressing group-interest, i.e., tribal interest or class interest or national interest.

Normally, a society's values are embodied in the art it patronizes. Works that are deemed important in a society fit into its philosophy and history and are explicable in terms of an aesthetic, or accepted standard of beauty and/or appropriateness expressing the society's outlook and objectives and the values that are bound up with its sense of identity.

This conservative aspect of culture may be summed up as "tradition." But new forms and ideas and artifacts from alien cultures may be assimilated into a tradition, provided they can be reconciled with its prevailing standards. This often involves adaptation of the tradition itself. In this respect, living traditions serve as a basis for change, modification, even revolution, while ensuring the survival of the community itself. For example, with the appearance of a southern market for Inuit sculpture, a traditional precision skill used for centuries to fashion the implements on which life in the north depended was adapted to a new purpose, and a new word, *sennengoarpok*, was invented to describe it.

Official Culture, for its part, could appreciate these carvings as bona fide sculpture once they had been rationalized according to contemporary theories of space and form and the subconscious. Their apparent resemblance to modern abstract styles only made the task easier.

The same thing happens with the certification of new art forms. The movies, for instance, were once considered vulgar entertainment for lumpenproletarians and their children, and are now officially accepted as a legitimate and full-fledged artistic medium. This may be promoted by changes in the relative strength and prestige of the classes within a society; in any case, the principle is the same. Acceptance depends on the appreciation of, and reflects the self-interest of, those who set the standard.

But what, exactly, is going on, then, when a nation's cultural leaders are proponents of an aesthetic standard that judges the bulk of the artistic output of its own citizens to be inferior and for that reason unworthy of official recognition? Such an aesthetic bias cannot be in the national interest; it can only be advocated by those who do not believe in, or do not want to see, their nation as a sovereign community.

In Canada, the organs of Official Culture address the local scene as if it were extraneous. Canadian art is treated as foreign art, acceptable only if it can be reconciled with the prevailing standards of other countries. The progress of this peculiar mental disorder has been well documented by Franz Fanon, the psychiatrist who diagnosed the effects of colonial oppression on the mental health of non-white people in *Black Skins, White Masks*:

> Every colonized people—in other words every people in whose soul an inferiority complex has been created by the death and burial of its local cultural originality—finds itself face to face with the language of the civilizing nation; that is with the culture of the mother country. The colonized is elevated . . . in proportion to his adoption of the mother country's cultural standards.

To the colonial mentality, the problem of identity rears its ugly head in the form of a dilemma: dependence or inferiority? The Canadian who looks to the cultures of bigger and more powerful nations for a definition of excellence inevitably concludes that "Canadian" and "excellent" are contradictory terms. The colonial lives a shadow existence where, as Fanon says, "The goal of his behaviour will be the Other . . . for the Other alone can give him worth." This is the limbo into which Canadian arts organizations in the main have withdrawn, while developing programs alienated from Canadian history, from Canadian goals, and even from Canadian modes of expression. Long ago, they settled for a drab diet of imitation, which Michael Cross, former editor of *The Canadian Forum*, described in 1973 as "old, foreign, and politically neutered," forsaking the chance to be creative, cultural forces in their communities.

The solution is to grab the bull by the horns, because the monster after all is an imaginary one. More and more of our artists are starting to explore that fabulous, hitherto invisible country inhabited by the vast majority of Canadians, and in so doing they are discovering that they are not the only ones who feel unwelcome in the palaces of Official Culture.

Most Canadians harbour a distinct impression, no doubt well founded, that the fine arts are not for them. During interviews with a cross section of Torontonians about attitudes to modern art, I frequently heard hints that galleries were considered to be off limits for ordinary folk. People feel inhibited by the trappings of big-C Culture—museum marble, opera-house plush, and fancy balls—because, even though top hats and tails at opening night are no longer *de rigueur*, arts events are still society events. This is borne out by the continuing use of pretentious architecture for cultural institutions. It is evident in the way opera and ballet are televised on the CBC as "special events" in the manner of a royal tour. And it is apparent in the attitude of the patrons—as, for instance, when the women's auxiliary of one of our largest symphony orchestras held a gala champagne-and-strawberries fund-raising ball and invited the orchestra to give a "benefit" concert at the party. When the performance was over, the musicians were ushered into a back room for beer and cheese.

Arts organizations receiving heavy government support are not generally available to Canadians as vehicles of their cultural expression. Far from it. By and large, our fine arts experts have ignored or discounted the fine arts of all but a minority, an élite who are basically ashamed of being Canadian. This outlook permeates the approach, presentation, and, of course, the content of the programs, which tend to be oriented to a rootless North American middle-class audience. "Democratization of access to cultural resources" has therefore literally meant "taking Official Culture to the masses." The masses are expected to assimilate an aesthetic which, in terms of both class and nationality, postulates their inferiority. This is why sovereignty is the first step towards true cultural democracy in Canada, just as cultural democracy itself has become a prerequisite for Canadian sovereignty.

MASS CULTURE: INSIDE THE U.S. EMPIRE

The fine arts in Canada in their present form, being the culture of a minority, are only a small part of Canadian culture as a whole. There are as many cultures as there are classes and ethnic groups, and there are manifold ways in which these find expression. Television, the press, movies, and recordings are, in their way, the arts organizations for mass or popular culture. In North America, these constitute actual commercial industries, and it is generally understood, because of the common misconception of the word culture, that this means commercial *as opposed to* cultural. The two are supposed not to mix. The fine arts, which are non-profit, are not expected to be commercial (or commercialized) and, by the same token, purely commercial enterprise is not identified as cultural.

But, while these industries may indeed be run like businesses (and, for that matter, so is a large symphony orchestra), their most important value to society is cultural. They are, practically speaking, public communication networks for unofficial culture.

In countries where Official Culture engages the interest of only a minority, one expects to find, and usually finds, a healthy and active popular mass culture. Masses of Americans do not listen to the Metropolitan Opera, but they do have their own music: Mantovani, Frank Sinatra, and the Mormon Tabernacle Choir. In Canada, mass cultural systems are saturated with the products of U.S. popular culture but not with the culture of average Canadians. To find it, you have to go outside the main networks. This is why Canadian culture is invisible, and it may also explain why popular culture in Canada tends to be strongest in outlying regions and rural communities that have not yet been totally plugged into and transformed by the media.

In Canada, the cultural industries are dominated by U.S. corporations, usually acting here through their various branch plants. Over the past decades, the Canadian market for cultural goods has been steadily annexed by the domestic U.S. market, with the result that the economic prognosis for native Canadian operations is deteriorating, day by day. Broadcasting, the only cultural industry that has been regulated by a government agency, remains in Canadian hands; even so, the U.S. influence on the content of radio and television programs is overwhelming.

In 1973, just 2 percent of all the records sold in this country were produced by Canadian firms. Canadian musicians have had little choice but to record on U.S. labels. Moreover, only the large U.S. recording companies command a vast continental distribution empire and have the resources to promote performers like Paul Anka and Joni Mitchell to stardom. But for Canadians there are real drawbacks to the U.S. system. Because it is based on a continental market, artists who have been writing or performing for a specifically Canadian audience must also compete for a U.S. audience. To get wide distribution in Canada requires acceptance in the States.

In this situation of dependence, our cultural industries have not been able to keep pace with the talent. Our artists have been hampered by the fact that, though Canada lies within the U.S. system, their access to its benefits is normally only through a side door, so the lure to try the main entrance has been hard to resist. Traditionally, Canadian singers, actors, and writers have had the choice of underexposure and hard times in Canada, or a chance of big success in the States. Some, like Mary Pickford, Hank Snow, Robert Goulet, and Rich Little, followed the yellow brick road to fame and fortune in the glittering capitals of U.S. culture and never returned. The others just disappeared. Either way Canada lost.

Everyone knows today how, in those formative years after World War II, U.S. money with Canadian government co-operation sought out a controlling interest in Canada's resource industries and manufacturing. Now we are discovering that our creative talent has been exchanged for U.S. movies, books, and television, just as our natural resources have been swapped for manufactured goods—and with identical results: the colonization and dependence, and eventually by the disappearance of the Canadian industry. In the cultural sphere, U.S. money with the same government co-operation is aborting Canadian initiative, capturing a part of our minds, and imposing an alien mythology.

As a colony of Britain, Canada grew up in a condition of economic dependence, and because one of the characteristics of a colony is the habit of looking for cultural leadership in the same place that it looks for loans and preferred markets, Canadians read Kipling, sang Gilbert and Sullivan, and named their dogs after British governors general. We adopted the

British parliamentary system, common law, and Twining's tea. After we had officially ceased to be a colony in 1931, the cultural ties remained for some time. The psychological conditioning of colonial attitudes lived on, particularly among the leading classes, who began looking for a replacement for Mother Britain. It was not a prolonged search. Our trading ties had already switched to New York and Washington, and, almost before we knew it, we were watching Archie Bunker, reading *Time* magazine, and taking the kids to McDonald's.

The effect of this psychological dependence is as harmful to a group as it would be to an individual. Canadians as a cultural group have lost touch with their past, as many Indian tribes have. We do not value the traditional ways. We denigrate our own cultural achievements, accepting them only when they are given certification elsewhere. (So, rock musicians become stars when they crash the U.S. charts, and a symphony orchestra becomes great when it tours internationally and draws praise from foreign audiences and critics.)

We may like to think that the tide has turned because of the encouraging surge of nationalist concern in recent times, accompanied by a revived interest in our culture and our roots. It is true that we are hearing more about Canadian culture, and more of it is working its way to the surface than ever before, but it comes at the moment of disaster, when broadcasting and educational systems are under the heaviest influence of Americanization, and when unprecedented numbers of gallery directors, theatre managers, CBC public relations officers, corporation arts consultants, and deans of fine arts faculties are arriving from the U.S. to direct Canadian cultural institutions.

Although the architects of the Canadian sell-out have been sitting on the boards of arts organizations all along, the U.S. influence arrived first through the media, and it affected popular culture long before it touched Official Culture. In fact, the upper classes in Canada resisted it at first, deploring Americanization, not so much on patriotic grounds as because they believed it to be vulgar and commercial. Still, the Royal Commission on National Development in the Arts, Letters, and Sciences (the Massey Commission) warned Parliament of the impending invasion:

> In meeting influences from across the border, as pervasive as they are friendly, we have not even the advantage of what soldiers call defence in depth. . . . Our military defences must be made secure; but our cultural defences equally demand attention.

WHAT IS A
CANADIAN PLAY? [*]

KEN GASS

○

Once it became clear to writers that the alternate theatres really were interested in staging their works, plays did emerge. In 1974, critic Connie Brissenden edited a collection of early plays produced by Ken Gass (b. 1945) at the Factory Lab Theatre. This is Gass's introduction to the volume.

What is a Canadian play? What is a Factory play? Since the Factory Theatre Lab subscribes to the by-line, "Home of the Canadian Playwright," one might rightly expect an anthology of Factory plays to provide some answers.

What is an Elizabethan play? "Hamlet?" "Titus Andronicus" is surely more typical of the period than Shakespeare's best plays. Should we try to characterize an age by its mainstream of writing or by its most notable exceptions? Should we try to characterize this so-called new wave of Canadian playwriting at all? What new "ism" (aside from Neo-Nationalism and Neo-Naturalism) can we add to the parade of twentieth-century critical catch-phrases to capture the flavour of our new playwrights? Well, if Esslin can coin a phrase to link such diverse stylists as Pinter and Genet, surely somebody's going to find a way of putting John Palmer and David French in the same sentence.

Because the advancement of the Canadian playwright was such a sudden and recent movement, it cannot help but be a little self-conscious. Future historians will obviously summarize the activity according to what they think is best worth remembering. From the viewpoint of Artistic Director of the Factory, I am loathe to try to categorize so diverse a collection of stimulating playwrights as exist in Canada today. This is not to say

[*] *The Factory Lab Anthology*, ed. Connie Brissenden (Vancouver: Talonbooks, 1974), 7–10.

that common factors are not present. I can't justify it, but I find myself wanting to say that the plays in this volume could not have been written or first produced anywhere else. Perhaps it is best, therefore, to start with what I think the plays are not.

I don't think the plays belong to any international theatrical trend. When the Factory began in 1970 with a commitment to do only Canadian plays, it seemed an extravagantly foolish ideology for the time. The policy, however, did not stem from any passionate nationalism. Rather, it was a simple and arbitrary way of escaping the Canadian theatrical rut of following fashion. Regional playhouses were (and, largely, still are) shaping their seasons to reflect the fashions of Broadway and the West End, and, young directors like myself in Studio or University companies were modelling our work after "Tulane Drama Review" descriptions of Off-Off-Broadway and Eastern Europe. By limiting the Factory to only new Canadian plays, we were forced to abandon the security blanket of our colonial upbringing. We found ourselves in a vacuum, without roots, and, indeed, without playwrights. The plays soon surfaced, happily, many of them bouncing to life after years of neglect. We also discovered to our surprise that the country was indeed ready for a surge of nationalism in many fields and that we were on the crest of a timely wave. Ours was not the arise-and-conquer-the-world breed of nationalism, however. The problem of living in a vacuum without roots still plagues many of our writers. I think our writers feel this sense of waywardness, this absence of conscious tradition. Thus, common factors that the plays include are a feeling of frustration, a sense of inertia, and yet the struggle to make something happen—even something fantastic happen. It is very much an unfinished struggle and many of the plays lack conclusive endings. True, this ambience is characteristic of a great deal of other twentieth century writing, but the uniqueness of Canadian writing is as unique as the country is itself. We are a large and important country, yet we do not have a war to renounce or a dominant history and mythology to question. We hardly know that we exist as a nation, except through our rejection of British and American paternalism. The Quebecois have at least a sense of culture and repressed nationhood. Even English-speaking audiences have no difficulty translating Michel Tremblay's kitchen-sink squabbles into political realities. But when George Walker writes about living in a cultural desert and banging one's head against an increasingly grotesque wall, English Canada thinks he's writing a fantasy.

I wish we could claim that Factory plays had something important to do with factory workers in Canada, but our overall repertoire does not allow us to make such a claim. In our first season, we produced a number of strong political works, such as "Branch Plant" by Harvey Markowitz and "Creeps" by David Freeman. However, the Factory has insisted on an eclectic outlook and tried to respond to writers and directors with a wide variety of backgrounds and personal viewpoints. I remember being berated by a University of Toronto student prior to our first production for remaining politically ambiguous and not declaring ourselves a theatre dedicated to revolution. This same student stormed out of our production of "We Three,

You and I" by Bill Greenland in a fit of anger, tearing her blouse on the barbed wire set. I found her action ironic because "We Three, You and I" is probably the most powerful political document we have ever produced. It has precipitated violent reactions of all sorts. When we produced it in England in 1973 as part of the Factory Festival of Canadian Plays, I forewarned the British actress playing the part of the Matron to anticipate the possibility of strong audience reaction. She replied that such things probably happened because of our relatively naive audiences in Canada, but, in London, audiences were used to the Open Space and would not get so involved. As it turned out, the charity-conscious British reacted most violently of all, literally rioting, calling the police, attacking myself and the actors and demanding a discussion of the play. "We Three, You and I" investigates the theatrics of our public platforms and, as such, has found the perfect form for its subject matter. The play attacks the way in which fund-raising campaigns exploit our sense of guilt to make us feel guilty about things that, yes, in the final analysis, we know we should feel guilty about. The Matron finds no solution to her daily frustrations but to become more and more ruthless in her quest, and Cathy, a pawn and a doomed child, screams out for life and humanity.

While the first Factory season gravitated towards works with a political basis, the second season seemed to find an unusual number of comedies, ranging from the grotesque, biting comedy of Larry Fineberg's "Stonehenge Trilogy" to the kooky nostalgia of Louis del Grande's "Maybe We Could Get Some Bach." One of our most successful works in this vein was "Brussels Sprouts" by Larry Kardish. On the surface, the play is an easy-to-take, naturalistic sex comedy about a charming menage-a-trois. But the key to what Kardish is really trying to write lies, I think, in two aspects of the play that many observers simply found an unnecessary intrusion: Charlotte's long fantasy speech about Persia and the bizarre "curtain raiser" at the end of the play. Is the "curtain raiser" a surrealistic look on how the Brussels relationships are remembered several years later? I think it is more likely that the "curtain raiser" represents the real world to Kardish: the kitchen, the wife and the pounding of one's frustrations into the typewriter. Brussels has become a faraway memory and the orgiastic weekend an impossible dream. Charlotte herself becomes most real when she fantasizes about her mad Persian abductors. In the rest of the play, she is elusive. When she leaves, even after stealing the motorbike, it feels as if she was never there. What is operative within the play is the way in which fantasy—or reality that now feels like fantasy—affects Ernie and, particularly, Moby. The unabashed musical beds comedy makes the play's serious reflections on fantasy and frustration all the more poignant.

George Walker is another playwright who explores his most serious concerns through comedy. Indeed, he is probably the wittiest and most thoroughly comic writer in Canada. Despite his natural humorous bent, Walker avoids conventional farce and comedy forms and creates his own style. "Ambush at Tether's End" is a fairly early play, produced near the beginning of our second season. A few months earlier, Walker made an impressive debut at the Factory with "The Prince of Naples," an unusual comic encounter of a young pseudo-prophet of the sixties trying to replace the rational, conventional thinking of an older man with a hip interpretation of Nietzschean madness. Walker's skill turns what could be a cerebral exercise into a zany life and death struggle between two obsessed individuals. "Ambush" develops further the serious game of philosophical one-upmanship. Here the superior being is Max, the corpse, who has demonstrated his intellectual supremacy through an artfully arranged suicide. His rival, Jobeo, tries to outwit Max by preparing the stage for a rational homicide. Our real concern, however, is with the two pawns of the game, Galt and Bush, little men embodying only the stereotypes of businessman and sportsman. The comic interest lies in watching their patterns of evasion. They are outwitted in this aspect though by Max's parents, the Cranes. When Jobeo flees the scene, Galt and Bush find themselves concerned. Their misdemeanours have been publicly exposed and they have no alternative but to join the philosophical race and embark on a colorful suicide attempt to redeem their everyday triviality. Walker always manages to balance extravagant farce with serious character desperation and their ultimate failure is both hysterically funny and painful. The Factory has produced five major Walker pieces within a three-year period. It is satisfying to reread his earlier works, not only to see how well they stand up, but also to observe how he develops his themes from play to play. It is further satisfying to note that while three years has seen Walker growing in leaps and bounds, he is still at the beginning of what should be a major literary output.

How to talk about Raymond Canale's "The Jingo Ring?" The Factory has always had a penchant for plays that are unusual, that defy conventional forms and approaches. Like "Ambush at Tether's End," in fact, "The Jingo Ring" was ignored when first produced in our second season. It is a slippery play to digest, as it seems to be constantly shifting its groundwork. The core of the play is actually quite straightforward: an enigmatic stranger visits a small town and plays on the minds of the townsfolk through simple powers of suggestion. The town pursues an illusion; there are casualties along the way. When the illusion fails to materialize, they return to their primitive pastimes. In the chase, absurd escapades of falling off precipices into dung-heaps in search of gold are juxtaposed to the trivial killing of a peon. The play is frightening: success is an illusion and inertia is the only state of well-being. What is troublesome about the play is its surface, the comic send-up tone that seems to grate against the tough, poetic vision at the play's centre. Yet it is precisely this tension created by playing the cruel central action in an almost camp style that gives the play its rich texture and its theatrical effectiveness.

"Strawberry Fields" by Michael Hollingsworth is another directorial challenge. Like "The Jingo Ring," it was premiered with a dynamic production by Paul Bettis. "Strawberry Fields" is the only play here from our third season. It was one of the most popular and controversial plays to come out of "Works," the mad Factory Festival of Short Plays. "Works" was a direct reaction against developments in the Toronto theatre scene where it was thought that theatres (including the Factory) were losing their creativity and giving in to pressures to produce commercial "hits." Thus, every two days for two weeks, we presented fourteen unusual short plays with fourteen directors and fourteen casts. The Canadian theatre machinery reacted against this exercise: critics hated it, although almost every play received rave reviews from different critics; the union, Actors Equity, withdrew their performers and closed down the theatre and, as a result, the Factory lost a major grant and nearly collapsed. Was the exercise worth it? Very definitely—and worth doing again. As with the theatre itself, by creating a new outlet for new short plays, we discovered new exciting talent. "Strawberry Fields" was submitted as a loose, short play which, through rehearsal process, developed into its present form. Hollingsworth has since gone on to write two other plays, including "Clear Light" which was produced by the Toronto Free Theatre and closed down by the city's morality squad. "Strawberry Fields" repulsed a lot of people and many audience members walked out. Yet the play is as fresh as it is horrific and it demands serious attention. Hollingsworth is a very gentle person, the play explores uncompromisingly the acid decadence of rock scene followers. Hollingsworth is a romantic nihilist exploring the aftermath of civilization, curious about the composition of the shit and the leftovers. The circus is over, yet the barren surface of the play hides infinite energy and frustration. The play is a tour de force that demands daring improvisational aliveness from its three actors. Is the play a reflection of Canada? Two young Canadians get mindfucked by a giant American, but they kill him in the end and then start in on each other. Positive action at last is possible! We will survive though it seems we will lose our humanity in the process.

I am honestly too nearsighted to know what these plays add up to, or whether they make any statement about Canadian writing or the Factory. Other works belong in the picture as well, such as John Palmer's "Touch of God in the Golden Age" which is too long for this anthology, and the following, all of which are available in other published editions: "Creeps" by David Freeman (Toronto, The University of Toronto Press, 1972), "Death" by Larry Fineberg (Toronto, The Playwrights Co-op, 1972), and "Foul Play" by Lawrence Russell (in "Penetration—Five Plays by Lawrence Russell," Mission City, The Sono Nis Press, 1972). What the plays really need at this point, however, is less commentary and more productions by adventurous directors. Only then will they find their true place in the context of contemporary Canadian theatre.

HENRIK IBSEN ON THE NECESSITY OF PRODUCING NORWEGIAN DRAMA ◇

JOHN PALMER

○

What exactly constituted a Canadian play? Even the playwrights themselves couldn't resist getting in on this debate. With his tongue planted firmly in his cheek, playwright John Palmer (b. 1943) put his own Henrik Ibsen on the stage in 1977 to discuss the issue of Canadian—oops, make that Norwegian— drama. The whole play appeared in 1977 in Canadian Theatre Review. *What follows is an excerpt only from Ibsen's lecture to his audience.*

IBSEN: There seems little doubt as to what is French drama or German drama or English drama; it is often what we see on the stage in France, Germany and England. . . . And though it seems odd to me to raise the question as to what is Norwegian drama, it is not I who have raised it, but, even more oddly, those who claim it does not exist, thereby placing themselves in the rather untenable position of demanding a definition of nothing. Since I know that it does exist I shall not insult anyone's intelligence by trying to define a self-evident term such as "Norwegian drama" except to observe that it may not portray sardines or fjords, may or may not transpire in Norway itself, even may or may not portray Norwegians; it is the sensibility that is Norwegian, not the cut of the maid's apron.

Other hysterics have prophesied that the production of new Norwegian drama will mean the demise of the classics and the best of contemporary foreign drama. Do they infer that once our new drama is widely produced, nothing can compete with it? Whatever their idiotic fear may be, it has been

◇ Canadian Theatre Review 14 (Spring 1977): 48–49. Reprinted by permission of the author.

trumped up by those who know they are incompetent in dealing with new work. There is no precedent for these prophesies in 2000 years of history.

During the following paragraph he dabs himself with his handkerchief.

Why has the lie been propagated that there are no Norwegian play-wrights who are any good? I think for the same reason that there are suppos-edly no women playwrights of merit. Well, there are very few Jews in the Vatican; if you want more you have only to advertise stipulating the salary.

The Norwegian theatre is paid for by the Norwegian people in taxes yet it is largely run by Germans and Englishmen who are bent on giving the Norwegian people German and English versions (I refer here to an all important sensibility) of German and English plays. I suppose we must be thankful they have sometimes bothered to have them translated into Norwegian.

I must here timidly inquire as to the purpose served by performing Norwegian in an English accent. Am I supposed to be impressed by that air of rigid respectability? I find it odd to live a Norwegian life the way I do and enter a Norwegian theatre to find not a jot that is Norwegian. Why do we not simply tour entire productions from England and Germany 52 weeks a year? Better the real thing than a copy of it? Why is our largest the-atre controlled by a foreigner? Why are many regional theatres, all subsi-dized as well by Norwegian taxpayers, similarly manacled? Why is this not tolerated in any other nation on earth? Why do these aliens overwhelm-ingly produce drama originating in any other nation than Norway? Why is their much touted genius not automatically used in the development of Norway? We, after all, are employing them at the disastrous expense of ignoring those who have consistently pledged themselves to precisely that indigenous labour which these carpet baggers disdain. *He crumples the hand-kerchief violently in his fist.* Who is using whom? Why is government condon-ing this state of affairs with subsidy and indifference? Why not subsidize Drury Lane directly? Why is this intolerable in any other nation on earth? What is suicide? *He picks up the glass and puts it down again.*

If the government were to heavily subsidize the importation of sardines and allow our own fishing industry to fend for itself as best it could, the nation's economy would collapse. Do not think that art has no relation to politics. It is the barometer of the times. In a healthy society, art is a minister created by the people, answerable only to the nation and before whom kings and presidents tremble alike. Why is the barometer in Norway being ignored? The main reason, as I have stated, is that Norwegians are not able to see it since our stage is at present cluttered with the lords and ladies of other lands, whose glitter, ambience and humour are irrelevant to Norway.

THEATRE IN CANADA: THREE STATEMENTS[◇]

GEORGE RYGA

o

Without doubt, the most distinguished and passionate Canadian drama-
tist of the late 1960s and 1970s was George Ryga of Summerland, BC.
Author of the groundbreaking The Ecstasy of Rita Joe, *Ryga, when not*
writing for the stage, radio, or television, contributed a series of essays on
theatre in Canada to the Canadian Theatre Review.

A VIEWPOINT ON ITS DEVELOPMENT AND FUTURE

In Canada, the quality of our lives is largely determined by the amount of
snow that falls annually on our landscape. By cutting through it—going
over it, creating a lore of seeming indifference about it, and just learning to
live with it as a reality for much of our lives—we manage to survive. Until
eventually the thought of living without snow of one form or another
becomes unthinkable in our mystique. Because of this, the folk expression
"snow job" has a particular poignancy when taken off the landscape and
applied to such things as the evolution of our national consciousness.

For we are all the victims of a colossal "snow job" perpetrated on us by
the makers of a history that often borders on being non-history—by definitions of ourselves which have succeeded in making near strangers of each
of us to the other—and by so-called resolutions to these problems which are

---

◇ "Theatre in Canada: A Viewpoint on Its Development and Future" is from
Canadian Theatre Review 1 (Summer 1974): 28–32; "Contemporary Theatre and Its
Language" is from *Canadian Theatre Review* 14 (Spring 1977): 4–9; "The Need for a
Mythology" is from *Canadian Theatre Review* 16 (Fall 1977): 4–6.

often-times worse than the original problems themselves. It was a process of fragmentation and systematic chaos with the culture of a people that was never attempted during the hey-day of colonialism in Angola or Mexico. In Canada it succeeded beyond the wildest expectations of its exploiters. The results were cultural subservience and a feeling of inadequacy that to this day bedevils the dedicated cultural worker in this country. In terms of economic and political manipulation, the cultural disorientation of our people has paid handsome dividends for the dominant economic sector. While the cultural energy of our people was distracted into hollow disputes on the artificial two-nations question, the same forces that have screwed both English and French-speaking Canadians for a century—the C.P.R. and its handmaiden, the Bank of Montreal—with the corporation of its American cousins, pulled off the coup of the century in the Columbia River give-away—an act, which in the words of a Calgary newspaperman and commentator, constituted nothing less than a crime, and possibly, treason had it been executed by a private *and not* a corporate citizen. There is more and it is much more frightening. While we debate as to how many angels or dollars can dance on a theatre director's head—the forces that steer us to preoccupy ourselves with smallness are profitably busy elsewhere. In Brazil at this moment, the reputation of our country and people is besmirched by an exercise in imperialism—Canadian imperialism—of which the average Canadian knows nothing. Through the Canadian-based multi-national corporation, Brascan, racial genocide is reportedly being practiced against the Indians of the Amazon basin, a race of people that once numbered over 3 000 000 and have now been decimated to less than 80 000.

Brascan owns 50 percent of Brazil's aluminum smelting and fabricating capacity. It now wants the entire Amazon basin—an area half the size of this country—for full and effective control of that nation's economy. Through the military junta, it already has effective political control in friendly hands. And to make certain it stays that way, you and I, through a federal government grant of a quarter-million dollars to the new International Centre of Comparative Criminology at the University of Montreal, are also reportedly paying for a specific program of counter-insurgency towards training and research which specifically aids the Brazilian police in safeguarding the investments and influence of Brascan!

So what has this to do with theatre in Canada, its development and future? If you have been snowed to the point of indifference, then it has nothing at all to do with anything, and I'm wasting my time. You've already lost your ability to think and speak in the rhythms of your parents. Another decade, and the folk song collections of Edith Fowke, Barbeau and Dr. Helen Creighton will vanish into oblivion. Our folk dances never did appear in the repertoire of the National or Royal Winnipeg ballet companies, for we were too infatuated with the court exercises of a Europe the Europeans cannot remember and we cannot forget. While the rest of the world, even the most poverty-stricken nations, pride themselves on their folk and cultural attainments, we take Shakespeare to Warsaw and Moscow with the full-muscled support of the Canada Council, External Affairs and

God alone knows who else. (I have a recurring nightmare in which the Peking Opera plays the National Arts Centre with a production of *Anne of Green Gables* and Don Messer's *Jubilee* and mistaking their sarcasm for art, we rose to our feet as one person in the audience and gave them a fifteen minute standing ovation.)

Our theatre is an accurate reflection of our economic and political reality. During the days of British imperial dominance, the English theatrical accent was the passport to all manner of theatre absurdities in this country. It took two courageous men—one a Swede and the other a Jew—to deflate that bladder to size in Canadian radio drama which in my estimation, was the real beginning of a Canadian theatre. Esse Ljungh and the late Rupert Caplan did more to stimulate good apprenticeship, reorientation and rebellion for new style and content in dramatic craft than all the efforts of funding agencies and professional and amateur so-called theatre prior to, and since their time. The beginnings of my contribution started with them. I did not know of Canadian Theatre when I began writing drama. Fifteen years later, I still know nothing of a Canadian theatre. There is a collection of theatre literature—of which a company here and there periodically produces an item—but there is no Canadian theatre I know of. There is a lot of transplanted English and American theatre of illusion to which a small percentage of our population—notably, those who have never known the biting eloquence of unemployment or enforced welfarism—cling like aging wolves to an arthritic moose.

But a national theatre, a full-bodied, dynamic theatre of people for people, is not going to happen in English-speaking Canada until we clear our heads and move forcefully beyond the outer limits of restriction imposed by the funding agencies through the proliferation of theatrical charlatans and economically-vested boards of directors. We have been trapped 40 years behind actual history. A viable national theatre must strive for nothing less than a vanguard position in expression of national ideals and international humanism. In this, we have a long way to go, for we are easy victims of our own lack of confidence in our heritage and quickly dazzled by seeming advances which are no advances at all.

In this latter context, I wish to cite what appears to be an interest in our regional theatres towards encouraging indigenous drama. In actual fact, the picture is grimmer today than it was three years ago, when the issue became a public one as a result of my confrontation with the Playhouse Theatre in Vancouver over *Captives of The Faceless Drummer*, a period when the gloves were off for the first time in a struggle that was to begin a definition of what really was meant by a Canadian theatre—for what end, and for whom. Fighting desperately against imposition of a Canadian-content quota, the regional theatres gave tacit recognition to the need for inclusion of more Canadian works in their programming. In return for this weak retreat, the class-based structure of theatre control was retained by the same people who had initiated the Playhouse controversy. And, of course, the Canada Council and provincial funding agencies chided the regional theatres, then backed them with continued support on an obscene scale—most of this funding being absorbed into management and operating expenses—and almost none of it trickling into creation of Canadian drama.

What followed was two-fold: the beginnings of sabotage productions of Canadian works—plays designed, interpreted and promoted in ways that would discourage both audiences and champions of Canadian theatre. And the rise of what I call "beggars theatre"—productions of Canadian drama under impossible conditions in garages, church basements, etc. led by dedicated, well-meaning people who failed to see the significance of what they were embarking on—the dangerous possibility that what we might call Canadian theatre might from its inception be a crippled, pathetic exercise in futility. I refused, and continue to refuse, to allow my works to be produced under these conditions. For while dinosaurs like the Stratford Festival and the self-indulgent thing at Niagara continue to be lavished with endless resources to produce Molière, Shakespeare and Shaw, I demand the right to equal auspices, for I too, am an artist of world stature. I refuse to endorse the cheap, diversionary and divisive tactics of the Canada Council and the regional theatres to delight their book-keepers in announcing vast numbers of productions of Canadian works—when in reality, nothing more than public rehearsals occur.

Because I refuse to divorce theatre from the larger issues of life confronting us, I get punished. My plays are produced less frequently in the regional theatres today than they were five years ago. Words written by me have been bastardized and rearranged beyond recognition, yet my name has been left on the playbills. Last summer I had to endure the agony of witnessing the dedication of talents of many people, as well as my text of a new play—being employed to give credence and dignity to the Banff School of Fine Arts and its hitherto invisible racial and social policies. So the cause of viable Canadian theatre has reeled under the counter-attack of a social and political system that viciously defends itself against all criticism and examination. Certainly, I've been hurt. And because I've been hurt, so have you. Because I do no more than reflect your experiences, thoughts and possibilities through my art.

But I am not a pessimist. I survive because I refuse to be contained. So will you, and perhaps twenty years from now we can discuss theatre in Canada as a substantial ingredient in our daily lives and not as some abstraction that provides a living for its teachers and administrators, and less than half a living to its practitioners. And as far as the rest of the population is concerned—a thing of no consequence, a private club where working men and women and enquiring youth are neither invited, nor made welcome.

Yet we all pay through public funding for this madness. But we have no say over ownership or direction of theatre as it exists. That is in the hands of the interlocked corporate structure that has moved in on public or semi-public institutions by the same means they use to control the means of production—through the boards of directors. They are empowered to hire or fire artistic directors, dictate policy, and even influence what goes onto the stage of a theatre. In other words, the company that pays you wages for your labor indirectly ends up determining what you might be allowed to see in a publicly-subsidized regional theatre. This is in line with a long process of Canadian reflection, beginning with the early vandals who ravaged our landscape for ore, furs and head-counts of Indian dead, writing their own history of these events, thereby destroying truth for all time.

What of the future for theatre? And what can we do about determining that future?

Well, for one thing, we can marvel at the variety and volume of snow that comes our way. Or we can, as part of our theatre experience, begin examining from our community outward just what is it we are doing and for what reason and whether this energy cannot be used in better ways. I know it can, or I wouldn't be saying these things.

The role of theatre as I see it is to give light, color and nobility to the quality or our lives. All else is adequately and disasterously covered by television. The history of theatre has few moments of serenity and, as I explained earlier, our times are no exception. Hardship is no problem. Control systems are. And they function only as long as people allow them to. As a result, a priority in future development of theatre in Canada is for the theatrical artists of this country to insist on direct control of theatre institutions subsidized by the state. From where came this god-given dictum that an artist has to answer to committees of businessmen and management professionals? And if government insists, then I demand parity for artists—that we make board members answerable to us for their enterprises! The entire question is absurd, and the Canada Council is remiss in not coming to grips with it by demanding a total change in the artist-community relationship. A change of this nature would no doubt quickly be followed by a drastic reallocation of funds to creative endeavour towards stimulating creation of an indigenous Canadian theatre that has to take second-place to nobody. This is not an abstract suggestion. From personal experience I can assure you that when we manage to take our home-grown theatre product into the outside world, it holds up well indeed!

Herbert Whittaker in a recent statement suggests that the Viet Nam war was the turning point in our theatre awareness—when we realized we did not want to be identified with the United States or its cultural values. To this, I say bravo, Herb Whittaker! But to reject, we must understand what we reject and replace the vacuum of unacceptable values with values based on our own humanity.

I don't know what the future of theatre holds. But it will be exciting and challenging. Learn all you can about theatre crafts, but alongside of that, study this country, its people, traditions, folklore, languages, myths and customs, for this is the stuff of which all good art is made.

Fortified with these qualities, none of us need have an identity crisis.

In closing, I would like to comment on charges made in the past year that I am an anti-classicist bent on destroying traditions, particularly in theatre. To lump my attacks on the Stratford and Shaw Festivals with anti-classicism is a deliberate misinterpretation of what I have consistently stated over the past six years. I stated that the Stratford and Shaw Festivals are not the national theatres of Canada—they cannot and they must never be—and I oppose those apologists who insult our sense of nation by maneuvering us for their own advantage into thinking otherwise. I would even predict that unless they retreat from their quaint, elitist and reactionary other-world stance, they may likely go the way of the Dominion Drama Festival—into well-deserved oblivion.

CONTEMPORARY THEATRE AND ITS LANGUAGE

It would be difficult and fruitless to address oneself to specific problems and qualities of contemporary Canadian theatre without reference to some framework which made contemporary theatre possible, and indeed necessary. The emergence of our contemporary theatre owes less to esoteric tradition than it does to political and economic realities outside the stage door.

This is not to suggest criticism of earlier Canadian theatrical literature—as literature, it offers valuable study. As theatre, it is unlikely to ever find acceptance again. As a dramatist, I wish it had been otherwise—that some continuity might have been maintained to enrich and deepen the field in which we work. That some additional light might have been thrown on the character, habits, agonies and laughter of those people who were our ancestors in the English-speaking parts of this country.

In a collection of *One-Act Plays by Canadian Authors* published in 1926, the following titles of plays appear: *The Maid . . . For The Empire . . . The Favours of My Lady Leone* and *The King*. I kid you not when I say the titles of those plays are also the content! For example, in *The Maid*, the heroine has the following monologue to be spoken "with considerable heat":

> If I were alive today I would not be content unless I were fighting the enemy all the time. And I am only a woman. Surely you, a man, and an Englishman at that, cannot be content to sit here waiting for regulations to allow you to fight? That is not like the English of the old days. They fought too well then, as we remember. You have ten hundred times more means at your disposal than we had in my day, and yet you sit here doing nothing when there is work to be done. Bah! I am going back to my countrymen.

Leaving Charters, the befuddled hero of the piece, no recourse but to abandon his trench and single-handedly attack the German trenches in this item of World War I madness. Interestingly enough, the hero has a French companion in the trenches—a man called Dechaux, whose final line in the play is "Mon Dieu, these English are all mad." . . . And on those words, Dechaux goes "back to sleep."

A racial cliché . . . a piece of romantic nothingness. Yet it was a published play, written by a so-called "prominent Vancouver dramatist" who went on to better things as an actor in Montreal. The play is interesting from various points of view. It is interesting for its unbashful stereotyping of characters as mouthpieces for the value-system of the British Empire at the time. It is interesting for its second-hand infatuation with the imperial war of 1914–18, which for the majority of Canadians did not have as profound an emotional influence as our previous historians would like to have us believe. It is interesting because nowhere in the play is there any indication the play was written by a person residing among people in this country. The language and metaphors are east of mid-Atlantic. The setting is European. The sentiments ready-made by the bugles of Westminster.

Anyway, the play was published and available to theatres. Which throws some insight on the *custodians* of Canadian theatre in the 1920s. And the powerful political and social influence they might have exerted as a class on the development and direction of earlier dramaturgy in this country. Certainly the conditions for a dynamic social theatre existed during this period. But by some process, theatre was isolated from people—a problem still bedevilling us in theatre a half century later.

The Maid was published in 1926. Twenty-four years earlier, in British Columbia where the play was written, the mine and smelter workers of the east Kootenays were organized into one of the most militant unions in North America. Despite years of agitation, blacklisting and company murders of membership, they survived the most vicious attacks against their ranks and pioneered the legislated eight-hour workday. A year later, the province wrote the Workmen's Compensation Act—both milestones for labor in North America. In the same period Gagnon, the inventor, successfully flew the first airborne machine (a crude prototype of today's helicopter) in Rossland, British Columbia, almost two years before the Wright Brothers flew the Kitty Hawk into aviation history—a place which rightfully belonged to an obscure, poor mineshaft mechanic from Quebec, whose place and time of death are impossible to ascertain now.

It cannot be argued that there was no place to perform theatre in British Columbia. The mining towns of Sandon, New Denver, Grand Forks, Greenwood and Rossland—among many others, not only had good recital halls in their heyday—most of them had opera houses for visiting opera companies from San Francisco and the eastern seaboard of the United States. From the 1860s to well past the turn of the century, folk songs were no longer created in this region of English Canada, as this was the period when the music-hall production of Stephen Foster began to stifle the fragile Celtic wellspring of music through which ordinary people expressed their experiences, longings and lives.

Illiteracy was widespread, and as a result, the tales of natural storytellers among the miners, fishermen and woodworkers are now largely lost to us. The literate people—like the dramatist who wrote *The Maid*—either chose to or were forced into isolation from the people . . . nurtured and sheltered by the custodians of theatre to write plays like *The Maid*, and thereby damning one of the most vibrant times of our history into obscurity. This is one of the saddest penalties we have paid in our experience with colonialism. Pray God it never happens again!

Brendan Behan once remarked that "being born in a stable doesn't necessarily make you a horse." Being force-fed colonial history and colonial styles of dress and speech doesn't mean the feeding digests well. Or that one emerges a colonial stereotype. Given the right set of circumstances, quite the opposite can occur, as the British—and more recently, the American empire-builders have discovered. If a house becomes suffocating, a point is reached where you no longer ask for repairs to the windows—you demand an entire new house with a wraparound patio!

Cultural rejuvenation, like political evolution, either works with systems or in opposition to them. Contemporary theatre in Canada—the contemporary theatre of the left—developed in opposition to official mythology. It had to—there was no other option.

If you were born in the early thirties in what was predominantly a so-called "ethnic" community, you were quickly faced with a series of absolutes. Language absolutes which were to have a profound influence on your life and thoughts. The people around you, as well as small merchants in town—the poolhall operator, restaurant waitress, blacksmith and grain elevator operator—spoke with the accent and phraseology you yourself used. But the ticket seller at the railway station, the social worker, the postmaster, and the old prick who fought in the first world war and now walked around town at night with a club in his hand in his capacity as town constable—all these spoke with an English accent. So when you heard an English accent, you heard state or civic authority or a lacky for the C.P.R. It was as clear-cut as that—there was "them" and there was "us." In "their" presence, you were guarded, tightlipped and careful. Among yourselves, you mimicked the accent and manners of the rulers. You sang your songs and turned language this way and that until it sat more comfortably in your mouth, your thoughts and your landscape. "A mite chilly" became "it's goddamned cold today!"

The language took the form of the land—uncompromising, hard, defiant—for three seasons of the year. The long months of winter isolation made the desire for human contact a constant ache. When you met another person, the meeting times were short and infrequent—there was much to say—the thoughts were no longer leisurely. You found the collective speech patterns becoming more rapid the further north you went—the consonants dropping or muted. This is a phenomenon which likewise developed in a parallel form in the outbacks of Australia.

And along with that, something else was happening. Here and there, individual people and entire families were becoming Anglicans. Certain foods began vanishing from festive dinners to be replaced by more expensive and less nourishing canned goods prepared by McDonald's Consolidated of the U.S.A. A small percentage of your boyhood friends suddenly acquired uniforms and a new identity in the Boy Scouts, where a deranged scout master spent Sundays with them teaching them how to blow up a bridge with four sticks of dynamite! Then one day, in later years, you saw the same lads in the Air Cadets, saluting the Union Jack and a water-stained portrait of the King of England, in a rundown old warehouse now turned into a cadet hall. The officer in charge was, of course, the old prick of a town cop we had all ridiculed privately only a few years earlier.

You wanted to, but you could not join them. Somewhere, at some unexplainable moment, the separation had taken place. You needed them and what they acquired. In later years, the positions would be reversed. For the flag was downgraded by legislation. And the portrait of old George the Sixth went the way of all old portraits.

All that was a prelude. Every contemporary dramatist in Canada had her or his prelude. But the crises were no longer esoteric or abstract. They were problems of physical or spiritual survival. Because much of the foundation for a substantial Canadian theatre was missing or misdirected, we had to instinctively work on a more elaborate canvas than we might otherwise have chosen.

Throughout the forties and fifties, much tentative work was done, particularly in radio drama, in exploring the altered social state of affairs as a result of political dislocations resulting from the war. A cultural and economic vacuum was occurring into which American investment and influence were channeled to displace the British loss. Buttressed with fear and despair for the serious artist, as American expansionist muscle came into play during the Korean war, coupled with the paranoia of McCarthyism on the U.S. mainland—whose repercussions were widely felt in Canada—writers like Gwen Pharis, James Reaney, Elsie Gowan, Lister Sinclair, Mavor Moore and Len Petersen, among others, were exploring directly or obliquely the changing times and social dislocations.

It was a difficult and provoking period—for both writer and performer. A period of honing crafts and trying to reckon out the possibilities. The tension snapped with an unlikely and peculiar event—the coming to power of John Diefenbaker's outdated yet effective conservative populism, and the death of the Duplessis regime in Quebec. A dedicated monarchist, a cartoonist's delight . . . a man remarkably unskilled in the sophistry of international dealings, Diefenbaker blundered into a confrontation position vis-a-vis the U.S. over the Cuban missile crisis. Open questions, awareness and quiet resentment over U.S.-Canadian relationships began to surface in a new current of national self-respect.

Almost on the heels of this development, a new Canadian theatre came to life with John Herbert's "Fortune in Men's Eyes"—the ice-breaker in the channel. A different theatre, rooted in an inescapable reality and of a dimension which would not be harnessed into a nice Sunday afternoon. For it dealt with prisons, and people who were not nice—the people on the other side—the "them." And now they had voice and language—and they were not only eloquent, they were excruciatingly poetic.

It was a play crying for reform and compassion, It was social theatre—late in coming, but powerful on arrival. Not that John Herbert altered the nature of Canadian theatre in the English speaking part of the country. Established theatres did not perform him. But serious playwrights realized what had happened, and the attempt by established theatres to isolate the politicized theatre of Quebec from the rest of the land was only partially successful. The next crop of dramatists in English Canada were no longer apologists or obscurantists.

In the early to mid-sixties, CBC television did much to popularize the underlying currents of the upcoming theatre styles and content. Particularly through two television dramas by M. Charles Cohen—"Flipside" and

"David, Chapter Two" and a production of mine titled "Indian." These three productions had a powerful impact on Canadians never previously exposed to drama, because the language, symbolisms and experiences being interpreted were uniquely their own. And it gave a greater legitimacy to dramatic writing through wide critical acclaim in Canada and abroad.

One wishes the CBC had exercised more courage and pursued with production of new Canadian works more widely, rather than falling prey to opinions and pressures of self-styled keepers of the public good! It would certainly have made for easier development and greater audience exposure to our works.

A qualitative change is taking place in the language of our theatre. The common speech of people, carefully studied and reproduced, is now being elevated into theatrical poetry. Regional speech mannerisms are no longer treated as aberrations—they are examined and integrated into emotional lines not previously explored. For indeed, without the language differences, some emotional lines were not attainable. One only has to hear the commonplace thoughts of Newfoundland fisherpeople translate into the soaring poetry of Michael Cook to understand why there will not . . . must not be, a return to one acceptable accent or language form for this country.

With the return to sources and regions, the dramatist discovers something the drama schools have yet to come to terms with—the affect of climate and atmosphere on movement in Canadian plays. The way we dress—the dimensions and style of our housing—the pace at which we must work to survive—all these things condition the internal person. There is nothing more ludicrous than watching a Toronto actor portraying a heavily dressed man entering his home, which has chilled to twenty below zero in his absence. At best, he resembles an overdressed Toronto actor moving uncomfortably through a badly designed set in a Toronto television studio. Theatre language is not merely the spoken word—it is the personality functioning in a specific environment.

And as the dramatist stops consciously considering the universal play, and concentrating on the regional, local drama with universal implications, he must care for those of whom he speaks, and of the audiences to whom he addresses his art. There can be no sham or treachery, or we have failed our obligations.

Mike Cook worries about the take-home pay and living conditions of the fishermen of whom he writes, and for whom, ideally, he would like to write. John Herbert's work on prison reform extends throughout this continent. There are numerous examples of personal and artistic contributions to social change, understanding the betterment of life.

Today's drama to a large extent concerns itself with a vanishing landscape. The fisherman working depleted waters . . . the Nova Scotian family leaving its ancestral fields . . . the Indian torn between two worlds—these seem to be paramount sources of concern, and the real content of contemporary plays. Certainly these are critical regions of social anxiety. But what is the larger contribution we are instinctively making? Perhaps we are defining the more visible details of a canvas on which our national hopes and frustrations are enacted. Perhaps we are doing what our earlier theatre should have done but failed in undertaking—recording in a human way the agonies and triumphs of yet another transition when nature or economics beat us back and alter the course of our destiny as a people.

Contemporary theatre and the makers of it take into account the small but constant advances in the lives of average people. The health and education of children, care for the aged, improved social services, medicare, public ownership of resources, cultural access to all no matter where they live—the preservation of authentic history—these are qualities of our lives which were dearly bought and will reflect itself in our theatre in days to come. Radical contemporary theatre came to life in opposition to forces which destroy life and personality. This is a commitment it must never surrender.

The struggle goes on to create a theatre in a vanguard of national expression and aspirations. It goes on against the stranglehold of multi-national corporations, and the comintern of these nation killing organizations—The Trilateral Commission, with its Canadian members—Jean Luc Pepin and Robert Bonner. There is mounting suspicion that already his world-wide organization of super economic giants has focused on undermining the more liberal provincial governments in this country. The dramatic and human implications of this are mind-staggering. But our sense of self-worth in recent times is also formidable. Which brings us back to the people as the fountainhead of all things worthwhile. As well as the field on which the worthy things we do are cultured and cared for by others as their own.

THE NEED FOR A MYTHOLOGY

Despite the fact that for generations the reasonably cultivated Canadian of means purchased his wines from France, his porcelain and silver from Britain, his woolens from Scotland, his entertainment and hardwood furnishings from the U.S.—despite the fact that acquisition of a pseudo-English accent adequately fed a national inferiority-superiority complex for longer than one cares to remember—despite the fact that as a nation we appeared to voluntarily submit into a position of cultural subservience by cultivation of tastes which depend entirely on importation of literature, music, drama and dance—despite all this, all is not as it should be in paradise. Very late in the day, in an atmosphere of impending crisis, our leaders—who understand their economic influences better than they understand their own people, turn to the sources of their inspiration and are dismayed to find deaf ears. Rene Levesque goes to New York to solicit investments for a Quebec aspiring to independence, and is rebuffed. Trudeau, in a startling display of uncertainty, meets with President Carter in Washington and asks for support on domestic issues in which the Americans should have neither influence or concern. He fares no better than Levesque—yet.

It appears that the cultivation which we imported and consumed much as we import and consume fig bars, is not adequate to sustain the spirit in times of stress. And it is a crisis of spirit we are experiencing as we slide through the millstones of history. The aspirations of Quebec are not the problem—this question has been with us for over a century. Our inability to cope with the problem is the problem. Our inability to cope with *any* problem is a source of potential satire and humour for generations to come. Faced with the choice of either destroying our Indian people or giving them an opportunity for life, we could do neither. Faced with the problem of defining immigration policies beyond the immediate future, we restrict immigration from the third world and allot grants for Canadian-born middle-class youngsters to publicly practice their Germanness, or Ukrainianness, or Hungarianness!

Sometimes our leaders turn wistfully to the Americans to draw from their experience. But that is a futile exercise, because our neighbors to the south were born out of, and tempered by, a revolution and a civil war which involved most, if not all of the people in a wrenching experience which was to shape their character, spirit and relationship to their land in a no-nonsense way. Americans have no crisis of identity or purpose. They know who they are and where they are going, for right or wrong. The language and cadence of their culture reflects this.

In Canada, our learning institutions are proud when they establish something called Canadian literature courses. Apologetically proud, as if what they were nurturing was a mild disease. Do any of us think that in Chinese secondary schools or universities there are tiny, equivalent studies titled Chinese literature studies? Or that an emerging country like Angola would permit a minor, peripheral status for a study of its heritage? Only in Canada. . . .

I was recently called into a school meeting in Summerland, where discussion of educational programs was the main point of agenda. I noticed the outline paper did not include study of Canadian history—which I felt might be mandatory, at least, for a student born and educated in Canada. The chairman of the meeting became flustered, then called for a motion to include the course on the agenda. The motion was made and seconded. Then began a lengthy and bizarre discussion, during which arguments were raised to what was more useful—history or study of welding techniques. The matter finally came to a vote—30 people voted for Canadian history to be included in high-school studies, six voted against and two abstained. There will be other, further studies made, and the last word was that the course would be included in curriculum—sometime in the future.

Among the best-fed, best-dressed, best-housed and best taken care of people in the world, we suffer from an embarrassing lack of understanding of ourselves. We live with the myth of the superiority of others, and the inadequacy of ourselves. This has hampered our political and economic sensibilities, has made our children increasingly turn to exotic and unworkable philosophies and religions of the far east, and has caused pain and exile to our finest and most sensitive artists who attempt to reflect the reality of our own lives, myths and worth. With the exception of Quebec, where cultural expression has long been integrated into national survival, the rest of Canada, the second richest country in the world, is among the poorest in its cultural deprivation. And because of this, we remain ripe as a dumping ground for the commercial cultural refuse of the world. Even worse, we mimic it, as in the case of a popular composer born and raised in the

Maritimes writing a song lamenting the loss of his childhood beside a river in Texas!

The remedy to this problem will not come from a local, provincial or federal level of government granting more funds to undisturbed artists and book publishers who are noted for their caution. It comes only through awareness of educators, parents, writers, unionists, composers, politicians and others that the key to self-reliance is self-understanding. That it is too late to dally with self-indulgent, elitist experiments . . . that the issue in national survival is development of a popular, genuine people's culture . . . whether it be literature, theatre, music or film.

And foremost in this is a re-examination of our history and lore for discovery of that distinctive mythology which reflects in our habits and ways a popularly agreed-on interpretation of who we are and how we got that way. Past experiences, climate, the distances of our geography, the role of winter . . . the colour, nature and tone of our storms and sunlight—determine the nature of our language, speed of movement and potential of our physical and spiritual appetites. This is at the core of who we are. Nobody can provide us with or sell us a substitute. And we should never accept substitutes, either at discount prices—or wrapped in colourful packaging.

It always comes to me as a surprise that to be honest in our society is somehow dangerous and not a thing to do. That people with such energy in their language and mythological references in things unsaid should be so bedevilled by theatre which bears little or no relevance to their lives . . . the same with ballet and concert music . . . the same of much of our literature written by accountants. Where in hell is the home-grown stuff that excites and ignites the imagination? Where are the raging, possessed poets and novelists whose obligation is to become not only writers but the "second government" of a nation, expressing the authentic fears, preoccupations and exaltation of the people? How many writers roared their disapproval at the arrogance and adventurism of proclamation of the War Measures Act during the October crisis? Who will remind our governments that opportunism, political juggling, and invitations for foreign influence will not resolve the dynamic problems of a two-nation, two-language, two-culture confederation. That a culture is a living thing, into which the problems of racial inequality, inflation, foreign ownership of resources and unemployment will and must reflect itself. That it pleases and refreshes by amusing. But that it also pleases and refreshes by isolating problems and proposing resolutions based on a daily contact and examination of people by the artist.

I am not going to beg the cause of Canadian authors or Canadian books here. That sort of plea would be humiliating and self-defeating. Rather, I would score the sort of complacency which has brought us all to the dangerous brink where the phrase "Canadian literature" gives some of us the vicarious delight of the defeated. Where the work "fuck" (unless appearing in a novel by an American novelist) automatically removes a novel from the reading list, irrespective of the fact that the novel may be of world stature, written out of this country, as has happened to Margaret Laurence. In one effective move, a generation of youth has lost access to a part of themselves and their land. I use this only as an example of the awesome power of the complacent educator in thoughtlessly assuming the posture of censor rather than partisan and advocate of deepening and more complex cultivation of a people equipped for changing times.

It would probably be a more pleasant world to live in if all things were structured to meet with our biases, approval and aging sense of serenity. But to accomplish this state of dying self-indulgence, we would be required to stop making children. Once we have opted for children, and the only promise of immortality left to us, the obligations to history, to a piece of this earth, to the generations to come, begins. We are caught in the business of the spinning earth even beyond the grave. Only madness exempts us from the responsibilities and rewards of changing the landscape and changing ourselves.

There is no time or need for complacency. We do what we have to do— and as long as we don't retreat against our better instincts, that is enough.

THE PLAYWRIGHT:
TWO STATEMENTS*

MICHAEL COOK

o

Out of Newfoundland came the eloquent, poetic voice of Michael Cook (1933–94). Author of stage plays (produced in both Canada and abroad) as well as radio plays (that won awards outside the country), Cook was hurt deeply by continuing rejections from some of the country's biggest theatres, which seemed to him uninterested in truly trying to establish a Canadian repertory. Both of the following essays were written in 1976.

IGNORED AGAIN

One of the most unpleasant aspects of being a playwright in this great country of ours is having to endure, almost daily, a variety of opinions from critics, directors and simple cultural bagmen about the state of the playwright. Very rarely do the playwrights get to speak for themselves. They can be personally abused and vilified by reviewers, yet denied even the right of reply. Their work provides expense account luncheons and booze parties far in excess of their own earnings. The reason for their neglect is obvious. The industry they generate is understandably nervous about releasing the source of their income without ensuring that they are suitably gagged, caged, or otherwise made innocuous.

I don't know how many playwrights are actually surviving on an income derived from writing plays in Canada. David French, David Freeman, George Ryga, Carol Bolt? Michel Tremblay, of course. There are obviously

* "Ignored Again" is from *Canadian Theatre Review* 10 (Spring 1976): 87–91; "The Painful Struggle For the Creation of a Canadian Repertory" is from *Performing Arts in Canada* 13, 4 (Winter 1976): 26–29.

others in French Canada but the Quebecois must excuse my cultural ignorance. They at least have a culture, we are staggeringly in retreat from ours
which possibly is one of the reasons they find it difficult to communicate
with us. Peering through the bars at the Quebec border they must sometimes
think they are looking at a bunch of orangutangs. I've long understood that it
might be possible to earn a living in Quebec, that superbly civilised, if politically bizarre province, by standing at a street corner sandwiched between
placards which read: "Starving English Language Playwright." They would
feel sorry for my persuasion but understand the cause.

This year, I have high hopes of earning between $7000 and $8000.
Cultural welfare. I can survive on that too, with dignity and pride intact. At
least I'm working at my craft, and am not desperately trying to snatch odd
hours between other jobs. I'm also asking my wife and three children to survive on that too, of course, with dignity, but they are understanding, and
the value of my presence at home, which others might consider onerous is,
by them, taken with the proper spirit of levity.

But I digress. I'm speaking of playwrights. The reason for theatre. Their
survival in this country is not taken too seriously. After all, culture occurs,
the reasoning runs, when the participants in cultural revolutions are dead.
What is of critical importance to those who wish to demonstrate, to themselves mainly, that English Canada has a culture are the great, plush
houses, the policies and philosophies they speak to, and their administrators and artistic directors. Providing such edifices, and their incumbents,
can survive and be seen to flourish, we may assure ourselves that, despite
living in a country noted for its resistance to truth, and ultimately, art, that
we are indeed alive and well, and able to contribute to the Olympic Games.

How do we survive? Playwrights?

The majority of us by churning out scripts for tv, radio and film. There's
nothing derogatory about that, you might say, and thank God for that, but
it does mean that the task of earning a living superimposes itself upon the
task of writing stage plays. Some of the best writers in this country are now
so much out of touch with theatre that they would find it difficult, almost
impossible to write for that form. They needed to survive. They needed outlets for their dramatic expression. But often, what began as an example of
diversification becomes the dominating fact of artistic life. Yet their initial
and overriding impetus was to write plays for the stage, a stage that neither
wanted them, cared for them, or in any way, encouraged them. There are
obvious and honourable exceptions to this generalisation, but the essential
fact remains. It is difficult to earn a living in this country as a playwright,
writing plays for the stage.

I can hear the Directors, and the critics, screaming now. Like a nation-
wide Barbers' Quartet, they intone, "The great majority of self-styled playwrights are unable to produce quality scripts."

Now we come to it. The magic words. Quality. Excellence.

We spend millions producing mediocre garbage on television, created
by people whose talent and vision is essentially dedicated to mediocrity
and who believe that the public aren't worthy of anything other than mediocrity. It's an example of a cultural attitude and a personal contempt of the

greatest magnitude, unparalleled since Hitler employed Goebbels to subvert the masses to one popular belief.

We do find it difficult, however, to commission any one playwright, of proven worth for $5000 and give him or her a year to create a play. On the other hand, a gaggle of lacklustre producers and performers in other media earn in excess of $30 000 a year and up.

But the playwrights lack quality. Even John Hirsch was moved to comment reflectively, in an earlier issue of *CTR*, that perhaps the playwrights hadn't suffered enough, that life was too easy. And in any event, by whose standards do we lack quality? Shakespeare's? Ibsen's? Chehov's? Shaw? What double standard makes it possible to tolerate and tout the lowest common denominator in other media, other art forms, then demand, from the height of Olympian detachment, that we must have only work of the highest international standards in another? And what's more, proceed forthwith to fill the theatres with imported plays that signally fail to qualify for these exacting standards—tired ex-Broadway and London hits, plays lacking relevance, humanity, dignity.

It might be of passing interest to note that all of the playwrights mentioned wrote mediocre plays, but, echoing out of a distant culture, another time, we are advised that the work is of interest. They were, after all, geniuses, and who would dare to suggest that there is such a thing extant in Canada. Greatness is one of the cardinal sins of the age. It must be negated, destroyed, neglected. Above all, it must not be allowed to show any hint of its strength, for were it to do so, the mediocrities would be shown up for the worthless pulp manufacturers that they are, and, with their direct access to millions of dollars from the public purse, there is an obvious conflict of interest at work.

Simply because we are a politically mediocre nation, it is not enough to demand that we must all bleat like lambs and believe accordingly that we are capable of no other form of expression. It is not for nothing that the most successful Canadian books of the past 20 years have been about Canadian politicians, the true inheritors of Chamberlain, whose pursuit of compromise as an art has distinguished and coloured and obscured the true strength of this country. A strength which astoundingly, lies in its art. Which is of its people.

What has aroused my ire is the tenor of a speech delivered by Robin Phillips, artistic director of the Stratford Festival, to a group of businessmen in Ottawa and reprinted, word for pristine word, in *Bulletin*, the Canadian Conference of the Arts newsletter. Not only was it reprinted, but it was prefaced by the following:

"*Bulletin* thanks Robin Phillips for permission to share his views with our readers, and is certain you will find them nothing short of inspiring."

I find them nauseating.

The basic thrust of the article is that Canada become the seat of English language theatre in the world. That is, that Stratford become the seat of English language etc. etc. And that the most revolutionary occurrence in Canadian theatrical life was the creation of the thrust stage at Stratford.

How does Mr. Phillips suggest that he accomplish this goal? By creating a film and television producing industry in Stratford that will not only attract major performing artists from abroad, but will spread its glow, like a hurricane lamp, to the dark corners of the world.

"What we have on call in Stratford," says Mr. Phillips, "is an incredibly advanced human technology, an ensemble of actors, directors, designers and, eventually, writers, who have the knowledge, experience, the instinct and the talent to make that machinery hum to creative life." Ho-hum. Eventually, the writers. But without writers, there is no indigenous theatre. What goes on in that strange mind that puts every talent before that of the writer? I think it's obvious. The writers Mr. Phillips will be concerned with are other, great, writers. They are not Canadian writers. Eventually, there might be Canadian writers, but first they must be dead. They must not be around to interfere with that creative ho-humming machinery.

There is more.

I quote: "Each year we have an array of directors, designers, actors, composers and theatre technicians whose total talent, if it could be quantified and measured on a scale of one to 10, would lift the scale into orbit somewhere around Saturn." Significantly, again, writers are not in evidence. And in any event, I think we should really be concerned with reaching the vastness of our country first before taking off on theatrical space projects.

But he begins to cut even deeper as he proceeds.

"A man may see himself as the greatest playwright in the world, but unless he gets the greatest play in the world out of his head and onto the page so that it can take shape in a theatre, who will believe him?" Who indeed, in the name of suffering Jesus? With Phillips' stated philosophy and more obvious practice, who will help him? Nobody at Stratford. We're right back to square one, where I came in.

Let's examine his phraseology again. He describes Stratford as a resource of human technology. What's human about technology? What art will be be beaming to the four corners of the Globe if and when Stratford becomes a great television and film producing centre? Just how much of an appallingly-limited artistic budget available to the media and the arts, does he propose to swallow? And will he be producing Canadian art? None, of course. That comes after the event. Eventually. First produce your chicken. Parade it. Colour it. Nurse and nurture and cherish it. But make sure the damned thing is sterile. There are after all, enough eggs in the world without adding something that might not be immediately recognisable as an egg.

A magnificent technological chicken.

Shakespeare bereft of roots and dignity.

Theatre bereft of religion and ritual.

Leaving us, a country, the supposed centre of the English language theatre, dedicated to the preservation of a standardised English language theatre culture, a dictionary beyond commonality, beyond sense, beyond meaning or significance.

I marvel at Mr. Phillips.

The theatre he serves, the playwright it was dedicated to serve, is much more than a thrust stage. Significantly, Shakespeare, with others, formed a company to produce his plays. The company's success depended to a great extent on the ability of the playwright to keep churning out those scripts. Brecht, a profound student of theatrical and social history, also formed a company to produce his plays.

Ah, I hear you cry, once again. Canadian plays and playwrights have no quality. They lack art. It's quite possible that some do. In all great ages of the-atre there have always been more playwrights than the principle star in the firmament. It takes a total theatre consciousness, in which all degrees and perversities of talent exist side by side to create a climate which makes the emergence of great plays, a great playwright, possible. It might also be worth noting, in passing, that Shakespeare wrote English plays for Englishmen. As I mentioned earlier, in Quebec there are a dozen good playwrights writing Quebec plays for Quebecois. But they are light years away from us in their comprehension and obsession with roots, and the eternal contemplation of the experience of life in a country they know and understand.

It is strange that we have a Canadian Radio and Television Commission that mediates control over Canadian content, and yet no agency that enforces it on theatres—notably Stratford. It is strange that the living kernel of the art of entertainment, the living theatre, is not even a handmaiden, but a whore afflicted with the pox, standing interminably on a street corner begging for charity. It is, granted these circumstances, that theatre, Canadian theatre, a universal theatre of known and recognisable people, struggling with dignity to assert their frail independence upon a vast and brooding landscape, a wretchedly unconcerned political and social environ-ment, should continue to exist and triumphantly assert itself. A theatre born, not perhaps of greatness, but of need.

One final quote from Mr. Phillips.

"Today, if I were to take a television camera to a street in St. John's, Newfoundland to a pedestrian and startle him half out of his mind by thrusting a microphone in his face and asking, "What sir, do you consider Canada's most significant contribution to the performing arts?" I doubt very much if the reply, "the thrust stage of the Stratford Festival" would spring immediately to his lips. The name Gordon Pinsent might, I expect. A few wits might even answer Joey Smallwood, but I'd stand a long time on a windy corner before I got the reply I was seeking."

You're damned right Mr. Phillips.

You'd stand for eternity.

The reply might well be, The Mummers Troupe, and their performance of *Buchans, A Mining Town*. Or *Dying Hard*, a play based upon the recollec-tions of miners dying from silicosis, their wives bereaved, or about to be bereaved. You see, there is a theatre of relevance, speaking to a people about themselves, in their time. Speaking in their language. As Shakespeare spoke. As all the great playwrights have spoken.

The playwrights in this country are a fact of life. Not an eventuality. To deny them existence or validity is to castrate the real Canadian theatre before it reaches manhood. To deny them existence is to impose alien academic and cultural values upon material that speaks directly to the landscape and its people. To deny the expertise Phillips speaks of to those struggling to create theatre is to ignore the fact of both the artists' and the country's existence.

It might well be that what is occurring in this country, at this time, at levels beyond Mr. Phillips and alas, many other's experience who should know better, is the last great flowering of the English Language theatre. But it's not a place, a building, a recreation. It is an original flowering, an original theatre.

For it is a fact that a theatre without playwrights, living, breathing, surly, cantankerous, loving, dedicated playwrights is a dead theatre. The future of Canadian theatre depends upon their cultivation, and recognition. Anything less, based upon no matter what human and technological resources employed in the service of no matter what or whose art, is to deny this country the theatre and truth of its own experience.

THE PAINFUL STRUGGLE FOR THE CREATION OF A CANADIAN REPERTORY

I had been cutting wood all day, that the winter might not catch us by surprise. After supper I went fishing, hungry for a freezer full of the gap mouthed cod. The wind came up Eastern. The water turned blood red. The sun paused for a moment in its weltering descent, then dropped, with the awful suddenness of fall. I stayed awhile longer, though the wind was cool and wraiths of mist went hunting for the last lone boats, but there were no fish. I came home carefully, at half throttle, the moon at my shoulder, the patched water silver and black like the vestments for a funeral service. Not inappropriate, for my mind had not been on the water or the trees, no, not even the fish, but on the painful struggle for the creation of a Canadian Repertory, of which I am a part, a canon illuminating the petty and giant destinies of Canadian humanity.

Now, no doubt, you have been warned. Here comes another frantic piece of rhetoric deploring cultural exploitation, and demanding, with all the frenetic passion of self-interest, that the theatre be devoted entirely to Canadian works for the next 25 years or, as a very minimum, the lifetime of the writer.

But this is not to be the case.

If there has been and continues to be, cultural exploitation, then it is because we wish it to be so, and, as T.S. Eliot pointed out, a nation gets the art it deserves.

No. Like the fisherman fighting for the 200-mile limit and a decent day's pay, I'm concerned with the recognition and survival of a valuable resource, theatre, and those who are its servants, and if there is an obvious element of self-interest at work, it is no more than that of the craftsman or labourer pressing for better working conditions that he or she might survive in Canada with dignity and freedom, while at the same time making a positive contribution to society.

My definition of repertory means simply an available stock of Canadian plays, a warehouse to which directors and dramaturges regularly repair each year when planning the next season. Such a repertory already exists, but unfortunately, few repair to it, or are even aware of its existence. Whereas this practice makes us unique, in a distinctly Canadian way, it also unfortunately has the effect of banishing the repertory to Purgatory, which in this country is either a series of Ph.D. theses or, perhaps more meaningfully, moving it in its echoing warehouse to an abandoned CN spur line in Northern Alberta.

In an effort to shed light upon the problem, I have solicited the aid of several illustrious dramatists from other countries who all have, it seems, faced similar problems at one time or another.

Oh dear. This raises a lot of uncomfortable spectres. It assumes, firstly, a dynamic belief in theatre as ritual, celebration, communion, theatre as revelation both sacred and profane. A belief in theatre as the ultimate art of the people and as the progenitor of a myriad of revolutions.

It is possible that, living in a time of utter confusion the chaotic resurgence of medieval style set against the collapsing edifice of 19th century manners and morals, that we are living artistically in a no man's land where everything can flourish but nothing can survive. If it is true, as McLuhan has argued, that the great bulk of the established generations, the wielders of power political, social and economic are busily trying to re-create the golden age of their imaginings, then it is also true that they will search for, and encourage, an art that is historic and nostalgic, one that relates to a past and not a present reality or a possible future.

We don't need to go to the States to find analogies there. Pierre Berton has been tapping that resource for a decade. Theatre too, apparently *avant garde* in style, limits itself to the romantic vision. One thinks of *Ten Lost Years . . . The Farm Show*. The political lessons to be drawn are less significant than the mood surrounding the recreation. In the sense that such theatre, such documentary drawing, presents us in many cases with an unknown or forgotten past it is of immense value, but only if it exists within a structure that is most powerfully of the truth of our time. The warehouse again.

And yet it is precisely against such a set of circumstances, an apparently secure order confronting a period of moral and philosophical chaos, that great ages of theatre do flourish. When Queen Elizabeth I died, the medieval world died with her. Shakespeare destroyed a play, *Measure for Measure*, by attempting to fuse the warring and irreconcilable philosophies of love and justice, and finally turned his back upon the future, the New World, in *The Tempest*, leaving it to the poetic beast to make or mar as he would. But he was a repertory in himself, and reduced all things to the familiar, the known realities of his time and place. Danes, Italians, Venetians, Moors, were all Elizabethans inhabiting a rural countryside of which they were an integral part, whose capital was a dirty, brawling city of a mere 100 000 people.

Although we inhabit an entirely different set of circumstances, the sense of confrontation, breakdown and impending chaos is not dissimilar. Unlike Shakespeare and his fellow dramatists however, standing on the back of Piers Plowman, we had no recourse to tradition, since we were strangers in a land already inhabited, with its own peoples and cultures. South of the border, our European brothers were in a similar predicament, and so, in our different ways, we set out, using dead Crusading ethics as an expedient, to destroy the native peoples. And when the land and its peoples were sufficiently tamed, and it became necessary to assume the trappings of civilization, both nations set out to re-create culturally the glories that existed in past homelands. But cultures only transplant as they adapt to environment, become grafted on to an existing root, become metamorphosed.

Full fathom five thy father lies;
Of his bones are coral made;
Those are pearls that were his eyes:
Nothing of him that doth fade
But doth suffer a sea change
Into something rich and strange.

The simple act of revolution in America made cultural metamorphosis possible. It served American roots from the Mother Country. The spiritual energies that gave rise to art were freed then to draw from the Dionysian source of all such energy, the environment, and the struggle of people to come to terms with the blind Heavens, the naked rock. Caliban, rapist and poet of the wilderness, masterless, coming to grips with his own soul.

But in Canada there was no revolution.

It is as if we have lived in the country by default, taking our spiritual nourishment from elsewhere (I hasten to exempt Quebec from this statement), and although we have made certain gains in the visual arts, music, dance, and particularly in the private vision of the novel, in theatre, the one art that requires the conspiracy of collaboration, we have barely progressed beyond the sentiment, glitter and bombast characteristic of the Opera Houses of the Gold Rush which in their ruin, like the one at Sandon, B.C., stand as mute testimonies to a people reaching out for an expression denied them.

It would appear that only a nation secure in itself (however falsely) can create, participate, joy and sorrow in a theatre that speaks to itself at no matter what cost. Lorca referred to the great age of Spanish Theatre, when author and actor did have authority, but it was an authority granted by the collaborators, the people. And if such authority is denied the artists and their collaborators, then there is nothing anyone can do about it.

o

From the esoteric to the particular.

In Canada at this moment in time, the annual repertory is almost exclusively non-Canadian. It is true that increasingly, playhouses are beginning to incorporate one new play into their repertory per season . . . a sop to Cerberus. In addition, by claiming it as a world premiere and shoving it to a second, third or fourth stage, there's a chance that it won't cost too much in either funds or subscriber alienation. Attempts to increase their commitment beyond this meet resistance, derision, occasionally downright aggression. Canadian content, the reasoning runs, will rise to the surface when it is good enough. The closest analogy to this process I can conjure up at this moment is that of the witch in the Middle Ages who, on being accused of witchlike conduct by friends and neighbours, would be attached to sacks of large rocks and unceremoniously dumped into a river or lake. If she rose . . . she was obviously not guilty, and would be freed to practice more witchery. If she sank . . . well, the shrug was not invented by Trudeau.

But the paradox is that without exposure there can be no Canadian repertory. Shakespeare, Calderon, Molière did not rise out of a firmament specializing in German, Italian or Russian plays. They rose out of the warehouse. This problem is basic to the problem confronting the playwright, and should be a major topic of concern to all those who love both the art, and their country, for we have never cut the umbilical cords that bind us, spiritually and physically, to cultures that, for all their magnificence, are unable to create for us a specific and recognizable sense of being.

Our fear of America, for instance, arises as much from a sense of guilt as from outrage. Americans possess the energy, will and belief to conspire to create, for conspiracy is an integral part of the artistic as well as the political process. And, if we find ourselves being raped, it is because we have failed to conspire to create a matching vision of our own nation manifest in its culture.

There appears to be a basic inferiority at work in the Canadian psyche as it applies to art, to theatre in particular, an inferiority aggravated by the fear of the primitive, the abundance of dialect, and the excesses of the environment itself. Almost from the beginning, we began to turn our back upon it, did not see in its artifacts, as the Indian and Eskimo see, the Spirit of the land struggling for release. We retreated instead to the cities and the comforting re-creations of civilizations that, even if they occasionally reflected passion and disorder, sprang at least from a known order and a comforting sense of tradition. We began to reject each other, considering as historical oddities or source material for jokes those who, living on the outer edges of the country, fought it, loved it, came to grips with it, learning not to fear it or the passions in themselves which it nurtured. We are, it seems, not merely ashamed of our mythology but are actively pursuing policies, political and artistic, that will effectively ensure its failure to surface into our consciousness at all.

Perhaps it's of significance that many major artists in this country, in every medium, are working out of specific and narrow localities, exploring the universal as it manifests in a closely observed rural experience. As the old are betrayed, the usefulness of their days denied; as the young are educated to believe that their own mythology is either non-existent or, at best, insignificant, then I suspect, increasingly, the artists will stand beyond the edge of contemporary society, creating a testament which has to endure for the future generations who will come to understand, will come to look for, the origins that have been denied them.

If I keep wandering from the specific to the general, I apologize, but I believe that my particular problems and concerns are akin to those faced by other artists and I am not so desperate yet as to believe that I function in isolation, Simon Stylites perched, piles and all, upon some upthrusting Newfoundland rock.

What can be done about the situation, if anything.

Well . . . we could, perhaps, create grants for artistic directors to give them the freedom to read plays, at home of course, instead of giving them grants to travel in order to import more plays. We could have crash training programmes for boards of directors, preferably on Fogo Island in November where they can't escape, on the importance of sublimating their prejudices for say, one-third of the year at least, and considering the future not merely of their theatre but the future of the theatre in the country, if any.

Perhaps it might be simplest to revise the policy of the National Arts Centre, insisting that it devote its entire season, every year, to the production of extant and original Canadian works. It would be critical that a feature of this programme would be to provide grants for artistic directors, boards of management, producers, everyone actively working from a power base, to attend the NAC productions. This would take the pressure from the regional houses, would unite the theatrical community into, at least, an awareness of the repertory as it exists and its possible future, and would turn the Centre in fact, into a kind of Globe serving artists and nations.

Please pick yourself up from the floor. I think the idea has merit, for we are, it seems, trapped into perpetuating a theatre paid for by the people, yet one which, by not speaking to them about themselves, confirms them in their own inferiority as objects of artistic attention. As my two-year-old says, when confronted by a piece of adult trickery, bullshit.

And yet one can't apportion blame. Some of my best friends are artistic directors and they wouldn't be seen dead near one of my plays because, as they admit, they are trapped into a set of political, economic and social circumstances which limit them artistically. Another friend, possibly the most sensitive script developer in the country, was recently moved to comment to me: "You know, soon, we must consider writing scripts for our audiences."

The implications of that remark I leave to your imagination. And my reaction to it is quite simple. I am not a box of assorted chocolates.

Although I agree with Synge in principle, I think he was being a little premature. I have written several plays which I consider (it's a personal opinion, of course) to be rich and wild. Unfortunately, they have been greeted with various suggestions ranging from vengeful comments that I give up writing entirely, to a healthier proposition that I be dumped, together with a few stones, in St. John's Harbour. (You see . . . medieval imagery lives on.) Perhaps the most positive response to one, however, came from Stratford, from a dramaturge who has since been replaced. The play, *Head, Guts and Sound Bone Dance*, a play of ritual, celebration and death as it concerns two old fishermen, a dialect play, was returned with the enthusiastic suggestion that, although it was not suitable for Stratford it would be absolutely marvellous for the Newfoundland National Theatre.

I have thought about that letter a lot.

It would be marvellous to have a Newfoundland National Theatre.

We have enough playwrights to start it. There's Al Pittman and Tom Cahill and Grace Butt and Ted Russell, who is father to us all, and perhaps, if we ever have the courage to secede from Confederation, declare a 200-mile limit exclusively for our own use and revert once more to our traditional and only source of real riches, the sea, then we could actually afford one, like Iceland.

I hardly think I'll live to see the day, but it's still not too late for a National Theatre of Canada, and I must believe with Synge that, even if vast numbers of our audience have not turned their backs upon what Peter Brook has called the Deadly Theatre, there does exist a vast untapped audience waiting to be called to that space before the cathedral.

၁

And so, without being, I hope, stridently nationalistic, a few final suggestions.

If, as I've suggested, the confident survival of theatre in other countries is based firmly upon the acceptance of their own repertory, why is the process ignored here? Examine carefully the content of repertory seasons in America, Britain, France, Sweden, Ireland, Germany. The bias, on average, is two indigenous to one play from other countries. When I suggest that we do that here I am informed that my attitude is extreme. I can only assume that at some time or other in those countries' various theatrical developments there must have been a lot of extremists around or a lot of dumb critics, or simply a lot of people who didn't know a Neil from a Beverley Simons. And just went happily along anyway.

No art can exist in isolation, but when we proceed on the assumption that everything that comes from away, as they say here in Newfoundland, is superior to the native product, then we simply become importers, rather than seeking a cultural balance of payment.

I would make a plea that the Canada Council suggest to all our regional theatres that one-third only of the budget allocated by them be devoted to Canadian work. I don't think this is an outrageous, or super-nationalistic proposition. If the companies don't want to do this, then let them pursue commercial properties which would make that portion of their programme self-sufficient. If it's what they, and the public want, then surely, it should become self-supporting. I would make a plea that our major festivals—Stratford, Charlottetown and Shaw—revise realistically, their funding processes. All three are essentially tourist attractions, and commercial propositions. It follows then, that the Canada Council is underwriting to a substantial degree, the economies of the towns in which those festivals operate, and quite possibly, judging from the amount of funding, are actually subsidizing tourist ticket prices. Surely, if such operations are unable to become self-sufficient (and granted the proliferating expenses of all artistic ventures I realize that's a near-impossibility) their funding at least should come from provincial and federal tourist agencies, with much greater support from organizations such as boards of trade that benefit from their operation. Money freed from such projects, wisely used, could seed what is apparently a less attractive theatre . . . even my proposal for the Arts Centre.

Theatre is the most neglected art form in this country, and I believe, the playwright the most neglected species.

Perhaps it's our own fault, for we have failed to master the process of gaining adequate political representation. Significantly, those areas of art that have powerful unions and organizations have mastered the mechanics of cultural politics, which goes far to explain why their continued and exhilirating growth is ensured. I refer to the composers, and musicians, and visual artists . . . perhaps there are more. But the playwrights have no such organization to represent them. They are few after all and, although often acutely political animals, have a poor sense of *realpolitik*. The revolution goes down on paper, and sometimes actually appears on stage but that is as far as it goes, and their death cries go unheeded.

For make no mistake about it . . . there is agony and death in the playwriting community.

Without production, a playwright dies.

Without active support from all levels of the public, the artistic directors, critics, audiences, all funding agencies, the playwright dies . . . even if the support is merely to recognize the importance of their existence. Without the creation of a climate which fertilizes and waters and recognizes the need for and will support the creation of a Canadian Repertory, then our own theatre will die.

And I wonder if anyone really gives a damn. After all, theatre is a universal art, and if every other country has its own, and Canada hasn't bothered to develop it, then it is perhaps too late to be hauling all these old chestnuts out of the fire when there are at least six smash hits waiting to come in from the States and Britain and the classics to fall back on.

One small point, a personal observation I admit, but it might illustrate the process of personal frustration which occasionally makes us froth too hysterically at the mouth.

Debit. During the past year I have not had one paying production of a stage play.

Credit. During the past year I have written three new plays.

Debit. During the past year I have sent out a dozen or more scripts to Canadian artistic directors, and, with one exception received neither reply nor acknowledgement of script.

Credit. During the past year I have sold a play in Germany, and have expressions of interest from two other European countries, currently being pursued.

It seems that I should have learned from John Herbert a long time ago, that to survive, artistically, I must sell abroad. Why, he said, writers are even respected in other countries. It's something of a culture shock, but you can quite enjoy getting used to it.

But listen out there . . . George and Beverley and John and Henry and Tom and David and David and Anee and Herschel and Ted and Sharon and James and—Hell, whoever is writing, whoever is listening, whoever cares at all.

I want it to happen here. In my country.

(Exits, pursued by a bear.)

WHY WE DON'T WRITE ◇

MARGARET HOLLINGSWORTH

○

Female playwrights have been heard from in Canada on only an occasional basis for most of this century. Among the few were Gwen Pharis Ringwood (1910–84), Elsie Park Gowan (b. 1905), Patricia Joudry (b. 1921) and Ann Henry (b. 1914). But even in the 1970s, only a relatively small proportion of the produced plays were written by women. Playwright Margaret Hollingsworth (b. 1942) speculated on why in this essay from the Canadian Theatre Review.

The question I am asked most frequently in formal and informal discussions about theatre is "where are the women playwrights?" It's a question I always dread—it can't be dealt with glibly; there is no single answer. And to answer it fully would take longer than any question period would allow.

"Why is it," I am asked, "that there have been great actresses from the time when women have been allowed on the stage, but no great women playwrights?" (That's significant—*from the time that women have been allowed on the stage*). There have been great women dancers, great instrumentalists, but few great women choreographers or composers. Why have women excelled in the *interpretive* arts?

The answer, of course, is that women have excelled in all the arts. Historians are discovering that many women were writing plays in the 17th and 18th centuries although Aphra Behn is the only woman acknowledged to have been writing in that era. Women were also writing music and painting pictures. The problem was, and is, that while their works were not censored, they were suppressed—gently, insidiously suppressed. Women were encouraged to think of themselves as supportive, rather than deserving of

◇ *Canadian Theatre Review* 43 (Summer 1985): 21–27.

support. The people who were considered to have artistic judgement were then, as they are now, men.

It was not that men went out of their way to promote work by members of their own sex; it was just that they understood it better and therefore valued it higher; they shared the point of view and perspective of their fellows, they did not have to go out on a limb, or put themselves out greatly to know what the potential of the work might be. Besides, it was more comfortable for them to work with talented young men than with talented women. It was, and is, difficult to ignore the sexual element in these working relationships, and to find a way of working with women which would not be termed "paternalistic."

Men were responsible for creating and nurturing the theatrical form, and for centuries they made sure the territory was not impinged upon by women. (The ancient Japanese forms of Kabuki, Noh and Bunraku, which are still popular today, exclude women entirely, as does the Indian Kathakali theatre.) I believe that men still have an unconscious wish to ward off the challenge from women in what has always been their province, a challenge which would prove a threat to what they know and understand.

In the past, young women were discouraged from entertaining the idea that they could ever be anything but dilettantes in a field that required arduous training to achieve mastery of the form. As actresses they were encouraged to excel, and they found it easy to go out in public, in disguise you might say, playing a role created by a man, not having to take responsibility for the ideas or thoughts behind the role. Women are still learning to go out in public, to defend their ideas and speak up for themselves.

Drama is the most social form of writing and this is perhaps the key reason why there are still so few women willing to get their feet wet. Unlike the novel, the play is public; the playwright is required to fight for her ideas, and defend them in the forum of workshops, rehearsals, and, after the production, in the media. Her critics will be harsh, particularly if she is a feminist playwright. The media has very little understanding of the art of playwriting; most critics can't tell the difference between the script and the performance; in fact many don't even have any interest in the theatre. Yet the drama critic's reaction, unlike that of the critic of prose, will have a direct effect on whether anyone goes to see her play, whether she makes any money from it (playwrights receive a percentage of the box office unlike other workers in theatre), and whether she will ever be asked to write another play. It's a tough way to make a public debut, and most women are woefully ill-equipped to handle it.

With a few notable exceptions, women in the past have been encouraged to stay away from the realm of ideas, particularly when they are called on to defend themselves in public. When they have elected to ignore this advice it has been mainly in the fields of religion or social and political reform, where they can distance themselves personally from the ideas they are defending.

We are told that a good play depends on conflict: for most women, conflict takes place behind closed doors in one-on-one situations; we are not strangers to the concept, but it does not have the same universal resonance for us as it does for men. A good play works on many levels; it speaks on a large and a small scale in a personal and collective way to every member of the audience. To write such a play requires a breadth and depth of experience that has simply not been in the range of a women's possibility until fairly recently. It is only in the last 20 years that most women have been freed from the limitations of constant child bearing and child rearing, and have had the opportunity to stick their noses outside their homes and take the first tentative steps towards discovering that there is the possibility of making an impression on the world. As Angela Carter, the English novelist, puts it, "we are a new kind, sexually active, yet voluntarily sterile." We need all the encouragement we can get if we are to move with confidence in a world where men play power games.

The English-Canadian theatre is dominated by men who are fighting for their audiences, their budgets, and their professional reputations. It is one of the most conservative institutions in Canada, and it is the exceptional artistic director who will take a chance on a young woman whose work has not already been sanctioned by the public, and who is writing in anything but the most acceptable style. A support network for women, such as is gradually growing in the business sector for those who want to assume leadership roles without assuming the male stance, simply does not exist in theatre. Hardly any women have made it to positions of power; the foothold of those who have is precarious, and few are able to offer anything more to other women than the odd encouraging word; they too are victims of the "accepted style."

What is the "accepted style" in playwriting? What would a woman left to her own devices bring to a play that a man would not?

For a start she would probably bring more women's roles. It's true that men have created wonderful starring roles such as Hedda Gabler and Medea, but the lives of most of their female characters are filtered through the eyes of the men who surround them. Even in a play which has no male characters such as *Waiting for the Parade*, women are shown as living through and for their men, dependent on them, generally passive and in need of support even when they don't know it. When they are independently active, this shows itself in a negative, manipulating light. They suffer, they are victims, they are trapped into perpetuating acts of violence, either against their aggressors or against themselves. Most audiences find this perfectly acceptable.

Over the centuries women have been socialized and schooled to identify with male views of the world, even male views of women, to the extent that it is now hard for them to make the distinction. They have only to switch on the TV to see that whenever an expert is called to give a view on some current or far-reaching topic, the expert is almost invariably a man, while the interviewer is often a woman. Men are still the authority figures and their images dominate all areas of our lives, except perhaps those concerned with home and family. Women are so used to identifying with the male point of view that they have no trouble with plays about war, prison, male homosexuality, plays which have no female characters, and completely ignore the woman's perspective. If a play or movie deals with a man's attempts to escape the scheming clutches of a woman (*One Flew over the Cuckoo's Nest*), there's no outcry about the woman being painted too black. If a wife or mother is offstage for the entire play and is only referred to peripherally (*Master Harold and the Boys*), it would be silly to demand that we should hear from her.

When the tables are turned, silliness reigns. Men, unused to identifying with the woman's point of view, often become extremely uncomfortable when there are no male characters in a play, or when those who are on stage are not shown in a particularly pleasant light; their discomfort becomes tangible when the women speak openly about sex or deeply held feelings, particularly when these are for another woman. Their wrath is vented in their reviews (the majority of reviewers are men). One has only to read the reviews of films such as Margarethe Von Trotta's *Sheer Madness* to confirm that this is true, and it's not a new phenomenon.

In Britain, the renowned advocate of birth control, Marie C. Stopes's play *Vestia* was banned in 1925; in her preface to the play, published in 1926 under the title *Censored—a banned play and a preface on the censorship*, she says that in a male-controlled society it is allowable to write about the excesses of oversexed, licentious, radically diseased men; but when a play points to the undersexuality of a man it is promptly suppressed. *Vestia* was a rewrite of the 1923 version of the play, *Married Love*, (also banned). The rewrite omitted reference to the "secret sin" which was the cause of the husband's impotence, but even this could not be allowed. But Marie C. Stopes, and other playwrights whose work was similarly banned, had one advantage over playwrights working today. Even if it was not performed she was given the chance to defend her work in print. So few plays are published today that the idea of publishing a play which has not been successful, let alone not been performed, is unthinkable.

There isn't space here to discuss whether or not there is a woman's aesthetic emerging in playwriting; but one need only read women's plays to discover that many of them do not have a leading or star character. They tend to be written for ensembles, always a stumbling block to smooth production, given the exigencies of the three-week rehearsal period allotted to most new work! Margarethe Von Trotta pointed out in a recent interview in *The Globe and Mail* that there is a tendency in women's films to treat events, large and small, with the same emphasis and to give them the same importance. This makes it difficult for playwrights to structure their work in an accepted dramatic mode, and meet the demands of our main stages.

I was asked recently why women don't give us more heroines in their plays? If a man could create Antigone, why wouldn't a woman writer come up with an equally laudable dramatic character? The questioner pointed out that Antigone was androgynous, and suggested that was the key to creating new heroines. It seems to me that most of the "heroines" in men's plays are androgynous. When they're not, they're manipulative, "bad" women. Personally I don't care for androgyny—it's boring. I'd rather see a full-blooded, sexy woman on the stage, willing to talk about the joys and problems of her sexuality, even if some of the men in the audience still cringe with embarrassment.

Do we need heroines anyway? The concept of a hero is perhaps a male invention, a male need; it is men who have stirred our blood with valorous acts, acts preceded or followed by violence. Maybe women feel that the real heroines are women like the ones across the street, whose old man has skipped town and is living in another province to avoid paying child support, leaving her to raise three kids on welfare. Maybe that's what women want to write about; maybe they want to explore the inner states and tensions which this situation engenders. The trouble is, it doesn't fit neatly into an accepted dramatic form, and they're told that it's the stuff of fiction, not of drama.

What artistic director in his right mind would take a chance on a play which is likely to provoke a hostile or uncomprehending reaction, not only from a portion of the males in the audience, but from some of the females who still identify with the male point of view as well? Theatre works best when it's provocative, but provocation isn't safe. The theatre is in a precarious financial position; plays must break even at the box office; women are told that they must learn to write *successful* plays, that there's no room for failure. Product is what counts; process is only useful when it leads to success. As one artistic director put it to me: "Give me a play I can make money on, I'll produce any woman's work." Success becomes synonymous with quality. Over and over again, boards, artistic directors and juries state that they are not prejudiced against women, they are looking for *quality*. If a woman produces quality she has just as much chance as a man. But quality is a value judgement based on all the prejudices and hang-ups that I've already outlined.

What does a woman who wants to write a play from even a mildly feminist perspective do? She must either work within the system and take her play to an established theatre (in which case she will probably have written a historical drama which is almost entirely unthreatening, like *The Fighting Days*), or she will decide to work outside the system. But there is only one professional woman's theatre in English Canada that I know of and its members, for reasons of mutual support and growth, have chosen to work mainly collectively. (Many women's theatres have taken this route, and it leaves women who wish to develop their craft in some other way with few alternatives.) The small fringe theatres are often (though not always), more open to women's work, but there's no money for the playwright, and no real resources to develop or produce a play that is at all ambitious in terms of cast or structure. (The situation in French Canada seems much healthier, and I can only conclude that this is because there are more women in key roles in québécois theatre.)

If audiences in English Canada were to ask, "where are the plays about social issues like abortion and incest, where are the satires and send-ups of both sexes written by women?" nobody can answer. (I suspect that the question hasn't even been asked.) In Great Britain and the U.S., women have been writing provocatively on these issues for 10 years but in Canada, alas, we're content to merely import their work.

Thirty percent of the membership of the Playwrights Union of Canada is female, yet only one play in 10 seen on the main stages of our theatres is by a woman. What are all these women writing then? The answer isn't hard to find. They are writing children's plays. Children's plays are not threatening to anyone, except those whose opinions don't count, and there are far more women in positions of power in children's theatres, so it's easier to get a hearing. A children's play written from a feminist perspective, where male/female role differences are diminished, is perfectly acceptable. Maybe our kids will make a different kind of theatre as a result but, meanwhile, the woman who feels she must write from her heart will probably choose another genre—short story, novel, or poem. Here she is less likely to be ridiculed, and therefore she need not be so rugged. A woman who writes plays is considered eccentric. She doesn't even have the support of writers in other genres who, in this country at least don't seem to consider drama as a form of writing, and exclude her from anthologies, surveys, and conferences on women's writing.

What can be done about all of this? Do we have to sit back on our heels and wait for Canada to catch up with the rest of the world, or is there any way that we can help women to help themselves by spawning new theatres, or trying to crack the current male hegemony, so that women have more than support roles in the theatrical hierarchy?

In the current fiscal climate new theatres are probably not the way to go, and there is also a danger of ghettoizing women. It should be possible to find ways of supporting those who finally reach leadership roles, so that they feel free enough to express themselves in their own styles rather than imitate male examples. It will take a lot of education, a lot of persuasion, a long time—and none of it can be accomplished if there is no interest.

The problem is that most men in positions of power don't see it as a problem. Why should they? Somehow their minds must be changed, and the only means to this is by affirmative action. Granting bodies and juries should be laying down guidelines whereby significantly more—dare I say 50 percent of those chosen for jobs, grants, residencies etc.—are women. Special programs should be set up to train women directors; they may not be well attended at first, they may even seem unnecessary, but someone at the top must have the tenacity and vision to see what the long-term results could be. Women must be canvassed to apply for jobs and for grants; their lack of training and experience must not be held against them for this merely promotes the vicious circle that already exists: if no one will give a woman the chance to gain experience, she will never be "qualified" and she'll never have any "quality" work behind her. It's a difficult circle to break, but it can be broken; and I feel the lead should be taken by the granting agencies. Money is a language of its own, and need have no sexual connotations.

As Adrienne Rich put it in *When we dead awaken*, woman, (the reader and the audience) . . . "is looking eagerly for guides, maps, possibilities; and over and over . . . she comes up against something that negates everything she is about. . . . She finds a terror and a dream . . . La Belle Dame Sans Merci . . . but precisely what she does not find is that absorbed, drudging, puzzled, sometimes inspiring creature, herself."

How much longer must this go on?

THE MEANING OF IT ALL [*]

RICK SALUTIN

○

The following interview with playwright Rick Salutin, author of Les Canadians *and* 1837, *was done by freelance writer Peter Copeman, an Australian then living in Calgary. The interview was done in June 1981.*

You have been involved with the evolution of the contemporary Canadian theatre. What do you feel is the state of that theatre at this moment?

SALUTIN: I find it quite confusing. In some ways, the big battle of a few years ago may have already been won, but it might have been a victory the way that nobody expected. The big battle was for Canadian plays and indigenous theatre, and to some extent one still has that battle, but less and less there's this kind of rap about how you can't have, and don't need, Canadian plays. In terms of the history of theatre in this country, the big difference in the last 10 years has been the rise of Canadian playwriting.

The previous movements in theatre, of which there were a number, had a lot of passion and commitment—in Toronto in the post-war period there was an indigenous theatre movement, with people like Mavor Moore at the centre, with a lot of other people, a lot of actors, some directors, and there were some writers. Morley Callaghan wrote some plays, and Lister Sinclair, and of course Mavor, but they didn't conceive of the Canadian play as the centre of the problem and they didn't really think that without Canadian plays you couldn't really have a Canadian theatre. They somehow thought you could manage with other people's plays. Foreign plays. Before that, there was some Canadian theatre, but most of it was not professional. The professional stuff was touring companies, and that had gone on since time immemorial.

[*] *Canadian Theatre Review* 34 (Spring 1982): 190–97.

It's hard to imagine it was only 10 years ago that Ken Gass founded the Factory Theatre Lab. That was the first time that anyone had set up a theatre which was exclusively dedicated to doing only Canadian plays. It was considered mindless at the time. People thought he was crazy—there was just no way you could do it. Within four years there was a season when there were 80 or 90 new Canadian plays produced in Toronto.

In numbers, it's dropped away, but in social acceptability it's definitely increased, so that now the notion of a Canadian play is not a joke. When I was growing up in Toronto, we had Wayne and Schuster, the comedy team. They went to the States, and went on the Ed Sullivan Show sometime in the 50s. The night they appeared it was like a national event. I remember CBC ran a news special following the show, in which they got a New York TV critic to comment, and he was inane, but it was a demonstration of our lack of confidence. We're still not that far from it: it's still big news when a Canadian play goes to Broadway, but it's not quite as bad these days.

We have a similar reaction in Australia, when any of our new works gets taken up on Broadway or the West End.

SALUTIN: Yes, but I get the impression that culturally it's a much better situation. The development of Australian literature, theatre and films, is well beyond that of English-Canada.

Obviously, in order to believe that there is a need for an indigenous theatre, you must believe that there is an identifiable indigenous culture, or that there is one in the making.

SALUTIN: Well there's a society, so there's got to be some sort of a culture. It is a different society from the U.S., so there are bound to be elements, and you just take what's there. There are some things that are distinctive, but when you're actually working, it's kind of irrelevant to specify it. You just go in and take what you find, and you say what you have to say. It's not an important question to me, so I'm afraid I haven't much to say about it.

When I was in Mozambique a couple of years ago, it was really refreshing. The country was maybe three or four years old at the time, and there'd been no Mozambique prior to that, except as part of the Portuguese empire. The indigenous peoples had 12 or 15 different languages, different territories, different traditions, but they just decided it would be a good idea to have a country, so they went ahead and did it. They were making up a culture. And they were very proud of it. They were going to create Mozambiquean dance, and Mozambiquean music, and you didn't find people saying things like "is there such a thing as a Mozambiquean identity." Since they were out to develop the kind of society they all wanted to live in, they were just going to go ahead and do it. I think it would be good here, instead of this obsessive national soul-searching about whether there is such a thing as a Canadian identity, to simply decide that it would be a good idea, and go ahead and acquire it. I know cultural nationalism often seems like a kind of archeological activity, unearthing, trying to discover—I've done lots of that, it's what *1837* is like—but I think it should be a project of the future rather than the past. You're trying to create something, and you just grab anything you can to do it with for the sake of building something for the future.

But the past, the archeology you refer to, provides a kind of perspective on the present and future.

SALUTIN: To some extent, as long as it doesn't get metaphysicalised, so that you're trying to discover your soul, as if it really exists back there, and all you have to do is scrape away the layers, or dig in the right spot.

In that context, and in the sense of the realisation of this "good idea" of developing a national identity, are you conscious at all of a role in achieving that goal?

SALUTIN: I think I'm more interested in political questions than strictly cultural issues. And have more of a contribution to make in that.

In what way is there a distinctively Canadian political outlook?

SALUTIN: I think you get a unique perspective on imperialism in Canada. I think in a lot of ways Canada is an extremely colonized place, in many ways more so than any banana republic in Latin America. Culturally, economically, and politically, it's sort of underdeveloped, but at the same time quite privileged in terms of the pay-off to the people from the degree of development it has. So it's just very odd. I continue to think that the real Canadian contribution to world culture would be some kind of statement from this unique position. I was reading the *Raj Quartets* by Paul Scott, about the end of the British empire in India, a wonderful theme, and when you're living in a place as a writer, you're looking for some way to encapsulate what's going on, what the meaning of it all is. There's something of that in how I feel about Canada. It's such an odd place, I think unlike any other. And if you could just say that. . . .

But obviously, it's not as easy as that.

SALUTIN: Obviously, or I would have done it more completely, although my plays are searching for it. The *Nathan Cohen* play I wrote was a sort of point of view. . . . In this country, culture is such an important issue, because of the domination, the position of the empire, the imperial domination that it's experienced, in the past, but even more now. The culture becomes *the* question of politics, because the historical question was the cultural question.

Do you find that the current cultural imperialism is British or American?

SALUTIN: American, but the British is still quite strong, especially in the theatre.

As witnessed by the major theatre festivals of Shakespeare and Shaw?

SALUTIN:Yes, it's bizarre. All these announcements last summer about Stratford that this is our most important and prestigious theatre. . . . I really think it's our least important theatre. Nothing could be less important to the future of Canadian theatre than that mausoleum out there. As I said in the diary of 1837, it's another country's national playwright, not ours.

Is there a national playwright in Canada yet?

SALUTIN: No. A friend of mine has a theory that theatre develops as the last stage in culture: it's the sign of a real maturing. You can have all the other art forms prior to theatre, but you have to have a relatively well-developed society to have a theatre.

Getting back to the last 10 years, did the 1967 Centennial celebrations for federation have some kind of catalytic role in the acceptance of Canadian plays?

SALUTIN: I don't know. Everybody says so. I was in the States at the time, so I really haven't a clue. I think it had a lot more to do with the war in Vietnam. And as well, there was an acceleration of the American take-over of this country at that time, I think as a result of the maturing of American capitalism, the heyday of U.S. multi-nationalism, just gobbling up everything at an extraordinary rate, and there was a kind of 11th hour reaction that set in.

What kinds of subjects interest you most?

SALUTIN: I'm working on a play that's set in Mozambique, and really I think it's about the possibility of change.

How do you choose your subject matter?

SALUTIN: I got interested in Mozambique because a friend of mine who was in quite close contact with it told me that the eight guys on the governing council, in fact the polit-bureau, five or six of them were major published poets, and I started reading some of the stuff. They're just very sharp on the cultural stuff. That was how I got interested in that. I arranged to go over. I thought there would be something to learn. And there was.

Did you speak to these poets in the polit-bureau?

SALUTIN: I never got to see them. I stayed an extra week to meet them, because I wanted to write about poetry and revolution. They were all just too busy. I know they made great efforts to try to get me an interview with at least one of them, but the president and vice-president were both involved in a huge crisis over agricultural policy. The People's Assembly had been held in extra session to deal with it, and they had just fired the Agriculture Minister, with huge conflict between the Soviet advisors and the indigenous politicians. The guy who was the head of the bank was dealing with the take-over of the biggest sugar estate in the country, and the head of the armed forces was dealing with the raids from Rhodesia at the time. They just went down the list for me, and every one was busy with some kind of national crisis.

Are you consciously setting out to help write the new history? To establish new heroes and mythology?

SALUTIN: No, I just do what I do. I don't think that kind of academic approach is really possible.

But isn't it a little like the Mozambique situation, in as much as they are trying to stimulate the process artificially?

SALUTIN: I don't think they're trying to hurry up a process, it's just that practically speaking, they want it.

Well, isn't this the same thing in Canada: a matter of recognising the need and being aware of fulfilling it?

SALUTIN: I just don't think you can create stuff that actually works that way. The stuff that actually works will be stuff that you feel strongly about and have some sort of relationship to. Then that is what becomes myth, and not by looking for stuff.

But are you not raising a pride in certain aspects of history?

SALUTIN: Yes, but it's just what's here, and what's interesting. It's the natural course. I mean, what are you going to write about, American culture? You just have to do your own work. I think the thing about heroes is a bit mystifying too. I mean, of course I write about people. I wrote a book, it was published about a year ago, it's the biography of a labour leader. It's called *The Organizer*. And that's a hero—in fact, the last chapter is called "On the Treatment of Canadian Heroes" or something. But what those people are is just people who did things before the time when everybody could behave that way. They're human behaviour before its time. They lived their lives in terms of the issues that are important to everybody, but not everybody can get a hold of, because they're too busy making their money, or just staying alive. It's not an abstraction. People become heroes because there's something important about what they do, not because we want to have heroes, because it's a good idea.

But often there are a lot of "unsung" heroes, and do I not perceive a deliberate consciousness in what you do, in raising a general awareness of people who should be known, but aren't? And that, in its own way, contributes to the mythology.

SALUTIN: Sure. You find that there were these people in our midst, and you point out that they were different from our official leaders, and they make them look sick.

Do you find that when you write, there are sufficient and adequate directors and performers to give your work the sort of treatment you envisage?

SALUTIN: Actors yes, directors no. That's the problem.

So there's a dearth of good directors.

SALUTIN: For what I'm interested in, yes.

What exactly are you interested in, in terms of directing style?

SALUTIN: I don't know how to express it. It's a sort of theatrical, descriptive, analytical, metaphorical, non-naturalistic style, that tries to find images that reveal something about the way the world we live in works. A sort of dialectical theatre.

Do you find Paul Thompson approaches that style?

SALUTIN: Paul's specialty is the collective. That's been the area of his real contribution, not in the scripted stuff.

Do you always attend rehearsals for the first productions of your plays?

SALUTIN: Sure.

Do you find yourself rewriting a lot, and are you flexible when it comes to actors' contributions? I'm referring to the fully scripted plays, of course.

SALUTIN: Well, there are a lot of changes that take place as a result of the work you do with the actors. I think everybody finds that, that they rewrite madly during rehearsals of the first production.

An immediate impression I have with your plays when I read them is that they are terse and economical. Do you generally cut a lot in rehearsal?

SALUTIN: Yeah, cutting is the most important part of writing, I think. There's a technical thing that happens because of the nature of theatre, because you're dealing with actors. When you write a line, I think you're better to over-write it to make your intention clear, and then if the actor can manage it with many fewer words, then you cut them, because it's much more interesting for an audience to get the meaning through voice and gesture and, you know, raised eyebrow, and through things *not* being said. The most interesting parts of plays are the things not said, the transitions between speeches, and the real interaction between characters. As in any conversation. It's the jumps that form the real interest, the intricate parts.

Have you actually had any formal training as a writer?

SALUTIN: I got a B.A. at Brandeis University in Boston in Near-Eastern and Judaic Studies, got an M.A. at Columbia, New York, on the New Testament, and I just narrowly escaped a Ph.D. in Phenomenology at the New School of New York.

What do you mean by "narrowly escaped"?

SALUTIN: I think that writing a Ph.D. is disastrous. It just kills any spontaneous or personal light. It infantilises you. You worry about people approving of you. It's very unimaginative. You usually start off with one, more or less, imaginative idea that you get in about 15 minutes, then you spend two or three years footnoting it. You have to become an expert in the field. I think it's disastrous.

Do you find that your Jewishness influences your writing?

SALUTIN: I'm told that all my plays end Jewishly. They end with a question.

Do you have any special attitudes to things, as a result of being Jewish? To sin, or morality, or anything like that.

SALUTIN: I don't think so. Of course what I tried to do with *Nathan Cohen*, had to do with the fact that Cohen's sensitivity to culture derived from being Jewish, but it also had to do with being a member of a small Jewish community on Cape Breton, where they were surrounded by non-Jews who had a real sense of the importance of having your own culture. But also he had a real sensitivity to the Gaelic culture that was there, and the working-class culture, so that there was a real sense of the importance of it to Canada, because there were a lot of Canadians who grew up without any reference points or benchmarks of that sort.

Do you think the same thing applies to you?

SALUTIN: To some extent.

Did you grow up in a strict Jewish household?

SALUTIN: No. Very, sort of, unstrict. I did all the Jewish things, but very casually.

I grew up in a working-class district, but when I was about nine or ten we moved out to a Jewish suburb, where you were supposed to go because they had such great education. That was a real class shift. We didn't really belong very well because my dad wasn't a boss, he was just a salesman. We rented and everybody else owned, and we didn't go south in the winter and everybody else did. I felt a bit alienated, a bit marginal. Unclear about what and who I was. I knew I didn't belong there, but I didn't feel I belonged anywhere else either.

You didn't identify with this area either?

SALUTIN: No, because my family hadn't. A salesman is a completely anomalous character socially. Just adrift. Terrible for any sense of social belonging.

In the Willy Loman sense?

SALUTIN: Oh I think so. There were always threats that we'd be out on the street, and nobody else had that. Had we stayed here there would have been lots of people who had it, and you wouldn't have felt like you had a curse. Just a rough time like all the others.

Are you a rebel in the family? Doing things that your parents wouldn't approve of?

SALUTIN: I suppose so, although it's not that unusual, being a writer is quite a bourgeois thing, the arts have become the new professionalism among the bourgeoisie. They're all dying to be in the arts. If they can't be writers or artists they're producers, or P.R. people, gallery owners. The expansion of leisure activities and affluence has meant that the arts are now a thoroughly integrated part of bourgeois society. Also, the economy has stagnated in the previously productive areas, so that that investment is seeking an outlet in new areas.

To move on to another item. Do you consciously experiment with form and style in your writing?

SALUTIN: I'm not preoccupied with form at all. I just look for something that works. If you get a chance sometime, you might have a look at a film I did. I did a naturalistic TV film called *Maria* that the National Film Board distributes. And the CBC, I suppose. It was shown on TV three or four times, and it's in release constantly. It's about an organising drive in a textile factory in Toronto, contemporary setting. It's a very different style from my usual—straight, naturalism. Because it was film. The CBC won't do anything else.

Did you find it difficult to write naturalistically?

SALUTIN: No, easy as hell. There are bits in the *Cohen* play that are just straight naturalistic dialogue. In all my plays. It's not hard to do.

Do you have any role models in playwriting history? Any gurus?

SALUTIN: Well, it may sound a bit . . . but I really love Shakespeare. When we were doing *1837*, I used to just read the histories—*Henry IV, Henry V.* Let's face it, those are the best historical plays.

The style is very different.

SALUTIN: But they're historical plays.

But although there are poetic elements perhaps in your plays, they could hardly be called verse drama. Is it the treatment, the episodic nature of Shakespeare that attracts you?

SALUTIN: I guess so. I hadn't thought of it to that extent, but you're probably right. I'm also beginning to think there might be a possibility for more outright poetry in modern plays. . . .

Would that include future works of your own?

SALUTIN: It might. Look out for it.

CANADA'S PLAYWRIGHTS: FINDING THEIR PLACE [◇]

SHARON POLLOCK

o

One of the most outspoken of the new generation of women writers was former actress Sharon Pollock (b. 1936). She recalled her perilous journey from stage to page in this essay published in the Canadian Theatre Review *in 1982.*

If 10 Canadian playwrights were to speak on Canadian playwriting today, there would be 18 points of view. My views are highly subjective and endorsed by no one but myself. My personal position has been described by some people as being slightly left of Trotsky, and by others as slightly right of Genghis Khan. Neither are Canadians, which makes me highly suspect by the nationalist; and my preoccupation with Canadian things, and worse still, regional Canadian things, means that I'm scorned by the internationalists as well.

I'm only one among approximately 156 playwrights who are members of our national service organization. Playwrights Canada, but let me tell you how I at least decided to put all my eggs in the playwright's basket. I was working as an actress back in 1971. I was touring Western Canada with *Come Blow Your Horn* or *Mary, Mary* or something similar, and I'd played almost every grain elevator town in the West. On this occasion I was in Acne, Alberta—that's actually the name of the place—population 250, and we had about 256 out to the show, which was nice. I was changing after the performance in a basement locker room. The air was rich with the scent of runners and stale jock straps. That was an aroma I'd grown to know if not to love on tour. I was an actress, and I naively thought I was going to change the world and that the theatre was the place to do it. I was going to alter men's minds by touching their hearts. Anyhow, as I was removing my

---

◇ *Canadian Theatre Review* 32 (Spring 1982): 34–38.

make-up, it began to dawn on me that changing the world with Neil Simon was a long-range project to which I was not prepared to commit my life. As I was taking in this stunning thought, there was a knock at the door. There was a girl of 14 or 15 standing there. She wanted my autograph and as I moved the old runners out of the way and leaned on the locker to sign my name on her program she said to me, "Miss Pollock, how did you get where you are today?" I answered, "By bus." But then I thought. "You deserve better than this, and God damn it I sure do." Thus was a Canadian playwright born.

I wanted to talk directly to that girl about things that I thought counted to both of us, with my own voice, a Canadian voice. I've since come to understand that although the production and consumption of theatre is generally viewed as good for you, theatre does not exist to serve the worthy ends of education and social betterment. It's not created for those ends, but it does serve them, I believe. For me the theatre is a way of knowing reality, and at its core is a single vision—the playwright's.

Now in 1971 when I began writing, the Canadian playwright had some difficulty getting anyone to read, let alone produce his singular vision. Canadian culture was an import commodity and still is to a degree. Toronto was a mecca for playwrights, because there Canadian directors and playwrights were establishing their own theatres to produce and direct their own work. They had got tired of knocking on doors and had taken another direction. The Garret Theatre, Passe Muraille, Factory Lab, Toronto Free were all part of an explosion of small theatres with a Canadian content mandate. The movement was helped by two conferences held in 1971 attended by Canadian playwrights—the first in the Gaspé—which came out with a demand for 50 percent Canadian content. The second was held in Niagara-on-the-Lake. For the first time a sense of community began to develop among playwrights. This led to the establishment of the Playwrights' Circle which in time became Playwrights' Co-Op which then turned into Playwrights Canada.

I was told when I started that if I was serious about writing, I had to move to Toronto. I chose not to leave the West. Eventually we began a number of small theatres dedicated to Canadian work, such as the New Play Centre in Vancouver, Alberta Theatre Projects in Calgary, Northern Lights, Theatre Network, and Twenty-Fifth Street House. Whether in the long run the small Canadian theatre producing only Canadian plays has worked for or against the playwright is debatable. It certainly took the pressure off the larger regional theatres to do Canadian work. While the playwright did hone his art and craft in the studio theatre, he was denied the opportunity to see and learn from productions on the main stages. At the same time, we suffered financially because we couldn't make money in the small houses.

Now that has changed, at least somewhat, more in some locales than in others. But there still is that attitude that persists. I was talking about my play *Blood Relations* to someone in Halifax, and he told me that the Neptune Theatre was not doing any "experimental" work, meaning Canadian work. In some parts of this country even the most traditional Canadian plays are still considered experimental. As I said, things have improved. We have finally made it into the regional theatres. Now some of the smaller theatres have started to produce works from the international canon in addition to Canadian plays.

Even though we are being produced in the major theatres and the small, the playwright remains outside the stage door. Seldom is he seen as an essential or integral component of the theatre process, and he suffers from his isolation. Playwright-in-residence positions are few and far between, and while a resident designer designs and a resident director directs, it is rare indeed that the resident playwright actually gets much time to write. There are often other tasks that appear to justify his ongoing existence in the company, such as providing dramaturgical services, writing critiques, and holding playwriting workshops. All this is done for a fee that presupposes an income from some other sources. In 1978, Canada Council was providing $5000 for playwrights attached to a company for an eight-month season.

For most playwrights interaction with a company takes place only during rehearsals. "Interaction" may not be the right word at all for too often the playwright is cast in the role of spectator, and if he rejects this role, he risks being ejected from rehearsals. Of course contracts are negotiated that assure your right of attendance. However, the sense of playwright-as-intruder cannot be overcome through contracts. In reaction to this, the playwright who has got within but still feels without, cannot help feeling hostile towards the producing company and seeing the artistic director and management as self-serving exploiters of his work. This situation is as deadly as isolation.

Creative energies are wasted in drawing up better contracts rather than in writing another play or a better play. Playwrights get caught up in political action that dissipates what it is we should be doing. I served on the Advisory Arts Panel for the Canada Council and I remember, in Charlottetown, bumping into John Hirsch who had just come from what he said was the best theatre he'd seen in years. He'd been at the Saturday night wrestling in town. He asked me what I was doing there. I guess I thought I was working on behalf of the artists of Canada. He said, "Then go home and write. That's what you're supposed to be doing. Don't get co-opted into the bureaucratic process. Your job is to write the best plays you can." I suddenly realized how much of my energy had been spent attending meetings and writing papers. I knew then I had to get back to playwriting, talking to people, communicating with them through the theatre.

Eventually after you are inside the door and your play is being produced, you have to ask yourself whether you respect the people you are working with. I always work with people I respect. That is very important, because so often you can find yourself in situations when rehearsing a new play when only good will and respect between you and the people you are working with will get you through the day.

I often wonder whether theatre schools are training actors for a Canadian theatre. In many cases I fear they're not. Canadian plays are most often ignored. This past year the National Theatre School, after almost 20 years in existence, has finally implemented a playwriting program in the English section. However this is still called "a pilot project." I know that we're uncertain how to train playwrights, but I do know that you don't do it by ignoring them. The Black Report on Theatre Training in Canada quotes a speech teacher telling a student, "Please, don't talk like that, you sound so Canadian." All too often I'm working with people who are speaking in an English accent with an English rhythm. I've even had to rewrite two characters because the English actors who played them couldn't accommodate the speech rhythms. There may be many weaknesses with my plays, but most people say that I write dialogue that is easy to speak and learn—for Canadians.

There is an interesting letter in the Black Report written by an actress, who had graduated from the National Theatre School. She says, "An average student or graduate is expected to be able to field auditions for Shaw, Tennessee Williams, Shakespeare and Ibsen, all of which is fine and right. Canadian actors do handle these situations with great regularity. The problem is the English actor has his home base to work from, i.e., a natural feeling for Shaw and Shakespeare. The American has at least Williams, Albee or Simon, the Irishman has O'Casey, while the Canadian is sent rushing around trying like hell to cover all the bases of modern or classical drama, all the while knowing there's someone else who's got the accent better. So, you don't try to be Canadian. You simply compete. But if Canadian theatre schools cannot in themselves compete with Julliard, R.A.D.A., or whatever, what are the student actors left with? If the situation doesn't improve they'd probably be better off going to Julliard or across the ocean. You'd be better trained for most of the theatre that goes on in this country if you did." That's a terrible statement from someone who's working in our theatre.

I'm told we have a theatre tradition that goes back 400 years, give or take. I think it's take. And traditionally, the playwright has been isolated from it. We have that to overcome. There's another isolation that bothers me far more and it doesn't have anything to do with the working conditions in our theatres. It has to do with the seeming isolation or disconnection that we have with this place, wherever your place is. I believe the best work is rooted in a strong specific: you have to be passionately connected to something. We seem to spend all of our time searching after the elusive Canadian identity. My theory is that there is no Canadian identity. I stopped looking for it a long time ago. I see Canada as a bureaucrat's name for a geographical area. What we do have is British Columbia, Alberta and Quebec. I look at Quebec and I see the desire for a political entity because they have a cultural entity. The cultural entity came first. Today, in Canada, we talk about Western separatism. I see that as a positive thing. I believe that we're finally starting to look at the roots of where we happen to be. We're tentatively trying to discover who we are. We need the maturity and strength to look at ourselves and to realize we're interesting.

What about international standards? I believe in excellence, but it doesn't hover over the golden triangle of Montreal, Ottawa and Toronto, which is what you feel when you live in the West. Nor does it hover over New York. Excellence is far more complicated than that because it changes. There are no universal standards floating around. But we Canadian playwrights are only going to remain immigrant playwrights until we form an organic and passionate relationship with ourselves and where we live. We must stop looking for acceptance outside. When is a Canadian play going to make it big in New York? Who cares. When we know where we are we'll know where we're going. Until then what we must do is keep writing.

THE TORONTO MOVEMENT*

DON RUBIN

○

As the wave of nationalistic fervour of the late 1960s and 1970s passed, new attitudes and new financial concerns began to emerge. A 1983 assessment on the state of theatre in Toronto from th pages of the Canadian Theatre Review.

In all exploratory behaviour, whether artistic or scientific, there is the ever-present battle between the neo-philic and neo-phobic urges. The former drives us on to new experiences, makes us crave for novelty. The latter holds us back, makes us take refuge in the familiar. . . . This state of conflict does not merely account for the more obvious fluctuations in fashions and fads . . . ; it is also the very basis of our whole cultural progression. We explore and we retrench, we investigate and we stabilise.

Desmond Morris, *The Naked Ape*

No one who is the least familiar with the recent history of Canadian theatre would deny, I think, the theatrical energy in the city of Toronto between about 1969 and 1974 and its significance to the theatrical life of the rest of the country at and since that time. Four theatres in particular—Passe Muraille, the Factory, Tarragon and Toronto Free—contributed a number of things of great importance: among them, at least five playwrights of note— David Freeman, David French, James Reaney, Rick Salutin and George F. Walker as well as a link to the fascinating dramaturgy of Quebec, particu- larly the work of Michel Tremblay; several deeply-committed visionaries who helped shape our national theatrical aesthetic—Jim Garrard, Ken Gass, Bill Glassco, Paul Thompson and, though his contributions go back prior to this period, Tom Hendry; and at least four talented directors who continue

* *Canadian Theatre Review* 38 (Fall 1983): 8–17.

to work actively in theatre and other media—Glassco, Thompson, Martin Kinch and the more experimental Hrant Alianak. As well, the Toronto scene of this time produced its share of fine young actors—Clare Coulter, the late Brenda Donohue, David Fox, Nick Mancuso, Eric Peterson and Saul Rubinek, to name just a few who come to mind immediately. It also produced designers and administrators and even a few critics of note.

Although many of these people are still an active and important part of the city's theatre scene, Toronto in the last 10 years has lost its centrality in the Canadian theatre; its once inspiring spirit has diminished into mere respectability. The reasons for this are many and varied ranging from the declining energies of its leaders to the diminishing financial resources that accompany a recession, from a need to find new challenges to simple artistic maturation and growth. There is also, if the zoological claims of Desmond Morris have any validity, the neo-phobic need to retrench and stabilize following an extraordinary period of neo-philic cultural exploration and progression.

But the fact remains that theatre in Toronto has quieted down to become a generally conservative activity—affirming rather than challenging social values. The fact that the four theatres mentioned have achieved a centrality within the Toronto community that they did not seek or want when they began is important to note. It seemed to critic Ronald Bryden, then fairly new to the Toronto scene, that even in 1978—as he said in the *Canadian Forum*—these companies would "rather be in opposition than in power,"[1] Indeed, that was the aesthetic which brought most of them into theatrical life.

I suppose that those who were part of what I will call the Toronto Movement (a Movement far larger than the four theatres and people I have mentioned) today might be tempted to move into the future feeling quite content about their accomplishments. Certainly it was through their efforts that Canadian theatre—that is, theatre created by artists with a specific rather than a generalized world view, with a view unique to that time and this place—won a role in the country's cultural life. But as tempting as this is, it would be counter-productive for it would suggest that the hard work of creating a viable and meaningful theatrical culture is somehow completed. And nothing could be further from the truth. If Toronto is no longer the central battlefield in English-language Canadian theatre, it remains a battlefield nevertheless and, as such, it is a microcosm of all that is both encouraging and discouraging across the country. The fact that Toronto theatre cannot assume any long-term commitment from either government or audience continues to suggest that Canadian theatre is a shaky growth at best. At any moment, funds could be pulled and key theatres could close. Toronto humorist Ben Wicks, quite brilliantly I think, captured this rather precarious state of the arts in Canada in one of his recent cartoons. In it, two rather fashionable ladies stand admiringly in front of a painting by a member of the Group of Seven. The first is effusive in her praise, calling the work "strong and vibrant and symbolic of the people. It makes one wish," she says, "that all Canadians were as aware as we are." The second then asks which one of the Group of Seven painted it, to which the first can only reply, "Number Six."[2]

Need this be said more directly? I think so. We have come far in recent years toward realizing our national cultural dreams; but we must not confuse growth with maturation. Culture in Canada, particularly the theatre, is not yet secure or mature enough, though it is, without doubt, more secure and more mature than ever before in our history. We have gained roots but we must not forget that they are not yet so very old or so very firm.

And lest anyone think that even these roots were easily achieved, it might be pointed out that even at the time of their being laid down, some of our best critics had their doubts about their efficacy. I recall a trade publication which flourished in Toronto in the early 70s called *That's Showbusiness*, a professional information report on theatre and the performing arts which appeared regularly in a simply written, newspaper format. Its most interesting critic was designer/theatre consultant Brian Arnott who was writing regularly for the publication under the *nom de plume*, Brian Boru. Arnott spoke authoritatively and supportively about theatre in Toronto and across the country during this period but he also was one of the first to question whether or not the national theatre in general and the Toronto Movement in particular was losing sight of its goals. He went so far as to suggest in 1974 that perhaps the Movement didn't exist, perhaps the child we thought had been born was really only an hysterical pregnancy.

Arnott was not the only one to suggest something like this. In the 1978 *Canadian Forum* article that I referred to earlier, Ronald Bryden told the story of an old French fisherman who came upon a tourist doing rather violent push-ups on a deserted beach. "Having observed in silence as long as he could bear," wrote Bryden, "the old fisherman eventually blurted: 'Mais m'sieu . . . mademoiselle est partie!'"[3] As a comment on theatre in Toronto circa 1978, this certainly made its point. Like Arnott's image of the hysterical pregnancy, it also suggested that perhaps theatre in Toronto never was there at all—at least not in the way so many of us had believed.

Looking back from 1983, however, I don't think that even Arnott and Bryden could deny that something new was born at that time, something fundamentally different from all that had come before.

How did it differ?

First, and perhaps most importantly, the Toronto Movement created a conscious interest in the notion of *Canadian theatre* as something distinct from the more traditional notion of *theatre in Canada*. It suggested that at the very least there should be a special place in our theatrical repertoires for plays by Canadian dramatists. Other movements had dreamed of such "alternative" notions in the past. With the Toronto Movement, however, the idea took root in both the city's and the country's theatrical imagination.

Second, the Movement differed in its ability to find and creatively use state subsidy for its goals. The Toronto Movement was never shy about subsidy. It took public money from wherever it could and, when it wasn't available from traditional funding agencies in the beginning, it took full advantage of federal make-work programs such as LIP (Local Initiatives Program) and OFY (Opportunities For Youth). It was subsidy—its existence and its use—that allowed those in the Movement to believe that a professional career was not just a dream but an idea that could be a reality. And this became a third characteristic of the Toronto Movement, a determination by those involved to develop professional rather than amateur careers in the theatre.

A fourth difference was the idea of *professional* awards—substantial cash awards in some cases—for achievement in various aspects of theatre art. Of particular significance in this was the creation of the annual Floyd S. Chalmers Playwriting Award. By attaching $5000 to this Award for an Outstanding Play which was produced in the Toronto area each year (plus smaller but still significant amounts for the runners-up), Chalmers helped the Movement gain greater credibility with the public at large.

A fifth difference between the Toronto Movement and others that had come before was the emergence of an extraordinary number of professional associations and service organizations. These began with the Playwrights Circle (which became the Playwrights Co-op and, later, Playwrights Canada) and eventually included a separate Guild of Canadian Playwrights. At the same time came the Toronto Drama Bench, an association of theatre journalists that eventually gave birth to a national organization, the Canadian Theatre Critics Association. Within just a few years there was also the Toronto Theatre Alliance, a loosely-knit group of theatres in the city which became a useful lobbying group and which would, some years later, be one of the motivating forces behind the 1981 Toronto International Theatre Festival; the Professional Association of Canadian Theatres (PACT), an organization representing national theatre managements and which helped to bring into being a new Canadian Centre of the International Theatre Institute; the Association of Canadian Designers; the Association of Cultural Executives; the Council for Business and the Arts; and the list goes on and on. Clearly, the development of such a superstructure was unique in our theatre history. It was, in some measure, this new sense of professional community that encouraged Toronto's major newspapers to support the Movement's activities and to assign critics and space in greater numbers than ever before. This too was different.

One could probably add to the catalogue of differences the appearance at this time of a relatively large number of publishing ventures which were devoted exclusively or almost exclusively to theatre. Again, these all helped widen the net of public support. I am thinking particularly of play publishing houses such as the Playwrights Co-op in Toronto, Talon in Vancouver and Leméac in Montreal as well as newspapers such as *That's Showbusiness* and *Toronto Theatre Review* and journals such as *Canadian Theatre Review* and, later on, *Scene Changes* and *Canadian Drama/L'Art dramatique canadien*.

Important as well in this development was the change in attitude that one could sense in the playwrights themselves. No longer would they stand quietly by while being ignored. Writing well, they began to *demand* production. At one point they called publicly for 50 percent Canadian content on the nation's subsidized stages. They never did manage this particular percentage but Canadian plays did start to be produced in increasing numbers from this period. Today, few major theatres would be foolhardy enough to ignore Canadian work in planning their seasons and even the Canada Council now asks about Canadian content in its grant applications.

Finally in this regard, never before did a Canadian theatre movement so clearly pass on a *vision*, an ideal sense of itself. That vision may still need clarification but it is here nonetheless. Mademoiselle, to return to Bryden's fisherman, may have gone but conception did take place and mademoiselle did leave a child, a child which today is no longer creeping unsteadily but which is taking solid steps toward self-realization and maturity. And it will continue to grow, I'm sure, unless we forget that the young continue to need our support for a very long time.

WHERE ARE WE NOW, AND HOW DID WE GET HERE?

I suppose the logical place to begin to answer any question about the state of any theatre community is to consider the state of the money that surrounds it. For in theatre, dreams always seem able to outstrip our ability to realize them. Unfortunately, it is only when realization becomes a possibility that theatre is able to make the move from personal vision to social reality.

In the late 60s and early 70s, money—our once and future culprit—seemed not to be such a problem. For the young and the visionary, it seemed not even necessary to have much; indeed, many seemed to pride themselves on apparently resisting its lure. The money necessary to make theatre at the time always seemed to come from somewhere. And people *would* work cheap then. Even when the unions began showing up at their doors, the companies always seemed able to pay, even if it meant in reality that on payday the actors would have to "kick back" some or all of it. Not every company operated this way but the practice was quite widespread and it was appropriate somehow to the ambiance created in the warehouses and church halls that many of the Toronto Movement theatres then called home. It was appropriate too for the audiences which seemed not to mind much sitting on floors or mats or pews, their long hair cascading, their headbands of many colors, their breasts occasionally exposed to better nurse the infants so often brought to the theatre with them. This was Toronto to be sure—the new Toronto of the late 60s—but it was also Vancouver and Montreal and, in the 70s, it became other cities as well.[4]

I think it was somewhere in the middle of the 70s when financial reality started setting in. Audiences, for one thing, started to tire of bleacher seats and cushions—the novelty was wearing a bit thin—and many Toronto theatres began to search for more permanent and comfortable homes. This was a natural development but one that would unfortunately cost money. And money was not so easy to find by 1975. LIP and OFY programs were just about gone by this time and the national political situation was also changing. In 1976, Rene Levesque's separatist Parti Québecois came to provincial power and federal priorities subtly shifted. Grants to Quebec, particularly in the arts, increased in an effort to shore up the sagging federal fortunes there. This financial change, coming when the national economy was taking

a strong downturn (the Canadian dollar fell by 35 percent in the months following the Quebec election in 1976), had severe effects on theatre in
Canada. I am not suggesting here that Quebec caused Canada's financial
problems in the post-'76 period anymore than I am suggesting that Canada
caused Quebec's. We both, as Jean-Claude Germain of Montreal's Théâtre
d'aujourd'hui, one of Quebec's most important alternative companies has
said, go to the same well for our water. I am simply saying that financial
priorities and fiscal realities caused changes that made the economy a major
factor in Canadian theatre. No one—Quebecois or Canadian (to use the distinction our Quebec colleagues prefer)—ultimately had enough, just as no
one has nearly enough today.

In the worsening economic and political climate the Canada Council's
ability to stimulate theatrical research and development of new plays, new
forms and new audiences—as opposed to its assumed mandate to simply
help companies maintain a certain level of production—was clearly affected.
By 1983, more Canadians were out of work than at any time since the 1930s,
and the Canadian dollar fell to near all-time lows against the American dollar. Subsidy began falling behind inflation rates. At the same time that theatres were trying to upgrade their quarters and their quality, audiences were
also becoming more choosy about what they would spend their money to
see. No longer was it enough to simply offer them something Canadian.
Plays now had to be both Canadian *and* good. Theatres began searching for
plays which seemed to have a higher entertainment quotient. In time, it was
this entertainment quotient itself which began to take precedence. The price
for failure at the box office was becoming increasingly clear: too many failures and a theatre's grant could be cut. Modest success was no longer
enough; higher production costs made anything with even an element of
risk something to be feared, even in theatres with strong subscription bases.

In just a few years, the mood had obviously changed from ecstasy to
caution, from commitment to compromise. As the Councils began to apply
more stringent standards with their ever-decreasing sums of funds to give
out, subsidy rules remained essentially the same but interpretations of those
rules began to change. "How many people," the Councils began to ask, "are
actually going to this particular theatre?" The question required many theatres to re-think their mandates with both good and bad results. As "commercial success" became important for increased or even continued
support, many of the small theatres that had intentionally kept audiences
small to suit their material or the realities of their spaces either stretched
themselves into virtually unrecognizable shapes or sought *formulas* for success. Tarragon's seasons—though still of import—became as predictable as
those at the St. Lawrence Centre, Passe Muraille's as predictable as the
Royal Alexandra's. Toronto's "hits" continued to be picked up by other theatres across the country but it was clear that the vision and commitment
that once had made these important were slowly slipping away.
Experiment and social criticism, among other things, began to disappear
from the work. While overall production levels continued to rise, the work
they served was much less interesting. Risk, as a theatrically viable concept,
was clearly disappearing from the scene.

A few of the small theatres, it must be noted, refused to compromise. At the Factory, for instance, much of Ken Gass' work became even angrier and more critical of the status quo. In fact, with hindsight, *Winter Offensive*, Gass' viciously satirical statement about art and humanity, seems to sum up the whole situation. The play, set during a party at the home of the Nazi leader Adolf Eichmann, included just about everything one could use to offend an audience—sexual abuse, violence, grotesque language, an anarchic plot and a truly black vision of mankind. But its conception was honorable for Gass intended it as a warning to Canadian society that it was treading on dangerous ground; it was a plea for human and artistic understanding. Unfortunately, the concept was lost in sloppy dramaturgy and an unfocussed production. The reviewers, giving Gass no credit for his vision, went after both him and the Factory with a vengeance. Audiences stayed away in droves as everything from Gass' aesthetics to his general sanity was questioned. That was November 1977. Toronto theatre certainly had changed in a very few years.

By about 1979 these changes were even more clear. Many of the city's small theatres had either moved into or were in the process of trying to find new homes. More importantly, each was trying to carve out a clear identity for itself. Strategies ranged from Passe Muraille's Canadian mythmaking (generally through collective creations) to Toronto Arts Productions' attempts to offer a little bit of everything to everyone (which usually meant little of interest to anyone); from Tarragon's usually worthwhile seasons of Freeman, French, Tremblay and Reaney to Theatre Second Floor's often self-conscious experiments in form; from Toronto Truck Theatre's blatantly commercial forays into popular world drama to Theatre Plus' attempts to prove that people's minds do not go flat each summer. Since then, even with the advent of new Artistic Directors at Tarragon, Passe Muraille, Toronto Free and The Factory, not much has changed. The identities of these theatres have grown clearer as their physical spaces have improved.

In truth and fairness, the Toronto theatre scene today—certainly in comparison to many other cities—still looks good. At least there still is ample choice. In comparison to 1973, however, there is less interesting theatre in Toronto and certainly much less Canadian-written theatre. In both the 1971–72 and 1972–73 seasons, for example, more than 200 new Canadian plays received full-scale productions. During 1981–82, only 32 new plays were produced in the city, a drop of some 85 percent.[5]

WHERE, THEN, IS TORONTO THEATRE GOING?

Not too much further I would suggest unless some major problems are solved. Some of these are beyond the control of the theatre community—the economy, for example. But others are presumably within its control. And though I don't pretend to have ready answers, it may be of some use to try and identify some of the problems facing Toronto theatre today.

One of our major problems—and this is probably true right across the country—is a tremendous lack of directors with an interest in and an ability to read new scripts. It is surely a special technique to be able to distinguish between the possibilities of a script in-potential and one whose problems have already been solved. As well, there seems to be a dearth of directors with the nerve—or perhaps the ability—to do more than simply shuffle actors around a stage, to dare a genuine, perhaps even a new, theatrical concept. With the possible exception of Richard Rose, Hrant Alianak, Paul Thompson and on occasion, Guy Sprung, there are few directors whose work one goes to see with any real hope of being surprised. My intention here is not to denigrate directors or to hold up "surprise" as an artistic guideline. It is rather to recognize a certain sameness and safety about most of the work I see. Too many of our directors—whether dealing with text or staging—seem to inherently distrust new vision, especially when those visions come from Canadian playwrights. Too often, they appear to force new plays into traditional forms even when the play is clearly moving in some other direction. In doing so, they often manage to make what is most intense in a new play seem safe, recognizable, acceptable. As a result, there probably exists a worse relationship between Canada's playwrights and directors now than there was a dozen years ago. We may see a higher quality product now but it is also an infinitely less interesting one. Our directors must begin to trust new work more and to risk in each production at least as much as our writers.

There is also, I'm sorry to say, a real problem with theatre reviewers. This is always a sore point for theatre people and it probably always seems to be "worse than ever." It does seem today, however, that there is even less interest on the part of our reviewers in discovering new work, confronting new ideas or trying to come to grips with new approaches. This begs the question, of course, of the critic's special role in a developing theatre. And, again, our theatre, taken as a whole, *is* still developing. *Do* our reviewers and critics have a special role to play in this regard? I think so and in saying that I am not implying any diminution of standards; I am speaking simply of a willingness to recognize new possibilities and perhaps even to develop new critical vocabularies.

But perhaps this suggests an even larger problem: the fact that we tend to be, when it comes down to anything that is called Canadian in the arts, an especially ungenerous people, ungenerous to the present and especially ungenerous to the past. When it comes to supporting our own creations in almost any field, we have many kilometres to go before the patronizing smile will finally be put to sleep. I cannot, for instance, understand why we seem so reticent to acknowledge that Ryga, Herbert, Simons, Cook, Walker, French, Freeman, Hardin, Ritter, Reaney, Murrell, Salutin, Alianak, Malliet and—if one is permitted here to include Quebec—Gélinas, Dubé and Tremblay, have all written world-quality plays, many of which have already been translated into other languages and have been played with success in other countries. These writers are national cultural treasures. We seem almost annoyed to learn that many of them are now the subject of dissertations and coursework in American, British, French and Italian universities.[6] Some years ago, I spoke at a Canadian studies colloquium at the University of Bologna. Before I began, I remember looking around at the tremendous number of people there and saying, "I know now that Canadian culture is safe . . . in Italy." In Canada, there are still too few exceptions within our own country who show the commitment, knowledge and enthusiasm necessary to make our arts central to the national experience and the national vision.

The problem, I am suggesting, is larger than simply our critics. It is as large as the country itself and as old as our history. We do not want, it seems, to have our artists (perhaps anyone, but for now we'll limit it to our artists) succeed. We seem determined to ensure that no one will stand out; if someone dares to do so we seem to take genuine delight in being able to put them down or, when dealing with the primary creators in the performing arts (the playwrights, the composers, the choreographers) turning our backs on them.

Finally, I suppose, a nation's theatre is only as great as the people in it. If we continue to reject the notion that Canadian artists and Canadian art can be great, then they never will be—in our eyes. That is why I am suggesting that even now when the vision of the Toronto Movement seems almost anachronistic, we still have much reason to retain its artistic hope and faith. If the Toronto theatre community today seems depressed, perhaps it's only because those in it know how close they really were to victory and how much victory seems to be retreating from them day by day. Back in the late 60s and early 70s, dreams were still acceptable and visionaries could be found dotted across the landscape. Now one is hard-pressed to find a genuine visionary—much less a visionary with resources and commitment—anywhere in our theatre, unless one accepts vision as being the lowest common denominator in the world of art—commercialism.

We have obviously lost our theatrical innocence over the last decade, not only in Toronto but all across the country. The less generous among us—the most Canadian among us?—might say that in losing that innocence we may have also lost our nerve, our defiance, our commitment and, perhaps, even our ideal of art as a meaningful role-player in society. But even were that so, even if age or expediency or whatever has stolen that from us in recent years, I do believe that the essence of the vision we shared for a moment can still be nurtured and restored.

We have not failed in the last 10 years. We have begun to mature. We must struggle to retain something of our earlier innocence, something of its openness, its freedom. I retain my own faith and optimism because, I suppose, I have seen it, I have lived with it, and I know that it is, in its highest and most difficult purpose, a vision worth pursuing.

NOTES

The opening quotation is from Desmond Morris, *The Naked Ape* (Chapter Four - "Exploration"), Toronto: Bantam Books, 1967, 122–23.

1. Ronald Bryden, "Toronto Theatre: Mademoiselle est partie," *Canadian Forum*, Aug. 1978, 8.

2. Ben Wicks, "The Outcasts, in *The Toronto Star* of 8 Oct. 1982.

3. Bryden, 8.

4. It should probably be stated at this point that I am generally ignoring Quebec in this consideration, though

much of what has been said clearly relates to the Quebec experience as well. The fact is, the French-language experience pre-dates the recent experiences in English-language Canada by five to 10 years and, in the case of the Toronto Movement, actually had great influence on it, especially in the work of Paul Thompson and Bill Glassco. To give it proper respect, the subject obviously needs an essay of its own, if not a full book. In a similar way, some of the activities which took place in Vancouver in the years just prior to 1967 and indeed during the whole period of the Toronto Movement must also be given credit for their importance and influence.

5. Ontario Arts Council statisti piled for use by the Toronto Bench in judging the Floyd S. Chalmers Playwriting Award each year.

6. It may surprise some to learn that active Canadian Studies Programs exist at the University of Bordeaux and the University of Bologna as well as at several major American universities including Harvard, and in Edinburgh, Scotland. Details on many of these programs can be obtained from the Department of External Affairs, Academic Affairs Division in Ottawa.

TORONTO'S ALTERNATES: CHANGING REALITIES *

KEN GASS

o

*While taking issue with the idea that earlier theatrical energies were fading,
director-writer Ken Gass tried to figure out where Toronto was theatrically,
what was coming next and, perhaps most importantly, what was needed.*

If one swallow doth not a summer make, then one might easily say in
response to Don Rubin's prognosis (that Alternate Theatre in Toronto is
dying) that one lame production of *Julius Caesar* doth not a general malaise
make. There's a cliché in the theatre that you're only as good as your last
show, which explains as well as anything why some theatres are regularly
described as failing or floundering if they haven't had a recognizable hit in
recent months. And by the same token, theatres like the Factory and
Theatre Passe Muraille who have had the privilege of reading their own
obituaries in the entertainment columns, are this season said to have
revived, their public image buoyed by a single successful production (*Lucky
Strike* at the Factory, *Les Maudits Anglais* at Passe Muraille). In truth, the
death knell has sounded over the Alternate Theatre movement every two or
three years for the past decade.

Having thus rejected Rubin's pessimism let me risk contradiction by
articulating some of my own alarmist sentiments. First, let me say that I
believe the notion of "alternate theatre" in Toronto is an archaic one, and
the phrase no longer describes current realities. Toronto is a very conservative community and it is not surprising to find this reflected in its theatre-
going habits. Audiences, critics and arts councils—perhaps even the
theatres themselves—want more of the *status quo*. They simply are not looking for alternatives.

* *Canadian Theatre Review* 21 (Winter 1979): 127–35.

In the early 1970s, "alternate theatres" (the phrase was coined by Tom Hendry and usually capitalized to suggest something formal), grew up in opposition to the regional theatre network which represented the bulwark of professional theatre in Canada at that time and also commandeered most of the financial resources available from the arts councils. The validity of the Alternate movement stemmed from its two-fold aims: a) Political—a redistribution of economic resources by giving significant funds to groups and individuals who wanted to work in smaller, independent environments, even if this necessitated dismantling the larger organizations, and b) Artistic—the development of new theatrical experiences, particularly in terms of new Canadian plays, which the regional theatre system had markedly discouraged.

In many Canadian cities, the polarity between the local regional bastion and the opposition alternate theatres still exists. In Toronto, and to a lesser degree, Vancouver, the balance has shifted so that the mainstay of the city's theatre scene is now those theatres that used to be described as Alternates. The main audience expectations here in Toronto are with Tarragon, an Alternate with nearly 3000 subscribers; TWP, which had a number of runaway hits last season; Open Circle's commercial successes: New Theatre's extravaganzas; Young People's Theatre's family shows; and Toronto Free Theatre's highly-polished productions. And there remains a curious regard for Theatre Passe Muraille and Factory Theatre Lab, often fanned into genuine excitement for individual shows. Audiences also flock to Toronto Truck Theatre, where *The Mousetrap* has been running a year and local productions of Broadway-style hits are filling its larger second theatre; and, they go to Phoenix which has pursued a similar policy, but has also made commercial successes of Edward Bond and Van Brugh. And of course, there is the Royal Alexandra, which has over 40 000 subscribers for its Broadway and West End touring shows, and the O'Keefe Centre, which strives vainly to keep pace.

In this milieu, it is impossible for Toronto Arts Productions (TAP) at the St. Lawrence to follow the easy programming formula of most regionals: two or three Broadway/West End hits; one old classic, one recent classic; one serious modern play, if possible and; also, *if* possible, a small-cast Canadian play. (Manitoba Theatre Centre, the dean of the regionals, is a good example.) In Toronto, the classics are best done at nearby Stratford; the commercial shows are done everywhere else; and the so-called Alternates do the best job of Canadian plays. Thus, TAP (albeit this season which includes three Canadian works, is less typical) appoints itself the role of providing the City with its only *real alternate*, a serious diet of modern pieces, neglected classics, and other missing fibres from the theatrical canon. Theatre Plus, at the adjoining space in the summer, has also taken on the role of shoring up our European sensibilities, often with greater success.

Of the dozen or so other professional companies in Toronto, such as Redlight Theatre, or Black Theatre Canada, they play to special communities, and their programming is often fragmented and seriously underfunded. Thus, to get back to Rubin's argument, Theatre Second Floor has been able to claim—particularly at any time that Factory and Passe Muraille

...ppeared to be operating below par—that *they* were Toronto's only genuine Alternate theatre. By producing limited shows with limited seating and charging only a dollar, they thwarted any commercial expectations that might creep in from the arts councils, just as Toronto Free Theatre used to do with its free performances. More importantly, Theatre Second Floor, under Paul Bettis, has been committed to performance experiments and even when unsuccessful or, more often, just unfulfilled, the productions have always been novel and innovative and, occasionally, startlingly good. Thus, when Theatre Second Floor serves up a traditional play and the nature of the experiment deals with the dynamics of traditional Elizabethan performance, and the result happens to be both an artistic and popular flop, too many critics mourn the passing of Alternate Theatre in Toronto.

The point, as I hope I have made clear, is that the Alternate movement is still alive and searching in Toronto and some of these companies are really quite successful.

One such is Open Circle, a company which originally gained fame, though not riches, from a tough entertaining show about lead pollution, and another work, also in a docu-drama format, about the plight of the Toronto Island homesteaders. Open Circle became known as a group with a social conscience, backed up by a talent and style directors Ray Whelan and Sylvia Tucker had cultivated in their years at Toronto Workshop Productions. Last season they produced an ambitious piece dealing with the Chilean situation, but their real connection with Toronto audiences has been through their highly popular Israel Horovitz shows, *Primary English Class*, and, recently, *Mackerel*, which opened their handsome new premises in the Adelaide Court. There is, of course, no reason why Open Circle shouldn't branch out and try to encompass both avenues, particularly if their directors are so inclined. The only sad admission that one must make is that there is little incentive for Tucker and Whelan to pursue what I know they consider their most important work, and to develop theatrical experiences that could become truly original as well as socially provocative. Given the scale of their productions, Open Circle are not well-funded and one cannot really blame them for lifting themselves out of the docu-drama ghetto and into an arena that offers tangible rewards.

Toronto, though it would like to think of itself as the cultural mecca of Canada, is simply not a conducive environment for serious theatrical experimentation. Even Paul Thompson, who has spawned the most vibrant Canadian collective creations, admits this by concentrating his energies outside the city. His productions have been major events all across the country but have been very much hit or miss affairs in Toronto. Only by giving first priority to his audiences elsewhere has Thompson managed to avoid the conservative coercion that the city seems to bring to bear.

Toronto Workshop Productions was the city's main alternate theatre throughout the 1960s, long before the phrase was coined. Under George Luscombe's firm hand, TWP provided a rich counterpoint to the ups and downs (mostly downs) of Theatre Toronto, our dearly-departed regional theatre of that time. After a year's absence, Luscombe bounced back last fall with a sell-out production of Rick Salutin's *Les Canadiens*. However, it was runs of an American show, *The Club*, and Lindsay Kemp's company from England that the theatre chose to extend and make into wholehearted commercial success. The challenge now is whether or not TWP can garner the same kind of support for a home-grown season in the old Luscombe style. If not, it would be one more telling example of how success can kill you in Toronto.

Does anyone remember Studio Lab? Their production of *Dionysus in '70* ran for a full year, and then, unable to repeat the success, they soon died as a Toronto producer. Similarly, after *Primary English Class*, when Open Circle tried to return to basics with two small-scale productions of plays on contemporary issues—one dealing with nuclear energy—the company found itself with virtually no audiences at all, absolutely no spill-over from the thousands who had seen the Horovitz play.

Regional theatres too have gone through a parallel pattern. In their early years, they justified government subsidy to Neil Simon productions as part of an audience-building campaign, assuming that once they'd built up their subscribers they would be able to branch into more adventurous and original programming. Instead, what has happened is that they have merely trained their audiences to respond to British and American sensibilities, and some attempts to alter the formula have resulted in massive subscription cancellations and pressure from their respective boards of directors to return to the kind of theatre audiences have learned to like. (There are, of course, significant exceptions, such as the Centaur, to whom the generalization does not apply. And, to add another tangent, it will be interesting to observe the growth of audiences in Newfoundland where professional theatre is not equated with any regional edifice but with the Alternate-styled Codco and the Mummers.)

Another factor in the conservative commercialization of our theatres has been the acquisition of several new or smartly renovated premises. Companies without a permanent home complain about the difficulty in finding performance space and organizing their seasons, while companies with their own theatres complain about the killing effects of high overhead. Even a theatre like Toronto Free, which ideologically is in favor of experiment and original writing that lies beyond the mainstream, finds itself doing a delicate balancing act between the most imaginative new work available and work that is, to use the current phrase, "accessible" enough to fill the house. Originally, the pride of TFT was its dynamic resident company; now, too often, the pride seems reflected in the physical surroundings. And while Toronto Free, in its two theatres, still provides some of the best-produced and most original work in Toronto, the economic erosion caused by the physical plant has resulted in shorter seasons and like many theatres here, a search for small-cast plays.

Jonathan Stanley's New Theatre is an Alternate that seeks out new aggressive writing from abroad—Mamet, Babe, Shepard, Stoppard, though this season includes a revival of a John Palmer piece—and presents it in Toronto, often with the original New York director. To the cynic, this may appear to be Canadian colonialism on an off-Broadway scale, but Stanley produces his ventures with a great deal of un-Canadian commercial panache and some of his extravaganzas take place in the St. Lawrence, and this year, at the oversized O'Keefe. Hardly typical Alternate Theatre behaviour.

In the case of Tarragon, its current commercial success is not a departure from original policy, for Bill Glassco has always been able to win a strong commitment from audiences with works that are rooted in naturalism and in emotional conflicts that are readily identifiable. If he has tended not to stray too far from David French, Michel Tremblay, David Freeman and James Reaney for his hits, it is nonetheless to his credit that he has built his success upon Canadian works. His subscription series has simply consolidated his position with audiences and if the opener this year, Lillian Hellman's *Toys in the Attic*, was a relatively safe pot-boiler, it is only fair to point out that the season also includes a difficult Racine play and work by a new writer, Steve Petch. By Alternate Theatre standards, Glassco's approach *is* careful and conservative, but by regional theatre standards, the programming is radical and its unqualified success with Canadian works is something to be emulated.

Having just resigned as Artistic Director of the Factory Theatre Lab, I suppose I should try to place it within this perspective as well. I think that because the Factory has been one of the main catalysts in the Alternate Theatre movement, it has been, in practice, one of the least successful theatres in terms of building a consistent audience. In fact, the Factory has tended to fly in the face of success by consciously changing direction whenever it found itself on an agreeable plateau. After a highly-esteemed production of *Esker Mike and his Wife, Agiluk*, in late 1972, the Factory switched to the first of its chaotic WORKS Festivals, presenting 14 short plays over two marathon evenings instead of a single standard program. As a result, the Factory was closed by Actors Equity, lost a grant and nearly collapsed entirely under the strain. Again, after *Boy Bishop* in 1976, it was back to another WORKS Festival, culminating in 10 plays in a single day, and followed by six months of in-camera work. Artistically, this was extremely rewarding, but it was hell on the organization and audiences lost track of what we were doing. And it was difficult to follow through on this approach as well, for the Ontario Arts Council began making portions of their grant contingent upon greatly improved box office and the Factory was in the uncomfortable position of trying to find the Canadian middle road. Meaningful experimentation on one hand; public acceptability on the other. At present, under Bob White's leadership, the Factory is trying to strengthen support for its valuable Playwrights Workshop program, one of the few arenas open to new playwrights in Toronto, but one that is costly and without box office returns.

By making grants conditional upon box office and corporate fund-raising results, the arts councils undoubtedly think that they are adjudicating theatres on the basis of their community support. On one hand this may be so, but it is also a strong incentive to appeal to the lowest common denominator and to simply do what has been proven will sell. Since the corporate sector is extremely conservative by nature, dependence on this community for survival strongly discourages theatres from producing anything that might be considered outrageous or offensive. These policies mitigate against any serious challenge to Toronto the Good.

Another factor that must be singled out in the conservative erosion of the Alternate Theatres is the deplorable level of criticism in the current press. It would be nice to think that we serious-minded theatre artists were above that sort of concern, but the reality is that we live in a media-oriented society where the press is our most vital link to an audience. In fact, it was the excitement echoed in the papers in the early 1970s that helped launch the Alternate Theatre movement by creating a myth around several isolated endeavours. It wasn't that the ratio of bad versus good reviews was any different; for if Herbert Whittaker had a reputation for kindness in the Globe, his counterparts did not. It was that somehow the press exhuded a passion and a contagious excitement that made the work seem important. It mattered. I think the reason that many artists from the Alternate Theatre movement are currently leaving Toronto is that a belief prevails that it doesn't ultimately matter how a show is received here, it won't make or break a career. This may be part of a broader Canadian syndrome as well and I'm not suggesting that the press was exemplary a few years ago, or that critics across the board are rotten right now. But an objective summary look at the situation points out that the overall level of critical writing has slipped from fair to very bad.

One of the failings of the Alternate Theatre movement is that it didn't develop an alternate press. Several alternate outlets do exist but they are too fragmented and inconsistent to have a major impact. Many of the scattered examples of good theatre journalism appear well after a show has closed and hence contribute little towards fostering audiences. The college papers, while often sympathetic, are lucky to find a reviewer who is even moderately informed or who can string three consecutive meaningful sentences together. The lack of a wholehearted interaction between the Alternate Theatres and what one would assume to be our natural market, the colleges, is a long tale of regret and only partly attributable to the low level of writing in the university tabloids. In New York, Richard Schechner has built up a whole industry for himself by writing essays about his productions, teaching at university and having his students buy his books and see his shows.

Other publications: *Performing Arts in Canada* is an embarrassment. *CTR* is showing improvement, but its mandate is too wide and its publication too infrequent to have any impact on week to week events in Toronto. The glossy magazines like *Maclean's* and *Saturday Night* comment in a random, wayward manner, usually more enticed by the variety of imports than Canadian drama, and generally are surprisingly loath to be seriously critical or to show any leadership. Theatre Ontario's *Scene Changes* and *Toronto Theatre Review* are struggling to find a voice. But, again, aside from their infrequent appearances, they are finding that good intentions are not enough. Good, compact theatre criticism is damned difficult to write, especially since most writers have been conditioned by years of shallow daily reviews.

In summary, Toronto may be a bustling, chic metropolis with abundant resources and an active theatre industry, but it is also thoroughly conservative and not the most conducive environment for serious theatre work. It is this realization that has caused me, for one, to plan my future theatre work elsewhere.

But I would not imply that Alternate theatre is dead in Toronto. It is kicking vigorously, despite government cutbacks. We may have lost a wave of alternate venues, but we do have a dozen or more solid theatre operations, still underfunded but playing in medium-sized houses, whose repertoires average 50 percent original Canadian and 50 percent imported work. In many cities, this could be considered a relatively healthy state of affairs.

Like all movements—surrealism, futurism, whatever—Toronto's Alternate Theatre movement makes complete sense only when seen within its historical context, a decade spanning 1969 to 1978. And there will always be alternate theatre experiences available to Toronto, as long as individuals like Bettis continue to produce their personal experiments, and as long as the Factory and Passe Muraille mange to stay afloat and retain some of their experimental eclecticism. But by removing the label of Alternate from what is now clearly the mainstream of Toronto theatre, one is effectively opening the arena to the next generation which must arise with its own banner, be it Fringe, New Alternate, or whatever. Elements of such a movement may already exist in the framework of Cafe Soho, Videocabaret, Dream Factory, Nervous Breakdown, Joe's Bowling Academy and others. Perhaps the next generation of writers and directors are fragmented, timid and leaderless, as it admittedly appears right now to an oldtimer like myself. But all that is needed is the right catalyst: an underground festival, a couple of surprise hits, a sudden infusion of Job Creation funds, an articulate visionary with a media outlet. Then a new movement for the 1980s may take hold and thoroughly shake the old Alternate/now Establishment. May it come soon.

LIVING WITH RISK:
TORONTO'S NEW
ALTERNATE THEATRE ◊

PATRICIA KEENEY

ɔ

Where were the "new" alternative theatres going in the 1980s? Some were turning their eyes abroad once again. Others were moving into previously forbidden realms, exploring the full range of sexual relationships. Some directors and writers were moving toward interdisciplinary experiments and what came to be called image theatre. Others were moving toward a new type of theatrical poetry. Critic Patricia Keeney (b. 1943) attempted to reflect a rapidly fragmenting theatrical focus in this essay from a 1983 issue of the Canadian Theatre Review *that was devoted to new directions in Toronto theatre.*

If Toronto's established theatre is now one of architecture and playwrights, then its leading edge has begun to run on image and idea. Though performances often fall short of the mental ideal, conceptualization being far ahead of execution, they occasionally score a brilliant hit. For the people involved in what may be considered Toronto's new alternate theatre, however, exploration is their true purpose. They do not work to patent successful formulae, but rather to probe and search for new forms and directions. They treat "success" with a caution natural to those who live more fully, more productively, with risk.

The focus for much of this activity in Toronto is the Theatre Centre at 666 King Street West. Established in 1979 above a Greek disco on the Danforth strip, the Centre moved to its downtown location in 1981 where it offers better facilities to its visiting and resident companies. Founded as a cooperative venture between six Artistic Directors who needed affordable space to pursue their experimental interests, the Centre now houses four

◊ *Canadian Theatre Review* 38 (Fall 1983): 33–43. Revised article.

separate companies including Buddies in Bad Times, A.K.A. Performance Interfaces, Nightwood Theatre and Autumn Angel Repertory Company, a recent amalgamation of Theatre Autumn Leaf and Necessary Angel Theatre Company, Actor's Lab which was part of the original group has now left the Centre and Autumn Angel has moved to separate offices, although its Artistic Directors still are members of the Centre's Board of Directors which, among other things, reviews every application from outside companies wanting to use the space.

The Centre's developing reputation is protected carefully. Amateur productions are viewed with caution because, as publicist Paul Leonard notes, "though we're all aware that sometimes quite bad things go on here, they emerge from an attempt to do something good." Intention and motivation are crucial terms at the Centre; seriousness of purpose is a constant. Those who experiment must at least be qualified to do so, no matter what the outcome of testing. Britain's 1982 Company, for example, made a positive impression with its evocation of a 20th century Latvian female writer, Aspazija, called *The Silver Veil*, early this year. Surprising largely Latvian audiences of a traditional generation, the company created stunning images and startling connections with Latvia's rich and troubled history. Actors interchanged parts in Aspazija's simple folk tale of a young woman who gains the powers of prescience through the gift of a silver veil. Bare feet in the sand denoted a landlocked peasantry; in a ceremonial depiction of history's cycles, a veil was undulated slowly down to the ground and up again; snuffed candles told of individual deaths; a vocal countdown backwards from the present intoned personal and international events that impinged on the writer's and actors' lives, and Latvia's.

Sky Gilbert, Artistic Director of Buddies in Bad Times, discusses his company's purpose with the articulate intensity typical of the Centre's founding directors. Buddies "was formed in 1979 to explore the relationship of the printed word to theatrical image in the belief that with the poet-playwright lies the future of Canadian theatre." Gilbert's conviction is not so far-fetched: in the beginning, of course, poetry was drama. Many of his shows are based on the poetry of individual writers, scenes built around poems to create, in the best, a network of interconnection by psychological/imaginative association. *Cavafy*, a show based on the work of the 20th century Greek poet, was one of the best. Cavafy interested Gilbert "because he puts his roots down into his own misery, thereby discovering to what extent his self-disgust was determined by his unauthentic, bourgeois environment."

Gilbert does not choose easy material. An equally enigmatic and difficult figure is Paolo Pasolini, Italian filmmaker and writer who became the subject of Gilbert's latest show, *Pasolini/Pelosi*, an investigation into the murder of Pasolini at the hands of his magnificent obsession, 17-year-old Guiseppe Pelosi. Gilbert's combination of lyricism, violence and broad satire was impressive in image after image in this show, evoking the indolence of Italian youth to the manipulative love/hate bond between Paolo and his favourite actress who, after a wonderfully vitriolic argument of equals, is hoisted, smiling like a seraphic Christ in full flight to end the first act. The acting of Arlene Mazarolle was splendid throughout, though some of her best moments took place around the rather superficial bourgeoisie-bashing of the second act. Problems built into this kind of production have to do with the diffusion of theatrical energies—why is *that* particular scene going on in *that* corner—and with the necessary assumption that the audience knows a lot about Pasolini or Cavafy or whatever poet is being presented.

Officially, "the intent of A.K.A. Performance Interfaces is to promote the integration of technological and live performance, and to represent the complexities of the urban situation." Under the directorship of Richard Shoichet, A.K.A. pursues the integration of various performance techniques utilizing live action, video, audiotape, etc. A "world tour of the modern age," their recent *The Road Show* combined dance, movement, video and electronic music. Whereas Gilbert's material may be historical, Shoichet's is quintessentially modern. For instance, in *The Road Show,* a city girl picks up a young boy in a bar and returns to his home in the suburbs for the night. Come morning, he must go to church with his parents, so it is decided that she will remain in bed and leave after the family has gone. The twist is that she gets disoriented; she thought the suburbs were all squares and blocks, geometrically logical; instead, she finds herself in a variation of the original labyrinth.

Of the several directors working out of the Theatre Centre, Shoichet is the one most explicitly concerned with entertaining. *The Road Show,* for example, was conceived as something of a spectacle. Video monitors showed ribbons of road from the driver's point of view; Margaret Dragu's choreography included jogging, exercising and javelin throwing. Eventually, the audience laughed though it didn't quite know whether it was supposed to. Based on the diaries of four of the performers who recorded urban life over a period of months, the script for this show was never truly brought to book, however; it remained a pile of pages containing an outline, stage directions, monologues and dialogues, only some of which were used.

Nightwood Theatre's expressions are many: adaptations of novels, such as *The True Story of Ida Johnson,* or *The Yellow Wallpaper;* the paintings of visual artists such as Alex Colville in *Glazed Tempera.* These subjects inspired what Artistic Director Cynthia Grant calls a "theatre of images." Collaborations with the Latin American and Greek communities have produced heady mixtures. Nightwood, together with Los Campañeros, for example, created *Flashbacks of Tomorrow,* a show built from Marquez' Nobel-winning epic, *One Hundred Years of Solitude.* One of their latest shows, *Mass/Age* has been called McLuhanesque but, as Grant readily acknowledges, it owes more to Mabou Mines, a New York company with which she apprenticed.

The biggest problem for Nightwood Theatre is honing a piece; there are always too many ideas and never enough time for the experiments to gestate properly. *Mass/Age* was big and busy. Einstein, da Vinci, Merlin—those seminal figures that Grant calls the Purists of Knowledge—people this production, each with their own appropriate music composed by Phillipp Glass. Images ranged from the cryptic and the witty to instantaneous disclosures that crept in at ground level to become part of the foundation: a

Tom and Jerry sort of hospital experiment (cartoon lobotomy?); the body of one actor in blue/silver light creating stellar patterns (Ursus Major) over two others below; Plato's cave and shadows; Merlin joining in a beachball game that includes kicking around the globe itself. As Cynthia Grant puts it, they did not want to create something definite but, rather, the *atmosphere* of insanity. As a result, they ended with a post-apocalypse banquet scene, people clicking into what they could remember of humanity: *did you eat the telephone*? Finally, the actors became TV ads there were seven different takes of *It might be possible, but would it make sense*?

Although Grant doesn't believe they've stretched their style sufficiently yet, *Glazed Tempera*, based on the paintings of Alex Colville was a virtually unqualified success. "It coalesced much more easily than other work we've done," she admits. Perhaps the concept was more clear and singular. Colville's cool moods flowed through the stage presentation to create a moving canvas of the painter's exact and compelling "magic realism." The piece used both taped commentary and original material worked up by the company. Slides of Colville paintings were juxtaposed with still figures behind scrims to produce a flat light effect uncannily similar to the artist's. They had some fun too; in one scene, actress Maureen White shoots her silhouette across a slide of Colville's "Stop for Cows!" while Kim Renders looks fixedly out at the audience through binoculars; and in the famous "Horse and Train" painting, a little toy train comes chugging along; the Canadian coin series evoked animal noises. There was magic in these colour-washed atmospheres that dabbled in fantasy, tinkered detachedly with perception and constantly surprised.

The reason for the merger between Thom Sokoloski's Theatre Autumn Leaf and Richard Rose's Necessary Angel Theatre Company was largely an artistic one. The two Artistic Directors had known each other through work at the Theatre Centre during the five previous years. The dynamics of *Tamara*, Rose's first popular success, were so good that Rose feels they should have continued into a second production immediately following it. The cast, however, was exhausted from working on a show that allowed the audience members to separate and follow whichever character they chose into whichever corner of Toronto's Strachan House they wished in this stylish Mussolini-era political farce. After Necessary Angel's next show, *Passchendaele*, a cinematically realized tale of love and violence that moved from the mud-and-fire poetry of the trenches to the pristine hypocrisy of the mandarin classes with the aspirations of an epic, Rose knew that a cycle was over. A certain pattern had become too set; the scale of vision both shows epitomized had taken years to understand: now the vision needed altering. As a result, Sokoloski and Rose collaborated and produced *Censored*, a fantastical version of Molière's life based on Bulgakov's *A Cabal of Hypocrites*. The production combined Rose's sense of moving spectacle with Sokoloski's emphasis on commedia dell'arte and mask.

It was his reading of the Greeks that opened Richard Rose to the nature of the epic. As he puts it, "their domestic stories covered it all—religion, sexuality, government." True enough, but life was simpler then, and unity of being not an invention of psychoanalysis. The gods did have great roles to play in love and war, for which they were rewarded handsomely. All aspects of living existed on a logical grid of cause and effect. By now, the connections are badly frayed. Consequently, any attempt to express total consciousness, the shifting sands of multiple viewpoint in one extended moment, is an overwhelming task. His early productions of *Electra and Boom* found Rose "looking at one picture in all its manifestations." Then came *Tamara*, which, he agrees *starred* Strachan House, a wonderfully complicated character seen from all perspectives. The impetus for this type of theatre, says Rose, is the desire for democracy, both among the actors who might play the king one moment and his clown the next, and for the audience for whom the fourth wall is totally eliminated. By the time he got to *Passchendaele*, his theatre of images had become too realistic, he feels; he neglected the more purely theatrical for a kind of docu-drama, although it still had a multiple focus. *Censored* allowed him to combine the realism of the backstage business of a Molière production with lofty ritual and vaulting church architecture. Attention was concentrated on individual moments; you might have an actor weeping beside you, then swivel on your bench to watch the Sun King declaim through his rigidly imperial face mask from a distant balcony.

Richard Rose wants to kick old habits of perception, change its structure. Mask work is a current challenge. Directing masked actors is like choreographing a dance, he claims. You cannot psychologize. Mask sets its own limitations. If anything, Rose's goal now is to become more theatrical, to create events that will draw people away from watching themselves on their own video screens. He hates formulae. He still thinks in epic proportions. The National's *Nicholas Nickleby* or their earlier productions of *The Romans* have inspired him to think big. For that sense of life's rich and shifting flux, he also turns to Canadian examples: *Billy Bishop, Maggie and Pierre* and *Balconville* exemplify multiple viewpoint. *Yankees at York*, the company's summer project based on the 1813 American invasion of Toronto, used 14 songs and dances, 20 actors, a boat "like Noah's ark—or maybe just the front end," two horses and 50 puppets. The extravaganza turns on many issues: British vs. American imperialism, the Canadian garrison mentality in its formative stages, the loyalties of expedience. It also turns on the figure of Bishop Strachan, by whose election the Americans maintained civic control and whose quick negotiating powers gradually gained Canadian independence.

The other founding company of the Theatre Centre, Actor's Lab, continues with its Grotowski-influenced physical emphasis under the Artistic Directorship of Richard Nieoczym, although it is now a separate company working out of its own space. Patricia White's one-woman show, *Passages*, began its life here, two hours of physical activity distilled into images that resonate with particular and general female history. Beginning with an object full of the past—her grandmother's patchwork quilt—and using music that ranges from Irish jig to rock and roll, White expresses many special feelings: a response to ageing provoked by the fragile delicacy of translucent skin; the regret that surrounds missed opportunities; excitement over conversations that could never take place except in the imagination. Exploring female mythology, she will add a section dealing with modern middle age, a time of life when her mother's generation slipped into dormancy and during which her own generation is just waking up.

Because of its strong aesthetic and its physical base (working out a role from the details of body), Actor's Lab is time-consuming and, so, not cost efficient. But it has produced some very exciting work. Its *Richard III* was visually interesting and true to text even though it condensed the play to one hour and 45 minutes (and one act) by excising all the foreshadowing, many of the messengers and long speeches. It also effectively used mixed casting. Pat White playing both King Edward who grew from an "insipid little twerp" to an exercise in cold executive veneer, and the Duchess, "a woman who had lost all and must confront the source of her miseries in her own son." The company continues to hold open auditions, regarding itself as a training base for continuing ensemble work. Despite the economic problems of maintaining a core of actors, Richard Nieoczym believes in the continuum of physical discipline: it is the raw material of his theatre.

As it is for Steven Rumbelow, Artistic Director of Triple Action Theatre, another of Toronto's new alternate theatres. This company first appeared during the Toronto Theatre Festival, Onstage 81, under the sponsorship of Actor's Lab, with a muscular and inventive adaptation of Joyce's *Ulysses*. Anyone who saw it will not easily forget the coffin thumping loudly on one end like the heavy pendulum of a gigantic clock as conceived by some Poe-ish mind; or Molly Bloom's lascivious ramblings in an upright bed. Last year at Theatre Passe Muraille, the company performed a wounding *Bridal Polonaise* that took much of its research from Toronto's Polish community. The piece began as an authentic Polish wedding, the audience becoming guests, and went on to utilize every available space including the lane outside and the workshop downstairs where tools became as menacing as machine guns. Having opened his first seed show, a *Cabaret*-style black comedy called *Matrimonium* at Queen Street's Blue Angel bar, Rumbelow, while continuing to accept the international invitations that keep rolling his way, confirms he is in Toronto to stay.

Besides the Theatre Centre and the companies it has spawned (or, more correctly, that have spawned it), other Toronto theatres continue to provide alternate fare. And, it must be noted, both Factory Theatre Lab and Theatre Passe Muraille are still active in this area. The Theatre Centre's annual Rhubarb series is, in fact, an imitation of the Factory's annual Brave New Works series; both provide space and money for staged readings and workshop productions of new plays by aspiring writers and give the opportunity for directors and actors to experiment with new styles. In some instances— as with the one-man shows of David Roche—productions even move between the two series. This last year, the Factory, now without its own theatre, utilized Theatre Passe Muraille's tiny Backspace for Brave New Works. The choice was appropriate for at the Backspace, TPM also continues to care for new work. In fact, Clarke Rogers, brought in by Paul Thompson to foster new scripts in this laboratory, has followed a fearless artistic policy since assuming full Artistic Directorship of the theatre. This last season, TPM, like the Factory, mounted *only* new Canadian plays. Although varying widely in aim and effect, some were particularly notable for their experimental nature—specifically Rogers' painstakingly careful production of *D and C* and Bob White's meticulous reading of Stephen Petch's *South*.

Other new theatres continue to emerge to expand alternate offerings even as existing theatres like NDWT and Open Circle fold. And with them, new approaches to production and subsidy continue to evolve. The Mercury, one of Toronto's newest theatre companies, deliberately eschews government funding, for example, thereby guaranteeing greater freedom even though a financially unpredictable life. Artistic Director Jon Michaelson who knows the welfare of his theatre must depend on audience, goes for substance *and* entertainment. Last season's opener, Albee's *Seascape*, a surreal fantasy based on the simple but outrageous situation of lizards talking to people, set a mental landscape that consistently interests Michaelson. Stephen Poliakoff's *Hitting Town* explores the latent sexuality of a brother/sister relationship realized in a setting of discos, back alleys and shoe-box apartments. Young, British and with a precocious talent, Poliakoff with his imaginative appeal to brooding youth is a favourite writer of Michaelson.

Though currently housed in the Poor Alex Theatre, Mercury collaborated with Peter Peroff's Bayview Playhouse to produce *Lee Harvey Oswald* last April, a sombre investigation of what made Lee Harvey tick. Dated and confusingly written, the play was barely saved by the riveting performance of Amanda Plummer (who did an earlier reading in New York at Michaelson's persuasion), and the diligence of other cast members Marion Gilsenon and James Kidnie. The Mercury wants to sparkle and shine; with two shows prematurely closed (due to various non-artistic contingencies), however, this may take a little time. As one company spokesman acknowledged, "the advertising isn't there, and that requires big money." He added, in a combination of irony and euphemism, "our funding policy is evolving."

Another response to economic austerity is the rise of the independent producing company. Michael Macina, writer, producer and lead actor of a colourful semi-cabaret saga called *Johnny Bananas*, the largely biographical story of an Italian immigrant family, tells a history of the project that is revealing. As part of its New Works series, Passe Muraille gave the script a staged reading in 1978. Macina got favourable responses from several theatres who could not afford to produce it. Thus in 1980, the script was adapted for film. In its 15th draft, the script was then reconceived as six one-hour segments for TV. The piece still was not produced. As Macina observes, the established theatres kept faith with their "subscription" writers before trying anything new. Thoroughly frustrated by the overlong development process, Macina struck a co-production agreement with Equity whereby a collective of actors put the show on the road for under $12 000. Macina feels this is the only viable way to get new work produced. He abhors the high production costs incurred by most theatres, and he believes in the efficacy of smart marketing. Reaping the benefits of direct telephone sales and exhaustive marketing research, targeting large segments of the Italian population, Macina ran his show in three different locations, thereby avoiding a pet peeve of his, the three-week assembly-line run.

Another example of this phenomenon is Gei/Smits Productions. Frustrated with trying to fit into someone else's idea of good theatre, and wanting to work together, actresses Sonja Smits and Angela Gei started looking for scripts themselves. Response from the theatre community to their desire for independence was enthusiastic. They expressed a need felt by many who began in theatre with the simple notion of sharing instincts and ideals. Again, Passe Muraille was interested in their script suggestions but had to defer to scheduling problems. *Later*, a straightforward script in which a widow and her daughters learn who they are without husband and father, consequently opened to good reviews at Toronto Free Theatre's upstairs space under its series of alternate programming called New Directions. What did the actress/producers learn from this experience? How easy the process can be, how willing people are to listen, how it is an excellent way to prevent spaces from going empty (which they still do over certain blocks of time), that committed people can still find the money and space to explore their own ideas.

These are lessons that the alternate theatre always has taught us but lessons that we obviously still need to learn. Appreciation of new talent, particularly talent which eschews popular taste, is still insufficient in Toronto. For Cynthia Grant of Nightwood Theatre, it's how we treat our artists that spins the roulette wheel of gains and losses. Des McAnuff had to go to New York to become appreciated. After Joe Papp spotted his talent, he won an Artistic Directorship in La Jolla and now can easily freelance in Canada, which he did at Stratford this summer. Hrant Alianak, laments Cynthia, should have gone to Europe where his structuralist theatre would warrant greater respect. She points out we still lack both foresight and hindsight, a strong enough reason for *doing*, for *seeing* the potential of what we're lucky enough to have happening here. In terms of government financing, there is no practical division between experimental and commercial theatre. Similar pressures will eventually produce similar products. For Pat White of Actor's Lab, experimental theatre suffers from the "scatter" effect: it lacks a centre. She suggests the case of Arturo Fresolini as an example: an Argentinian whirlwind of macho energy in the theatre, he hung around Toronto for five years before going off to develop his own ideas; most recently he returned to perform *Judicum Ultimum*, his anti-war "poem" for a nuclear age, at VideoCabaret, Toronto's adamantly fringe theatre which, under Artistic Director Michael Hollingsworth, continues to pursue its unique integration of ideas and imagery—and, incidentally, to demonstrate the viability of living with risk.

Image, idea, risk, the vital components of Toronto's alternate theatre also unite with sound in many of the city's most innovative productions. The centrality of music to VideoCabaret's aesthetic might also be a key to that company's success—a possibility that more and more alternate artists are considering. Two recent shows especially have been made by music. Allen Booth's punk rock score for *Sid's Kids*, directed by Thom Sokoloski, gave the show its power centre and caused the action to happen. Much cooler, but with language and mood just as dependent on music, was Steven Bush's new wave musical satire, *Life on the Line*. This also utilized an Allen Booth score, one crisp, clean and physically unpredictable as it adroitly counterpointed both the angst and banality of contemporary experience. Bush and Booth are yet another example of performer/writers who have founded their own production unit, Mixed Company, espousing, among other things, "an unapologetic bias towards music theatre."

Toronto's new alternate theatre combines techniques old enough to recall dithyramb and masks with the newest technological gadgetry of video and electronic music. For better or worse, life is no longer people moving through plot lines; it is multidimensional existence—sensual and perceptual bombardment, multiplicity of choice, the crudely comic underside of tragedy, the surrealistic base of ordinary event, the isolation of the heart. This is a hard won and reluctantly accepted understanding that the new alternate theatre is attempting to express honestly and comprehensively. They're mining a vein of enormous creative potential.

ON NATIVE MYTHOLOGY[*]

TOMSON HIGHWAY

ɔ

Canada's First Nations people found an eloquent and original voice in Tomson Highway (b. 1951) in the mid- and late-1980s. By the 1990s, his plays were being seen in commercial runs at large and prestigious venues across the country.

"Native theatre"—for lack of better terminology—has been around for only about ten years, if that. By "Native theatre," I mean theatre that is written, performed and produced by Native people themselves and theatre that speaks out on the culture and the lives of this country's Native people.

The Indian painters made their first big statement in the early 1960s with the explosion onto the Canadian scene of such names as Norval Morrisseau, Daphne Odjig and others. This event—and particularly in the case of Morrisseau—marked the first time Indian people made available for public consumption their mythology, a mythology considered too sacred, by their own people, for this purpose and, in fact, so potent in its meaning that Christian missionaries did all they could to replace this mythology with their own. Twenty years later, it appears the writers are now finally ready to take the step taken earlier by the visual artists.

If Canada, as a cultural entity, is slowly succeeding in nurturing a literary tradition that has a distinctly and uniquely Canadian voice—albeit, one fashioned out of the melding of any number of other traditions—then the Indian people of this country have a literary tradition that goes back thousands of years. As a people, we are very much aware of the fact that there were mythologies that applied—and applied in a very powerful manner—to this specific landscape since long before the landmark year of 1492. But this literary tradition is an oral tradition, not a written one and these ancient

---

[*] *Theatrum* 6 (Spring 1987): 29–31.

stories were passed down generation to generation—in Cree, in Ojibway, Mohawks—until they reached us, the present generation, the first, as a group, to have a reasonable grasp of the English language.

But why not write novels? Why not short stories? Why the stage? For me, the reason is that this oral tradition translates most easily and most effectively into a three dimensional medium. In a sense, it's like taking the "stage" that lives inside the mind, the imagination, and transposing it—using words, actors, lights, sound—onto the stage in a theatre. For me, it is really a matter of taking a mythology as extraordinary and as powerful as the human imagination itself and re-working it to fit, snugly and comfortably, the medium of the stage.

The only thing is, this mythology has to be re-worked somewhat if it is to be relevant to us Indians living in today's world. The way these stories go, they were meant for a people who lived in a forest environment; we—our family—were all born in tents, grew up travelling by dog-sled and canoe, etc. But, today, as a adult, I am urban by choice. So in order for these myths to be relevant to my life, to my own system of spiritual beliefs, I have to apply these myths, this mythology to the realities of city living. So, "Weesageechak" the trickster figure who stands at the very centre of Cree mythology and who is a figure as important to Cree culture as Christ is to Western culture, still hangs round and about the lakes and forests of northern Manitoba, yes, but he also takes strolls down Yonge Street, drinks beer, sometimes passes out at the Silver Dollar and goes shopping at the Eaton Centre. You should have seen him when he first encountered a telephone, an electric typewriter, a toaster, an automobile. I was there.

Greek drama fascinates me because I feel that the basis for much of that drama is the mythology of that culture: the creatures, beings, the gods and events that inhabit the spiritual world in the Greeks play a central role. In much of Western literature, Christian mythology acts as a central underpinning. And I believe that for "Native literature" to achieve any degree of universal resonance or relevance, any degree of performance, Indian mythology must lie at its very root.

The difficulty Native writers encounter as writers, however, is that we must use English if our voice is to be heard by the large enough audience: English and not Cree. The Cree language is so completely different and the world view that that language engenders and expresses is so completely different—at odds, some would say—that inevitably, the characters we write into our plays must, of necessity, lose some of their original lustre in the translation. So, of necessity again, we are very conscious of the fact that we are working with a language that we must reshape to our own particular purpose. I suppose it's a little like trying to imagine what Chekhov's *The Three Sisters* must look and sound and feel like in the original Russian performed by a Russian company of actors and then seeing it performed in "Oxford" English. We get the general drift, maybe more, but I don't think we get the total reality of it, in the end. At any rate, the English language, as any language does, is changing constantly and we have a say in the changing of that language. It will be interesting to see where we get with it in the next few decades.

Indian mythology is filled with the most extraordinary events, beings and creatures. These lend themselves so well to visual interpretation, to exciting stage and visual creation: the cannibal spirit Weetigo (Windigo in Ojibway) who devours human flash (in one show, we had him dining out at a Yuppie restaurant in Yorkville); the young man Ayash who encounters a village populated by women with teeth in their vaginas and has to deal with them as part of his vision quest, the woman who makes love to a thousand snakes; and so on and so forth. Not only are the visuals powerful, the symbolism underlying these extraordinary stories is as basic and as direct as air. And they come from deep, deep within the flesh and blood of a people who have known this particular landscape since time immemorial and who are so close to it they have become an integral part if it, like rock.

A recent Toronto production provides a good example. In *The Rez Sisters*, the story, essentially, is of the lives of these seven extraordinary Ojibway women, their passions, their tragedies, their exhilarations and of their bizarre and fantastical adventure with a game called bingo, a game otherwise tawdry and mundane as laundry day on an Indian reservation (the "Rez" to us Indian folk). But on a larger scale, the story is of the Trickster, Nanábush—the Ojibway equivalent of the Cree Weesageechak— and his adventure with these women, the fun he has in "monitoring" the spiritual dimension of their lives. As this spirit figure is the one who straddles the consciousness of Man and that of God, the intermediary between the Great Spirit and his people—he informs the cancer victim among this group of women, Marie-Adele Starblanket, that "it is almost time for you to come with me," all the while disguised as a seagull who shits on Marie-Adele's lawn, swings from her clothesline as she does laundry, etc. Marie-Adele, in some dark corner of herself, knows somehow that she is dying and sort of, though not quite, recognizes the spirit inside the beckoning bird.

Later, as the women are in the van, driving down the highway to Toronto to take part in "the biggest bingo in the world," they stop for a flat tire. In the darkness, Nanabush, now in the guise of a nighthawk, makes another appearance. And he and Marie-Adele have this violent confrontation through which Marie-Adele realizes, for certain now, that she is going to die soon. When the women get to the bingo palace, Nanabush appears to Marie-Adele for the last and final time, this time in the guise of the bingo master—"the master of the game," as Marie-Adele now addresses him— who finally takes her hand at the climax of the game and proceeds to escort her into the spirit world. The other six women, who meanwhile have had varying degrees of awareness with this creature throughout, are left weeping and mourning at her grave. The Trickster has played his "trick" and he chortles. The play, in fact, becomes the tale of small and petty doings of men/women on this earth while only half-aware of some grander, larger "design" that rules their lives.

The mythology of a people is the articulation of the dreamworld of that people; without that dreamlife being active in all its forms—from the most extreme beauty to the most horrific and back—the culture of that people is dead. It is a dead culture and it is, in effect, a dead people we speak of. And, ironically, enough, with the threat of nuclear annihilation facing us square in the face, we could be a dead culture and a dead people sooner than we think.

So I suppose that we Indian people writing for the stage ultimately want to be heard so the dreamlife of this particular people, this particular landscape, can achieve some degree of exposure among general audiences. They just may learn, we keep hoping, something new and something terribly relevant and beautiful about that particular landscape that they too have become inhabitants of.

NATIONAL THEATRE, NATIONAL OBSESSION [*]

ALAN FILEWOD

o

While the production of Canadian plays in Canadian theatres was apparently an issue consigned to the past, at least one of the "old" issues was still debated from time to time: is it possible in such a regional country as Canada to have a National Theatre? The question was reexamined in this 1990 Canadian Theatre Review *essay by theatre scholar Alan Filewod (b. 1952).*

Why have Canadian theatre critics been so obsessed with the absence of a national theatre? The question of what kind of national theatre might be most appropriate to this country has worried cultural pundits for a century, and occupies most of the deliberations on theatre in the Massey Report, the seminal document presented to Parliament in 1951 that shaped the develop-ment of the arts in Canada over the subsequent four decades. The Massey Report didn't invent that obsession. Since the 1890s theatre critics in Canada have wrestled with what appeared to be a simple problem: if we have a Canadian nation, then a Canadian drama must be one of its proofs; there-fore we must have a national theatre to advance the national drama.

This logic is not as self-evident as it might appear, because there are many countries that do very well without a national theatre. Certainly, Great Britain has a nominal one, and a case can be made that the Comédie Française is the national theatre of France (although many would argue against it). But the United States does not have one; nor does the USSR; nor do either of the Germanies. In fact it can be argued that the idea of a national theatre is a rhetorical construct that predates the concept of the modern state which redefines the idea of nation. If this is the case, the rea-

[*] *Canadian Theatre Review* 62 (Spring 1990): 5–10.

son that we have never succeeded in establishing a national theatre in Canada is that the very idea is a historical anachronism inapplicable to this country. But then, if that is the case, why does the subject keep coming up? The answer, I suggest, lies in Canada's complex experience of colonialism, in which the theatre has been identified throughout our history as a site for a debate on the nature of nationhood. What makes this complex is that the evolution of the theatre as an expression of post-colonialism coincides with the historical transformation of the theatre as a cultural industry.

Throughout this century critics around the world have bewailed the displacement of the theatre as a mass art by the cinema. That was certainly true of the first decades of the 20th century, when the movies destroyed the centralized theatre touring industry. Ironically however the marginalization of the theatre has also coincided with the greatest burst of theatrical activity—and in the commercial theatre sector, the greatest profits—this country has even known. Fifty years ago Vincent Massey could see only a slim sign of hope in the (erroneous) fact that "Canadian drama ... at present represents no more than twelve or fifteen produced plays";[1] today we know that thousands of Canadian plays have been produced, most of them never published and irretrievably lost. Yet, from these relatively few which have been published, some critics are attempting to establish a canon; others are questioning not only the concept of one but also questioning the ideological function of anthologies and university courses that canonize particular playwrights and modes of theatrical production. The sheer volume of plays written in this country would amaze the critics of five decades ago; it surpasses their wildest hopes. What would amaze them more is that our present theatrical culture has evolved without a consensual recognition of a national drama, and without the one thing that most critics of the past identified as necessary to the evolution of the drama: a specifically defined national theatre.

The idea of a national theatre was initially proposed as a means of recuperating Canadian theatre from American cultural expansion. It was an idea predicated on a model of national culture that few would subscribe to today. It can be argued that our theatrical culture evolved to its present vigorous, if financially tenuous, state precisely because it didn't fall into the trap of working towards a centralized National Theatre dedicated to the performance of a National Drama.

The obsession with a Canadian identity is not a modern phenomenon; it can be traced to the early years of the last century, and it fuelled the movement of romantic poetic drama that produced the ponderous pseudo-Shakespearean tragedies which plague today's students of Can Lit. When Charles Mair wrote his epic *Tecumseh* in 1886, he called for a national drama "tasting of the wood." The 19th century anthropomorphized culture according to the ideas of "radicalism" so prevalent at the time. If Canada is a unique nation, this argument went, then it must reflect a national character. As Carl Berger points out in his landmark study of the Canada First movement, *A Sense of Power*, this character was originally proposed as rugged, nordic, pure, and Anglo-Saxon to the bone. The notion of the Canadian character was revised, and is still revised, according to the ideological fashions of the day. (Few outside Quebec considered the French factor in this equation. In *Tecumseh* Mair wrote the Québecois out of the history of the War of 1812 to prove that the war was one between American "mobocracy" and British constitutional liberty.) For all of Vincent Massey's snobbery and his allegiance to British cultural models, as an essayist and a cultural politician he did more than perhaps any other individual to create the conditions in which Canadian theatre could flourish.

Before looking at Massey's effect on the idea of a national theatre, we have to retrace our steps to examine how that idea became inextricably entwined with the idea of a national drama. For that we must look at the turn of the century, when the stage in Canada was a branch-plant extension of the novel American discovery that if theatre was business, then it could be big business; in fact it could be organized as a monopoly trust. By 1910 almost every playhouse in Canada was owned directly or contractually locked into the American theatrical syndicates, a condition that alarmed nationalistic critics only after it was well entrenched. This early experiment in theatrical free trade created a situation in which Canadian playwrights were effectively denied access to the theatre—a situation with uncomfortable parallels to the problems of Canadian film distribution today. The first alarms sounded against this colonizing monopoly were not raised in objection to the American lock-out of Canadian theatre artists, but rather questioned the cultural effects of subjecting Canadian audiences to a steady diet of what amounted to American propaganda. In 1896, the young Hector Charlesworth, taking his cue from the growing agitation for public theatres in Britain, suggested that perhaps the only alternative to the deleterious diet of banal American sit-coms on the stage was "some form of public subsidy".[2] This radical suggestion was of course unheeded at the time, but it grew in the minds of the more perceptive critics of the day. In the first decade of this century, B.K. Sandwell, who like Charlesworth rose to become editor of *Saturday Night*, wrote a slew of articles and speeches in which he decried "the annexation of our stage."[3] The problem was clear: even as Canada was stumbling towards autonomous nationhood, it was in danger of cultural absorption by the vast commercial power of the United States. How to preserve Canadian identity? What in fact *was* Canadian identity? These were the questions that our dramatists could answer, if only they could be found. Charlesworth and Sandwell were among the first to recognize the relationship between cultural identity and the economic conditions of the stage.

The first proposed solutions to this American influence may seem in retrospect to be regressive but they were inevitable. Canadians—English Canadians—saw themselves as citizens of a "Vaster Britain," in the phrase coined by the arch-Imperialist poet Wilfred Campbell. The antidote to Americanism was plainly Imperialism, a renewed emphasis on the "British Connexion." When theatre critics sought alternatives to the American monopoly control, they naturally turned to the British example, at a time when writers like Granville-Barker, William Archer and Bernard Shaw were advocating a public National Theatre for Britain. If such a scheme could work in the Mother Country, then it was a natural for provincial Canada. There were of course dissenters, like Frederick Robson, who in 1908 advised readers of *The Canadian Magazine* that "it will be impossible for many years to have a Canadian 'style' or a Canadian drama."[4]

Popular mythology of the first half of this century advanced the thesis that Canadian nationhood was won on the battlefield, not on Queenston Heights, as Mair and his contemporaries would have it, but in the trenches of Flanders and Vimy Ridge. Perhaps Canadians were envious of the forged-in-battle myths of Agincourt and Valley Forge that justified the expansionist ideology of our big cousins. Canadian critics leapt upon the Canadian victories of the Great War as proof of nationhood, with a typically colonial twist. In 1915, when the first self-declared National Theatre in Canada emerged out of the amateur Drama League of Ottawa, its advent was greeted with hysterical rapture by *Maclean's*, which screamed, "In the agony of the present conflict, Canada has given birth to a national consciousness. . . . By the living God, we're British! Canada had found herself."[5] The writer, Arthur Beverly Baxter, saw the formation of the Canadian National Theatre (which incidentally proved still-born) as a decisive indication of cultural maturity; he wanted to see a Canadian nation that held up its end of the Empire, martially and culturally. He concluded that "Canada must seek artistic expression. It is the law of nations, and the law of individuals and the law of Nature."

For Baxter, as with many of his day, Canadian drama must necessarily be a celebration of Canadian nationhood; Canadian culture was an extension of British culture. In this he differed little from the writers of the previous generation. Mair's *Tecumseh* is predicated on the seemingly rational assumption that an Indian warrior speaking blank verse is no more ludicrous than Shakespeare's Romans and Celts. Tecumseh would take his stand beside Caesar and Lear.

The idea that Canadian national drama was an appropriation of British cultural models gathered strength in the years after the Great War, and led directly to the model of public regional theatres advocated by the Canada Council in the 1960s. The key figure in this was the man who most successfully combined Canadian nationalism and arch anglomania, Vincent Massey. His nationalism was not the same as the nationalism that inspired the post-war generation; it was not predicated on the post-colonial sense of difference that identified the Canadian experience as unique, but rather on a concept of civilization. To Massey, a flourishing Canadian drama was a mark of cultural maturity, but his understanding of culture maintained the British axis of the generations that preceded him. His was a concept of culture that expressed the ideals of the proprietary class schooled at Oxford and infused with the genteel British attitudes of power, privilege, and cultural purity. This brought with it a polite anti-semitism; one of Massey's disparagements of the New York-based theatre syndicates noted that the producers had "Old Testament names."[6] Any foreign influence other than British was to him alien to the natural tendencies of Canadian cultural evolution. And even so he doubted the value of British imports unless they were "the best."

Massey used his social privilege to advance the cause of Canadian drama materially, by his founding of Hart House Theatre in 1919, his anthologies of Canadian plays produced there, and his numerous articles advocating the Canadian dramatist. Ironically, the first important playwright to emerge out of the Hart House experiment argued an antithetical nationalism. Merrill Denison's 1928 article, "Nationalism and the Drama" went against the main current to propose that Canadian drama was an essentially regional American drama. (Denison doesn't mention in the article that he himself had dual citizenship; is this why he could assert that "life in Cleveland and Toronto is identical?") But Denison's was a dissenting voice, barely heard amidst the clamour for a national theatre, an ideal to which Massey still aspired. His belief that an institutional theatre was a necessary precondition of a national drama shaped public policy in the theatre thereafter.

The 1930s and 40s saw repeated attempts to raise the national theatre idea to the level of action rather than rhetoric. By the end of the 40s, when Massey and his Royal Commission heard the briefs of arts organizations across the country, the idea of government intervention was not just acceptable, but inevitable. This was in large part a consequence of the Depression and the Second World War, struggles that were won because of massive government intervention in what was soon to be known as the "private sector." The legitimation of a "public sector" in social policy made the idea of government funding for the arts feasible. In fact the Massey Report equates cultural funding with national defence; in ponderous cold war logic the report introduces its recommendations with the admonition that "we must strengthen those permanent institutions which give meaning to our unity and make us conscious of the best in our national life. . . . Our military defenses must be made secure; but our cultural defenses equally demand national attention; the two cannot be separated."[7] In other words, a national arts policy is a necessary defence against un-Canadian communism. Small wonder that the Massey Report's survey of Canadian theatrical achievements omits any mention of the workers' theatres of the preceding decade.

The Massey Report's remarks on theatre are a masterful example of fence-sitting. The report implies the necessity of a national theatre, and even proposes the founding of a national theatre school as an adjunct of such a company. It questions the idea of a single centralized national theatre, but finds merit in the idea of a touring company. The reports seem to favour the construction of playhouses as a means of bringing professional theatre to cities across the country, but also notes that "whether this would mean a renaissance of the theatre in Canada has been sharply questioned."[8] On one issue the Commission was clear: a national theatre could "give counsel" to local dramatic societies, and would uplift "gifted amateurs." In a passage of brilliant ambivalence, the report notes that

> It would of course be disastrous to conceive of the National Theatre merely as a playhouse erected in the capital or one of the larger centres; but it seems apparent that the national company of players would require a base for their operations. . . .[9]

Massey was inspired in large part by the example of the Dominion Drama Festival, which the report endorses enthusiastically, and which had in the years immediately preceding the Commission's inquiry moved to establish just such a company. In fact, in the years immediately preceding the Massey Commission it seemed that the DDF would successfully initiate a National Theatre plan. Under the leadership of Earle Grey (not to be confused with the earlier, titled, Earl Grey, the Governor General who left such an indelible mark on Canadian football) and the Arts and Letters Club of Toronto, this scheme, initiated in 1945, proposed a national organization of regional affiliates. Despite the endorsement of names such as John Coulter, Brian Doherty (who later founded the Shaw Festival), Lister Sinclair and Father Legault, the scheme floundered for several years before collapsing under the weight of divergent interests. Some, like Coulter, called for a national touring company; others argued for a National Theatre Association comprised of professional, amateur and university theatres. Again the problem of location proved insuperable. But in good committee procedure the DDF planned and generated numerous reports, articles in *Saturday Night*, and bylaws. As early as 1945 the committee had circulated a proposal that outlined the structure of a national council and even suggested a title for a national theatre newsletter (to be called, not surprisingly for a committee decision, *The National Theatre News*).

The DDF plan was unable to surmount the paradoxes that informed it from the beginning; much like the Meech Lake Accord (and for that matter, Confederation) it was an attempt to reconcile the irreconcilable. What is of particular interest in retrospect is that the plan completely ignored the material conditions that gave evidence of a national theatre movement in the making. The proposal proceeded from an imposed model of what a national theatre meant; and because it emanated from the amateur theatre it found its evidence in the Little Theatres that made up the DDF. It was the product of a particular class that could not accommodate opposing models. But the closest that Canadians came to a true national theatre was the workers' theatre movement of the preceding decade. The workers' theatres were themselves oriented towards a foreign model, but they were an authentic populist movement generating plays out of the experience of the community. The workers' theatre was not just a left-wing mirror of the DDF; it differed in that it generated a dramatic literature out of its own experience, even though that literature (the classic example being *Eight Men Speak*) was marginalized by contemporary critics. The workers' theatre movement anticipated later developments in that its plays repudiated traditional notions of literary drama in favour of a textuality of performance. The very negation of the workers' theatre movement and its successors, such as Toronto Workshop Productions and today's popular theatres, as marginal, as outside the "mainstream" of Canadian theatrical development, proved its fundamental assertion that theatre in Canada was an expression of class interests.

The social orientation of the national theatre idea was nowhere more evident than in its next manifestation following the implosion of the DDF plan. With the founding of the Stratford Festival in 1953 and the Canada Council in 1957, the Massey Commission's implied concept of a national theatre acquired a material basis and a political structure. The Stratford Festival presented the country with just the classic repertory company the Commission envisioned as the basis of a national theatre. On the one hand, Stratford's offshoot, the Canadian Players, fulfilled the model of a touring national company; on the other the Festival itself aspired to National Theatre status. This aspiration grew even as it was challenged by the alternative theatres of the 1970s that rejected Stratford as the ultimate expression of a colonized theatre. In the midst of the debate over nationalism in the arts in the 70s, the Festival briefly renamed itself the Stratford National Theatre of Canada when on tour, promoting critics abroad to ask why Canada's national theatre was devoted to the canon of a foreign country.

Stratford's claim to national theatre status was in effect a minor historical trope. What was more important during the post-war decades was the *de facto* realization of the Massey Commission's alternative suggestion of a decentralized national theatre. This is in effect the situation we are left with today. With the founding of the regional theatres during the 1950s and 60s, the dream of a professional theatre movement emerging out of the amateur theatres was fulfilled, and by the 1970s, there seemed to be a network of regional civic theatres that could in effect be called a national theatre. It fulfilled all the expectations of the earlier generation: these companies were generously subsidized, and they brought professional standards and the international repertoire to cities across the country. What they didn't bring was a vision of Canadian theatre; they accepted the 19th century premise that a national drama would emerge out of the nurturing influence of international "mature" repertoires. An exposure to Ibsen, the logic went, would eventually result in a Canadian Ibsen. This was the logic that John Palmer so brilliantly parodied with his 1976 monodrama, *Henrik Ibsen on the Necessity of Producing Norwegian Theatre*.

In retrospect it seems easy to point out that the authentic English-language national theatre developed in the alternative theatre movement, in the plays of groups like Theatre Passe Muraille, The Mummers Troupe and 25th Street House. The historic success of these companies in validating the voice of the Canadian playwright (who was often the Canadian actor equipped with a tape recorder) may have proved the case that a national theatre emerges from the engagement of the theatre with the living culture of its audience, but it also attenuated the idea of a National Theatre to the point where it became a tautology: the theatre is a national expression, therefore it is a national theatre. By this point the term effectively disallows itself. This was a point made but unheard as early as 1933 when Archibald Key wrote in the pages of *Canadian Forum*, "I foresee Canada's National Theatre in the form of a little red schoolhouse, a Ford Sedan with trailer, a few drapes, props and an elementary lighting set."[10]

Key's voice was prophetic but his point was made too soon. In fact, it still hasn't sunk in: the hegemonic idea of a monumental National Theatre continues to recur. It surfaced in 1968 with the original aspirations of the National Arts Centre, whose dream of a central showcase fell apart with the disbanding of its English-language theatre company after the 1983–84 season. And it surfaced again in 1987 when Toronto Free Theatre and CentreStage merged to form the Canadian Stage Company. When the merger was announced CentreStage's artistic director Bill Glassco proudly informed *The Globe and Mail* that the new theatre could be the seed of a "national theatre company." Once again the point of reference was British, even though Canadian Stage subsequently moved its sights from the National Theatre of Great Britain to the more recent identification with the English Stage Company of the Royal Court Theatre.[11]

A century after it was first proposed, the recurring obsession of a national theatre remains with us. But it is an obsession that may be impossible to gratify because its primary term of reference, the idea of a nation itself, is taken entirely from the cultural experience of another country. "National theatre" is a rhetorical idea that expresses particular values of nationhood and the theatre's place as a nation's "shining glory." Inscribed in it is an idea of national culture that can be rendered topographically as a pyramid: the national drama is the summit of the national culture, which takes its vertical structure of "low" popular culture and "high" educated culture from the historical arrangement of wealth and power. When critics of past decades spoke of raising the level of Canadian culture, they meant it literally: they meant raising the artistic consciousness of the bottom levels of the social pyramid to meet that of the educated elite at the top. The very idea of a national theatre rests upon the hegemonic idea of a nation that can be expressed in simple cultural codes. Vincent Massey's idea of Canadian nationhood was very different than mine is today; and mine is very different than Brian Mulroney's. The rhetorical proposal of a national theatre in effect means the canonization of a theatre and drama that reflects the national ideals of the governing elite.

NOTES

1. Vincent Massey, "The Prospects of Canadian Drama," *Queen's Quarterly* 30 (Dec. 1922): 197.

2. Hector Charlesworth, "Touchstone," *News*, Toronto, 5 June 1897.

3. B.K. Sandwell, "The Annexation of Our Stage," *Canadian Magazine* 38 (Nov. 1911): 22–26. See also "Canada's Adjunct Theatre," *Canadian Club Addresses* (Hamilton, The Canadian Club, 1913–14), 94–104.

4. Frederic Robson, "The Drama in Canada," *The Canadian Magazine* 31 (May 1908): 58–61.

5. Arthur Beverly Baxter, "The Birth of the National Theatre," *Maclean's Magazine*, 29 Feb. 1916, 27–29.

6. Massey, "The Prospects of Canadian Drama," 197.

7. Royal Commission on National Development in the Arts, Letters and Sciences, *Report* (Ottawa: Queen's Printer, 1951), 275.

8. Ibid., 197.

9. Ibid., 198.

10. Archibald Key, "The Theatre on Wheels," *Canadian Forum* 13 (Sept. 1933): 462.

11. Ann Wilson, "Stages and Doubles: The English Stage Company Visits the Canadian Stage Company," *Queen's Quarterly*, in press.

FURTHER READING

○

Beyond the many books and articles included in the current volume, the following is a list of publications that those working in the field might find particularly useful.

BIBLIOGRAPHIES, ENCYCLOPEDIAS, AND RESEARCH GUIDES

Ball, John and Richard Plant, eds. *Bibliography of Theatre History in Canada: The Beginnings Through 1989.* Toronto: ECW Press, 1993.

Ball, John, and Plant, Richard eds. *A Bibliography of Canadian Theatre History 1583–1975.* Anton Wagner, gen. ed. Toronto: Playwrights Co-op, 1976.

———. *A Bibliography of Canadian Theatre History Supplement 1975–1976.* Toronto: Playwrights Co-op, 1979.

Benson, Eugene and L.W. Conolly. *English Canadian Theatre.* Toronto: Oxford University Press, 1989.

Buller, Edward. *Indigenous Performing and Ceremonial Arts in Canada: A Bibliography.* Toronto: Association for Native Development in the Performing and Visual Arts, 1981.

Report of the Federal Cultural Policy Review Committee. Ottawa: Information Services, Department of Communications, Government of Canada, 1982.

Rubin, Don, ed. *Canada on Stage: Canadian Theatre Review Yearbook*, 8 vols. Downsview, ON: CTR Publications, 1974–1982. Since 1982 various organizations have been involved in keeping this archival series more or less up-to-date. Check under the series title for later volumes.

———. *World Encyclopedia of Contemporary Theatre: Volume Two—The Americas.* London: Routledge, 1996. Includes an extended section on both French and English-Canadian theatre.

Wagner, Anton, ed. *The Brock Bibliography of Published Canadian Plays in English 1766–1978.* Toronto: Playwrights Press, 1980.

MEMOIRS, SURVEYS, AND OVERVIEWS

Brask, Per, ed. *Contemporary Issues in Canadian Drama.* Winnipeg: Blizzard, 1995.

Conolly, L.W., ed. *Theatrical Touring and Founding in North America.* Westport: Greenwood Press, 1982.

Doucette, Leonard E. *Theatre in French Canada: Laying the Foundations 1606–1867.* Toronto: University of Toronto Press, 1984.

Edwards, Murray D. *A Stage in our Past. English-language theatre in Eastern Canada from the 1790's to 1914.* Toronto: University of Toronto Press, 1968.

Evans, Chad. *Frontier Theatre: A History of Nineteenth-Century Theatrical Entertainment in the Canadian Far West and Alaska.* Victoria: Sono Nis, 1983.

Filewod, Alan. *Collective Encounters: Documentary Theatre in English Canada.* Toronto: University of Toronto Press, 1987.

Godin, Jean-Cléo and Mailhot, Laurent. *Le Théâtre québécois: Introduction à dix dramaturges contemporains.* Montréal: Hurtubise HMH, 1970.

————. *Le Théâtre québécois II: Nouveaux auteurs, autres spectacles.* Montréal: Hurtubise HMH, 1980.

Johnston, Denis. *Up the Mainstream: The Rise of Toronto's Alternative Theatres.* Toronto: University of Toronto Press, 1991.

Knelman, Martin. *A Stratford Tempest.* Toronto: McClelland & Stewart, 1982.

Lee, Betty. *Love and Whisky: The Story of the Dominion Drama Festival.* Toronto: McClelland & Stewart, 1973; reprint, Toronto: Simon & Pierre, 1982.

Mews, Diane, ed. *Life Before Stratford: The Memoirs of Amelia Hall.* Toronto: Dundurn, 1989.

Moore, Mavor. *Reinventing Myself.* Toronto: Stoddart, 1994.

Much, Rita, ed. *Women on the Canadian Stage: The Legacy of Hrotsvit.* Winnipeg: Blizzard, 1992.

Nardocchio, Elaine. *Theatre and Politics in Modern Quebec.* Edmonton: University of Alberta Press, 1986.

Orrell, John. *Fallen Empires: Lost Theatres of Edmonton 1881–1914.* Edmonton: NeWest Press, 1981.

Ostry, Bernard. *The Cultural Connection: Culture and Government Policy in Canada.* Toronto: McClelland & Stewart, 1978.

Pettigrew, John and Jamie Portman. *Stratford: The First Thirty Years.* 2 vols. Toronto: Macmillan, 1985.

Ryan, Toby Gordon. *Stage Left: Canadian Theatre in the Thirties.* Toronto: CTR Publications, 1981; reprint, Toronto: Simon & Pierre, 1985.

Saddlemyer, Ann, ed. *Early Stages: Theatre in Ontario 1800–1914.* Toronto: University of Toronto Press, 1990.

Sainte-Pierre, Annette. *Le Rideau se lève au Manitoba.* Saint-Boniface: Editions des Plaines, 1980.

Smith, Mary Elizabeth. *Too Soon the Curtain Fell: A History of the Theatre in Saint John 1789–1900.* Fredericton: Brunswick Press, 1981.

Stuart, Ross. *The History of Prairie Theatre: 1833–1982.* Toronto: Simon & Pierre, 1984.

Usmiani, Renate. *Second Stage: The Alternative Theatre Movement in Canada* Vancouver: University of British Columbia Press, 1983.

PLAYWRITING

Althof, Rolf et al., eds. *Inter-Play: Works and Words of Writers and Critics*. St. John's: Breakwater, 1994. Includes plays by Andre, Beissel, Cook, French, Griffiths, Reaney and Rubess as well as criticism.

Anthony, Geraldine, ed. *Stage Voices: Twelve Canadian playwrights Talk About Their Lives and Work*. Toronto: Doubleday, 1978.

Bessai, Diane. *Playwrights of Collective Creation*. Toronto: Simon & Pierre, 1992.

Brissenden, Connie, ed. *The Factory Lab Anthology*. Vancouver: Talonbooks, 1974.

———. *Spotlight on Drama: A Teaching and Resource Guide to Canadian Plays*. Toronto: The Writer's Development Trust, 1981.

Dramatic Voices from England, Canada and New Zealand. Berlin: Cornelsen: 1989.

Filewod, Alan, ed. *The CTR Anthology: Fifteen Plays from* Canadian Theatre Review. Toronto: University of Toronto Press, 1993.

Glaap, Albert-Reiner, ed. *Das englische-kanadische Drama*. Dusseldorf: Schwann, 1992. In German. An English-language version with slightly different material was scheduled for publication by Breakwater (St. John's) in 1996.

Moore, Mavor. *4 Canadian Playwrights*. Toronto: Holt, Rinehart, 1973.

New, William H. *Dramatists in Canada: Selected Essays*. Vancouver: University of British Columbia Press, 1972.

Rubin, Don and Alison Cranmer-Byng, eds. *Canadian Playwrights: A Biographical Guide*. Downsview: CTR Publications, 1980.

Rudakoff, Judith and Rita Much, eds. *Fair Play: 12 Women Speak: Conversations with Canadian Playwrights*. Toronto: Simon & Pierre, 1990.

Staines, David ed. *The Canadian Imagination: Dimensions of a Literary Culture*. Cambridge: Harvard University Press, 1977.

Wagner, Anton, ed. *Contemporary Canadian Theatre: New World Visions*. Toronto: Simon & Pierre, 1985.

Wallace, Robert and Zimmerman, Cynthia. *The Work: Conversations with English-Canadian Playwrights*. Toronto: Coach House Press, 1982.

PLAY COLLECTIONS

Perkyns, Richard, ed. *Major Plays of the Canadian Theatre 1934–1984*. Toronto: Irwin, 1984.

Plant, Richard, ed. *Modern Canadian Drama*. Markham: Penguin, 1984.

Wagner, Anton, ed. *a Vision of Canada: Herman Voaden's Dramatic Works (1928–1945)*. Toronto: Simon & Pierre, 1993.

Wagner, Anton and Plant, Richard eds. *Canada's Lost Plays*, 4 vols. Downsview: CTR Publications, 1978.

Wallace, Robert, ed. *Making Out: Plays by Gay Men*. Toronto: Coach House Press, 1992.

Wasserman, Jerry. *Modern Canadian Plays.* 2

Wright, Richard and Endres, Robin, eds. *E*
Canadian Worker's Theatre. Toronto: N

INUIT AND NATIVE STU

Ernst, Alice H. *The Wolf Ritual of t*
Oregon Press, 1952.

Hofman, Charles. *Drum Dance.* To.

Macnair, Peter L. "Kwakiutl Dance
1973–Jan. 1974.

———. "Potlatch at Alert Bay," *Artscanada*, Dec. 19

DRAMA IN EDUCATION AND THEATRE FG.
THE YOUNG

Courtney, Richard. *The Dramatic Curriculum.* London: Faculty of Educa.
University of Western Ontario; New York: Drama Book Specialists and
London: Heinemann Educational Books, 1980.

———. *Play, Drama and Thought: The Intellectual Background to Drama-in-*
Education. 3rd ed. New York: Drama Book Specialists, 1974.

Baker, Jane Howard. *A Teacher's Guide to Theatre for the Young.* Vancouver:
Talonbooks, 1978.

———. Barnieh, Zina, with Beauchamp, Hélène. *A Mirror of Our Dreams:*
Children and the Theatre in Canada. Vancouver: Talonbooks, 1979.

THEATRE CRITICISM

Bryden, Ronald with Boyd Neil, eds. *Whittaker's Theatre, 1944–1975.* Toronto:
University of Toronto Press, 1985.

Conolly, L.W., ed. *Canadian Drama and the Critics.* Vancouver: Talonbooks, 1987.

Edmonstone, Wayne. *Nathan Cohen. The Making of a Critic.* Toronto: Lester and
Orpen, 1977.

Wallace, Robert, *Producing Marginality: Theatre and Criticism in Canada.*
Saskatoon: Fifth House, 1990.

JOURNALS

The following journals are also good sources of criticism and documentation.
All are indexed.

Canada Drama/L'art dramatique Canadienne, Canadian Theatre Review, Essays in
Theatre, Jeu, Modern Drama, Theatre History in Canada, Theatre Research in
Canada/Recherches Théâtrales au Canada.